SERVICE MANAGEMENT AND MARKETING

Managing the Service Profit Logic

Fourth Edition

CHRISTIAN GRÖNROOS

Library of Congress Cataloging-in-Publication Data
Grönroos, Christian, 1947-
    Service management and marketing : managing the service profit logic / Christian Grönroos. —
Fourth edition.
        pages cm
    Includes index.
    ISBN 978-1-118-92144-9 (pbk.)
  1. Service industries — Marketing.   2. Customer services.   I. Title.
    HD9980.5.G776 2015
    658.8–dc23
                                                                2015005386
ISBN: 9781119159865 (CourseSmart)
ISBN: 9781119092841 (ePUB)

A catalogue record for this book is available from the British Library.

Typeset in 10/11pt Bembo by Aptara Inc., New Delhi, India.
Printed and bound in Great Britain by TJ International Ltd., Padstow, Cornwall

CONTENTS

PREFACE

This book is about the *service perspective* in business, that is, *how to adopt service logic in management*, regardless of whether the core of the offering is a service or a physical product. It is a *how-to-think* rather than a *how-to-do* book. Therefore, it is not a traditional textbook with all the usual chapters. It is intended to help readers – students and practitioners alike – to realize the importance of service in today's competitive environment, and to see the opportunities for creating and maintaining a sustainable competitive advantage in any kind of market.

The text takes a unique approach to management and marketing from a service logic perspective. Previous editions have served well in academic education, especially on masters and doctoral levels. The book has also been used successfully by top- and middle-level managers, at board level, and in executive education to introduce the service perspective on business as well as service management and marketing in service competition for service firms and manufacturing firms alike.

Services exist alongside goods and other types of resources of course, but following the research on *service as logic* rather than as a category of products only, here service is first and foremost considered a way of approaching customers and facilitating their life and business processes by supporting their everyday practices rather than only delivering products and services as resources for their use.

Customers integrate anything they buy in their consumption or usage processes, that is, they use it in a process which can be characterized as a service process. Hence, customers consume and use goods, services or any resource *as service* to achieve something. As a consequence, firms will be better off directing their activities and processes towards facilitating these customer processes in a value-supporting manner. This requires service logic to be adopted in the firm, and that management thinking and attitudes, and management behaviour are geared towards this perspective. A service perspective cannot be adopted by implementing conventional manufacturing-oriented management attitudes and models. New service-focused thinking and, to a large extent, new management models and instruments are needed. The term *service management* is used for this new attitude to management and the new theories and models that go with it. This is what this book is all about.

Service logic and a service perspective require that the firm knows its customers well enough to be able to support their processes successfully. Although customers are by no means always right – they do not always have enough information to be able to make optimal purchasing decisions – the obligation of a firm is to help their customers to achieve their goals as well as possible. This makes the firm meaningful to its customers. To be able to implement such a service approach to customers requires that the firm's processes and activities are indeed customer-focused throughout the organization. Therefore, *service management is a truly customer-focused management approach*. This has consequences for marketing.

Traditionally, when delivering resources such as consumer goods, marketing is treated as one business function alongside other functions, and in business practice marketing is implemented as an isolated process in the firm. However, facilitating customers' life and business processes by successfully supporting their everyday practices, requires that all processes of a firm, which one way or the other have an impact on this, are focused on the customer. In other words, all such processes must be implemented in a marketing-like manner, with the interest of the customer in mind. Otherwise the customers will become unsatisfied with the firm's way of supporting them.

Hence, marketing is more a customer-focused attitude than one separate business function only. Such a customer-focused attitude is needed throughout the organization. This means that *the customer becomes a top management issue*. The importance of marketing-like attitudes in the whole organization – in managerial decision making and implementation alike – is the reason for the title of this book: *Service Management and Marketing*.

Every firm, regardless of whether it is a one which is traditionally categorized as a service firm or as a product manufacturer or as any other type of organization, faces what can be labelled *service competition*. Service competition can be defined as a competitive situation where the core of a firm's offering – a physical product or a service concept – is a prerequisite only for a sustainable competitive advantage, but where the firm, by taking a service perspective, competes with an *integrated offering* – or more accurately an *integrated service offering* – which also includes all additional resources and activities needed to facilitate the customer's processes in a satisfactory, value-supporting way. If the firm does not function like this, it will not act in a way its customers are expecting. Then the firm's logic and the customers' logic will collide. Firms that manage to support their customers' processes more effectively and efficiently than their competitors will survive in this competitive situation. The challenges are the same for firms operating on business-to-business and business-to-consumer markets, and for firms in what are traditionally called service industries and manufacturing industries. As a matter of fact, the biggest challenge of all is for traditional manufacturers to manage to transform themselves into service businesses and learn how to adopt service logic in management.

In management and marketing books, service firms have always been considered a special case, if considered at all. However, now we are approaching a point where the scale is tipping in the other direction. Service as a perspective on management is becoming the norm, and goods-based logics special cases that may sometimes apply. We are not there yet, and it may still take more time than firms deserve until management attitudes have changed. It is fascinating, and unfortunate, how steadfast the grip of the traditions from the industrial era is on management and all its subfields, and how slowly old and outdated corporate cultures let go. However, in the not-too-distant future the service-led environment and service economy in which firms have already competed for a long time will break down the resistance of the old world attitudes, and management approaches will change. *Inside-out management will be replaced by outside-in management.*

As national statistics demonstrate, in the developed world and beyond, services and what is labelled the service sector dominate economies and employment. No statistical proof is needed anymore to justify a book on service management, and therefore, there are no such statistics in these pages. However, official statistics do not tell the whole truth. Instead they underestimate the role of services. For example, the official figures do not include the many service activities which manufacturing firms produce and perform and which may amount to a remarkable value. If these service activities are removed from the manufacturing sector in the statistics, this sector shrinks dramatically, and the service sector grows correspondingly. Furthermore, when putting statistics aside and considering how large a part of product manufacturers and organizations in the agricultural sector, in reality faces service competition, the importance of service, and of understanding service management, grows even more.

It is my intention that this book will help students and managers to cope with the competitive environment – service competition – which is already here, but which is not yet properly recognized. Furthermore, it will help them to understand the nature and scope of a service perspective and the role of customer relationships therein, the characteristics of service competition, and what adopting service logic demands from management and from the whole organization. The book also demonstrates what it takes to manage the firm and to take care of the firm's customers from the perspective of service logic.

For this fourth edition, in addition to an upgrading of the content warranted by new research, some structural changes have been made. For example, the two first chapters of the previous edition have been merged into a new introductory chapter, where service logic and strategic and tactical aspects of a service and relationship strategy are discussed. The *service profit logic* and the corresponding need for an *outside-in management* approach form the foundation of the service perspective. The chapter on return on service and relationships has been updated with models of *reciprocal return on relationship* (ROR_R), and metrics needed for calculation of reciprocal returns are presented. The use of ROR_R is illustrated with a case study based on research by *Pekka Helle* at Hanken School of Economics. The discussion of the marketing implications of service logic has been further developed. Marketing is understood as customer-focused management with the ultimate goal to *make a firm meaningful to its customers*. The chapter on internal marketing has been restructured. In the chapter on how to transform a manufacturing firm into a service business, a major new case study illustrating such a process has been added. In other chapters some new short cases have also been included. A totally new chapter on *social media in service* written by *Johanna Gummerus* at Hanken School of Economics has also been included. I want to thank her especially for contributing this important chapter.

I also want to thank Aaro Cantell, Ray Fisk, Peter Murphy and Kaj Storbacka, who have contributed to this book with cases and illustrations. I also appreciate the continuous support that Steve Hardman, Georgia King and Juliet Booker from John Wiley & Sons have provided throughout the writing process. Last but not least I would like to acknowledge the support I have received from colleagues at Hanken School of Economics, Finland and from my wife Viveca throughout this endeavour.

Please note that 'he' and 'his' have been used in this book to mean 'he/she' and 'his/her'. This is intended to ensure that the text flows more smoothly and is not meant to be sexist.

Christian Grönroos
Tölö, Finland

CHAPTER 1
THE SERVICE AND RELATIONSHIP IMPERATIVE: MANAGING IN SERVICE COMPETITION

" Everyone faces service competition. By providing service, firms make themselves meaningful for their customers. "

INTRODUCTION

In this introductory chapter the logic of service as a business perspective and the relationship between service and customer interactions are discussed, and the concept of service competition is introduced. Service as a strategy in comparison with other strategic approaches is considered in detail. Strategic and tactical implications of a service strategy and of a relationship approach to customers are outlined. The concept of service logic and its implications for the value generation process and value co-creation are then presented. Further, the meaning of a customer relationship approach and a number of aspects of customer relationships are discussed. Finally, some central aspects of the book are presented as guidelines for the reader. After having read this chapter the reader should understand the logic of service and the characteristics of a service strategy, and know which strategic and tactical implications follow from such a strategy. It should also be clear how value evolves for customers as value-in-use and what roles the firm and customer have in the value process.

ONCE UPON A TIME: A CASE OF SERVICE AND CUSTOMER RELATIONSHIPS

In a village in ancient China there was a young rice merchant, Ming Hua.[1] He was one of six rice merchants in that village. He was sitting in his store waiting for customers, but business was not good.

One day Ming Hua realized that he had to think more about the villagers, what they were doing, their needs and desires, and not just distribute rice to those who came into his store. He understood that he had to provide the villagers with something that was more valuable for them, and something different, from what other merchants offered. He decided to develop a record of his customers' eating habits and ordering periods and to start delivering rice to them. To begin with Ming Hua walked around the village and knocked on the doors of his customers' houses asking:

- how many members there were in the household;
- how many bowls of rice they cooked on any given day; and
- the size of the rice jar in the household.

Then he offered every customer:

- free home delivery; and
- a service to replenish the household's rice jar automatically at regular intervals.

For example, in one household with four persons, every person would consume on average two bowls of rice a day, and therefore the household would need eight bowls of rice every day for their meals. From his records Ming Hua could see that the rice jar of that particular household contained rice for 60 bowls, or approximately one bag of rice, and that a full jar would last for 15 days. Consequently, he offered to deliver a bag of rice every 15 days to this house.

By establishing these records and developing this new service, Ming Hua managed to create more extensive and deeper relationships with the villagers: first with his old customers, then gradually with other villagers. Eventually the size of his business increased and he had to employ more people: one person to keep records of customers, one to take care of book-keeping, one to sell over the counter in the store, and two to take care of deliveries. Ming Hua spent his time visiting villagers and handling contacts with his suppliers, a limited number of rice farmers whom he knew well. Meanwhile his business prospered.

THE NATURE OF SERVICE AND CUSTOMER RELATIONSHIPS

The story of Ming Hua, the rice merchant, demonstrates significant aspects of a service perspective on business, and includes all basic elements of a relationship approach to customers. Key aspects of service are:

- Service is support for customers' individual processes in a way that facilitates their value creation,[2] and this support is enabled when knowledge and skills are used on resources.[3]
- The ultimate goal of service-based business is to facilitate value creation for the customer, which in return enables the service provider to capture value from the relationship,[4] with service as a mediator.
- Service is a process, where the service provider's resources and the customer often interact to some extent.

- To become a service provider, the resources of the firm's offering can be of any kind, such as physical goods (e.g. rice), service activities (services), information, or combinations of these and other types of resources.

Key relationship-based characteristics are:[5]

- The service provider and customer engage in long-term business contact.
- The relationship requires that the service provider gains insight into the customer's everyday processes.
- The goal of the relationship is mutual value creation, i.e. a win–win situation.

As demonstrated, Ming Hua created a process for supporting the villagers' cooking, which made their cooking process easier and acquiring rice more convenient, thus increasing value in their life. At the same time, the rice merchant's business improved, i.e. he managed to capture more value than before from serving the villagers. For this to take place, he had to gain enough knowledge about the villagers' cooking habits and cooking equipment, such as the size of each family and their rice bowls and jars. Once he had this insight, he could develop long-term contact with the villagers and engage them with his new service process. Finally, this arrangement became a win–win situation for both parties.

The story about the rice merchant, shows how, through what today would be called a relationship marketing strategy, he changed his role from a transaction-oriented channel member to a service-providing, value-supporting relationship manager. In that way he created a competitive advantage over rivals who continued to pursue a traditional strategy. Three important *strategic requirements* of a relationship strategy can distinguished:[6]

1. Redefine the business as a *service business* and the key competitive element as *service competition* (competing with service and a total service offering, not just the sale of rice alone).
2. Look at the organization from a *process management perspective* and not from a functionalistic perspective (to manage the process of supporting and facilitating value creation for the villagers, not only to distribute rice).
3. Establish *partnerships* and a *network* to handle the whole service process (close contacts with well-known rice farmers).

As can be seen from the story, three *tactical elements* of a relationship strategy are included:[7]

1. Seek direct contacts with customers and other business partners (such as rice farmers).
2. Build a database covering necessary information about customers and others.
3. Develop a customer-centric service system.

The three strategic requirements set the strategic base for the successful management of relationships. The three tactical elements are required to successfully provide service and implement customer management.

Later on in this chapter, strategic requirements and then the tactical elements will be discussed in some detail. However, using Ming Hua's new service-based relational business as an example, an analysis of the commercial focus of service providers and product distributors will first be made and discussed.

A COMMERCIAL ANALYSIS: FROM PRODUCT-FOCUSED TO SERVICE-FOCUSED MANAGEMENT

A first customer satisfaction-based analysis of a service strategy, Ming Hua's tale, clearly shows that the customers were satisfied, the customer base grew, and the business prospered. However, a customer satisfaction analysis is not enough to understand the effect of a service approach and the implementation of a service strategy. We also have to do a commercial analysis. Basically, the commercial outcome of a business can be described with three elements, namely *revenues, costs and capital*. A firm's profitability is a function of all three elements, whereas the *profit level is a function of the revenue generation capability and the cost level*. Finally, the revenue generation capability is dependent on how well the firm understands its customers and their processes, and how well it manages to gear its resources, such as skills and knowledge, technologies, systems, products and service activities, towards supporting its customers' processes and goals in life (consumer markets) or business (business-to-business markets). In the continued analysis, we exclude the influence of capital, and analyse the impact on the profit equation of various management approaches.

In Chapter 3 on *the service profit logic and service management principles*, the profit logic in service is analysed in detail. At this point we only note that a service provider's revenue generation capability is not only dependent on sales and traditional marketing of a more or less standardized product. Because the customer interface is much broader than that, the customers' interest in paying for the firm's service is influenced by a whole host of other activities and processes managed by the service provider. For example, in the rice merchant's story, selling rice is not enough for the new service strategy to succeed; the rice delivery system supported by the customer information system as a service process is the most important reason why customers wanted to buy from Ming Hua.

For understanding the business from a commercial point of view, therefore, two variables are enough, namely the *profit variable* and the *process variable*. A chart for analysing the business from a commercial perspective based on these two variables is illustrated in Figure 1.1, with the profit variable as the vertical scale and the process variable as the horizontal scale.

The end points of the profit and resource variables, respectively, are the following:

- Dominating focus on *revenues and revenue generation*, or dominating focus on *costs*.

- Dominating focus on *the firm's resources and processes*, or dominating focus on *the customers' resources and processes*.

It is important to realize the customers' focus is always, with few exceptions, in the *upper right quadrant* of Figure 1.1, 'focus on revenues (and revenue generation)/focus on the customers' resources and processes'. The reason for this is simple. Customers are interested in the *price* they are requested to pay for a solution, and of course also in *their own processes* which they want to have supported: for example, in what life or business processes are they involved and what do they wish to achieve, what skills and knowledge to make use of a solution offered to them do they hold and what complementary resources required to make use of the solution offered do they have access to? Hence, *a firm's customers are always interested in the firm's revenues and revenue generation capability*. It is ironic that far too often firms are more interested in their cost level and in focusing on cost efficiency, and consequently, a clash with the customers' interests occurs.

Frequently, another clash between firms and their customers also happens. The customers are, of course, more or less only interested in their own resources and processes. Firms, on the other hand,

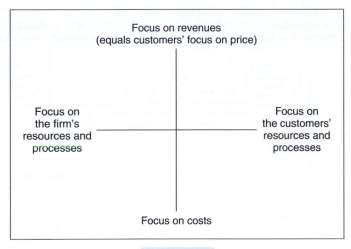

FIGURE 1.1

Chart for analysing commercial focus.

are often predominantly focused on their own resources and processes, and gather only too-superficial market research data about their customers, but limited insight into the customers' processes, goals, and thoughts which steer their buying and usage/consumption behaviour.

If these conflicts occur, a firm – its management and the whole organization – is mentally positioned in the *lower left quadrant* of Figure 1.1, whereas its customers are mentally positioned in the *upper right quadrant*. First of all, *it is a mental positioning*, which reflects, respectively, the dominating thoughts and dominating focus of interest of a firm and its management, and of the customers. However, this mental focus influences how the firm is managed and how its processes are implemented, and it reflects the customers' buying behaviour as well.

SERVICE MANAGEMENT REQUIRES AN OUTSIDE-IN MANAGEMENT APPROACH

In the four parts of Figure 1.2, various positions of firms in the commercial analysis chart of Figure 1.1 are depicted, depending on their mental managerial and operational foci. In the upper left corner of Figure 1.2 *(Part A)* customers' typical mental focus is positioned in the upper left quadrant, with a dominating interest in their own resources and processes as well as in the price they are required to pay, and therefore also, indirectly, in the firm's revenue generating capability.

In *Part B* of the figure, in the upper right corner, the different mental foci and the corresponding business approach of the rice merchants in the village are illustrated, as examples of typical firms' positions. The focus of the traditional merchants is in the *lower left quadrant*, where the business is based on an interest in the firm's own resources (rice) and processes (rice-selling shops), and a focus on the costs of running the business is dominatant, i.e. the business is based on selling the product (rice). Ming Hua, however, moved his focus towards the *upper right quadrant* by turning to a strategy of developing relationships with his customers and providing service to them. Doing this required a shift of interest from his old processes of selling rice from a shop to understanding the customers'

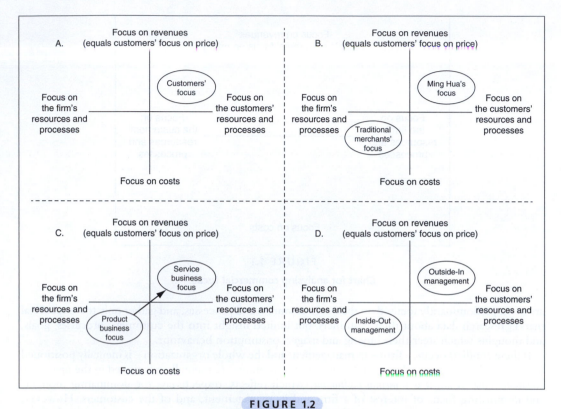

FIGURE 1.2

From product-focused inside-out management to service-focused outside-in management.

relevant processes and resources, such as their cooking routines and sizes of rice cups and jars. Based on this customer insight, he adjusted his own processes from selling rice from a shop to servicing the customers by delivering rice to their homes according to a customized schedule, and to creating a network of rice farmers to make sure that he had products to deliver. To make his business prosper, which it did, he of course also had to adjust his cost level to the revenue generation capability of the new service strategy.

In the lower left corner of Figure 1.2 *(Part C)* the two strategies described above are summarized. If, as illustrated by the *lower left quadrant of Part C*, management's and the organization's mental focus is dominated by an interest in the firm's own resources (e.g. technologies and products) and processes, and by an overwhelming concern for costs and cost efficiency, the firm's business approach will be driven by its resources, and overly focused on delivering such resources to its customers. This can be characterized as a *product business focus*, regardless of whether the core of the offering is a physical good or a service activity, such as rice or, say, transportation. In the *upper right quadrant of Part C*, a *service business focus* is positioned. Such a business approach is characterized by a dominating focus on gaining in–depth insight into the customers' processes and resources (e.g. skills, capabilities and access to complementary resources) and on how revenues are generated for the firm.

Firms are often mentally in the lower left quadrant and take a product business focus. This applies equally to so–called service firms, such as banks, insurance companies, airlines and those in hospitality industries, and organizations in the public sector, and to goods manufacturers. It is not the core of the offering that determines what kind of business a firm is conducting; *it is the mental focus of management and the organization that counts.* A firm that wants to move towards adopting a service strategy and pursuing a service perspective in its business performance must follow the black arrow in *Part C* of the figure, and change its mental focus and corresponding behaviour accordingly. In this way any firm, regardless of its business or industry, can transform itself into a service business.

Finally, in *Part D* of Figure 1.2, in the lower right corner, the underpinning logic of, respectively, a product business and a service business is characterized. A *service business logic* is basically grounded in *a dominating interest in thoroughly understanding the processes and resources of the firm's customers, and in its revenue generation capabilities.* Of course, this does not mean that a focus on the firm's own resources and processes and on cost efficiency would be less important than otherwise. In absolute terms they are equally important as before but, *relatively speaking*, focus on the customer and revenues is more important. Hence, service business management can be characterized as *outside-in management.* In contrast, product business management with its dominating interest in issues internal to the firm, such as the firm's resources, processes and costs, can be characterized as *inside-out management.*

In conclusion, *service management requires a mental focus on customers and revenues, and an outside-in management approach.* In Table 1.1 fundamental differences between a service-focused outside-in management approach and a product-focused inside-out approach are summarized.

In view of the preceding discussion, the two first rows of the table – core competence and core process – are self-explanatory. However, the two sales-related issues require some clarification. In conventional product selling based on an inside-out approach, the technical specifications qualify the offering. However, as there often are several competitors offering similar technical solutions, price becomes the distinguishing sales argument. In *service selling*, regardless of whether the core of the offering is a physical good or a service concept, the aim of the total offering is to provide value-creating support for the customers' processes and thereby contribute to their goal achievement. Hence, the offering's *value-creating support becomes the qualifying characteristic.* As price is only one element of customer value (this is developed further in Chapter 6 on *return on service and relationships*),

---

TABLE 1.1

Fundamental differences between outside-in and inside-out management.

	Outside-in management	Inside-out management
Core competence	Understanding customers' everyday processes and how they affect their life/business goals.	Understanding technology, products and production processes.
Core process	Providing value-creating support to the customers' everyday processes, which contributes to their life/business goals.	Production of goods and/or services.
Major sales pitch	Value-creating support.	Product (goods or services) specifications.
Determining sales argument	Long-term value for customers relating to their life/business goals.	Price.

other sacrifice-related or revenue-related elements may well compensate for a high price. For example, an unattractive price can be balanced by lower operational and/or administrative costs in the long run, and also by the prospect of growing sales and/or increasing revenues. Therefore, *long-term value is the determinant sales argument*.

In the following sections, the strategic and tactical requirements of a service strategy based on customer relationships referred to above will be discussed in some detail. The three strategic requirements – redefining the firm as service business, taking a process management perspective, and developing partnerships and networks – set the strategic base for the successful management of relationships. The three tactical elements – seeking direct contacts with customers, building customer insight, and developing a customer-focused service system – are required to successfully implement customer management.

DEFINING THE FIRM AS A SERVICE BUSINESS

A key requirement in a service and relationship strategy is that a manufacturer, wholesaler, retailer, service firm or supplier has a thorough insight into the customers' everyday processes, and into the relationship between them and the customers' life or business processes, and the long-term needs and desires of their customers. Another requirement is that value-supporting service is offered based on the technical solutions imbedded in consumer goods and industrial equipment, or in service activities. The core of a service firm's offering is by definition a service activity, but if it takes an inside-out management approach, such a firm may nevertheless operate as a product business.

The service approach to customers applies to any type of firm, and if they choose to do it, any firm – so-called service firms and goods manufacturers alike – can adopt a service strategy. *Customers do not only look for goods or services, they demand a much more holistic service offering,* including everything from information about how best to use a product, to delivering, installing, updating, repairing, maintaining and correcting solutions they have bought. Moreover, they demand all this, and much more, to be delivered in a friendly, trustworthy and timely manner.

In a customer relationship that goes beyond a single transaction of goods or services, the product itself as a technical solution involving goods, service activities or industrial equipment becomes just one element in the *holistic ongoing service to the customers*. For a goods manufacturing firm, the physical good is a core element of the service offering, because it is a prerequisite for a successful service. For a service firm it is the service concept. In today's competitive situation this core is very seldom sufficient to produce successful results and a lasting position in the marketplace. What counts is the ability of the firm, regardless of its position in the distribution channel, to manage the additional elements of the offering better than its competitors. Moreover, the core physical product or service concept is less often the reason for dissatisfaction than the elements surrounding the core. For example, when buying a car, the car is seldom the reason for customer dissatisfaction; the after-sales service is the main reason. Or in a restaurant, the meal may be good but poor service is the reason for dissatisfaction. In other words, competing with the core product or service concept is not enough; competing with the total offering, where the core of the offering is only one element of a total service offering, is what counts. The transition from the product or service concept as the dominating element of the offering to management of human resources, technology, knowledge and time in order for the firm to create successful market offerings is evident.

In Figure 1.3 the thick black arrow from the factory or back office of a service firm out towards the customer demonstrates the traditional product-oriented approach, where the factory (and the management of what takes place in the factory) is considered the key to success in the marketplace.

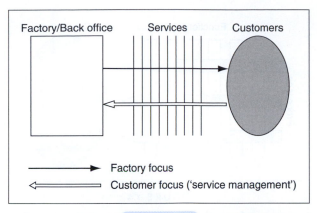

FIGURE 1.3

A customer focus: the firm as a service business.
Source: Grönroos, C., Relationship marketing logic.
Asia–Australia Marketing Journal, **4**(1); 1996:
p. 13. Reproduced by the permission of the ANZMAC
(The Australasia and New Zealand Marketing Academy).

For a manufacturing firm, services are considered add-ons to the factory output. In service firms interactions in the service process are often considered less important to the customer than what is produced in the back office. This management approach is based on a factory or back office focus. Although this approach to management may have been highly successful in the past, it does not reflect the current competitive situation, where a new management perspective is needed. As indicated by the second arrow in the figure, from the customer towards the factory or back office, the various service elements of the firm are the first elements of the output of the firm that the customer encounters and experiences. These service processes support the customer's perception of value, whereas the factory or back office output is only a prerequisite for value.

A growing number of industries, manufacturers and service firms now face a competitive situation for which we have coined the term *service competition.* They have to understand the nature of *service management* as a management approach geared to the demands of the new competitive situation. *The solution to customer problems seen as a total service offering thus becomes service,* and this total offering becomes service provision, instead of mere delivery of a physical product or a service. When service competition is the key to success for everybody, the firm has to offer service, irrespective of its traditional business, and consequently *every business is a service business.*

A PROCESS MANAGEMENT PERSPECTIVE

An ongoing relationship with customers, where customers look for value support by the total service offering, requires internal collaboration among departments that are responsible for different elements of the offering, such as the core product (goods or services), advertising the product, delivering the product, taking care of complaints and rectifying mistakes and quality faults, maintaining the product, billing routines, product documentation, etc. The whole chain of activities has to be co-ordinated and managed as a total process. Moreover, from profitability and productivity perspectives only activities that support value for customers should be carried out. Other resources and activities should

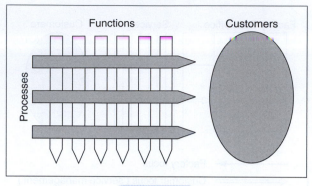

FIGURE 1.4

A process focus: the firm as a value-generating operation.
Source: Grönroos, C., Relationship marketing logic.
Asia–Australia Marketing Journal, **4**(1); 1996: p. 14.
Reproduced by permission of the ANZMAC
(The Australasia and New Zealand Marketing Academy).

be excluded from the process. In a traditional functionalistic organizational setting this cannot be achieved. Therefore, *a service and relationship approach to customers requires a process management approach.*

A process management perspective is very different from the functionalistic management approach. A functionalistic organization allows for sub-optimization, because every activity and corresponding department within a company is more oriented towards specialization within departments than collaboration between them. As indicated in Figure 1.4, the various departments do not necessarily direct their efforts towards the demands and expectations of the customers. This does not necessarily support customers' total requirements. Customers do not look for a combination of sub-optimized outputs of different departments of a firm that is not supporting total value for them. For example, an outstanding technical solution and a cost-effective transportation system may be optimal from the supplier's point of view, but for the customer it is often equivalent to an unreliable supplier. An unreliable supplier equals low value for the customer.

Project and task force organizations are first attempts to break free from the strait-jacket of a functionalistic organization, so that the various departments are geared towards working according to the horizontal arrows in the figure. However, in order to be able to create maximum total value in a coordinated relationship with customers, the firm should strive to go further. A process management approach should be taken. In such an approach traditional departmental boundaries are torn down and the workflow (including, for example, traditional sales and marketing activities, production, logistics, general administration and distribution activities with a host of customer contact activities involved) is organized and managed as a value-supporting process that enables and strengthens relationship-building and management.

PARTNERSHIPS AND NETWORKS

A service and relationship approach to customers is based on cooperation. Service providers and customers will not view each other from a win–lose perspective but will rather benefit from a win–win situation, where the parties involved will be best off as partners. Furthermore, frequently manufacturing and service firms will find that they cannot by themselves supply customers with a total offering needed, and that it is too expensive to acquire the necessary additional knowledge and resources to produce the required elements of the offering themselves. Hence, it may be more effective and profitable to find a partner who can offer the complementary elements of the offering needed to develop a successful relationship with a customer. *Partnerships and networks of firms are formed horizontally and vertically in the distribution channel and in the supply chain.* Although firms compete with each other, they may sometimes find it effective and profitable to collaborate in some areas to serve mutual customers. This of course demands the existence of one key ingredient of relationship marketing; *trust* between the parties in a network. Otherwise they will not feel committed to the mutual cause.

The next sections turn to the tactical elements of relationship marketing.

SEEKING DIRECT CONTACTS WITH CUSTOMERS

A service and relationship approach to customers is based on a notion of trusting cooperation between the business partners. Hence, firms have to get to know their customers much better than has normally been the case. In an extreme situation, which is quite possible in many consumer service markets such as household insurance and industrial markets such as merchant banking and industrial equipment provision, a firm can treat each customer individually. At the other extreme of consumer goods and mass markets, customers cannot be identified in the same way. However, the manufacturer or retailer should develop systems that provide them with as much insight about their customers' processes and behaviours as possible so that, for example, advertising campaigns, sales contacts and every interaction with customers can be made as relationship-oriented as possible. Modern information technology provides the firm with ample opportunities to develop ways of showing a customer that he is known and valued. Also, traditional advertising campaigns become too expensive and ineffective if they are not directed towards customers so that a dialogue can be initiated. One-way market communication costs too much and produces too little.

Regardless of how close a firm can get to the situation of knowing and treating customers as individuals, one should always use face-to-face contacts with customers or means provided by information technology to get as close as possible to customers. In every face-to-face service encounter, regardless of whether there is a mass market of customers or not, *the firm interacts with each customer as an individual* and should treat the customer as an individual and not as a member of a mass. In addition, each such encounter is a source of insight into the customer's processes, thoughts, needs, wishes and values. This is a source of customer information which most often is unused.

DEVELOPING A CUSTOMER DATABASE

Traditionally, marketing operates with limited and incomplete information about customers. In order to pursue a relationship marketing strategy, a firm cannot let such ignorance last. A customer information database must be established, which can be turned into actionable knowledge about the customers. If such a database does not exist, customer contacts will only be handled partially in a relationship-oriented manner. If the person involved in a particular interaction with a customer has first-hand information about the customer and knows the person he is in contact with, the interaction may go well. However, in many situations – for example, employees who answer customers' phone calls, meet customers at a reception desk or make maintenance calls – they will not personally know the customer. A well-prepared, updated, easily retrievable and easy-to-read customer information file is needed in such cases to make it possible for the employee to pursue a relationship-oriented customer contact. In addition, a good database will be an effective support for cross-sales and new product offerings.

In addition to their primary use to maintain customer relationships, databases can be used for a variety of marketing activities, such as segmenting the customer base, tailoring marketing activities, generating profiles of customer types, supporting service activities and identifying likely purchasers.

A customer information database should also include profitability information, so that one knows the long-term profitability of customers in the database. If such long-term profitability information is lacking, the firm may easily include segments of unprofitable customers in its customer base.

CREATING A CUSTOMER-ORIENTED SERVICE SYSTEM

Successful customer management demands that the firm defines its business as a service business and understands how to create and manage a total service offering, i.e. it adopts a service strategy. The organization's processes thus have to be designed to make it possible to serve customers and produce and deliver a total service offering. In other words, the firm has to know and practise *service management*. The philosophy and principles of service management are in many respects different from those of a traditional management philosophy. In Chapter 3 we will discuss such differences. Four types of resources are central to the development of a successful service system: customers, technology, employees and time.

Customers take a much more active role than they normally do. The perceived quality of the service offering partly depends on the impact of the customer. The service system is increasingly built upon *technology*. Computerized systems and information technology used in design, production, administration, service and maintenance have to be designed from a customer-oriented perspective, and not only from internal production and productivity-oriented viewpoints. The success of relationship marketing is highly dependent on the attitudes, commitment and performance of the *employees*. If they are not committed to their role as true service employees and are not motivated to perform in a customer-oriented fashion, the strategy fails. Hence, success in the external marketplace requires success internally in motivating employees and making them committed to the pursuit of a relationship marketing strategy. Marketing based on a service and relationship strategy is, therefore, highly dependent on a well-organized and continuous *internal marketing* process. Internal marketing will be discussed in some detail in Chapter 14. *Time* is also a critical resource. Customers have to feel that the time they spend on their relationship with a supplier or service firm is not wasted. Badly managed time creates extra costs for all parties in a relationship.

CUSTOMER VALUE AND VALUE CREATION

Value is an elusive concept, and it has been approached and defined in many different ways. In some situations, especially but not only in business-to-business markets, it can be measured in monetary terms. In other contexts, mostly in consumer markets, value is merely a perception. However, even when value is calculated in monetary terms, there is often this element to it, for example perceived ease of doing business with a firm, or trust in a firm. A value perception can be based on experiences with a service provider in a variety of different ways.[8] Here we do not go into the various ways value can be calculated or perceived. Instead we define value in a simple but practical way as *'being better off'*. More value means that a customer, after having been supported by a service provider, is or feels better off than before.[9] What 'better off' means in any given situation must be analysed and, if possible, calculated. In Chapter 6, *Return on service and relationships*, how to calculate value for both a customer and the service provider is discussed and appropriate metrics presented. It should be observed that a customer does not always have positive experiences, and sometimes the customer may also be 'worse off', which means that value deterioration has taken place, at least temporarily.

Service management requires a customer-focused outside-in approach. Value for customers, and the service provider's capability to support its customers' processes in a way that enables the customers to create value and achieve their goals, are key aspects of outside-in service management. In marketing, value for customers has for decades been considered a key aspect of service management,[10] which has been re-emphasized during the past few decades.[11]

Traditionally, value creation is seen as a value chain,[12] which is dominated by various activities of a supplier, whereas the role of customers is marginalized and often neglected. This model of value creation is based on a labour theory view of value, according to which value is gradually worked on in the supplier's processes, or in a wider context in a supply chain's different processes. As a result, value is considered embedded in the supplier's output, and materializes when customers pay money for this output. Therefore, this value concept is labelled *value-in-exchange*. Normann and Ramírez, suggesting a *value constellation* model,[13] were the first to criticize this view as being provider-centric, excluding the important impact on value by other parties in the supplier-customer ecosystem, and by the customers as users of the output.

As we have demonstrated, all kinds of resources can be offered as service, and as Gummesson[14] points out, *are used by customers as service that renders value for them*. This is supported by Normann and Ramírez,[15] who emphasize that a defining aspect of a service perspective is '. . . the role (or roles) that the seller plays in helping customers to create value for themselves'. According to the contemporary view, *value for customers is created by the customer in the customer's processes, supported by the resources and processes of service providers*. This notion leads to an alternative value concept based on utility theory labelled *value-in-use*, meaning that value for a customer is created during usage. Another notable difference between value-in-use and value-in-exchange is that value-in-exchange materializes at one particular point of time, i.e. when a sale is concluded and money is paid for the resource, whereas *value-in-use evolves over time during the usage or consumption process*.[16]

Another important difference between the two concepts is that value-in-exchange is always positive on some level determined by the price paid, whereas the evolvement of value-in-use can be *both positive, 'value creation; better off', and negative, 'value destruction; worse off'*.[17]

In conclusion we may state that customers do not buy goods or services, or any other resources or resource constellations as such, but instead the service the resources can provide them with, which enables value creation in their processes.[18] *Resources provided to customers over time in a relationship are only facilitators of value*. As service providers get in touch with their customers and direct interactions between the provider's resources and the customer occur, the service provider will engage with the customer's processes and have opportunities to influence them. Consequently, we can conclude that *value for customers is created throughout the relationship by the customer, partly in interactions between the customer and the supplier or service provider*.[19] The focus is not on the resources, such as goods or services, but on the customers' processes where value creation occurs.[20]

VALUE CREATION AND THE VALUE-GENERATING PROCESS

In 1993 Normann and Ramírez pointed out that several parties, such as a supplier, subcontractors to the supplier, financing institutions and the customer itself, contribute to the value that in the end emerges for the customer.[21] Some ten years later, Vargo and Lusch stated the same conclusion in their *service-dominant logic* of value creation and marketing by claiming that customers and firms are always co-creators of value.[22] However, as service–dominant logic is more of a systemic approach on a societal level, discussing value co-creation in a metaphorical manner, it is less applicable for management practice. Here we use the management-oriented view of value creation of the *service logic* approach instead. It provides concepts and instruments that help managers to understand the different roles and goals in value creation of service providers and customers, respectively.[23] In Appendix 1, similarities and differences between service logic and service-dominant logic are summarized.[24]

As value for a customer is defined as value-in-use and created by the customer, from a management point of view it is important to clearly define *what the service provider does* and *what the customer does* in the total process of creating value for the customer. This total process can be labelled *value generation*. The value-generation process and its sub-processes are illustrated in Figure 1.5.

As the figure demonstrates, the value generation process can be divided into three spheres: a *customer sphere*, a *provider sphere*, and a *joint sphere*. From a management point of view, keeping these value creation spheres apart is important, because the roles and goals of the service provider and customer respectively differ between spheres.

The customer's creation of value-in-use takes place in the customer and joint spheres. In the *customer sphere* two types of value creation take place:

- The customer creates value independently from the service provider.

- The customer engages in social value co-creation with members of his ecosystem, such as family, friends, business associates, or social media connections.

Independent value creation means that the customer makes use of acquired resources, such as goods or services or combinations of these and other resources, and integrates them with other available and

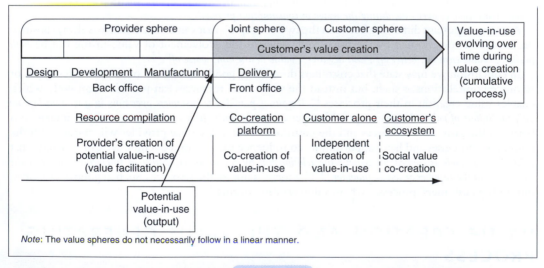

Note: The value spheres do not necessarily follow in a linear manner.

FIGURE 1.5

Value generation process: value creation and co-creation according to the service logic.
Source: Adapted from Grönroos, C. and Voima, P., Critical service logic: making sense of value creation and co-creation. *Journal of the Academy of Marketing Science*, **41**(2); 2013: p. 136. With kind permission from Springer Science and Business Media.

needed resources in a usage process. The customer *interacts only indirectly* with the firm through its products and non-interactive systems which do not respond in more than one way when operated on by the customer. Most products and systems, but of course not all, are like that.

Social value co-creation means that a customer interacts with people in his social ecosystem, and during these interactions the value that evolves for the customer from using goods and services may change in any direction. The customer may become better off or worse off.[25]

The *joint sphere* refers to the part of the service process where the customer *directly interacts* with the service provider. During these direct interactions the provider's process and the customer's process do not run in parallel *but merge into one interactive, collaborative and dialogical process*. In this merged process the two parties relate to each other, work together and communicate in a dialogical fashion. The two parties in the process engage with each other's processes.[26] Hence, they may directly influence each other's perception of value created in the interactions through communication, actions and reactions. During this merged interactive process a *co-creation platform* is formed. On this co-creation platform such interactions occur, and they enable *the service provider to engage with the customer's value-creating process and influence this process, and thus co-create value together with the customer*.

From a management standpoint, value co-creation between the customer and the service provider occurs *only* when a co-creation platform has been formed and direct interactions between the two parties take place. Furthermore, it should be observed *that it is the customer who drives and is in charge of the value creation process*. On the co-creation platform the service provider can be invited to join this process as a value co-creator, but if the customer does not want to listen to the provider, and to communicate and work with the provider, no co-creation takes place. It is the customer's decision.[27] For example, in a restaurant, a guest may choose to listen to the waiter's explanation about why an item on the menu is missing, and based on a dialogue with the waiter moderate a negative feeling of value, or he may choose not to listen and his value experience will remain negative. In the former situation, the customer invites the provider to co-create value with him, but in the latter situation he does not allow co-creation.

Other than value co-creation in such direct interactions, what is the service provider's role and goal in the value generation process? In the *provider sphere* the firm compiles resources, such as products, services, information and other types, or resource constellations, which are offered to customers. These offerings include *potential value-in-use* as an output from the firm's resource compilation process. The service provider's *goal* is *to facilitate the customer's creation of value-in-use* by providing value-supporting resources as *potential value-in-use*, which this customer may convert into *realized value-in-use* in their own sphere.[28] If and only if a co-creation platform of direct interactions exists or can be established, in addition to the role of value facilitator the service provider may also co-create value-in-use with its customers.[29]

In conclusion, according to a *service logic*:

- The customer is the *value creator* (of value-in-use) *in the customer sphere* and *in the joint sphere* (if such a sphere has been established).

- The service provider is fundamentally a *value facilitator in the provider sphere* through resource compilation aimed at provision of potential value-in-use.

- Provided that direct interactions between the firm and the customer occur or can be created, a co-creation platform is formed, and the service provider has an opportunity to engage with the customer's value-creating process and *co-create value with the customer* as well *in the joint sphere*.

- If interactions between the customer and people in his ecosystem occur, *social value co-creation* takes place *in the customer sphere*.

In the following section the co-creation platform will be discussed and two models of value co-creation presented.

MODELS OF VALUE CO-CREATION

There have been some attempts to develop models of value co-creation, but this has turned out to be difficult, probably because co-creation has been considered an omnipresent phenomenon in the relationship between a firm and a customer, where everything is co-creation. In this section we present models of value co-creation, which are based on the *service logic* view, according to which co-creation of value requires a co-creation platform of direct interactions between a service provider and a customer. Value co-creation is a reciprocal process. On the co-creation platform it is not only the firm that may influence the customer's value creation; it works the other way as well. In addition to the price paid for service, the customer may also provide other value-supporting service in return, such as feedback about how the provider's systems function and information about how to improve them to make them more competitive.

Hence, two models of value co-creation are presented, one about *value for the customer*, and a reverse model about *value for the service provider*. In Figure 1.6 a model of co-creating value for the customer,

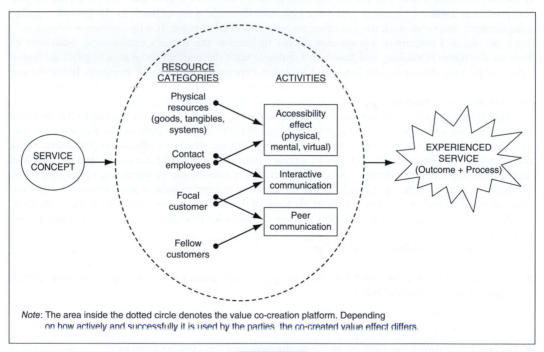

Note: The area inside the dotted circle denotes the value co-creation platform. Depending on how actively and successfully it is used by the parties, the co-created value effect differs.

FIGURE 1.6

Value co-creation: value for the customer.
Source: Grönroos, C., Conceptualising value co-creation: a journey to the 1970s and back to the future. *Journal of Marketing Management*, **28**(13–14); 2012: p. 1528. Reproduced by permission of Taylor & Francis.

based on the *servuction model* by Eiglier and Langeard and the *interactive marketing model* by Grönroos, is illustrated.[30] The servuction model provides the *resource categories* to the left in the circle in the middle of the figure. The different *activities* to the right in this circle are suggested in the interactive marketing model.

The model moves from the left to the right. The starting point is a governing *service concept*, which states what the service provider attempts to do for its customers. There are four resource categories: *physical resources*, including goods, other tangible elements and systems, and of course also IT-based technologies,[31] *contact employees* interacting with the customers, the *focal customer*, for whom service is provided, and *fellow customers* simultaneously present in the service process.

In the direct interactions between the resources on the co-creation platform, three types of influence on the focal customer's value creation may take place. *The physical resources* and *contact employees* create an *accessibility effect* in the service process, which makes the service easier or more complicated to access and use, and therefore influences the customer's perception of the service. This effect may be physical, mental, or even virtual. *The contact employees* and *the focal customer* engage in a dialogical *interactive communication*, which also influences the focal customer's perception of the service. Finally, *the focal customer* and *fellow customers* may communicate with each other *(peer communication)*, which can have a similar effect. These influences on the service have a continuous separate and/or combined effect on the focal customer's *service experience*, both with the outcome of the service process and with the process itself (in Chapter 4, *Service and relationship quality*, the quality effects of the outcome and the service process will be further discussed). The focal customer's co-created value perception is grounded in this experience, and *may continue to evolve* during an independent value creation and social value co-creation phase that may follow.

As an example, we can think about a restaurant. The waiter (contact employee) and the various physical resources and systems, such as the food, tables and chairs, atmospheric artefacts, menus and serving and paying systems, and other resources, together make the restaurant service *accessible* both from a physical and mental standpoint. In the interactions between the restaurant guest as the focal customer and the waiter, the guest asks, for example, clarifying questions about items on the menu, the waiter responds and makes suggestions, and on top of that non-task related communication may take place. These discussions form *interactive communication* between the guest and the contact employee. If there are fellow customers in the restaurant, the guest may discuss the restaurant or the menu with them, or the behaviour of fellow customers may in many other ways communicate something, good or bad, about being in the restaurant. For example, too noisy a company at a nearby table may create negative communication. All this is *peer communication*.

The various activities exemplified above in a restaurant context form a co-creation platform with direct interactions. These various types of interactions form the restaurant guest's, the focal customer's, experience with the restaurant service. This experience makes the customer better off in various degrees, or in a negative situation, worse off. Hence, *value-in-use co-created by the resources on the co-creation platform emerges*. After the customer has left the restaurant, this value may evolve further, for example, when he continues to think about it or about an element of it, such as the excellent food or impeccable service.

However, continuing the restaurant example, value is not only co-created for the customer. Co-created value may flow in the other direction as well, forming a reverse value co-creation model. Figure 1.7 includes a model of *co-creating value for the service provider*.

In this model, as illustrated by the figure, the value process moves from right to left. The starting point is the *customer's participation* in the restaurant's service process. In this reverse value co-creation model there are three resource categories: *physical resources and systems*, the *customer*, and *contact employees*. The activities in the value co-creation process are *accessibility* of customer feedback and

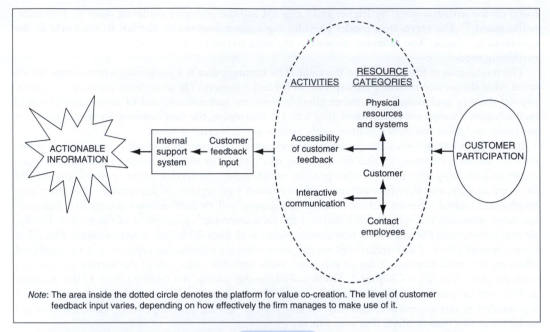

Note: The area inside the dotted circle denotes the platform for value co-creation. The level of customer feedback input varies, depending on how effectively the firm manages to make use of it.

FIGURE 1.7

Value co-creation in service: value for the service provider.
Source: Grönroos, C., Conceptualising value co-creation: a journey to the 1970s and back to the future. *Journal of Marketing Management*, **28**(13–14); 2012: p. 1530. Reproduced by permission of Taylor & Francis.

interactive communication. The output of this reverse model is *actionable information* which the firm can use for developing its resources, systems and processes, and even its service concept. The amount of information depends on how prepared the firm is to register *customer feedback.* There must be some kind of *internal support system* – either formal or informal, but still supporting an internal flow of customer feedback – for registering feedback and analysing it and turning it into actionable information and knowledge.

In the restaurant example, the customer interacts with the waiter and other employees, and *interactive communication* occurs. This communication may include either direct complaints or direct suggestions about improvements, or it may in a more subtle way include ideas for future use. If the contact employees are encouraged to gather such information, and have the skill to do it, and if there is a system for registering it for management use, this is *co-created value for the restaurant.*

Furthermore, in addition to interactions with the waiter, the customer also interacts with and perceives the many physical resources and systems of the restaurant. Sometimes the customer does not voice his perceptions of these interactions with contact employees and physical resources and systems in interactive communication with employees, but still he wants to make them known to the service provider. In order to make such feedback information *accessible* to the restaurant, or any firm, an easily usable system for customer complaints and feedback through various means should be used. Internet-based systems for gathering *customer feedback* are frequently used, but old-fashioned paper-based systems can also exist. The important thing is that customers who did not want to give feedback directly, for example in the restaurant, or who later came to think about something to communicate, should be offered an easily accessible feedback system, which in turn makes the feedback information *accessible to the firm*.[32]

If the firm manages to register customer feedback information either based on interactive communication *during* the service process or from a feedback system that makes it easy to give feedback *after* the service process, then actionable information to be used to change or improve the service process or some part of it, or to develop the service concept, is accessed. This is a reverse value co-creation process, which gives the provider valuable means for improving its operations.

THE SERVICE PERSPECTIVE

Here and in the following sections we will discuss in more detail what a service perspective on business means, and contrast this perspective with three other strategic perspectives.

Many firms fall into the trap of competing with low prices, which may sometimes be effective, but most often is a way of giving away the revenue that is needed to create and maintain a sustainable advantage over the competition. Price is never a sustainable advantage. As soon as a competitor can offer a lower price, the customer will be gone. Every firm, regardless of whether its core product is a physical good or a service, or whether the firm is operating in consumer markets or business-to-business markets, has the option of taking a service perspective. A service perspective will enable management to see different opportunities to create a competitive advantage compared with other strategic perspectives, and more importantly, it forces the firm to get closer to its customers and acquire much more insight about the customers' life and business than is normally the case. *By adopting a service perspective and providing service, the likelihood that a firm becomes meaningful for its customers increases.*

THE SERVICE PERSPECTIVE COMPARED WITH OTHER STRATEGIC PERSPECTIVES

Firms can choose from a number of strategic perspectives, of which a service perspective is one. For example, four major strategic perspectives can be distinguished as follows:

- Service perspective.
- Core product perspective.
- Price perspective.
- Image perspective.

First, the three comparison perspectives will be described briefly, followed by the service perspective.

A *core product perspective* is a traditional scientific management-based approach,[33] where the quality of the core solution is considered to be the main source of competitive advantage. A firm that, for example, has a sustainable technological advantage can benefit from applying such a perspective. The core product is supposed to be the sole or major carrier of potential value for customers. In such cases, services or singular service activities may be included as necessary elements in customer relationships, but their role is not strategic. A firm that adopts a core product perspective without having a technological advantage often falls into the price trap. In the long run, this is not a sustainable strategy. Such a core product perspective is often also adopted by service firms, such as banks and insurance companies, where the core service, for example a loan concept or an insurance policy, is considered the key source of competitive advantage. In a competitive situation, this seldom works well. Such a service firm reverts to being a product firm taking an *inside-out management* approach.

Taking a *price perspective* means that the firm considers a continuously low price to be the major means of competition. If a sustainable cost advantage can be achieved and maintained, this is a possible perspective to take. The firm may still obtain an acceptable profit margin so that it can invest in its future. However, if the cost advantage is lost, a strategic approach based on a price perspective becomes dangerous. Prices are pressed further down by the competition, and the firm loses its chance to develop for the future. Adopting a price strategy leads to an *inside-out management* approach. Such a strategy works if the customers accept the lower level of service which goes with the lower price.

An *image perspective* will make the firm use mostly marketing communications to create imaginary values in addition to the potential value of the core offering. For some types of goods and services – for example, fashion products such as designer clothes and perfumes, some consumer packaged goods such as soft drinks and some service such as fast-food restaurants – an image approach has been effective. Such a strategic approach requires there to be an attractive and functioning core product as a starting point. The offering also easily becomes very dependent on the imaginary extras created by the firm's marketing strategy. If the firm stops reinforcing them, they may eventually deteriorate to just another physical product or service in the marketplace. Therefore, pursuing an image strategy demands continuous heavy investment in marketing communication. If the firm cannot afford this, the offering (consisting of a core physical good or service and a weakening image-boosting support) will lose its attractiveness, and competitors who can continue to invest extensively in marketing communication will take over. Also in an image strategy management is easily dominated by *an inside-out approach*.

A service perspective is based on an outside-in management approach, whereby the firm aims to support its customers' everyday processes in a way that facilitates value creation in individual customers' life processes and business-to-business customers' business processes. The core solution, whether a physical good or a service, has to be good enough to provide a competitive advantage, but this is not enough for success in the marketplace, or in the digital marketspace. What creates a sustainable competitive advantage is the development of every element of the customer relationship, including all types of resources and processes, into one overall service offering. The driving force is the service perspective, according to which customers are served with a value-supporting combination of goods and services, additional separately billable services, such as repair and maintenance, and other non-billable services, such as invoicing, complaints handling, advice and personal attention, information and other value-supporting components. This situation can be described as service competition.[34] This is a competitive situation where the core solution is the prerequisite for success, but where the management of a number of other required resources, together with the core solution, forms a total service offering, aiming at supporting customer processes. The total service offering determines whether or not the firm will be successful. This book is about how to manage an organization and its customer relationships in service competition.

The central requirement of management in service competition is to appreciate the service perspective as a strategic approach and understand how to manage the firm in order to develop a total service offering. This is called *service management*, and can be seen as an alternative management approach to scientific management,[35] geared to the demands of service competition. Service management as a management focus will be discussed in detail in Chapter 3 on *the service profit logic and service management principles* and in subsequent chapters.

HIDDEN AND RECOGNIZED SERVICES

In order for firms to develop a total service offering successfully, they must observe that two kinds of service elements are included in such an offering:

- Recognized services.
- Hidden services.

Recognized services, such as repair and maintenance and consultancy, are thought of as service activities by management. Sometimes, but not always, they are billable, which means that a price can be put on them. These services form only a part of the service offered to customers. For example, all customers, individual consumers as well as organizations and business-to-business customers, note the way a firm handles invoicing, takes care of quality problems, mistakes and service failures, manages complaints, offers documentation and directions for the use of goods and services, offers customer training on how to use machines, equipment and software, handles queries and answers questions and e-mails, pays attention to customers and their special requests and wishes, keeps promises and delivers promptly, etc. The clarity and accuracy of invoices, speed and efficiency in managing failures and complaints, the attention that employees show customers and the promptness with which actions are taken all influence a customer's perception of the value of being a customer of a given supplier or service provider. In addition, this also creates more or less costs for the customer, for example costs of processing invoices and following up on complaints, and corrections of the problems causing the need to complain. They either make it easier or more troublesome to be a customer and also frequently help the customer to save money. The way these services function contributes to making it worthwhile for customers to continue purchasing from the same firm, and prevents customers from considering alternative options. Hence, these normally *non-billable* types of service components also contribute to the creation of a competitive advantage.

The problem with *hidden services* such as invoicing, complaints handling, documentation and customer training is that they are seldom perceived as service by management, and therefore are frequently not designed and managed as value-supporting service to customers. Instead, they are managed as administrative, legal or operational routines with internal efficiency criteria and cost consideration as the main guidelines. As a result, customers generally do not perceive most of these as value-enhancing activities. However, the use of hidden services in customer relationships is a powerful way of setting apart a firm from its competitors and of supporting a sustainable competitive advantage.

CHOOSING STRATEGIC PERSPECTIVE

A firm can choose any one of the perspectives discussed above. Following this choice it will develop a strategic approach which differs from the approach that would have been taken if another strategic perspective had been adopted. Choosing one strategic perspective does not mean that aspects of the other perspectives are not important. However, the choice of a perspective determines the way a firm will develop resources and competencies. For example, choosing a service perspective as the main strategy does not mean that less attention than otherwise will be paid to production technologies and the technical quality of the core solution. Elements from perspectives other than the dominating one, however, have always to be geared to the requirements of the dominating perspective. The fine-tuning of a strategic approach varies, of course, but Table 1.2 shows in a simplified way the strategic orientation of the four strategic perspectives.

TABLE 1.2

Characteristics of strategic perspectives.

Strategic perspective	Characteristic of a corresponding strategic approach
Service perspective	The firm takes the view that a service offering is required to support the customer's value creation, and that the core solution (a physical product, service or combination of goods and services) is not sufficient to differentiate the offering from those of competitors. Physical product components, service components, information, personal attention and other elements of customer relationships are combined into a *total service offering*. Because it provides service to the customer, the offering is labelled a service offering, although the core solution may be based on a physical product, because all elements of the offering are combined to provide a value-supporting service for customers. Developing such a total service offering is seen to be of strategic importance and therefore given highest priority by management. *Hidden services*, both billable and non-billable, are considered part of this offering and supportive to the customer's value-creating processes. Price is considered less important for customers than long-term costs. A firm that adopts a service perspective will consider itself a *service business*.
Core product perspective	The firm concentrates on the development of the core solution, whether this is a physical product or a service, as the main provider of value for the customer's value-creating processes (the customer's use of solutions to create value for himself or for an organizational user). Additional services may be considered necessary but not of strategic importance, and therefore they have a low level of priority. *Hidden services*, especially non-billable ones, are not recognized as value-enhancing services. The firm differentiates its package from others through providing an excellent core solution.
Price perspective	The firm takes the view that price is the dominating purchasing criterion of its customers, and that being able to offer a low price is a necessity for survival in the marketplace. Price is seen as the main contribution to the customer's value-creating processes. The provision of additional services is not considered value-enhancing and is therefore of lower priority than the capability to offer a low-price solution. Price is considered more value-enhancing than the long-term cost effects of a solution. The firm is differentiating its offering by being the cheapest alternative available, or one of the cheapest.

Image perspective	The firm differentiates its offering by creating imaginary extras (a brand image) around its core product. Such extras are mainly created in the minds of customers by advertising and marketing communication. The core solution is seen as a starting point for the development of customer value, but the brand image that is created by marketing is considered to be the major contribution to the customer's value-creating processes.

A CUSTOMER RELATIONSHIP PERSPECTIVE

Service as a perspective and service activities *are inherently relational*. A service encounter, where a customer, for example, is a restaurant guest or has a machine repaired, is a process. At some point in this process the service provider is normally present, interacting with the customer. Even a single encounter includes relational elements. If several encounters follow each other in a continuous or discrete fashion, and if both parties want it, a relationship may emerge. If a customer feels that there is something special and valuable in his contacts with a given firm, a relationship may develop. Perceived relationships are not enough to make customers loyal, but they are a central part of loyalty, and loyal customers are normally, but not always,[36] profitable customers.

Relationship marketing has emerged, or rather re-emerged, as a marketing paradigm.[37] Marketing and management based on customer relationships is seen as an alternative to focusing on transactions or exchanges of goods and services for money. Firms choosing a service perspective as their strategic approach almost inevitably have to focus on relationships with their customers and other stakeholders, such as suppliers, distributors, financial institutions and shareholders. Thus, *understanding relationship marketing and how to manage customer relationships becomes a necessity for understanding how to manage a firm in service competition*. Hence, the approach to managing in service competition taken in this book is geared towards a customer relationship–based view as a dominating marketing perspective.

THE LOGIC OF SERVICE COMPETITION

Service competition is nothing new. Service firms such as banks, hotels, restaurants and transportation companies have always faced such situations. They have not always realized what this requires of them, and therefore sometimes reverted to a product strategy and inside–out management. However, firms in more and more industries, regardless of whether they are traditionally categorized as service or manufacturing industries, now find themselves in a situation where the core product only offers a starting point for the development of a competing advantage, but does not guarantee it any more. In such a situation a service perspective offers an approach to the strategic reorientation. The development of the core product into a service offering, including product elements and recognized and hidden services, may make the firm competitive again. *Service competition has become a reality for most firms.*

There are at least three reasons for the need to focus on service. The demand for adopting a service perspective, and thus for learning how to cope with service competition, is partly *customer-driven*, partly *competition-driven* and partly *technology-driven*. First, customers in a greater number of markets demand more than a mere technical solution to a problem provided by a service firm or a manufacturer. Customers are gradually becoming more sophisticated, more informed and, consequently, more demanding. By and large, they are looking for more comfort, fewer problems, lower additional costs and less trouble caused by the use of goods and services; in short, they are looking for better value. Second, this demand by customers is constantly enhanced by competition, which is becoming increasingly global. In the pursuit of more valuable offerings for their customers, firms turn to service, and thus force competitors to appreciate the importance of service too. Third, technological developments, especially in the area of information technology and digital solutions, enable firms to create new service more easily. An early example of this was the just-in-time approach to logistics, which to be successfully implemented required high-powered computerized information systems. More recently, the development of the Internet and e-business and mobile commerce has also made it possible to create new service. The Internet is a highly relational tool, making it possible for firms to develop interactive and relationship-building contacts with their customers, thus enhancing the value support of their core solution. The emergence of mobile commerce reinforces this trend. By and large, new information technology often makes it easier to maintain relationships with customers, as well as creating new ways of doing so.[38] At the same time electronic and mobile technologies make it possible for customers to maintain contact with service providers and use their service free from time and spatial restrictions, thereby providing the everyday activities of customers who appreciate this with additional value-creating support.[39]

When new elements are added to the goods and service components of customer relationships, these relationships are expanded. Traditionally, marketing and sales organized in marketing and sales departments have been responsible for customers. The other departments of the firm were involved only to a limited extent. As the relationship grows in scope, more functions are in immediate contact with customers: for example, bank tellers and ATMs, service technicians involved in the repair and maintenance of machines and equipment, telephone receptionists, call centre and contact centre systems, people in R&D departments. Responsibility for developing and maintaining customer relationships, which is normally called 'marketing', is no longer solely related to the marketing department and the marketing director. In the organizational structure this new shared responsibility for the customer has to be recognized and accepted.

As mentioned, in the literature there are two major ways of understanding the service perspective on business, *service logic* and *service-dominant logic*. Because the latter approach tends be basically systemic and societal and advances the understanding of the service perspective on a systemic level, in this book, which is about service management, we follow the service logic approach. Service logic takes a management-level approach to understanding and managing a service perspective.[40] In Appendix 2 *the managerial principles of service logic* are summarized. Table 1.3 provides a comparison between some central elements of *service logic* and *goods logic* relating to, respectively, a service perspective and product perspective on business.

Finally, it is important to realize that although customers' experiences with service and a service provider is considered important for value creation, most service situations are very *ordinary* and mundane, such as travelling on a bus, operating a vending machine or making a phone call. Although experiences sometimes can be enhanced and made exclusive, as suggested by Pine and Gilmore,[41] the ordinary service situations must also be handled successfully, such that the customer's processes are supported successfully.

WHAT IS A RELATIONSHIP?

Relationships occur between two or more parties. In much of the management and marketing literature on the subject the questions 'what is a relationship?' or 'when do we know that a relationship has developed?' are not discussed.

TABLE 1.3

Service logic versus goods logic.

Service is a holistic process aiming at supporting customers' processes.	Goods are resources delivered to customers for their use.
Value evolves over time during the customers' use of resources.	Value is embedded in resources.
Direct interaction between the firm and its customers exist and form a co-creation platform.	Customers interact only indirectly with the firm through their use of products and non-interactive systems. No co-creation platforms exist.
The firm may co-create value with its customers on the co-creation platform.	Firms cannot co-create value with its customers.
By compiling resources to be used by its customers, the firm provides potential value-in-use for them. Through co-creational and independent value creation as well as social value co-creation, the value potential is realized by the customers as value-in-use which evolves during the value creation process.	Value for customers is embedded in resources, and materializes as value-in-exchange at the point and time of purchase.
The firm can go beyond promising value for its customers, and influence its customers' value creation directly and actively on the co-creation platform, and thus marketing breaks free from its traditional restriction of only being able to make promises offered through value propositions.	Because a co-creation platform is missing, the firm is restricted to making promises about customer value only, through offering value propositions.

One thing is quite clear: a relationship with a customer has not been established only because the marketer has said it has, or believes it has. Far too often marketers state that they have turned to relationship marketing and believe that their marketing efforts are relationship-oriented, without making sure that the customers see it in the same way. In reality, if one asks the customers, much of what marketing practitioners call relationship marketing has very little to do with creating or maintaining customer relationships.[42] A firm may provide more tailor-made direct mail, customized e-mail or mobile contacts, membership of a loyalty club or the like, but for the customer this may mean the same slow service and uninterested service personnel, no or late responses to e-mails or phone calls, or slow complaints handling. The customer may benefit from improved direct contacts and membership in a loyalty club, but this is not relationship-based customer management, and no relationship has developed. *A relationship can develop only when all, or at least most, important customer contacts and interactions are relationship-oriented.*

One way of defining when a relationship has developed is to measure how many times a given customer has made purchases from the same firm. If there have been a number of continuous purchases, or a contract has been effective for a certain period of time, one might say that a relationship with this customer has developed. Repetitive purchases by a customer can be a sign of the development of a relationship between the firm and this customer, but this measure is not a good way of assessing whether a relationship has developed or not. There are many reasons for a customer to continue buying from one supplier or service provider for some time without perceiving that he has a relationship with that firm. Low prices may be one such reason. When a competitor offers a better price, the customer will turn to that firm. Convenient location may be another such reason. For example, a supermarket may be conveniently placed on a person's way home from work and is therefore patronized by him.

There are a number of other *bonds* that keep a customer attached to a firm, even though the customer does not feel that there is any relationship with that firm. If these bonds are removed, there is a high likelihood that such a customer will be lost. Such bonds may, for example, be technological, geographical or knowledge-based in nature, or they may be of some other type.

Therefore, it is important that one has some other conception of what a relationship is. A relationship is by and large related to an attitude. A relationship is not only manifested by the customer's purchasing behaviour; their hearts and minds must also be devoted to the relationship and the relationship partner.[43] A person or a group of people feel that there is something that ties them to another party. This feeling does not develop out of nothing. *It has to be earned* by the supplier or service provider. The relationship is earned by the way customers are treated. Hence, a firm should create interaction and communication processes that facilitate a relationship, but it is the customer, not the firm, who determines whether or not a relationship has developed. This is further discussed in Chapter 9 on *marketing and customer-focused management*.

The following attitude-oriented description of a relationship may be useful for an understanding of a relationship: a relationship has developed when a customer perceives that a mutual way of thinking exists between customer and supplier or service provider.[44]

From the customer's point of view this can be stated in another way: 'I am not there for the supplier only, the supplier is there for me as well.' A mutual way of thinking means that there is two-way commitment. The firm should understand its customers and continuously demonstrate this by actions. Loyalty[45] does not only mean that the customer should stay loyal to the firm, but that the latter should stay loyal to the former as well. This mutual way of thinking develops over time. This development process includes *interactions* between the supplier or service provider and the customer and *communication* between them. Interaction includes all sorts of exchanges of goods, recognized and hidden services, information, administrative, legal and operational routines; in fact, any contact that occurs between the two parties. Communication takes place as part of all interactions, but in addition, a series of separate planned communication efforts, such as direct mail, advertising, sales negotiation, etc. occur. Interaction and communication activities and processes continue over time and become integrated into one value-creating relationship process. If they do not develop in that way, a relationship will not emerge. In Chapter 10 we shall go into these interaction and communication issues in more detail.

It is of course not an easy task to measure whether or not a relationship has emerged based on this description. However, the marketer should measure the existence of a relationship on this level as well. Even though an ideal measurement instrument cannot be developed, this is not an excuse for not trying to create an instrument that comes as close as possible.

The inherent mutuality in the relationship perspective creates a *win–win* situation, where both parties should gain something. Effective collaboration in a long-term relationship between a supplier or service provider and a customer can continue only if the parties involved feel like 'winners', or at least feel that they continuously gain more from the situation than from any other option available.[46] An adversarial situation, where the marketer aims at doing something *to* the customer and not *with* and *for* the customer, which is far too common in much marketing practice, is not part of relationship marketing. Hence, correctly understood and implemented relationship marketing can foster mechanisms that create ethical values in an organization and support ethical decision-making.[47]

WHEN IS THE CUSTOMER A CUSTOMER?

In a transactional approach to marketing the customer is considered a customer when he (or the buying organization) is the target of marketing and sales efforts. According to the relationship perspective, the situation is different. A relationship is an ongoing process. From time to time transactions of goods, services, information and other resources for money take place, *but the relationship exists all the time*, including the time in between such transactions. Customers should continuously feel that the other party is there to help and support them, not just when they make a purchase. Hence, *once a relationship has been established, customers are customers on a continuous basis – and they should be treated as such regardless of whether at any given point in time they are making a purchase or not*. Firms that understand this, and perform like this, treat their customers as *relational customers*.

For several years SAS Scandinavian Airlines showed that they understood the meaning of their most valued customers, holders of the most prestigious frequent traveller cards, and hence the most frequent users of the airline's service, and regarded them as *relational customers*. Such card holders were invited to use the airline's lounges regardless of whether they travelled on a flight operated by this airline or not. Customers felt that they were respected as relational customers and frequent users of the airline's service. It is not always possible to use a given firm's service all the time. As all frequent travellers know, access to airport lounges is a real value-supporting service. For some reason, this policy was suddenly abolished. 'Why should we bear the extra costs of serving other airline's customers?' may have been the question asked by somebody in a top management position. The result is that customers now know that they are no longer relational customers but are treated as valued passengers only when they actually use the airline's service. In other situations they are nobodies for the firm.

To sum up, unless customers are treated as customers between purchases as well, the firm does not show a genuine *relational intent*.

ARE ALL CUSTOMERS INTERESTED IN RELATIONSHIPS?

Not all customers are always interested in relationships with a firm. Generally speaking, customers are interested in either a relational or transactional contact with a firm. Thus, in a given marketing situation the customer is either in a *relational mode* or in a *transactional mode*.[48] Some customers who, for example, buy books from Amazon.com or any other bookstore on the Internet welcome continuous information about new books that fit their past purchasing history. Others only get annoyed by such messages showing up in their e-mail inbox.

Furthermore, consumers or users in a relational mode can either be in an *active* or a *passive* relational mode.[49] For example, marketers of canned juice can provide web page and e-mail addresses, or fax or telephone numbers on the can, so that customers have an opportunity to get in contact with the

TABLE 1.4

Relational and transactional customers

Customer mode	Customers' expectations
Transactional mode	Transactional customers are looking for solutions to their needs at an acceptable price, and they do not appreciate contacts from the supplier or service provider in between purchases.
Active relational mode	Active relational customers are looking for opportunities to interact with the supplier or service provider in order to get additional value. A lack of such contacts makes them disappointed, because the value inherent in the relationship is missing.
Passive relational mode	Passive relational customers are looking for the knowledge that they could contact the supplier or service provider if they wanted to. In this sense they too are seeking contact, but they seldom respond to invitations to interact.

firm, give feedback, make suggestions, file complaints, etc. Customers in an active relational mode seek contact, whereas customers in a passive relational mode are satisfied with the understanding that, if needed, the firm will be there for them. They will not make use of the contact opportunity, but if it is missing they will nevertheless feel disappointed. For customers in a passive relational mode, a relationship-oriented marketing strategy is important, although it may not seem so. In Table 1.4 the different customer modes are summarized.

CUSTOMER BENEFITS IN A RELATIONSHIP

Why people enter a relational mode and choose to react favourably to a relationship marketing approach by a firm is a topic that has not been studied very much. It could be that the primary reason is to reduce choice. After having found a reliable relationship partner, other alternatives are less attractive for the customer in a relative sense and thus do not have to be considered on a regular basis.[50] Another reason is that by entering a relationship customers can more effectively fulfil goals that they had earlier committed to or tentatively committed to, such as profitability, cost reduction, comfort, health or self-esteem. Finally, for some customers being involved in a relationship is an end in itself.[51]

In a study of the benefits for customers of maintaining a relationship with a service provider, Gwinner et al.[52] concluded that benefits can be of three types.

- *Confidence*: reduced anxiety, faith in the service provider, feeling of trustworthiness of the service provider.

- *Social benefits*: personal recognition by employees, customer being familiar with employees, the development of friendship with employees.

- *Special treatment*: extra services, special prices, higher priority than other customers.

The *confidence* types of special relational benefits were considered most important by customers across all categories of services studied. This means that customers feel more secure by their choice than they would feel by patronizing any other firm. In this way *cognitive dissonance*, or a feeling of having made a less than optimal choice after all, can be minimized or altogether eliminated.

The other types of relational benefits are also important. Wherever interpersonal contacts exist, *social benefits* can be developed. Customers may, for example, have a sense of 'my own contact employee' or in some other way feel that there is a special connection to employees. Clearly, this also has a positive effect on the *confidence* type of relational benefits. Although *special treatments* were also considered important by customers, their role was found to be less important in this study.

The ultimate benefits for customers of being involved in a relationship should be financial. Especially in business markets such benefits can be calculated, whereas individual consumers may perceive them. The financial benefits are of two kinds:

- Increased wealth and/or revenue-generating capability.

- Lower costs of being a customer.

In a well-functioning relationship a business customer can, on a continuous basis, and with the support of a relationship partner, run its (for example, production, administrative or sales) processes in a way that generates a higher or steadier flow of revenues. For example, a supplier that can guarantee that a manufacturer will never be out of raw material or components can support its customer's production process in that way. Due to the well-functioning and trustworthy relationship partner the risk of standstill is eliminated or at least minimized and potential lost sales avoided. In this way the customer's financial result will be improved.

A supplier that, for example, can guarantee that quality problems will not occur, or that lengthy and time/cost-consuming complaints handling procedures will be replaced by smooth service recovery processes, will eliminate unwanted and unnecessary costs for the customer, thus improving the financial result of the customer.

Both types of benefit can occur simultaneously or sometimes only one of them will be achieved. Often firms do not calculate these financial effects, and in sales negotiations they are not always pointed out. However, they should be calculated and sales representatives should develop means of demonstrating the financial effects of functioning relationships for their negotiation partners.

In consumer markets it is more difficult to calculate financial effects of relationships. For example, in the case of financial service or insurance service, individual consumers may be able to calculate similar financial effects of a relationship. In other situations such effects are more or less only sensed. In many situations the benefits of a relationship are perceived as convenience, increased comfort and special treatments only.

TRUST, COMMITMENT AND ATTRACTION

In the literature the concepts of trust, commitment and attraction play an important role. However, in spite of numerous studies, especially of trust and commitment, it is not clear how these concepts function. One reason for this may be the effect of other variables in the customer relationship, such as bonds between a customer and a supplier or service provider, or boredom, inertia and curiosity on the part of the customer.

Trust in another party can, for example, be described as one party's expectation that the other party will behave in a certain predictable way in a given situation. If the other party does not behave in the expected way, the trusting party (for example the customer) will experience more negative outcomes than they otherwise would.[53] Another commonly cited definition of trust states that trust is a willingness to rely on a business partner in whom one has confidence.[54]

Trust can stem from different sources.[55] *Generalized trust* is derived from social norms. For example, a customer knows that a large supplier can be expected to stay in business and offer the same components and parts in the future due to its size and reputation; he therefore trusts this supplier to be the continuous source of the components that he is looking for. *System trust* depends on laws, industry regulations and contracts but also on the professionalism of the other party. If a customer, for example, has entered into a long-term contract with a supplier, the customer trusts that the supplier will perform according to expectations. *Personality-based trust* is based on the human tendency to rely upon another person to behave in a predictable way according to expectations because of personality traits. If a person considers that he can rely upon the word or statement of another person representing a supplier or service provider, trust exists and the customer is prepared to continue a business relationship with that other party. Finally, *process-based trust* follows from experience of business and contacts that have taken place over time in an ongoing relationship between two parties.

Trust partly depends on *past experiences* from interacting with another party; partly on other factors, such as *contracts, regulations and social norms* on the one hand, and *personality factors* on the other hand, which can be expected to make the other party in a relationship behave in a predictable way according to expectations. The existence of trust in a relationship is a kind of insurance against risks and unexpected behaviour by the other party in the future.

How trust develops in the marketplace is a debated issue. Is trust built in an ongoing relationship, or must there be trust in a supplier for a potential customer to engage in a business relationship with this supplier? There are no clear answers to these questions. However, recent research indicates that if a supplier is considered trustworthy, it will be easier for this firm to connect with potential customers and establish a relationship with them.[56]

Commitment means that one party in a relationship feels motivated to some extent to do business with another party. Commitment has also been defined as an enduring desire to maintain a valued relationship.[57] A customer is committed to a supplier, for example, because the latter has proved to be trustworthy and has shown that it is able to offer solutions that successfully support value creation. A manufacturer may feel committed to a repair and maintenance provider who has consistently proved that it can offer skilful and timely service of its production machines. If the service provider has taken extra trouble to do so, for example in spite of excess demand for its service at some point in time, the sense of commitment is even deeper.

A third key concept in relationship marketing is *attraction*.[58] This means that there should be something that makes a supplier interesting to a given customer, or the other way round. Attraction can be based on, for example, *financial, technological* or *social* factors. A globally operating certified accountant will probably find a large firm with affiliations in several countries an attractive potential customer, which offers large financial opportunities. In the same way a supplier of the latest technology for a manufacturing process is an attractive partner for a manufacturing firm. Even social contacts that are highly appreciated may form a source of attraction that can lead to a business relationship. If attraction between two parties exists, there is a basis for a relationship to develop. If attraction is lacking, the parties will probably not start doing business with each other.

The relation between trust, commitment and attraction and the development of commercial relationships is not clear.[59] However, it seems as if the existence of trust in a business partner and commitment to that partner (probably in consumer as well as in business-to-business markets) may be more important for customers who see more value in the relationship itself. Such relationship-oriented customers may appreciate the existence of trust and commitment more than being satisfied with every single exchange in an ongoing relationship, whereas customers who are more transactionally-oriented demand that every transaction should be satisfactory.

Long-term relationships should increase business between two parties. It is, however, not clear that this is always the case. There may also be negative effects of long-standing relationships that make customers look for alternative solutions. Curiosity or boredom may be such reasons. The customer wants to experience other alternatives for a change. There may also be good reason for customers to look for alternatives. Overlong relationships with one supplier or service provider may create blindness. The customer may not see, for example, new technologies or new financial opportunities developed by competing suppliers. The existing relationship partner may not have been able to follow the developments that have taken place, and as a consequence the customer is locked up with a low-quality or old-fashioned supplier. The trust and commitment in the relationship partner has remained, but the customer has observed that the financial or technological attraction that initially may have been the reason for the relationship to start to develop does not exist anymore. In relationships, customers must always be aware of this risk. It has sometimes been called 'the dark side of a relationship'.[60]

The relationship philosophy in business relies on cooperation and a trusting relationship with customers and other stakeholders and network partners instead of an adversarial approach to customers; on collaboration within the company instead of specialization of roles and the division of labour only; and on the notion of marketing as a customer-focused management approach, where marketing is spread throughout the organization, rather than as a separate function for specialists only.

THE OBJECTIVE AND APPROACH OF THIS BOOK

The main objective of this book is to describe the nature and scope of *customer-focused management in service competition* in an innovative way. It takes a management approach and a strategy focus; therefore, tactical issues and instruments are only discussed briefly. Instead, the strategic issues are discussed in greater detail. It is not a 'what to do' handbook, but a *how to think* and *what to think* book. Topics such as personal selling and pricing, which are typical parts of standard textbooks, are not addressed here, other than as parts of larger strategic issues.

Although this text is based on international research into various areas of service management and marketing, it is geared to the service-based school of thought, which has internationally been labelled the *Nordic School*.[61] The main characteristic of this school of thought is the notion that, in service as well as relationship contexts, marketing decisions cannot be separated from overall management and the management of other business functions. Neither top management decisions nor decisions concerning any business functions can be made without considering the external implications of such decisions. On a research-oriented note, the Nordic School has encouraged qualitative research and conceptual development, rather than jumping into theory testing when there is no theory to test. When appropriate, theory testing and quantitative research approaches have of course been used. The position of the Nordic School has always been that the sound development of context-oriented theories is a prerequisite for any meaningful testing of theories. No *quantum leaps* are made based on quantitative testing of pre-existing theories; only conceptual work can provide new perspectives suited to new or changing conditions.

This book is intended for people who, as educators, researchers, students or practitioners, are interested in how to cope with service competition in a customer-focused manner. It is not a book for service firms only. It is equally intended for manufacturers of physical goods operating in business-to-business or consumer markets, because the importance of service to success is constantly growing for such firms. Finally, because service and relationships are interrelated, the present book is as equally based on customer relationships and relationship management as it is on service management and managing customers in service contexts.

Today, the traditional context of consumer goods still dominates but the scale is tipping. The importance of service has already been extended far beyond what are traditionally termed service industries and the service sector. In fact, it can be argued that *everybody* is in service. The service perspective has slowly won more ground and will soon, in the form of service management, take over and become the norm.[62]

SUMMARY

In this introductory chapter the nature of service competition and customer relationships were presented, and the differences between outside-in management and inside-out management were analysed. The reasons for taking a service perspective were discussed, and this perspective was contrasted with other business perspectives. The logic underpinning the service perspective on business was described. Then value creation and models of value co-creation were presented. In the final part, relationships, who decides when a relationship has been established, and what relationship benefits there are, were discussed.

QUESTIONS FOR DISCUSSION

1. What is the difference between outside-in management and inside-out management? Why does a service perspective on business require an outside-in management approach?

2. Which are the three strategic requirements for the implementation of a relationship-based service approach? What challenges for an organization are created by them?

3. Which are the three tactical elements of a relationship strategy?

4. Describe the spheres of the value generation process, and how the firm and the customer respectively contribute to value for the customer.

5. Which is the nature of value-in-use? How does it differ from value-in-exchange?

6. Which are the differences between a service logic and a goods logic?

7. What benefits are customers in any given industry looking for that can be offered by a relationship-based strategy?

NOTES

1. I was told the story of Ming Hua, the Chinese rice merchant, by a student attending a course on service management that I was teaching in an executive programme at Thammasat University in Bangkok. This story is a true relationship marketing case, which illustrates the nature of service and demonstrates the ingredients of a relationship perspective, and also shows that service and relationship marketing are not new.

2. See, for example, Grönroos, C. & Gummerus, J., The service revolution and its marketing implications: service logic versus service-dominant logic. *Managing Service Quality*, **24**(3), 2014, 206–229, and Grönroos, C., Value co-creation in service logic: a critical analysis. *Marketing Theory*, **11**(3), 2011, 279–301.

3. See Vargo, S.L. & Lusch, R.F., Service dominant logic: continuing the evolution. *Journal of the Academy of Marketing Science*, **36**(1), 2008, 1–10, where service is defined as using skills and knowledge on resources for the benefit of someone (or oneself).

4. Grönroos, C & Ravald, A., Service business logic: implications for value creation and marketing. *Journal of Service Management*, **22**(1), 2011, 5–22.

5. Grönroos, C., Value-driven relational marketing: from products to resources and competencies. *Journal of Marketing Management*, **13**(5), 1997, 407–420.

6. Grönroos, C., Relationship marketing logic. *Asia-Australia Marketing Journal*, **4**(1), 1996, 7–18.

7. Grönroos, 1996, *op. cit.*

8. See, for example, Holbrook, M.B., Introduction to consumer value. In Hobrook, M.B. (ed.), *Customer Value. A Framework for Analysis and Research*. London: Routledge, 1999, pp. 1–28, and Sánchez-Fernández, R., Iniesta-Bonillo, Á. M., & Holbrook, M. B., The conceptualisation and measurement of consumer value in services. *International Journal of Market Research*, **51**(1), 2009, 93–113.

9. Grönroos, C., Service logic revisited: who creates value? And who co-creates? *European Business Review*, **20**(4), 2008, 208–314, where value in this way is defined as follows: 'Value for customers means that after they have been assisted by a self-service process (cooking a meal or withdrawing cash from an ATM) or a full-service process (eating out at a restaurant or withdrawing cash over the counter in a bank) they are or feel better off than before.' (303).

10. Already Wroe Alderson called for 'a marketing interpretation of the whole process of customer utility' (p. 69). See Alderson, W., *Marketing Behavior and Executive Action*. Homewood, IL: Richard D. Irwin, 1957. In Rust, R.T. & Oliver, R.L., Service quality: insights and managerial implications from the frontier. In Rust, R.T. & Oliver (eds), *Service Quality: New Directions for Theory and Practice*. Sage: Thousand Oaks, CA, 1994, pp. 1–20, the authors claim that

'. . . ultimately it is perceived value that attracts a customer and lures away a customer from a competitor' (p. 7). See also Sheth, J.N, & Uslay, C., Implications of the revised definition of marketing: from exchange to value creation. *Journal of Public Policy & Marketing*, **26**(2), 2007, 302–307.

11. In the American Marketing Association's two attempts in 2004 and 2007 to redefine marketing, value for customers was explicitly included. Also in research into service as a perspective, value for customers has been emphasized. See, for example, Vargo, S.L. & Lusch, 2008, *op. cit.* and Grönroos, C., Adopting a service logic for marketing. *Marketing Theory*, **6**(3), 2006, 317–334.

12. See Porter, M.E., *Competitive Advantage*. New York: The Free Press, 1985.

13. See Normann, R. & Ramírez, R., From value chain to value constellation. *Harvard Business Review*, **71**(Jul–Aug), 1993, 65–77.

14. Gummesson, E., Relationship marketing: its role in the service economy. In Glynn, W.J. & Barnes, J.G. (eds), *Understanding Service Management*, New York: John Wiley & Sons, 1995, pp. 244–268.

15. Normann, R. & Ramírez, R., A theory of the offering: toward a neo-industrial business strategy. In Snow, C.C. (ed.), *Strategy, Organization Design, and Human Resource Management*, Greenwich, CN: JAI Press, 1988, pp. 111–128 (quote on p. 116).

16. See, for example, Grönroos, 2008, *op. cit.* and Grönroos, C. & Gummerus, J., The service revolution and its marketing implications. Service logic versus service-dominant logic. *Managing Service Quality*, **24**(3), 2014, 206–229. It is interesting to note that more than two millenia ago Aristotle, in his value theory, defined the value-in-use and value-in-exchange concepts, and claimed that the former is the more important one to understand market activities, because value-in-exchange is a function of value-in-use. See Gorden, B.J., Aristotle and the development of the value theory. *Quarterly Journal of Economics*, **78**(1), 1964, 114–128.

17. Echeverri, P. & Skålén, P., Co-creation and co-destruction – a practice theory based study of interactive value formation. *Marketing Theory*, **11**(3), 2011, 351–373.

18. Gummesson, 1995, *op. cit.*

19. See Grönroos, C., *Service Management and Marketing. A Customer Relationship Management Approach*. Chichester: John Wiley & Sons, 2000, p. 24.

20. As is the norm in the management and marketing literature, and in this book, the expression *value creation* is used. However, because this phrase implies that value is instrumentally created through deliberate actions by a customer, it is not really an accurate expression. Obviously, value is sometimes instrumentally created, but often *value emerges* for customers, without any deliberate value-creating steps by them. Hence, the reader must observe that value creation in this book, as

in other contemporary publications, may mean either instrumentally created value or value that just emerges for customers. The notion that value rather emerges than is created is emphasized by the *customer-dominant logic* literature. See, for example, Heinonen, K., Strandvik, T. & Voima, P., Customer dominant value generation in service. *European Business Review*, **25**(2), 2013, 531–538.

21. Normann & Ramírez, 1993, *op. cit.*

22. Vargo & Lusch, 2008, *op. cit.,* and Vargo, S.L. & Lusch, R.F., Evolving to a new dominant logic for marketing. *Journal of Marketing*, **68**(Jan), 2004, 1–17.

23. See, for example, Grönroos, 2008, *op. cit.*, Grönroos, 2011, *op. cit.*, Grönroos & Ravald, 2011, *op. cit.*, Grönroos, C. & Voima, P., Critical service logic: making sense of value creation and co-creation. *Journal of the Academy of Marketing Science*, **41**(2), 2013, 133–150, and Grönroos, C. & Gummerus, J., 2014, *op. cit.*

24. This comparison between service logic and service-dominant logic was first published in Grönroos & Gummerus, *op. cit.*

25. The importance of the customers' ecosystem for value creation is pointed out in the customer-dominant logic field of research. See Heinonen, Strandvik & Voima, *op. cit.*

26. Grönroos & Voima, 2014, *op. cit.*

27. Unlike in service-dominant logic, in the *service logic* approach to the service perspective, it is observed that the value-in-use concept, where the customer is the value creator, requires that the customer is in charge of value creation and can invite the service provider to engage. See, for example, Grönroos, 2011, *op. cit.* and Grönroos & Voima, 2013, *op. cit.* Service-dominant logic claims that the customer is invited to engage with the service provider as co-creator of value. See, for example, Vargo & Lusch, 2008*, op. cit.*

28. Grönroos & Voima, 2014, *op. cit.* See also Grönroos & Ravald, 2011, *op. cit.*

29. In service-dominant logic the whole value generation process is treated as an *all-encompassing value creation process*, and the firm and the customer as value co-creators throughout this process, without specified roles and goals. This functions metaphorically as an eye-opener for researchers and practitioners, showing that it is not only the firm that creates value for the customer, and for a systemic analysis on a societal level it makes sense. However, it does not offer a meaningful and useful instrument on a management level to understand the roles and goals of the service provider and customer, respectively, and hence is less useful for planning and decision making on this level.

30. The models of value co-creation are based on two service marketing and management models from the early years of modern service research, namely the *servuction model* by Pierre Eiglier and Eric Langeard in France and the *interactive marketing model* by Christian Grönroos in Finland. See Eiglier, P. & Langeard, E., Une approche nouvelle du marketing des services. *Revue Française de*

Gestion, **2**(Nov), 1975, 97–114, and Grönroos, C., A service-orientated model of the marketing of services. *European Journal of Marketing*, **12**(8), 1978, 588–601.

31. ICT (Information and Communication Technology) is of course used to an extended degree in service encounters, and such systems may have a positive effect on customers' value perceptions. See Polo Pena, A.I., Frías Jamilena, D.M. & Rodriguez Molina, M.A., Value co-creation via information and communication technology. *The Service Industries Journal*, **34**(13–14), 2014, 1043–1059.

32. However, creating functioning feedback systems, and making the information created in such systems accessible in a way that leads to actionable information and corresponding actions turns out to be difficult. See, for example, Höykinpuro, R., *Service Firms' Actions Upon Negative Incident in High Tough Services. A Narrative Study*. Helsinki: Hanken School of Economics, Finland, 2009.

33. Taylor, F.W., *Scientific Management*. London: Harper & Row, 1947 (a volume of two papers originally published in 1903 and 1911, and a written testimony for a Special House Committee in the USA in 1912).

34. Grönroos, C., *Service Management and Marketing. Managing Moments of Truth in Service Competition*. Lexington, MA: Lexington Books, 1990.

35. Grönroos, C., Service management: a management focus for service competition. *International Journal of Service Industry Management*, **1**(1), 1990, 6–14.

36. See Storbacka, K., *The Nature of Customer Relationship Profitability – Analysis of Relationships and Customer Bases in Retail Banking*. Helsinki/Helsingfors: Swedish School of Economics Finland/CERS Centre for Relationship Marketing and Service Management, 1994.

37. Gummesson, *op. cit.* and Sheth, J.N. & Parvatiyar, A., The evolution of relationship marketing. *International Business Review*, **4**(4), 1995, 397–418.

38. Sisodia, R.S. & Wolfe, D.B., Information technology. Its role in building, maintaining, and enhancing relationships. In Sheth, J.N. & Parvatiyar, A. (eds), *Handbook of Relationship Marketing*. Thousand Oaks, CA: Sage Publications, 2000, pp. 525–563. See also Zeithaml, V.A., Service excellence in electronic channels. *Managing Service Quality*, **12**(3), 2002, 134–138 and Meuter, M.L., Bitner, M.J., Ostrom, A.L. & Brown, S.W., Choosing among alternative service delivery modes: an investigation of customer trial of self-service technologies. *Journal of Marketing*, **69**(2), 2005, 61–83.

39. Heinonen, K., Temporal and spatial e-service value. *International Journal of Service Industry Management*, **17**(4), 2006, 380–400. See also Baron, S., Patterson, A. & Harris, K., Beyond technology acceptance: understanding consumer practice. *International Journal of Service Industry Management*, **17**(2), 2006, 111–135.

40. Grönroos, C. & Gummerus, 2014, *op. cit.*

41. Pine, B.J. & Gilmore, J.H., *The Experience Economy: Work is Theatre & Every Business a Stage.* Cambridge, MA: Harvard Business School Press, 1999.

42. A discussion of the misuse of the relationship marketing concept can be found in Fournier, S., Dobscha, S. & Mick, D.G., Preventing the premature death of relationship marketing. *Harvard Business Review*, Jan/Feb, 1998, 42–51.

43. Storbacka, K. & Lehtinen, J.R., *Customer Relationship Management.* Singapore: McGraw-Hill, 2001.

44. This description is adapted from a definition used by Håkan Håkansson and Ivan Snehota in a discussion of relationships in a business-to-business context. They, however, interpret the definition in a somewhat different way. See Håkansson, H. & Snehota, I., *Developing Relationships in Business.* London: Routledge, 1995.

45. For an extensive discussion of the loyalty concept see Nordman, C., *Understanding Customer Loyalty and Disloyalty – The Effect of Loyalty-supporting and Loyalty-repressing Factors.* Helsinki, Finland: Hanken Swedish School of Economics Finland/CERS, 2004.

46. Gummesson, E., Internal marketing in the light of relationship marketing and virtual organizations. In Lewis, B. & Varey, R. (eds), *Internal Marketing.* London: Routledge, 2000.

47. Kavall, S.G., Tzokas, N.X. & Saren, M.J., Relationship marketing as an ethical approach: philosophical and managerial considerations. *Management Decision*, **37**(7), 1999, 573–581.

48. Grönroos, 1997, *op. cit.*

49. Grönroos, 1997, *op. cit.*

50. Sheth, J.N. & Parvatiyar, A., Relationship marketing in consumer markets: antecedents and consequences. *Journal of the Academy of Marketing Science*, **23**(4), 1995, 255–271.

51. Bagozzi, R.P., Reflections on relationship marketing in consumer markets. *Journal of the Academy of Marketing Science*, **23**(1), 1995, 272–277.

52. Gwinner, K.P., Gremler, D.D. & Bitner, M.J., Relational benefits in service industries: the customer's perspective. *Journal of the Academy of Marketing Science*, **26**(2), 1998, 101–114. See also Dimitriadis, S. & Koritos, C., Core service versus relational benefits: what matters most? *The Service Industries Journal*, **34**(13–14), 2014, 1092–1112, where the relationship between the core service and additional relational benefits is discussed.

53. See Johnson, D.S. & Grayson, K., Sources and dimensions of trust in service relationships. In Swartz, T.A. & Iacobucci, D. (eds), *Handbook of Services Marketing & Management.* Thousand Oaks, CA: Sage Publications, 2000, pp. 357–370.

54. Moorman, C., Deshpandá, R. & Zaltman, G., Factors affecting trust in market relationships. *Journal of Marketing*, **57**(Jan), 1993, 81–101.

55. Johnson & Grayson, *op. cit.* and Lane, C. & Bachmann, R., The social construction of trust: supplier relations in Britain and Germany. *Organizational Studies*, **17**, 1996, 365–395.

56. See Sekhon, H., Ennew, C., Kharout, H. & Devlin, J., Trustworthiness and trust: influences and implications. *Journal of Marketing Management*, **30**(3–4), 2014, 409–430, where it is concluded that if a service provider is considered trustworthy, this has a favourable impact on the cognitive dimension of trust, but also, to a lesser degree however, on the affective dimension.

57. Moorman, C., Zaltman, G. & Deshpandá, R., Relationships between providers and users of market research: the dynamics of trust within and between organizations. *Journal of Marketing Research*, **29**(Aug), 1992, 314–329.

58. Halinen, A., *Relationship Marketing in Professional Services: A Study of Agency–Client Dynamics in the Advertising Sector*. New York: Routledge, 1997.

59. See Garbarino, E. & Johnson, M.A., The different roles of satisfaction, trust, and commitment in customer relationships. *Journal of Marketing*, **63**(Apr), 1999, 70–87, who studied satisfaction, trust and commitment as mediating constructs between attitudes and future purchasing intentions in a repertory theatre environment.

60. Grayson, K. & Ambler, T., The dark side of long-term relationships in marketing services. *Journal of Marketing Research*, **36**(Feb), 1999, 132–141. See also Moorman, Zaltman & Deshpandá, *op. cit.*

61. See Berry, L.L. & Parasuraman, A., Building a new academic field – the case of services marketing. *Journal of Retailing*, **69**(1), 1993, 13–60, where the Nordic School is described as one of three main approaches to service marketing research. The scope and history of the Nordic School is discussed in Gummesson, E. & Grönroos, C., The emergence of the new service marketing: Nordic School perspectives. *Journal of Service Management*, **23**(4), 2012, 479–497, and in Grönroos, C., *In Search of a New Logic for Marketing. Foundations of Contemporary Theory*. Chichester: John Wiley & Sons, 2007.

62. We have elaborated on this argument in, for example, Grönroos, C., Service reflections: service marketing comes of age. In Swartz, T.A. & Iacobucci, D. (eds), *Handbook of Services Marketing & Management*. Thousand Oaks, CA: Sage Publications, 2000, pp. 13–16.

FURTHER READING

Alderson, W. (1957) *Marketing Behavior and Executive Action*. Homewood, IL: Richard D. Irwin.

Bagozzi, R.P. (1995) Reflections on relationship marketing in consumer markets. *Journal of the Academy of Marketing Science*, **23**(1), 272–277.

Baron, S., Patterson, A. & Harris, K. (2006) Beyond technology acceptance: understanding consumer practice. *International Journal of Service Industry Management*, **17**(2), 111–135.

Berry, L.L. & Parasuraman, A. (1993) Building a new academic field – the case of services marketing. *Journal of Retailing*, **69**(1), 13–60.

Brown, S.W. (2005) Marketing renaissance: opportunities and imperatives for improving marketing thought, practice, and infrastructure. *Journal of Marketing*, **69**(4), 1–25.

Dimitriadis, S. & Koritos, C. (2014) Core service versus relational benefits: what matters most? *The Service Industries Journal*, **34**(13–14), 1092–1112.

Echeverri, P. & Skålén, P. (2011) Co-creation and co-destruction – a practice theory based study of interactive value formation. *Marketing Theory*, **11**(3), 351–373.

Eiglier, P. & Langeard, E. (1975) Une approche nouvelle du marketing des services. *Revue Française de Gestion*, **2**(Nov), 97–114.

Fournier, S., Dobscha, S. & Mick, D.G. (1998) Preventing the premature death of relationship marketing. *Harvard Business Review*, Jan/Feb, 42–51.

Garbarino, E. & Johnson, M.A. (1999) The different roles of satisfaction, trust, and commitment in customer relationships. *Journal of Marketing*, **63**(Apr), 70–87.

Gorden, B.J. (1964) Aristotle and the development of the value theory. *Quarterly Journal of Economics*, **78**(1), 114–128.

Grayson, K. & Ambler, T. (1999) The dark side of long-term relationships in marketing services. *Journal of Marketing Research*, **36**(Feb), 132–141.

Grönroos, C. (1978) A service-orientated model of the marketing of services. *European Journal of Marketing*, **12**(8), 588–601.

Grönroos, C. (1990a) *Service Management and Marketing. Managing Moments of Truth in Service Competition*. Lexington, MA: Lexington Books.

Grönroos, C. (1990b) Service management: a management focus for service competition. *International Journal of Service Industry Management*, **1**(1), 6–14.

Grönroos, C. (1996) Relationship marketing logic. *Asia-Australia Marketing Journal*, **4**(1), 7–18.

Grönroos, C. (1997) Value-driven relational marketing: from products to resources and competencies. *Journal of Marketing Management*, **13**(5), 407–420.

Grönroos, C. (2000) *Service Management and Marketing. A Customer Relationship Management Approach*. Chichester, UK: John Wiley & Sons, p. 24.

Grönroos, C. (2000) Service reflections: service marketing comes of age. In Swartz, T.A. & Iacobucci, D. (eds), *Handbook of Services Marketing & Management*, Thousand Oaks, CA: Sage Publications, pp. 13–16.

Grönroos, C. (2006) Adopting a service logic for marketing. *Marketing Theory*, **6**(3), 317–334.

Grönroos, C. (2007) *In Search of a New Logic for Marketing. Foundations of Contemporary Theory*. Chichester, UK: John Wiley & Sons.

Grönroos, C. (2008) Service logic revisited: who creates value? And who co-creates? *European Business Review*, **20**(4), 208–314.

Grönroos, C. (2011) Value co-creation in service logic: a critical analysis. *Marketing Theory*, **11**(3), 279–301.

Grönroos, C. & Gummerus, J. (2014) The service revolution and its marketing implications: service logic versus service-dominant logic. *Managing Service Quality*, **24**(3), 206–229.

Grönroos, C. & Ravald, A. (2011) Service business logic: implications for value creation and marketing. *Journal of Service Management*, **22**(1), 5–22.

Grönroos, C. & Voima, P. (2013) Critical service logic: making sense of value creation and co-creation. *Journal of the Academy of Marketing Science*, **41**(2), 133–150.

Gummesson, E. (1995) Relationship marketing: its role in the service economy. In Glynn, W.J. & Barnes, J.G. (eds), *Understanding Service Management*, New York: John Wiley & Sons, pp. 244–268.

Gummesson, E. (2000) Internal marketing in the light of relationship marketing and virtual organizations. In Lewis, B. & Varey, R. (eds), *Internal Marketing*. London: Routledge.

Gummesson, E. & Grönroos, C. (2012) The emergence of the new service marketing: Nordic School perspectives. *Journal of Service Management*, **23**(4), 479–497.

Gwinner, K.P., Gremler, D.D. & Bitner, M.J. (1998) Relational benefits in service industries: the customer's perspective. *Journal of the Academy of Marketing Science*, **26**(2), 101–114.

Håkansson, H. & Snehota, I. (1995) *Developing Relationships in Business*. London: Routledge.

Halinen, A. (1997) *Relationship Marketing in Professional Services: A Study of Agency–Client Dynamics in the Advertising Sector*. New York: Routledge.

Heinonen, K. (2006) Temporal and spatial e-service value. *International Journal of Service Industry Management*, **17**(4), 380–400.

Heinonen, K., Strandvik, T. & Voima, P. (2013) Customer dominant value generation in service. *European Business Review*, **25**(2), 531–538.

Holbrook, M.B. (1999) Introduction to consumer value. In Holbrook, M.B. (ed.), *Customer Value. A Framework for Analysis and Research*, London: Routledge, pp. 1–28.

Höykinpuro, R. (2009) *Service Firms' Actions upon Negative Incidents in High Touch Services. A Narrative Study*. Helsinki: Hanken School of Economics, Finland.

Jaakkola, E. & Alexander, M. (2014) The role of customer engagement behavior in value co-creation: a service system perspective. *Journal of Service Research*, **17**(3), 247–261.

Johnson, D.S. & Grayson, K. (2000) Sources and dimensions of trust in service relationships. In Swartz, T.A. & Iacobucci, D. (eds), *Handbook of Services Marketing & Management*. Thousand Oaks, CA: Sage Publications, pp. 357–370.

Kavall, S.G., Tzokas, N.X. & Saren, M.J. (1999) Relationship marketing as an ethical approach: philosophical and managerial considerations. *Management Decision*, **37**(7), 573–581.

Lusch. R.F. & Vargo, S.L. (2006) *The Service-Dominant Logic of Marketing: Dialog, Debate, and Directions*. Armonk, NY: M.E. Sharpe.

Meuter, M.L., Bitner, M.J., Ostrom, A.L. & Brown, S.W. (2005) Choosing among alternative service delivery modes: an investigation of customer trial of self-service technologies. *Journal of Marketing*, **69**(2), 61–83.

Moorman, C., Deshpandá, R. & Zaltman, G. (1993) Factors affecting trust in market relationships. *Journal of Marketing*, **57**(Jan), 81–101.

Nordman, C. (2004) *Understanding Customer Loyalty and Disloyalty – The Effect of Loyalty-supporting and Loyalty-repressing Factors*. Helsinki: Hanken School of Economics, Finland/CERS.

Normann, R. & Ramírez, R. (1988) A theory of the offering: toward a neo-industrial business strategy. In Snow, C.C. (ed.), *Strategy, Organization Design, and Human Resource Management*. Greenwich, CN: JAI Press, pp. 111–128.

Normann, R. & Ramírez, R. (1993) From value chain to value constellation. *Harvard Business Review*, **71** (Jul–Aug), 65–77.

Pine, B.J. & Gilmore, J.H. (1999) *The Experience Economy: Work is Theatre & Every Business a Stage*. Cambridge, MA: Harvard Business School Press.

Polo Pena, A.I., Frías Jamilena, D.M. & Rodriguez Molina, M.A. (2014) Value co-creation via information and communication technology. *The Service Industries Journal*, **34**(13–14), 1043–1059.

Porter, M.E. (1985) *Competitive Advantage*. New York: The Free Press.

Rust, R.T. & Oliver, R.L. (1994) Service quality: insights and managerial implications from the frontier. In Rust, R.T. & Oliver, R.L. (eds), *Service Quality: New Directions for Theory and Practice*. Sage: Thousand Oaks, CA, pp. 1–20.

Sánchez-Fernández, R., Iniesta-Bonillo, Á.M., & Holbrook, M.B. (2009) The conceptualisation and measurement of consumer value in services. *International Journal of Market Research*, **51**(1), 93–113.

Sekhon, H., Ennew, C., Kharout, H. & Devlin, J. (2014) Trustworthiness and trust: influences and implications. *Journal of Marketing Management*, **30**(3–4), 409–430.

Sheth, J.N. & Parvatiyar, A. (1995) Relationship marketing in consumer markets: antecedents and consequences. *Journal of the Academy of Marketing Science*, **23**(4), 255–271.

Sheth, J.N. & Parvatiyar, A. (1995) The evolution of relationship marketing. *International Business Review*, **4**(4), 397–418.

Sheth, J.N. & Uslay, C. (2007) Implications of the revised definition of marketing: from exchange to value creation. *Journal of Public Policy & Marketing*, **26**(2), 302–307.

Sisodia, R.S. & Wolfe, D.B. (2000) Information technology: its role in building, maintaining, and enhancing relationships. In Sheth, J.N. & Parvatiyar, A. (eds), *Handbook of Relationship Marketing*. Thousand Oaks, CA: Sage Publications, pp. 525–563.

Storbacka, K. (1994) *The Nature of Customer Relationship Profitability – Analysis of Relationships and Customer Bases in Retail Banking*. Helsinki/Helsingfors: Hanken School of Economics, Finland/CERS Centre for Relationship Marketing and Service Management.

Storbacka, K. & Lehtinen, J.R. (2001) *Customer Relationship Management*. Singapore: McGraw-Hill.

Taylor, F.W. (1947) *Scientific Management*. London: Harper & Row (a volume of two papers originally published in 1903 and 1911, and a written testimony for a Special House Committee in the USA in 1912).

Vargo, S.L. & Lusch, R.F. (2004) Evolving to a new dominant logic for marketing. *Journal of Marketing*, **68**(Jan), 1–17.

Vargo, S.L. and Lusch, R.F. (2008) Service dominant logic: continuing the evolution, *Journal of the Academy of Marketing Science*, **36**(1), 1–10.

Zeithaml, V.A. (2002) Service excellence in electronic channels. *Managing Service Quality*, **12**(3), 134–138.

APPENDIX 1

SERVICE LOGIC (SL) VERSUS SERVICE-DOMINANT LOGIC (SDL): SIMILARITIES AND DIFFERENCES

Source: Grönroos, C. & Gummerus, J., The service revolution and its marketing implications. Service logic versus service-dominant logic. *Managing Service Quality*, **24**(3); 2014: 213–214.

Similarities

Objective	A perspective on value creation for business and marketing.
Meaning of service	Application of knowledge and skills to resources to support someone's value creation.
Resources used	The type of resources used by a provider (goods, service activities, information, or any other type of tangible or intangible resources) are not important for the implementation of a service perspective.

Differences

	SL	SDL
Level of perspective	Managerial; defined concepts.	Systemic; abstract; metaphorical.
Goal of the service perspective	Value creation, where service functions as a facilitator; through service, the user's value creation gets facilitated, which enables the provider to capture value by providing service.	Service is exchanged for service.
Value	Defined as value-in-use.	Value used with different meanings in different contexts.
Value generation process	A process including all actions by all actors involved, which ultimately leads to value for a user (as exemplified by the customer).	Not explicitly discussed; implicitly, an all-encompassing value creation process including all actors (e.g., provider, customer, others) involved.
Locus of value creation	Customer's creation of value-in-use.	Not explicitly defined; implicitly, an all-encompassing process including actions by providers, customers, and other actors.
The nature of value as value-in-use	Evolving as value-in-use in a cumulative process, with favourable and unfavourable phases throughout the customer's value creation.	

(continued)

(continued)

	SI	SDL
Value in use: contextual influence	The qualifying dimension of a utility-based value concept evolving during use; when social, physical, mental, or other contextual factors are altered, the level of value-in-use changes.	Sometimes replaced by the expression value-in-context, which disguises the qualifying aspect of value-in-use as being created during the many forms of use.
Value spheres	Three, distinctly different, value spheres: a provider sphere closed to the customer, a customer sphere closed to the provider, and a joint sphere where customers and providers directly interact and may co-create value.	Not explicitly included; implicitly, one value sphere for an all-encompassing value creation process, in which all actors involved co-create value.
Interaction	Explicitly defined with a clear, conceptual distinction between direct and indirect interactions; direct interactions with intelligent resources (people, intelligent systems) enable co-creation; indirect interaction with non-intelligent resources (most products and systems) do not.	Not explicitly defined, only implicitly addressed through foundational premises.
Co-creation	A joint directly interactive process in which the actors' (e.g., provider's and customer's) processes merge into one collaborative, dialogical process, such that a co-creation platform forms.	Actions taken by all actors involved in a process (e.g., providers, customers), regardless of how they relate to each other.
Value co-creation	Actions taken by the actors on a co-creation platform, where the actors may directly and actively influence each other's processes (e.g., supplier service process and customer consumption and value creation processes).	Actions contributing to value for customers during an all-encompassing value creation process by all actors involved (e.g., providers, customers, others), regardless of how they relate to one another or the process.
Driver of value creation	The customer drives value creation and is in charge of it.	The provider drives value creation and is in charge of it.

Division of roles in value co-creation	The provider may engage with the customer's value creation and co-create value with the customer.	The customer may engage with the provider's process and co-create value with the provider.
Value creation: customer's role	The customer both creates and determines value (as value-in-use).	The customer only determines value (as value-in-use).
Value creation: provider's role	The provider compiles resources embedded with potential value-in-use through which the customer's value creation is facilitated.	The provider co-creates value.
Value co-creation: customer ecosystem's role	During interactions with persons in the social ecosystem, the customer may socially co-create value with them.	Abstract; not explicitly discussed.
Marketing: making promises through value propositions	The provider can go beyond making promises by offering value propositions and undertake direct, interactive actions on a co-creation platform to actively and directly influence the customer's value creation and value fulfilment.	The provider can only offer value propositions.
Marketing: keeping promises	By co-creating value with its customers, the provider may extend the keeping of promises beyond product performance; from passive to active promise keeping.	Not explicitly discussed.
Reinventing marketing	Marketing extends beyond a single-function, one-department process of making promises and creating brand awareness; it may become an organization-wide promise management process.	Not explicitly discussed.

APPENDIX 2

SERVICE LOGIC. TEN MANAGERIAL PRINCIPLES ABOUT SERVICE PROVIDER-CUSTOMER RELATIONSHIPS

Source: Grönroos, C. & Gummerus, J., The service revolution and its marketing implications. Service logic versus service-dominant logic. *Managing Service Quality*, **24**(3); 2014: 222–223.

1. In a value generation sphere closed to the service provider (a customer sphere), customers, or any users, create value in the form of value-in-use, emerging out of or being created from integrating new resources with existing resources and applying previously held knowledge and skills.

2. Value (as value-in-use) evolves in a cumulative process, or is sometimes destroyed, throughout the customer's value-creating process.

3. Value (as value-in-use) is uniquely, experientially and contextually perceived and determined by customers.

4. Firms as service providers are fundamentally value facilitators in a value generation sphere closed to the customer (a provider sphere), such that they develop and provide potential value-in-use for customers and other users.

5. If a platform of co-creation exists or can be established through direct interactions among actors in the value generation process, the service provider can engage with customers' value creation, and opportunities for co-creation of value among actors arise.

6. Between the customers and individuals in their ecosystem, social value co-creational activities that influence the customers' independent value creation process may take place.

7. Service is the use of resources in a way that supports customers' everyday practices – physical, mental, virtual, possessive – and thereby facilitates their value creation.

8. The goal of marketing is to engage the service provider with customers' processes to enable reciprocal value creation among the actors, with service as a facilitator.

9. As service providers, firms are not restricted to making promises through value propositions.

10. In direct interactions, using a platform of co-creation, through interactive marketing, firms as service providers can directly and actively influence customers' value fulfilment and thereby keep promises made, as well as contribute to the establishment and maintenance of customer relationships; marketing is extended beyond a predominantly promise-making function.

CHAPTER 2
THE NATURE OF SERVICE AND SERVICE CONSUMPTION, AND ITS CUSTOMER MANAGEMENT IMPLICATIONS

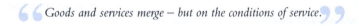

Goods and services merge – but on the conditions of service.

INTRODUCTION

In this chapter the nature and characteristics of service are discussed. The consequences of the process of how service is consumed and used as well as the difference between process consumption and outcome consumption are also covered. Finally, the implications of process consumption, which characterizes service and the content and scope of marketing, are described. After having read this chapter the reader should understand the nature of service and of service consumption as compared to the consumption or use of physical products, as well as the scope and content of marketing in service contexts compared to goods marketing. The reader should also understand what main sources of competitive advantage exist for service businesses.

WHAT IS A SERVICE? AN ATTEMPT TO DEFINE THE PHENOMENON

A service is a complicated phenomenon. The word has many meanings, ranging from personal service to service as a product or offering. The term can be even broader in scope. A machine, or almost any physical product, can be turned into service to a customer if the seller makes efforts to tailor the solution to meet the most detailed demands of that customer. By adopting a service logic a firm can turn any resource into service for customers. A machine is still a physical good, of course, but the way of treating the customer with an appropriately designed machine is service. Sir John Harvey-Jones, former chairman of ICI, said almost three decades ago, referring to some successful firms in the chemical industry, that they had developed an ability to provide a chemical service to customers, rather than selling chemical products.[1] The Kone Corporation, one of the world's leading elevator and escalator manufacturers, headquartered in Finland, has successfully transformed its manufacturing and service businesses into one business, 'dedicated to people flow'. A growing number of manufacturing firms have changed their focus and claimed at least that they are becoming service businesses.

Moreover, as we have discussed previously, there is a variety of administratively managed activities, such as invoicing and handling claims, which in reality are service to the customer. Because of the passive way in which they are handled, they remain 'hidden services' for customers. In fact, they are usually taken care of in such a way that they are perceived not as service but rather as nuisances. Obviously, this offers several opportunities to create a competitive advantage for organizations that can innovatively develop and make use of such 'hidden services' and integrate them with the core of the offering, such as a physical product or a service concept, into a total service offering.

A range of definitions of service have been suggested. Traditionally these definitions focus upon the service activity, and mainly include only those services rendered by so-called service firms.[2] As a criticism of the variety of definitions suggested, Gummesson, referring to an unidentified source, put forward the following definition: 'A service is something which can be bought and sold but which you cannot drop on your feet.'[3]

Although this definition in a way criticizes attempts to find a definition that could be agreed upon by everyone, it points out one of the basic characteristics of services; that is, that they can be exchanged although they often are not tangible as physical products.

Today, service carries at least two distinctly different meanings:

1. Service as a perspective on business and marketing (service logic).

2. Service as an activity.

Service as a perspective was discussed in Chapter 1. Here we discuss the latter meaning of service. One should, however, keep in mind that these two ways of understanding service are intertwined. When adopting a service logic (the perspective), all kinds of resources – goods as well as service activities and other types of resources – are presented to customers in a way resembling service activities. In principle, there is no difference between the beef in a restaurant's service activity and an elevator in an offering aiming at 'supporting people flow' (the Kone Corporation). They are both resources needed to provide service to customers. Hence, the discussion of service as activities is relevant for understanding service as a perspective. Since the 1980s much less discussion of how to define service as an activity has taken place, and no ultimate definition has been agreed upon. Nevertheless, in 1990 the following definition[4] was proposed (here slightly modified):

A service is a process consisting of a series of more or less intangible activities that normally, but not necessarily always, take place in interactions between the customer and service employees and/or physical resources or goods and/or systems of the service provider, which are provided as solutions to customer problems.

Most often a service does involve interactions of some sort with the service provider. However, there are situations where the customer as an individual does not interact with the service firm. For example, when a plumber using the main keys of an apartment complex goes into an apartment to fix a leak when the tenant is out, there are no immediate interactions between the plumber, his physical resources or systems of operating and the customer. On the other hand, many situations where interactions do not seem to be present nevertheless do involve interactions. For instance, when a car problem is taken care of at a garage, the customer is not present and interacting with anybody or anything. However, when the car is taken in by the garage and later delivered to the customer, interactions occur. These interactions are part of the service. Moreover, they may be extremely critical to the customer experience. The customer probably cannot properly evaluate the job done in the garage but can, however, evaluate it based on the interactions that occur at both ends of the service process. Sometimes, as in the case of Internet banking or phone calls, the customer interacts with an infrastructure and systems provided by the bank or telecom operator. Although customers tend to notice them only when they fail, these interactions are equally important to the success of this service as interactions with employees. Consequently, in service, interactions are usually present and of substantial importance, although the parties involved are not always aware of this. Furthermore, service is not a thing, it is a process or activities, and these activities are more or less intangible in nature.

Since 1990 the importance of information technology to service has increased dramatically. Systems indicated in the definition of service are increasingly based on IT and Internet-related solutions and mobile technologies.

The most important contribution to marketing theory and practice by service research, especially emphasized by the Nordic School, is the notion of *interaction* instead of exchange as a focal phenomenon.[5] Without including interactions between the service provider and the customer during the consumption process as an integrated part of marketing, successful marketing cannot be implemented and realistic marketing models cannot be developed. Although at some point exchanges have taken place, it is successful management of interactions that makes exchanges possible. A first exchange may occur, but without successful interactions continuous exchanges will not take place. Moreover, as service is a process rather than an object of transaction it is impossible to assess at which point in time an exchange takes place. Money can be transferred to the service provider either before the service process or after the process, or continuously on a regular basis over time.

SOME COMMON CHARACTERISTICS OF SERVICE

Service, both as a perspective and an activity, has specific characteristics. A whole range of characteristics has been suggested and discussed in the literature. Traditionally service is compared with physical goods.[6] This is, however, not a very fruitful way of developing service models. Service and the nature of service management and marketing should be understood in their own right.

The specific models and concepts of service management and marketing follow from the fact that the customer is present to a certain degree in the service process, where service is produced and provided to him, and that the customer also participates in the process and perceives how the process functions at the same time as the process develops. This is the case also when customers are serviced seemingly on their own, such as paying invoices using an Internet banking option or a vending machine to get a cup of coffee. The customer is involved in a service process, interacting with systems and infrastructures provided by the service firm and, as in the case of making a phone call, also with another customer. In these interactions as a co-producer the customer influences the progress of the service process and the outcome of it just as much as when having dinner in a restaurant. One of the reasons that understanding service management is of interest to manufacturers of goods is that customers are now more involved in various processes of the manufacturer such as the design of goods, modular production, delivery, maintenance, helpdesk functions, information sharing and a host of other processes which, in today's competitive environment, have become important for the creation of a competitive advantage. When manufacturers take a *lifecycle approach* to managing their customer relationships, i.e. set out to take care of their customers' varying needs of support over time instead of only selling products or delivering services to them at a discrete point in time with a transaction approach, taking care of their customers becomes a *service management* issue.

For service in general, *three* basic and more or less generic characteristics can be identified:

1. Service is a *process* consisting of a *series of activities*.

2. Service is at least to some extent *produced and consumed simultaneously*.

3. The *customer participates* as a *co-producer* in the service production process at least to some extent.

By far the most important characteristic is the *process* nature of service and service activities. Service is a process consisting of a series of activities where a number of different types of resources – people as well as goods and other physical resources, information, systems and infrastructures – are used, often in direct interactions with the customer, so that a solution is found and thus value emerges for the customer. Because the customer participates in it, the process, especially the part in which the customer is participating, becomes part of the solution. Most other characteristics follow from the process characteristic. In later sections we shall go into the implications for management and marketing of this process nature of service.

Because service is not a thing but *a process* consisting of a *series of activities – produced and consumed simultaneously* (this is also called the 'inseparability' characteristic) – it is difficult to manage quality control and to do marketing in the traditional sense, since there is no pre-produced quality to control before the service is sold and consumed. Of course, situations vary, depending on what kind of service is being considered. A hairstylist's service is obviously almost totally produced when the customer is present and receives it. When delivering goods, only part of the service (production) process is experienced and, thus, simultaneously consumed by the customer. Most of the process is invisible for the customer. However, in both cases, one should realize that *it is the visible part of the service process that matters in the customer's mind*. As far as the rest is concerned, he can only experience the outcome; but the visible activities are experienced and evaluated in every detail. Quality control and marketing must therefore take place at the time and place of simultaneous service production and consumption. If the firm relies on traditional quality control and marketing approaches, the part of the service process where the customer is involved may go uncontrolled and include negative quality and marketing experiences.

The third basic characteristic of service points out that the customer is not only a receiver of the service; the customer participates in the service process as a production resource as well. Hence, the customer co-produces the service and when there are interactions with the firm's resources he may also co-create value with the firm.

In addition to the three basic characteristics, other important aspects of service can be distinguished. For example, it is not possible to keep service in stock in the same way goods are. If an airplane leaves the airport half-full, the empty seats cannot be sold the next day; they are lost. Instead, capacity planning becomes a critical issue. Even though service cannot be kept in stock, one can try to *keep customers in stock*. For example, if a restaurant is full, it is always possible to try to keep a customer waiting in the bar until there is a free table.

In much of the service literature *intangibility* is said to be the most important characteristic of a service. However, physical goods are not always tangible either in the minds of customers. A kilo of tomatoes or a car may be perceived in a subjective and intangible way. Hence, the intangibility characteristic does not distinguish service from physical goods as clearly as is usually stated in the literature. And intangibility is certainly not *the* most important characteristic. However, service is characterized by varying degrees of intangibility. Normally service cannot be tried out before it is purchased. One cannot make a trial trip on a new airline or try out an inclusive tour before buying it. Furthermore, being on a holiday at a resort is largely an experience or a feeling that as such cannot be captured in a physical way.

Service is normally perceived in a subjective manner. When service is described by customers, words such as 'experience', 'trust', 'feeling' and 'security' are used. These are highly abstract ways of formulating what service is. The reason for this, of course, lies in the intangible nature of service. Often service include highly tangible elements as well: for example, the bed and amenities in a holiday resort, the food in a restaurant, the documents used by a forwarding company, the spare parts used by a repair shop. The essence of service, however, is the intangibility of the phenomenon itself. Because of the high degree of intangibility, it is frequently difficult for the customer to evaluate a service. How do you give a distinct value to 'trust', or to a 'feeling', for example? Therefore, it is often suggested in the literature that one should make service more tangible for the customer by using concrete, physical evidence, such as plastic cards (in banking) and various kinds of atmosphere-related artefacts (in a restaurant). However, many physical goods, such as a sports car or luxury cellular phone, are equally intangible and perceived in a subjective way by customers.

Furthermore, many definitions imply that service does not result in *ownership* of anything.[7] Normally this is true. When we use an airline's service, we are entitled, for example, to be transported from one place to another, but when we arrive at our destination, there is nothing left but the boarding card. When we withdraw money from our current account we may feel that the bank's service resulted in our ownership of the withdrawn money. After the service process, we undoubtedly have the sum of money in our hands and we own it. However, the bank's service did not create this ownership. We, of course, owned the money all the time. On the other hand, retailing is service, and after using service provided by, say, a grocery store, the customer undoubtedly owns the groceries.

Finally, because of the impact of personnel and customers or both, on the service production and delivery process, it is often difficult to maintain consistency in the process. Service to one customer is not exactly the same as the 'same' service to the next customer. If nothing else, the social relationship in the two situations is different and the customer may act in different ways. The service a customer receives by using an ATM may differ from the 'same' service received by the next customer because, for instance, the second person has a problem understanding the instructions on the screen. The inconsistency in service processes creates one of the major problems in service management; that is, how to maintain an evenly perceived quality of the service rendered to customers.

CLASSIFICATION SCHEMES FOR SERVICE

In many publications from the early days of service marketing research, service was classified in a number of different ways.[8] Here we are only going to discuss two classifications:

1. High-touch/high-tech service.
2. Discretely/continuously rendered service.

First, service can be divided into *high-touch* or *high-tech*. High-touch service is mostly dependent on people in the service process, whereas high-tech service is predominantly based on the use of automated systems, information technology and other types of physical resources. This is of course an important distinction to make. However, one should always remember that high-touch also includes physical resources and technology-based systems that have to be managed and integrated into the service process in a customer-oriented fashion. While high-tech service, such as telecommunications or Internet shopping, by and large is technology-based, in critical moments, such as complaints situations or technology failures, or in built-in contacts with service employees representing, for example, helpdesk operations, the high-touch characteristic of the technology-based service takes over. In fact, one can say that high-tech service is often even more dependent on the service orientation and customer-consciousness of its personnel than high-touch service, because human interactions occur so seldom and when they occur they do so in critical situations. If these high-touch interactions of the high-tech service process fail, there are fewer opportunities to recover the mistake than in high-touch processes. In these cases high-touch contacts are true moments of truth for a firm, making it possible to secure a favourable quality perception in the end.[9]

Second, based on the nature of the relationship with customers, service can be divided into *continuously rendered service* and *discrete transactions*. Service such as industrial cleaning, security service, goods deliveries, banking, etc. involve a continuous flow of interactions between the customer and the service provider. This creates ample opportunity for the development of valued relationships with customers. For providers of discretely used service, such as hair stylists, many types of firms in the hospitality industry, providers of *ad hoc* repair service to equipment and so on, it is often more difficult to create a relationship that customers appreciate and value. However, as we know from many hair stylists, hotels and restaurants and other providers of discretely used service, this is possible and is considered a profitable strategy. Firms that offer service which are used on a continuous basis cannot afford to lose customers, because the cost of finding new customers is often high. On the other hand, firms offering service that is used in a discrete fashion may also develop a profitable business based on transaction oriented strategies, although a relationship orientation is probably to be recommended in most cases.

The models and concepts of service management discussed in this book are intended to be useful for all types of service firms and manufacturers for which service competition is important, and therefore useful for high-touch as well as for high-tech service, and for continuously rendered service as well as for discretely used service. However, service is always in some respect unique, and when developing strategies and implementing them this should be taken into consideration.

THE CONSUMPTION OF SERVICE: PROCESS AND OUTCOME CONSUMPTION

The focus on the interactions between the service firm and its customers in service research made consumption of service an important marketing issue. In traditional marketing models consumption is not a central issue. Marketing is geared towards sales and making customers buy. In goods-oriented models consumption is more or less a black box. In service marketing research the black box of consumption was opened up and explored. From a marketing point of view, consuming service is seamlessly integrated with buying service.[10] *Interactive marketing* (which will be explored further in Chapter 9) is the part of total marketing that is geared towards managing interactions with the customer during the consumption process in a value-supporting way, in order to increase the likelihood that the customers decide to stay with the firm.

In service research there has been no attempt to define the scope of the consumption process. In reality it is difficult to determine when consumption and customers' value creation starts and ends. For example, depending on how broadly consumption is defined, the consumption of an inclusive tour to a tourist destination may begin already when the customer starts thinking about taking the trip, or when the first interaction with an advertisement by the tour operator is seen. There may be a mental pre-consumption even before interactions with the tour operator's processes commence. Also, it may be difficult to determine when consumption ends. A similar mental post-consumption may take place. Using the inclusive tour example, one could say that consumption does not necessarily end when the customer returns home, but when memories of the trip are not brought up in discussions or entering the person's mind anymore.[11]

In order to understand service management and the marketing of service it is critical that one realizes that the consumption of service is *process consumption* rather than *outcome consumption*. In the case of physical goods, customers consume the *outcome* of the production process. In contrast, when consuming service customers perceive the process of producing service to a greater or smaller degree, but always to a critical extent, as well as take part in the process as co-producers. Thus, the consumption of the service *process* is a critical part of the service experience.

As service quality research demonstrates (see Chapters 4 and 5), experience of the process is important for the perception of the total quality of a service, even though a satisfactory outcome is necessary and a prerequisite for good quality. Often the service firm cannot differentiate its outcomes from those of its competitors. Withdrawing a given sum of money from a current account leads to the same result; the customer gets the requested amount, regardless of which bank is rendering the service. Flying from one place to another takes the passenger to the destination, regardless of which airline he patronizes. In some situations customers take the quality of an outcome for granted, and in many situations it is difficult for a customer to evaluate the quality of the outcome of the service process. For example, it is difficult to evaluate whether an Internet website provided by one firm is better than that which another firm could have offered. However, in every situation customers take part in the service processes and interact with the employees, physical resources, technologies and system of the service provider to some extent. The process easily distinguishes one service from another. Because of this inseparability of the service process and the consumption of a service, the process can be characterized as an *open process*. Hence, regardless of how the customer perceives the outcome of a service process, service consumption is basically *process consumption*.

In Figure 2.1 the nature of the consumption of physical goods (outcome consumption) and the consumption of service (process consumption) is illustrated. The relationships between production, consumption and marketing are shown in the figure. In the case of outcome consumption of physical goods, which is illustrated in the upper part of the figure, production and consumption are processes that are separated from each other in time and space. The traditional role of marketing, which is defined by the requirements of consumer goods, follows from this situation. A bridge between production and consumption that closes the gap between these two processes is needed. This bridge has, since the early twentieth century, been labelled marketing.

In the lower part of the figure, process consumption of service is illustrated. Production and consumption are simultaneous processes with interactions between the consumer and the service provider's production resources – people, physical resources, operational systems and infrastructures, information technology, etc. The obvious conclusion that can be drawn from this is that *there is no gap between production and consumption that needs to be closed by a separate activity or function.* There is no room for marketing's traditional bridge-building role in this situation. This can be considered to be the essence of service marketing. Marketing has to be included in the system in a different way than in traditional models. *The heart of marketing service is how the service (production) process and service consumption process match each other, so that consumers perceive good service quality and value-creation support, and are willing to continue the relationship with the service provider.*[12] Of course, some activities of a bridge-building nature remain. For example, market research, as well as efforts, such as pricing, advertising and other kinds of marketing communication, to create an interest among potential customers in the

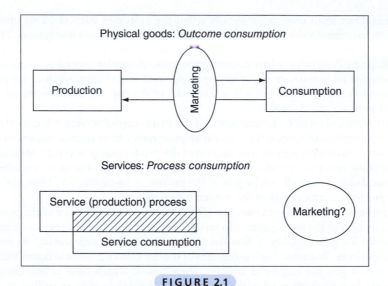

Physical goods: *Outcome consumption*

FIGURE 2.1

**The nature of consumption of physical goods and services and
the role of marketing.**

service provider and its service offerings and to create trial purchases, is still required. However, the major part of marketing, managing the firm's customer relationships and other market relationships, becomes an integral part of the simultaneous service production and service consumption processes.

Thus service consumption and production have interfaces that are always critical to customers' perception of the service and consequently to their long-term purchasing behaviour. For example, in the bank and airline examples used earlier, the location and security of an ATM or the interaction process in a bank, as well as the check-in, in-flight and luggage claim processes in an airline experience, have a decisive effect on customers' perception of the service and its quality. Hence, for the long-term success of a service firm the customer orientation of the service processes is crucial. If the process fails from the customer's point of view, no traditional marketing efforts, and frequently not even a good outcome of the service process, will make them stay with a company in the long run, if they can find an alternative.

It is interesting to observe that in the production of a variety of physical goods, everything from cars and computers to jeans and dolls, customers can be drawn into the planning of goods and the manufacturing processes of the factory, through the use of modern information technology and the Internet, and modern design and modular production techniques. This enables *mass customization* and interactions between the manufacturer and marketer on the one hand and the customer on the other.[13] Levi Strauss makes jeans to order, and Mattel offers customized 'friends of Barbie' dolls. One can buy a customer–ordered BMW, and even made–to–order vitamin pills.[14] In manufacturing in general this is the case both for consumer markets and business–to–business markets. The physical goods become more and more service–like, and service marketing knowledge and a service management framework are required to successfully manage the business.

Thus it seems inevitable that understanding service processes is becoming an imperative for all types of business, not only for what used to be called service firms. One central reason for management to understand the logic of service management is the fact that the main sources of competitive advantage are different for a service business as compared to a traditional product business.

SOURCES OF COMPETITIVE ADVANTAGE IN SERVICE

The main sources of competitive advantage are different in service compared to a product business. For a product business there are of course also other sources of competitive advantage, but the most basic and generic one is *standardization* and the possibility to produce an item on a large scale with a guaranteed quality. If a product with standardized and to some extent unique features can be developed, it can be reproduced as many times as the available production capacity allows. The drawback is of course rigidity, and any customer who prefers something even slightly different will not buy.

The sources of competitive advantage are different for service businesses mainly because of the process nature of service. Service as a business perspective and also as an activity are ongoing processes which are inherently relational. Relational processes include both social and physical interactions, which are difficult to standardize. Attempts to do that normally leads to a rigid process, which neither the customers nor the firm's employees feel comfortable with. Employees become frustrated and in the end demotivated to provide good service. Customers see the quality of the service deteriorate, become frustrated and are demotivated to continue buying from the service provider. Unsatisfied customers defect, and business is lost. Lost customers must be replaced by new ones, which increases the firm's customer acquisition costs. Price pressure may also develop.

Further, service processes have to be systematized in some way, so that unnecessarily complicated and bureaucratic parts can be avoided. However, *systematizing is not the same as standardizing*. For example, an elevator repair process can be systematized, for example to avoid overlapping activities and delays caused by the wrong sequence of activities, without standardizing the process. Unfortunately, firms often mistake systematizing processes for creating standardized processes.

Service processes can, and should, be systematized, but without destroying the two key sources of competitive advantage of service businesses. These are:

1. Flexibility when designing service processes.

2. Adaptability when situations which differ from the normal procedure occur.

Flexibility means that a service process is designed such that it allows for deviations from a normal, or standard, procedure. Flexibility must be built into the service process However, it must be planned, so that limits of allowed deviations are known. Otherwise, employees do not know how far from the standard they are allowed to go. The limit of flexibility is a strategic decision. Refunding customers who want to return something they have bought 'no questions asked' is one extreme flexibility limit. On the other hand one can go even further. In the management literature there is a supposedly true anecdote about the Nordstroms stores in the US. This is a top end department store, and when a person returned four new tyres with the wrong dimensions for his car, he was refunded. However, Nordstroms do not sell tyres. Most flexibility limits are of course less extreme. For example, in a restaurant with set menus the waiters can suggest or allow some combinations between menus and à la carte lists. An airline employee knows how to compensate passengers for flight delays or lost luggage, what can be offered automatically, and when a decision by a supervisor is required.

To make sure that customers will get good quality, flexibility must be a forethought, not an afterthought. If it is an afterthought, inconsistent behaviour will follow and customers will be lost. Lack of in-built flexibility leads to rigidity, and one of the central sources of competitive advantage is lost.

Adaptability relates to *ad hoc* situations that occur in a service process, and is therefore required for successful implementation of flexible processes. Flexibility means that a service process is designed in a certain way. Adaptability means that employees and systems can observe the need for out-of-the-normal behaviour in customer contacts. This requires that customer contact employees have the skills and knowledge to register a need for deviations from the normal procedure and to perform their tasks accordingly in a flexible manner, and are motivated to do so. Systems in the service process must be designed to support adaptability and not to make it impossible. For example, if a waiter observes that a restaurant guest is uncomfortable with the items on the menu, he could ask whether the guest has some special wishes, and then try to offer something that meets the guest's requirements.

If service processes are standardized, flexibility and adaptability are lost, and the offering reverts to a standardized product. As a consequence, the service firm becomes a product business. On the other hand, if a goods manufacturer adds flexibility to its ways of taking care of its customers, for example in deliveries or maintenance or in hidden services such as invoicing and complaints handling, it moves away from being a product business towards becoming a service business and makes use of sources of competitive advantage in service. (Chapter 16 discusses at length how a manufacturing firm can transform into a service business.)

CASE STUDY

COFFEE SHOP: THE IMPORTANCE OF AVOIDING INFLEXIBILITY

Early one morning a guest in a coffee shop asked for a ham omelette, although the menu did not include such an item. The waiter responded that the coffee shop did not serve ham omelettes. But the guest really fancied such a dish and asked whether they had ham and eggs and other required ingredients in the kitchen. The waiter admitted that all ingredients were available. 'Then ask the kitchen to make a ham omelette,' said the guest. To this the waiter, at this point clearly feeling awkward, responded that it was impossible. 'Why is that? You have all the ingredients,' the guest prompted. The final words in this dialogue were voiced by the waiter: 'We have no code.'

It turned out that the coffee shop had preprogrammed the prices of all available dishes in the computer, and there was no way of calculating a price for anything outside this predetermined list of items.

Flexibility was removed from the process, the waiter had no means of adapting to the situation, and the customer left and never came back. However, through word-of-mouth the story lives.

CUSTOMER MANAGEMENT IN A PHYSICAL GOODS CONTEXT: THE TRADITIONAL GOODS MARKETING TRIANGLE

In this and the following section we shall explore how the role of marketing differs between a physical goods and a service context. As a means of illustration we use a marketing triangle. This way of representing the field of marketing is adapted from Philip Kotler,[15] who introduced it, to illustrate

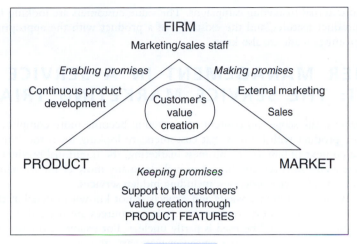

FIGURE 2.2

The product marketing triangle.
Source: Adapted from Grönroos, C., Relationship marketing
logic. *Asia-Australia Marketing Journal*, **4**(1); 1996: p. 9.
Reproduced by the permission of the Australasian and New
Zealand Marketing Academy.

the holistic concept of marketing suggested by the Nordic School approach to service marketing and management. This triangle's sides represent *making promises*, *keeping promises* and *enabling promises*.

A physical product, in the traditional sense, is the result of how various resources, such as people, technologies, raw materials, knowledge and information, have been managed in a factory to incorporate a number of features that customers in target markets are looking for. The production process can be characterized as a *closed process*, where the customer takes no direct part. Thus a product evolves as a pre-produced package of resources and features ready to be exchanged. The task of marketing (including sales) is to find out what product features the customers are interested in and to make promises about such features to a segment of potential customers through external marketing activities such as sales and advertising campaigns, and to take the product to locations where customers are willing to purchase it. If the product includes features that customers want, it will fulfil the promises that have been made to them. This marketing situation is illustrated in the *product marketing triangle* in Figure 2.2. Customers' willingness to buy a product and satisfaction with the product are due to how well it supports their value creation, which is indicated by the circle in the centre of the triangle.

In the figure the three key parts of marketing in a goods context are shown. These are the *firm*, represented by a marketing and/or sales department, the *market*, and the *product*. Normally, marketing (including sales) is the responsibility of a department (or departments) of specialists or full-time marketers (and salespeople). Customers are viewed in terms of markets of anonymous individuals. The market offering is a pre-produced physical product. Along the sides of the triangle three key functions of marketing are displayed, to *make promises*, to *keep promises* and to *enable promises*. Promises are normally made through external mass marketing, and in business-to-business marketing, as well as through sales. Promises are kept through a number of product features and enabled through the process of continuous product development based on market research performed by full-time marketers and the technological capabilities of the firm. Marketing is very much directed towards making promises through external marketing campaigns. The value customers are looking for is guaranteed by appropriate product features, and the existence of a product with the appropriate features will make sure that promises made are also kept.

CUSTOMER MANAGEMENT IN A SERVICE CONTEXT: THE SERVICE MARKETING TRIANGLE

For a service business, the scope and content of marketing become more complicated. The notion of a pre-produced product with features that customers are looking for is too limited to be useful here. Also, in the context of business-to-business marketing, the traditional product construct is too restrictive, because a customer relationship often includes many more elements than physical goods, normally various types of service processes, including hidden services.

In many cases what the customer wants and expects is not known in detail at the beginning of the service (production) process or, consequently, what resources are needed, to what extent and in what configuration they should be used is partly unclear. For example, the service requirements of a machine that has been delivered to a customer may vary; the need to provide training for the customer's personnel and the need to handle claims may vary; a bank customer may only realize what his needs actually are during interactions with a teller or a loan officer. Thus, the firm has to adjust its resources and its ways of using its resources accordingly.

In Figure 2.3, the *service marketing triangle*,[16] marketing in a service context is illustrated. As can be seen, compared to the goods marketing triangle in Figure 2.2 most elements are different. Customers' willingness to buy service and satisfaction with it are due to how well the service supports their value creation, which is indicated by the circle in the centre of the triangle.

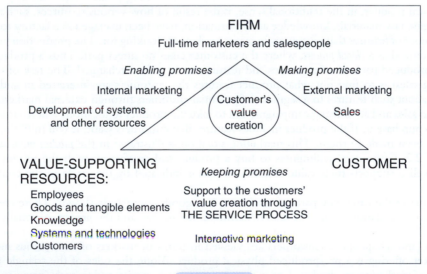

FIGURE 2.3

The service marketing triangle.
Source: Adapted from Grönroos, C., Relationship marketing logic.
Asia-Australia Marketing Journal, **4**(1); 1996: p. 10. Reproduced by the permission of the Australasian and New Zealand Marketing Academy.

The most important change from the goods marketing situation is the fact that the *pre-produced product is missing*.[17] In process consumption, no pre-produced bundle of features that constitutes a product can be present. Only service concepts and preparations for a service process can be made beforehand and partly prepared service can exist. In many service contexts, such as fast-food restaurants or car rental service, physical product elements with specific features are also present as integral parts of the service process. These product elements are sometimes, as in the case of car rental, pre-produced, and sometimes (as in the case of the hamburger in a fast-food operation) partly pre-produced, partly made to order. However, such physical products have no meaning as such, unless they fit the service process. They become one type of resource among many other types that have to be integrated into a functioning service process. A bundle of different types of resources creates value for customers when these resources are used in their presence and in interactions with them. Even if service firms try to create products out of the resources available, they cannot come up with more than a standardized plan to guide the ways of using existing resources in the simultaneous service production and service consumption processes. Customer-perceived value follows from a successful and customer-oriented management of resources relative to customer sacrifice, not from a pre-produced bundle of features.

The firm may still have a centralized marketing and sales staff, the full-time marketers, but they do not represent all the marketers and salespeople of the firm. In most cases the service firm has direct contact with its customers, and information about each and every customer can be obtained on an individual basis. This is beneficial because, in many cases, customers (business-to-business customers and individual consumers and households alike) like to be treated individually.

In Figure 2.3, the pre-produced product is replaced by an offering consisting of a set of value-supporting resources functioning together with the customer in a service process. These resources of a firm are divided into five groups: personnel, technology, goods, knowledge, and the customer. Many of the *people* representing the firm influence the customers' perception of quality and value creation in various service processes, such as deliveries, restaurant service, customer training, claims handling, repair and maintenance, etc. Their way of handling their tasks influences the customers' perception of quality and willingness to do business with them and the organization they represent in the future as well. Thus, their way of serving customers has a decisive marketing impact. Gummesson has called these customer contact service employees *part-time marketers*.[18] In many service firms they outnumber the full-time marketers many times. In addition, they have customer contacts during the crucial moments of truth when the service is produced for the customer, often together with the customer, something that full-time marketers seldom have.

In addition to part-time marketers, other types of resource influence the quality and value perceived by the customer and are hence important from a marketing perspective. *Technologies*,[19] *goods*, the *knowledge* that employees have and that is embedded in technical solutions, and the firm's way of managing the *customer's time* are such resources. By participating in the service process, the *customers* as individual consumers or as users representing organizations often become a value-creating resource.

In summary, from the customer's point of view, in process consumption the solutions to their problems are formed by a process and a *set of resources* needed to create a good customer-perceived service quality. In addition, the firm must have *competencies* to acquire and/or develop the resources needed and to manage and implement the service process in a way that creates value for each customer. Thus, a *governing system* is needed for the integration of the various types of resources and for the management of the service processes. In the service marketing literature, the way these resources are managed and implemented in interactions with the customers is called the *interactive marketing* function. We shall return to this concept in Chapter 9 on *managing marketing or customer-focused management*.

Promises made by sales and external marketing are fulfilled through the use of all types of resources. In order to prepare an appropriate set of resources, continuous product development in its traditional form is not enough, because the service process encompasses a large part of the activities of the service firm. Instead, to enable the fulfilment of promises, continuous *resource development* including *internal marketing* and a continuous development of the competencies and the resource structure of the firm are needed. Internal marketing will be discussed in depth in Chapter 14.

SERVICE MANAGEMENT AND MARKETING: A CASE OF A MISSING PRODUCT

The conclusion of the discussion in the previous sections is that service businesses – service firms and product manufacturers adopting a service logic – do not have products (understood as pre-produced bundles of resources and features); they only have processes, including a set of resources of many kinds, to offer their customers. Of course, these processes also lead to an outcome that is important for the customer. However, as the outcome of, for example, a management consultancy assignment or hotel accommodation cannot exist without the process, and because from the customer's perspective the process is an open process, it is fruitful to view the outcome as a part of the process. Both the process and its outcome have an impact on customer perception of the quality of service and consequently on customers' value creation.

A major challenge for service providers is, therefore, to develop innovative ways of managing processes as solutions to customer problems. The value support that a firm can offer is not embedded in the resources used in the service process, but it emerges in customers' consumption or usage processes, when they use these resources in interaction with the service provider in order to achieve an outcome for themselves. Models and concepts of service management – perceived service quality, customer-perceived value, service production systems, internal marketing and other models and concepts – have been developed to help managers cope with this challenge.

CUSTOMER-TO-CUSTOMER COMMUNICATION: EXPERIENTIALIZING SERVICE PROCESSES

The customers have many roles in the service process. In the previous section customers interacting with the service provider's resources were considered participants in the process as co-producers. Furthermore, customers experience the service process and perceive the service they get. These are the traditional customer roles in service processes. However, with the emergence of Internet and mobile-mediated ways of interacting and communicating, such as Facebook and Twitter, customers can also interact during a service process while consuming the service. Twitter especially provides a means of on-the-spot interactions through live tweeting, where tweets can be responded to instantly or forwarded immediately to other persons. This, of course, has a dramatic effect on word-of-mouth, where customers can share experiences with a huge number of peers for their further consideration when looking for purchasing options. However, it also has an effect which changes the nature of service experiences and therefore also of service processes, and the perception of the service.

Kai Huotari, who has studied the use of Twitter during TV shows and ice hockey games on TV, introduces the term *experientializing* for this phenomenon.[20] A group of people sharing an interest in, for example, a given TV show, who watch the show in different locations, establish a contact with Twitter and, using *live-tweeting*, share their experiences with others in the group. In this way *the personal service experiences change due to the experience sharing* throughout the process, through customer-to-customer communication. *Because the service provider has no control over how the service is experientialized,* the service experiences and how they are developing and changing through experientializing may cause new challenges. Of course, experientializing has existed before, for example when a group of people gather at home or in a bar to watch a TV programme, but Twitter and live-tweeting add a totally new dimension to this phenomenon.

The experientializing concept also helps to understand other consumption situations, where consumers interact, either in person or through live-tweeting or any other similar means, and even where a single consumer without any C2C interactions adds an aspect to the service process which is not originally part of the planned service. For example, a person reading a newspaper or book during a bus or train trip experientializes the travel process, and the experience is different from a trip without a newspaper or book, and therefore the service is also different.[21] For example, cafés, train companies and airlines have offered newspapers and magazines to their customers, in order to make their service experience more enjoyable.

CASE STUDY

THE MISSING PRODUCT IN AN ELEVATOR REPAIR AND MAINTENANCE FIRM

This case study of a firm providing elevator repair and maintenance service is an illustration of how the missing product of a service provider has been replaced by a quality-generating service system to promote enduring customer relationships. The case company is a large elevator manufacturer, and repair and maintenance provider, operating globally. Its repair and maintenance business had, however, been unprofitable for some time and it had problems in maintaining its customer relationships.[22]

To find out the reason behind the loss of customers, a large-scale survey was conducted among the firm's customers. The questionnaire was based on the assumption that the company offered a product that could be described as the outcome of repair and maintenance activities. This quantitative study indicated that the repair and maintenance service of the firm was low quality and that its prices were considered high. This result led to great consternation among top management and the marketing and sales group, because they knew that the firm as a major service provider had by far the best-trained service technicians, the best possible instruments for diagnosing problems, the best tools and equipment for taking care of any repair and maintenance job, and the widest possible assortment of spare parts. Everybody in the firm considered it to have the best service on the market, and they could not understand why the customers considered the quality of the repair and maintenance service to be low. High prices were easier to understand because being a large company, it had high overhead costs and had to maintain a high price level.

Because top management had difficulty in accepting the results of the study, a second, qualitative study was initiated. One hundred former customers, mostly representing business customers such as office buildings and institutions but also residential buildings, were interviewed in an unstructured fashion. The main interview question could be phrased as 'What went wrong?'

In spite of some variations in results, the average lost customer expressed the following opinion:

We realize that you have the best capabilities on the market to repair and maintain elevators, and in most cases you do a good job. However, we do not feel comfortable with the way you are doing the job. We cannot trust your service technicians to start doing the repair or maintenance task according to what has been promised, and quite often you do not give exact promises about when the job will start. Although some of your people are attentive and show an interest in our concerns regarding the elevator and its problems, most of them could not care less about us as people and the need for information that we sometimes have. Sometimes we do not even recognize them as your employees. Quite often the service technician just leaves a job unfinished and we do not know why or when he will be back to finish it. Because we cannot always trust your way of doing the job and because it is therefore complicated for us to be your customers, we think that the quality of your service is low and that we, therefore, pay too much for them.

The implications of the second study were quite obvious. Top management and the marketing and sales group thought that the company had ready-made products to be delivered to their repair and maintenance customers (more or less equalling the outcome of repair and maintenance), whereas the customers considered the company to be offering processes. Furthermore, although the customers recognized that the processes had to include a successful outcome, their concerns regarding the repair and maintenance service and its quality were associated with the process and with problems occurring in the process.

The second study helped management to understand that the object of the elevator repair and maintenance business was the service process, and that it really was a case of a missing product. It was realized that the solution to the customers' problems consisted of the outcome of the service process as well as of the process itself. Moreover, the customers clearly indicated that the outcome had to be of on acceptable quality, but when this was the case the outcome (the successful result of the repair and maintenance process) was obvious to the customers and the service process became the issue. Both the outcome and the process have to be carefully planned and well implemented, if the repair and maintenance service is to be considered good. Both the outcome and the service process have to be of good quality. It turned out that the former was perceived by the customers as a prerequisite, and in the final analysis it was the quality of the process that counted.

Clearly the firm thought that it was offering and delivering pre-produced products to its repair and maintenance customers, whereas the customers considered the offering to be quite different. They saw a process which created quality and value for them, and no ready-made solution. Although the outcome of the service process had to be good, it was the quality of the service process and the value provided by it that determined whether or not the repair and maintenance service was considered good. This case will be continued in Chapter 13. In that context the actions taken to improve the perceived quality of the service as a process will be discussed.

SUMMARY

This chapter discussed the characteristics of service and observed that their processes form their major feature. The difference between process consumption and outcome consumption was analysed, and it was concluded that the consumption or use of service can be characterized as process consumption. Sources of competitive advantage in service due to their process nature were then discussed. Finally, implications for marketing of the process nature of service was discussed at some length. It was concluded that the scope of marketing is different in services to that in physical goods.

QUESTIONS FOR DISCUSSION

1. Why is the process nature of services their most important feature? What other distinguishing characteristics of service can be identified?

2. What impact does the process nature and other characteristics of service have on the scope and content of marketing?

3. What are the differences between outcome consumption and process consumption?

4. Which sources of competitive advantage exist for service businesses? How do they differ from those of a product business?

5. What are the major managerial consequences of the fact that service to a critical extent is consumed at the same time as it is produced?

6. What is meant by experientializing, and how is a given service experientialized, for example, through live tweeting.

NOTES

1. Harvey-Jones, J., *Making It Happen. Reflections on Leadership*. Glasgow: Fontana/Collins, 1989.

2. A range of such definitions is discussed in Grönroos, C., *Service Management and Marketing. Managing the Moments of Truth in Service Competition*. Lexington, MA: Lexington Books, 1990.

3. Gummesson, E., Lip services – a neglected area in services marketing. *Journal of Services Marketing*, **1**, 1987.

4. Grönroos, 1990, *op. cit.*

5. See Grönroos, C., Adopting a service logic for marketing. *Marketing Theory*, **6**(3), 2006, 317–333.

6. Since the beginning of systematized research into service marketing in the 1970s, four generic characteristics of services that distinguish services from physical goods have invariably been

included in articles and textbooks; that is, intangibility, heterogeneity, inseparability and perishability. This set of characteristics and the fact that services are described in relation to goods have seldom been disputed. In the Nordic School research this set of characteristics has never been used as such. However, lately the relevance of this way of describing services has been criticized. See, for example, Lovelock, C.H. & Gummesson, E., Whither service marketing? In search of a new paradigm and fresh perspectives. *Journal of Service Research*, **7**(1), 2004, 20–41 and Edvardsson, B., Gustafsson, A. & Roos, I., Service portraits in service research: a critical review. *International Journal of Service Industry Management*, **16**(1), 2005, 107–121.

7. For a recent discussion of the ownership issue, see Lovelock & Gummesson, 2004, *op. cit.*

8. A comprehensive discussion of classification schemes can be found in Lovelock, C.H., Classifying services to gain strategic marketing insights. *Journal of Marketing*, **47**(3), 1983, 9–20. See also Grönroos, 1990, *op. cit.*

9. Wünderlich, N.V., von Wangenheim, F. & Bitner, M.J., High tech and high touch: a framework for understanding user attitudes and behaviors related to smart interactive services. *Journal of Service Research*, **16**(1), 2013, 3–20. See also Berry, L.L. & Parasuraman, A., *Marketing Services. Competing Through Quality*. New York: Free Press, 1991.

10. Grönroos, C., What can a service logic offer marketing theory? In Lusch, R.F. and Vargo, S.L. (eds), *The Service-Dominant Logic of Marketing: Dialog, Debate, and Directions*. Armonk, NY: M.E. Sharpe, 2006, pp. 354–364.

11. As observed in the customer-dominant logic research stream, the question of when consumption starts and when it ends has not been problematized in the service management and marketing literature. See Heinonen, K, Strandvik, T. & Voima, P., Customer dominant value formation in service. *European Business Review*, **25**(2), 2013, 104–123.

12. See Grönroos, C., Service reflections: service marketing comes of age. In Swartz, T.A. & Iacobucci, D. (eds), *Handbook of Services Marketing & Management*. Thousand Oaks, CA: Sage Publications, 2000, pp. 13–16.

13. Peppers, D. & Rogers, M., *Enterprise One-to-One*. London: Currency/Doubleday, 1997.

14. See Schonfeld, E., The customized, digitized, have-it-your-way economy. *Fortune*, 28 September, 1998, 69–74.

15. Kotler, P., *Marketing Management. Analysis, Planning, Implementation and Control*, 8th edn. Englewood Cliffs, NJ: Prentice-Hall, 1994. However, Kotler only included people in his triangle model and omitted the physical resource (technology, goods and systems) elements of the Nordic School approach to service marketing.

16. In a service context the marketing triangle issue has been developed by Mary Jo Bitner and Christian Grönroos. See Bitner M.J., Building service relationships: it's all about promises. *Journal of the Academy of Marketing Science*, **23**, 1995, 246–251 and Grönroos, C., Relationship marketing: strategic and tactical implications. *Management Decision*, **34**(3), 1996, 5–14. Since then the service marketing triangle concept has been applied in several contexts. See, for example, Yadav, R.K. & Dabhade, N., Service marketing triangle and GAP model in hospital industry. *International Letters of Social and Humanistic Sciences*, **8**, 2013, 77–85.

17. See Grönroos, C., Marketing services: a case of a missing product. *Journal of Business & Industrial Marketing*, **13**(4–5), 1998, 322–338.

18. See, for example, Gummesson, E., *Total Relationship Marketing. Rethinking Marketing Management: From 4Ps to 30Rs*. London: Butterworth-Heinemann, 1999.

19. Parasuraman has also recognized the importance of adding technology to the product marketing triangle, which he illustrates using a pyramid metaphor. See, for example, Parasuraman, A. & Grewal, D., The impact of technology on the quality–value–loyalty chain: a research agenda. *Journal of the Academy of Marketing Science*, **28**(1), 2000, 168–174.

20. Huotari, K., Experientializing – how C2C communication becomes part of the service experience. The case of live-tweeting and TV-viewing. Helsinki: Hanken School of Economics, Finland, 2014.

21. See Huotari, *op. cit.*

22. This case is based on a situation that occurred roughly 25 years ago. However, because it is pedagogically the best case about the 'missing product' in a service operation that the author knows about, it is used here. Moreover, although the case company successfully solved their problems, situations like the one presented in the case study are not uncommon today.

FURTHER READING

Berry, L.L. & Parasuraman, A. (1991) *Marketing Services. Competing Through Quality*. New York: Free Press.

Bitner M.O. (1995). Building service relationships: it's all about promises. *Journal of the Academy of Marketing Science*, **23**, 246–251.

Edvardsson, B., Gustafsson, A. & Roos, I. (2005) Service portraits in service research: a critical review. *International Journal of Service Industry Management*, **16**(1), 107–121.

Grönroos, C. (1990) *Service Management and Marketing. Managing the Moments of Truth in Service Competition*. Lexington, MA: Lexington Books.

Grönroos, C. (1996) Relationship marketing: strategic and tactical implications. *Management Decision*, **34**(3), 5–14.

Grönroos, C. (1998) Marketing services: a case of a missing product. *Journal of Business & Industrial Marketing*, **13**(4–5), 322–338.

Grönroos, C. (2000) Service reflections: service marketing comes of age. In Swartz, T.A. & Iacobucci, D. (eds), *Handbook of Services Marketing & Management*. Thousand Oaks, CA: Sage Publications, pp. 13–16.

Grönroos, C. (2006a) What can a service logic offer marketing theory? In Lusch, R.F. and Vargo, S.L. (eds), *The Service-Dominant Logic of Marketing: Dialog, Debate, and Directions*. Armonk, NY: M.E. Sharpe, pp. 354–364.

Grönroos, C. (2006b) Adopting a service logic for marketing. *Marketing Theory*, **3**(3), 313–337.

Gummesson, E. (1987) Lip services – a neglected area in services marketing. *Journal of Services Marketing*, **2**(1), 19–24.

Gummesson, E. (1999) *Total Relationship Marketing. Rethinking Marketing Management: From 4Ps to 30Rs*. London: Butterworth–Heinemann.

Harvey-Jones, J. (1989) *Making It Happen. Reflections on Leadership*. Glasgow: Fontana/Collins.

Heinonen, K, Strandvik, T. & Voima, P. (2013) Customer dominant value formation in service. *European Business Review*, **25**(2), 104–123.

Huotari, K. (2014) *Experientializing – how C2C communication becomes part of the service experience. The case of live-tweeting and TV-viewing*. Helsinki: Hanken School of Economics, Finland.

Khalifa, A.S. (2004) Customer value: a review of recent literature and an integrative configuration. *Management Decision*, **42**(5), 645–666.

Korkman, O. (2006) *Customer Value Formation in Practice. A Practice-Theoretical Approach*. Helsinki: Hanken Swedish School of Economics, Finland.

Kotler, P. (1994) *Marketing Management. Analysis, Planning, Implementation and Control*, 8th edn. Englewood Cliffs, NJ: Prentice-Hall.

Lovelock, C.H. (1983) Classifying services to gain strategic marketing insights. *Journal of Marketing*, **47**(3), 9–20.

Lovelock, C.H. (1991) *Services Marketing*. Englewood Cliffs, NJ: Prentice-Hall.

Lovelock, C.H. & Gummesson, E. (2004) Whither service marketing? In search of a new paradigm and fresh perspectives. *Journal of Service Research*, **7**(1), 20–41.

Parasuraman, A. & Grewal, D. (2000) The impact of technology on the quality–value–loyalty chain: a research agenda. *Journal of the Academy of Marketing Science*, **28**(1), 168–174.

Peppers, D. & Rogers, M. (1997) *Enterprise One-to-One*. London: Currency/Doubleday.

Prahalad, C.K. & Ramaswamy, V. (2004) *The Future of Competition: Co-Creating Unique Value with Customers*. Boston, MA: Harvard Business School Press.

Ravald, A. & Grönroos, C. (1996) The value concept in relationship. *European Journal of Marketing*, **30**(2), 19–30.

Schonfeld, E. (1998) The customized, digitized, have-it-your-way economy. *Fortune*, September 28, pp. 69–74.

Wünderlich, N.V., von Wangenheim, F. & Bitner, M.J. (2013) High tech and high touch: a framework for understanding user attitudes and behaviors related to smart interactive services. *Journal of Service Research*, **16**(1), 3–20.

Yadav, R.K. & Dabhade, N. (2013), Service marketing triangle and the GAP model in hospital industry. *International Letters of Social and Humanistic Sciences*, **8**, 77–85.

Zeithaml, V.A. & Bitner, M.J. (2000) *Services Marketing. Integrating Customer Focus Across the Firm*, 2nd edn. New York: McGraw-Hill.

CHAPTER 3
THE SERVICE PROFIT LOGIC AND SERVICE MANAGEMENT PRINCIPLES

In service, costs and revenues are inseparable. The same resources, activities and processes drive both costs and revenues — and ultimately profits.

INTRODUCTION

This chapter will discuss the nature of a service strategy, based on the service profit logic, and the importance of customer perceived quality. This includes a discussion of the pitfalls for service organizations of strategic management from a traditional manufacturing perspective, and the development of a service-oriented view of the business logic. Thus, the importance of a service-oriented approach to strategy and management is emphasized. Finally, service management as a management philosophy is defined and principles of this approach to management are discussed. After having read this chapter the reader should understand the Service Profit Logic and how it differs from a conventional manufacturing profit logic, and be familiar with the pitfalls of a traditional management approach in service contexts. Finally the reader should know how to apply a service logic to management and service management principles.

SOME TRADITIONAL AND POTENTIALLY DANGEROUS STRATEGY LESSONS FROM MANUFACTURING

For a manufacturer of goods, conventional managerial thinking generally includes, among other elements, three rules of thumb to follow in order to strengthen or maintain the competitive edge of a firm:

1. Decrease production and administration costs, to decrease the unit cost of products.

2. If needed, increase the budget for traditional marketing efforts such as advertising, sales and sales promotion in order to make the market buy the goods produced.

3. Strengthen product development efforts.

For conventional product manufacturing, these rules of thumb usually make sense. If production costs can be decreased, lower prices can be offered, or higher margins can be obtained. The consumption of physical goods can be characterized as *outcome consumption* – the customer consumes the outcome of the production process – and, regardless of the new, more effective and efficient production technologies and methods used, the outcome and the product quality remains the same. Economies of scale normally pay off. Moreover, sales and marketing efforts usually have a positive effect on demand. Continuous product development is of vital importance to manufacturing.

Assuming that the management of capital is sound, the long-term business success of any business is to manage revenues and costs successfully, such that a positive economic outcome is achieved. It is simplistic to say that profit equals revenues minus costs, but the business implications of this are far from simplistic. Misunderstanding these implications may turn out to be fatal. For conventional product manufacturing the business implications can be illustrated as the *Manufacturing Profit Logic* in Figure 3.1.

As illustrated by the Manufacturing Profit Logic, and the ground rules for product management outlined earlier, *revenues are driven* by sales and conventional external marketing mix activities – traditional marketing such as product design and packaging, advertising and other means of marketing communication, pricing and distribution. Marketing and sales are given the responsibility for successful external impact in the marketplace and marketspace. Production and a whole host of production-related and administrative processes, such as R&D, product development, manufacturing, logistics, order-taking, invoicing, complaints handling, human resource management, accounting and budgeting processes, and general administration are considered *cost driving*. Their immediate impact on revenues is thought to be minimal, and mostly only indirect through the manufactured products. This is due the fact the most of the manufacturing firm's processes are closed to the customer. In other words, the *internal efficiency* of the firm's processes, how the firm's production and many administrative functions work, are considered to drive costs only, but not revenues, other than indirectly through the quality of the goods produced. The firm's *external effectiveness*, how customers perceive the quality of products and why they are willing to purchase them, is mainly considered the responsibility of traditional marketing and sales.

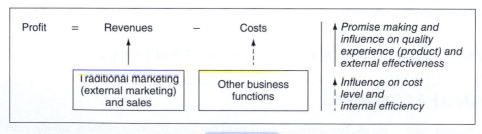

FIGURE 3.1

The Manufacturing Profit Logic.

Internal efficiency and external effectiveness can be defined and described in the following way:

- *Internal efficiency*: efficient use of production (and administrative) resources; what traditionally, but not totally accurately, is called 'productivity'.

- *External effectiveness*: the external effectiveness of the firm's operations as perceived by its customers (in the form of customer perceived quality and customers' willingness to pay a given price for an offering).

Internal efficiency is related to the way a firm operates and the productivity of labour and capital. It can, for example, be measured by the unit cost of the production output. External effectiveness, on the other hand, is the way customers perceive the processes and the process outcomes of the firm, or in other words, how customers perceive quality.

In conventional product manufacturing, *internal efficiency* and *external effectiveness* are treated as separate management issues, and *cost drivers are not considered revenue drivers*. Conventional management models are based on the situation described by the manufacturing profit logic. In conventional product manufacturing it works.

To sum up, according to this profit logic, sales and marketing are expected to be promise making, and therefore to acquire paying customers, as indicated by the thick arrow in Figure 3.1. By producing products for sales and marketing, business function other than these functions create costs and determine the firm's level of internal efficiency (indicated by the dotted arrow in the figure).

Profit orientation is needed in service, too. However, if lessons from the manufacturing sector, and the Manufacturing Profit Logic, are followed unchanged, there is a risk that the firm will fall into a *strategic management trap*, or what Richard Normann called a *vicious circle*.[1] Before we discuss the strategic management trap further, it is important to define the commercial foundation of service, or the *Service Profit Logic*.

THE SERVICE PROFIT LOGIC

According to the characteristics of service and the service quality models (see Chapters 4 and 5 where perceived service quality is discussed in detail), resources and activities that have an impact on customer perceived quality and future buying and consumption behaviour can be found in most departments of the service firm. Production and other business functions traditionally considered internal to the firm affect customers' behaviour. In service, operations management, management of human resources and marketing management are interrelated. Peter Drucker's view that marketing, from the customer's point of view, is too important to the firm's economic result to be treated as a separate function is very valid indeed.[2]

As a consequence, other than partly, the profit and cost drivers in service are not the same as in product manufacturing. Because of this, managers in service business must consider the *Service Profit Logic* as a starting point for any strategies and business decisions. As Figure 3.2 shows, the Service Profit Logic is dramatically different from the corresponding Manufacturing Profit Logic.

We demonstrate in Figure 3.2 that decisions concerning business functions other than traditional marketing and sales, such as production and those functions responsible for a variety of customer contacts and what, in the previous chapter, was labelled recognized and hidden services, not only affect internal efficiency and costs, but also have a decisive impact on external effectiveness and revenues. *Recognized services* such as repair and maintenance, as well as *hidden services*, such as invoicing and recovering failures and quality problems, not only drive costs but often have a major impact on the firm's power to generate revenues. *Thus, the profit logic and how profit is formed through revenue*

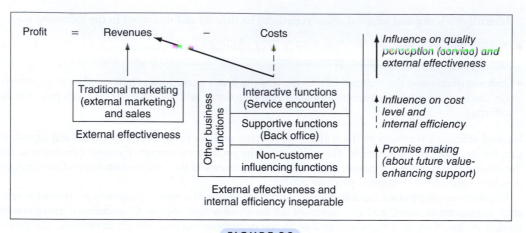

FIGURE 3.2

The Service Profit Logic.

and cost drivers change altogether. Decisions regarding internal efficiency and costs are to a large extent intertwined with external effectiveness decisions affecting the firm's ability to generate revenues. In strategic management and in strategic as well as tactical planning processes, the revenue-generating effects of business processes other than conventional marketing and sales must be included.

As further shown by the Service Profit Logic, decisions that simultaneously influence internal efficiency and external effectiveness should not be made before both the revenue-generating effects (external effectiveness) *and* the cost-generating effects (internal efficiency) of such decisions have been taken into consideration and analysed.

Because revenue-generating costs are needed to maintain a level of perceived service quality which makes customers willing to become and remain customers, revenue-generating costs and costs which predominantly enhance bureaucracy should be kept apart and treated in different ways. Moreover, from a business point of view, *in relative terms*, the effects on external effectiveness of planning the firm's many processes is more important than the cost efficiency aspect, which of course must not be neglected either. *In the long run at least, revenue generation is more important than cost consideration.* Of course, in the short run, a firm's situation may at times require more attention to costs. However, in the final analysis, external effectiveness and customer perceived quality drives revenues *and* profit. Costs have to be adjusted to meet this level of external effectiveness.

In other words, strategic planning and management should begin with the revenue-generating implications of a given decision, but of course, as an integrated process, cost implications should be considered. This is *not* to say that costs are of minor importance. Although perceived quality drives revenues, profits suffer if the service is produced with too high costs. Saving costs, in particular costs that *do not* contribute to the generation of revenues, is necessary in most firms, and monitoring costs is always of crucial importance. Sometimes the cost level can be reduced by encouraging customers to change their consumption habits. For example, banks have persuaded customers to use ATMs, and computer-based and Internet-based payment of bills instead of withdrawing money at bank counters, which costs more for the bank to administer. Airlines and airports are persuading travellers to use check-in machines instead of going to check-in encounters. And as research into the use

TABLE 3.1

The profit logic in manufacturing and in service organizations.

Manufacturing	Service
Internal efficiency and external effectiveness are separable.	Internal efficiency and external effectiveness cannot be separated other than partly.
Revenues and costs are driven by different processes.	Revenues and costs are largely driven by the same processes.
Decisions regarding internal efficiency and external effectiveness can be taken separately, i.e. they can be managed as different processes by different business functions.	Decisions regarding internal efficiency and external effectiveness cannot be taken separately, i.e. they have to be managed in an integrated process.

of information technology in service shows, customers often appreciate the freedom from time and space restriction offered by Internet and mobile technologies.[3] However if, for example, a cost-saving decision can be expected to have a negative impact on quality and revenues which is bigger than the cost reduction, it should probably not be made.

Not all production and administration resources and processes can be expected to have effects on revenue. As shown in Figure 3.1, there are *interactive functions*, with which customers have direct contact, and *supporting functions*, such as warehousing, information processing and other back-office activities, that through internal service indirectly influence perceived quality. Such functions are critical because *they drive both revenues and costs*. However, there are functions that, from the customer's point of view, are totally invisible – such as some back-office and general administration processes. These functions are only cost-generating.

The differences in the profit logic between traditional manufacturing and service organizations are summarized in Table 3.1.

Standardization of service production, *industrialization* in a manufacturer-like manner, can be done in the truly invisible part of the organization. In the other parts of the organization, industrialization has to be implemented much more carefully if one wants to make cost savings without damaging perceived quality and the generation of revenue, and avoid destroying the competitive advantage of service (flexibility and adaptability; see Chapter 2).

Traditionally, external marketing activities and sales are considered to be more or less solely responsible for revenues. However, this is not true as far as service is concerned, and firms offering projects and any manufacturers of goods with extensive customer contacts by non-marketing persons face a new service-based reality as well. If the organization produces bad service quality, marketing communicaton and selling will not satisfy customers and make them buy again from that organization. The scope of marketing will have to be broadened. If the firm has to increase its traditional marketing and sales budget to maintain revenues and profit, this causes additional costs, as indicated in Figure 3.2.

To sum up, in addition to creating costs and influencing internal efficiency, as the thick arrow in Figure 3.2 indicates, other business functions than sales and marketing have an impact on the customers' quality perception and willingness to pay a given price (external effectiveness), and thereby contribute to the firm's revenue-generating capability in a decisive way. Sales and marketing make promises (the thin arrow) about the potential quality and value-creating support the firm intends to provide.

The Service Profit Logic has much more far-reaching management implications than for marketing only. The interconnectedness of revenue and cost drivers – external effectiveness and internal efficiency intertwined – influences, often even to a dramatic extent, at least the following management areas, which will be discussed in separate chapters in this book:

- Quality management (Chapters 4 and 5).
- Offering management (Chapter 7).
- Productivity management (Chapter 8).
- Marketing management (Chapter 9).
- Marketing communication management (Chapter 10).
- Brand management (Chapter 11).
- Human resource management (Chapters 14 and 15).

In the following sections we will first demonstrate the pitfalls of following a goods profit logic in service organizations (the strategic management trap), and then discuss how to avoid falling into this trap by implementing a service-oriented strategy based on the Service Profit Logic.

THE STRATEGIC MANAGEMENT TRAP

When the goods profit logic and manufacturing-based rules of thumb for management are followed, the consequences for a service provider may be those illustrated in Figure 3.3. We may assume, for example, that the service firm or any service organization, for example in the public sector, either has financial problems or foresees such problems, or is facing increasing competition, or both. Or the firm may for some other reason, for example in order to please shareholders, want to improve its internal efficiency. Irrespective of the impact of technology, labour costs are high in most service operations. In order to control costs, strategic decisions concerning personnel are often made: personnel reductions, a hiring freeze, full-time employees replaced by temporary staff, a greater degree of customer self-service, people being replaced by machines, and so on.

In manufacturing, such decisions should improve production efficiency, lower costs, yet have no effect on the output. They may even improve the quality of the goods produced. A favourable effect on productivity could be expected. In a service context some of this may happen. However, far too often none of these effects will occur, at least not in the long run.

As we have noted, in traditional manufacturing, the interrelationship between internal efficiency and external effectiveness is less important. Customers only perceive the physical output of the production process. In service organizations the situation is different. The consumption of service is *process consumption* and, according to the basic characteristics of service, the customer as a co-producer is involved in the production process and perceives not only the output of the process but parts of the process itself. In a service process an efficient manufacturing orientation, focusing primarily on internal efficiency, may easily alienate the customers, make the customers' perception of quality deteriorate and in the end chase customers away. Hence, opportunities are missed to sell more and obtain repeat business in ongoing customer relationships. However, in back-office processes, where customers are not involved and which are not visible to them, a manufacturer-oriented approach

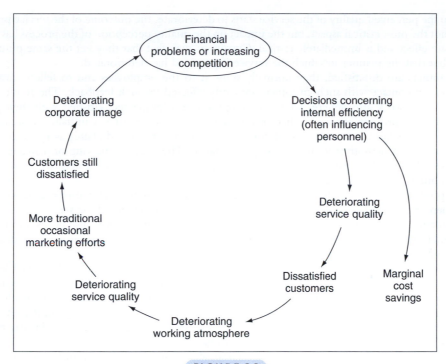

FIGURE 3.3

The strategic management trap.
Source: Grönroos, C., *Strategic Management and Marketing in the Service Sector.*
Cambridge, MA: Marketing Science Institute, 1983, p. 41. Reproduced by
permission of the Marketing Science Institute.

to developing the processes may pay off.[4] On the other hand, improved back–office efficiency may make the internal support to those who serve external customers deteriorate. In that case the effect on external effectiveness and customer perceived quality is probably negative.

Management decisions concerning the production process in a service context are too often thought of as having an impact only on internal efficiency. This often leads to operations and reward systems supporting the wrong actions. For example, restaurant managers are frequently rewarded for low food costs, which are of no interest to customers, who are looking for good food *and* attentive service. Doing what is important to customers and means value for them should be rewarded instead.

In reality, the external effectiveness issue is highly relevant. If only internal efficiency goals are pursued, the perceived service quality changes; too often it deteriorates. Thus, an improved internal efficiency may in service operations lead to a negative shift in perceived quality. Personnel have less time for a single customer, or for paying attention to the customer, and solving the customer's problems are not rewarded. This may increase waiting times, decrease the employee's likelihood of penetrating to the problems of a given customer, and leave less time for employee flexibility. Self–service procedures and technology, which may be introduced as a substitute for personal service, may help the customer. Information technology may also improve the service. However, often this unfavourably changes the perceived quality, because the customer either does not accept the new system or is not prepared, trained or motivated to operate it.

When the perceived quality of the service starts to deteriorate, the outcome of the service process is usually not the most critical aspect, but the impact on the quality perception of the process has a more immediate effect and is immediately critical. Customers may feel that they get the same outcome as before, but that the manner in which the service is provided has deteriorated.

If customers are dissatisfied, they normally show it to the employees and to fellow customers. Employees in contact with such customers are easily affected by such feedback. The result may be a deteriorating work atmosphere, where the employees no longer feel satisfied with their jobs or as motivated to provide service to the customers as they may have been initially. Moreover, the direction of decisions taken in the organization, where people are treated mainly as a cost-generating burden, also has a demotivating impact on performance. The decision-making of management has a negative effect on the employees. The service employees become under a negative pressure from both customers and management.

This process may be fatal to the service operation and the whole service organization. As the atmosphere in the workplace is affected, the customer perceived quality of the service may continue to deteriorate. Employees may have less time to perform well, but they may also be less motivated to do so. Such negative sequences of management decisions easily lead to a *vicious circle*.[5] Once a firm has entered into such a circle, its growth potential may be seriously affected.

The destructive process illustrated here and in Figure 3.3 seems to be caused by a lack of understanding of how the service profit logic differs from the traditional goods logic, and of the interrelationship between internal efficiency and external effectiveness in service organizations. Decisions made to help cost savings have an unexpected external effect. The output of the service operation, the service and the quality of the service are not the same as they were, or as they are supposed to be according to traditional management thinking from manufacturing.

At this point the firm sometimes turns to traditional external marketing in order to keep its customers. A temporary boom may be achieved by, for example, heavy advertising, but in the long term the new customers as well as the old ones will observe the decrease in quality and become dissatisfied with what they receive. If external marketing campaigns make unrealistic promises, which in situations like this are not uncommon, disappointment will be severe among newcomers who wanted to give the firm's service a try. Furthermore, unrealistic promise-making has a negative and discouraging internal effect as well.

Consequently, in spite of traditional marketing efforts, in the long term one often ends up with dissatisfied customers. At the same time the firm's corporate image will change. Decreasing perceived quality and unrealistic promises by external marketing efforts have a negative impact on image. Moreover, a growing number of dissatisfied customers and ex-customers creates a substantial negative word-of-mouth effect on image, as well as on purchase decisions.

In the end one will probably find that the decisions taken may have caused varying degrees of damage. In the worst case, service quality has decreased, the work atmosphere has deteriorated, word of mouth has become a problem instead of a support, negative comments in social media explode, the corporate image has been affected, and finally, the problems caused by the financial problem or increased competition have not been solved. In summary, *a bad situation has become even worse*.

A VICIOUS CIRCLE: AN EXAMPLE

What is going on in many hospitals with their for-profit service providers seems to be an example of a bad situation becoming worse, caused, to a greater or lesser extent, by the wrong management approach and a lack of understanding of the characteristics of service. If there are financial problems, doctors are urged to concentrate on professional and technical issues, which they do, and nurses are requested not to interact too much with patients and maybe not at all with family members. The intention here is, of course, to achieve a more effective use of time and, as a consequence, to cut costs.

The consequences of these actions are a lower level of service quality as perceived by the customers – the patients and their relatives and friends. But this approach from management has a much more severe internal effect, which is eventually perceived by the customers as well. The employees, probably the nurses and staff personnel first, start to feel a role conflict. Patients and relatives demand more, but management says no. They are not encouraged or authorized to give good service. This quickly affects the working atmosphere, which in turn leads to a deterioration of the customer perceived quality of the service. At this point, external marketing communication and PR activities communicating a 'we care' image have no significant positive effect on customers or potential customers. They know better, or will soon find out what the truth is. Moreover, they will create a substantial amount of bad word of mouth.

However, in one respect, such promotional campaigns clearly have an effect. This effect is not normally recognized by managers, or by communications people. It is an *internal effect*, and it is *negative*. Employees realize that management has deliberately attempted to fool customers and potential customers. It may, in reality, not be deliberate, it may just be a result of bad and thoughtless management, but it is easily perceived as deliberate. For example, nurses know that they cannot fulfil the promise 'we care'. They just do not have the time, and they are encouraged not to do so. This, of course, by itself hurts morale and damages the internal atmosphere even more. Second, nobody wants to deliberately take part in lies and cheating, which such promotional efforts are in this situation. It goes against the ethics of most people, and increasingly damages the working atmosphere. Consequently, good employees start looking for another job and eventually quit; they have no interest in helping the employer, and quality continues to deteriorate. If the financial problems were initially minor, they grow as the internal crisis deepens and the service quality (the reason for the external crisis) decreases. A few wrong management decisions can easily lead to a downward spiral, a negative trend which gains momentum once it has started.

COST EFFICIENCY AND THE RISK OF FALLING INTO THE TRAP

Initial cost savings often turn out to be marginal in the long run. Employee absence due to illness or other reasons such as job dissatisfaction tends to increase. Extra personnel, without proper training, have to be hired. The work surroundings and the technology used may not be handled with appropriate care by less motivated and temporary personnel.

The process illustrated in Figure 3.3, and in a sketchy way by the hospital example above, is a true and real *strategic management trap*. By making the wrong decisions based only on product manufacturing know-how and models, the organization may be thrown into a *vicious circle*[6] or negative downward spiral, which weakens the competitiveness of its operations and causes or intensifies the financial problems that are often the reason for making inappropriate decisions in the first place.

Why does it go wrong? Why do conventional wisdom and guidelines from manufacturing not help? The main reason is the fact that a service organization is not a traditional manufacturing firm. Instead it is an organization with characteristics of its own where a different profit logic forms the commercial basis of management and a different service-based management logic should, therefore, be adopted. Service consumption is *process consumption*, not outcome consumption. The service production process is a partly open system, where at the same time as he perceives and consumes a service the customer also participates in the process as a co-producer. The nature of service and service competition requires a different approach to strategic thinking and management.

In traditional management thinking the productivity of capital and labour, and internal efficiency considerations, are the factors that predominantly drive profit. However, a service firm, or any service operation, is different in some vital aspects. As noted earlier in this chapter, external effectiveness, how the organization performs and the output of its operations – in short, the perceived service quality with both its process- and outcome-related features – is what customers experience and evaluate. Actions to improve internal efficiency and productivity as traditionally measured can easily have a negative external impact on perceived quality. For service organizations, external effectiveness and *customer perceived service quality drives profit*, provided of course that customers consume the service in such a way that the cost of producing the service does not exceed revenues from that service.[7] Conceptually and operationally, productivity has to be treated differently in service than in manufacturing. We shall return to this issue in Chapter 8.

However, this does not mean that decisions which are only or predominantly related to internal efficiency always lead to negative consequences. This also does not mean that cost savings and the more effective use of resources are wrong and should not be attempted. On the contrary, improved productivity of resources – labour as well as capital, and information – and better internal efficiency should always be an objective, and new technology and production processes that save costs should be used. Moving from one technology level to another, for example from traditional face-to-face bank service to Internet banking, often improves internal efficiency and external effectiveness and customers' quality perception at the same time. However, there may be a time lag before customers learn to appreciate a new technology. The main point here is that internal developments aimed at improving internal efficiency should be based on the characteristics of service, so *that the interrelationships between the internal and external effects are taken into account*. It should be emphasized that all costs are not equal. There is a difference between various types of costs which has to be taken into account. Some costs are revenue-generating, some are not.

A SERVICE-ORIENTED STRATEGY

Figure 3.4 illustrates schematically a favourable process which may occur if a *service strategy*, and a service-based management approach, is followed.[8] Figure 3.4 can be compared with Figure 3.3, which demonstrates the strategic management trap. To give an example, if financial problems or problems with increased competition make it necessary to change the strategies of, say, an airline company, cost considerations and internal efficiency should not govern the strategic thinking in the firm. Instead, management should focus upon the interactions with customers and customer relationships. Effects on external effectiveness and customer relationships should primarily guide the decisions to be made. Of course, cost considerations and the implications for internal efficiency must not be overlooked. Concern for internal efficiency can be given priority in the part of the organization invisible to customers. Moreover, a distinction between revenue-enhancing costs and bureaucracy-caused costs should always be made.

External effectiveness and service quality concerns should be given top priority in the interactive functions. In an airline, for example, improving buyer–seller interactions in the service encounters, for instance, by increasing seat size in planes, paying attention to in-flight services, and offering the employees appropriate customer contact training, to mention a few possibilities, would probably lead to improved perceived quality from the customers' point of view.

Such decisions may or may not necessitate more personnel, or more advanced technology, but if the effects on revenues make up for the additional costs, such revenue-creating cost increases should

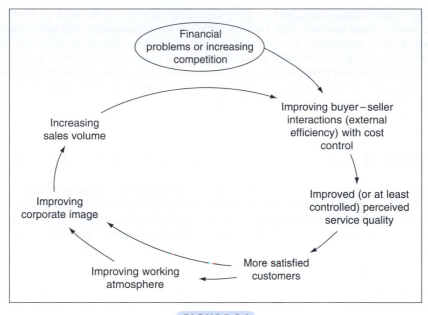

FIGURE 3.4

A service-oriented approach.
Source: Grönroos, C., *Strategic Management and Marketing in the Service Sector*. Cambridge, MA: Marketing Science Institute, 1983, p. 58. Reproduced by permission of the Marketing Science Institute.

obviously be allowed. Here, difficulties in calculating the effects on revenue are no excuse for ignoring the effects on external effectiveness. It should be noted that improved service quality often does not require additional costs. The only thing that is needed, in many cases, is a better understanding of customer relationships, how quality is perceived, and finally, the importance of the process-related quality dimension. Once these points are made clear, internal arrangements for using existing resources in a more systematic and market-oriented way can usually be made. Service quality management will be discussed in detail in Chapters 4 and 5.

To return to Figure 3.4, improved quality usually means greater customer satisfaction, which in turn has a twofold effect. Internally, the work atmosphere will probably improve. Increased customer satisfaction is noticed by the employees. The positive effects are often very obvious. This favourable trend is supported by the service-oriented strategic direction that is chosen by management. Decisions directed towards improving the service encounters and service quality imply that management is prepared to accept the revenue-generating power of the employees and to support it. Such a strategic attitude has a considerable positive effect on the internal environment of the firm and on employee motivation. Employees are encouraged by both management and customers. Again, this results in increased internal efficiency. In some situations the service process can of course be improved by introducing technology-based solutions, in which cases fewer personnel may be needed and/or the role of employees may change. Customers of insurance companies are often requested to ask routine questions over the phone or to use the Internet instead of visiting an office in person, whereas service employees are supposed to provide customers with more knowledge-intensive service, such as financial advice. In such situations a critical challenge for management is to maintain and even improve the work atmosphere for personnel.[9]

Improved customer satisfaction also has other external effects. Favourable word of mouth is created. Existing customers may increase their business with the service provider and new customers will be attracted to the organization. The corporate image and/or local image are enhanced by positive customer experience and by favourable word of mouth and positive comments in social media.

Finally, sales volume will probably increase. If internal efficiency, external effectiveness and service quality are controlled simultaneously, a larger volume of sales can be expected to have a sound financial effect and to improve the firm's competitive position. Such a positive trend may well continue. The improved atmosphere in the company makes the buyer–seller interactions even better, and the firm will generate more financial resources to be used to back up this trend.

CUSTOMER BENEFITS OF A SERVICE STRATEGY

Good service means certain benefits for the customer. Especially in business-to-business markets, customers may be able to calculate these benefits and see the results on the bottom line. For example, reliable and timely repair and maintenance service may reduce downtime costs, which otherwise could amount to considerable sums. Such costs can easily be calculated. Individual consumers may sense these benefits more than see them. Such cost effects will be discussed in Chapter 6.

The better the total customer relationship is taken care of, the better the quality impact of the service process will be, and the less complicated it is for the customer to maintain the relationship with the service provider. Co-operation between the two parties becomes easier. For example, the buyer can rely on the seller that deliveries will always be made on time, technical service will be good and personal contacts will be accessible when needed, claims will be handled promptly and with the buyer's interest in mind, and social contacts will be satisfactory. Not only is it more convenient for the buyer to do business with a service provider who can be trusted in all respects, in many situations such a relationship equals a cost reduction for the buyer as well.

If the level of perceived quality is high and co-operation between the two parties is smooth, three sources of cost reduction for the customer can be distinguished:

1. *Fewer resources/personnel* are needed to maintain contact with the service provider.

2. The person involved in contacts with the provider will *need less of their time* for handling these contacts.

3. It is psychologically less demanding to maintain contact with the provider, which in turn *increases the mental capacity* of personnel to be used for other tasks.

In many cases the cost reductions that can thus be achieved are easy to calculate. The psychological effects of good service may be less so, but the other effects can easily be transformed into euros, pounds sterling or dollars – money that, for the buyer/customer, can be used productively elsewhere. The service provider, in turn, can transfer some of this cost reduction to the price. The benefits of improved customer relationships by a service strategy can thus be shared between the buyer and the seller. This should have a favourable impact on profitability.

THE BUSINESS MISSION AND SERVICE CONCEPT

Every service provider needs some performance guidelines. Overall, the concept of a *business mission* is used to determine in which markets the firm should operate and what kinds of problems it should try to solve. In generic terms a business mission, or service vision, for any firm that wishes to be a true service organization can be formulated as follows:

The firm's business mission is to provide target customers with service that supports their everyday activities and processes, thereby contributing to their goals in life or business in a value-enhancing way.

The expression 'supports . . . in a value enhancing way' means that the service provided should impact a customer's activities and processes so that value emerges for the customer, i.e. the customer is better off than before the service had been produced and used. A firm can develop a service-focused, and customer-focused, business mission based on this generic formulation by specifying:

1. Which process or processes in a customer's everyday activities it aims to support.

2. How this support is intended to enable and enhance value creation in the customer's life or business.

3. With what resources, processes and interactions the customer's process should be supported.

3. What should be achieved for the customer (value-in-use; goal achievement) and service provider (value capture) respectively.

In Figure 3.5 a business mission formulation based on service logic is schematically illustrated. In the figure an example from car rental, further discussed in Chapter 7, is also included.

Within the framework of the business mission, concrete guidelines for developing service offerings have to be developed. These can be called *service concepts*. The service concept is a way of expressing the notion that the organization intends to solve certain types of problems in a certain manner. This

The Firm
Facilitate *(add how)*
Its customers' *(add a description of customer segments)*
Life processes/Business processes *(define the processes; if appropriate, add what everyday processes facilitate these life/business processes)*
By supporting their appropriate everyday process or processes *(define which everyday process/processes)*
By operating in a given manner *(add in what manner, through what processes; both outcome-related and process-related aspects)*

Such that the Customers achieves *(add in value terms (monetary and/or other) what the firm wants the customers to achieve)*

Such that the Firm achieves *(add what the firm should achieve; financially and otherwise)*

An example from car rental (excluding outcome- and process-related aspects of how to operate)

"The firm aims at providing immediately accessible solutions to temporarily occurring transportation problems"

The customers' everyday process: Temporarily occurring transportation problems
Base for value perception in everyday life: An immediately accessible solution
Which type of customer (which segment): Business travellers

FIGURE 3.5
Service logic-based business mission.

means that the service concept has to include information about *what* the firm intends to do for *a certain customer segment, how* this should be achieved, and with *what* kinds of *resources*. If there is no service concept agreed upon and accepted, the risk of inconsistent behaviour is high. Supervisors do not know what should be achieved and what priorities to set. The same goes for other personnel. A situation would develop in which different parts of the organization perform inconsistently. This, of course, adds to confusion. And in an Internet-based virtual organizational setting with more or less loosely connected network partners, a clear and easily communicated service concept is of utmost importance.

The service concept should be as concrete as possible so that it can be understood by everybody. To give an example, in a car rental company case discussed in Chapter 7, the firm stated their service concept as follows: '*To offer immediately accessible solutions to temporary transportation problems.*' This service concept states that since problems are immediate and temporary, therefore the solutions to them must be quick and easy to obtain. This firm became very successful.

Depending on how differentiated the operations are and how many different customer segments exist, there can be one or several service concepts. It is, however, important that they all fit the overall service vision or business mission. Before a service concept can be determined, careful market research must be carried out, otherwise there is always a risk that there will be an insufficient market for service produced according to the service concept.

INCREASING THE SERVICE IMPACT IN CUSTOMER RELATIONSHIPS

Implementing a service strategy requires appropriate action at the operational level. Here one should notice that a service strategy can be pursued by actions of many kinds. However, what is often needed is a new way of thinking, i.e. adopting a new logic. Old rules and ways of thinking may misguide management and leave opportunities unexploited.

The service impact on customer relationships can be increased in three ways:

1. Developing *new services* to offer to the customer.

2. Activating *existing but hidden services or service elements* in a business relationship.

3. Turning the *goods component into a service element* in the customer relationship.

Too often only the first possibility is taken into account, but there are many additional opportunities for strengthening customer relationships through a better service impact.

Increasing the service impact by adding new services. The first category of activities literally means that new services are added to the offering. *New services* are typically various consultancy services, information services, repair and maintenance services, software development, websites, logistical services, customer training or joint R&D activities. Clearly, this may be a powerful means of differentiating one firm's offering from that of the competition. Such efforts should be used whenever appropriate. However, such new services require new investments and increase the cost level. These must be justified by expected additional revenue.

Increasing the service impact by activating existing but hidden services. The second type of activity seems much less dramatic and is therefore frequently not thought of as a strategic issue that should initiate major changes in the customer relationship. It may, nevertheless, have a dramatic impact on the offering, perhaps even more of an impact than the first type. It is a matter of *actively using existing but hidden, often non-billable, service elements in the relationship between the buyer and the seller* in order to differentiate the offering and increase the support provided to the customers' processes, and thus make use of these services as a means of competition.

Such service elements in customer relations are, for instance, casual advice, order taking, deliveries, claims handling, invoicing, demonstration of manufacturing processes, technical quality control, call centres, help desks and telephone reception services, and frequently asked questions on a website. *Customers do pay for these services, too,* although one seldom thinks about it. However, such service elements are far too often perceived as nuisances rather than as services by most customers. The reason for this is, of course, that they are frequently *handled as mere administrative routines and not as actively rendered services.* If these service elements are thought of as service and the value support that can be provided by them is recognized, the firm may improve its position and strengthen its competitive edge.

It is important to realize that these potential services *already exist in the customer relationships* – they only have to be managed in a different way so that their value-supporting possibilities are utilized, and customers start to experience them as service. For example, complaints handling is far too often managed as an administrative task with the seller's interest as the top priority. Instead a complaint could be taken care of in a *service recovery* fashion, quickly, preferably even before a formal complaint has been made by the customer, with the customer's interest as the first priority. In the former situation, customers consider the complaints-handling process a nuisance, which in addition may cause considerable sacrifice for them. In the latter situation, the quality problem or service breakdown is recovered in a way that the customer perceives as quality-enhancing and most often also cost-saving. Changed invoicing systems may also have similar effects.

Many of the services that are managed as administrative routines, or in some other way without taking the customer's interests into account, are truly *hidden services.* On the one hand, service firms or manufacturers do not see them as potential value-creating service. On the other hand, customers often do not think of them as anything other than a necessary evil. Hence, the firm that manages to turn such hidden services or 'non-services' into real service to its customers can easily provide them with a series of positive surprises, and enhance perceived quality in the minds of the customers. From this should follow strengthened customer relationships.

Developing hidden services often does not demand big investments or extra costs. Rearranging existing resources and routines may frequently be all that is needed. In fact, more service-oriented invoicing and complaints handling may ensure that these activities are more effectively dealt with internally as well, and operating costs can thus be saved. The customer benefits that can be achieved frequently exceed the additional efforts. Furthermore, hidden services, which are managed as non-service – for example, invoices including mistakes or failures managed with delays – cause costs for the customer and the firm alike. If they are not activated and turned into true value-supporting service for customers, they remain a cost burden for both parties, and the service provider loses the revenue potential of improved overall service.

Increasing the service impact by turning goods components into service. If the goods component is offered in a flexible manner and tailor-made to fit the needs and wishes of the customer, or made easy to install, maintain and upgrade, it is turned into service for the customer. Consequently, it is turned into a service element in the customer relationship. A good salesperson uses such a sales strategy. However, turning the goods component into a service goes far beyond sales. In production, logistics, installation, IT applications, and so on the same approach is required.

A manufacturer of industrial equipment may try to tailor its goods as much as possible to the specific needs of its customers and make them easy to understand and easy to maintain. A restaurant may cook meals and even add seasoning according to the wishes of a specific customer. In both cases, *the goods component is transformed from being a physical thing to customized service.*

SERVICE MANAGEMENT: ADOPTING A SERVICE LOGIC IN MANAGEMENT

Having demonstrated the nature and characteristics of a service strategy, we now turn to the principles of management which guide decision-making and managerial behaviour in service competition. This approach to management has been labelled *service management*.[10] It is a methodology in which management procedures are geared to the characteristics of service and the nature of service competition. Service management is also very much a customer-oriented approach. Often the term 'service management' is used instead of the term 'service marketing'. Sometimes the phrase 'service marketing and management' is also used in the literature to describe this field.[11] The use of the term 'service management' indicates the cross-functional nature of marketing in service contexts. Marketing is not a separate function, but in the management of all business functions the interests of the customer, i.e. a *customer focus*, has to be taken into account. It is a matter of *customer-oriented or market-oriented management*. Chapter 9 discusses marketing in service competition and the relationship between marketing and customer-oriented management.

Service management is understanding how to manage a business in service competition, that is, in a competitive situation where service is the key to success in the marketplace, regardless of whether the core of the offering is a service or a manufactured product.

Service management can be described as follows:[12]

1. Understanding the value that emerges for customers by consuming or using the offerings of an organization and knowing how service, provided through goods, service activities, information, and other resources, and combinations of such resources, contributes to this value.

2. Understanding how total quality is perceived in customer relationships to facilitate such value and how it changes over time.

3. Understanding how an organization (people, technology and physical resources, systems and customers) will be able to produce and deliver this perceived quality and support customers' value-creation, and during direct interactions also co-create value with customers.

4. Understanding how an organization should be developed and managed so that the intended perceived quality and value are achieved.

5. Making an organization function so that this perceived quality and value are achieved and the objectives of the parties involved (the organization, the customers, other parties, etc.) are met.

This means that the firm has to understand the following:

1. The perceived quality and value in their everyday activities and processes customers are looking for in service competition.

2. How to create that value support for customers.

3. How to manage the resources available to the organization to be able to support such service-based value creation.[13]

This description of service management is rather exhaustive. Shorter definitions lose some of the information content, but may still be clear to readers, and they are easier to remember. According to another definition in the literature, 'service management is a total organizational approach that makes quality of service, as perceived by the customer, the number one driving force for the operation of the business'.[14] Applying service management principles means that service is considered *the* organizational imperative.[15]

'Organization' in these contexts, of course, refers to the bundle of quality-supporting resources involved in producing the service, that is, people (personnel and customers alike) as well as technology and physical resources, and information and operating systems, and administration. As organizations increasingly move towards being network organizations, many of these resources are outside the boundaries of traditional organizational constructs. It is also important to observe that the definition of service management requires a dynamic approach to management. It is not enough to understand which values or benefits customers are seeking; one must also understand that the benefits customers are looking for will change over time, and that the customer perceived quality and value which is produced has to change accordingly.

A service management perspective changes the general focus of management in service firms as well as in manufacturing firms adopting a service logic in the following ways:[16]

1. From product-based value ('value-in-exchange') to *total value* emerging in customers' processes ('value-in-use').

2. From short-term transactions to *long-term relationships*.

3. From core product (goods or services) quality (the quality of the outcome only) to *total customer perceived quality* in customer relationships.

4. From production of the technical solution (of a product or service) as the key process in the organization to *developing total perceived quality and supporting customer value as the key process*.

The expression *value-in-exchange* refers to the view that value for a customer is embedded in a pre-produced product. *Value-in-use* means that value for a customer evolves in the customer's activities and processes.

SERVICE MANAGEMENT: A SHIFT IN MANAGEMENT FOCUS

Two basic shifts in focus are implicit in the service management principles when compared with the traditional management approach used in manufacturing. These are:

1. A shift from an interest in the internal consequences for the firm of performance to an interest in the *external* consequences for customers and other parties.

2. A shift from a focus on structure to a focus on *process*.

These two shifts imply a shift of focus *from inside-out management to outside-in management*, as discussed in Chapter 1, and they are of paramount importance. A service strategy, to be successfully implemented, *requires both*. As a management philosophy, service management is predominantly related to managing processes in which the underlying structures are of less importance. If the structures take over, the flexibility of operations and the handling of customer contacts suffer. The encouragement and support of managers and supervisors decreases, and thus motivation among personnel suffers as well. In the following phase, the perceived service quality starts to deteriorate and customers are probably lost. The new emphasis on process and external consequences changes the focus on (1) the profit logic as the driving force of a business, (2) decision-making authority, (3) organizational structure, (4) supervisory control and (5) reward systems; and when there is a shift in the focus on reward systems, other tasks and types of achievement have to be (6) monitored and measured. These *six principles of service management* are summarized in Table 3.2 and discussed below.

TABLE 3.2

Principles of service management: a summary.

Principle		Remarks
1. The service profit logic as business driver	Customer perceived service quality drives profit.	Decisions on external efficiency and internal efficiency (customer satisfaction and productivity of capital and labour) have to be totally integrated.
2. Decision-making authority	Decision-making has to be decentralized as close as possible to the organization–customer interface.	Some strategically important decisions have to be made centrally.
3. Organizational structure	The organization has to be structured and functioning so that its main goal is the mobilization of resources to support frontline operations.	This may often require a 'flat' organization with no unnecessary layers.
4. Supervisory control	Managers and supervisors focus on the encouragement and support of employees.	As few legislative control procedures as possible, although some may be required.
5. Reward systems	Producing customer perceived quality should be the focus of reward systems.	All relevant facets of service quality should be considered, although they cannot always all be built into a reward system.
6. Measurement focus	Customer satisfaction with service quality should be the focus of measuring achievements.	To monitor productivity and internal efficiency, internal measurement criteria may have to be used as well.

The service profit logic as the driver of business. As discussed in some detail in this chapter, the *general economic focus* or the *business logic* is shifted from managing internal efficiency and the productivity of capital and labour to *managing total business effectiveness*, including both internal efficiency and external effectiveness considerations, where customer perceived quality drives profit. However, there are several interrelated factors influencing how, and indeed if, perceived quality leads to sound economic results. Service management appreciates the importance to success of managing external effectiveness and customer relationships. Internal efficiency needed to function profitably is an inevitable issue, but it is not a top priority in itself. It must be totally integrated with external effectiveness issues and geared to managing customer perceived quality. As soon as the internal perspective begins to dominate, an interest in costs and managing internal efficiency will take over, but without a simultaneous consideration of the quality implications. Inside-out management starts to dominate at the expense of outside-in management. Issues related to creating and maintaining excellence and revenue generation will then become secondary and receive less or no management attention.

Decision-making authority. Because of the characteristics of service (e.g. the inseparability of critical parts of production and consumption) and the facets of customer perceived service quality (e.g. a demand for flexibility and recovery capabilities), decisions concerning how a service operation should function have to be made *as close as possible to the interface between the organization and its customers*. Ideally, customer contact employees who are involved in service encounters should have the authority to make prompt decisions. Otherwise sales opportunities and opportunities for service recovery, correcting quality mistakes and problems will not be used intelligently. If the moments of truth in the service encounters go unmanaged, service quality deteriorates quickly. Of course, a contact employee, for example a bank clerk or a service technician, cannot always have the professional knowledge required if a customer wants, for example, a sophisticated financial solution for his international business or an estimate of expected future repair costs. However, the customer contact employee should nevertheless have the decision-making authority, for example, to ask for assistance from the back office and support staff professionals.

If the employees in customer contacts are not given authority to think and make decisions for themselves, they become victims of a rigid system. Customer contact employees may be demotivated by rigid rules and systems which hamper them instead of empowering them to handle deviations from standard operational procedures. 'Empowering' personnel is a powerful way of motivating people (empowerment will be discussed in Chapter 14 on internal marketing). It means that employees are encouraged, and trained, to recognize the diversity of customer contact situations and to use their judgement in handling situations and solving problems following on from deviations from standard procedures so that customer satisfaction is created.

Thus, *operational decision-making needs to be decentralized*. However, some strategically important decisions have to be kept centralized; for example, decisions concerning overall strategies, business missions and service concepts. The unique knowledge among contact personnel of aspects of the business that are vital to making such strategic decisions should, however, always be used in central decision-making. First, this improves the quality of decisions, and second, it creates a stronger commitment to these decisions among those who will have to live with them and carry them out.

The 'local' manager, whether he is the head of a branch of a multi-outlet organization, such as a bank or hotel chain, or the head of a department in a firm which produces service has, of course, the overall responsibility for his team. The manager is also responsible for the total operation, service consciousness and profitability of his 'local' organization. One can say that the manager has dual responsibility: responsibility towards the customers and towards the corporation. Svenska

Handelsbanken, a nationwide and internationalizing retail and commercial bank based in Sweden, has formulated the following ground rule for their local branch managers: 'The local manager is responsible for perceived service quality and value for the customers and for profitability for the corporation.' This bank is probably the most decentralized and customer-oriented bank in Scandinavia. It is also one of the most profitable banks and has invariably been rated highest by customers in satisfaction studies.

Organizational structure. Traditionally, the *organizational focus* is geared to building up and maintaining a structure in which management decisions are cascaded through processes involving legislative control. This often creates a lack of flexibility, fuels centralization tendencies, and can be a hindrance to the vertical flow of information in the organization. Service management shifts management focus away from structure and control procedures towards improved external efficiency with acceptable internal efficiency. This requires a more flexible organizational solution, where the *mobilization* of resources – management, staff, systems – to support customer contact activities is imperative. The organizational structure that suits this requirement may differ from situation to situation, but some common principles can be identified. Organization for service will be discussed in more detail in Chapter 13.

Supervisory control. In traditional management approaches, supervisory systems are closely related to monitoring the capability of the organization and its various departments in performing their tasks according to predetermined standards. If such standards are met, the employee, or a group of employees, has performed satisfactorily, and may be rewarded.

However, such a supervisory control system does not fit the nature of service and service production very well. By its very nature, service cannot often be completely standardized. Moreover, for employees to deliver quality service, some degree of flexibility is needed to meet the special wishes of customers or to successfully recover negative situations in service encounters. Here, guidelines and visions are better than rigidly defined standards. Only the technical quality aspects of service can be monitored by standards; whereas, from a competitive standpoint, the highly important process-related quality aspects are not well suited for the development of traditional standards. Process-related quality-creating performance cannot easily, if at all, be monitored by comparing it with predetermined standards. Instead, service management requires that the supervisory focus be on the support and encouragement of employees. This may require new management and leadership methods. Subsequent chapters on *service culture* and *internal marketing* will touch upon this issue to some extent.

Reward systems. Normally, *reward systems* are geared to the focus of supervisory control. What is monitored can be measured, and what is measured can be controlled and rewarded. Of course, not all, if any, of the tasks and factors that are controlled are geared to reward systems. However, a shift in supervisory focus requires a corresponding shift of focus on rewarding. Generally speaking, service management requires that *producing perceived service quality and supporting customers' value creation* at some level – excellent or otherwise acceptable – should be rewarded, not just compliance with predetermined, easily measurable standards.

Measurement focus. What is controlled and rewarded has first to be measured. The focus here must of course also be shifted, or at least expanded. The ultimate signs of success are customer satisfaction with total perceived quality, loyal customers and improved profits. Thus, according to service management principles, for service-oriented supervisory approaches and reward systems, customer satisfaction with *service quality* as well as tasks that boost satisfaction and loyalty has to be measured. Measuring how standards are met and the bottom line are not enough. Internal efficiency criteria may have to be used as well, so that internal efficiency is kept under control. However, the external effectiveness criteria always dominate.

SUMMARY

There are clear and well-defined customer benefits in pursuing a service strategy. However, doing so requires different knowledge on the part of management as well as those implementing a service strategy. The service profit logic has to be understood, and the issues of quality, marketing, human resource management, productivity and profitability have to be addressed differently from a traditional manufacturing context. This, of course, is due to the characteristics of service and service consumption, and the nature of customer relationships in service contexts. What is standard in managing a traditional manufacturing firm may turn out to be inappropriate and even counterproductive for a service business or for a manufacturer pursuing a service strategy. A 'service imperative' and the management of service quality are at the heart of service management.

QUESTIONS FOR DISCUSSION

1. How could traditional management wisdom from manufacturing become a trap for a service firm?

2. Discuss the profit logic and the factors influencing its components in service and manufacturing respectively. What are the specific characteristics of the service profit logic?

3. What characterizes service management as a management approach?

4. Discuss how applying the service management principles would change the strategic focus, structure and governance systems of a firm.

NOTES

1. Grönroos, C., *Strategic Management and Marketing in the Service Sector*. Cambridge, MA: Marketing Science Institute, 1983 (first published in 1982 as a research report by Hanken Swedish School of Economics, Finland). Compare Richard Normann's discussion of how it is possible to get into a good circle and avoid falling into such a trap. See Normann, R., *Service Management*. New York: John Wiley & Sons, 1984, where he uses the expression *vicious circle* for this trap.

2. Drucker, P., *Management: Tasks, Responsibilities, Practices*. New York: Harper & Row, 1973.

3. Heinonen, K., Temporal and spatial e-service value. *International Journal of Service Industry Management*, **17**(4), 2006, 380–400.

4. Chase, R.B. & Haynes, R.M., Service operations management: a field guide. In Swartz, T.A. & Iacobucci, D. (eds), *Handbook of Services Marketing & Management*. Thousand Oaks, CA: Sage Publications, 2000, pp. 455–471. The classic article on the manufacturing orientation of service processes is Levitt, T., Production-line approach to service. *Harvard Business Review*, **50**(Sept–Oct), 1972, 41–52.

5. See Normann, *op. cit.*, where the existence of – and internal effects of – such vicious circles are discussed extensively.

6. Normann, *op. cit.*

7. In a major study in the financial services sector in Scandinavia, Kaj Storbacka has demonstrated that 20% of the customers do not stand for 80% of profits but for 180% to 200% of profits. Other customers do not contribute to total profits or are directly unprofitable, thus eroding the total profitability accumulated by the group of profitable customers. Moreover, many of the unprofitable customers or customers who do not contribute to profits are what he calls 'satisfied small customers' and sometimes also big customers, that is customers who are satisfied with the perceived service quality but who consume the services in such a way that the cost of producing them exceeds the revenues from those services. See Storbacka, K., *The Nature of Customer Relationship Profitability – Analysis of Relationships and Customer Bases in Retail Banking*. Helsinki/Helsingfors, Finland: Hanken Swedish School of Economics, Finland/CERS, 1994.

8. Compare Richard Normann's discussion of how, by strengthening peripheral services, it is possible to get into a good circle and avoid a vicious circle. See Normann, *op. cit.*

9. This effect is discussed and pointed out by Heskett, J., Guru's View. Notes from the search for deep indicators in services. *Journal of Service Management*, **25**(3), 2014, 298–309.

10. Grönroos, C., Service management: a management focus for service competition. *International Journal of Service Industry Management*, **1**(1), 1990a, 6–14. This service management concept should not be mixed up with the concept of service management, which is used to denote the management of service operations. See, for example, Fitzsimmons, J.A. & Fitzsimmons, M.J., *Service Management*. San Francisco, CA: McGraw-Hill, 2006.

11. The title of the handbook in the field, *Handbook of Services Marketing and Management*, is a good example.

12. See Grönroos, C., *Service Management and Marketing. Managing the Moments of Truth in Service Competition*. Lexington, MA: Lexington Books, 1990b.

13. Grönroos, 1990a, *op. cit.*

14. Albrecht, K., *At America's Service*. Homewood, IL: Dow Jones-Irwin, 1988.

15. Schneider, B. & Rentsch, J., The management of climate and culture: a futures perspective. In Hage, J. (ed.), *Futures of Organizations*. Lexington, MA: Lexington Books, 1987.

16. See Grönroos, 1990b, *op. cit.*

FURTHER READING

Albrecht, K. (1988) *At America's Service*. Homewood, IL: Dow Jones-Irwin.

Chase, R.B. & Haynes, R.M. (2000) Service operations management: a field guide. In Swartz, T.A. & Iacobucci, D. (eds), *Handbook of Services Marketing & Management*. Thousand Oaks, CA: Sage Publications, pp. 455–471.

Drucker, P. (1973) *Management: Tasks, Responsibilities, Practices*. New York: Harper & Row.

Fitzsimmons, J.A. & Fitzsimmons, M.J. (2006) *Service Management*. San Francisco, CA: McGraw-Hill.

Grönroos, C. (1983) *Strategic Management and Marketing in the Service Sector*. Cambridge, MA: Marketing Science Institute.

Grönroos, C. (1990a) Service management: a management focus for service competition. *International Journal of Service Industry Management*, **1**(1), 6–14.

Grönroos, C. (1990b) *Service Management and Marketing. Managing the Moments of Truth in Service Competition*. Lexington, MA: Lexington Books.

Heinonen, K. (2006) Temporal and spatial e-service value. *International Journal of Service Industry Management*, **17**(4), 2006, 380–400.

Heskett, J. (2014) Guru's view. Notes from the search for deep indicators in services. *Journal of Service Management*, **25**(3), 298–309.

Levitt, T. (1972) Production-line approach to service. *Harvard Business Review*, **50**(Sept–Oct), 41–52.

Normann, R. (1984) *Service Management*, 2nd edn. New York: John Wiley & Sons.

Schneider, B. & Rentsch, J. (1987) The management of climate and culture: a futures perspective. In Hage, J. (ed.), *Futures of Organizations*. Lexington, MA: Lexington Books.

Storbacka, K. (1994) *The Nature of Customer Relationship Profitability – Analysis of Relationships and Customer Bases in Retail Banking*. Helsinki/Helsingfors: Hanken Swedish School of Economics, Finland/CERS Centre for Relationship Marketing and Service Management.

CHAPTER 4
SERVICE AND RELATIONSHIP QUALITY

> *An acceptable outcome is a prerequisite for good perceived quality and a satisfied customer, but an excellent service process creates customer satisfaction and a distinct and sustainable competitive edge.*

INTRODUCTION

Based on the discussion of the characteristics of service and service consumption, and on the customer management approach to marketing in the previous chapters, this chapter explains how the quality of service is perceived in service encounters as well as in ongoing relationships. The *perceived service quality model* is presented as a basic model of the perception of total service quality. The characteristics and determinants of good service quality, such as the *seven criteria of good perceived service quality*, are then discussed, followed by a description of instruments for measuring perceived service quality. Attribute-based approaches, such as the SERVQUAL instrument, are presented as well as the *critical incident* approach. In the latter part of the chapter, dynamic approaches to understanding service quality in a relationship context are described. After having read the chapter, the reader should understand the nature of perceived service quality and the determinants or criteria of service quality as well as know how to measure perceived service quality. The reader should also understand how perceived service quality develops into relationship quality in a long-term relationship context.

RESEARCH INTO SERVICE QUALITY

Chapter 2 illustrated the complexity of service and most service activities. Consequently, the quality of service is complex, too. The quality of goods is traditionally related to the technical specifications of the goods, although, even in a goods context, a firm using an image strategy, for example, tries to add to the quality of their goods component by creating imaginative extra value for their customers using, for example, fashion, status or lifestyle aspects.

Service as a process and a series of activities, where production and consumption cannot be totally separated, and where the customer often actively participates in the production process, is bound to be perceived as extremely complex. In order to develop service management and marketing models, it is important to understand what customers are really looking for and what they evaluate.

When the service provider understands how service is perceived and evaluated by the users, it will be possible to identify ways of managing these evaluations and influencing them in a desired direction. The relationship between the service concept, the service offered to customers and customer benefits has to be clarified.

Grönroos introduced a service-oriented approach to quality in 1982 (in English) with the concept of *perceived service quality* and the model of total perceived service quality.[1] This approach is based on research into consumer behaviour and the effects of expectations concerning goods performance on post-consumption evaluations. The perceived service quality approach with its *disconfirmation construct* (that is, it measures how well experiences of the service process and its outcome meet expectations) still forms the foundation of most ongoing service quality research.[2]

The original perceived quality model was developed as a conceptual guideline to help managers and researchers understand what constitutes service in the minds of customers. Goods have physical features which can be perceived and evaluated. Service does not exist before it is consumed. When a customer asks for service the service production process can begin. Eventually it ends and the customer is left with an outcome. Features of service emerge during the simultaneous service production and consumption processes. In the model that was developed the term 'quality' was used. In the same way as a marketer of physical goods needs to know how customers perceive the quality of product features, the service marketer has to assess how customers perceive the quality of the 'service features' implied by the perceived service quality framework. The perceived service quality model was introduced as a conceptual framework that describes how customers perceive the 'features' of service. Originally there was no intention to develop quality measurement models based on a service quality model. Once it is known how customers perceive the quality of the 'service features', normal customer satisfaction studies can be conducted to find out how satisfied customers are with a certain service. Customer satisfaction measurement models are also based on the disconfirmation construct and fit service well. However, research into service quality took another avenue, and parallel models for the assessment of service quality were developed.

In addition to research into service quality, there is also an existing quality management establishment with roots that go a long way back in the twentieth century. During the 1990s this took the form of total quality management. However, this quality movement is overwhelmingly devoted to issues related to goods quality. Because of the characteristics of service, much of the goods-related quality know-how is not directly applicable in service organizations.

Of course, on the other hand, much of this is useful for service, too. This should not be forgotten, although this chapter concentrates on what is unique to quality and quality management in service contexts.

QUALITY IS WHAT CUSTOMERS PERCEIVE

Quality has to be defined and how customers perceive quality understood before decisions about quality development can be made. Otherwise quality decisions only become paying lip service to service quality improvement. In service quality literature it is noted that the quality of a particular product or service is *whatever the customer perceives it to be*.

If quality is defined too narrowly, quality programmes become too narrow in scope. For example, the technical specification of a service, or a product, is frequently considered the only or the most important feature of the perceived quality. The more technology-oriented the firm is, the bigger this risk tends to be. In reality, customers perceive that quality is a much broader concept and moreover, features other than technical ones frequently dominate the quality experience. One has to *define quality in the same way customers do*, otherwise the wrong actions may be taken and money and time may be poorly invested. It should always be remembered that *what counts is quality as it is perceived by customers*.

QUALITY DIMENSIONS: WHAT AND HOW

Service is a more or less subjectively experienced process where production and consumption activities take place simultaneously. Interactions, including a series of moments of truth between the customer and the service provider, occur. What happens in these interactions, so-called *buyer–seller interactions* or *service encounters*, will obviously have a critical impact on the perceived service.

Basically, the quality of a service as it is perceived by customers has two dimensions: a *technical outcome-related dimension* and a *functional process-related dimension*. The hotel guest will be provided with a room and a bed to sleep in, the consumer of a restaurant's service will get a meal, the airline passenger will be transported from one place to another, the client of a business consultant may receive a new organization scheme, a factory may have its goods transported from its warehouse to a customer, the bank customer may be granted a loan, the servicing of a machine may be taken care of by the manufacturer, a claim by an unsatisfied customer may be settled by a retail store, and so on. All of these outcomes of service processes are obviously part of the quality experience.

What customers receive in their interactions with a firm is clearly important to them and their quality evaluation. Internally though, this is often thought of as *the quality* of the service. However, this is not the whole truth. It is merely *one* quality dimension, called the *technical quality of the outcome* of the service production process. In service management literature the term 'outcome quality' has also been used for this dimension. It is *what* the customer is left with, when the service production process and its buyer–seller interactions are over. Frequently, but by no means always, this dimension can be measured relatively objectively by customers, because of its characteristic as a technical solution to a problem.

However, as there are a number of interactions between the service provider and the customer, including various series of moments of truth, the technical quality dimension will not count for the total quality that the customer perceives he has received. The customer will obviously also be influenced by the way in which the technical quality – the outcome or end result of the process – is transferred to him. The accessibility of an ATM, a website, a restaurant or a business consultant, the appearance and behaviour of waiters, bank clerks, travel agency representatives, bus drivers, cabin attendants, repairmen and service and maintenance technicians, and how these service employees perform their tasks, what they say and how they do it, also influence the customer's view of the service.

Furthermore, in the case of self-service, the more customers accept and understand self-service activities or co-production routines, the better they will, probably, regard the service. Also, other customers simultaneously consuming the same or similar service may influence the way in which a given customer will perceive a service. Other customers may cause long queues, or disturb the customer; on the other hand, they may have a positive impact on the atmosphere of the buyer–seller interactions in these service encounters.

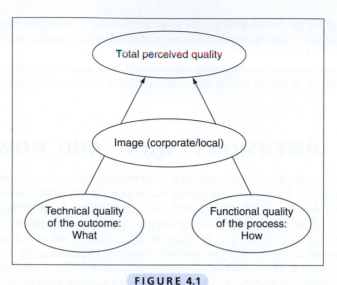

FIGURE 4.1

Two service quality dimensions.

In summary, the customer is also influenced by *how* he receives the service and how he experiences the simultaneous production and consumption process (the service encounter). This is another quality dimension, which is related to how the moments of truth of the service encounters are taken care of and how the service provider functions. Therefore, this is called the *functional quality of the process*. In the literature this dimension is also labelled 'process quality'. Hence, as illustrated in Figure 4.1, we have two basic quality dimensions, namely, *WHAT* the customer receives and *HOW* the customer receives it; the technical result or outcome of the process (technical quality) and the functional dimension of the process (functional quality).[3] It is easy to see that the functional quality dimension cannot be evaluated as objectively as the technical dimension; frequently, it is perceived very subjectively.

Moreover, unlike goods consumption, in most cases the customers knows which organization produces the service. *Company and/or local image* is therefore of utmost importance to most services. It can affect the perception of quality in various ways. If the provider is good in the minds of the customers, that is, if it has a favourable image, minor mistakes will probably be forgiven. If mistakes often occur, the image will be damaged. If the image is negative, the impact of any mistake will often be considerably greater than it otherwise would be. As far as the quality perception is concerned, *image can be viewed as a filter*.

The two quality dimensions, that is, *what* and *how*, are not only valid for service activities. The technical solution for a customer – provided by, for example, a machine or another good – is part of the overall technical quality perceived by this customer. But attempts to tailor the machine according to the specific demands of a customer are an additional value of a functional nature and therefore part of the overall functional quality which this customer experiences.

It should be observed that hidden services, such as invoicing and complaints handling, have a quality impact on customers as well. For example, if a claim is settled with satisfactory results for the customer, the outcome of the claims handling process has good technical quality. However, the total customer influence of the claims handling process also depends on how the process flows. For instance, if it was complicated and time-consuming to get results, the functional quality of the claims handling process has been low and *total perceived quality* lower than it otherwise would have been.

ADDITIONAL DIMENSIONS

Quality dimensions other than the two basic ones (what and how) have been suggested in the literature. Rust and Oliver discussed the need for explicitly recognizing the physical environment of the service encounter as a third dimension.[4] Thus, the *where* of the service quality perception would be added to the *what* and *how*.[5] In the perceived service quality model the service processes include the environment of the process, and thus the *functional quality* perception is influenced by elements of the physical environment. Therefore, the *where* aspect is part of the *how* dimension, which is logical because the perception of the process is clearly dependent on the context of that process. For example, shabby decor influences the perception of the service process in a restaurant. However, as a way of increasing the clarity of the model, if needed a distinction between 'how' and 'where' could very well be made. Hence, a third basic dimension (not counting image) would be introduced into the model. This dimension could, for example, be labelled *servicescape quality*, using the term 'servicescape'[6] introduced by Bitner to describe various elements of the physical environment of the service encounter.

The economic consequence is another aspect of perceived service quality that Holmlund has suggested in a business-to-business context.[7] *Economic quality* would denote the perceived economic consequences of a certain solution. It is not directly a question of price or other kinds of sacrifice for a customer, but rather the perception of, for example, possible economic sacrifice caused by a solution. In some situations, not only in industrial markets, it may very well be justified to take this aspect of perceived service quality into account.

QUALITY AND THE COMPETITIVE EDGE

Quality is often considered to be one of the keys to success. In service contexts, quality is often the foundation of creating a competitive advantage, but which quality dimension (*what* or *how*) is the vital part of excellent total quality? If this question is not answered correctly, the wrong actions may be taken, and the company would lose its chance to achieve a stronger competitive position.

Too often technical quality considerations are thought of as the paramount quality issues. A technical quality strategy is successful if a firm succeeds in achieving a desired technical outcome that the competition cannot match. Today, this is rarely the case; there are a number of firms that can produce approximately the same technical quality. Creating a technical advantage is difficult because, in many industries, competitors can introduce similar solutions relatively quickly. In service, creating a technical advantage seems to be even more difficult than in manufacturing. For example, in financial service or insurance competitors often launch a similar service in a technical sense in response to competition within weeks or even days. Even when an excellent solution is achieved, the firm may be unsuccessful, if excellent technical quality is counteracted or nullified by badly managed or handled service encounters; that is, by an unsatisfactory functional quality of the process.

Implementing a service strategy is a viable option for most firms, service firms and manufacturers of physical goods alike. This means, in principle, that improving the service process and service encounters becomes the basis for quality programmes. Developing the functional quality dimension may add substantial value for the customers and thus create the necessary competitive edge. To state this in a more simplified way, you can beat the competition if you provide your customers with more and better service where functional quality is emphasized. Of course, this does not mean that technical quality issues are not important, and that technical quality should not be developed as well.

The technical quality of the outcome of a service process is normally *a prerequisite for good perceived quality*. It has to be at an acceptable level. The definition of an acceptable level depends on the strategy of a firm and the needs and expectations of its customers. However, once the outcome is good enough, this becomes transparent. *Good technical quality alone does not mean that customers perceive that the service quality is good*. If customers are to consider total service quality good, functional quality has to be good as well. In a situation where a number of firms are competing with similar outcomes or technical quality*, the functional quality impact of the service process counts*. In that situation, firms compete with their service processes and the functional quality impact created by them. However, if technical quality fails, total perceived quality fails as well.

In conclusion, the technical quality has to be good enough, as defined by the firm's strategy and its customers' needs and expectations, but a service provider competes with functional quality, that is, with how its service process is experienced by its customers.

THE PERCEIVED SERVICE QUALITY

In previous sections we discussed the two basic quality dimensions – the *what* and the *how*. We also noted that quality is to a large extent perceived subjectively. However, the quality perception process is more complicated. It is not just the experiences of the quality dimensions that determine whether quality is perceived as good, neutral or bad.

Figure 4.2 illustrates how quality experiences are connected to traditional marketing activities resulting in a *perceived service quality*. Good perceived quality is obtained when the *experienced quality* meets the expectations of the customer; that is, the *expected quality*. If expectations are unrealistic, the total perceived quality will be low, even if the experienced quality measured in an objective way is good. As shown in Figure 4.2, the expected quality is a function of a number of factors, namely marketing communication, word of mouth and discussions in social media, company/local image, price, customer needs and values. *Marketing communication* includes, for example, advertising, direct mail, sales promotion, websites, Internet communication and sales campaigns, which are under the direct control of the firm. *Image, social media* and *word of mouth*, as well as public relations, are only indirectly controlled by the firm. Image also includes a customer's *prior experiences*. External impact on these factors may also occur, but they are basically a function of the previous performance of the firm, supported by, for example, advertising. Finally, the *needs* of the customer as well as the values of the customer that determine his choice also have an impact on his expectations.

A service quality programme may be unsuccessful, or even lead to deteriorated perceived quality, if the firm simultaneously runs advertising campaigns that promise too much or are inadequate in some other respect. The level of total perceived quality is not determined simply by the level of technical and functional quality dimensions, but rather by the *gap between the expected and experienced quality* (the disconfirmation notion). Consequently, every quality programme should involve not only those involved in operations, but also those responsible for external marketing and market communication.

Image plays a central role in customer perception of service quality, and is as important to a service firm as to any other organization. Hence, it is imperative that image be managed in a proper

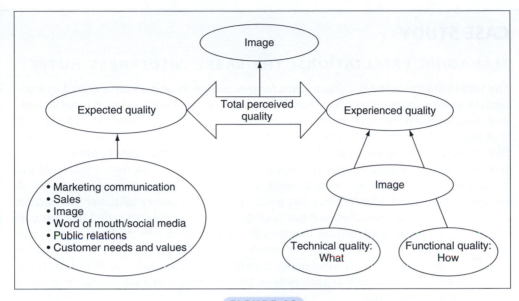

FIGURE 4.2

Total perceived quality.

manner. The issues of how image develops and what causes image problems are not always very well understood. Therefore these issues will be dealt with at length in Chapter 11 on managing brand relationships and image.

MANAGING EXPECTATIONS TO SECURE THE QUALITY PERCEPTION

As the perceived service quality model shows, customer expectations have a decisive impact on customers' quality perceptions. If a service provider overpromises, it raises customers' expectations too high and, consequently, customers will perceive that they get low quality. The level of quality may very well still be high, objectively measured, but as customer expectations were not in balance with experiences, the perceived quality is nevertheless low. Many quality development processes are destroyed by too much promise of improved service, too early. The marketer has to be very careful when designing external marketing campaigns and activities, so that he avoids making promises that cannot be kept. Indeed, it may be wiser to try to keep promises on a lower level than actual customer experiences. In that way customers will at least not be dissatisfied with the quality they perceive. At the same time it allows the service provider to offer its customers unexpected surprises, which much more effectively create loyalty and repurchases than simply satisfactorily perceived quality. We shall return to this issue in the next chapter.

In conclusion, from a marketing point of view it is better to underpromise in order to be sure that the organization can fulfil the promise that has been given. *It is even better to underpromise and overdeliver.*

CASE STUDY

MANAGING EXPECTATIONS: THE SABEL WILDERNESS HOTEL

The Sabel Wilderness Hotel is situated in a large natural park and wilderness area in Scandinavia. Several other hotels operate in the vicinity. The Sabel is a hotel with some 80 beds and is well known for its high standard of service. The hotel has invested in large and well-furnished rooms as well as in a cosy restaurant serving local and international dishes. Over the years it has invested substantial sums in training its employees to offer excellent service to the hotel guests in a personal and flexible way. The most recent theme of the managing director's regular meetings with the employees has been service recovery. A support system for service recovery has been developed. In every customer satisfaction study made over the years the Sabel has been given the best possible rating by most customers. Over 75% of the guests say that they are very satisfied with the hotel overall, and under 5% indicate that they are less than satisfied. Almost all guests who stay at the Sabel and who come back to the national park area make new reservations at the Sabel. However, as the area continuously attracts new visitors, the Sabel has a substantial number of first-time guests every year.

The management of the Sabel was recently offered an opportunity to upgrade the hotel to the highest class in the unofficial rating system used for hotels in the country. However, Mr Leopold, the managing director, also directly responsible for marketing and customer service, turned down this offer. He did not want hotel guests to expect the best, although he is convinced that the hotel indeed offers its guests the highest quality service. Says Mr Leopold, 'It is much better that guests come to us with lower expectations based on our next-to-highest rating, because then we can always surprise them with better service than they thought they would get.' He continues, 'I believe it is much better for us to underpromise and overdeliver.' According to Leopold, guests perceive that they get a better quality this way, and this has a favourable impact on the image of the Sabel. In addition, it reinforces positive word of mouth behaviour.

THE MOMENTS OF TRUTH AND QUALITY

As noted in this chapter, the situations in which the customer meets and interacts with the service provider's resources and processes are critical to the quality experience. In these interactions most or all of the technical quality of the outcome is transferred to the customer, but often even more importantly, these buyer–seller interactions or service encounters determine the level of the functional quality. In service management such situations are often called *moments of truth*, to use a term that was introduced into the service management literature by Richard Normann.[8]

The 'moments of truth' concept literally means that this is the time and place when and where the service provider has the opportunity to demonstrate to the customer the quality of its service. It is a true *moment of opportunity*. In the next moment the opportunity will be lost. The customer will have gone, and so will the moment of opportunity. If a quality problem has occurred, it is too late to take corrective action. In order to do so, a new moment of truth has to be created. The service provider can, for example, actively contact the customer to correct a mistake or to at least explain why things went wrong. This is, of course, much more troublesome and probably less effective than a well-managed moment of truth.

In reality, the customer will experience a whole series of moments of truth when patronizing a service organization. When using the service of an airline the passenger goes through a number of such moments, beginning with arrival at the airport and ending with baggage claim and transportation away from the airport.

The service process must always be planned and executed so that no badly handled moments of truth take place. If such situations go unmanaged there is an evident risk that unexpected quality problems may occur.

THE EFFECT OF EMOTIONS AND MOOD

Emotions that customers feel when consuming a service have not been included in the perceived service quality model, or in models for measuring satisfaction with service quality. However, it is quite obvious that felt emotions, such as anger and depression, guilt or happiness, delight and hopefulness, somehow affect the pure cognitive perception of service processes. Some services, such as theatre or an ice hockey game, should arouse emotions, but emotions also form either a filter mediating experiences of the service process, or are variables that influence the experiences alongside cognitively perceived quality elements.

Managers should always bear in mind the potential effects of emotions on perceived service quality. There have been some minor studies of the effects of emotions on satisfaction with service quality. One such study indicated that negative emotions may have a stronger effect on satisfaction with quality than positive emotions.[9] However, no conclusive guidance for management has yet been found.

Mood is a related concept, which may also have a decisive effect on how the quality of a service is perceived. Previous research on consumer behaviour has shown that customers' mood – positive or negative – has an effect on their evaluations and behavioural responses to, among other things, service encounters.[10] As with emotions, research into the effects of mood on how service quality is perceived is very scarce. However, based on existing research, it seems that mood may only have a limited impact on how customers perceive service encounters.[11]

MEASURING SERVICE QUALITY

Customers' perception of the quality of service features must, of course, be assessed. The natural way of doing it would be to measure customers' satisfaction with the quality they have perceived, as was originally intended with the perceived service quality model. However, a major part of service quality research has been geared towards the development of instruments for measuring service quality directly. In the literature, two types of measurement instruments have been discussed and used.

1. Attribute-based measurement instruments: measurement models based on attributes describing the features of a service.

2. Qualitative measurement instruments: for example, measurement models based on the assessment of critical incidents.

Attribute-based models are the most widely used measurement instruments in academic research as well as in business practice. The most well-known instrument is the SERVQUAL instrument. According to this measurement approach a number of attributes that describe the features of a service are defined, and after that respondents are asked to rate the service on these attributes.

Qualitative measurement approaches are used to a much lesser extent. Here respondents are asked to describe their perception of the service or the service encounters. The critical incident method is the most often used qualitative method. In a subsequent section this method will be described.

ATTRIBUTE-BASED MODELS: SERVICE QUALITY DETERMINANTS AND THE SERVQUAL INSTRUMENT

How service quality can be measured using attribute-based models has been studied extensively. In the mid-1980s. Berry and his colleague began to study service quality determinants and how customers evaluate the quality of service based on the perceived service quality concept.[12] In Figure 4.3 the results of their initial study, the 10 service quality determinants, are summarized.

The 10 determinants were found to characterize customers' perception of the service. One of the determinants, *competence*, is clearly related to the *technical quality* of the outcome, and another, *credibility*, is closely connected to the *image* aspect of perceived quality. However, it is interesting to observe that the rest of the determinants are more or less related to the process dimension of perceived quality. The importance of the *functional quality* dimension is very much stressed by these findings.

As a result of a later study the 10 determinants of service quality were decreased to the following five:[13]

1. *Tangibles*. This determinant is related to the appeal of facilities, equipment and material used by a service firm as well as to the appearance of service employees.

2. *Reliability*. This means that the service firm provides its customers with accurate service the first time without making any mistakes and delivers what it has promised to do by the time that has been agreed upon.

3. *Responsiveness*. This means that the employees of a service firm are willing to help customers and respond to their requests as well as to inform customers when service will be provided, and then give prompt service.

4. *Assurance*. This means that employees' behaviour will give customers confidence in the firm and that the firm makes customers feel safe. It also means that the employees are always courteous and have the necessary knowledge to respond to customers' questions.

5. *Empathy*. This means that the firm understands customers' problems and performs in their best interests as well as giving customers individual personal attention and having convenient operating hours.

SERVQUAL is an instrument for measuring how customers perceive the quality of a service. This instrument is based on the five determinants above and on a comparison between customers' *expectations* of how the service should be performed and their *experiences* of how the service is rendered (disconfirmation or confirmation of expectations). Usually 22 attributes are used to describe the five determinants and respondents are asked to state (on a seven-point scale from 'Strongly Disagree' to

1. *Reliability* involves consistency of performance and dependability:
   - the firm performs the service right the first time
   - accuracy in billing
   - keeping records correctly
   - performing the service at the designated time
2. *Responsiveness* concerns the willingness or readiness of employees to provide service:
   - timeliness of service
   - mailing transaction slips immediately
   - calling the customer back quickly
   - giving prompt service
3. *Competence* means possession of the required skills and knowledge:
   - knowledge and skills of the contact employees
   - knowledge and skills of operational support personnel
   - research capability of the organization
4. *Access* involves approachability and ease of contact:
   - the service is easily accessible by telephone
   - waiting time to receive service is not extensive
   - convenient hours of operation
   - convenient location of service facility
5. *Courtesy* involves politeness, respect, consideration, and friendliness of contact personnel:
   - consideration for the consumer's property
   - clean and neat appearance of contact personnel
6. *Communication* means keeping customers informed in language they can understand and listening to them:
   - explaining the service itself
   - explaining how much the service will cost
   - explaining the trade-offs between service and cost
   - assuring the consumers that a problem will be handled
7. *Credibility* involves trustworthiness, believability, honesty, and having the customer's best interests at heart:
   - company name
   - company reputation
   - personal characteristics of the contact personnel
   - the degree of hard sell involved in interactions
8. *Security* is the freedom from danger, risk, or doubt:
   - physical safety
   - financial security
   - confidentiality
9. *Understanding/Knowing the Customer* involves making the effort to understand the customer's needs:
   - learning the customer's specific requirements
   - providing individualized attention
   - recognizing regular customers
10. *Tangibles* include physical evidence of the service:
    - physical facilities
    - appearance of personnel
    - tools or equipment used to provide the service
    - physical representations of the service (cards, etc.)
    - other customers in the service facility

FIGURE 4.3

Determinants of perceived service quality.
Source: Parasuraman, A., Zeithaml, V.A. & Berry, L.L., A conceptual model of service quality and its implications for future research. *Journal of Marketing*, **49**(Fall); 1985: p. 47. Reproduced by permission of the American Marketing Association.

'Strongly Agree') what they expected from the service and how they perceived the service. Based on the discrepancies between expectations and experiences over the 22 attributes, an overall quality score can be calculated. The more this score shows that experiences are below expectation, the lower the perceived quality.[14] However, more important than calculating the overall score may be the scores on the individual attribute scales.

There has been some controversy regarding the use of the SERVQUAL instrument. In many studies the determinants have been reported to be stable over various types of service, but in other studies the set of five standard determinants has not been found. Moreover, sometimes in a factor analysis one set of determinants emerges for expectations and another set for experiences. In addition, the 22 attributes used in the original instrument do not always accurately describe all aspects of a given service.[15]

The SERVQUAL scale should be applied carefully, and the determinants and attributes of the instrument should always be reassessed in any situation, before the instrument is used. The services, as well as markets and cultural environments, are different. It may be necessary to add new aspects of the service to be studied to the original set of determinants and attributes, and sometimes to exclude some from the measurement instrument used. From a managerial point of view, when trying to understand what constitutes a given service, the five determinants, and also the original 10 determinants, give a valuable starting point for the development of an understanding of what aspects characterize the service that is provided. However, when using a SERVQUAL-type approach to measuring perceived service quality one should always carefully customize the set of determinants and attributes used to the specific situation at hand.

PROBLEMS WITH EXPECTATIONS/EXPERIENCES MEASUREMENTS AND COMPARISONS

There has been a considerable amount of debate regarding what kind of expectations the real experiences of a given service should be compared with. In the original SERVQUAL instrument, customers were asked what they expected from the service they had consumed, so the expectations and experiences measurements related to the same service. Later the measurement method was changed so that customers were asked what they expected from an excellent or *ideal* service in the same category as the one they had consumed. The original perceived service quality model from which the expectations/experiences comparison originates in service quality contexts was developed to help managers and researchers understand how customers perceive features of a given service. Hence, the expectations concept in that model is quite clearly related to the same service that is also experienced. Following the original model, the expectations should be measured as the expectations of the service that is consumed.

However, independent of what one wants to know about a given service, different kinds of expectations could be measured. If one wants to assess how good a given service is considered to be compared with the best in its category, expectations of the best-in-the-category service or an ideal service should be measured. On the other hand, if one wants to find out how customers perceive the quality of a given service, both expectations and experiences regarding this particular service should be measured.

There is another problem with measurement instruments that are based on comparisons between expectations and experiences over a number of attributes. This is because there are certain validity problems related to the measurement of expectations. These problems can be summarized in the following three points:[16]

1. If expectations are measured after the service experience or at the same time as the experiences occur, which for practical reasons they often are, then what is measured is not really expectation but something that has been biased by experience.

2. It does not necessarily make sense to measure expectations *prior* to the service experience either, because the expectations that customers have beforehand are perhaps not the expectations with which they will compare their experiences. The customer's experiences of the service process may change his expectations, and altered expectations are ones with which the experiences should be compared to determine the actual quality perception of a customer.

3. Measuring expectations is not a sound way of proceeding in any case, because experiences are perceptions of reality, and inherent in these perceptions are prior expectations. Consequently, if first, one way or the other, expectations are measured and then experiences are measured, then the expectations are *measured twice*.

When measuring perceived service quality, the problems described above are not easy to solve. *Theoretically*, a comparison of experiences and expectations still makes sense, because expectations clearly influence the perception of quality. Managers need to observe the management of expectations when developing quality programmes. However, *in practice* we may have to find alternative ways of measuring perceived quality.

In her study on the restaurant industry, Liljander[17] compared a number of different standards to relate experiences to, expectations being one of them. Her conclusion was that making no comparisons at all seems to be a good approach to measuring perceived service quality. This means that *by measuring experiences only* over a set of appropriate attributes, one can get a good approximation of the perceived quality. In a North American study, based on similar arguments as Liljander's, a measurement instrument called SERVPERF (service performance only) was suggested.[18] Indeed, measuring customers' experiences only may be the best and most valid way of assessing perceived service quality. Thus, the researcher develops a set of attributes that describes the service as conclusively as possible and only measures how customers experience the service on scales that measure these attributes. This way of measuring perceived service quality is also much easier to administer and the data is easier to analyse.

STUDYING CRITICAL INCIDENTS: A QUALITATIVE APPROACH TO MEASURING SERVICE QUALITY

An alternative to attribute-based methods to study how customers perceive the quality of a given service is the *critical incident method*. This method has been used a great deal in various studies in the service field.[19]

The methodological approach is to ask respondents, in this case customers with experiences of a given service, to think of situations where the service, or any part of the service process including the outcome of that process, clearly deviated from the norm, either in a favourable or unfavourable way. These are *critical incidents*. Then the respondent is asked to describe, in as much detail as possible, *what happened* and *what made him consider the incident critical*. Finally, the researcher analyses the descriptions of the critical incidents and the reasons for them in order to find out what kind of quality problems exist and why these problems occur. Favourable quality perceptions and the reasons for them are also categorized in the same fashion.

A study using critical incidents gives the marketer rich material indicating problem areas and strengths as well as what should be developed in order for the firm to improve the perceived quality of its service. One may find out, for example, that a lack of resources, problems with the technical skills of service employees or negative attitudes towards customers are frequently occurring reasons for negative critical incidents, causing low service quality perception. If needed, the marketer can use these findings as a basis for further research on actions necessary to improve service quality. Frequently the findings from a critical incident study give direct indications about what actions need to be taken.

PERCEIVED SERVICE QUALITY VERSUS CUSTOMER SATISFACTION

Customer satisfaction with a physical product is often measured using an instrument where a given physical product is described by a set of attributes that reflect key product features. A comparison of experiences with prior expectations is also often made. Probably because the development of measurement models for perceived service quality included similar elements to models for measuring satisfaction with goods features, the question whether there is a difference between service quality and customer satisfaction has been debated in the literature. Furthermore, if there is a difference, the question whether quality is perceived first and then satisfaction, or satisfaction with a service comes first and then leads to a quality perception has also been discussed. This discussion has been extensive and even heated at times; however, it is quite unnecessary.

The perceived service quality model is intended to offer a conceptual framework for understanding the features of a service, including its outcome, process and image dimensions. It is not a measurement model. Instead it should give the researcher and marketer a basis for developing a service offering with a certain quality. In the same way as a customer first perceives the quality of the features of a physical product, and only then, perhaps taking into account price and other sacrifice-related issues, finds out whether or not he is satisfied with the product, a person consuming a service first perceives the quality of the dimensions of the service, and only then, again perhaps considering other issues as well, is either satisfied or not with the quality of that service.

A logical analysis clearly shows that a perception of service quality comes first, followed by a perception of satisfaction or dissatisfaction with this quality.

A SUMMARY: THE SEVEN CRITERIA OF GOOD PERCEIVED SERVICE QUALITY

There has been a range of studies of service quality conducted in many countries. From them various lists of attributes or factors of good quality can be collated. Such lists are useful as starting points for managers who want to develop an appropriate list of attributes or features that describe a given service. However, in order to make such lists of determinants or factors of good service quality useful for managerial purposes, they have to be short, yet still provide a comprehensive list of aspects of

1. **Professionalism and Skills**
   Customers realize that the service provider, its employees, operational systems, and physical resources have the knowledge and skills required to solve their problems in a professional way (outcome-related criteria).
2. **Attitudes and Behaviour**
   Customers feel that the service employees (contact persons) are concerned about them and interested in solving their problems in a friendly and spontaneous way (process-related criteria).
3. **Accessibility and Flexibility**
   Customers feel that the service provider, its location, operating hours, employees, and operational systems are designed and operate so that it is easy to get access to the service and are prepared to adjust to the demands and wishes of the customer in a flexible way (process-related criteria).
4. **Reliability and Trustworthiness**
   Customers know that whatever takes place or has been agreed upon, they can rely on the service provider, its employees and systems, to keep promises and perform with the best interest of the customers at heart (process-related criteria).
5. **Service Recovery**
   Customers realize that whenever something goes wrong or something unpredictable happens the service provider will immediately and actively take action to keep them in control of the situation and find a new, acceptable solution (process-related criteria).
6. **Servicescape**
   Customers feel that the physical surrounding and other aspects of the environment of the service encounter support a positive experience of the service process (process-related criteria).
7. **Reputation and Credibility**
   Customers believe that the service provider's business can be trusted and gives adequate value for money, and that it stands for good performance and values which can be shared by customers and the service provider (image-related criteria).

FIGURE 4.4

The seven criteria of good perceived service quality.

good quality. Figure 4.4 provides such a list. These seven criteria of good perceived service quality are an integration of available studies and conceptual work. Some of these studies have been discussed in this chapter. One of the seven, *professionalism and skills*, is outcome-related and thus a *technical* quality dimension. Another criterion, *reputation and credibility*, is *image*-related, thus fulfilling a filtering function. However, four other criteria, *attitudes and behaviour*, *accessibility and flexibility*, *reliability and trustworthiness* and *service recovery*, are clearly process-related and thus represent the *functional* quality dimension. Finally, following the conceptual work by Bitner *et al.*,[20] the impact of the *servicescape* is introduced as a seventh criterion. This is clearly a process-related, functional quality criterion.

These seven criteria of good perceived service quality can be viewed as guidelines based on a solid body of empirical and conceptual research as well as on practical experience. Therefore, they should be useful as managerial principles. Of course, the list is not exhaustive. In various industries and for various customers certain criteria are more important than others. And of course, there may in specific situations be other determinants of good quality that are not covered by these criteria.

The role of *price* in a quality context is not very clear. Normally, however, the price of a service can be viewed in relation to the quality expectations of customers or to their previously perceived service quality. If the price of a service is considered too high, customers will not buy. Price also has an impact on expectations. But in some situations price seems to be a quality criterion. A higher price level may equal a better quality in the minds of customers, especially when the service is highly intangible. In many cases professional service is an example of such service.

RELATIONSHIP QUALITY: A DYNAMIC APPROACH TO PERCEIVED QUALITY

The perceived service quality model is basically static, although the *image* factor adds dynamism to it. Most service quality models and instruments are static. As service is a process and inherently relational, clearly customers' quality perceptions develop and undergo change over time as the relationship continues. Even if there is only one single service encounter, this encounter is a process that includes a series of moments of truth and the customer's quality perception develops in a dynamic fashion throughout this interaction process. The need for dynamic models to further develop the understanding of how service quality is perceived by customers was expressed at the beginning of the 1990s.[21] Driven by service quality research, an interest in *relationship quality* emerged.[22] Relationship quality can be described as *the dynamics of long-term quality formation in ongoing customer relationships*. In the last part of this chapter models that describe how long-term quality perceptions can be understood and analysed are described.[23]

From the customer's point of view, relationship quality is their continuously developing quality perception over time. However, as a relationship includes at least two parties, the supplier or service provider and the customer, a quality perception is really developing on both sides. The supplier or service provider forms an impression of the quality of the customer and, especially in business relationships, there may be ongoing reciprocal business developing over time with continuous quality perceptions by both parties related to the two-way exchanges of goods, service activities, information or other items of value.

A RELATIONSHIP FRAMEWORK FOR THE ANALYSIS OF RELATIONSHIP QUALITY

In any commercial relationship between two parties, *interaction* is the key concept. Interactions are the basic phenomena in quality and customers' value creation.[24] The perception of *relationship quality* occurs in ongoing interactions, which may be either continuous, such as in security and cleaning services, or discrete, such as in bank service or goods transportation. Maria Holmlund has developed a framework for understanding and analysing ongoing interactions.[25] Such interactions may be very different depending on the type of marketing situation involved. Some contacts are between people, some between customers and machines and systems, and some between systems of the supplier and customer, respectively. In every case interactions are involved. The framework is equally valid for describing and analysing relationships in consumer markets and in business-to-business markets.

The framework consists of a continuous flow of *acts*, *episodes* and *sequences*, which form the *relationships*.[26] Figure 4.5 illustrates this *relationship framework*.

Acts are the smallest unit of analysis in the interaction process. Examples of *acts* could include phone calls, factory visits, service calls and hotel registration. These are moments of truth. Acts may be related to any kind of interaction elements, physical goods, services, information, financial aspects or social contacts.

Interrelated acts form a minor part of a relationship. These are called *episodes* (or *service encounters* to use a concept frequently used in the service management literature) and examples of these include paying bills from a home computer or visiting a bank office to withdraw money, a negotiation, a shipment of goods, or dinner at a hotel restaurant during a stay at that hotel. Every episode includes a series of acts, and consequently a series of moments of truth. For example, a shipment may include such acts as the placement of an order by telephone, assembling and packing the products, transporting the products, unpacking them, making a complaint, and sending and paying an invoice.

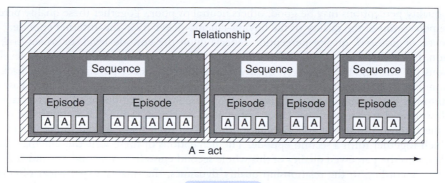

FIGURE 4.5

A relationship framework: interaction levels in a relationship.
Source: Holmlund, M., *Perceived Quality in Business Relationships.* Helsinki:
Hanken Swedish School of Economics, Finland/CERS, 1997, p. 96. Reproduced by
permission.

Interrelated episodes form the next level of analysis in the interaction process, a *sequence*. Sequences can be defined in terms of a time period, a product offering, a campaign or a project, or a combination of these. The analysis of a sequence may contain all kinds of interactions related to a particular project, which may take up to a year or even longer. As an example, in a hotel context, a sequence comprises everything that takes place during one stay at a particular hotel, including episodes such as accommodation, eating in the hotel restaurant and using the hotel's gym or pool. Sequences may naturally overlap, so that episodes belonging to one sequence may also be part of another sequence.

The final and most aggregated level of analysis is the *relationship*. Several sequences form a relationship. Sequences may follow each other directly, may overlap or may follow after longer or shorter intervals depending, for example, on the type of business or on whether the service is of a continuous or discrete nature. This way of dividing the interaction process into several layers on different levels of aggregation gives the marketer a detailed enough instrument to be used in the analysis of interactions between a supplier or service provider and his customers. All different types of elements in the interaction process – goods and service outcomes, service processes, information, social contacts, financial activities, etc. – can be identified and put into their correct perspective in the formation of a relationship over time.

PERCEIVED QUALITY IN A RELATIONSHIP FRAMEWORK

The more or less static models of perceived service quality describe how quality is perceived at the episode (or service encounter) level, and the measurement instruments that have been developed measure perceived quality on that level. From a dynamic perspective, quality is perceived at every level of the relationship framework, thus accumulating to an overall perception of quality at any given point of time. The quality perception at a certain time reflects on the perception of quality in, for example, single acts and episodes, for example by continuously forming and reforming the customer's image of the service provider. Thus, single acts such as visiting a movie theatre's website, buying tickets for a certain movie and finally paying for the tickets over the Internet form the episode (or service encounter) of buying cinema tickets. The customer forms a perception of the quality of an act, and this perception, or image, is reflected in the expectations of and perceptions of the next act. Some of these quality perceptions may be good, others neutral or poor. Together these quality perceptions form the perception of the quality of the buying-cinema-ticket-over-the-Internet episode.

Act-level, or *first-level*, quality perception reflects upon the episode level, or *second-level*, quality perception. However, the dynamics of relationship quality formation then make upper-level quality perceptions (in this case the perceived quality of the Internet ticket purchase) reflect back on the perception of lower-level acts of following episodes. The quality perception of the purchase episode forms customer expectations and the image of the firm, and these influence the perception of following lower-level acts; in this case, the act of picking up tickets at the ticket counter of the movie theatre, the comfort of the seat and visibility of the screen from the seat, and the movie experience itself, which together form a second episode. The perceptions of these visit-the-cinema-related acts accumulate into the perceived quality of this whole second episode as a second, second-level quality perception. According to the relationship quality dynamics, the quality experiences of continuous episodes, some good, some neutral or poor, accumulate into an overall *third-level* quality perception of the whole sequence of going to the movie theatre on a particular evening, including buying the tickets over the Internet and going to the movie theatre to see the movie. This third-level quality perception then reflects back on continuing lower-level perceptions of episodes and acts in the relationship between a given customer and this particular movie theatre in the future.

Finally, the quality perceptions of sequences of episodes accumulate into a *fourth-level* quality perception; that is, into *relationship quality*. This quality perception in turn, following the logic of relationship quality dynamics, reflects back on how quality is perceived in the future on lower levels.

The dynamics of relationship quality are illustrated schematically in Figure 4.6. The arrows indicate how perceptions of quality reflect up onto higher levels and then back again in the form of image and expectations. For the sake of clarity, the figure does not show all influences. The grade of shading of the boxes depicting acts, episodes, sequences and the relationship illustrate whether the quality is

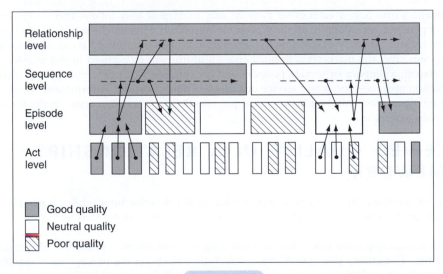

FIGURE 4.6

Inherent dynamics in the formation of quality in a relationship.
Source: Adapted from Holmlund, M., *Perceived Quality in Business Relationships*. Helsinki: Hanken Swedish School of Economics, Finland/CERS, p. 160. Reproduced by permission.

perceived as good, neutral, or poor. For the sake of simplicity, only a three-grade scale is used here to show the level of the quality perception. As the figure shows, the level of quality may vary and this influences the formation of the quality perception on higher levels. In practical quality management it is of course important to build as much consistency and continuously good quality perceptions as possible into the process, because unfavourable quality experiences always have a negative effect, which in turn will reflect on future quality perceptions.

The strength of this relationship framework, with its four levels of analysis, is that it enables the supplier or service provider to study in detail the development of a relationship with a customer and also makes it possible to understand and analyse how the development of a series of customer contacts adds to an overall relationship quality. It clarifies the multi-faceted dynamics involved in customers' perceptions of quality. An analysis of the relationship demonstrates the multitude of acts and episodes (service encounters) that contribute to the long-term formation of quality and makes managers more aware of the range of customer contacts that have to be managed from a quality perspective. It shows which acts or episodes are relationship-breaking and which are less critical for the continuation of the relationship. It does not, however, go into the detailed aspects of the dynamics in long-term quality formation. The next section deals with this issue.

THE LILJANDER–STRANDVIK MODEL OF RELATIONSHIP QUALITY

The Liljander–Strandvik model of relationship quality includes four important aspects:[27]

1. It makes a distinction between *episode-level quality* (the perceived quality of a service encounter) and *relationship-level quality*.

2. It incorporates satisfaction and customer perceived value in a quality framework.

3. It enables an extension of the traditional limited disconfirmation notion used in static models of perceived service quality to include a range of comparison standards.

4. It includes customer behaviour variables.

The model is illustrated in Figure 4.7. Concepts used in the model are described in Table 4.1. The lower part of the Liljander–Strandvik model is related to the perception of service quality in a single service encounter (*episode-level quality*). *Episode performance* – that is, the service experienced in one service encounter – can be compared with any *comparison standard*, not only predictive expectations as is traditionally the case in service quality models (see Table 4.1), or it can be compared with no comparison standards, depending on what seems to generate the most valid result. By comparing the *episode quality* that emerges with the customer's perceived *sacrifice* (such as price, queuing time, lost earnings opportunities and standstill costs), the customer forms his (or the organization's) perception of the *value* for him (or the organization) provided by the episode. This in turn leads to *satisfaction* (or *dissatisfaction*) with the service. The *zone of tolerance* is an accepted variation in performance levels.

The satisfaction with a given service encounter (episode) influences the future behaviour of the customer. The customer's behaviour is dependent on his feelings of loyalty and commitment to the firm. However, there are also other factors that have an impact on behaviour. These are *bonds* that exist between the customer and the service provider. Some bonds, such as *legal*, *economic*, *technological*, *geographical* and *time-related* bonds, often constitute barriers to exiting from the relationship. Other bonds, such as *knowledge-related*, *social*, *cultural*, *ideological* and *psychological* bonds, may glue the customer

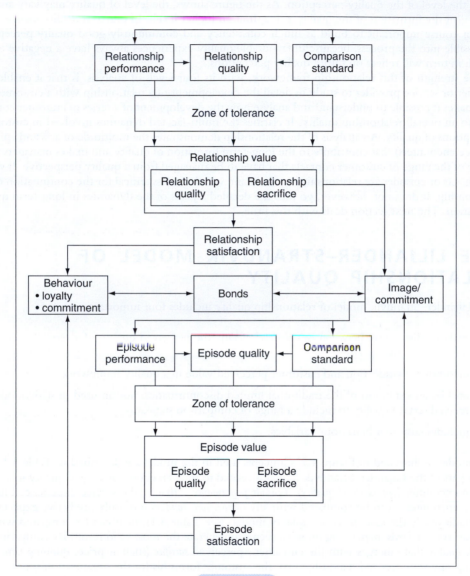

FIGURE 4.7

The Liljander-Strandvik relationship quality model.
Source: Adapted from Liljander, V. & Strandvik, T., The nature of relationships in services. In *Advances in Services Marketing and Management*, Vol. 4. Greenwich: CT: The JAI Press, copyright ©1995, p. 143 with permission from Elsevier.

TABLE 4.1

The Liljander–Strandvik model of relationship quality.

Concept	Episode level	Relationship level
Comparison standard	All comparison standards suggested in the literature (e.g. predictive expectations, brand norm, adequate, product norm, best brand norm, excellent service, ideal, competitor).	All comparison standards suggested in the literature except predictive expectations.
Disconfirmation	Direct or inferred disconfirmation of any comparison standard.	Direct or inferred disconfirmation of any comparison standard except predictive expectations.
Performance	Perceived performance of one particular episode.	Perceived performance across all episodes in the relationship.
Zone of tolerance	The accepted variation in performance levels. A plateau in the quality function.	The accepted accumulation variation in the performance within the relationship.
Quality	Customers' cognitive evaluation of the service of one episode compared with some explicit or implicit comparison standard.	Customers' cognitive evaluation of the service across episodes compared with some explicit or implicit comparison standard.
Sacrifice	Perceived sacrifices (price, etc.) connected to the service episode compared with some explicit or implicit comparison standard.	Perceived sacrifices (price, etc.) across all service episodes in the relationship compared with some explicit or implicit comparison standard.
Value	Episode quality compared with episode sacrifice.	Relationship quality compared with relationship sacrifice.
Satisfaction	Customers' cognitive and affective evaluation based on the personal experience of one service episode.	Customers' cognitive and affective evaluation based on the personal experience across all service episodes within the relationship.
Image	The holistic perception of a service provider that filters performance evaluations and can in itself constitute a comparison standard. It is also the attitudinal component of commitment in a relationship. All types of bonds can affect the image positively or negatively. Image itself is more likely to affect and strengthen the psychological bonds.	
Commitment	Commitment is defined as the parties' intentions to act and their attitude towards interacting with each other. High relationship value will positively affect commitment.	

TABLE 4.1
(continued)

Concept	Episode level	Relationship level
Behaviour	Purchase behaviour and communication behaviour (word of mouth, complaints). Loyalty, which is based also on positive commitment by the customer, indicates a stronger relationship than if it is based on mere repetitive purchase behaviour. The behaviour is also affected by the bonds between the customer and the service provider. By using the same service provider the bonds may be strengthened.	
Bonds	Exit barriers that tie the customer to the service provider and maintain the relationship. These are legal, economic, technological, geographical, time-related, knowledge-related, social, cultural, ideological and psychological bonds.	

Source: Adapted from Liljander, V. & Strandvik, T., The nature of relationships in services. In *Advances in Services Marketing and Management*, Vol. 4. Greenwich, CT: The JAI Press, copyright © 1995, p. 144 with permission from Elsevier.

to the service provider in a positive fashion. The 10 different types of bonds are described in some detail in Table 4.2.

The customer-perceived episode-level value, as well as bonds that exist in the relationship, influence the customer's *image* of the service provider. As in the image concept in the basic perceived service quality model, the image incorporates the customers' old and recent experiences with the firm and builds a bridge to the relationship level of the model. The image functions as a filter when the customer perceives the next episode or service encounter. As in the model of perceived quality described in the previous section, perceptions of quality and value of episodes or service encounters following each other accumulate into perceived quality of the relationship. According to the Liljander–Strandvik model the customer compares the firm's ongoing performance in subsequent service encounters (*relationship performance*) with a comparison standard and, based on that comparison, *relationship quality* emerges. When the customer compares this quality perception perceived long-term sacrifice (*relationship sacrifice*), the value of the relationship at a given point in time is perceived (*relationship value*). This affects long-term satisfaction with the service provider (*relationship satisfaction*), which in turn feeds into the image on the one hand and into future behaviour (loyalty and commitment) on the other hand.[28]

From a management point of view this model of relationship quality offers a good description of the mechanisms of relationship quality. It demonstrates how customers proceed through the service process over time and perceive their relationship with a service provider. The model includes several concepts, such as *bonds*, *value* and *sacrifice*, and connections between concepts which help managers understand the process and determine where action should be taken. Some of these concepts will be discussed further in Chapter 6. The major strength of this model is its multi-faceted nature. It demonstrates to managers how perceived quality is formed and accumulates over time as the relationship evolves, and describes which factors need to be taken into account when managing quality in an ongoing relationship context. It should guide managers towards a comprehensive approach to understanding relationship quality and quality management to make customer-oriented decisions.[29] However, it is not a measurement model.

TABLE 4.2

The Liljander–Strandvik model of relationship quality.

Type of bond	Examples
Legal bond	A contract between the customer and service provider (e.g. telephone company, cable TV, electricity, bank services).
Economic bond	Lack of resources may force the customer to buy a service that fits the customer's budget; price reductions based on relationship.
Technological bond	The purchase of a specific product that requires the use of a specified deal for repairs/maintenance and/or original spare parts from manufacturer or retailer.
Geographical bond	Limited possibilities to buy the service from other than one or a few service providers because of distance and/or lack of transportation.
Time-related bond	A service provider may be used because of suitable business hours or because of a flexible appointment system. Customers are limited by business hours set by service providers (e.g. child care from 8 am to 4 pm) or employers (office hours and limited lunch hour).
Knowledge-related bond	The customer may have an established relationship with a doctor who knows the customer's medical history. A customer's relation to a bank teller may be strong because of the teller's knowledge about the customer's business which facilitates the transactions. It also works the other way, so that the customer gains knowledge about the service provider (e.g. the scripts of how to behave are known to the customer, which reduces uncertainty).
Social bond	Social bonds exist when the customer and the service personnel know each other well. Contact is easy, there is mutual trust (services can be handled by phoning the bank, the customer does not have to go there personally).
Cultural bond	Customers may identify themselves with a subculture (e.g. language, country) and therefore relate more strongly to certain companies or products made by certain countries.
Ideological bond	Customers may be inclined to prefer some service providers because of certain personal values (e.g. environmentally friendly products, avoiding companies that exploit nature, support local or national products over imported products).
Psychological bond	The customer is convinced of the superiority of a certain service provider (brand image).

THE DYNAMICS OF EXPECTATIONS

The Liljander–Strandvik model of relationship quality implies that a range of comparison standards can be used by customers to compare their experiences of quality attributes. As has been noted earlier, it may often be best to use no comparison standard at all, but simply to measure customers' experiences of various quality attributes. However, customers' expectations do *theoretically* form an important factor influencing perceived service quality both on an episode (service encounter) level and on a relationship level. Regardless of whether expectations are measured or not, in order to understand how quality is perceived in an ongoing relationship, one has to understand how expectations develop throughout the relationship. This is important for several reasons. First, customers' expectations should be managed, so that they do not expect the impossible. Second, it is critical to understand that customers may not expect the same aspects of quality at a later stage in the relationship as they do in the beginning, and why this change has taken place. Third, one has to know the inherent mechanisms of the dynamics of expectations to be able to manage expectations.

Jukka Ojasalo[30] studied the way the quality of professional service develops in a customer relationship over time. Although this study was carried out in the professional service area, the *dynamics of expectations* revealed in the study seem to be valid for any types of service in customer relationships. Figure 4.8 illustrates the expectations model.

In the long term, three different types of expectations can be identified: *fuzzy*, *explicit* and *implicit* expectations. These can be characterized in the following way:[31]

- *Fuzzy expectations* exist when customers expect a service provider to solve a problem but do not have a clear understanding of what should be done.

- *Explicit expectations* are clear in customers' minds in advance of the service processes. They can be divided into *realistic* and *unrealistic* expectations.

- *Implicit expectations* refer to elements of a service that are so obvious to customers that they do not consciously think about them but take them for granted.

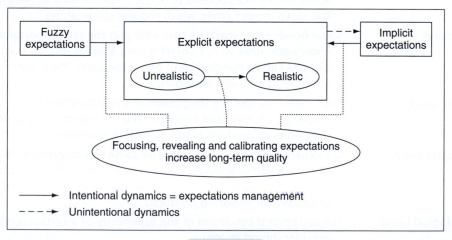

FIGURE 4.8

A dynamic model of expectations.
Source: Ojasalo, J., *Quality Dynamics in Professional Services*. Helsinki: Hanken
Swedish School of Economics, Finland/CERS, 1999, p. 97. Reproduced by permission.

FUZZY EXPECTATIONS

It is essential for a service provider to understand which *fuzzy expectations* customers may have, because even though customers cannot consciously formulate such expectations, they still have an impact on satisfaction with quality. Customers may feel that there is a need for service or for a change of their current state in general, but they do not have a clear understanding of what would fulfil this need or change the current situation. Such fuzzy expectations are very real, because customers expect something to be done. If the service rendered by the service provider does not fulfil such fuzzy expectations, customers are disappointed. They feel that something is missing, and they do not understand why they are not satisfied. Fuzzy expectations remain fuzzy.

The service provider should be aware of the existence of such expectations and try to make them surface in the form of explicit expectations. Only then can it be sure that a satisfactory service is provided. Otherwise the service organization may be faced with unhappy and frustrated customers. The existence of such fuzzy expectations has been recognized for a long time in professional service.[32] Similar situations also occur in other types of service to organizations and individuals alike.

A manufacturing firm that looks for security service does not necessarily understand what needs to be done to provide full security, for example, for its plants. A provider of security service makes an offering that seems appropriate but the manufacturer may still feel that more could be done. The customer may not know what could or should be done and cannot make his expectations explicit, but he still expects something more, and customer remains unsatisfied. For example, restaurant customers often have unclear fuzzy expectations about what they want from an evening at a restaurant. They know that they want to have a good time, but not what will make them feel that they are having one. If the evening does not offer experiences that fulfil this unspecified wish for a good time, they will leave the restaurant disappointed. In all these examples, fuzzy expectations exist. If the service provider *can make these explicit for the customer and for itself*, there is a greater opportunity to satisfy the customer.

EXPLICIT EXPECTATIONS

Customers actively and consciously assume that *explicit expectations* will be met. However, some of these expectations may be unrealistic. For example, a customer who believes that a financial advisor will always be able to manage his funds so that their value grows may one day be very disappointed. It is important for service providers to help customers *adjust unrealistic expectations into more realistic ones*. If this is done, the likelihood that a service is provided which will meet customers' expectations will be much higher. In the beginning of a relationship, but of course also as it continues, the service provider should be very careful in what promises it makes. The more vague promises are, the bigger the risk is that customers will form unrealistic explicit expectations. Such 'implied-in-fact' promises[33] are extremely dangerous, because the customer is led to believe that the service offered will include features that in fact are not included. Unclear and deliberately vague sales messages easily lead to such 'implied-in-fact' promises, and to possibly unrealistic explicit expectations.

IMPLICIT EXPECTATIONS

Customers may take for granted that a service provider will fulfil their *implicit expectations*, because these are so obvious that they are never clearly expressed. Because of this, the service provider may neglect them and not include elements that are required to fulfil such expectations in the service offering. Often customers do not even consciously think about implicit expectations, as long as they are fulfilled. However, the existence of such expectations becomes obvious when they are not met by the service provided, and in that situation dissatisfaction occurs. It is important that service providers make sure that no implicit expectations remain undetected, so that the service offering can be designed to meet all expectations, not only the explicit ones.

Referring back to Figure 4.8, the thick arrows demonstrate *intentional dynamics*; that is, how the service provider can and should actively manage expectations. Fuzzy and implicit expectations should be detected and made explicit. Fuzzy expectations become less fuzzy if they are focused on by the service provider. As the relationship continues, the service organization knows what to do and the customer learns what to expect. Implicit expectations become explicit if they are not fulfilled. Unrealistic expectations should be detected and customers should be made aware of what is realistic to expect.

The dotted lines in the figure indicate what could be called *unintentional dynamics*; that is, shifts in the nature and range of expectations that take place over time without interference from the service provider as the relationship proceeds.

Customers calibrate fuzzy expectations into explicit ones and unrealistic expectations into realistic ones as time goes by, and they learn what they explicitly need and want as well as accept what it is unrealistic to expect. Of course, the effect of these unintentional dynamics processes is not always positive in the sense that customers accept that unrealistic expectations really are unrealistic. They may shift to another firm, which may have the capability to fulfil expectations that were considered unrealistic by the previous service provider.

The dotted arrow in the figure (from explicit expectations towards implicit expectations) demonstrates another type of learning process that creates unintentional expectations dynamics. As customers get used to a certain level of quality in a relationship, some expectations that were originally explicitly expressed become implicit. Customers do not think of them any more and, as long as everything continues as before, no problems occur. However, if the service provider changes something in the service offering – for example, a new service employee takes over a task in the relationship and starts to carry it out in a different way to what the customer is used to – the customer may become disappointed. The implicit expectation becomes explicit once again.

A FRAMEWORK FOR MANAGING CUSTOMER EXPECTATIONS

Jukka Ojasalo offers a framework for managing expectations, which is illustrated in Figure 4.9.[34] The goal is to find ways of avoiding pitfalls created by incorrect or inaccurate expectations. If the

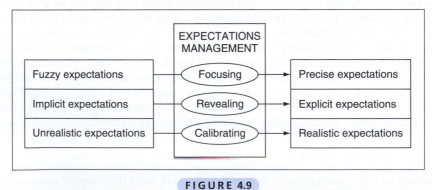

FIGURE 4.9

A framework for managing customer expectations.
Source: Ojasalo, J., Managing expectations in professions services. *Managing Service Quality*, **11**(3); 2001: 206. Reproduced by permission of Emerald Group Publishing Ltd.

customers' expectations are fuzzy, the marketer should help them *focus* their expectations and make them as *precise* as possible. On the other hand, if expectations are implicit, and there is a risk that they will have a negative effect on customers' perceptions at a later stage, marketers need to make customers *reveal* such expectations and make them *explicit*. Finally, unrealistic expectations held by customers should be *calibrated* by marketers, such that they become *realistic*.

SUMMARY

In this chapter we first discussed the nature of perceived service quality and presented the *perceived service quality model* as a basic model of service quality. The *technical quality (what)* and *functional quality (how)* dimensions of the model, as well as *image* as a quality filter, were discussed. Extensions of this model (a possible *servicescape*-related *where*) as well as determinants of service quality were then discussed. Measurement approaches, such as the attribute-based SERVQUAL instrument and the *critical incident model*, were presented. In the latter part of the chapter, models of *relationship quality* and a dynamic approach to managing expectations in service contexts were discussed.

QUESTIONS FOR DISCUSSION

1. Why is quality of service understood as perceived quality?

2. Which dimensions of perceived service quality have to be recognized, according to the *perceived service quality model*? Why? Which additional dimensions could be included?

3. Discuss various determinants and criteria of perceived service quality.

4. What are the strengths and weaknesses of the SERVQUAL instrument as a measurement model? What are those of the critical incident approach?

5. What are the different layers in which quality is formed and perceived in an ongoing relationship context? How does quality develop?

6. Discuss the dynamics of the Liljander–Strandvik model of relationship quality. Which are its strengths and weaknesses for practical use?

7. Discuss how various kinds of expectations influence the perception of quality in a relationship context. What are the risks of not clarifying a customer's expectations?

8. Discuss how the quality of one or several services offered by your firm, or the quality of any given service, is perceived by a specified group of customers. What problems exist? What needs to be improved?

NOTES

1. Grönroos, C., *Strategic Management and Marketing in the Service Sector*. Helsinki/Helsingfors: Swedish School of Economics, Finland, 1982 (published in the USA in 1983 by Marketing Science Institute and in the UK in 1984 by Chartwell-Bratt). See also Grönroos, C., A service quality model and its marketing implications. *European Journal of Marketing*, **18**(4), 1984, 36–44. Evert Gummesson was probably the first service marketing researcher to express the quality of services as perceived quality: in the context of professional services he concludes that '(quality) becomes a matter of subjectively *perceived* quality' (emphasis as in the original publication). See Gummesson, E., *Models of Professional Service Marketing*. Stockholm, Sweden: Liber/Marketing Technique Centre, 1979, p. 9.

2. There is, however, some criticism of the use of customers' expectations as the only comparison standard in models and measurements of perceived service quality. See Liljander, V., *Comparison Standards in Perceived Service Quality*, diss. Helsinki/Helsingfors, Finland: Hanken Swedish School of Economics, Finland/CERS, 1995.

3. The importance of the process-related functional quality alongside the outcome-related technical quality was first observed in a service context in Grönroos, C., A service quality model and its marketing implications. *European Journal of Marketing*, **18**(4), 1984, 36–44. The impact of these two quality dimensions have been studied in various contexts, recently as explanations of customer happiness. Both dimensions are found to have an impact on happiness. See De Keyser, A. & Lariviere, B., How technical and functional quality drive consumer happiness: moderating influences of channel usage. *Journal of Service Management*, **25**(1), 2014, 30–48.

4. Rust, R.T. & Oliver, R.L., Service quality: insights and managerial implications from the frontier. In Rust, R.T. & Oliver, R.L. (eds), *Service Quality: New Directions in Theory and Practice*. Thousand Oaks, CA: Sage Publications, 1994.

5. See Brady & Cronin Jr., Some thoughts on conceptualizing perceived service quality: A hierarchical approach. *Journal of Marketing*, **65**(Jul), 2001, 34–49.

6. Bitner, M.J., Servicescapes: the impact of physical surroundings on customers and employees. *Journal of Marketing*, **56**(Apr), 1992, 57–71. The *servicescape* consists of the physical resources, technology and other physical elements surrounding the service process. It helps to create the ambience of the service process. Thus, it is expected to have an impact on the way service employees and customers behave and interact in service encounters.

7. Holmlund, M., *Perceived Quality in Business Relationships*, diss. Helsinki/Helsingfors, Finland: Hanken Swedish School of Economics, Finland/CERS, 1997.

8. Normann, R., *Service Management*, 2nd edn. New York: John Wiley & Sons, 1992.

9. Liljander, V. & Strandvik, T., Emotions in service satisfaction. *International Journal of Service Industry Management*, **8**(2), 1997, 148–169. See also Jang, S. & Namkung, Y., Perceived quality, emotions, and behavioral intentions: application of an extended Mehrabian–Russell model to restaurants. *Journal of Business Research*, **62**, 2009, 451–460, and Hume, M. & Sullivan Mort, G. The consequence of appraisal emotion, service quality, perceived value and customer satisfaction on repurchase intent in the performing arts. *Journal of Services Marketing*, **24**(2), 2010, 170,182.

10. White, C.J., Towards an understanding of the relationship between mood, emotions, service quality and customer loyalty intentions. *Service Industries Journal*, **26**(9), 2006, 837–847. See Also Gardner, M.P., Mood states and consumer behavior: a critical review. *Journal of Consumer Research*, **12**(Dec), 1985, 281–300.

11. Knowles, P.A., Grove, S.J. & Pickett, G.M., Mood versus service quality effects on customers' responses to service organizations and service encounters. *Journal of Service Research*, **2**(2), 1999, 189–199.

12. The conceptual and empirical results of their studies of service quality have been reported in a large number of articles. Key aspects are presented in Berry, L.L. & Parasuraman, A., *Marketing Services. Competing Through Quality*. New York: The Free Press, 1992 and in Zeithaml, V.A. & Bitner, M.J., *Services Marketing*, 2nd edn. New York: McGraw-Hill, 2000.

13. Parasuraman, A., Zeithaml, V.A. & Berry, L.L., SERVQUAL: a multiple-item scale for measuring consumer perceptions of service quality. *Journal of Retailing*, **64**(Spring), 1988, 12–40.

14. A detailed description of the SERVQUAL instrument as well as the attributes used to measure the five determinants can be found in Parasuraman, A., Berry, L.L. & Zeithaml, V.A., Refinement and reassessment of the SERVQUAL scale. *Journal of Retailing*, **67**(4), 1991, 420–450.

15. Murphy, P., Service performance measurement using simple techniques really works. *Journal of Marketing Practice: Applied Marketing Science*, **5**(2), 1999, 56–73.

16. Grönroos, C., Toward a third phase in service quality research: challenges and future directions. In Swartz, T.A., Bowen, D.E. & Brown, S.W. (eds), *Advances in Services Marketing and Management*, Vol. 2. Greenwich, CT: JAI Press, 1993, p. 56.

17. Liljander, *op. cit.*

18. Cronin Jr., J.J. & Taylor, S.A., Measuring service quality: a re-examination and extension. *Journal of Marketing*, **56**(Jul), 1992, 55–68. See also Cronin Jr., J.J. & Taylor, S.A., SERVPERF versus SERVQUAL: reconciling performance-based and perceptions-minus-expectations measurement of service quality. *Journal of Marketing*, **58**, 1994, 125–131.

19. Roos, I., Methods of investigating critical incidents: a comparative review. *Journal of Service Research*, **4**(3), 2002, 193–204. See also, for example, Bitner, M.J., Booms, B.H. & Tetrault, M.S.,

The service encounter: diagnosing favorable and unfavorable incidents. *Journal of Marketing*, **54**(Jan), 1990, 71–84 and Edvardsson, B., Service breakdowns: a study of critical incidents in an airline. *International Journal of Service Industry Management*, **3**(4), 1992, 17–29.

20. Reimer, A. & Kuehn, R., The impact of servicescape on quality perception. *European Journal of Marketing*, **39**(7–8), 2005, 785–808. See also Bitner, *op. cit.* and Rust & Oliver, *op. cit.*

21. Grönroos, 1993, *op. cit.*

22. Athanasopoulou, P., Relationship quality: a critical literature review and research agenda. *European Journal of Marketing*, **43**(5–6), 2009, 583–561. Evert Gummesson introduced the *relationship quality* concept in 1987 as part of a study of quality in an Ericsson quality programme. With this concept he drew attention to the fact that relationships are part of customer perceived quality. See Gummesson, E., *Quality – The Ericsson Approach*. Stockholm, Sweden: Ericsson, 1987.

23. Relationship quality has been studied to a very limited extent. Therefore, general attributes or antecedents of relationship quality cannot be presented. There are some studies that give valuable indications. From a consumer brand perspective, see Gifford Jr., D., Moving beyond loyalty. *Harvard Business Review*, **75**(Mar–Apr), 1997, 9–10 and Fournier, S., Consumers and their brands: developing relationship theory in consumer research. *Journal of Consumer Research*, **24**(4), 1998, 343–373 and from a business relationship perspective, see Leuthesser, L., Supplier relational behavior: an empirical assessment. *Industrial Marketing Management*, **26**(3), 1997, 245–254. For a recent study see Roos, I., Gustafsson, A. & Edvardsson, B., Defining relationship quality for customer-driven business development. *International Journal of Service Industry Management*, **17**(2), 2006, 207–223.

24. This observation has always been evident in Nordic School research into service marketing, and it has become more and more evident as the relationship aspect of buyer–seller interactions in services and in any types of business is studied. See Gummesson, E., Total relationship marketing: experimenting with a synthesis of research frontiers. *Australasian Marketing Journal*, **7**(1), 1999, 72–85 and Grönroos, C., A service-orientated approach to the marketing of services. *European Journal of Marketing*, **12**(8), 1978, 588–601.

25. Holmlund, 1997, *op. cit.* Although this framework was originally developed in a business-to-business context, it is equally suited for understanding and analysing relationships in consumer markets.

26. In the context of services the interaction process has been studied in terms of *acts*, *episodes* and *relationships*. According to Liljander and Strandvik an episode is, for example, a visit to a bank office to discuss a loan, whereas an act is the meeting with the loan officer during the visit. Several interactions related to, for example, withdrawal of money, payment of bills, etc. form a relationship. See Liljander, V., Introducing deserved service and equity into service quality

models. In Kleinaltenkamp, M. (ed.), *Dienstleistungsmarketing – Konzeptionen und Anwendungen*. Berlin, Germany: Gabler Edition Wissenschaft, 1994, pp. 1–30. In German. See also Liljander, V. & Strandvik, T., The nature of customer relationships in services. In Swartz, T.A., Bowen, D.E. & Brown, S.W. (eds), *Advances in Services Marketing and Management*, Vol. 4. Greenwich, CT: JAI Press, 1995, pp. 141–167. Holmlund has added a *sequence* level and has, based on these concepts, offered a relationship framework. See Holmlund, 1997, *op. cit.*

27. Liljander & Strandvik, *op. cit.*

28. Compare also Andreassen, T.W. & Lindestad, B., The effect of corporate image in the formation of customer loyalty. *Journal of Service Research*, **1**(1), 1998, 82–92.

29. In ongoing relationships a two-party situation is formed. When developing instruments for the measurement of relationship quality, especially in business-to-business markets, this fact should be taken into account: the quality perception of both parties in the relationship should be measured. An interesting conceptual foundation for such an instrument is developed in Holmlund, M. & Strandvik, T., Perception configuration in business relationships. *Management Decision*, **37**(9), 2000, 686–696.

30. Ojasalo, J., *Quality Dynamics in Professional Services*. Helsinki/Helsingfors: Swedish School of Economics Finland/CERS, 1999. This analysis of the nature and management of expectation has been further developed in Ojasalo, J., Managing customer expectations in professional services. *Managing Service Quality*, **11**(3), 2001, 200–212.

31. Ojasalo, *op. cit.*

32. See, for example, Wittreich, W.J., How to buy/sell professional services. *Harvard Business Review*, Mar–Apr, 1966, 127–138, where the author discusses confusion relating to clients who wish to purchase marketing communication and management consultancy services.

33. The term 'implied-in-fact' promises is used by Henrik Calonius to indicate unclear promises by marketers that create unrealistic expectations. See Calonius, H., The promise concept. In Blomqvist, H.C., Grönroos, C. & Lindqvist, L.-J. (eds), *Economics and Marketing. Essays in Honour of Gösta Mickwitz*. Helsinki/Helsingfors: Swedish School of Economics, Finland, 1992, pp. 37–56.

34. Ojasalo, *op. cit.*, 2001, 206.

FURTHER READING

Andreassen, T.W. & Lindestad, B. (1998) The effect of corporate image in the formation of customer loyalty. *Journal of Service Research*, **1**(1), 82–92.

Athanasopoulou, P. (2009) Relationship quality: a critical literature review and research agenda. *European Journal of Marketing*, **43**(5–6), 583–561.

Berry, L.L. & Parasuraman, A. (1991) *Marketing Services. Competing Through Quality*. New York: The Free Press.

Bitner, M.J., Booms, B.H. & Tetrault, M.S. (1990) The service encounter: diagnosing favorable and unfavorable incidents. *Journal of Marketing*, **54**(Jan), 71–84.

Brady, M.K. & Cronin Jr., J.J. (2001) Some thoughts on conceptualizing perceived service quality: A hierarchical approach. *Journal of Marketing*, **65**(Jul), 34–49.

Brogowicz, A.A., Delene, L.M. & Lyth, D.M. (1990) A synthesized service quality model with managerial implications. *International Journal of Service Industry Management*, **1**(1), 27–45.

Calonius, H. (1992) The promise concept. In Blomqvist, H.C., Grönroos, C. & Lindqvist, L.-J. (eds), *Economics and Marketing. Essays in Honour of Gösta Mickwitz*. Helsinki/Helsingfors: Swedish School of Economics, Finland, pp. 37–56.

Cronin Jr., J.J. & Taylor, S.A. (1992) Measuring service quality: a re-examination and extension. *Journal of Marketing*, **56**(Jul), 55–68.

Cronin Jr., J.J. & Taylor, S.A. (1994) SERVPERF versus SERVQUAL: reconciling performance-based and perceptions-minus-expectations measurement of service quality. *Journal of Marketing*, **58**, 125–131.

De Keyser, A. & Lariviere, B. (2014) How technical and functional quality drive consumer happiness: moderating influences of channel usage. *Journal of Service Management*, **25**(1), 30–48.

Edvardsson, B. (1992) Service breakdowns: a study of critical incidents in an airline. *International Journal of Service Industry Management*, **3**(4), 17–29.

Fournier, S. (1998) Consumers and their brands: developing relationship theory in consumer research. *Journal of Consumer Research*, **24**(4), 343–373.

Gardner, M.P. (1985) Mood states and consumer behavior: a critical review. *Journal of Consumer Research*, **12**(Dec), 281–300.

Gifford Jr., D. (1997) Moving beyond loyalty. *Harvard Business Review*, **75**(Mar–Apr), 9–10.

Gronroos, C. (1978) A service-orientated approach to the marketing of services. *European Journal of Marketing*, **12**(8), 588–601.

Grönroos, C. (1982) *Strategic Management and Marketing in the Service Sector*. Helsinki/Helsingfors: Swedish School of Economics, Finland (published in the USA in 1983 by Marketing Science Institute and in the UK in 1984 by Chartwell-Bratt).

Grönroos, C. (1984) A service quality model and its marketing implications. *European Journal of Marketing*, **18**(4), 36–45.

Grönroos, C. (1993) Toward a third phase in service quality research: challenges and future directions. In Swartz, T.A., Bowen, D.E. & Brown, S.W. (eds), *Advances in Services Marketing and Management*, Vol. 2. Greenwich, CT: JAI Press, pp. 49–64.

Gummesson, E. (1979) *Models of Professional Service Marketing*. Stockholm, Sweden: Liber/Marketing Technique Centre.

Gummesson, E. (1987) *Quality – The Ericsson Approach*. Stockholm, Sweden: Ericsson.

Gummesson, E. (1993) *Quality Management in Service Organizations*. New York: ISQA, International Service Quality Association.

Gummesson, E. (1999) Total relationship marketing: experimenting with a synthesis of research frontiers. *Australasian Marketing Journal*, **7**(1), 72–85.

Holmlund, M. (1997) *Perceived Quality in Business Relationships*. Helsinki/Helsingfors: Hanken Swedish School of Economics, Finland/CERS Centre for Relationship Marketing and Service Management.

Holmlund, M. & Strandvik, T. (1999) Perception configuration in business relationships. *Management Decision*, **37**(9), 686–696.

Hume, M. & Sullivan Mort, G. (2010) The consequence of appraisal emotion, service quality, perceived value and customer satisfaction on repurchase intent in the performing arts. *Journal of Services Marketing*, **24**(2), 170–182.

Jang, S. & Namkung, Y. (2009) Perceived quality, emotions, and behavioral intentions: application of an extended Mehrabian–Russell model to restaurants. *Journal of Business Research*, **62**, 451–460.

Knowles, P.A., Grove, S.J. & Pickett, G.M. (1999) Mood versus service quality effects on customers' responses to service organizations and service encounters. *Journal of Service Research*, **2**(2), 189–199.

Leuthesser, L. (1997) Supplier relational behavior: an empirical assessment. *Industrial Marketing Management*, **26**(3), 245–254.

Liljander, V. (1994) Introducing deserved service and equity into service quality models. In Kleinaltenkamp, M. (ed.), *Dienstleistungsmarketing – Konzeptionen und Anwendungen (Service Marketing – Conceptualization and Implementation)*. Berlin, Germany: Gabler Edition Wissenschaft, pp. 1–30. In German.

Liljander, V. (1995) *Comparison Standards in Perceived Service Quality*, Helsinki/Helsingfors: Hanken Swedish School of Economics, Finland/CERS Centre for Relationship Marketing and Service Management.

Liljander, V. & Strandvik, T. (1995) The nature of customer relationships in services. In Swartz, T.A., Bowen, D.E. & Brown, S.W. (eds), *Advances in Services Marketing and Management*, Vol. 4. Greenwich, CT: JAI Press, pp. 141–167.

Liljander, V. & Strandvik, T. (1997) Emotions in service satisfaction. *International Journal of Service Industry Management*, **8**(2), 148–169.

Murphy, P. (1999) Service performance measurement using simple techniques really works. *Journal of Marketing Practice: Applied Marketing Science*, **5**(2), 56–73.

Normann, R. (1992) *Service Management*, 2nd edn. New York: John Wiley & Sons.

Ojasalo, J. (1999) *Quality Dynamics in Professional Services*. Helsinki/Helsingfors: Swedish School of Economics, Finland/CERS Centre for Relationship Marketing and Service Management.

Ojasalo, J. (2001) Managing customer expectations in professional services. *Managing Service quality*, **11**(3), 200–212.

Parasuraman, A., Berry, L.L. & Zeithaml, V.A. (1991) Refinement and reassessment of the SERVQUAL scale. *Journal of Retailing*, **67**(4), 420–450.

Parasuraman, A., Zeithaml, V.A. & Berry, L.L. (1988) SERVQUAL: a multiple-item scale for measuring consumer perceptions of service quality. *Journal of Retailing*, **64**(Spring), 12–40.

Reimer, A. & Kuehn, R. (2005) The impact of servicescape on quality perception. *European Journal of Marketing*, **39**(7–8), 785–808.

Roos, I. (2002) Methods of investigating critical incidents. A comparative review. *Journal of Service Research*, **4**(3), 193–204. Roos, I., Gustafsson, A. & Edvardsson, B. (2006) Defining relationship quality for customer-driven business development. *International Journal of Service Industry Management*, **17**(2), 207–223.

Rust, R.T. & Oliver, R.L. (1994) Service quality: insights and managerial implications from the frontier. In Rust, R.T. & Oliver, R.L. (eds), *Service Quality: New Directions in Theory and Practice*. Thousand Oaks, CA: Sage Publications.

Schneider, B. & White, S.S. (2004) *Service Quality. Research Perspectives*. Thousand Oaks, CA: Sage Publications.

White, C.J. (2006) Towards an understanding of the relationship between mood, emotions, service quality and customer loyalty intentions. *Service Industries Journal*, **26**(9), 837–847.

Wittreich, W.J. (1966) How to buy/sell professional services. *Harvard Business Review*, Mar–Apr, 127–138.

Zeithaml, V.A. & Bitner, M.J. (2000) *Services Marketing*, 2nd edn. New York: McGraw-Hill.

CHAPTER 5
QUALITY MANAGEMENT IN SERVICE

> *It is important for a firm to manage service quality well, but it is critical for it to manage service failures even better.*

INTRODUCTION

After discussing the nature of service and relationship quality in Chapter 4, We now turn to various models for the management of quality in service contexts. In this chapter the gap analysis framework and other holistic models for service quality management are discussed. The tolerance zone concept and the shape of the quality function are also described. Then quality management is considered at some length, in situations where a service failure or another problem has occurred. Service recovery, as opposed to traditional complaints handling, as well as elements of a service recovery process, are discussed. In addition, the timing of service recovery and various timing strategies are put forward. After having read the chapter the reader should understand how quality can be managed in service; for example, by using the gap analysis approach and following a quality development structure, and he should know how service recovery should be taken care of in situations where a service failure has occurred.

WHY MANAGERS HESITATE TO INVEST IN SERVICES AND SERVICE QUALITY

Managers often believe that developing and offering services with 100% quality is impossible. Consequently, the organization accepts that mistakes happen, and failures are allowed. Psychologically, the battle for excellent performance is over before it has even begun.

Tom Gillett, when Director of Services of the telecommunications firm GTT, used to tell his employees the following anecdote when they argued that in the complex telecommunications business top quality could not be achieved and thus could not be offered to their customers: 'Imagine a large international airport with hundreds of take-offs and landings each day. If they accepted a quality level of 99%, they would have a number of accidents every day. That just cannot be allowed to happen. And can you imagine a more difficult and technically complicated service and service production system than that of an airport!' The conclusion is, of course, that if an airport can offer and maintain a 100% quality level, you can do it as well, whatever your business is.

Saying and perhaps even believing that a particular firm's service is so complex and difficult that to produce that top quality cannot be achieved is just an excuse for not trying hard enough. True, hard work and long-term effort may be required, but it is never impossible.

SOME REASONS WHY QUALITY IMPROVEMENT PROCESSES FAIL

In spite of the obvious benefits of improving quality, many firms that have implemented quality programmes feel that it did not pay off. Normally, the problem is in a firm's approach to quality improvement. If it is only considered as a project, if a limited time frame is given to the effort, and it is perceived by everybody in the organization, top management and all other employees alike, as simply a tactical issue, the risk of failure is high. For some managers, quality improvement is a matter of time-and-motion studies or investment in machinery or equipment that allows the firm to reduce its labour force. For others, it means a training programme, or introducing a new monetary reward system.

While all these elements can be part of a quality improvement process, as isolated activities they are bound to fail in the long run. The main problem is in the approach. Quality development must not be considered as a project, or even worse as a campaign, but has to be an ongoing *process*. A continuous appreciation of the importance of quality and an understanding of how to influence good service quality is required of every individual in the organization, and this has to be *constantly reinforced by management*. Quality, and hence quality improvement and quality management processes, are strategic issues, which require continuous attention by top management.

HOW GOOD SHOULD QUALITY BE?

A question that is often asked is how good should the optimal quality of a given service be? First of all, the answer depends on the strategy of the firm and the expectations of the customers for whom its service is intended. And these two factors are dependent on each other. A service provider, where the strategy is to be the best on the market and cater to customers demanding excellent service, should first create such expectations among its potential customers, and second provide a service quality that is perceived as excellent. The strategy of another firm may be to provide a less demanding target group of customers with service of a lower quality, at a lower price. In this case, the level of service quality can be lower, but the expectations that the customers are given should not deviate from the real level of quality. If, in this situation, expectations and experiences meet, *the perceived quality is still good*.

There is an often-mentioned ground rule that customers should be surprised by getting a little bit more than they expect. Acceptable quality (confirmed quality where expectations are met but no more) satisfies a customer but does not necessarily make him feel that this is a relationship with a service provider that must not be broken. It does not make the customer talk about his experiences to friends, neighbours and business associates, and write positive comments in social media. Perceived quality which exceeds expectations to some extent, which is sometimes also called *customer delight*, may make customers more interested in continuing the relationship with the service provider, and this also creates good word-of-mouth benefits. The positively surprised customer remembers the experience and often likes to talk about it.[1]

Critics of this ground rule argue that customers learn from their experiences and the next time their expectations are higher. This will lead to an upward spiral where the firm in the end cannot, profitably at least, produce a quality level that meets the increased level of expectations. However, surprising customers does not necessarily mean providing them with something that raises expectations. Normally the surprise effect can be achieved by a small gesture that does not cost anything and leads to a similar positive feeling on the part of the customer every time. It is also important to note that customers' expectations can be exceeded and customers can be surprised regardless of the level of the quality of a given service. The same positive effects on loyalty and on word of mouth can be achieved by small surprises in situations where the level of service quality is low. It does not matter whether the level of expectations is high or low or in between.

Service providers should not, however, provide customers with a surprising effect once, and then revert to a previous quality level. Rust and Oliver call this 'hit-and-run delight'.[2] According to them, a firm which does this will be worse off than if it had not, because a one-time rise in quality experience will increase expectations, and the next time customers will be dissatisfied. Dissatisfaction causes more negative effects than the positive effects created by one-time surprise. However, when a higher level of experiences is constantly offered, customers may forget the surprise element from one occasion to another. The surprise-creating element may be remembered, but the feeling of surprise it causes is not. Then the same feeling of surprise can be repeated again, and the same positive quality effect be achieved every time.[3]

CASE STUDY

GO THE EXTRA MILE TO MAKE THE CUSTOMER'S DAY

The Shangri-La Hotel in Bangkok is one of the region's luxury hotels. In spite of the fact that the number of employees attending to guests during breakfast and happy hour in the Horizon Club (the hotel's executive floor) seems to be much smaller than it was 10 years ago and that the employees seem to be constantly overworked, Ms Tippawan, one of the employees, found the time to show special concern for a guest whom she found out was temporarily ill with a nasty cold and high fever. She insisted that she fetched hot soup from the kitchen for the guest and served it in his room. Said Ms Tippawan, 'Hot soup in the morning is good for this illness.' Every morning she brought a different kind of soup, until the guest was up on his feet again after a few days. By showing this extraordinary care and concern, she made the guest's day, and he was positively surprised every time.

MANAGING SERVICE QUALITY: THE GAP ANALYSIS APPROACH

Berry, Parasuraman and Zeithaml have developed what they call a *gap analysis model*, which is intended to be used for analysing sources of quality problems and for helping managers understand how service quality can be improved.[4] The model is illustrated in Figure 5.1.

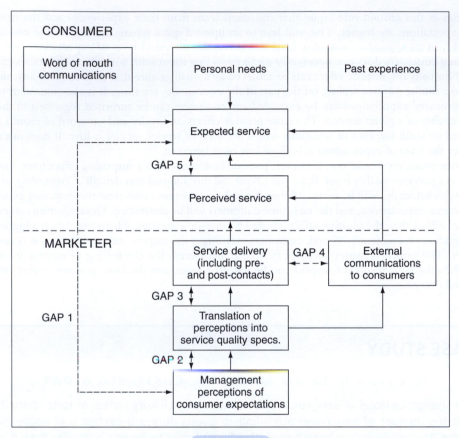

FIGURE 5.1

The gap analysis model of service quality.
Source: Parasuraman, A., Zeithaml, V.A. & Berry, L.L., SERVQUAL: a multi-item scale
for measuring consumer perceptions of service quality. *Journal of Retailing*, **64**(1);
1988: p. 36. Reproduced by permission of the New York University.

First of all, the model demonstrates how service quality emerges. The upper part of the model
includes phenomena related to the customer, while the lower part shows phenomena related to the
service provider. The *expected service* is a function of the customer's *past experience* and *personal needs*
and of *word of mouth communication* from various channels. It is also influenced by the firm's *market
communication*.

The service experienced, which in this model is called the *perceived service*, on the other hand, is the
outcome of a series of internal decisions and activities. *Management perceptions of customer expectations*
guide decisions about *service quality specifications* to be followed by the organization, when *service delivery*
(the execution of the service process) takes place. The customer, of course, experiences the service
delivery and production process as a process-related quality component (creating a functional quality
impact), and the technical solution received by the process as an outcome–related quality component
(creating a technical quality impact). As is illustrated, *marketing communication* can be expected to
influence the perceived service as well as the expected service.

This basic structure demonstrates the steps that have to be considered when analysing and planning service quality. Possible sources of quality problems can then be detected. In Figure 5.1 five discrepancies between the various elements of the basic structure, so-called *quality gaps*, are illustrated. These quality gaps are the result of inconsistencies in the quality management process. The ultimate gap – that is, the gap between expected and experienced (labelled 'perceived' in the model) service (Gap 5) – is, of course, a function of the other gaps that may have occurred in the process. The five gaps, their consequences and implications for management, and the reasons why they occur are discussed in the next section.

MANAGING THE QUALITY GAPS

THE MANAGEMENT PERCEPTION GAP (GAP 1)

This gap means that *management perceives the quality expectations inaccurately*. This gap is due to:

- Inaccurate information from market research and demand analyses.

- Inaccurately interpreted information about expectations.

- Non-existent demand analysis.

- Bad or non-existent upward information from the firm's interface with its customers to management.

- Too many organizational layers, which stop or change the pieces of information that may flow upwards from those involved in customer contacts.

There may be various cures. If problems are due to bad management, obviously either a change of management or an improvement in the knowledge of the characteristics of service competition on the part of management is required. Probably the latter action is more appropriate, because normally the problems have not occurred because of a genuine lack of competence but rather because of a lack of knowledge or appreciation of the nature and demands of service competition and service management among managers.

Part of any cure is always better research, so that the customers' processes and their needs and wishes are better observed and appreciated. The information obtained through market research and from internal flows of information from the customer interface is perhaps not good enough or only partly appropriate. New methods to gain deeper insight about the customers and their lives and businesses may be needed, and better ways of using customer feedback from service encounters or customer complaints systems may be required.

THE QUALITY SPECIFICATION GAP (GAP 2)

This gap means that *service quality specifications are not consistent with management perceptions of quality expectations*. This gap is a result of:

- Planning mistakes or insufficient planning procedures.
- Bad management of planning.
- Lack of clear goal-setting in the organization.
- Insufficient support for planning for service quality from top management.

Depending on the size of the first gap, the potential planning-related problems vary. However, even in a situation where there is enough and sufficiently accurate information on customer processes and expectations, planning of quality specifications may fail. A fairly normal reason for this is a lack of real commitment to service quality among top management, because quality is not considered an issue of highest strategic priority. An obvious cure in such a situation is to change a firm's priorities. Quality as perceived by customers is such a vital success factor today, certainly in service competition, that it is imperative that commitment to quality ranks high on management's priority list.

Of course, the problem may be in the planning process itself. Those providing service also have to feel a commitment to the quality specifications. This has to be taken into account in goal-setting and planning routines. Planning from the top without the collaboration of those who actually produce the service should be avoided. Ideally, goals and specifications should be agreed upon by the service providers as well as by the planners and management. Also, it is good to remember that too-rigid specifications damage flexibility and decrease the willingness of employees to take flexible actions involving risks. And again, this usually damages service quality.

In summary, commitment to service quality among management as well as service providers is far more important in closing the quality specification gap than any too-rigid goal-setting and planning procedure.

THE SERVICE DELIVERY GAP (GAP 3)

This gap means that *quality specifications are not met by performance in the service production and delivery process*. This gap is due to:

- Specifications that are too complicated and/or too rigid.
- Employees not agreeing with the specifications and therefore not fulfilling them.
- Specifications not being in line with the existing corporate culture
- Bad management of service operations.
- Lacking or insufficient internal marketing.
- Technology and systems not facilitating performance according to specifications.

The possible problems here are many and varied, and normally the reasons for the existence of a service delivery gap are complicated. There is seldom only one reason, and the cure is, therefore, usually complicated. The reasons for this gap can be divided into three categories: management and supervision, employee perception of specifications and rules/customer needs and wishes, and lack of technological/operational support.

Management- and supervision-related problems may also be varied. For example, supervisors may not be encouraging and supportive of quality performance, or the supervisory control systems may be in conflict with good service or even with quality specifications. In any organization where control and reward systems are decided upon separately from the planning of quality specifications, which is the case far too often, there is an inherent risk of a service delivery gap occurring. And this risk is not small. Too often non-essential or unimportant activities are controlled, perhaps even rewarded; and activities that contradict quality specifications are encouraged by the control system. They too may even be rewarded. Of course, this puts employees in an extremely awkward position. Control and reward systems partly determine the corporate culture, and goals and specifications that do not fit the existing culture tend not to be well executed. The cure here involves changes in the way managers and supervisors treat their employees, and in the way supervisory systems control and reward performance. Larger issues related to the culture of the firm and internal marketing may also have to be attended to. We will return to the issues of internal marketing and service culture in Chapters 14 and 15.

From what has been discussed above it follows, among other things, that employees may feel that their role as service providers is ambiguous. We have already mentioned the way in which performance requirements of the specifications, on the one hand, and existing control and reward systems, on the other hand, are in conflict with each other. An awkward situation could also occur for personnel when a customer contact person realizes that a customer requires different behaviour on the part of the service provider than what the company's existing specifications allow. The customer contact employee knows that the customer is not getting what he expects and may feel that the demands and wishes of the customer are justified and perhaps could be fulfilled, but he is not allowed to perform accordingly. This slowly but surely kills any motivation for quality-supporting performance among the service employees.

The cure in situations like these is to remove all reasons for ambiguity on the part of the personnel. This may, on the one hand, require changes in the supervisory systems so that they are in line with the quality specifications. It may, on the other hand, also require better employee training, so that they are aware of the limitations for performance due, for example, to strategic considerations or profitability reasons. Here again the issue of internal marketing is critical.

Further, the skills and attitudes of personnel may cause problems. It may be that the wrong people have been recruited in the first place. The firm may have people who cannot adjust to the specifications and systems that guide operations, however justifiable they are. The cure in this situation is, of course, to improve recruitment processes so that poor decisions can be avoided. Furthermore, the workload perceived by employees may be a problem. There may, for example, be too much paperwork or too many other administrative tasks involved, so that quality specifications cannot be fulfilled. Because of this, the service provider does not have time to attend to customers as expected.

The cure is to clarify the tasks of all personnel and find a solution where necessary tasks are dealt with without interfering with quality performance. Finally, problems may be caused because the technology or the systems of operating, including decision-making and other routines, cannot be successfully used by the employees. The problem may be the employees, of course, but it is more probable that technology and operational and administrative systems have been introduced in the wrong way. Perhaps technology and the company's systems do not support quality behaviour, or they have not been properly introduced to the employees who are expected to live with them. The remedy is either to make proper changes to technology and systems so that they are supportive of the execution of the quality specifications or, again, to improve training and internal marketing.

THE MARKET COMMUNICATION GAP (GAP 4)

This gap means that *promises made by marketing communication are not consistent with the service delivered*. This gap is due to:

- Marketing communication planning not being integrated with service operations.

- Lacking or insufficient co-ordination between traditional external marketing and operations.

- The organization failing to perform according to specifications, whereas marketing communication campaigns follow these specifications.

- An inherent propensity to exaggerate and, thus, promise too much.

The reasons for the occurrence of a market communication gap can be divided into two categories, namely, the planning and executing of external marketing communication and of operations, and a company's propensity to overpromise in sales and marketing communication.

In the first case, the cure is to create a system that coordinates planning and execution of external marketing communication with service operations. For example, every major campaign should be planned in collaboration with those involved in executing the service process. Two goals can be achieved by this. First, promises in marketing communication become more accurate and realistic. Second, a greater commitment to what is promised in external campaigns can be achieved, which also has the effect that more can be promised than would otherwise be the case.

The second category of problems, overpromising because of the very nature of marketing communication and sales where superlatives are far too easily used, can only be dealt with by improving planning of marketing and sales tasks. The cure may be better planning procedures, but closer management supervision also helps.

THE PERCEIVED SERVICE QUALITY GAP (GAP 5)

This gap means that *the perceived or experienced service is not consistent with the expected service*. This gap results in:

- Negatively confirmed quality (bad quality) and a quality problem.
- Bad word of mouth and negative comments in social media.
- A negative impact on corporate or local image.
- Lost business.

The fifth gap may, of course, also be positive, which leads either to a positively confirmed quality or overquality. If a perceived service quality gap occurs, the reason for this could be any of those discussed in this section, or any combination of these. Of course, there may also be other reasons in addition to those mentioned here.

The gap analysis model should guide management in finding out where the reason or reasons for the quality problem lie and in discovering appropriate ways to close this gap. Gap analysis is a straightforward and appropriate way of identifying inconsistencies in the market research, service process planning and execution, and external communication about the service. Addressing these gaps is a logical basis for developing service processes in which expectations and experiences consistently meet. In this way the likelihood of good perceived service quality will be increased.

MANAGING TOLERANCE ZONES

According to the perceived service quality model's disconfirmation concept – customers' experiences are compared with their expectations – customers' expectations of the level of a given service attribute are thought of and measured as one singular level of expectation. No variation in expectations is included. The *zone of tolerance* concept has been suggested by Berry and his colleagues,[5] because they considered the underlying assumption of this concept too simplistic.

The zone of tolerance concept assumes that customers do not have expectations of a service attribute on *one* given level. Rather, they can tolerate a variation in the real experiences and still consider them acceptable according to their expectations. This concept implies that customers' expectations exist on two levels, a *desired level* and an *adequate level*. The desired level reflects on what level the service *should* be, whereas the adequate level is what customers believe it *could* be. The latter level is the least acceptable level of the service experience. These two levels of expectations form the borders of customers' *zones of tolerance*. If the real experiences of a customer fall in between these borders, they are tolerated by him and the perceived quality is considered good.

The zone of tolerance can of course vary from customer to customer, and from service attribute to service attribute. It may also, for a given customer, vary from time to time. It is suggested that, in general, it is narrower for outcome-related service features and broader for process-related features. This means that customers generally tolerate more variation in the process (expectations related to the *functional quality* dimension) than in the outcome of the process (expectations related to the *technical quality* dimension). In addition, if there is a service failure which has to be corrected, the zone of tolerance diminishes, regarding both outcome-related and process-related service features.

Measuring the zones of tolerance of expectations and comparing them with the experiences of customers may give management useful information about where service quality problems exist, and where there is no need for immediate action. For those attributes where the experience measurement falls in between the desired and adequate levels of expectations, the level of perceived service quality is at least tolerable. Again, for those attributes where the experience measurement is lower than the adequate level, immediate corrections may be required, so that the overall level of perceived service quality does not decrease. It is of course more urgent to take action if such an attribute is considered central to customers' quality perception, than if its impact is only marginal.

THE SHAPE OF THE QUALITY FUNCTION

In the service quality models it is normally assumed that the quality function is linear; that is, as the performance of a service provider improves, the perceived quality increases at the same pace, and vice versa. In Figure 5.2 this assumption is illustrated at the left of the figure. In reality, this relationship varies between customers and between quality attributes, and probably also between one customer's perception of different service encounters. However, the quality function is probably not linear at all.[6]

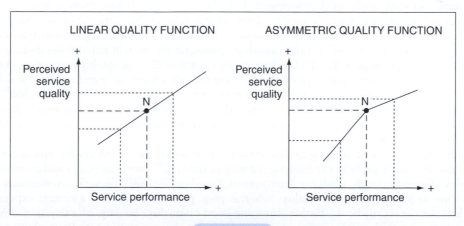

FIGURE 5.2
Linear and asymmetric quality functions.
Source: Expanded from Strandvik, T., *Tolerance Zones in Perceived Service Quality*.
Helsinki: Hanken Swedish School of Economics, Finland, 1994, p. 154. Reproduced by
permission of Tore Strandvik, Hanken Swedish School of Economics.

At the right of Figure 5.2 a typical quality function is illustrated. When the service firm performs better than normal (denoted by the letter N in the figure), perceived service quality increases at a lower pace than it decreases when the firm performs below its normal level. This *asymmetric shape of the quality function*[7] means, among other things, *that it is easier to make a bad impression when quality deteriorates than it is to please a customer with quality above the normal expected level.* Another conclusion is that it is dangerous for a service provider to let its overall performance, or performance on some critical attributes, drop below normal expectations, because the quality perception then decreases quickly. On the other hand, it is difficult to increase the quality perception above normal, because the service performance has to be improved (relatively speaking) much more to lead to significant results. As the figure demonstrates, a given increase in service performance has a much smaller effect on the perceived service quality than does a similar decrease.

For example, if an Internet shop responds to a customer's inquiry or order more slowly than this customer considers normal, speeding up the response time can be expected to have a rapid impact on the perceived quality. However, improving perceived quality by answering even faster than this normal level will have a much smaller impact on the customer's quality perception.

Another assumption that is often made in the literature is that all quality attributes are equally important. However, there may be a clear distinction between the effects on perceived quality of different attributes. Again, there is probably a difference between customers and between various types of services, but generally it seems as if different attributes have a different impact on the quality perception. The main thing is that some attributes may be necessary for a good perception of service quality, but if they are improved then this does not have a significant positive effect on perceived quality. Reliability, functionality and competence could be examples of such *hygiene factors*. A hygiene factor must be on a given level, otherwise quality is perceived as low, but increasing the level of a hygiene factor does not improve the quality perception.

Other quality attributes may be *quality-enhancing factors*, where a higher level of performance has a positive effect on the quality perception, whereas there is no significant additional negative effect once it has reached a certain low level. Friendliness, attentiveness, cleanliness and availability could be examples of such attributes. Improving such quality-enhancing factors above a minimum level improves the perception of service quality. There may also be quality attributes that influence perceived quality *both ways*. Comfort, communication and courtesy could be examples of such attributes.[8]

For example, the *reliability* of an airline assuring a passenger that he will arrive at the destination on time is an essential hygiene factor. Delays have major negative effects on quality perception. Arriving ahead of time probably has limited positive effect. On the other hand, the *friendliness* and *attentiveness* of the in-flight personnel and the cleanliness of restrooms are quality-enhancing factors that linearly increase the quality perception. However, when they have reached a certain low point, passengers will have become so frustrated or annoyed that an even worse performance will not further decrease their quality perception.

Another related way of studying quality attributes is to divide them into *satisfiers* and *dissatisfiers*.[9] According to a major study in the banking industry in the UK,[10] *attentiveness*, *care* and *friendliness* are examples of predominantly satisfying determinants. Good performance on such determinants causes an increase in perceived service quality, whereas poor performance below a certain expectations level does not necessarily have a further damaging effect on quality. *Integrity*, *reliability*, *availability* and *functionality* are examples of dissatisfiers. Good performance above a certain expectation level on such attributes does not increase the perceived service quality, whereas poorer performance has a negative effect on quality.

In this study *responsiveness* was found to be both a satisfier and dissatisfier. This is a crucial observation, because this quality attribute is often considered to have a decisive impact on satisfaction with

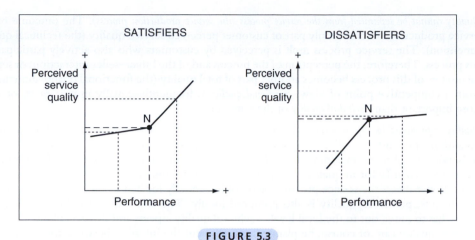

FIGURE 5.3

Service quality attributes: the effects of satisfiers versus dissatisfiers.

quality. The different ways satisfiers and dissatisfiers work are illustrated in Figure 5.3. On the left one can see how changes in the performance level of satisfiers impact perceived quality, whereas the reverse effects of dissatisfiers are shown. The normal expected level of quality attributes is denoted by the letter N.

The research results reported in this section are somewhat contradictory, which may be a result of cultural or industry differences or different ways of measuring quality. However, it is important for managers responsible for service quality to bear in mind that various quality attributes or factors may function in different ways. The examples mentioned are relevant for some service and some customers, and function in this way in some cultures, but in other cases other attributes may function as hygiene, quality-enhancing or two-way factors, and as satisfiers or dissatisfiers. Investing in further improvement of hygiene factors and neglecting investments in quality-enhancing or two-way factors, or investing in dissatisfiers above the acceptable expectations level, are clearly ineffective strategies and a waste of money. Such investments are, however, easily made, if one does not have a clear picture of the quality-influencing nature of various quality attributes.

LESSONS OF SERVICE QUALITY AND QUALITY MANAGEMENT RESEARCH

The models and frameworks of customer perceived service quality and how to manage service quality presented in this chapter demonstrate a number of important lessons learned from research into service quality. Some of these issues have also been focused on in studies of good quality management. The lessons are as follows.

1. *Quality is what customers perceive.* Quality cannot be determined by management alone; it has to be based on customer needs, wishes and expectations. Moreover, quality is not what is planned in objective measures; instead it is how customers subjectively perceive what is delivered.

2. *Quality cannot be separated from the service process (the service production process).* The outcome of the service production process is only part of customer perceived service quality (the technical quality dimension). The service process itself is perceived by customers who also actively participate in this process. Therefore, the perception of the process and of the buyer–seller interactions or service encounters of this process becomes another part of total quality (the functional quality dimension). From a competitive point of view, *functional quality* is frequently equally important as, or even more important than, *technical quality* of the outcome.

3. *Quality is produced locally in a series of moments of truth of service encounters or buyer–seller interactions.* Because of the existence of the important functional quality dimension of total service quality, the service encounters, including a number of moments of truth (or moments of opportunity) become a pivotal factor in quality perception. Since service encounters take place locally, where the customer meets the service provider, and not in centrally located quality design and planning departments, perceived quality is also produced locally. Therefore, the planning and design of quality has to move out to the local level. Technical quality aspects and the overall design of how to create quality can, of course, be planned centrally, but the interface between the organization and its customers has to be involved in quality management and design as well. Otherwise, well-designed quality may remain a desk product that does not materialize in good customer perceived quality.

4. *Everyone contributes to customer perceived quality.* As quality is created and produced in buyer–seller interactions of service encounters, a large number of employees become involved in the production of quality. Since these customer contact employees who handle customer contacts in order to serve their customers well are dependent on the support of people beyond them in the service process, these 'support' people also become responsible for the ultimate customer perceived quality. Hence, most employees contribute to quality. If someone in the customer services department or beyond the direct customer interface fails, quality suffers.

5. *As co-producers in service processes customers have to be managed as a quality-producing resource.* A central characteristic of services is the fact that customers participate as co-producers in the service production process. In that capacity they can influence both the process and its outcome, and hence, their own as well as fellow consumers' perception of quality. Therefore, the firm should guide the customer through the production process so that he does not, by mistake or because of a lack of knowledge or motivation, behave in a way that has a negative impact on quality. Customers may have to be informed about what is required of them and motivated to act in a certain manner. Sometimes customers may even have to be trained to make a positive contribution to quality.

6. *Quality has to be monitored throughout the organization by the whole organization.* As quality is produced by a large number of people and departments throughout the organization, quality performance has to be monitored and assured at the point where a quality contribution is produced. A centrally located quality control and management staff cannot normally do this. The task is overwhelming; and having a separate department for this has a negative effect psychologically on the people in the organization. The mere fact that such a department exists can easily draw the attention of those producing quality away from quality assurance. It is easy for other employees to stop worrying about the tricky issue of constantly producing, maintaining and monitoring quality when there is a group of specialists to turn to, and to blame when problems occur. In the final analysis, the organization itself has to do the job of assuring quality.

7. *External marketing has to be integrated into quality management.* Customer-perceived quality is a function of expectations as well as of real experiences. Therefore, improvement of quality experiences

may be counteracted by, say, a marketing campaign that gives customers reason to believe that improvements will be greater than they really are. Customer expectations which are not met by reality will be created. The perceived quality will be bad, although quality improvements, objectively measured, may have taken place. Such negative external marketing effects may have far-reaching consequences, for example, because this creates negative publicity and the image of the firm may be damaged. If marketing campaigns are planned in collaboration with those responsible for the quality improvement process, these mistakes can be avoided. Hence, external marketing, marketing communication and sales have to be integrated with quality management.

A SERVICE QUALITY MANAGEMENT PROGRAMME

In this chapter we have discussed concepts and models of perceived service quality, in order to develop an understanding of how service quality is formed and perceived by customers, as well as an understanding of how important aspects of service quality can be managed. In the present section we will sum up these concepts and models in the form of a management-oriented *service quality management programme*. This programme is intended to help management implement a service strategy to respond to the challenges of the constantly increasing service competition. If the organization has decided to pursue a service strategy, the service quality management programme should, for managerial purposes, give adequate guidance in what to do. Such a programme must, of course, be grounded in sufficient insight about target customers' everyday processes and goals, and about their needs and expectations.

The service quality management programme consists of seven *subprogrammes*. These are:

1. Service concept development.

2. Customer expectations management programme.

3. Service outcome management programme.

4. Internal marketing programme.

5. Physical environment (servicescape) and physical resources management programme.

6. Information technology management programme.

7. Customer participation management programme.

These will now be described separately in more detail.

1. *Service concept development.* The establishment of customer-oriented service concepts which guide the management of resources and activities to be used in the service process is, of course, the first task in the service quality development process. The service concept must clearly indicate the intended *customer benefits*.

2. *Customer expectations management programme.* Traditional external marketing and sales activities should never be planned and implemented in isolation. They should always be related to the experiences the service provider is willing and able to provide to its customers. Otherwise, there will always be a quality problem, irrespective of the other quality development subprogrammes. Therefore, managing *customer expectations* must always be an integral part of any quality programme. This makes, for example, managing external marketing communication and sales part of quality management.

3. *Service outcome management programme.* The outcome of the service process (i.e. what customers get as a *technical quality* of the service) is part of the total service experience. The outcome of the service production process has to be developed and managed according to the service concepts agreed upon, and the specific needs of the target customers.

4. *Internal marketing programme.* As we have demonstrated, the *functional quality* of the process (i.e. how the service process is perceived by customers) is the key in most cases to an excellent service quality and to achieving a winning competitive edge. Most frequently this quality dimension is predominantly due to the courtesy, flexibility and general service-mindedness of the customer contact employees, and to their ability and willingness to perform in a customer-focused fashion. Hence, the employees, customer contact employees, managers and other employee categories, have to be considered a first, *internal market* of the service provider. A continuous and strategically backed up internal marketing process is, therefore, a vital part of any quality development and management program. (Internal marketing will be discussed in detail in Chapter 14.)

5. *Physical environment (servicescape) and physical resources management programme.* The physical resources, technology and computing systems of service organizations are too frequently developed according to internal efficiency standards. The external effects of, for example, a computer system failure are seldom taken into account to a proper degree. Consequently, these resources, which constitute a technology base for service production as well as the physical environment for service consumption, may have a negative impact on customers' perception of the service process. Hence, a physical environment and physical resources management programme should be part of an overall quality programme, to support the *functional quality* perception.

6. *Information technology management programme.* Customers make increasing use of information technology-based systems; for example, using a website on the Internet to get access to information, feedback or support from a service firm, to making purchases on the Internet or to use Internet and mobile applications as part of a service process. Therefore, the service provider must invest in appropriate information technology and must upgrade software and hardware as technology and applications advance. Hence, an information technology management programme is required. This is needed to secure both a good *technical quality and functional quality* impact.

7. *Customer participation management programme.* Customers should be advised how to act in the service process, so that they have a favourable impact on the process themselves. Especially *functional quality*, but sometimes also *technical quality,* can be destroyed by customers who either do not know what to do or do not want to perform according to the service provider's intentions. Negative effects of fellow customers, causing queues, for example, must also be avoided, if possible. Eliminating unfavourable effects on the service process of a misfit between customer segments and individual customers is also part of a customer participation management programme.

SERVICE RECOVERY: MANAGING QUALITY WHEN SERVICE FAILURES OCCUR

The real test of the customer orientation of a service provider takes place when a service failure has occurred. Ideally, quality should be high all the time and failures should not occur. However, employees make mistakes, systems break down, customers in the service process may cause problems for other customers, or a customer may not know how to participate in the process or may change his mind regarding some aspect of the service during the process. As a consequence, the planned service process will not lead to a good result for the customer. The intended level of quality is not achieved. It is important to realize that such a failure does not always result from mistakes made by the service provider; the customer or fellow customers can also cause service failures. However, regardless of whether the firm, the customer, or something else is to blame, every problematic situation for a customer is an opportunity for the service provider to demonstrate its commitment to service.

Hence, regardless of the reason for a failure, the service provider has to take care of the situation and is responsible for solving the problem in a way that satisfies the customer. Unless this is done, the customer will feel that he received poor quality, and the risk of losing that customer grows. Or, if complaining customers feel that their complaint is not handled quickly enough and with enough attention and empathy, the quality of the whole relationship will deteriorate. If there is a quality problem in the service process, the recovery of the problem has to be performed very carefully and accurately.[11] Research shows that service providers are often offered a second chance to create a positive quality perception by customers even though a service process has broken down.[12] The way a firm manages service recovery forms a platform for strengthened or weakened customer relationships. A well-managed recovery has a positive impact on the development of a trusting relationship between a firm and its customer and it also may deepen the customer's commitment towards the service provider.[13]

As discussed in the previous chapter, service recovery is a factor influencing perceived service quality. It is a process-related service criterion that can have a positive effect on functional quality. After a good recovery, satisfaction with services can be increased.[14] It has even been claimed that good service recovery can make angry and frustrated customers more satisfied with service quality than they would have been if no problem had occurred in the first place.[15]

SERVICE RECOVERY VERSUS COMPLAINTS HANDLING

Service recovery is a concept that was introduced in the service management literature to help firms manage service failures and complaints in a service-oriented way.[16] The traditional way of handling service- or goods-related failures is complaints handling, where customers who have experienced problems are requested to make formal complaints. Such complaints are analysed and handled by the firm usually following legal and administrative procedures. Frequently it seems as if the objective of complaints handling is to make sure that, regardless of who caused the failure, the firm does not have to compensate the customer unless absolutely necessary. Complaints handling has a significant effect on customers' perception of the service orientation of a service firm or a manufacturer, and the complaints-handling approach is inherently non-service-oriented. *Service recovery is a service-oriented approach to managing the same situations that, in an administrative way, are managed by complaints-handling routines.*

For traditional complaints handling *internal efficiency*, keeping costs as low as possible and not compensating a customer unless this cannot be avoided for legal reasons, seems to be the standard. The result is unsatisfied customers and lost business. For service recovery *external effectiveness*, good perceived quality, is the main guideline. *The objective of service recovery is to satisfy customers in spite of a service failure as well as to maintain and possibly improve long-term relationship quality, to retain customers and long-term profitable business rather than short-term cost savings.*

Tax and Brown[17] define service recovery in the following way:

Service recovery is a process that identifies service failures, effectively resolves customer problems, classifies their root cause(s), and yields data that can be integrated with other measures of performance to assess and improve the service system.

Customer problems caused by a service failure or some other problem are usually twofold; *factual* problems and *emotional*[18] problems. Both have to be attended to by the firm.

In a problematic situation when service recovery is called upon, customers are often frustrated and also tend to have a narrower *zone of tolerance* than normal.[19] Service recovery may therefore be risky.[20] It has to be managed well. It seems that the more committed the employees of a firm feel to the firm's visions, strategies and service concepts, the better their service recovery performance will be. Moreover, employees who are *empowered to make independent decisions* can be expected to do better in recovery situations; they are inclined to deal quickly and effectively with service failures.[21] It is important that customers who have suffered from a service failure or some other mistake in the service process feel that they are treated fairly by the firm. The service recovery process should therefore be developed and exercised to maximize fairness as perceived by the customer.[22]

SERVICE RECOVERY AND PERCEIVED FAIRNESS

Since the late 1990s, following the initial work by Stephen Tax, there has been a stream of studies on how customers perceive service recovery in terms of perceived fairness or justice.[23] In most of the studies the term 'justice' is used. However, as this term has a legal meaning, the term *fairness* is more appropriate in a service management context and is used here as a synonym.

According to this model customers' perception of a service recovery process is divided into three parts, which describe three different aspects of how fair or unfair the process is considered:

1. *Distributive fairness*: the degree to which the outcome of the service recovery process equals what the customer thinks he deserved or needed, including the level of compensation and apology.

2. *Procedural fairness*: the degree to which customers feel that they could influence the recovery process, and the convenience and timeliness of the process.

3. *Interactional fairness*: the degree to which customers consider interpersonal interactions during the process to be fair, honest and empathetic, including fair communication and behaviour.

The three types of perceived fairness represent different aspects of the service recovery process and its outcome. It is important to realize that customers assess the fairness of the recovery process in more than one dimension. If the process itself and the interactions and communications taking place during the process are perceived as unfair, it is not enough to provide customers with a fair outcome in terms of compensation that recovers a factual loss and apology that reduces the emotional stress felt by the customer. As a well-managed and favourably perceived recovery is a way of turning a quality disaster into a positive overall experience of the service provider's way of operating and thus into a positive quality experience, it is important for firms to develop service recovery procedures that make customers feel that they are treated well on all fairness dimensions and thus perceive total fairness.[24]

GUIDELINES FOR SERVICE RECOVERY

Service recovery is a strategy for managing mistakes, failures and problems in customer relationships. It can be applied by all types of organizations, regardless of the firm's core business. A manufacturer or an organization in the public sector can benefit from this approach in the same way as a service firm, and the customers of any firm will certainly benefit from an organization that takes a service recovery approach instead of a traditional complaints-handling approach to managing mistakes and quality problems. Unlike traditional complaints handling, service recovery offers a service-oriented approach to managing problems. Below is a list of guidelines for the development of an effective service recovery process.

- It is the organization's responsibility to spot service failures and other types of mistakes or quality problems. Customers should only have to notify the firm about the situation or make a complaint if the firm has been unable to do so.

- If formal complaints are required, it should be made as easy as possible for the customer to complain. The complaints procedure should be made as unproblematic and free from bureaucracy as possible. Written complaints should be used only when absolutely necessary, for example for legal reasons or when large amounts of money are involved. Remember that most customers who are dissatisfied do not bother to complain; they just take their business away without saying what went wrong.

- The organization should take the initiative to inform the customer about the failure or mistake and, in cases where immediate corrections cannot be made, keep the customer up-to-date about the progress of rectifying the mistake.

- The organization should actively take measures to correct failures and mistakes, and not wait until the customer demands action. Corrections should be made as quickly as possible. Every mistake or failure should be rectified immediately it occurs, if possible.

- The customer should be compensated immediately and, in cases where immediate compensation cannot be given, no unnecessary delays should be allowed. A lost customer, if profitable, has a greater negative effect on long-term profits than an overcompensated, satisfied customer who continues his relationship with the firm and probably also contributes to favourable word-of-mouth communication.

- If for some reason, legal or otherwise, a customer cannot be compensated for the problem that has occurred, a swift and service-oriented recovery process may still make the customer feel satisfied with the relationship, because a positive functional quality impact has been created in this situation. However, this requires that customers perceive the procedures and interactions as having been fair. For long-term profitability it may be wise to compensate customers even when they are wrong or have caused the failure themselves. Taking short-term losses for the sake of long-term revenues in strengthened customer relationships often makes sense.

- Emotional reactions, such as anxiety and frustration, which customers often feel because of a service failure or some other mistake, must also be managed, in addition to recovering the problem itself. Such emotions should be attended to first.

- Apologizing is important, but is not enough in most situations. Customers must also be compensated for losses they feel they have suffered and the failure must be dealt with.

- To make full use of the potential of successful recovery, a systematic service recovery system should be developed. In such a system empowered employees such as customer contact employees, customer-oriented supervisors and managers as well as support persons, are in a central position.

- Complaints departments and managers of complaints-handling departments often only impede customer-oriented service recovery. However, a service recovery manager may be needed to develop and support the recovery system.

CASE STUDY

THE RITZ-CARLTON HOTEL: SERVICE RECOVERY

A group of four executive MBA students from Europe had attended a service marketing seminar at the Ritz-Carlton Hotel in Phoenix, Arizona. Before leaving for the airport in the evening, they wanted to spend a few hours of leisure time in the 'Valley of the Sun' at the swimming pool of the hotel. However, when coming down to the pool in the mid-afternoon, they were politely told that the pool area was closing, because the area was about to be prepared for an evening reception and dinner. Upon the students' explanation that during their stay at the hotel this was their only time to spend by the pool before returning to the freezing temperature of their home country and that they had very much looked forward to this opportunity, the waiter asked them to wait while he sorted out the situation. After a short while a supervisor arrived and informed the group that the hotel unfortunately did have to close the whole pool area right away to get ready for the evening event in time. However, he added, a limousine waited for them outside the main entrance to take them and their luggage to the Biltmore Hotel, where the pool area would be at their disposal. The limousine was at the Ritz-Carlton's expense, of course.

The group was delighted by this solution, and their already favourable perception of the hotel was improved even more. They have also engaged in a considerable amount of positive word-of-mouth communication.

SERVICE RECOVERY PROCESSES

Customer contact employees may spot problems and service failures and take action but, as stated in the previous section, to make full use of the potential of successful service recovery the firm should develop a *recovery system*. The following guidelines may be helpful in developing such a system.[25]

1. *Calculate costs of failures and mistakes.* Customers who defect because they are dissatisfied have to be replaced by new customers, and in addition they often engage in negative word of mouth. Acquiring new customers is always several times more expensive than keeping existing customers. Negative word of mouth also has a damaging effect on image. This makes the acquisition of new customers more difficult and expensive. Correcting mistakes and recovering problematic situations adds costs that could have been avoided had the service functioned well in the first place. However, management too seldom realizes the financial effects of bad service. Therefore, careful measurements of the costs involved may warn management of the negative financial effects of badly managed service processes. In view of the high cost of losing customers, the need for a service recovery system is easily appreciated and the cost of compensating, and even overcompensating, customers for their losses becomes marginal.

2. *Solicit complaints.* Most customers never tell a firm about problems with services or goods that they have faced. They just disappear to a competitor. It is important to get information about failures that occur, mistakes that are made, systems that do not function in a service-oriented way, and

other reasons for poor perceived quality and dissatisfaction. Employees, especially those in contact with customers, should be able to monitor the service processes for mistakes and service failures, so that the firm realizes there is a problem, if possible even before the customer does. However, many problems are first and perhaps only perceived by the customer. Because dissatisfied customers form a firsthand source of information regarding what needs to be improved, it must be made as easy as possible for customers to complain about quality problems and failures in the service system. Some firms use information technology to help customers inform the firm about a mistake that has occurred.[26] When customers complain, they must be shown respect and attention by the employee to whom they make the complaint.[27]

3. *Identify recovery needs.* Mistakes can happen and failures can occur almost anywhere. However, by carefully analysing the service process, human resources, systems used in the process and customers' need for information and guidance, it is possible to spot areas with high risk of failure. Situations where one error can lead to a chain reaction (for example, a delayed incoming flight) are particularly problematic. Complicated IT systems are another risky area. The introduction of new systems is always critical. By being aware of such areas where the risk of mistakes is especially high, management can prepare the organization for taking care of possible failures.

4. *Recover quickly.* An old rule of thumb says that disappointed customers tell 12 others about their negative experiences, whereas satisfied customers tell much fewer about their positive experiences. With the introduction of social media, these effects can be much more dramatic today. The more slowly a problem is attended to and corrected, the more negative word of mouth is created. In addition, the impact of a slow recovery process on a damaged quality perception is much greater than if there is a quick recovery. We shall turn to this aspect of service recovery in the next section.

5. *Train employees.* Customer contact employees must understand why service failures need to be attended to and recovered quickly, and they need to understand and appreciate why they, in the front line, have a responsibility, *first of all*, for spotting problems, mistakes and customers who seem to become disappointed with the service process or who do not understand how to participate effectively in the process. *Second*, they need to understand and accept their responsibilities for taking action to manage a disappointed customer's frustration and make efforts to quickly correct mistakes and compensate the customer for his losses. Training is required so that employees have the service-oriented perspective needed to take care of problematic situations and also the skills required in these situations. Without this perspective the employees may have a different view of recovery needs to the customers.[28] This is part of internal marketing, which will be discussed at length in Chapter 14.

6. *Empower and enable customer contact employees.* Training gives employees a better understanding of the situation and their central role in service recovery, and also the knowledge and skills for doing the job. However, to handle dissatisfied and frustrated customers, employees need authority to make decisions about what to do and how much to compensate. They also need to know how far their authority goes and when the recovery of a failure has to be handed over to someone else in the organization, or when a formal written complaint needs to be made. Employees have to be *empowered* with authority and *enabled* with access to information, databases and compensation systems, such as vouchers, free tickets or money. In Chapter 15, empowerment and enabling are discussed at length.

7. *Keep the customer informed.* The customer should always be told that the failure or mistake has been acknowledged and that the recovery process is underway. If a recovery cannot be made on the spot and if the process takes time, customers must be kept informed about its progress. Finally,

when a problem has been corrected, the customer should be notified about the result but also about what the firm has learnt from the failure and which corrective actions they have taken to improve the service process.

8. *Learn from mistakes*. The firm must have a system for using service recovery experiences in a productive way. Service failures, quality problems and other mistakes can often be traced back to either a structural problem in some process in the organization or to employee or management attitude. It is important that the firm analyses the root cause of a problem and corrects the underlying processes or attitudes. Situations that have led to problematic situations must be handled better the next time they occur.[29]

In summary, a system for effective service recovery includes three areas of focus:[30] constantly monitor service processes to identify problems, solve problems effectively and learn from problems and the recovery process. Table 5.1 shows the necessary recovery steps expected by customers.[31]

TIMING OF RECOVERY PROCESSES

In addition to correcting the mistake, quick response and adequate compensation are usually considered crucial elements of service recovery.[32] This final section of Chapter 5 will discuss some effects on perceived service quality resulting from various timing strategies.[33] The *relationship framework*, including episodes (or service encounters) consisting of singular acts, sequences of interrelated episodes and the overall relationship itself, is used to illustrate various timing strategies. The three strategies

TABLE 5.1

Customer expectations when service failures or problems occur.

Action expected	How action should be handled
Apology	Delivered in person, even if the firm did not cause the problem (however, apology is often not enough).
Fair compensation	Reasonable compensation on the spot from customer contact employee.
Caring treatment	By showing empathy and treating each customer as an individual; attending to emotional problems.
Value-added atonement	Customer gets something as a symbol of appreciation of value as customer (sometimes a fair compensation may serve as such a symbol).
Kept promises about recovery	Contact employee describes what will happen and when, with confidence that it actually will happen that way (negative information is better than no information or wrong information; it is better to hear once that a flight is 60 minutes delayed than to hear four times that there is a 15-minute delay).

Source: Amended from Zemke, R. (1992) Supporting service recovery: attributes for excelling at solving customers' problems. In Sheuing, E.E., Gummesson, E. & Little, C.H. (eds), *Selected Papers from the Second Quality in Services (QUIS 2) Conference*. New York: St. John's University and ISQA, International Service Quality Association, p. 46.

are labelled *administrative* (a passive approach), *defensive* (an active approach) and *offensive* (a proactive approach), respectively. A lost-luggage situation is used as an example. A family of three is arriving by air at a distant beach resort for four days of vacation. Upon arrival they realize that all their checked-in luggage has been lost. This means that the family does not have more than their travelling clothes at their disposal. The need for service recovery is evident.

An *administrative service recovery* (passive approach to service failures) is shown in the top part of Figure 5.4. The airline agent does the required paperwork and gives the family a standard voucher for a nominal amount of money. The family realizes immediately that this sum will not cover more than a fraction of the purchases necessary to save their vacation. They are informed that if that is the case they will have to make a formal complaint to the airline after their vacation. The recovery of the service failure will thus be taken care of afterwards when this complaint has been duly processed. The recovery is managed as a separate *service sequence* following the *main service sequence* (the vacation consisting of, for example, three *episodes*: flight to the vacation resort, stay at the resort, and flight back). This configuration of the relationship is illustrated in the upper part of Figure 5.4. This way of handling service failure can be labelled *administrative recovery*, because the service failure is not fully recovered at all. Instead the responsibility to seek redress is left to the customer as a separate process (sequence). This type of recovery is similar to traditional complaints handling.

Furthermore, the emotional effects of the failure are not addressed, which will probably negatively influence the customer's perception of service quality. Also, the damage to the perceived service quality caused by the failure is not likely to be diminished, even if the customer is fully compensated after the complaints-handling process.

A *defensive service recovery* (active approach to service failures) is illustrated in the middle part of the figure. Following this timing strategy the airline company suggests to the family that they buy what they need at their own expense and then get their purchases reimbursed at the airline's office after the return trip. In this way the recovery of the failure is managed as a separate recovery episode, but as part of the main service sequence (as part of the vacation). This approach to managing service failures can be called *defensive recovery*, because there is a clear attempt to recover the situation without any formal complaints procedure. In this sense it is an active approach. However, it is defensive, because it leaves the customer to sort out the problem for himself first. The formal recovery is taken care of later, however, as part of the main service sequence.

The emotional problems following the service failure are probably not managed very well in this way either, although they will have less influence on the perceived service quality than the administrative service recovery. As the customer knows from the beginning that he will be able to make the purchases required without economic consequences for himself, the intended service quality perception can probably be restored.

An *offensive service recovery* (proactive approach to service failures) is shown at the bottom of the figure. The airline company could also make the recovery of the service failure immediately as part of the episode where the failure occurred. The agent could, for example, offer the family the opportunity to make all the purchases they need at the airline's expense in a number of listed shops at the resort. The firm takes a proactive approach to managing the problems caused by the failure, by removing all additional annoyance and problems. The recovery act becomes part of the episode where the failure took place, although some of the recovery-related activities (buying clothes, for example) are part of a later episode.

In this way the emotional problems caused by the service failure are much more likely to be diminished. The customer is likely to be surprised by the positive way the negative situation is handled by the service provider, and there is even a possibility that the originally intended level of perceived service quality will be exceeded.

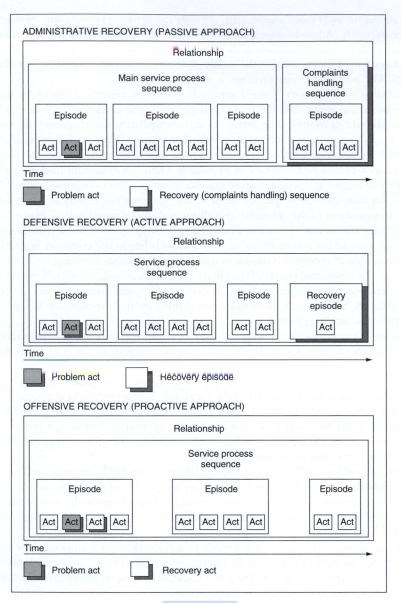

FIGURE 5.4

Timing of service recovery in a relationship framework.
Source: Grönroos, C., The role of service recovery: administrative, defensive and offensive management of service failures. In Fisk, R. & Glynn, L. (eds), *Jazzing Into the New Millennium*. 1999 SERVSIG Services Research Conference, Chicago, IL: American Marketing Association; 1999: pp. 40–42. Reproduced by permission of the American Marketing Association.

MANAGING SERVICE FAILURES AND QUALITY PROBLEMS: A SUMMARY

Some quality problems and failures cannot be corrected immediately. However, the customer's emotional concerns, anxiety and frustration should always be attended to right away. Most failures can be taken care of and recovered on the spot, if there is a *functioning recovery system* in the firm and if the customer contact employees are *empowered* with authority, knowledge and skills, and *enabled* to perform with easily retrievable information, an appropriate compensation system and, when needed, supportive superiors.

Timing is essential. As a ground rule, the quicker recovery can be made, the better. A quick recovery will make the customer *more satisfied with service quality* than otherwise. In addition, a prompt recovery will *cost the firm less* than a slow recovery or a traditional complaints-handling process. First, the costs of handling recovery, including compensation paid, will probably amount to a smaller sum, and second, quick recovery will increase the likelihood of positive word of mouth and also of customer retention. If customers stay in the relationship, the much higher costs of getting new customers to replace lost ones can be avoided. Patrick Mene, Director of Quality at the Ritz-Carlton Hotel Company, an early Malcolm Baldrige Quality Award-winning service firm, coined the '1–10–100 rule of service recovery'.[34] What costs the firm one pound, euro or dollar to fix immediately will cost 10 tomorrow and 100 later on. This is the financial logic of service recovery in a nutshell.[35]

SUMMARY

In this chapter the reasons why firms hesitate to invest in improved service quality were described. Then, quality management models for service organizations were discussed: these include the gap analysis model to close gaps in the quality generation processes of the firm, and programmes for holistic management of service quality. In the latter part of the chapter service recovery, as an alternative to traditional complaints handling, was described and service recovery processes were explained.

QUESTIONS FOR DISCUSSION

1. Why are managers often hesitant to invest in quality improvements in services?

2. How can reasons for quality problems be traced using the gap analysis framework?

3. Why is the management of quality a holistic issue in service contexts?

4. What are the benefits (for the customer and the firm) of a service recovery approach to handling mistakes or quality problems compared with a traditional complaints-handling system?

5. How can effects of service recovery be understood as customer perceived fairness?

6. How could a proactive service recovery system be installed in your organization, or in any given organization?

NOTES

1. See Yang, C-C., Identification of customer delight for quality attributes and its applications. *Total Quality Management and Business Excellence*, **22**(1), 2011, 83–98, where a customer delight barometer is developed. However, see also Correira Loureiro, S.M., Miranda, F.J. & Breazeale, M., Who needs delight? The greater impact of value, trust and satisfaction in utilitarian, frequent-use retail. *Journal of Service Management*, **25**(1), 2014, 101–124, where the authors claim that in a retailing context at least delight may be less important for customers than perceived value, trust and satisfaction.

2. Rust, R.T. & Oliver, R.L., Should we delight the customer? *Journal of the Academy of Marketing Science*, **28**(1), 2000, 86–94.

3. Rust & Oliver, *op. cit.*

4. The gap analysis model as well as reasons for gaps and ways of managing gaps are discussed in Parasuraman, A., Zeithaml, V.A. & Berry, L.L., A conceptual model of service quality and its implications for future research. *Journal of Marketing*, **61**, 1985 and Zeithaml, V.A., Berry, L.L. & Parasuraman, A., Communication and control processes in the delivery of service quality. *Journal of Marketing*, **64**(Apr), 1988, 35–48.

5. See Berry, L.L. & Parasuraman, A., *Marketing Services. Competing Through Quality*. New York: The Free Press, 1991. See also Yap, K.B. & Sweeney, J.C., Zone-of-tolerance moderates the service quality–outcome relationship. *Journal of Services Marketing*, **21**(2), 2007, 137–148, and Wu, L-W. & Wang, C-Y., Satisfaction and zone of tolerance: the moderating roles of elaboration and loyalty programs. *Managing Service Quality*, **22**(1), 2012, 38–57.

6. In a large study of the restaurant industry Tore Strandvik demonstrated that in general customers seem to show a loss aversion. See Strandvik, T., *Tolerance Zones in Perceived Service Quality*. Helsingfors/Helsinki: Swedish School of Economics, Finland, 1994.

7. See Strandvik, *op. cit.*

8. This classification of quality attributes and the examples of various types of attributes were suggested by Silvestro and Johnston. See Silvestro, R. & Johnston, R., The determinants of service quality: hygiene and enhancing factors. In Sheuing, E.E., Gummesson, E. & Little, C.H. (eds), *Selected Papers from the Second Quality in Services (QUIS 2) Conference*. New York: St. John's University and ISQA, International Service Quality Association, 1992, pp. 193–210.

9. Johnston, R., The determinants of service quality: satisfiers and dissatisfiers. *International Journal of Service Industry Management*, **6**(5), 1995, 53–71.

10. Johnston, *op. cit.*

11. Berry & Parasuraman, *op. cit.*

12. Boshoff, C. & Leong, J., Empowerment, attribution and apologising as dimensions of service quality. *International Journal of Service Industry Management*, **9**(1), 1998, 24–47 and Andreassen, T.W., *Dissatisfaction with Services. The Impact of Satisfaction with Service Recovery on Corporate Image and Future Repurchase Intentions.* Stockholm, Sweden: Stockholm University, 1997.

13. Tax, S.S., Brown, S.W. & Chandrashekaran, M., Customer evaluation of service complaint experiences: implications for relationship marketing. *Journal of Marketing*, **62**(Apr), 1998, 60–76.

14. Spreng, R.A., Harrell, R.A. & Mackoy, G.D., Service recovery: impact on satisfaction and intentions. *Journal of Services Marketing*, **9**(1), 1995, 15–23.

15. Kelley, S.W. & Davis, M.A., Antecedents to customer expectations for service recovery. *Journal of the Academy of Marketing Science*, **22**(1), 1994, 52–61.

16. An early publication where service recovery was suggested as a way of managing service failures is Hart, C.W.L., Heskett, J.L. & Sasser Jr., W.E., The profitable art of service recovery. *Harvard Business Review*, Jul/Aug, 1990, 148–156.

17. Tax, S.S. & Brown, S.W., Service recovery: research insights and practices. In Swartz, T.A. & Iacobucci, D. (eds), *Handbook in Services Marketing & Management.* Thousand Oaks, CA: Sage Publications, 2000, p. 272. See also Lovelock, C.H., *Product Plus.* New York: McGraw-Hill, 1994.

18. The emotional aspects of service failures and how they can be handled by service recovery procedures do not seem to be discussed very much in the literature. The emotional effects of how failures are recovered have been studied in Shoefer, K. & Ennew, C., The impact of perceived justice on consumers' responses to service complaint experiences. *Journal of Services Marketing*, **19**(5), 2005, 261–270. See also Chebat, J.-C. & Slusarczyk, W., How emotions mediate the effects of perceived justice on loyalty in service recovery situations: an empirical study. *Journal of Business Research*, **58**(5), 2005, 664–674, and DeWitt, T., Nguyen, D.T. & Marshall, R., Exploring customer loyalty following service recovery: the mediating effects of trust and emotions. *Journal of Service Research*, **10**(3), 2008, 269–281.

19. Tax, Brown & Chandrashekaran, 1998, *op. cit.* See also Zeithaml, V.A., Berry, L.L. & Parasuraman, A., The nature and determinants of customer expectations of services. *Journal of the Academy of Marketing Science*, **21**(1), 1993, 1–12.

20. Smith, A.K. & Bolton, R.N., An experimental investigation of customer reactions to service failure and recovery encounters. *Journal of Service Research*, **1**(1), 1998, 65–81.

21. Boshoff, C. & Allen, J., The influence of selected antecedents on frontline staff's perception of service recovery performance. *International Journal of Service Industry Management*, **11**(1), 2000, 63–90.

The authors of this article suggest that managers must be prepared for their staff to make mistakes and that 'they must adopt an "it's better to try and fail than not to try at all" attitude' (p. 82).

22. de Ruyter, K. & Wetzels, M., Customer equity considerations in service recovery: a cross-industry perspective. *International Journal of Service Industry Management*, **11**(1), 2000, 91–108.

23. See Tax, S.S., Brown, S.W. & Chandrashekaran, M., *op. cit.* Studies following the justice approach are, for example, Yim, C.K., Gu, F.F. & Tse, D.K., Justice-based service recovery expectations: measurements and antecedents. *Journal of Satisfaction, Dissatisfaction and Complaining Behavior*, **16**, 2003, 36–47; Mattila, A.S. & Cranage, D., The impact of choice on fairness in the context of service recovery. *Journal of Services Marketing*, **19**(5), 2005, 271–279; Shoefer, K. & Ennew, C., *op. cit.*; and and Liao, H., Do it right this time: the role of employee service recovery performance in customer-perceived justice and customer loyalty after service failures. *Journal of Applied Psychology*, **92**(2), 2007, 475–489.

24. See Tax, S.S., Brown, S.W. & Chandrashekaran, M., *op. cit.*, p. 72. See also del Rio-Lanza, A.B., Vasquez-Casielles, R. & Diaz-Martin, A.M., Satisfaction with service recovery: perceived justice and emotional responses. *Journal of Business Research*, **62**(8), 2009, 775–781.

25. See Hart, Heskett & Sasser, *op. cit.*, Berry & Parasuraman, *op. cit.* and Tax, S.S. & Brown, S.W., Recovering and learning from service failure. *Sloan Management Review*, **40**(1), 1998, 75–88. In these publications service recovery systems are discussed at length. See also Wang, K-Y., Hsu, L-C. & Chih, W-H., Retaining customers after service failure recoveries: a contingency model. *Managing Service Quality*, **24**(4), 2014, 318–338, where the authors study ways of keeping customers after service recovery situations.

26. Tax & Brown, *op. cit.*

27. In a study of the food retailing industry Inger Roos observed that a lack of respect for customers' complaints had a decisive effect on customers' decisions to switch from one shop to another. See Roos, I., *Switching Paths in Customer Relationships*. Helsinki/Helsingfors: Swedish School of Economics, Finland, 1999.

28. In a study of the airline industry Edvardsson found a considerable difference between how employees and customers perceived critical incidents in the service process. See Edvardsson, B., Service breakdowns: a study of critical incidents in an airline. *International Journal of Service Industry Management*, **3**(4), 1992, 17–29.

29. Bill Marriott, Managing Director of Marriott Corp., says that he demands that his firm not only do whatever is necessary to take care of guests in normal situations, but that employees also track, measure and follow up on how to handle things better in the future. See Bowen, D.E. & Lawler III, E.E., Empowering service employees. *Sloan Management Review*, **36**(Summer), 1995, 73–84.

30. Compare Berry & Parasuraman, *op. cit.*

31. Zemke, R., Supporting service recovery: attributes for excelling at solving customers' problems. In Sheuing, E., Gummesson, E. & Little, C.H. (eds), *Selected Papers from the Second Quality in Services (QUIS 2) Conference*. New York: St. John's University and ISQA, International Service Quality Association, 1992, pp. 41–46.

32. See, for example, Johnston, R. & Fern, A., Service recovery strategies for single and double deviation scenarios. *The Service Industry Journal*, **19**(2), 1999, 69–82.

33. Grönroos, C., The role of service recovery: administrative, defensive and offensive management of service failures. In Fisk, R. & Glynn, L. (eds), *Jazzing Into the New Millennium. 1999 Servsig Services Research Conference*. Chicago, IL: American Marketing Association, 1999, pp. 39–43.

34. Patlow, C.G., How Ritz-Carlton applies 'TQM'. *The Cornell H.R.A. Quarterly*, August, 1993, 16–24.

35. See Stauss, B. & Seidel, W., *Complaint Management. The Heart of CRM*. Mason, OH: Thomson, 2004, where the authors demonstrate how well-handled customer complaints, following a service recovery system, help the firm save money and achieve sustainable revenues.

FURTHER READING

Andreassen, T.W. (1997) *Dissatisfaction with Services. The Impact of Satisfaction with Service Recovery on Corporate Image and Future Repurchase Intentions*. Stockholm, Sweden: Stockholm University.

Berry, L.L. & Parasuraman, A. (1991) *Marketing Services. Competing Through Quality*. New York: The Free Press.

Boshoff, C. & Leong, J. (1998) Empowerment, attribution and apologising as dimensions of service quality. *International Journal of Service Industry Management*, **9**(1), 24–47.

Boshoff, C. & Allen, J. (2000) The influence of selected antecedents on frontline staff's perception of service recovery performance. *International Journal of Service Industry Management*, **11**(1), 63–90.

Bowen, D.E. & Lawler III, E.E. (1995) Empowering service employees. *Sloan Management Review*, **36**(Summer), 73–84.

Chebat, J.-C. & Slusarczyk, W. (2005) How emotions mediate the effects of perceived justice on loyalty in service recovery situations: an empirical study. *Journal of Business Research*, **58**(5), 664–674.

Correira Loureiro, S.M., Miranda, F.J. & Breazeale, M. (2014) Who needs delight? The greater impact of value, trust and satisfaction in utilitarian, frequent-use retail. *Journal of Service Management*, **25**(1), 101–124.

de Ruyter, K. & Wetzels, M. (2000) Customer equity considerations in service recovery: a cross-industry perspective. *International Journal of Service Industry Management*, **11**(1), 91–108.

del Rio-Lanza, A.B., Vasquez-Casielles, R. & Diaz-Martin, A.M. (2009) Satisfaction with service recovery: Perceived justice and emotional responses. *Journal of Business Research*, **62**(8), 775–781.

DeWitt, T., Nguyen, D.T. & Marshall, R. (2008) Exploring customer loyalty following service recovery: the mediating effects of trust and emotions. *Journal of Service Research*, **10**(3), 269–281.

Edvardsson, B. (1992) Service breakdowns: a study of critical incidents in an airline. *International Journal of Service Industry Management*, **3**(4), 17–29.

Grönroos, C. (1999) The role of service recovery: administrative, defensive and offensive management of service failures. In Fisk, R. & Glynn, L. (eds), *Jazzing Into the New Millennium*. 1999 Servsig Services Research Conference. Chicago, IL: American Marketing Association, pp. 39–43.

Hart, C.W.L., Heskett, J.L. & Sasser Jr., W.E. (1990) The profitable art of service recovery. *Harvard Business Review*, Jul/Aug, 148–156.

Johnston, R. (1995) The determinants of service quality: satisfiers and dissatisfiers. *International Journal of Service Industry Management*, **6**(5), 53–71.

Johnston, R. & Fern, A. (1999) Service recovery strategies for single and double deviation scenarios. *The Service Industry Journal*, **19**(2), 69–82.

Kelley, S.W. & Davis, M.A. (1994) Antecedents to customer expectations for service recovery. *Journal of the Academy of Marketing Science*, **22**(1), 52–61.

Liao, H. (2007) Do it right this time: the role of employee service recovery performance in customer-perceived justice and customer loyalty after service failures. *Journal of Applied Psychology*, **92**(2), 475–489.

Lovelock, C.H. (1994) *Product Plus: How Product Service Affects Competitive Advantage*. New York: McGraw-Hill.

Mattila, A.S. & Cranage, D. (2005) The impact of choice on fairness in the context of service recovery. *Journal of Services Marketing*, **19**(5), 271–279.

Parasuraman, A., Zeithaml, V.A. and Berry, L.L. (1988) SERVQUAL: a multiple-item scale for measuring consumer perceptions of service quality. *Journal of Retailing*, **64**(1), 12–40.

Patlow, C.G. (1993) How Ritz-Carlton applies 'TQM'. *The Cornell H.R.A. Quarterly*, August, 16–24.

Roos, I. (1999) *Switching Paths in Customer Relationships*. Helsinki/Helsingfors: Swedish School of Economics, Finland/CERS Centre for Relationship Marketing and Service Management.

Rust, R.T. & Oliver, R.L. (2000) Should we delight the customer? *Journal of the Academy of Marketing Science*, **28**(1), 86–94.

Shoefer, K. & Ennew, C. (2005) The impact of perceived justice on consumers' responses to service complaint experiences. *Journal of Services Marketing*, **19**(5), 261–270.

Silvestro, R. & Johnston, R. (1992) The determinants of service quality: hygiene and enhancing factors. In Sheuing, E.E., Gummesson, E. & Little, C.H. (eds), *Selected Papers from the Second Quality in Services (QUIS 2) Conference*. New York: St John's University and ISQA, International Service Quality Association, pp. 193–210.

Smith, A.K. & Bolton, R.N. (1998) An experimental investigation of customer reactions to service failure and recovery encounters. *Journal of Service Research*, **1**(1), 65–81.

Spreng, R.A., Harrell, R.A. & Mackoy, G.D. (1995) Service recovery: impact on satisfaction and intentions. *Journal of Services Marketing*, **9**(1), 15–23.

Stauss, B. & Seidel, W. (2004) *Complaint Management. The Heart of CRM*. Mason, OH: Thomson.

Strandvik, T. (1994) *Tolerance Zones in Perceived Service Quality*. Helsingfors/Helsinki: Swedish School of Economics Finland.

Tax, S.S. & Brown, S.W. (1998) Recovering and learning from service failure. *Sloan Management Review*, **40**(1), 75–88.

Tax, S.S., Brown, S.W. & Chandrashekaran, M. (1998) Customer evaluation of service complaint experiences: implications for relationship marketing. *Journal of Marketing*, **62**(Apr), 60–76.

Tax, S.S. & Brown, S.W. (2000) Service recovery: research insights and practices. In Swartz, T.A. & Iacobucci, D. (eds), *Handbook in Services Marketing & Management*. Thousand Oaks, CA: Sage Publications, pp. 271–285.

Wang, K-Y., Hsu, L-C. & Chih, W-H. (2014) Retaining customers after service failure recoveries: a contingency model. *Managing Service Quality*, **24**(4), 318–338.

Wu, L-W. & Wang, C-Y. (2012) Satisfaction and zone of tolerance: the moderating roles of elaboration and loyalty programs. *Managing Service Quality*, **22**(1), 38–57.

Yang, C-C. (2011) Identification of customer delight for quality attributes and its applications. *Total Quality Management and Business Excellence*, **22**(1), 83–98.

Yap, K.B. & Sweeney, J.C. (2007) Zone-of-tolerance moderates the service quality-outcome relationship. *Journal of Services Marketing*, **21**(2), 137–148.

Yim, C.K., Gu, F.F. & Tse, D.K. (2003) Justice-based service recovery expectations: measurements and antecedents. *Journal of Satisfaction, Dissatisfaction and Complaining Behavior*, **16**, 36–47.

Zeithaml, V.A., Berry, L.L. & Parasuraman, A. (1988) Communication and control processes in the delivery of service quality. *Journal of Marketing*, **64**(Apr), 35–49.

Zeithaml, V.A., Berry, L.L. & Parasuraman, A. (1993) The nature and determinants of customer expectations of services. *Journal of the Academy of Marketing Science*, **21**(1), 1–12.

Zemke, R. (1992) Supporting service recovery: attributes for excelling at solving customers' problems. In Sheuing, E.E., Gummesson, E. & Little, C.H. (eds), *Selected Papers from the Second Quality in Services (QUIS 2) Conference*. New York: St. John's University and ISQA, International Service Quality Association, pp. 41–46.

CHAPTER 6
RETURN ON SERVICE AND RELATIONSHIPS

"Customers look for value. However, more value does not necessarily require new services but better service, meaning that all existing customer contacts are managed as value-supporting service for customers."

INTRODUCTION

Building on the discussions of perceived service quality and relationship quality in Chapter 4 and quality management in service in Chapter 5, this chapter now turns to the question of whether investing in service can be expected to pay off. The issues of relationship costs and long-term customer sacrifice are discussed, and various approaches to understanding customer perceived value are described. Then a model of *reciprocal return on relationship* (ROR) and metrics for calculating this ROR are presented. Finally, a model of customer relationship profitability is presented. After having read the chapter, the reader should understand how to justify investments in service quality and in service in customer relationships, and how to quantify the total benefits of a service offering as well as how reciprocal ROR and the profitability of customer relationships are calculated.

WHY CUSTOMERS ARE NOT PREPARED TO PAY FOR IMPROVED SERVICE QUALITY

Service competition is a fact for a growing number of firms and industries. Service firms have always faced service competition, whereas this situation is less familiar for most manufacturing businesses. In spite of this new competitive situation, one often meets the sceptical suspicion that, in the final analysis, developing service and capabilities to cope with service competition will not pay off after all. 'Customers are prepared to pay only for the core solution, a physical product or a service' and 'For our customers price is the only important factor, so it is no use to invest in services' are arguments which are frequently heard. In some situations, and for some customers, they may of course be true. However, in general they are certainly not valid. Improved service and the development of sustainable customer relationships usually pays off. The problem for most firms is that many customers, individual consumers as well as organizational, do not see how improved service means more value for them. The service provider has to make customers realize the value-enhancing potential of better service.

If customers do not appreciate the value to them of good service and are not willing to pay for service, there can be at least four reasons for this:

1. The service provider has not been able to demonstrate to its customers how they can benefit from the service offered in terms of added comfort, support, security, wealth and/or lowered costs.

2. The service provider has not managed to show the customers that long-term cost effects of a service offering are a more important decision-making criterion than price.

3. The service offering is not as customer-centric as it should be and does not offer the favourable benefits that customers are looking for.

4. A particular customer is not interested in value-enhancing additional services but is only looking for the core solution at as low a price as possible.

In this chapter we discuss how to cope with the first two reasons given above. The third reason is discussed in other chapters throughout the book. The fourth reason is not discussed in this context: a firm that has done its market research carefully enough should realize that such customers are in a transactional mode (see Chapter 2) and they should not be offered a total service offering at all but merely the core solution they want.

THE COST OF IMPROVING SERVICE QUALITY

Managers often feel uncomfortable at customer demands for better quality. They feel that improved service quality does not pay off. Two reasons why the firm cannot improve its quality are normally offered: improving quality costs more than can be achieved in additional revenues and new business, and improving quality means that productivity will suffer, which the organization cannot afford. Managers tend to believe that quality improvements come at the expense of productivity, and vice versa. Caught in this apparent dilemma, they often choose to concentrate on one of these issues.[1] Far too often attention to productivity is given priority, and how to improve quality remains an unsolved problem. In Chapter 9 the issue of productivity in service is discussed in some detail, and it is shown that, although it may be true for some firms, as a general rule productivity and quality do not counteract each other.

Both of these reasons for why quality cannot be improved are cost-related. To improve service and increase their quality requires too many resources and additional costs, and supposedly lowers productivity, which leads to higher costs per unit produced. Both reasons are invalid, and are based on an insufficient understanding of the relationships between quality and productivity on the one hand and the use of resources and the sources of costs and revenues on the other. Efforts to raise quality almost always result in better productivity and efforts to raise productivity can very well pay off through better quality. However, in order to achieve positive results, managers will have to rethink the relationship between costs and revenues, productivity and quality (see Chapters 1 and 8). If managers are able to define these relationships, they are probably able to exploit their strengths as far as production effectiveness, employee satisfaction and profitability are concerned.

QUALITY DOES NOT COST: A LACK OF QUALITY DOES

The belief that high quality implies higher costs is not based on fact. Normally, it is the other way around. Frequently the more important issue is that a lack of quality costs money. Philip Crosby coined the phrase 'quality is free'.[2] He based his statement on the notion that firms spend more than 20% of their sales revenue doing things wrong and then having to correct these mistakes.

These are facts from manufacturing. However, service organizations are probably no better. On the contrary, it has been suggested that up to 35% of their operating costs may be due to a lack of quality, having to repeat tasks and correct errors. This, of course, follows from the fact that service quality is a complicated phenomenon and that it is more difficult to monitor and assure quality in service than in manufacturing. Furthermore, manufacturing has a long history of quality control research and a whole collection of quality monitoring techniques, quality assurance and total quality management at its service.

Hence, improving quality by creating customer-oriented and foolproof systems and by training employees well is a way not to increase costs, but to get rid of unnecessary costs. If we assume that 35% of operating costs are unnecessary, because they are due to bad quality, quality improvement by removing these quality problems would save 35% of these costs. All of this would be visible on the bottom line. However, such an improvement would not go unnoticed by the market, and new business and additional revenues could be expected to be achieved. This would add even more to the bottom line, thus profits would be boosted by more than 35% of the original operating costs. Furthermore, if the firm spends this 35% on further improving quality, operating costs would remain on the same level as they were originally. This quality improvement process could be expected to bring in more business and perhaps, even probably, enable the firm to get a better price for its service. The effects on the bottom line are obvious.

BETTER QUALITY, HIGHER CUSTOMER RETENTION RATES, MORE PROFITS

Service is inherently relational. This does not mean that some service providers could not develop their marketing strategy in a transaction-oriented fashion. However, there is always the possibility for the development of customer relationships in service. Relationships between service providers and consumers and users of services normally continue over time. Hence, we start our analysis of return on service and relationships by discussing the effects of good service on customer retention and loyalty,[3] and the economic consequences of longer customer relationships.

What 'good service' means is a strategic issue. In many cases it means that the service is excellent in comparison with competing offerings and meets customers' expectations and other comparison standards. If this is the case, good service means that the service is genuinely good. However, in other cases it may mean a lower level of service, because the target group of customers may be looking for a lower quality level, for example because the correspondingly lower price better fits their budget. Then the lower level is 'good service' for those customers. For example, a couple spending the evening at a gourmet restaurant consider the quality of the restaurant service good if it meets their expectations of good food, attentive waiting staff, and so on. However, if the performance of a fast-food restaurant meets the different expectations they have when visiting such a restaurant, in a relative sense they will consider the quality of the service equally good.

THE RELATIONSHIP BETWEEN CUSTOMER SATISFACTION AND REPURCHASES AND LOYALTY

Even though a positive relationship between satisfaction with service and goods quality, on the one hand, and customers' willingness to continue the relationship or make repurchases, on the other, seems to exist, it is important to realize that this function is normally far from linear. Experiences from Xerox reported by Hart and Johnson[4] (see Figure 6.1) clearly indicate that there is a substantial *zone of indifference* including customers who claim that they are everything from 'so-so satisfied' to 'satisfied'. Only the 'very satisfied' customers show a high repurchasing rate and a high propensity for positive word of mouth. As the figure shows, the retention curve rises steeply at this point of the satisfaction scale. Evidence from other types of both goods and services supports these observations. Two obvious conclusions can be drawn from this:

- It is not enough to offer the quality of service that keeps customers in this *zone of indifference* as far as repurchasing behaviour is concerned; customers have to be offered a service offering which makes them *very* satisfied before they will repurchase. Therefore it is important to surprise customers in such a way that their quality perception is satisfactory enough to reinforce loyalty and make them repurchase.

- When reporting results from customer satisfaction and service quality studies, it is extremely important to keep those respondents who report that they are very satisfied apart from those who say that they are simply satisfied. The repurchasing and word-of-mouth behaviour, and therefore also

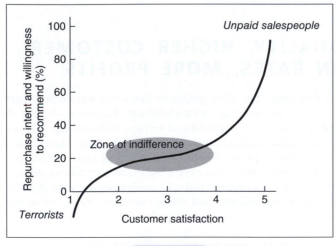

FIGURE 6.1

The satisfaction/repurchase function.
Source: Hart, C.W. & Johnson, M.D., Growing the trust
relationship. *Marketing Management*, American Marketing
Association, Spring; 1999: p. 9. Reproduced by permission of
the American Marketing Association.

the actions required to ensure enduring customer relationships, are totally different for these two groups of customers (normally, the responses of these two categories of customers are reported jointly in the 'satisfied or very satisfied' category. By so doing, the firm loses vital information needed to create profitable customer relationships.)

Hart and Johnson[5] draw the conclusion that a firm has to go beyond what normally can be described as good service to create loyalty. The firm must serve customers in such a way that they realize that the firm can be *trusted in every respect at all times*. This means that the firms should deliver consistently good service.

Another interesting conclusion that can be drawn from Figure 6.1 is the effect of customer satisfaction on word-of-mouth communication. Only very satisfied customers will engage in any substantial positive word-of-mouth endorsements and thus become 'unpaid' marketing and sales persons for the firm. On the other hand, very unsatisfied customers can be expected to create substantial negative word of mouth, and thus become 'terrorists' reinforcing negative but not totally unsatisfactory experiences by other customers and scaring away potential new customers. The development of social media makes such effects much more far-reaching than ever before.

Furthermore, there are indications that firms gain a larger share of customers' spending in their category if the customers are very satisfied with the service they have experienced than if the customers are less satisfied.[6]

In conclusion, there are a number of reasons why a firm should strive to provide consistently impeccable service.

THE RELATIONSHIP BETWEEN CUSTOMER LOYALTY AND PROFITABILITY

The largest published study of higher customer retention levels following better service quality and how this affects profit is one by Bain & Company. Although it is not new it is still very relevant. In this US study several service industries were studied. The effects on profits through improved customer retention and hence longer relationships with customers are astonishing. It was found, among other things, that the average profit per customer grew constantly over the first five years.

The reasons why the profit per customer increases over time are illustrated schematically in Figure 6.2. The economic effect of customer loyalty can be attributed to the following factors: acquisition costs, revenue growth, cost savings, referrals and price premiums.[7]

The vertical axis in the figure does not have a scale, because the effects on profits of the various factors differ from industry to industry, firm to firm, and even customer to customer. However, the height of the sections gives some general indications of the relative importance of these factors. Every firm should, however, take the time and trouble to study its accounting and reporting system in order to make the necessary calculations of the influence on total profits per customer of these and possibly other profit drivers. Because in most firms the figures needed are not readily available, this can be a time-consuming task. Revenues and costs are usually registered on a per product basis, not on a per customer basis. These factors are discussed below.

Acquisition costs. The active acquisition of new customers using sales and external marketing efforts is required in most businesses. As a rule of thumb, getting a new customer costs five to six times more than it costs on top of normal service operations (sales calls, providing information about new goods or services, etc.) to keep an existing satisfied customer. In other words, to keep an existing customer it costs only 15 to 20% of what has to be invested in getting a new customer. The economics

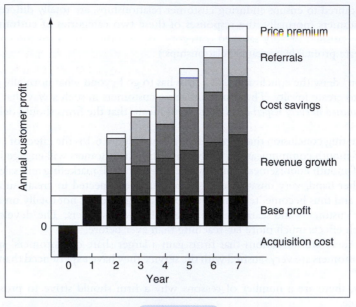

FIGURE 6.2

The profitability effect of loyal customers.
Source: Reichheld, F.F., *The Loyalty Effect. The Hidden Forces
Behind Growth, Profits, and Lasting Value*. Boston, MA: Harvard
Business School Press, 1996. Reproduced by permission of
Harvard Business Review.

of customer loyalty are very apparent. These figures of course vary from industry to industry, and situation to situation, but are nevertheless remarkable. In Figure 6.2 the acquisition cost per customer appears as a negative profit effect in the year before the customer relationship starts.

Base profit. In many service industries the price paid by customers during the first year or even first few years does not cover the costs of producing the service. In other cases the price covers costs and produces a profit per customer from the first year. This is the base profit in the figure. After some years, depending on the industry and other factors, the accumulated base profits have covered the initial marketing costs of getting the customer.

Revenue growth. In most situations a long-standing customer will bring more business to the same service provider. This means that, on average, customers can be expected to contribute more to a firm's profits as the relationship grows. The annual revenue per customer increases over the years, thus contributing to growing profits.

Cost savings. As the service provider and the customer learn about each other, about what to expect and how to perform, service processes will be smoother and take less time, and fewer mistakes that have to be corrected will be made. Thus, the average operating costs per customer will decrease, which in turn has a positive impact on profits.

Referrals. Long-standing and satisfied customers will create positive word–of–mouth communication and recommend the supplier or service provider to friends, neighbours, business associates and others. The customer takes over the role as marketer without any additional costs to the firm. A large number of businesses, especially smaller ones, thrive on good referrals by satisfied customers. In this way new customers are brought in with lower than normal acquisition costs, which has an extra favourable effect on profits.

Premium price. In many business, old customers pay a higher price than newcomers. Discounts that were initially given to new customers do not exist for older customers. In many cases introductory offers decrease prices for new customers. However, the main reason for the premium price effect can be attributed to the fact that long-standing customers realize the value provided by the firm and make cost savings by using the service of a service provider they know well. We shall return to this later in the context of relationship costs. In summary, this value offsets the negative effect of higher prices. Of course, it is not always the case that old customers pay a premium price. Sometimes long-lasting relationships have given the customer a bargaining position based on power or social relationships which keeps prices down. If this happens, a negative, profit-eroding effect occurs.

In the study by Bain & Company the economic effects of higher retention rates were calculated in the service industries studied. These results were also quite astonishing. In general, it was found that as the customer defection rate falls (i.e. as customer retention grows), profits increase. The variation between the industries in the study was remarkable. In retail banking at the time of the study operations profits improved by 85% as the customer defection rate decreased by five percentage points. Over the service industries in the study the impact on the economic result of a decrease of the defection rate of this magnitude varied between 25% and 85%.[8]

Again, the economics of customer loyalty are quite obvious. However, almost always separate studies of the revenue and cost flows are required, because accounting systems seldom produce the information needed for such calculations. The growth in customer retention rates and customer loyalty is probably not just caused by improved service. However, it is apparent that customer satisfaction with service quality is a central factor here. On the other hand, it is also clear that satisfaction as such does not necessarily create loyal customers. The sacrifice made by customers, in terms of price, comfort, timeliness and relationship costs, which may follow from these and other factors, as well as the value customers feel they get, are critical variables affecting loyalty and the length of customer relationships.

In the next sections we shall first discuss how to analyse customer sacrifice and then the customer-perceived value of service in a relationship.

CUSTOMER SACRIFICE: THE COST OF BEING A CUSTOMER

The view that improved service does not pay off for the service provider or for the customer is expressed quite regularly, as we have seen above. Nevertheless, as a general rule this is not true. Except for special cases, for example with highly transaction-oriented customers, there is always an opportunity to increase customer value and strengthen relationships with customers, *if the service provider understands the nature of service competition and the cost consequences for customers of good and bad service.* One has to realize that bad service creates costs for customers, and good service makes such costs decrease or eliminates them.

The usual problem is that marketers, salespeople and buyers think in terms of short-term exchanges or transactions, and they are therefore preoccupied with short-term sacrifice, or the price to be paid. Because the accounting systems of both the seller and the buyer are normally geared towards registering transactions and not towards following up on costs and revenues caused by suppliers, service providers and customers, neither party realizes the long-term cost effects of bad service; nor do they see the long-term gains of good service. Unnecessary costs caused by bad service and the cost gains of good service occur for the customer as well as for the service provider. In this section we shall concentrate on the effects on customers. Later on, effects on the supplier or service provider will be discussed.

Price is only a part of the total long-term cost of being a customer of a given service provider. *Price, including discounts and terms of payment, is a cost component which occurs in the short run, whereas other cost components occur in the long run as the relationship unfolds.* Thus, the total long-term customer sacrifice consists of price and additional costs occurring in the relationship. These additional costs are called *relationship costs.*[9] Hence, it is important to make a distinction between short-term and long-term sacrifice:

- Short-term customer sacrifice: price.

- Total long-term customer sacrifice: price, relationship costs.

Relationship costs are the additional costs on top of price that occur for a customer due to the fact that he has purchased something from a given supplier or service firm and entered into a relationship with this organization. The relationship costs are of three different types:[10]

1. Direct relationship costs.

2. Indirect relationship costs.

3. Psychological costs.

In the following sections these types of relationship costs will be discussed in more detail. Such costs occur in relationships with individual consumers and households as well as in business-to-business relationships. It may be easier to calculate them in the latter type of relationship, but they exist for individual consumers too.

DIRECT RELATIONSHIP COSTS

Direct relationship costs are costs that depend on the processes that the customer has to maintain because of the solution offered by the supplier. Such costs consist, for example, of investments in office space, additional equipment, personnel and software and depreciation costs over time. Direct relationship costs can be calculated either as gross or net costs. *Gross direct costs* are the total costs if the customer decides to purchase the solution offered. *Net direct costs* are any additional costs which are less than optimal from the customer's point of view. Both ways of calculating this cost component give the same result. A net calculation may be more useful when comparing two or more competing offerings, whereas a gross calculation gives more appropriate information when following up on the total long-term sacrifice in a given relationship with a supplier or service provider.

For example, Xerox once dominated the market in photocopying machines, and offered a service system that was efficient from Xerox's perspective. However, as the Japanese started to introduce photocopying machines that required little servicing, a new standard for optimal service costs was established. Any supplier who provided a solution that required higher service costs caused unnecessary direct relationship costs for the customer. Now, with digitized and computerized office systems there is a move back to favouring Xerox. A classic example of how to manage direct relationship costs is just-in-time logistics. By offering a delivery system that enables a customer to keep a minimum number of items in stock, a supplier can minimize the customer's need to keep capital tied up in inventories and also make it possible for the customer to invest in smaller and probably less expensive facilities. All this decreases the direct relationship costs of being a customer of this particular supplier, and that way the total long-term customer sacrifice also decreases. To take another example, in a relationship where an advertising agency requires the customer to add an additional person to its marketing staff, the extra cost for this person is a direct relationship cost.

A competitor who can offer a just-in-time delivery system that enables the customer to keep an even smaller inventory buffer, or can offer the same advertising services but without requiring the customer to tie up one person in the relationship, helps customers to decrease their long-term direct costs. If everything else is equal, these competing offerings mean more value for customers, because they involve less long-term sacrifice.

INDIRECT RELATIONSHIP COSTS

Indirect relationship costs caused by a relationship with a given supplier or service firm are due to the amount of time and resources that a customer has to devote to maintaining the relationship in case it does not function as it should. Hence, they are unexpected and unwanted costs. Standstill costs or other quality costs that follow from delays or low-quality repair, maintenance and delivery services or from goods and service that do not function as they are supposed to also cause indirect relationship costs. Complaints always cause such costs. On the other hand, a quick and well-managed service recovery is considered value-supporting by customers, because it keeps down indirect relationship costs caused by a service failure, mistake or other quality problem.

The less a supplier can be trusted to keep delivery times, or the more problems there are with maintenance service, invoices and other documents, the more resources the customers have to devote to the relationship. Documents have to be checked, re-checked, phone calls have to be made, e-mails have to be sent, complaints have to be filed and followed up, more checking is required and more phone calls and e-mails are needed, and so on. These costs are *indirect* relationship costs, because they are not directly due to the flow of the relationship, but to unnecessary and unwanted deviations from the intended processes.

The additional costs caused by this are often significant. Sometimes one or more employees have to spend a considerable amount of time taking care of problems like these, which are all caused by an unreliable supplier or service provider. Temporary personnel may have to be hired or additional personnel added. However, far too often the reasons for these costs go unnoticed by management. The internal report systems seldom show that such additional costs are caused by the poor service of a given supplier; hence, management is not alerted. Another type of indirect relationship cost is standstill costs, and the costs of lost business due to the poor service of a supplier; for example, late deliveries. Such costs can grow very high.

A competitor who provides higher quality service to the buyer creates less pressure, fewer problems and also minimizes standstill costs and other quality costs. Thus, the indirect relationship costs are lower. A company that can demonstrate to the customer that it can provide a service offering at such a quality level that indirect relationship costs are kept to a minimum will be able to show the buyer that in the long run it can support more value for the customer.

PSYCHOLOGICAL COSTS

Psychological costs are caused when the staff of a firm feel that they cannot trust a supplier or service provider. They worry about the relationship and feel that they have to take action to ensure acceptable service. They feel insecure and lack control. Their mental capacity to perform other tasks is constrained to some extent. They feel that they have to use some of their time to check that everything is in order with the supplier, that deliveries will not be delayed, that maintenance will take place as scheduled, and that complaints will be attended to in a timely and appropriate way. As a result, decisions are perhaps not taken as promptly as they should be or implemented as swiftly as intended, some tasks may be postponed or even forgotten, etc. This may again lead to indirect relationship costs in the form of increasing overtime, the need for part-time manpower, lost business opportunities, etc. Psychological relationship costs for a customer are not always measurable, but they are always felt by those who suffer from having to cope with suppliers or service providers who provide bad service, and they often create unnecessary additional measurable indirect relationship costs.

As general guidelines of how to handle the various kinds of relationship costs, the following advice can be used:

- Direct relationship costs: *minimize* investments and out-of-pockets costs required by the relationship.

- Indirect relationship costs: *eliminate* unexpected and unwanted costs occurring due to mistakes and quality problems, lack of information and service failures.

- Psychological costs: *avoid* causing a feeling of lack of control and other reasons for being worried.

PRICE, RELATIONSHIP COSTS AND TOTAL LONG-TERM COSTS AND SACRIFICE

Relationship costs – direct, indirect and psychological – are equally as important as the price paid for the buyer. Frequently, firms do not realize this and focus on the singular transactions and the cost of singular exchanges. The price becomes the only cost component they consider. However, price is only the *short-term sacrifice* for the customer, whereas what is interesting for a customer from a business point of view should be the *long-term sacrifice*:

$$\text{Short-term sacrifice} = \text{Price paid (including discounts and terms)}$$
$$\text{Long-term sacrifice} = \text{Price paid} + \text{Relationship costs}$$

Because of relationship costs, direct as well as indirect costs, the long-term sacrifice easily grows even far above the short-term sacrifice. To see this one has to take a long-term view of total costs. In Figure 6.3 the formation of total costs in a relationship is illustrated schematically.

The total cost or sacrifice over time may be much higher than price, as is indicated in the figure. Regardless of how high a proportion of total long-term cost is relationship cost, using price as the main or sole criterion for purchasing decisions is always misleading. When a buyer is evaluating the value of competing offerings, in addition to price the *net present value* of relationship costs that can be expected to occur over time should be calculated. As is illustrated in Figure 6.4, from a long-term perspective a lower price offering may well lead to higher total long-term costs than a higher-priced product. This should not come as a surprise, because a lower level of service is probably the reason why one competitor is able to offer a lower price. In the end this lower service level will, however, cause added relationship costs. Moreover, additional service that the customer may need over time is normally not included in the price. Hence, the customer will have to pay extra for such service.

The seller should always calculate what level of relationship cost, both direct and indirect and also psychological, can be expected to occur for a potential customer, to put price in a long-term cost perspective. This is a way of not only helping buyers to make better decisions, but also of justifying a higher price for better service. By carrying out such long-term cost calculations the seller can put a value on the service he provides, which the buyer can understand and appreciate.

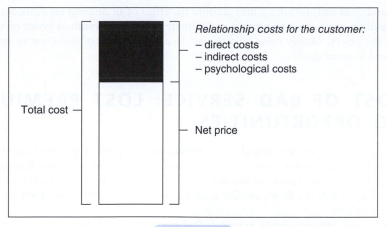

FIGURE 6.3

Relationship costs for the customer and their effect on total costs.
Source: Grönroos, C., Facing the challenge of service competition: the
economies of service. In Kunst, P. & Lemmink, J. (eds), *Quality
Management in Services*. Maastricht, the Netherlands: Van Gorcum,
1992, p. 133.

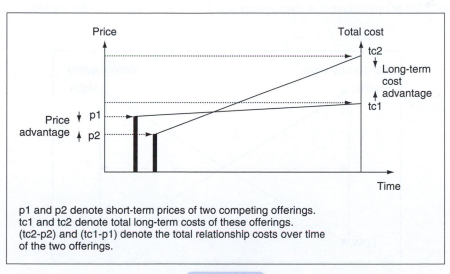

FIGURE 6.4

Price, relationship costs and total long-term costs of two offerings.

Going beyond costs and also taking into account the effect of an offering on a customer's revenue-generation capabilities we come to what is really interesting from a business point of view for both the seller and the buyer, namely *value for customers*. In a later section of this chapter customer value will be discussed in some detail.

THE COST OF BAD SERVICE: LOST PREMIUM PRICING OPPORTUNITIES

If a firm offers low-quality service, or makes an offering where a physical product constitutes the core with additional low-quality service such as late deliveries, slow recovery of problems and unreliable maintenance processes, unnecessary relationship costs will be incurred by the customer. However, as is illustrated in Figure 6.5, if a firm's service is high quality, relationship costs for the customer will correspondingly be low.

The less a potential customer thinks in terms of relationship costs and long-term sacrifice, the more important price will be as a decision-making criterion. However, there are firms who claim that they are able to price up to 10% and even 20% above market price. The reason for this is that these firms understand their customers and have been able to deliver an offering which keeps relationship costs at a minimum. Their service lowers any extra long-term costs of being a customer of this particular supplier or service provider. This provides the seller with a well-founded argument for selling his service at a higher price. The argument for a premium price is based on hard facts, i.e. cost savings. The trick is to learn how to calculate these costs and to teach customers to look for the impact of relationship costs on total long-term costs. The lower the relationship costs a firm can guarantee for a buyer, compared with competitors, the more opportunities exist for premium pricing.

If the additional long-term costs of bad service are not perceived by customers in a concrete way (based on facts, references and calculations) it will be difficult to make them pay for better service. In such cases, a lot of opportunities to earn money *both for the buyer and for the seller* are lost.

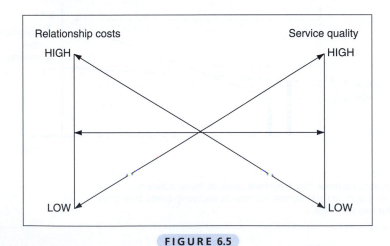

FIGURE 6.5

The relationship between service quality and relationship costs.

RELATIONSHIP COSTS FOR THE SUPPLIER

It is not only for the customer that poor service leads to unnecessary extra costs over time. As illustrated in Figure 6.6, the supplier receives a *net price*, after taking into account any discounts and terms of payment. According to the accounting systems of most firms, the margin between this net price and the *cost of producing* the solution for the customer is the direct economic result of the relationship. However, this is how it looks from a short-term, product-focused and transaction-oriented perspective.

From a customer relationship economics perspective the production costs, schematically illustrated in the lower part of Figure 6.6, are imaginary. The real cost of servicing a customer is much higher. To obtain the real cost of maintaining the relationship with a given customer, all other costs caused by the way the customer is served have to be added. Relationship costs occur for the supplier or service provider as well, and these costs decrease the *gross margin* between net price and production cost. If they add too much to production costs, what should be a good profit unexpectedly turns into a negative *net profit*. Because of the accounting systems used in many firms, management may not understand what causes this decrease in profit level.

Relationship costs for the supplier can be divided into the same types of costs as relationship costs for the customer. There are the *direct relationship costs* of maintaining a customer relationship caused, for example, by delivery systems, invoicing, complaints handling, technical service, customer training, etc., which the supplier uses. The more complicated, outdated and inefficient systems are and the more inappropriate the tools and equipment used, the higher the level of direct relationship costs will be for the supplier. Interestingly, the more inefficient, inappropriate and bureaucratic systems the supplier uses, *the lower the level of service quality* will be. Of course, the reverse also holds true.

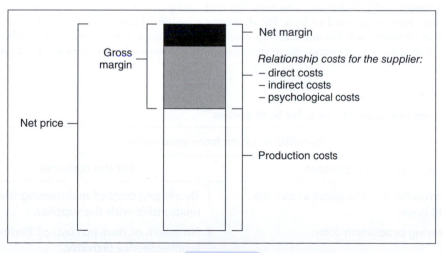

FIGURE 6.6

Relationship costs for the supplier and their profit-destroying effects.
Source: Grönroos, C. (1992) Facing the challenge of service competition: the economies of service. In Kunst, P. & Lemmink, J. (eds), *Quality Management in Services*. Maastricht, the Netherlands: Van Gorcum, 1992, p. 133.

There are also *indirect relationship costs* for the supplier in a relationship. Mistakes have to be corrected, complaints have to be attended to, inaccurate invoices have to be altered, problems have to be looked into, phone calls and e-mails have to be responded to, and so on. This leads to additional workload, the need for temporary employees, and possibly the need to employ more personnel, etc. All these costs are unnecessary and result from less than good service. These costs are also not easily detected and can be attributed to the fact that the firm does not take good care of its customers. However, *firms should always have an account for the costs of bad service rendered, preferably specified per customer or at least customer group*. If this account grows, management should perceive this as a warning signal. Finally, there are, of course, also *psychological costs* involved.

EXCELLENT SERVICE PAYS OFF TWICE: FOR BOTH PARTIES

The analysis of relationship costs for customers, suppliers and service providers clearly reveals that bad service causes problems and unnecessary costs *for both parties*. Moreover, it shows that by and large it is the same inefficient and untrustworthy service systems that lead to complicated procedures, service failures, quality problems and complaints, thus causing these extra and unnecessary costs. Improving service quality is, therefore, a *win–win strategy* in a customer relationship. Both parties will gain something to improve their profit margin. *Good service pays off twice: for the supplier as well as the customer*. This is illustrated in Table 6.1.

The supplier or service provider has an opportunity to raise prices above market price, and at the same time has considerable cost-saving opportunities, because improved service decreases additional relationship costs for the supplier. On the other hand, the customer can avoid substantial relationship costs if the service rendered is good. Moreover, if customers are satisfied with a given supplier or service provider and feel that they can trust the firm, and perceive that they get good value in the relationship, there is no need to look for alternative suppliers. Thus, the considerable search costs involved in changing supplier and start-up costs resulting from a new business relationship can be avoided. This does not, of course, mean that customers sometimes do not want to check alternative

TABLE 6.1

Excellent service pays off twice: for both parties.

Benefits resulting from good service	
For the supplier/service provider	For the customer
1. Opportunities to raise prices above the market price.	1. Decreasing costs of maintaining the relationship with the supplier.
2. Decreasing production costs	2. No search or start-up costs of finding new supplier/service provider.

Source: Grönroos, C., Facing the challenge of service competition: the economies of service. In Kunst, P. & Lemmink, J. (eds), *Quality Management in Services*. Maastricht, the Netherlands: Van Gorcum Assen, 1992, p. 139. Reproduced by permission of Van Gorcum, the Netherlands.

sources of goods and services, for example just out of interest or to check that their service supplier is keeping up-to-date with new technology. However, in a well-functioning relationship a trusted supplier or service provider frequently has the opportunity to upgrade its solutions to meet or exceed the standard that competitors are offering.

CUSTOMER PERCEIVED VALUE IN RELATIONSHIPS

Previous chapters discussed the perceived service quality concept and in this chapter customer perceived sacrifices have been analysed in terms of short-term sacrifice (price) and long-term sacrifice (relationship cost). In this and the next section we shall take the discussion one step further and analyse how customers perceive value in a relationship. As service is inherently relational, the value of a service offering will be discussed from a relationship perspective.[11] Such service offerings may include a service or a physical product as its core.

The starting point for understanding value is the observation that value is created and perceived by customers in their everyday activities and processes and in interactions with suppliers or service providers when consuming or making use of services, goods, information, personal contacts, recovery and other elements of ongoing relationships. Value emerges in the customer's processes. Unlike normal management jargon and the traditional view in the management and marketing literature, value is not produced in a factory or in the back office of a service firm.[12] According to the conventional, production–oriented view, value for customers is embedded in the goods or services delivered to customers, and it materializes as value-in-exchange at the time of purchase. However, in reality there is no real value before the customer can make use of a product or a service. Only then value emerges as value-in-use for the customer in the customer's processes.[13] The role of the firm is to support a customer's value creation.[14] The firm provides the customer with resources and service processes, where interactions between the firm and the customer occur. In this way, on top of the customer's creation of value, during direct interactions the firm also co-creates value with its customer.[15] All this makes value a complicated concept to understand and manage. However, it is a concept that cannot be ignored.[16] Here approaches to understanding customer perceived value in relationships will be discussed. Based on these approaches, value–destroying elements in a relationship can be detected and eliminated, value–enhancing elements can be spotted and reinforced, and ways of calculating perceived value can be developed.

First we present a ground model of customer perceived value:

$$(0) \; CPV0 = \frac{What \, (Technical \; quality; \; process) + How \, (Functional \; quality; \; outcome)}{Price + Relationships \; costs \, (Direct + Indirect + Psychological)}$$

The technical quality outcome (what) provided by a firm combined with the functional quality (how), i.e. how the service and relationship process contributes to the support to the customer's processes, are related to the price paid and the additional relationship costs accruing over a given period of time. Sometimes all or parts of the customer perceived value can be calculated in monetary terms, sometimes it is only perceived in some way. In business-to-business relationships monetary value can always, in principle, be calculated, whereas it is mostly, but not always only, perceived by individual consumers and households.

In addition, customer perceived value (CPV) can be described by the following five equations:[17]

$$(1) \ CPV1 = \frac{\text{Episode benefits} + \text{Relationship benefits}}{\text{Episode sacrifice} + \text{Relationship sacrifice}}$$

$$(2) \ CPV2 = \text{Transaction value} + \text{or} - \text{Relationship value}$$

$$(3) \ CPV3 = \frac{\text{Core solution} + \text{Additional services}}{\text{Price} + \text{Relationship costs}}$$

$$(4) \ CPV4 = \text{Core value} + \text{or} - \text{Additional value}$$

$$(5) \ CPV5 = \frac{\text{Long-term revenue-generation support}}{\text{Price} + \text{Relationship costs}}$$

The five equations above describe the same value concept as the general model CPV0 from varying angles. By taking them all into account, one finds a deeper perception of how customers perceive value, which factors contribute to this value, and how value can be managed.

The first equation (CPV1) demonstrates that value is created by elements in singular episodes or service encounters as well as by perceptions of the relationship itself. This means that inherently value-creating elements exist in a relationship. Such *relationship benefits* may be a feeling of trust in a supplier or service provider, or social and technological bonds that have been established between the parties. The level of such benefits can, of course, be high or low, or somewhere in between, and may vary over time. The point is that such relationship benefits are perceived as true value-creating benefits and not as feelings. In a similar way, *relationship sacrifice* exists in an ongoing relationship. The customer realizes that some sacrifices are related to a given relationship. For example, being the customer of a certain bank may yield a lower rate of interest on deposits, but the customer may accept this because he trusts the bank and likes the personal attention paid to him (relationship benefits).

Every episode, service encounter or purchase of a physical product produces a benefit (*episode benefit*), and requires a sacrifice (*episode sacrifice*), normally in the form of a price to pay. However, the important thing here is that the value of one service encounter cannot be judged solely on the benefit and sacrifice related to that episode. The benefits and sacrifice involved in the whole relationship also contribute to the total perceived customer value.

The second equation (CPV2) illustrates the same thing as the previous one. The episode benefits and sacrifices constitute a value emerging from the transaction of the core solution – a physical product or a core service – whereas the relationship benefits and sacrifices constitute the value that emerges from the existence of the relationship itself. Hence, the total perceived value has a transaction value component and a relationship value component.

The third equation (CPV3) takes a different approach. Benefits for a customer are divided into two parts, the benefit of a *core solution* and of *additional services*. The core solution (a financial transaction, a production machine, or transportation from one place to another) is perceived on a per episode level. In quality terms, the core solution creates the perception of the outcome-related *technical quality* or *what* dimension. Additional services may be related to the episode, such as personal attention, deliveries or meals served during transportation. They may also be part of the continued relationship, such as information support, social calls, or recovery of quality problems or other types of mistakes. In quality terms, such additional services are perceived as the process-related *functional quality* or *how* dimension.

The denominator is divided into a *price* component, which is perceived in the short term, and a *relationship cost* component, which emerges over time as the relationship develops. The sum of price, including discounts and terms of payment, and relationship costs constitutes the total long-term costs or sacrifice in the relationship, and thus equals the sum of episode and relationship sacrifice (see CPV1).

Customer-perceived value can, of course, be improved by adding benefits; that is, by increasing the nominator of the equation. By providing a better core solution or new additional service, such as consulting services, a firm can improve its value perception in an ongoing customer relationship.[18] However, it is equally important, and sometimes more important, to look at the denominator of the equation (CPV3). By decreasing the sacrifice perceived by a customer, the perceived value also improves.[19] The interesting aspect of decreasing sacrifice is not related to the price component, which should not be lowered, but to the relationship cost component of the equation. By making it easier and more cost-effective for a customer to be involved with a supplier or service provider, it can also create a positive effect on customer perceived value. This kind of effect is often perceived in a favourable way by customers. In the next section we discuss this issue further in the context of the fourth customer-perceived value equation (CPV4).

The fifth equation (CPV5) is actually the same as the third one (CPV3). It indicates the economic effect of the total offering (core solution plus additional services), which should be calculated as the net present value of the *total revenue-generating support* over time attributable to a solution divided by the long-term sacrifice to get this revenue-generation support. From a business point of view this is the most important calculation of value for the customer. However, this requires that the level of revenues can be assessed or at least estimated over a relevant period of time, and that both direct and indirect relationship costs over the same period of time can be calculated at least in an approximate manner.

VALUE AND THE MANAGEMENT OF VALUE DESTROYERS

The fourth equation (CPV4) describing customer perceived value takes yet another approach to the phenomenon. Here value is divided into a *core value* part and an *additional value* part. The core value means the benefits of a core solution compared with the price paid for that solution. Additional value is created by additional service in the relationship compared with the relationship costs that occur over time.

The interesting thing to observe is the fact that the additional value component can be both positive and negative. (Compare the relationship value component in CPV2.) If it is positive, for example because of quick delivery, attentive and supportive service employees or smoothly handled service recovery, it contributes favourably to total perceived value. However, if additional service causes unnecessary or unexpected relationship costs, the effect of the added value component is negative. Thus it is not an added value, but a negative value-eroding component.

Negative additional value is created by complicated systems, non-user-friendly technology, unfriendly or unskilful employees, late deliveries, incorrect invoices, badly handled complaints, delayed maintenance of equipment, complicated equipment documentation, long queues to be served, etc. If such contacts and processes in the customer relationships are not *managed as service* but as administrative routines, or are focused on as internal efficiency only, their effect on customer-perceived value is normally destructive. Even an excellent core value is quickly destroyed by late deliveries, lack of proper support and delayed maintenance, or unfriendly and untrustworthy personnel and a lack of interest in service recovery. Elements in customer relationships – additional services in CPV3 – which are not managed as services for the customers, but as administrative routines or in some other customer-aversive fashion, may easily become *value destroyers*. Because they create problems, a bad impression and unnecessary extra costs for customers, they decrease the value of the core solution (core value).

'Adding value' has been a buzzword in management for a long time. However, firms seem to have problems in realizing which services are really valuable for customers and add to their perceived value, i.e. create *additional value*. 'Added value' is almost always treated as something extra or new that is created for customers.[20] However, adding new services to a relationship which *already* includes value destroyers does not make much sense, because these value destroyers spoil the core value of the solution. *A much more effective way of adding value for customers is to improve what is already done for them, instead of creating something new.* By turning customer contacts and processes which are treated as administrative routines, and therefore perhaps create unnecessary and unexpected relationship costs, into services for customers, *by activating hidden services*, relationship costs for the customers are eliminated or at least minimized. At the same time the quality of these customer contacts increases. The additional value component in CPV4 becomes positive and starts to contribute favourably to total customer perceived value.

Detecting processes and customer contacts in relationships which make the value of the core solution (core value) deteriorate and taking corrective action are essential management tasks. In this way customer-perceived value is improved and the customer relationship will be strengthened. When value destroyers have been removed, if necessary, new value-adding goods or services can be included. However, at that point such extras will probably not be needed any more. Hence, *the trick is not to do new things for customers, primarily, but to improve what already exists in the customer relationship.*

Managers should define value-creating elements in their customer relationships and, based on the customer perceived value equations discussed in this section, develop models that in monetary terms represent the worth of the supplier's or service provider's offerings to the customers.[21] Without such models it may be difficult, or even impossible, to demonstrate to customers the value of a total service offering and how it develops over time.

QUANTIFYING THE VALUE OF A TOTAL SERVICE OFFERING

In order to quantify the value of a total service offering, the various features that distinguish a given offering from an existing one or from competing alternatives have to be explicitly demonstrated. Such *offering features* can be related to goods components, service components, or other components in the customer relationship, such as hidden services like complaints handling and invoicing. As is illustrated in Figure 6.7, both revenue and cost benefits as well as customer investments of each feature must be calculated for a relevant number of time periods (years, months or whatever is most appropriate).

Revenue benefits are sales increases that can be expected to be achieved if a customer chooses the offering. *Cost benefits* are cost savings that follow from the choice of the given offering. Both savings of *direct* and *indirect relationship costs* ought to be included and calculated. Customer *investments* are additional costs that customers have to accept in order to be able to use the offering. Such investments are normally direct relationship costs. Cost benefits are direct relationship costs that can be saved continuously over the whole relationship, whereas customer investments are extra direct costs that normally occur only at the start of the relationship. As the figure demonstrates, revenue benefits, cost benefits and customer investments have to be calculated for each offering feature for each time period. These figures can be calculated based on historical data, sales and revenue forecasts, and calculated anticipated cost effects of the features included. The total offering benefits for each period can be

OFFERING FEATURES		YEAR				
		1	2	3	4	... n
Feature 1:	Revenue benefit Cost benefit Investment					
Feature 1:	Revenue benefit Cost benefit Investment					
Feature 1:	Revenue benefit Cost benefit Investment					
Feature 1:	Revenue benefit Cost benefit Investment					
Total offering benefits						

FIGURE 6.7
Value quantification of benefits of a total service offering.

derived, and the *net present value* (NPV) of these total benefits over the whole time span can be calculated using an appropriate interest rate. The total offering benefits and their NPV offer a strong argument in planned marketing communication, development of offers and sales negotiations.

Figure 6.8 shows an example of the quantification of the value of a component in 'Salute's Salvation', a manufacturing process over a six-year time period, following the technological upgrading of a previous component ('Salute's Traditional') where a competitor is offering a similar solution at a considerably lower price. The values in the figure represent changes from using the old technology.

Three major offering features of 'Salute's Salvation' representing value-creating improvements are included. Two features are related to the manufacturing process of the customer – Goods feature 1: Multi-use process component and Service feature 1: Improved maintenance reliability.

One feature of the offering is related to changes in invoicing routines made by the supplier to make the previously highly internally-focused invoicing procedure a customer-centric service – Service feature 2: Monthly invoices specified by customer requirements.

The upgraded technology used in 'Salute's Salvation' (Goods feature 1) makes it possible for the customer to manufacture several grades of its product without changing the component (the *multi-use feature*). This means that downtime decreases substantially, which can be forecasted to result in additional annual sales and revenues of 30 (annual *revenue benefit* in a currency and magnitude of the reader's choice) over the six-year period (or any other relevant time span and scale). The upgraded technology also decreases costs for changing the component whenever a new product grade is manufactured in the process (thus diminishing *direct relationship costs*). The estimated annual cost savings, based on previous records, are 20 (annual *cost benefit*). The new technology requires substantial new

OFFERING FEATURES		YEAR					
		1	2	3	4	5	6
Goods features	Revenue benefit	30	30	30	30	30	30
1. Multi-use process component	Cost benefit	20	20	20	20	20	20
	Investment	−40	−10	0	0	0	0
Service features	Revenue benefit	20	20	20	20	20	20
1. Improved maintenance reliability	Cost benefit	15	15	15	15	15	15
	Investment	−25	−10	0	0	0	0
2. Monthly customer-specified invoices	Revenue benefit	0	0	0	0	0	0
	Cost benefit	5	5	5	5	5	5
	Investment	0	0	0	0	0	0
Total offering benefits		25	70	90	90	90	90

FIGURE 6.8

Calculation of relationship benefits of a total service offering including goods, services and other components.

skills among the employees involved in the process (additional *direct relationship costs*). Therefore, initial training costs have to be taken into account: 40 during year 1, 10 during year 2 and 0 during the following four years (annual *customer investments*).

The new technology also adds *improved maintenance reliability* to 'Salute's Salvation' (Service feature 1). The component requires substantially less maintenance, and the customer can take over follow-up maintenance. First of all, this means that even less downtime will occur, which will lead to additional annual sales and revenues of 20 (annual *revenue benefit*). Furthermore, improved maintenance reliability means lower maintenance costs (diminishing *relationship costs* including both a *direct* and an *indirect* portion), calculated to an annual amount of 15 (annual *cost benefit*). However, the customer will have to invest initially in employee training so that they learn how to handle maintenance-related tasks. These sums are calculated as 25 during year 1, 10 during year 2 and 0 thereafter, because newly hired employees are expected to be trained on the job by more experienced colleagues.

Because the relationship with this customer and others includes the regular shipment of materials in order to strengthen the relationship with its customers, the supplier has at the same time developed a new invoicing system, where the invoices are specified according to customer requirements. In addition, instead of sending an invoice for every shipment, which for larger customers may have meant several invoices per month, customers are now invoiced monthly only (Service feature 2: Monthly invoices specified by customer requirements). This is calculated to decrease the customers' cost of handling documents (annual *direct relationship cost*) by 5 every year.

When the revenue and cost benefits are added up and the customer investments subtracted, the total offering benefits for each year can be assessed. In this example they are 25, 70, 90, 90, 90 and 90 for the six years studied. Using the customer's normally applied interest rate, the NPV of the total benefits of the three new and distinguishing offering benefits can be calculated.

When this NPV is compared with a traditional solution and with the price savings offered by a competitor, the value of improved goods and service features can be put into perspective. A competing offering that does not offer these benefits will have to be priced considerably lower. Another consequence of a value quantification of a total service offering like the one illustrated here is that one can *put a price on services*. If the total benefits for the customer can be calculated in this way, it is possible to argue for the costs of the improved service that enables the customer to enjoy these benefits. Then a price increase which splits the total savings potential between the supplier and the customer may make sense.

CUSTOMER RELATIONSHIP PROFITABILITY

Offering good customer perceived value (as value-in-use) is critical, because good value will have a positive impact on customer loyalty, which in turn – through lower relationship costs and premium pricing opportunities – improves a customer's contribution to the firm's profit. However, value is, of course, not the only factor influencing profit. In the following sections a model of customer relationship profitability will be discussed, in order to help managers understand the mechanisms that make a customer profitable for a firm.

Analysing the profitability and profit contribution of customers and customer relationships is a problematic task in most firms, for individuals as well as for customer groups. Accounting systems are normally based on products, not customers. For a manufacturer of physical goods, it is possible to calculate revenues, costs, profits and even profitability per product and product group. In a service firm it is much more difficult to do the same, because of the difficulty of measuring and quantifying one unit of service. For both manufacturers and service firms it is almost impossible to find out information about revenues, costs, profits and profitability of customers or customer bases. Separate analysis almost always has to be done, and even then the information registered by the accounting system may not be enough.[22] The tradition of registering cash flow, revenue and cost per product comes from the industrial era, when production was the major bottleneck. In the post-industrial era where customers, and employees, are the bottleneck, customer profitability and registration of cash flows, revenues and costs per customer is more important for strategic as well as tactical management.

Figure 6.9 illustrates a *customer relationship profitability* model.[23] This model helps managers to see the mechanisms that make customers more or less profitable. A quick glance at the model demonstrates that the road from *customer perceived value* to customer profitability includes a considerable number of factors, which are areas that have to be planned, managed and monitored if a positive contribution to profit is to be expected. The model is conceptual, and should help managers realize the complicated mechanisms that influence customer profitability. Some of the factors, such as perceived sacrifice, some customer–firm bonds, patronage concentration, relationship length, relationship revenue and relationship cost can be measured in an objective manner using metric scales. Other factors, such as perceived quality and value, satisfaction, commitment, some customer–firm bonds and relationship strength can only be measured using attitudinal scales and/or qualitative data. The objective here is not, however, to develop a calculation model, but to show the reader what to take into consideration and *how to think*.

The *customer relationship profitability* model includes four links as well as factors that influence these links. The four links are:

1. From customer perceived value to customer satisfaction.
2. From customer satisfaction to relationship strength.

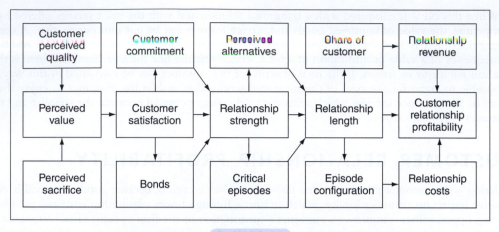

FIGURE 6.9

**The customer relationship profitability model: the mechanisms
behind profitable customers.**
Source: Storbacka, K., Strandvik, T. & Grönroos, C., Managing customer relationship for
profit: the dynamics of relationship quality. *International Journal of Service Industry
Management*, **5**(5); 1994: p. 23. Reproduced by permission of Emerald Insight.

3. From relationship strength to relationship length.

4. From relationship length to customer relationship profitability.

From value to satisfaction. As discussed earlier in this chapter, the total service offering includes core solutions and additional services. How the *quality* of this offering is perceived compared with the *perceived sacrifice* of customers, determines customers' perceptions of the value of this offering and, in ongoing relationships, the value of the relationship. Customers are satisfied with perceived quality provided that the sacrifice involved – price and relationship costs – is not too high. Hence, perceived value determines customer satisfaction.

Customer satisfaction has an effect on two factors that have an impact on the next link in the model. Satisfied customers may become *committed* to the supplier or service provider, because they trust the other party or are pleased with the level of sacrifice involved in the relationship. Customer satisfaction also contributes to the formation of *bonds* between the two parties. Bonds (which can be social, cultural, ideological, psychological, knowledge-based, technological, geographical, time-related, legal or economic) (see the discussion of bonds in Chapter 4) tie customers to the supplier or service provider, because they make it easier, more comfortable or more economical for the customer to continue to patronize the same firm.

From satisfaction to relationship strength. The next link shows how satisfaction has a favourable effect on the strength of a relationship. Strong relationships can make customers loyal. Customer satisfaction has a direct impact on *relationship strength*. However, the effect also applies to *customer commitments* and *bonds* between the two parties. The more committed a customer is to a firm and the more bonds that exist between them, the stronger the relationship will be. The model does not say anything about what degree of satisfaction and commitment is required to create relationships of a certain strength, since this varies from case to case. It is important to bear in mind that the degree of satisfaction and commitment and perceived bonds often may have to be quite high to have a definite impact on relationship strength. For example, it seems that customers who claim that they are satisfied with a solution are not always loyal. The percentage of customers who make repeat purchases can be as low as 30% or even lower. However, customers who claim that they are *very* satisfied with a solution seem to have a much stronger relationship with the seller. The repurchase percentage may increase to 80% or above.

Strong relationships influence the number of *alternative solutions* that a customer considers. A high relationship strength can be expected to make the customer think less of alternatives to the existing relationship, and vice versa. In addition, a strong relationship will probably include fewer *critical* service encounters or *episodes* (unfavourable incidents). First, customers are satisfied with and feel committed to the relationship, because no or only a few unfavourable incidents have occurred. Second, a strong relationship can be expected to make critical episodes look less unfavourable, provided that such incidents do not occur too often.

From relationship strength to relationship length. In the third link, relationship strength has direct and indirect effects on the *length of a relationship*. The stronger the relationship, the longer it will last. Customers do not see incentives to stop doing business with the same supplier or service provider. At the same time, a strong relationship makes customers perceive that *fewer alternatives exist*, and this lack of alternatives has a positive effect on the length of a relationship. Also, a lack of perceived *critical episodes* has a similar influence.

Longer relationships can be expected to have a favourable effect on two factors, which are critical for customers' contribution to profit. In continuing relationships, where customers are satisfied and feel strong ties to the other party, they can be expected to purchase more from this firm. A *patronage concentration* effect thus occurs. The supplier or service provider gets a 'larger share of the customer's wallet'. In ongoing relationships both parties also learn how to adjust to each other and how to collaborate so that the customer uses the offering in a more effective and personalized way. Fewer mistakes are made, so less recovery is needed. A more cost-efficient *episode configuration* should develop. Moreover, when there is a trusting enduring relationship, the firm can more easily suggest new ways of producing and using a service, moving to, for example, less expensive Internet-based contacts for information and payments. Hence, the service can be produced in a way that ties up less expensive resources without a perceived negative effect on quality and value.

From relationship length to relationship profitability. The final link shows how the length of a relationship influences the profitability of customer relationships. The length of a relationship by itself has a *positive effect on profit*, because costs of customer acquisition can be minimized and in many cases opportunities exist for premium pricing. A higher patronage concentration has a *positive effect* on the *revenue streams* in the relationship with any given customer. In addition, a more cost-efficient episode configuration, where unnecessary elements in relationships, such as answering customer questions and recovering service failures, can be avoided, and less expensive ways of performing a service can be introduced and accepted by customers, has a positive effect on *relationship costs*.

Hence, a stronger relationship can be expected to directly influence customer relationship profitability, and does this indirectly through improved revenue streams, higher relationship revenue, and more cost-efficient service processes and lower relationship costs.

If all favourable effects implied by the model occur, higher perceived service quality compared with customer sacrifice should lead to improved profitability in customer relationships. However, the links are not totally clear-cut; factors external to the model may influence some of the links or factors in an unexpected manner. A competitor who introduces a solution, for example, based on new technology, or who aggressively promotes a low price may change the links between the factors in the model. For example, a new much lower price option may make customers perceive episodes in existing relationships in a negative sense, because price may suddenly have become an issue. Or new technology offered by a competitor may untie a technology-based bond. In both cases, a new alternative may suddenly be considered realistic.

Managers must always follow up customer relationships, on individual relationship levels where possible, to monitor how the mechanisms in the model function. What can be measured using hard data should be measured. This requires that accounting systems are adjusted so that data on costs and revenues are available at a customer- or customer-base level. Factors that can be measured only by attitudinal measurement instruments or in other qualitative ways should also be monitored.

RECIPROCAL RETURN ON RELATIONSHIP

Relationship marketing is based on the idea that two (or several) actors, in the simplest case a supplier or service provider and its customer, are involved in a business engagement, where both parties should benefit from the relationship. A win–win situation should develop. It is, however, difficult to calculate the value of such a win–win situation. To understand this value the *return on relationship* (ROR) concept has been introduced. Relationships are reciprocal business engagements, and therefore, ROR should also be defined as a reciprocal concept. Grönroos and Helle define *reciprocal ROR* as follows:[24]

Reciprocal return on relationship (ROR_R) is the long-term net financial outcome emerging for all parties resulting from the establishment and mutual maintenance of a relational business engagement.

Reciprocal return on relationship is an outcome of a mutual reciprocal process, and it can be calculated as a joint return on the relationship level as well as separately for the relationship parties. In Figure 6.10 the underpinning model for mutual value creation is illustrated.[25] *Mutual value creation* includes activities by the supplier and customer respectively with the common goal of creating value for themselves out of their business engagement. Some of these activities are performed by the parties without direct interactions with each other (activities in the *provider* and *customer spheres*; see Chapter 1 and Figure 1.5 about value spheres). Some activities are co-created in direct interactions between the supplier and customer (activities in the *joint sphere*; see Chapter 1 and Figure 1.5).

The model and corresponding calculations are easier to comprehend in a business-to-business context, but in principle the situation is the same in business-to-consumer relationships. As demonstrated by the figure, value emerges for both parties (and in a network, for several parties) based on the business configuration the parties agree upon and implement.

In the centre of the figure the provider's and the customer's everyday processes required to run their businesses are schematically illustrated. Which processes are central to a customer's business and commercial process is, of course dependent on the context. As an example, in Figure 6.10 the following customer processes are considered central: *order-making, warehousing, production* (as an example of any type of core customer process to be supported)*, maintenance, information need, problem solving, and cost control.* Because these processes are central to the customer's business and commercial outcome, the supplier's corresponding provider processes, needed to support these customer's processes successfully, are *order taking, deliveries, product* (as the core of the offering)*, maintenance, call centre, service recovery, and invoicing system.*

After having assessed which the central processes on both sides are, the supplier and customer should engage in a process of *innovating and aligning their processes, resources and competencies* relating to these processes in order to find an optimal match between them. Because the provider and customer strive to match how they practise their processes, this is called *practice matching*.[26] As a result of the practice matching process the two parties adopt their processes to fit the other party's corresponding

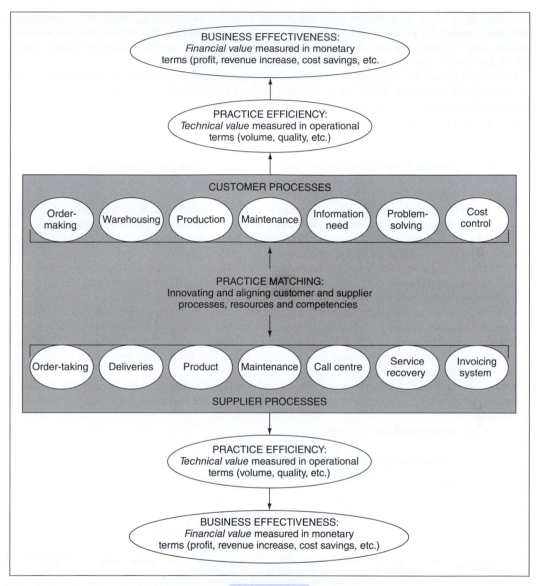

FIGURE 6.10

The mutual value creation model.

Source: Adapted from Grönroos, C. & Helle, P., Return on relationships: conceptual understanding and measurement of mutual gains from relational business engagements. *Journal of Business & Industrial Marketing*, **27**(5); 2012: 348. Reproduced by permission of Emerald Insight.

processes. Who adopts its processes more depends on a number of factors: e.g. the power–dependence situation between the provider and customer, the strategies of the respective parties, and the perceived need to adopt. In the ideal case, both the provider and the customer adopt to reach an optimal match, which has the best possible effect on future revenues and costs for both.

In the next phase, the implications of the matched processes for the customer's and firm's processes are assessed and calculated. The improved *practice efficiency* following the use of the renewed processes is calculated as a *technical value effect*. The technical value improvement can normally be measured in volumes (e.g. production volume per time unit; amount of scrap), quality (e.g. the technical quality of a production output), time (the standstill time caused by maintenance need or problem recovery), or other units.

Finally, the *business effectiveness* of the new way of maintaining the relationship should be calculated *in monetary terms*, which gives decision-makers a *financial value effect* of the new way of operating in the relationship measured. This means that the changes in the technical value due to the practice matching process are transformed into monetary revenue effects and cost effects. Revenue effects following from, for example, growth or premium pricing opportunities can only be projected, whereas real cost effects, for example cost savings or required additional costs in the various processes, can be calculated using real data, for example by applying activity-based costing (ABC).

In addition to the monetary value effects, there are also *value perceptions* which should often be considered. The parties may feel more comfortable with doing business with each other, find it easier to collaborate, and a growing level of trust and commitment may develop.

It is not self-evident that such practice matching processes and corresponding efficiency and effectiveness calculations can be undertaken. It requires a certain amount of trust between the parties to reveal their processes and, to make the monetary calculations, to open their books and show their cost and revenue drivers, and business models. However, when firms enter into such a process, they normally find it worthwhile.

Next, the way of calculating *reciprocal return on relationship* (ROR$_R$) is described.[27] The process is illustrated in Figure 6.11, and the corresponding calculations are shown in the case study at the end of this section.

The whole process includes six steps:

1. Adopting a service perspective.

2. Practice matching.

3. Joint productivity gain calculation.

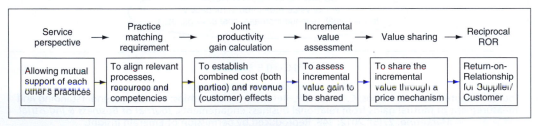

FIGURE 6.11

The reciprocal return-on-relationship assessment process.

Source: Adapted from Grönroos, C. & Helle, P., Return on relationships: conceptual understanding and measurement of mutual gains from relational business engagements. *Journal of Business & Industrial Marketing*, **27**(5); 2012: 350. Reproduced by permission of Emerald Insight.

4. Incremental value assessment.

5. Value sharing.

6. Calculating the reciprocal and separate return on relationship (ROR_R, ROR_P, ROR_C).

The *first* step for the supplier, or any service provider, is to strategically adopt a *service perspective* (service logic) in the management of the relationship, and set out to develop an offering which aims to support the customer's processes (practice efficiency) and, in the end, the customer's commercial and business goals (business effectiveness) in a value creating way. Without this service intention to support the other party's processes it will be difficult to get the process going.

The *second* step is to fulfil the *practice matching requirement* where the two parties go through the practice matching process and create appropriate process, resource and competence adjustment. Then cost effects for both the customer and the provider and projected revenue effects for the customer, following the new way of operating the relationship based on the practice matching, are calculated. The revenue effect for the provider is taken into account later, through a pricing mechanism, in the value sharing phase (the fifth phase).

The *third* step is to calculate the *joint productivity gain* of the renewal of the processes on both sides and the related new way of managing and operating the relationship. Firms in a relational business engagement which set out to develop the relationship together can often be expected to gain more than if the parties act independently.[28] 'Joint productivity' as an idea and concept was introduced and defined by Pekka Helle.[29] This concept is based on the service productivity concept (see Chapter 7), and means that instead of calculating productivity and productivity changes for providers and customers separately, the effects on revenues and costs which constitute productivity are pooled and calculated jointly. It turns out that this triggers new ways of operating for the two parties in a business relationship and enables new pricing models. As a consequence, the return on the relationship for both parties can improve even dramatically, as shown later in this chapter in the case study involving reciprocal return on relationship calculations.

The *fourth* step in the model is to assess the *incremental value* emerging from the joint productivity gain calculation. This means that one monetary value of the new proposed way of doing business is calculated by pooling the cost and revenue effects for the parties calculated in the previous phase (cost effects for both parties; revenue effect for the customer). This is the increase of the value of the relationship as such, without splitting it between the parties involved. It reflects the total value increase following the new way of managing and operating the relationship. In practice, this and the previous phase are intertwined.

The *fifth* step is the *value sharing* phase, where the incremental value calculated in the previous step is shared. In practice this involves *price negotiations* between the parties, where it is decided how the incremental value is shared between the provider and the customer. For example, a higher price means that the provider gets a larger share of the incremental value gain.

In the *sixth* and final step the return on relationship is calculated as a ROR_C for the customer and a ROR_P for the provider, and as a reciprocal ROR_R for the relationship as such:

$$ROR_{Relationship} = \frac{\text{Incremental value gain}}{\text{Provider's} + \text{Customer's investments in the relationship}}$$

$$ROR_{Provider} = \frac{\text{Provider's part of the incremental value gain}}{\text{Provider's investment in the relationship}}$$

$$ROR_{Customer} = \frac{\text{Customer's part of the incremental value gain}}{\text{Customer's investment in the relationship}}$$

In the case illustration which concludes this section, the six-step procedure and corresponding calculations will be illustrated.

Bigger firms engaged in close and ongoing relationships can probably benefit more than others from joint business development as suggested here. Moreover, firms which become intertwined with their customers in terms of roles, activities and perceived risks probably also benefit more. Also, firms that are innovative in their customer relationships and strive to determine their own markets may also find this approach beneficial. Industry innovators that do not restrict their business performance to existing offering constellations and market definitions will probably also find this kind of reciprocal relationship approach useful. Dynamic and uncertain business environments may also be supportive. On the other hand, if firms perceive a risk of opportunistic behaviour by the other party in a relationship, the willingness to engage in this type of business may decrease.

CASE STUDY

THE INDUSTRIAL DYAD CASE: RECIPROCAL RETURN ON RELATIONSHIP CALCULATION

A provider of technology-based equipment to an environmental control customer, with which it had been doing business together for some time already, had suggested a joint development of the business performance with an aim of supporting the customer's business more effectively (Step 1 in Figure 6.11: a service approach). This proposal was accepted, and the provider and customer set out to develop a new, more collaborative business process.

Step 2 (practice matching). The provider and the customer defined the customer's key everyday processes and the provider's corresponding processes, and looked at the firms' respective business models and cost drivers. After a practice matching analysis, changes in the way some of the key processes were conducted were agreed upon. Then cost savings or increases for the respective parties and potential revenue gains for the customer were calculated. For calculations, a three-year time frame was considered appropriate, and the corresponding net present values (NPV) of the cost and revenue effects were calculated:

Customer effects

The net effects of the customer's changes of processes were calculated as follows: in some processes an investment of 120 000 the first year was required, whereas the changed support by the provider combined with other actions lead to a total cost saving of 2 700 000 (NPV; three-year time frame), which amounts to a total of 2 580 000 in net costs savings (out of which the cost increase item of 120 000 is an additional investment in the relationship):

$$\Delta \text{Customer's Costs} = +120\,000 - 2\,700\,000 = -2\,580\,000 \text{ (net cost savings)}$$

The net present value of projected additional revenues was calculated to 975 000 (NPV over three years):

$$\Delta\text{Customer's Revenues} = +975\,000 \text{ (revenue increase)}$$

Provider effects

The net effects of required R&D efforts and development of some processes were calculated to an increase of 585 000 (NPV over three years):

$$\Delta\text{Provider's Costs} = +585\,000 \text{ (cost increase)}$$

Steps 3 and 4 (Joint Productivity Gain Calculation and Incremental Value Assessment): the next two phases are normally intertwined, although theoretically they are separate processes. The changes in costs for the customer and provider and revenues for the customer (the provider's revenue change is taken into account through price negotiations in Step 5) are put together, such that the jointly achievable productivity gain and incremental value gain to share are calculated as:

Incremental Value Gain (to be shared in Step 5)

$$= \Delta\text{Customer's Revenues} - \Delta\text{Customer's Costs} - \Delta\text{Provider's Costs}$$

$$= +975\,000 - (-2\,580\,000) - (+585\,000) = 2\,970\,000$$

Hence, the practice matching analysis and corresponding adjustments of the provider's and customer's processes are expected to generate a joint productivity gain which corresponds to a joint value increase (incremental value gain) of 2 970 000 calculated as NPV over a three-year time frame. The question that now arises is how this gain should be shared between the relationship parties.

Step 5 (Value Sharing): the jointly created incremental value is shared through a price mechanism. The provider and customer have to negotiate how large a part of this value gain the provider can keep in the form of price premium. In this case the parties decided that the incremental value be shared in a 30/70 proportion, such that the provider gets 30% of the incremental value gained through the joint productivity efforts following the practice matching process. The remaining part, 70%, benefits the customer:

Customer Value Creation $= 0.70 \times$ Incremental Value Gain $= 0.70 \times 2\,970\,000 = 2\,079\,000$

Provider Value Capture $= 0.30 \times$ Incremental Value Gain $= 0.30 \times 2\,970\,000 = 891\,000$

Step 6 (Calculation of Reciprocal and Seperate Returns on Relationship): The development starting with the practice matching can be seen as a joint investment in this relational business engagement. The additional costs paid by the parties (120 000 by the customer and 585 000 by the provider, respectively) represent the monetary value of the investment. The value created for the customer and captured by the provider, following the value sharing negotiation, represent the outcomes of the investment in the relationships. Consequently, the reciprocal return on this relationship investment (ROR_R) can be calculated in the following way:

Reciprocal Return on Relationship ROR_R

$$= \frac{\text{Customer Value Creation} + \text{Provider Value Capture} (= \text{Incremental Value Gain})}{\text{Costs paid by Customer and Provider}} \times 100$$

$$= \frac{2\,079\,000 + 891\,000}{120\,000 + 585\,000} \times 100 = \frac{2\,970\,000}{705\,000} \times 100 = 421\%$$

Return on Relationship for the Customer ROR_C

$$= \frac{\text{Customer Value Creation} (= 0.70 \times \text{Incremental Value Gain})}{\text{Costs paid by Customer}} \times 100$$

$$= \frac{0.70 \times 2\,970\,000}{120\,000} \times 100 = \frac{2\,079\,000}{120\,000} \times 100 = 1730\%$$

Return on Relationship for the Provider ROR_P

$$= \frac{\text{Provider Value Capture} (= 0.30 \times \text{Incremental Value Gain})}{\text{Costs paid by Provider}} \times 100$$

$$= \frac{0.30 \times 2\,970\,000}{585\,000} \times 100 = \frac{891\,000}{585\,000} \times 100 = 152\%$$

The return of the joint investment in the business relationship ROR_R is expected to be 421%, and when the business partners take their respective additional costs paid into account, the return of their investments are expected to amount to 1730% for the customer and 152% for the provider. Without taking the service perspective approach and engaging in joint practice matching with the customer, the provider could hardly have been expected to help the customer to such a business outcome. And the provider could not have expected such a good value capture opportunity.

Source: Helle, P, Re-conceptualizing value creation: from industrial business logic to service business logic. *Working Paper 554*. Hanken School of Economics, Finland, Helsinki, 2011, and Grönroos, C. & Helle, P., Return on relationships: conceptual understanding and measurement of mutual gains from relational business engagements. *Journal of Business & Industrial Marketing*, **27**(5); 2012: 344–359, where formulas and complete calculations can be found.

CUSTOMER EQUITY MANAGEMENT

Rust *et al.*[30] have introduced a model for the management of customer profitability, which can be labelled a *customer equity management* model. They define *customer equity* as 'the total of the discounted lifetime values over all the firm's customers'.[31] This more or less equals the profitability of a firm's customer base. The model has three components. Depending on the effect on customers' purchasing and consumption behaviour of each of these components, the customers decide to give more or less of their business to the firm, and thus form a more or less profitable customer base for the firm. The three components are:[32]

1. *Value equity*. The end customer's perception of value from the product.
2. *Brand equity*. The end customer's emotional and subjective assessment about the value of the brand.
3. *Retention equity*. The end customer's repeat purchase intention and loyalty towards the supplier.

According to this model, value for customers is derived from two sources – the product (a good or a service) itself and the perception of the brand. If the product functions well for the customer, he can capture a basic value from the use of the product (value equity). If he considers the product to own additional emotionally and subjectively felt qualities caused by the brand image of this product, this provides additional value support (brand equity). Both these components make the customer buy from the supplier of this product and thus generate cash flow for the firm. In addition, if the customer has a willingness to stay loyal to the firm and continue buying this product from it, the firm gets additional cash flow over time (retention equity).[33] Rust and his colleagues provide metrics to use for calculation of customer equity, using this three-component model, but when planning how to create a profitable customer base the model also functions as a conceptual support for marketers.

THE VALUE OF CUSTOMERS

Finally, firms should know the long-term value of their individual customers. The lifetime value of customers should be calculated. When managers have such information they realize that long-term customer relationships are valuable assets. It also helps marketers to realize the importance of keeping existing customers.

The calculation of customers' value should be based on information on *customers' current contribution to net profit*, not sales figures.[34] For each customer, or for customer groups, the direct costs of producing an offering, including relationship costs occurring for the seller, are deducted from revenues from this customer. What remains after this deduction, the net profit from a customer, should cover the firm's fixed costs.

A customer's contribution to net profit may vary substantially over the life of the relationship. New customers may be unprofitable or their profit contribution may be low, whereas long-standing customers frequently become more profitable as the relationship continues. Such considerations have to be taken into account when calculating the long-term profit contribution of customers. Therefore, it is essential that managers gain as much insight as possible into typical customer life cycles.[35]

The *lifetime value* of a customer relationship or, when individual figures cannot be obtained, the lifetime value of a relationship with a given customer group can be calculated as the *net present value of the net profits that can be expected over the years*. This lifetime value shows how important each customer is to a supplier or service provider. If such figures are not calculated, the value of existing customers will not be fully appreciated, and the loss of value that follows from departing customers will not be understood. By calculating the lifetime value of customers, managers obtain information on which customer relationships are critical to the firm, which are contributing less to total profitability, and which are not profitable. However, one should always remember that customers who are not profitable at a given time may become profitable in the future, for example as a result of a different episode configuration, increasing disposable income or changing needs.

CASE STUDY

ANALYSING CUSTOMER PROFITABILITY

Customer-base analyses, in which companies specifically focus on determining profitability distributions, show that certain parallels can be drawn between companies regardless of industry.

Most companies that have conducted customer profitability analyses have been surprised to discover how large a share of their customer base really is unprofitable. It seems to be the rule, rather than the exception, that more than 30% of customers are unprofitable. This uneven distribution of profits and losses between customers of course leads to a number of strategic and operational problems. A central strategic problem is that customers subsidize each other, i.e. cross-subsidization occurs in the customer base. Cross-subsidization makes a company vulnerable to onslaughts by competitors. Competitors usually try to attract the most profitable customer groups, and if only 30% of a company's customers are profitable, for example, the risk exposure is of course enormous.

Management literature often cites the Pareto rule, which claims that 20% of customers account for 80% of profits. This is, however, incorrect: 20% of customers may indeed account for 80% of volume but, with regard to profit, the distribution can be very different. This is because earnings can be negative of course and this leads to a distribution which is often very dramatic.

Source: This illustration was developed by Kaj Storbacka, Vectia Ltd.

CASE STUDY

THE PROFITABILITY PROBLEM OF MAJOR OFFICE MACHINE (MOM) LTD

Tom 'Jungle' Peterson had been with Major Office Machine Ltd (MOM) for four years when he was appointed Executive Vice President of the business unit selling office equipment and other technical equipment to retailers. In addition to the thrill of promotion, Tom was faced with a serious problem as the business unit had been incurring losses of half a million euros annually for several years. His job was to ensure that the unit at least broke even. His predecessors had tried many different restructuring methods but they had all failed. Tom chose to use an alternative method to solve the problem. He decided to start at the customer end and analyse the reasons behind the unprofitable situation.

Tom assembled a team to analyse the situation. The team consisted of an experienced consultant and his assistant, a controller at MOM, and *ad hoc* members from various departments at MOM who were involved in producing different types of customer encounters.

The development process consisted of three phases:

- *The customer profitability analysis phase*. The aim of this phase was to calculate customer profitability and analyse reasons for the losses.

- *The relationship strategy phase*. The aim of this phase was to differentiate the offerings and customer relationship processes on the basis of the data obtained from the analysis in order to ensure a satisfactory profit level.

- *The implementation phase.* MOM was an established company and had been operating for about 20 years. Tom was well aware that implementing the changes he envisioned would demand a considerable amount of work both within the company and with the customers.

1. The Analysis Phase

The business unit had 1201 retailers as customers; some belonged to chains, others were large companies, but a large share of the customer base consisted of relatively small retailers. In total the business unit was making an annual loss of about €0.6 million.

The analysis team carried out a customer profitability analysis in which all revenue and the total cost mass of the business unit were distributed among customers. The distribution of customer profitability in the business unit's customer base is depicted in Figure 6.12 (a so-called Stobachoff curve).[36]

The curve is based on the calculation of the profit for each individual customer. The customers are arranged in order of profitability, so that customer 1 is the most profitable and customer 1201 the least profitable. The profits from each customer are then added together. The curve shows how profit accumulates throughout the customer base.

On the basis of the curve, it was possible for Tom to draw several interesting (and dramatic) conclusions about his customer base:

- As long as the curve rises, profitable customers are added. This makes it possible to determine the number of profitable customers. To Tom's surprise only about 250 out of 1201 (i.e. 20%) were profitable. They accounted for approximately €1.5 million of revenue. These were later called the Protect group.

- Out of the unprofitable customers, two groups emerged. The first group consisted of the next 800 customers, who all seemed to be equally unprofitable since an almost straight line emerged between customers numbered 250 to 1050. Together, these customers created a loss of about €0.75 million. Tom found out in the analysis that these were small sales volume customers. These were later called the Develop group.

- The final 151 customers, who were the most unprofitable, created a loss of over €1 million. These customers were, to Tom's great surprise, very large and highly valued at MOM. He noticed the 'customer profitability paradox': only really large customers can be very profitable or very unprofitable! This group was later called the Change group.

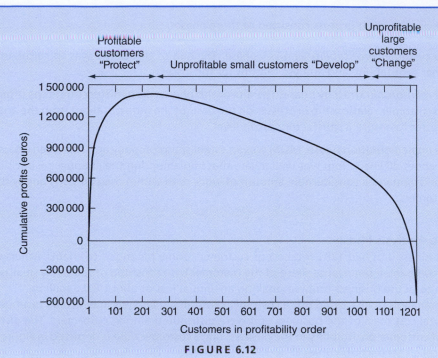

FIGURE 6.12

Case study of MOM: profitability of the customer base (1201 customers).
Source: Storbacka, J.: CRM Customer Relationship Management, Ltd.

Tom concluded that his customer base was especially sensitive to attacks from competitors. The company's existence depended on about 250 profitable customers! Also, there had to be serious problems with the strategy of the business unit since it allowed about 100 customers to be extremely unprofitable.

Finding The Profitability Potentials

It is tempting, based on the Stobachoff curve, to draw straightforward, simple conclusions. It might seem attractive to 'cut' the curve at around customer number 1000. Thus, it would seem to be possible to eliminate the most unprofitable customers. Even if the idea of terminating relationships is part of the relationship marketer's arsenal, a more developed analysis rapidly shows that this is not a simple solution to the profitability problems of a customer base. The termination of customer relationships should never be the main solution to improving customer profitability. The reason for this is obvious. Most costs in most businesses these days are fixed costs. When analysing customer profitability, fixed costs are divided among customers. Even if the most unprofitable customer relationships were terminated, the fixed costs remain, and these, in turn, have to be redistributed to the rest of the customers, leading to the emergence of an identical curve. Terminating customer relationships is thus not an optimal solution.

To work with customer profitability as a calculation exercise is in itself uninteresting. What is interesting is using customer profitability knowledge to identify profitability potentials within the customer base and implement changes which make it possible to benefit from this potential.

The information gathered can be used to conduct simulations of consequences of various changes in the relationships ('what-if' analyses). You can simulate a situation where, for example, you terminate certain relationships and redistribute all costs, raise prices (and assume that some customers will decrease their purchases), invest in marketing and simulate by how much sales have to increase for profitability to reach an acceptable level, etc. These analyses usually show dramatic results. Even small changes in customer purchasing behaviour can have very significant effects if you are able to change the behaviour of a large share of the customer base.

To identify profitability potential, you have to analyse the causes of unprofitability. Companies need to ask themselves what aspect of their operations encourages unprofitable behaviour. In principle there seem to be three causes of unprofitability.

1. *Work*. Most unprofitable customers are unprofitable because the service provider is investing too much in the relationship in proportion to the revenue derived from it. 'Work' includes all activities carried out within the relationship, both for the customer and with the customer. To benefit from the profitability potential, the provider should reduce activities for which it is not compensated. Typical activities that create large costs are all those performed in connection with the logistics process: order lines, deliveries, after-sales service. Customer service work in terms of sales, technical service, help desk and call centre activities also results in costs.

2. *Price*. Pricing is a complex issue, which is partly determined by the competitive situation, but which in surprisingly many cases includes a large component of creativity. Profitability analyses often indicate that really unprofitable customers are unprofitable because of pricing problems. A reason for this may be the fact that relationships with large customers are less symmetrical, i.e. large customers can negotiate prices that are favourable to them. But even in asymmetric relationships, where the provider's power is greater, the pricing system can lead to unprofitability. In such a case it is often a question of discount systems based on sales volumes. In certain cases the price is so low that the customer is no longer profitable. In other cases corrective actions can include other pricing issues such as the pricing of deliveries, after-sales service, interest on delayed payments and additional fees for small deliveries. In general, of all the measures a provider can take to influence customer purchasing behaviour, price is the most powerful. It is therefore important to ensure that pricing leads to the customer behaviour that is desired by the provider. A quick analysis often proves

that companies lack pricing policies with general principles about how price should influence customer behaviour. If a daily newspaper, for example, wants its customers to commit for longer periods, it has to ensure that this is advantageous to the customer from a pricing point of view. In most cases in the newspaper industry, however, it would seem that it is cheapest for the customer to subscribe periodically, taking advantage of the special rates that newspapers offer.

3. *Volume.* Even if volume in itself is not a good indicator of relationship value, it is clear that customers with greater volume are more interesting from the profitability point of view. In most customer bases, all small-volume customers are unprofitable because their volume is not sufficient to cover fixed costs. As a result, many providers have chosen to set volume limits which customers have to reach in order to enter into a relationship with the provider. Alternatively, transaction fees can be imposed in the form of an additional fee, for example, for small deliveries, which ensures that even minor orders can be sufficiently profitable. Choosing one's customers can thus also be a sound strategy.

Profitability potential can be identified on the basis of the analysis carried out in the Stobachoff curve. The grouping of customers has a direct effect on the profitability potential. Profitability potential includes:

- *Protecting profitable customers.* By protecting these customers a company can ensure that relationships become long-term and that it can maintain the positive cash flow from profitable customers. This creates security and a starting point for further business development.

- *Developing small customers.* This development can often involve both an increase in relationship revenue and a decrease in relationship costs. Revenue can be increased by changing the pricing policy or by setting a minimum volume limit for customers. Changing relationship strategies so that the amount of work invested in each relationship decreases can also cut costs.

- *Changing the behaviour of the most unprofitable customers.* These customers, taken individually, are the most interesting since they hold the potential to become very profitable. Individual analyses of the causes behind customer unprofitability can be carried out and individual solutions created for each customer with the aim of changing pricing (to increase relationship revenue) or changing relationship processes to reduce the work done for the customer (and thus cut costs).

All customers have profitability potential and are therefore of interest. Profitable customers are interesting because they constitute the backbone of the provider's cash flow and enable future development of the business. The most unprofitable customers taken individually are interesting since it is possible to rapidly transform them into profitable customers. Customers seldom wish to be unprofitable since they know that this will have adverse effects on the service they receive from the provider. Individual negotiations can therefore lead to dramatic results.

Even small customers are interesting, although perhaps they are more interesting as a group. This is because there are usually many of them and relationships with them are asymmetric. Asymmetry in this context refers to their ability and desire to oppose changes initiated by the provider. Implementing changes in pricing is often easier with small customers. In many of the cases we have observed, the largest profitability potential was found among the small customers.

2. The Relationship Strategy Phase

Existing MOM customer relationships were analysed with regard to their processes and the activities which MOM performed in these processes.

The analysis showed that MOM was serving its small customers 'too well', i.e. both large and small customers received the same level of service. It was also concluded that customers with the same purchasing volume could differ quite significantly in profitability – and this seemed to be true in most volume classes. To find out why customers with the same volume could vary so much regarding profitability, Tom compared the purchasing behaviour of some customers with the help of customer profiles, describing the behaviour behind the profitability figures. Tom focused on issues such as product mix, number of sales calls, number of calls to the call centre, number of orders, number of order lines, number of invoices, credit limit, number of returned products, number of service visits, number of deliveries and after-sales service.

First, Tom discovered that there were differences in the profitability of the different products, i.e. customers who bought products with a better sales margin were naturally more profitable than others. He also noted that some customers enthusiastically used MOM's free services. Service Support, Helpdesk and Customer Service were functions that demanded a lot of time and work and which cost a great deal. Personal contacts also affected profitability. Tom was forced to admit that his games of golf with the CEO of one of their biggest customers, fun as they were, had a negative impact on company profitability.

Tom also realized that certain customers bought products often but in small quantities. They seemed to be waiting for discounts and buying products sold at reduced prices. They often received cash discounts and goods in after-deliveries (additional product deliveries when not all products ordered were shipped at the same time). These customers also returned products more often than others did.

On the basis of this analysis, three alternative relationship strategies emerged: (1) partnerships, (2) contract-dealers and (3) regular customers. The relationship strategies were described in great detail in terms of offerings for respective customers, the processes necessary to produce the offering, and also how work would be organized with different customer types. A script was also created for each relationship strategy.

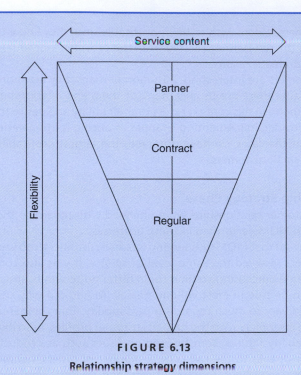

FIGURE 6.13
Relationship strategy dimensions

The relationship strategies differ in two ways (see Figure 6.13):

- Service content, i.e. the degree of service content. That is, all the support that MOM can give to retailers in terms of training, marketing support, alternative invoicing methods, strategic planning, etc. The service content is greatest for partners and smallest for regular customers, with contract-dealers in between.

- Flexibility, i.e. the willingness of MOM to find customer-specific solutions and adapt to retailer processes. The logic here is the same as with the service content. In other words, MOM is willing to make changes to their own processes for partners, whereas they are not interested in creating diverging solutions for regular customers. The regular customers are offered a standardized solution, while partners are offered company-specific solutions. Contract-dealers are offered some level of customization of the service offering.

Involving Employees in Changing Strategies
Change is always difficult to implement, and changes that aim to improve customer profitability are among the most difficult. This is because change often involves negative

aspects from the customer's point of view: prices are raised, delivery terms worsen, less personal service is offered, more self-service is required, etc. For customer contact employees this usually means more complaints from customers and unpleasant customer encounters. As a result, there will be resistance to change from both employees and customers.

It is therefore crucial that the change process is as smooth as possible and that key customer contact people are involved. Employees need to be aware of the profitability data and draw their own conclusions. They have to personally understand the strategic solutions the provider has chosen in order to be able to deal with the complex customer encounters that change often entails.

3. The Implementation Phase

The previous section discussed changing strategies, and ways to make the implementation of change as smooth as possible, for both staff and customers.

Tom decided to involve a large number of the business unit's personnel in the relationship strategy phase. By involving his personnel he hoped that the implementation phase would be made significantly easier.

What was the end result of the work carried out? Tom Peterson is pleased. The company was able to attain several goals at once with the systematic process they created. The business unit no longer incurred losses and personnel had embraced a new way of thinking. There was a much greater awareness of what drives profitability in a company like MOM. Most importantly, MOM had also succeeded in improving customer service as they improved customer profitability.

Unprofitable Customers

It is essential to maintain a positive attitude towards unprofitable customers. Unprofitable customers are not bad customers. Customers are unprofitable because the company's strategies make unprofitable customer behaviour possible. There are no bad customers, only bad strategies. Customer profitability is always a function of customer purchasing behaviour, and behaviour can be influenced in many ways. By changing strategies you can encourage customer behaviour, which in turn can have a positive impact on customer profitability.

Many companies dealing with customer profitability issues have drawn too simplistic conclusions from the results of the analyses. As a result, personnel often end up thinking that unprofitable customers are bad customers. This has direct consequences on how customers are handled, which further aggravates profitability problems. It is therefore important for companies to view unprofitable customers in a positive light. Unprofitable customers often represent the greatest profitability potential of a company.

MOM: Strategic development based on customer base analysis.[37]

Source: Kaj Storbacka, The University of Auckland Business School.

SUMMARY

In this chapter the issue of return on service and relationships between service providers and customers was discussed. Sellers have to be able to calculate the long-term value of their service offerings to make buyers appreciate the value of services. If such calculations are not made, buyers will frequently consider service elements in customer relationships to be of limited or no value for them. The concept of relationship costs occurring for customers, suppliers and service providers was discussed, and it was observed that unnecessary costs are created for both customers and suppliers due to the same reasons; for example, late deliveries, slow service, failures or quality problems. The profitability of customer relationships was then discussed, and a model of customer relationship profitability was described. Metrics for calculating reciprocal return on relationships ROR_R and corresponding case illustration were presented. Finally, a way of illustrating and calculating customers' contribution to profitability was presented.

QUESTIONS FOR DISCUSSION

1. Why are long-term costs more important to consider than price when making purchasing decisions?

2. What are relationship costs? Why do relationship costs occur? How can such costs be avoided?

3. What is meant by 'It is a lack of quality, rather than increasing the quality level, that becomes expensive for a firm'?

4. What is customer perceived value? How can it be calculated?

5. What is reciprocal return on relationship (ROR_R)? How can it be calculated?

6. What is meant by joint productivity and joint productivity gains? What are the benefits of joint productivity gains over separately calculated productivity?

7. Develop a customer value model for your business, or for any given business.

8. How can the value of an improved total service offering be quantified?

9. Which factors influence the formation of customer relationship profitability?

10. What is customer lifetime value? Why is it important to calculate this?

NOTES

1. Pickworth, J.R., Minding the Ps and Qs: linking quality and productivity. *The Cornell Hotel and Restaurant Administration Quarterly*, May, 1987.

2. Crosby, P.B., *Quality is Free*. New York: McGraw-Hill, 1979.

3. Customer satisfaction studies frequently demonstrate a clear relationship between customer satisfaction and retention. See, for example, Rust, R.T., Zahorik, A.J. & Keiningham, T.L., *Return on Quality: Measuring the Financial Impact of Your Company's Quest for Quality*. Chicago, IL: Richard D. Irwin, 1994 and Anderson, E.W. & Sullivan, M.W., The antecedents and consequences of customer satisfaction for firms. *Marketing Science*, **12**(Spring), 1993, 125–143. One should, however, remember that there are clear indications that this relationship is often only positive if customers are very satisfied and not merely satisfied. In a business-to-business context, Venetis and Ghauri demonstrate that service quality has a positive impact on customer retention. See Venetis, K.A. & Ghauri, P.N., Service quality and customer retention: building long-term relationships. *European Journal of Marketing*, **38**(11–12), 2004, 1577–1588. See also Bell, S.J., Auh, S. & Smalley, K., Customer relationship dynamics: service quality and customer loyalty in the context of varying levels of customer expertise and switching costs. *Journal of the Academy of Marketing Science*, **33**(2), 2005, 169–183 and Keiningham, T.L., Cooil, B., Aksol, L., Andreassen, T.W. & Weiner, J., The value of different customer satisfaction and loyalty metrics in predicting customer retention, recommendation, and share-of-wallet. *Managing Service Quality*, **17**(4), 2007, 361–384.

4. Hart, C.W. & Johnson, M.D., Growing the trust relationship. *Marketing Management*, Spring, 1999, 9–19.

5. Hart & Johnson, *op. cit.*

6. See Keiningham, T.L., Aksoy, L., Malthouse, E.C., Lariviere, B. & Buoye, A., The cumulative effect of discrete transactions on share of wallet. *Journal of Service Management*, **25**(3), 2014, 310–333.

7. See Reichheld, F.F., *The Loyalty Effect. The Hidden Force Behind Growth, Profits and Lasting Value*. Boston, MA: Harvard Business School Press, 1996.

8. Reichheld, F.F. & Sasser Jr., W.E., Zero defections: quality comes to services. *Harvard Business Review*, Sept–Oct, 1990, 105–111. Similar results from another study are reported in Heskett, J.L., Sasser Jr., W.E. & Schlesinger, L.A., *The Service Profit Chain: How Leading Companies Link Profit and Growth to Loyalty, Satisfaction, and Value*. New York: The Free Press, 1997.

9. Grönroos, C., *Service Management and Marketing. Managing the Moments of Truth in Service Competition*. Lexington, MA: Lexington, Books, 1990.

10. Grönroos, C., Facing the challenge of service competition: the economies of service. In Kunst, P. & Lemmink, J. (eds), *Quality Management in Services*. Maastricht, the Netherlands: Van Gorcum, 1992, pp. 129–140.

11. Value perception and value formation in relationships have not yet been studied to any considerable extent. See, for example, Ravald, A. & Grönroos, C., The value concept and relationship

marketing. *European Journal of Marketing*, **30**(2), 1996, 19–30 and Lapierre, J., What does value mean in business-to-business professional services? *International Journal of Service Industry Management*, **8**(5), 1997, 377–397. For excellent overviews, see Payne, A. & Holt, S., Review of the 'value' literature and implications for relationship marketing. *Australasian Marketing Journal*, **7**(1), 1999, 41–51 and Tzokas, N. & Saren, M., Value transformation in relationship marketing. *Australasian Marketing Journal*, **7**(1), 1999, 52–62. See also Hennig-Thurau, T., Gwinner, K.P. & Gremler, D.D., Understanding relationship marketing outcomes. An integration of relationship benefits and relationship quality. *Journal of Service Research*, **4**(3), 2002, 230–247.

12. Normann, R., *Reframing Business. When the Map Changes the Landscape*. Chichester, UK: John Wiley & Sons, 2001 and Storbacka, K. & Lehtinen, J.R., *Customer Relationship Management*. Singapore: McGraw-Hill, 2001. See also Normann, R. & Ramírez, R., From value chain to value constellation: designing interactive strategy. *Harvard Business Review*, July–Aug, 1993, 65–77 and Wikström, S., Value creation by company–consumer interaction. *Journal of Marketing Management*, **12**, 1996, 359–374. This is, of course, not an entirely new observation. Theodore Levitt expressed this point of view in the 1980s by noticing that value can only reside in the benefits of customer needs or expectations and that, therefore, only the customer can assign value to a physical product or a service. See Levitt, T., *The Marketing Imagination*. New York: The Free Press, 1986. By and large, Levitt's observation went unnoticed, or received only marginal interest, by practitioners as well as academics.

13. Vargo, S.L. & Lusch, R.F., Evolving to a new dominant logic for marketing. *Journal of Marketing*, **68**(Jan), 2004, 1–17. See also Woodruff, R.B. & Gardial, S., *Know Your Customers – new approaches to understanding customer value and satisfaction*. Oxford: Blackwell Publishers, 1996.

14. Grönroos, C. & Voima, P., Critical service logic: making sense of value creation and co-creation. *Journal of the Academy of Marketing Science*, **41**(2), 2013, 133–150. See also Grönroos, C., What can a service logic offer marketing theory? In Lusch, R.F. & Vargo, S.L. (eds), *A Service-Dominant Logic in Marketing. Dialog*. Armonk, NY: M.E. Sharpe, 2006, pp. 354–364.

15. Grönroos & Voima, *op. cit.* See also Prahalad, C.K. & Ramaswamy, V., *The Future of Competition: Co-Creating Unique Value with Customers*. Boston, MA: Harvard Business School Press, 2004, who discuss the idea of value co-creation, and Wikström, *op. cit.*

16. Wilson, D.T. & Jantrania, S., Understanding the value of a relationship. *Asia-Australia Marketing Journal*, **2**(1), 1994, 55–66 and Tzokas & Sarin, *op. cit.* Wilson and Jantrania offer a comprehensive discussion of the value concept.

17. Ravald & Grönroos, *op. cit.* and Grönroos, C., Value-driven relational marketing: from products to resources and competencies. *Journal of Marketing Management*, **13**(5), 1997, 407–419.

18. In a recent study, Dimitriadis, S. & Koritos, C., Core service versus relational benefits: what matters most? *The Service Industries Journal*, **34**(13–14), 2014, 1092–1112, the authors found that additional relational benefits are appreciated by customers, but they also found that the role of the core service may dominate over additional benefits in the customers' value perception. The relationship between the importance of the core service and benefits provided by additional services is to some extent controversial.

19. As Christopher Lovelock observes, 'creating value requires rigorous analysis of all possibilities on both the cost and benefit sides of the equation' (p. 61). See Lovelock, C.H., *Product Plus: How Product + Service = Competitive Advantage*. New York: McGraw-Hill, 1994.

20. As Anderson and Narus observe, 'instead of tailoring their packages of services to customers' individual needs . . . many suppliers simply add layer upon layer of services to their offerings' (p. 75). By doing so they do not necessarily create more real value for their customers. See Anderson, J.C. & Narus, J.A., Capturing the value of supplementary services. *Harvard Business Review*, **73**(Jan–Feb), 1995, 75–83.

21. See Anderson, J.C. & Narus, J.A., Business marketing: understand what customers value. *Harvard Business Review*, **76**(Nov–Dec), 1998, 53–61. They call such models *customer value models*.

22. Storbacka, K., *The Nature of Customer Relationship Profitability*. Helsinki/Helsingfors: Swedish School of Economics, Finland/CERS, 1994.

23. Storbacka, K., Strandvik, T. & Grönroos, C., Managing customer relationships for profit: the dynamics of relationship quality. *International Journal of Service Industry Management*, **5**(5), 1994, 21–38.

24. The definition is based on Grönroos, C. & Helle, P., Return on relationships: conceptual understanding and measurement of mutual gains from relational business engagements. *Journal of Business & Industrial Marketing*, **27**(5), 2012, 344–359. The first scholar to present a definition of ROR was Evert Gummesson, whose definition, however, only implicitly includes the reciprocity aspect of relationships. See Gummesson, E., *Total Relationship Marketing. Marketing Management, Relationship Strategy, CRM, and a New Dominant Logic for the Value-creating Network Economy*. Oxford: Butterworth Heinemann, 2008, p. 257.

25. The mutual value creation model is introduced in Grönroos & Helle, 2012, *op. cit.* Figure 6.10 and the explanation of the model are adapted from Grönroos & Helle, 2012, *op. cit.*, and Helle, P., Re-conceptualizing value creation: from industrial business logic to service business logic. *Working Paper 554*. Helsinki: Hanken School of Economics, Finland, 2011.

26. Grönroos, C. & Helle, P., Adopting a service logic in manufacturing: conceptual foundation and metrics for mutual value creation. *Journal of Service Management*, **(21)**5, 2010, 564–590. See also

Russo-Spena, T. & Mele, C., 'Five co-s' in innovating: a practice-based view. *Journal of Service Management*, **23**(4), 2012, 527–553.

27. The reciprocal return on relationship process and Figure 6.11 are adapted from Grönroos & Helle, 2012, *op. cit.*

28. Compare also Jap, S., Pie-expansion efforts: collaboration processes in buyer-seller relationships. *Journal of Market Research*, **(36)**4, 1999, 461–475.

29. Helle, P., *Towards understanding value creation from the point of view of service provision*. Conference report. EIASM Service Marketing Forum, Capri, 2009. See also Helle, *op. cit.* and Grönroos & Helle, *op. cit.*

30. Rust, R.T., Zeithaml, V.A. & Lemon, K.N., *Customer Equity Management*. Englewood Cliffs, NJ: Prentice Hall, 2004.

31. Rust, Zeithaml & Lemon, *op. cit.*, p. 4.

32. In the original version of the model 'relationship equity' was used instead of 'retention equity'. See Rust, R.T., Zeithaml, V.A. & Lemon, K.N., *Driving Customer Equity: How Customer Lifetime Value is Reshaping Corporate Strategy*. New York: The Free Press, 2000.

33. It is interesting to notice the resemblance between this three-component customer equity management model and the logic underpinning the second customer perceived quality equation (CPV2) discussed earlier in this chapter. Value equity equals the transaction value component in CPV2, whereas the relationship value component in CPV2 is divided into two components – brand equity and retention equity.

34. Rust, R.T., Zahorik, A.J. & Keiningham, T.L., Return on Quality (ROQ): making service quality financially accountable. *Journal of Marketing*, **59**(Apr), 1995, 58–70.

35. Stauss, B. & Friege, C., Regaining service customers: costs and benefits of regain management. *Journal of Service Research*, **1**(4), 1999, 347–361.

36. See Storbacka, 1994, *op. cit.* and Storbacka, K., Customer profitability: analysis and design issues. In Sheth, J.N. & Parvatiyar, A. (eds), *Handbook of Relationship Marketing*. Thousand Oaks, CA: Sage Publications, 2000, pp. 565–586.

37. This case was developed by Dr Kaj Storbacka, professor at The University of Auckland Business School and former research director of *CERS* (Centre for Relationship Marketing and Service Management) at Hanken Swedish School of Economics, Finland, based on his research on customer relationship profitability and his consultancy experience.

FURTHER READING

Anderson, J.C. & Narus, J.A. (1995) Capturing the value of supplementary services. *Harvard Business Review*, **73**(Jan/Feb), 75–83.

Anderson, J.C. & Narus, J.A. (1998) Business marketing: understand what customers value. *Harvard Business Review*, **76**(Nov/Dec), 53–61.

Anderson, E.W. & Sullivan, M.W. (1993) The antecedents and consequences of customer satisfaction for firms. *Marketing Science*, **12**(Spring), 125–143.

Bell, S.J., Auh, S. & Smalley, K. (2005) Customer relationship dynamics: service quality and customer loyalty in the context of varying levels of customer expertise and switching costs. *Journal of the Academy of Marketing Science*, **33**(2), 169–183.

Crosby, P.B. (1979) *Quality is Free*. New York: McGraw-Hill.

Dimitriadis, S. & Koritos, C. (2014) Core service versus relational benefits: what matters most? *The Service Industries Journal*, **34**(13–14), 1092–1112.

Grönroos, C. (1990) *Service Management and Marketing. Managing the Moments of Truth in Service Competition*. Lexington, MA: Lexington Books.

Grönroos, C. (1992) Facing the challenge of service competition: the economies of service. In Kunst, P. & Lemmink, J. (eds), *Quality Management in Services*. Maastricht, the Netherlands: Van Gorcum Assen, pp. 129–140.

Grönroos, C. (1997) Value-driven relational marketing: from products to resources and competencies. *Journal of Marketing Management*, **13**(5), 407–419.

Grönroos, C. (2006) What can a service logic offer marketing theory? In Lusch, R.F. & Vargo, S.L. (eds), *A Service-Dominant Logic in Marketing. Dialog,* Armonk, NY: M.E. Sharpe, pp. 354–364.

Grönroos, C. & Helle, P. (2010) Adopting a service logic in manufacturing: conceptual foundation and metrics for mutual value creation. *Journal of Service Management*, **21**(5), 564–590.

Grönroos, C. & Helle, P. (2012) Return on relationships: conceptual understanding and measurement of mutual gains from relational business engagements. *Journal of Business & Industrial Marketing*, **27**(5), 344–359.

Grönroos, C. & Voima, P. (2013) Critical service logic: making sense of value creation and co-creation. *Journal of the Academy of Marketing Science*, **41**(2), 133–150.

Gummesson, E. (2008) *Total Relationship Marketing. Marketing Management, Relationship Strategy, CRM, and a New Dominant Logic for the Value-creating Network Economy*. Oxford: Butterworth Heinemann.

Hart, C.W. & Johnson, M.D. (1999) Growing the trust relationship. *Marketing Management*, Spring, 9–19.

Helle, P. (2009) *Towards understanding value creation from the point of view of service provision*. Conference report. EIASM Service Marketing Forum, Capri.

Helle, P. (2011) Re-conceptualizing value creation: from industrial business logic to service business logic. *Working Paper 554*. Helsinki: Hanken School of Economics, Finland, Helsinki.

Hennig-Thurau, T., Gwinner, K.P. & Gremler, D.D. (2002) Understanding relationship marketing outcomes. An integration of relationship benefits and relationship quality. *Journal of Service Research*, **4**(3), 230–247.

Heskett, J.L., Sasser Jr., W.E. & Schlesinger, L.A. (1997) *The Service Profit Chain: How Leading Companies Link Profit and Growth to Loyalty, Satisfaction and Value*. New York: The Free Press.

Keiningham, T.L., Aksoy, L., Malthouse, E.C., Lariviere, B. & Buoye, A. (2014) The cumulative effect of discrete transactions on share of wallet. *Journal of Service Management*, **25**(3), 310–333.

Keiningham, T.L., Cooil, B., Aksol, L., Andreassen, T.W. & Weiner, J. (2007) The value of different customer satisfaction and loyalty metrics in predicting customer retention, recommendation, and share-of-wallet. *Managing Service Quality*, **17**(4), 361–384.

Lapierre, J. (1997) What does value mean in business-to-business professional services? *International Journal of Service Industry Management*, **8**(5), 377–397.

Levitt, T. (1986) *The Marketing Imagination*. New York: The Free Press.

Lovelock, C.H. (1994) *Product Plus: How Product + Service = Competitive Advantage*. New York: McGraw-Hill.

Normann, R. (2001) *Reframing Business. When the Map Changes the Landscape*. Chichester, UK: John Wiley & Sons.

Normann, R. & Ramirez, R. (1993) From value chain to value constellation: designing interactive strategy. *Harvard Business Review*, Jul–Aug, 65–77.

Payne, A. & Holt, S. (1999) Review of the 'value' literature and implications for relationship marketing. *Australasian Marketing Journal*, **7**(1), 41–51.

Pickworth, J.R. (1987) Minding the Ps and Qs: linking quality and productivity. *The Cornell Hotel and Restaurant Administration Quarterly*, May.

Prahalad, C.K. & Ramaswamy, V. (2004) *The Future of Competition: Co-Creating Unique Value with Customers*. Boston, MA: Harvard Business School Press.

Ravald, A. & Grönroos, C. (1996) The value concept and relationship marketing. *European Journal of Marketing*, **30**(2), 19–30.

Reichheld, F.F. (1996) *The Loyalty Effect. The Hidden Force Behind Growth, Profits and Lasting Value*. Boston, MA: Harvard Business School Press.

Reichheld, F.F. & Sasser Jr., W.E. (1990) Zero defections: quality comes to services. *Harvard Business Review*, Sept–Oct, 105–111.

Russo-Spena, T. & Mele, C. (2012), 'Five co-s' in innovating: a practice-based view. *Journal of Service Management*, **23**(4), 527–553.

Rust, R.T., Zahorik, A.J. & Keiningham, T.L. (1995) Return on Quality (ROQ): making service quality financially accountable. *Journal of Marketing*, **59**(Apr), 58–70.

Rust, R.T., Zeithaml, V.A. & Lemon, K.N. (2000) *Driving Customer Equity: How Customer Lifetime Value is Reshaping Corporate Strategy*. New York: The Free Press.

Rust, R.T., Zeithaml, V.A. & Lemon, K.N. (2004) *Customer Equity Management*. Englewood Cliffs, NJ: Prentice Hall.

Stauss, B. & Friege, C. (1999) Regaining service customers. Costs and benefits of regain management. *Journal of Service Research*, **1**(4), 347–361.

Storbacka, K. (1994) *The Nature of Customer Relationship Profitability*. Helsinki/Helsingfors: Hanken Swedish School of Economics, Finland/CERS Centre for Relationship Marketing and Service Management.

Storbacka, K. (1997) Segmentation based on customer profitability – retrospective analysis of retail bank customer bases. *Journal of Marketing Management*, **13**(5), 479–492.

Storbacka, K. (2000) Customer profitability: analysis and design issues. In Sheth, J.N. & Parvatiyar, A. (eds), *Handbook of Relationship Marketing*. Thousand Oaks, CA: Sage Publications, pp. 565–586.

Storbacka, K. and Lehtinen, J.R. (2001) *Customer Relationship Management*. Singapore: McGraw-Hill.

Storbacka, K., Strandvik, T. & Grönroos, C. (1994) Managing customer relationships for profit: the dynamics of relationship quality. *International Journal of Service Industry Management*, **5**(5), 21–38.

Tzokas, N. & Saren, M. (1999) Value transformation in relationship marketing. *Australasian Marketing Journal*, **7**(1), 52–62.

Vargo, S.L. and Lusch, R.F. (2004) Evolving to a new dominant logic for marketing. *Journal of Marketing*, **68**(Jan), 1–17.

Venetis, K.A. & Ghauri, P.N. (2004) Service quality and customer retention: building long-term relationships. *European Journal of Marketing*, **38**(11–12), 1577–1588.

Wikström, S. (1996) Value creation by company–consumer interaction. *Journal of Marketing Management*, **12**, 359–374.

Wilson, D.T. & Jantrania, S. (1994) Understanding the value of a relationship. *Asia-Australia Marketing Journal*, **2**(1), 55–66.

Woodruff, R.B. & Gardial, S. (1996) *Know Your Customers – New Approaches to Understanding Customer Value and Satisfaction*. Oxford: Blackwell Publishers.

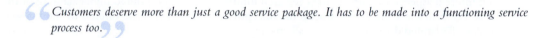

CHAPTER 7
MANAGING THE AUGMENTED SERVICE OFFERING

> **"** *Customers deserve more than just a good service package. It has to be made into a functioning service process too.* **"**

INTRODUCTION

Based on discussions of service quality in previous chapters, this chapter presents a conceptual model of how to develop service offerings that are geared to customers' perception of the quality of services. The conceptual model is called the *augmented service offering* model. It takes into account the impact of the outcome of the service processes (the *technical quality* of the service) and the impact of how customers perceive the processes (the *functional quality* of the process). The effects of brand image and marketing communication on the service offering are also discussed. Then, service design and a model of *designing for service* are presented, and finally a model of service offering development in the marketspace called the NetOffer model is discussed. After having read this chapter the reader should understand the complexity and scope of service as an offering and know how to develop a service offering. The reader should also understand what such an offering includes in a marketspace context. Finally, the reader should understand what designing for service means and what such a process includes.

THE MISSING SERVICE PRODUCT: SERVICES AS A BUNDLE OF OUTCOME- AND PROCESS-RELATED FEATURES

One of the essential cornerstones in developing service management models is a thorough understanding of the phenomenon to be studied. In other words, what is needed is a good model of services as offerings to be produced, marketed and consumed. Physical products are a bundle of features embedded in the ready-made product. However, as discussed in Chapter 2, services are different. Services are processes, where no pre-produced product to be marketed and consumed exists.

To understand service management and how to market services it is important to remember that all models and concepts are based on the fact that the service emerges in a process, in which the customer participates as a co-producer, and that the production of a service is not separated from the consumption of this service. Moreover, this process forms an essential part of the service. From the service provider's point of view, some of the service is produced in a back office, but from a quality perception perspective the most critical part of the service is produced at the time when the customer participates, perceives and evaluates the service process.

As discussed in previous chapters, instead of product features embedded in a pre-produced physical product, services consist of a bundle of features which are related to the service *process* and the *outcome* of that process. Neither of these exists before the customer initiates the service production process. These characteristics of services have to be taken into account when developing models describing services. We name the bundle of process- and outcome-related features a *service offering*, and the comprehensive model of a service offering described in this chapter is called the *augmented service offering* model.[1]

This chapter will not discuss a new service development process from idea generation to launch.[2] Instead, it will concentrate on the core of such a process, that is, how to understand and manage the object of development itself, the *service offering*. Without a thorough understanding of this core concept, every attempt to design and develop service will fail or at least be less effective.

Any attempt to conceptualize the service offering has to be based on a customer perspective. Far too often internal aspects, too little market research information, or too limited understanding of the customers' point of view guide the process of conceptualizing services to be offered to the market. However, well planned does not automatically mean well executed. The following sections are going to address, in detail, how to develop the service offering so that all aspects are thoroughly covered. This requires, among other things, that service production and delivery issues (that is, the service process) be incorporated as inseparable parts of the process of planning a service offering. Otherwise, well-planned service offerings may remain theoretical, unless the execution of plans is made an integral part of the undertaking to create a service offering.

THE SERVICE PACKAGE

According to the service package model, which is often used in the literature, the service is described as a package or bundle of different services, tangibles and intangibles, which together form the service.[3] The package is divided into two main categories: the *main service or core service* and *auxiliary services or extras*, which are sometimes referred to as peripherals or peripheral services, sometimes also as facilitator services. A hotel service may include the accommodation element as the main or core service, and reception service, valet service, room service, restaurant services and the concierge as auxiliary services or peripherals in the package. Such extras are often considered to be the elements of the service package that define it and make it competitive.[4]

Lovelock developed a model of the service offering which includes *supplementary services* in addition to a core service. Supplementary services resemble the idea of auxiliary services and extras.[5] This is a simple and realistic way of illustrating at least part of the nature of any service. However, it has a few weaknesses if it is to be used for managerial purposes. First, a service is more complicated than this model would suggest. From a managerial perspective auxiliary or supplementary services may be used for totally different reasons. This has to be recognized. Second, the main service/auxiliary service (core service/peripherals, supplementary) dichotomy is not clearly geared to the customer perception of a service and total service quality. Only *what* is supposed to be done for customers is recognized.

How the service process and the process-related features are to be handled (i.e. the *functional quality* aspects of a service) is not included.

A model of the service offering has to be customer-centric. It has to recognize all the aspects of a service that are perceived by customers. *How* customers perceive the interactions with the service provider (the functional quality of the service process) as well as *what* the customers receive (the technical quality of the outcome) has to be taken into account. In addition to this, the image impact on service quality perception also has to be recognized. What has to be planned and marketed and offered to customers is a comprehensive service offering.

MANAGING THE SERVICE OFFERING

Based on a thorough understanding of *the customers' everyday activities and processes* a well-defined *customer benefit concept*, which states the benefits or bundle of benefits customers appreciate, can be derived. Having gained this knowledge about target customers the firm can develop and manage *service offerings*. Managing a service offering requires four steps:

1. Developing the *service concept.*

2. Developing a *basic service package*.

3. Developing an *augmented service offering*.

4. Managing *image* and *communication*.

The *service concept* or concepts determine the intentions of the organization. The package can be developed based on this concept.

The *basic service package* describes the bundle of services that are needed to fulfil the needs of customers in target markets. This package, then, determines *what* customers receive from the organization. A well-developed basic package guarantees that necessary outcome-related features are included, and that the *technical quality* of the outcome will be good. However, even an excellent service package can be destroyed by the way in which the service process functions. Therefore, a good service package does not necessarily mean that the perceived service is good, or even acceptable. According to the quality models of services, the service production and delivery process, especially the customer perception of the buyer–seller interactions or the service encounter, is an integral part of the service. This is the reason why the basic service package has to be expanded into an augmented service offering before we have a description of the service as an offering.

In the *augmented service offering* model the service process and the interactions between the organization and its customers as well as customers' co-production efforts are included. In this way the model of the service offering is geared to the total customer perceived quality of services.

Finally, image has a filtering effect on the quality perception. Therefore, the firm has to manage its corporate and/or local *image* and its *marketing communication* so that they enhance the perception of the augmented service offering.

THE BASIC SERVICE PACKAGE

As noted previously, in the literature a distinction is often made between core services and supplementary/auxiliary/peripheral services. However, for managerial reasons, it is useful to distinguish between *three* groups of services:[6]

1. Core service.

2. Enabling services (and goods).

3. Enhancing services (and goods).

The *core service* is the reason for a company being on the market. For a hotel it is lodging and for an airline it is transportation. A firm may also have many core services. For example, an airline may offer shuttle services as well as long-distance transportation. A mobile phone operator may, for example, offer phone calls as well as an e-mail facility as its core services.

In order to make it possible for customers to use the core service some additional services are often required. Reception services are needed in a hotel, and check-in services are required for air transportation. Such additional services are called *enabling* or *facilitating services*, because they enable the use of the core service.[7] If enabling services are lacking, the core service cannot be consumed. Sometimes *enabling goods* are also required. For example, in order to be able to operate an automatic teller machine, a customer needs a bank card. However, it is often difficult to say whether the physical things involved in the service offering are goods given to the customer as part of the service production process or are physical production resources. For instance, the bank card can be considered a physical thing (an enabling physical good), but it can equally be considered a production resource. The ATM equipment, on the other hand, is definitely a physical production resource and not an enabling good.

The third type of service is *enhancing* or *supporting services*. These, like enabling services, are also auxiliary services, but they fulfil another function. Enhancing services do not facilitate the consumption or use of the core service, but are used to increase the value of the service and/or to differentiate the service from that of competitors. Hotel restaurants and airport lounges and a range of in-flight services related to air transportation are examples of enhancing services. Games and wake-up calls are examples of enhancing services offered by a mobile phone operator. In some cases physical things that can be considered *enhancing goods* are used to enhance the service offering. Shampoo and shoeshine in hotel rooms are such goods.

The distinction between enabling services and enhancing services is not always clear. A service that in one situation is enabling the core service – for example, an in-flight meal on a long-distance route – may become an enhancing service in another context, i.e. on a short flight.

From a managerial point of view it is important to make a distinction between enabling and enhancing services. Enabling services are mandatory. *If they are left out, the service package collapses*. This does not mean that such services could not be designed in such a way that they differ from the enabling services of the competitors. On the contrary, whenever possible enabling services should be designed so that they also become means of competition and thus help to differentiate the service. Enhancing services, however, are used as a means of competition only. If they are lacking, the core service can still be used. However, the total service package may be less attractive and perhaps less competitive without them.

The basic service package is, however, not equivalent to the service offering customers perceive. This package corresponds mainly to the technical outcome dimension of the total perceived quality. The elements of this package determine *what* customers receive. They do not say anything about *how* the process is perceived, which in the final analysis is an integral part of the total service offering customers experience and evaluate. In other words, no process-related features of the service have yet been taken into account.

As the perception of the service process cannot be separated from the perception of the elements of the basic service package, the process has to be integrated into the service offering. Therefore, the basic service package has to be expanded into a more comprehensive model, called the *augmented service offering* model.

THE AUGMENTED SERVICE OFFERING

The service process, the buyer–seller interactions or service encounters, are perceived in a number of ways, which differ from situation to situation. Due to the characteristics of most services, there are, however, three basic elements, which from a managerial point of view constitute the process:[8]

1. Accessibility of the service.

2. Interaction with the service organization.

3. Customer participation.

These elements are combined with the concepts of the basic package, thus forming an *augmented service offering* (see Figure 7.1). It is, of course, essential that these three elements of the service offering are geared to the *customer benefits* that were initially identified to be sought by customers in the selected target segments, and the *service concept* based on these benefits.

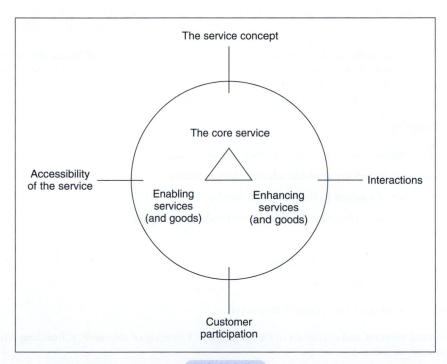

FIGURE 7.1

The augmented service offering.
Source: Developed from Grönroos, C., Developing the service offering – a source of competitive advantage. In Surprenant, C. (ed.), *Add Value to Your Service*. Chicago, IL: American Marketing Association, 1987, p. 83. Reproduced by permission of the American Marketing Association.

The *accessibility of the service* depends, among other things, on:

- The number and skills of the personnel.
- Office hours, timetables and the time used to perform various tasks.
- Location of offices, workshops, service outlets, etc.
- Exterior and interior of offices, workshops and other service outlets.
- Tools, equipment, documents, etc.
- Information technology enabling customers to gain access to the service provider and the service process, and to use the service.
- The number and knowledge of consumers simultaneously involved in the process.

Depending on these and other factors customers will feel that it is easy, or difficult, to get access to the services and to purchase and use them. If the telephone receptionist of a repair firm lets the customer wait before answering the telephone, or if he cannot find a service technician for the customer to talk to, there is no accessibility to the service. Even an excellent service package can be destroyed in this way. Even if the service package does not totally deteriorate, the perception of the service may be seriously damaged. Internet sites, help desks and call and contact centres are increasingly becoming accessibility issues for service providers.

For example, in a study of a for-profit laboratory in the southwest United States, the accessibility issue could be broken down into four parts: site accessibility, customer ease of use of the physical resources of the laboratory, contact personnel's contribution to accessibility, and ease of customer participation. The following variables were identified for each of the four aspects of accessibility:

1. Site accessibility

   - The convenience and ease of access from a major street.
   - The amount of parking available adjacent to the facility.
   - The number of medical facilities located nearby.
   - The relative ease of locating the laboratory inside the building.
   - Office hours.
   - The ease of getting an appointment.
   - The size of the waiting room.

2. Customer ease of use of the physical resources

   - The attractiveness and condition of the exterior and interior of the medical building where the laboratory is located.
   - The exterior of the laboratory facility.
   - The waiting room.
   - The patient rooms.
   - The restrooms.

3. Service employees' contribution to accessibility

- The response time to phone calls.
- The number of employees.
- The skills of employees.
- The response time to people walking in the front door.
- The response time to patients in the waiting room.
- The professionalism of the employees.
- The care taken to reduce unpleasantness of drawing blood.
- The billing procedures.
- The types of payment accepted.
- The insurance arrangements available.

4. Ease of customer participation

- The number and difficulty of forms to fill out.
- The instructions given to patients concerning procedures the patient must participate in or do alone.
- The difficulty of these procedures.

Interaction with the service organization can be divided into the following categories:

- Interactive communication between employees and customers, which in turn depends on the behaviour of the employees, on what they say and do, and how they say and do it.
- Interactions with various physical and technical resources of the organization, such as vending machines, computers, documents, waiting room facilities, tools and equipment needed in the service production process, etc.
- Interactions with systems, such as waiting systems, seating systems, billing systems, Internet sites and telecommunication systems, systems for deliveries, maintenance and repair work, making appointments, handling claims, etc.
- Interactions with other customers simultaneously involved in the process.

Customers have to get in touch with employees, they have to adjust to operative and administrative systems and routines of the organization, they may have to use websites, and they sometimes have to use technical resources such as teller machines or vending machines. Moreover, they may get in contact with other customers. All these interactions with human as well as physical resources and systems are part of the service perception. Again, if these interactions are considered unnecessarily complicated or unfriendly, the perceived quality of an excellent basic service package may be low.

In the same study interactions between the organization and its customers were broken down into the following parts:

- Interactions with medical personnel (their attitudes, attention to the customer, skill in drawing blood).

- Interactions with customer service department (attitudes, phone answering promptness, prompt and accurate answers to questions).

- Interactions with waiting room environment (space, cleanliness, crowdedness).

- Interactions with other customers (communication between patients).

- Interactions with payment or billing system (means of payment available to choose from, understandability of invoices and receipts).

- Interactions with scheduling systems (waiting time for service).

- Interactions between physicians (referring patients to the laboratory) and customer service department (attitudes, phone answering promptness, prompt and accurate answers to questions, calling results, follow-up).

Customer participation means that the customer has an impact on the service he perceives. Thus, he becomes a *co-producer of the service* and therefore also a *co-creator of value* for himself.[9] Often the customer is expected to fill in documents, give information, use websites, operate vending machines, and so on. Depending on how well the customer is prepared and willing to do this, he will improve the service or vice versa. For example, if a patient is unable to give correct information about his problems, the physician will not be able to make a correct diagnosis. The treatment may, therefore, be inappropriate or less effective than otherwise. The service rendered by the physician is thus impaired.

In the study the following questions were asked, to identify aspects of customer participation:

- Are patients knowledgeable enough to identify their need or problem?

- Do patients have a reasonable understanding of the time constraints involved?

- Is the patient willing to co-operate in the process?

- Can additional information be obtained quickly from physicians?

In the case of self-service, customers are required to take a more substantial and active co-producer role, using the systems and resources provided by the service firm.

Thus, in service encounters the core service, enabling services and enhancing services of the basic service package are perceived in various ways, depending on the accessibility of the services, how easily and well the interactions are perceived, and how well customers understand their role in the service production process.

Finally, in Figure 7.1, the *service concept* is seen as an umbrella concept, to guide development of the components of the augmented service offering. The service concept should thus state what kind of core, enabling and enhancing services are to be used, how the basic package could be made accessible, how interactions are to be developed, and how customers should be prepared to participate in the process.

The service concept should also be used as a guideline when, in the next phase of the planning process, adequate production resources are identified. In a going concern there are, of course, a set of human and physical resources as well as functioning systems already in place. They determine to some extent which resources are going to be used. However, the development of an augmented service offering requires a fresh analysis of the types of resources that are needed. Otherwise, existing resources may unnecessarily restrict the implementation of a new service offering. Existing resources must never become a hindrance to the successful implementation of new ideas.

In summary, developing the service offering is a highly integrated process. A new enhancing service cannot be added without taking into account the accessibility, interaction and customer participation aspects of that service. On the other hand, the well-planned introduction of an additional enhancing service, or an improved facilitating service, may become a powerful source of competitive advantage.

MANAGING IMAGE AND COMMUNICATION AND THE SERVICE OFFERING

As illustrated by the model of perceived service quality, *image* has an impact as a filter on the service experienced. A favourable image enhances the experience; a bad one may destroy it. Therefore, managing image and communication becomes an integral part of developing the service offering.[10] Because of the intangible nature of services, marketing communication activities not only have a communicative impact on customer expectations, but a direct effect on experiences as well. This latter effect is sometimes of minor, sometimes of major, importance.

In the long run, *marketing communications* such as advertising, websites, sales and public relations enhance and to some extent form images. However, even an advertisement or a brochure (which a customer notices and perceives at the point and time of consumption, or in advance) may have some impact on his quality perception of a service. Moreover, *word of mouth* is essential in this context. Peer communication between customers at the point and time of purchasing and consumption may have a substantial immediate effect as well as a long-term impact. In the same way, a negative comment from a fellow customer may easily change a given person's perception of the service he receives.

THE ROLE OF TECHNOLOGY IN SERVICE OFFERINGS

The development of information technology and the increase in Internet and mobile technology use has offered new opportunities for firms to develop their service offerings.[11] IT systems and improved databases from which customer information files are easier to retrieve, and which are less complicated to update than before, provide customer contact employees with improved support to help them to be customer-centric in interactions with customers. More accurate, easily retrievable and available information about customers enables employees to increase the quality of customer interactions. In addition, this use of technology also has a positive effect on the accessibility of services. The Internet may also improve employees' ability to handle customer contacts, for example, when routine interactions can be transferred to an Internet-based help desk.

New technology also gives customers the means to access the services of a manufacturer or service firm more quickly and easily. For example, using the website of a manufacturer, a customer can easily request supportive information about how to handle a problem with a production machine or make arrangements for the maintenance of the machine. The Internet and mobile technologies offer lots of opportunities to make a service more accessible than before, and it may also improve interactions. Of course, customers need to be trained and motivated to use a website for such purposes.

However, although some services, such as the purchase of movie theatre tickets, can be completed on the Internet, in most cases the customer will at some point also interact with employees and more traditional physical resources and technologies of the service provider. It should be kept in mind that well-functioning IT and Internet and mobile service interactions have to be supported by the 'real', personal interactions that also take place. Quick and easy arrangements to get a maintenance task done using the Internet have to be followed by prompt, skilful and attentive service, otherwise the high-quality perception of the service provider's use of new technology in the mind of a customer is destroyed by a low-quality perception created by traditional means of producing the service offering.

Finally, one should remember that new technologies used in service processes may not be accepted and appreciated by all customers of a given service provider. Some customers can be motivated to accept new technologies, for example after having been informed about their benefits or after having been trained to use them. Others may want to continue to use more traditional means of interacting with the service provider. In any case, the firm has to introduce new technologies carefully, otherwise their effect may be negative. Also, it is important to market new technologies internally, so that employees are motivated to use them. Employees too have to be properly informed and trained.

DEVELOPING THE SERVICE OFFERING: A DYNAMIC MODEL

The composition of the augmented service offering in Figure 7.1 is static. The model simply lays out the elements that have to be taken into account and introduces appropriate concepts. In this section the model of the augmented service offering will be placed in a dynamic framework, which illustrates more realistically how the service as a product emerges. Because services are processes in which consumption is inseparable from production and delivery processes, the service offering by definition is dynamic. The service exists as long as the production process goes on. Hence, any model of services, such as the augmented service offering, has to include a dynamic aspect

The framework can be divided into eight steps:

1. Analysing target customers' everyday activities and processes.

2. Assessing customer benefits required to support these activities and processes.

3. Defining overall features of an augmented service offering.

4. Defining a service concept which guides the development of the service offering.

5. Developing the core service, enabling and enhancing services, and goods of the basic service package.

6. Planning the accessibility, interaction and customer participation elements of the augmented service offering.

7. Planning supportive marketing communication.

8. Preparing the organization for producing the desired customer benefits in the service processes (*internal marketing*).

First, one has to analyse the customers' everyday activities and processes where they may benefit from a service that the firm can provide them with or develop for them. For example, Apple's launch of the iPhone was a result of thorough ethnographic studies of what people in large customer segments were doing and would like to do, for example with the support of a new kind of mobile device, combined with the firm's innovative knowledge of the possibilities of software technology. Then, an assessment of the *customer benefits* is needed, so that the development process is geared to customer experiences of total service quality. Next, the desired *features of a competitive augmented service offering* have to be defined as the basis of further planning. These features, following the model of Figure 7.1, should be related to the *service concept*, and structured according to the elements of the service package and the augmentation elements, as well as related to corporate and local image and market communication.

The next step is to plan the *basic package*, including the core service, enabling services and goods, and enhancing services and goods, according to the service concept. Then, the *augmented service offering* – which materializes through the *service process* – has to be developed, so that the service is made accessible in a way that reflects the service concept, and interactions and customer participation meeting the same criterion emerge.

The next step is to plan *supportive marketing communication*, which not only informs customers about the service and persuades them to try it but also has a positive impact on the consumption of the service and enhances a desired image.

If all steps so far are properly carried out, the result should be a concrete offering, which – in the basic package elements as well as in the accessibility, interaction and customer participation aspects of service production and delivery – includes the desired features, which then create the benefits customers seek. This, in turn, should provide the customers with value-creating support to their activities and processes. However, yet another step is required, and that is *preparing the organization* for producing the desired customer benefits through production and delivery of the augmented service offering.

One of the fatal mistakes that can be made is to believe that the service, once it has been planned, is automatically produced as planned. The discussion of customer perceived quality, and especially of the gap analysis model, in Chapter 5 demonstrated the problems and pitfalls present in producing excellent perceived service quality and showed how complicated a process it is. Hence, the preparation of the organization has to be made an inseparable part of any development of service offerings, otherwise even sound and customer-oriented plans can easily fail.

The preparation of organizations for a desired performance involves the *creation of sufficient resources* and *internal marketing* of the new offering to the employees, so that they first understand it, then accept it and feel committed to producing it. In Chapter 14 the concept and phenomenon of internal marketing is covered at some length.

To sum up this discussion of the dynamic model of the augmented service offering, the first stage is always analysis of the customers' activities and processes and an assessment of what benefits target customers are looking for and would appreciate. Proper market research and use of internal information, for example, from the interface between customers and the organization, should provide management with the necessary knowledge of what customers expect, so that corresponding features can be built into the service. However, innovative market research, such as using ethnographic methods, should be used as well.

The first four steps of the process, analysing the customers' activities and processes, assessing a customer benefit concept, determining the desired features of the service offering to be produced and defining the service concept, are separate processes. However, the next two phases, developing the basic package and planning the interaction, accessibility and customer participation elements of the augmented service offering in the service process, as well as the last phase, preparing the organization, are *inseparable processes*. They have to go together, otherwise there is a risk that a good plan will result in a mediocre service. The basic package may include the correct features, but the crucial importance of the accessibility, interaction and customer participation aspects of service production and delivery to total customer perceived quality will not be fully understood or appreciated. Moreover, the need to actively market the new service internally will be neglected, or not taken care of with sufficient attention to detail.

Next, a case study describing a successful development and launching of a new service will be described. The case includes most of the features of the models of the augmented service offering described earlier in this chapter.

CASE STUDY

DEVELOPING AN AUGMENTED SERVICE OFFERING: THE INTERRENT CASES.[12] THE COMPANY AND ITS SERVICE CONCEPT

Interrent-Europcar operates nationwide in Sweden in the auto rental market. Although it belongs to an international group, it is managed as an independent Swedish firm. It is one of the main auto rental companies in Sweden. Interrent has operated for a long time as a distinctly service-producing firm. Hans Åke Sand, retired CEO, said:

When this industry was starting to grow here, we realized that we should not just provide our customers with an automobile, if they ask for one, which our competitors were doing, and still to some extent seem to be doing. Instead we wanted to position our company as a provider of transportation service. We developed a service concept, according to which we provide immediately accessible transportation solutions to temporary transportation problems.

This service concept still holds and guides Interrent's new service development and marketing strategies.

Although the firm was doing well, the competition had increased substantially, and continued to do so. Therefore, it was decided that the auto rental service of Interrent should be developed in a more service-oriented direction. Hans Åke Sand said: 'The objective was to create a unique position for Interrent, where the most important keywords were trustworthiness and reliability.' According to Sand, Interrent wanted to be able to offer customer benefits that were more real and tangible than just 'we do it with a smile' or 'we try harder'.

The Elements of the Basic Service Package
The *core service* was a *transportation solution*. The basic ingredients of the service package were broken down into elements that needed to be designed and planned, so that an *'immediately accessible solution to temporary transportation problems'* would emerge as required by the service concept. Both *enabling services* and *enhancing services* were needed, and most of the necessary enabling services were designed so that they simultaneously served as enhancing services as well.

The elements considered were as follows (F denotes enabling (facilitating) service, S denotes enhancing (supportive) service):

- Information about terms (S).
- Reservation (F and S).
- Delivery of auto to customer (F and S).
- Customer use of auto (F and S).
- Return of car (F and S).
- Pricing (S).
- Billing (F and S).
- Payment (F and S).
- Handling complaints (S).

These were the major elements included in the service development process. Three important observations can be made at this point. First, it is interesting to note how elements such as billing and complaints handling, which are normally not considered service, just administrative routines, can be turned into service in a basic service package. Secondly, most or all enabling services, even payment and the actual use of the automobile, can also be thought of as enhancing services. Lastly, some traditional marketing variables, such as pricing in this case, can be transformed into enhancing service elements.

When all the elements of the basic package are there, the necessary outcome-related features of the service offering, that is, the *technical quality dimension* of the total customer perceived quality, have been planned. However, the way in which the basic package functions, that is, how the service process functions and is perceived by the customer, is yet to be planned.

Augmenting the Offering: Goals to be Achieved

At this point, the elements of the *basic service package* have been defined. The next step is to design these elements so that the basic package functions in a service-oriented way, so that the service concept is transformed into a well-functioning service or a successful *augmented service offering*. When this has been done, the *functional process-related quality* dimension of total perceived quality is also accounted for, not just the technical outcome-related quality. In the next phase, *accessibility* issues, *interactions* between customers and Interrent, and the *customers' role as co-producer during the service process* were looked into. Three general goals, expressed as service guarantees, are *features* the company decided to build into the new service. To plan the augmentation of the service package in the form of developing service guarantees is one way to ensure that a company focuses on the customer and what the customer considers important in the service offering. Moreover, it helps to set standards for employees. Offering guaran tees immediately creates service-related goals to employees, which helps management to make the organization perform as planned (close the fourth gap in the gap analysis model; see Chapter 5).[13] Of course, offering service guarantees should also have external effects. Research into service guarantees seems to be limited; however, research suggests that offering guarantees can reduce the risk customers perceive before purchasing a ser vice. The more variety there is in the quality of service in an industry, the more service guarantees can reduce customers' perceived pre-purchase risk.[14]

The service guarantees Interrent chose to offer were:

1. A *get to your destination* guarantee which addressed the operational security of the service.

2. A *lowest price* guarantee which addressed the issue of cost efficiency *for the customer*.

3. A *trouble-free service* guarantee which addressed any problems related to the conve nience, interactivity and accessibility of the service.

Get to your destination. To achieve this goal the automobiles must, of course, be in as good a condition as possible; but as there is always a chance of breakdown, a system for taking the customer to his destination if that were to happen had to be designed. It was decided that customers had to be on their way to their final destination not later than 45 minutes after they informed Interrent of the breakdown. Interrent entered into an agreement with a security firm which had a 24-hour telephone answering service. If the customer could not continue his trip without assistance, he was advised to call the security firm's number. The customer was guaranteed that *within 45 minutes he would be on the road again*. If no other solution could be found, a taxi was sent to pick up and transport the customer to his final destination at Interrent's expense, even if this cost could be expected to be high. This, of course, led to substantial internal discussions but as it turned out, this 'rescue service' has not been expensive. It has, however, created a lot of goodwill and positive word of mouth. Hans Åke Sand said: 'We wanted to create reliability in our booking and delivery commitment. Our customers have to be absolutely sure that there will be a service available; and we wanted to give our booking centre and locations and our partners a strong signal saying that a customer who has a reservation number is entitled to the service, either by car or taxi.'

Lowest price. To achieve this goal a well-integrated computer system was required, so that the lowest possible fee, taking into account the various ways of calculating the final price, could always be immediately given to the customer. The system also enabled Interrent to do this when the automobile was returned to a location other than where it had been picked up. Because of this system, customers did not have to figure out whether they should rent a car on a daily basis or for a weekend, or whether they should choose a no-mileage fee or not. Before the customer has used the service he will be quoted the lowest possible fee.

Trouble-free service. To achieve this goal, it was decided that picking up the car and returning it must be made as convenient as possible for the customer. First, Interrent decided that a car could be picked up at any Interrent location, or it could be delivered to company addresses, railway stations or hotels. Interrent also decided to promise that the car would be delivered *not later than five minutes* after the time agreed upon. If a customer had to wait any longer for a car, he would not be billed by Interrent. Hans Åke Sand said: 'The signal to the organization and to the market is clear: it is not acceptable to deliver a car 10 minutes late and offer explanations about unexpected traffic jams.' Second, customers are not required to return the car to the same place they got it, but to any Interrent location. They would be guaranteed the 'lowest price' quotation at any location, and immediately.

Developing the Augmented Service Offering

Once these goals were decided upon, the next phase was to develop the resources necessary for their implementation. Most of the resources existed already, but some had to be created. For example, the existing computer system could not fulfil the 'lowest price' goal, so it had to be developed further. The rescue centre did not exist and had to be developed. As mentioned earlier, a partner was engaged here.

The *accessibility* of the service was enhanced by the actions taken to fulfil the 'Get to your destination', 'Lowest price' and 'Trouble-free service' goals. The customers had to be informed about how to react in case of a flat tyre, motor breakdown or accident in order to be able to activate the 'rescue activities'. The *participation of the customers* was ensured by written information on how the three 'guarantees' functioned both in the cars and on the accompanying documents, as well as verbally by the employees. Information about these guarantees and the benefits they offered was also included in Interrent's market communication when the new service was launched. Interrent wanted to prepare the customers to be co-producers of the service as well as possible.

In order to make sure that the *interactions* with the systems and physical resources were favourable, the new auto rental service required some specific resources. As far as technology, systems and physical resources were concerned, Interrent already had a nationwide network, where locations operated in isolation from each other and Interrent's headquarters and were therefore used to making decisions on their own. Also, Interrent had its own computer system, but the pricing system had to be developed. Furthermore, the cars used by Interrent were of good quality and dependable, but they had to be maintained as well as possible to avoid unnecessary extra costs due to breakdowns. Support by the garage and the mechanics had to be secured. This was achieved by internal information, oral as well as written, to the mechanics, during the weeks before the new service was launched. The 'security alarm system', involving the subcontracted 24-hour telephone reception and rescue system, had to be developed and the staff of Interrent's partner had to be trained and motivated to accept the new commitments.

The customer contact people in the reservation centre and at the rental locations also had to be trained and motivated to fulfil the goals of the new auto rental service, so that customers experienced favourable and positive interactions with the employees. The 'five-minute maximum delay' commitment and the 'within 45 minutes on the road again' commitment caused some internal controversy, but the *internal marketing* approach, headed by the managing director, convinced the organization of the rationale behind the new service. Eventually, as the service turned out to function well and without significant extra costs, a total commitment seemed to have been achieved. This internal marketing process had to be squeezed into a 10-day period before the service was launched, so that no information would leak outside the organization ahead of time. Meetings, called 'service seminars', were arranged, which included oral and written information, where discussion and communication was encouraged. Hans Åke Sand himself, as CEO, took an active part in this process. The new service, the goals and the rationale behind the promises to the market were explained and discussed. Hans Åke Sand concluded that 'the people in the organization perceived the total programme we were to offer our customers as a challenge, but they also realized that the firm trusted them, and we achieved a commitment for the new service.'

When launching the new service offering, the external marketing campaign was directed at travel agencies, but there was also a short advertising campaign involving leading daily newspapers which focused on the three guarantees. Building upon its previous good image, Interrent wanted to create a *communicated image* of trustworthiness and real value and comfort for its customers.

The Results

Immediately after the service was launched sales increased considerably, improving 15% in the first month, 9% in the second month and 17% in the third month after launching the service offering. After a year, sales were 23% higher than during the same period the year before.

The costs of operating the new service had not gone up to any significant extent. The fear of enormous extra costs following the three guarantees turned out to be unwarranted. Positive and service-oriented standards have also been set for the organization: promises must be kept 100%, no unnecessary (more than five-minute) delays will be accepted, no customer must be left without help if a breakdown occurs (on the road not later than 45 minutes after a phone call to the alarm centre), and the lowest price must always immediately be quoted. The effects of these and other standards are even greater because of the trust that management showed in the organization. Goals cannot be fulfilled without decentralized decision-making authority. Top management supported this, and provided the employees with sufficient information, guidance and managerial backup. The pricing system also produced such support.

As Hans Åke Sand said: 'We wanted to get rid of general promises to our customers, such as "We do it with a smile" or "We try our best", and demonstrate real excellence and trustworthiness.'

SERVICE DESIGN OR DESIGNING FOR SERVICE

Service design has become an important management issue.[15] However, designing services or service activities is too limited a view. It is based on the thought that goods and services are different categories of products, and that service design is developed alongside product design. The service perspective on business, or service logic, does not make such a distinction. Instead it is based on the foundation that service is a way of approaching the firm's customers in a manner that supports the customers' everyday processes, in order to facilitate their value creation and contribute to their goal achievement in life or business. Service to customers can be implemented by a firm through any kind of resources or any resource constellations, including any combination of goods, service activities, information, etc.

Following the service logic, designing services is a special case of designing any resource or resource constellation in such a way that they support the customer's processes. The broader view of designing resources and processes is called *design for service*.[16] Anything, including physical products, can be designed for service, in other words, *to serve customers* or any users. The opposite is to design a resource, for example, for artistic merit or technical smartness only. However, designing for service does not mean that such goals could not be included in the design process as well.[17] Hence, we should distinguish between:

- Design for service.
- Service design.

The latter means designing service activities, whereas *design for service* means that anything – goods, service activities and constellations of these and other resources – are designed to fulfil the purpose of a service logic:[18] to serve the customer or any other user in a value-creating way. Thus, designing for service may include service design, but also design of product elements and other tangible items in an offering. For example, a teapot can be designed to look good, but when used it spills tea onto the table, or it can be designed to function properly without spilling tea outside the cup, and still look good in an artistic sense. In the former situation, the teapot is *design as a product* only; in the latter situation it is *design for service*, i.e. to service the user's tea-drinking habit in a value-supporting manner.

In Figure 7.2 a model of designing for service is schematically illustrated *(the designing for service triangle)*. The three basic parts of the model are the *customer/user*, whom the resource or offering is designed to serve, the *concept* guiding the design process, and finally the service *process*.

As the model indicates, a thorough understanding of the *customers' everyday processes and goals* forms the starting point. Such an insight can hardly be gained through traditional market research. Instead ethnographic and similar methods are normally required. The following questions have to be asked and thoroughly answered:

- Who is the user?
- What is the user doing?
- Why is the user acting in a certain way?
- What could the user achieve?

Answers to such questions help the designer understand what opportunities exist to serve the customer, and to serve better than before and perhaps in a totally new way.

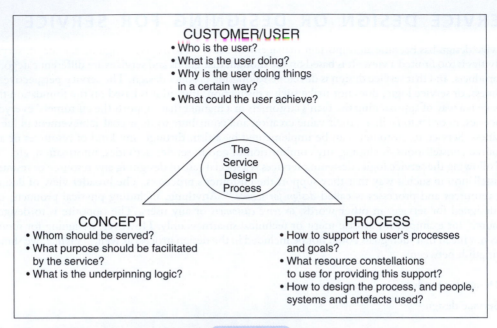

CUSTOMER/USER
- Who is the user?
- What is the user doing?
- Why is the user doing things in a certain way?
- What could the user achieve?

The Service Design Process

CONCEPT
- Whom should be served?
- What purpose should be facilitated by the service?
- What is the underpinning logic?

PROCESS
- How to support the user's processes and goals?
- What resource constellations to use for providing this support?
- How to design the process, and people, systems and artefacts used?

FIGURE 7.2

The designing for service triangle.

Then a customer-focused and service-based *concept* guiding the design process is established. Such a concept can be formulated by answering three simple questions:

- Whom should be served?

- What purpose should be facilitated by the service?

- What is the underpinning logic?

The two first questions provide basic facts for the design process. However, the third question, 'What is the underpinning logic?', is the most important one at this stage. Discussing this question and finding a new and unique answer to it, based on the answers to the two customer/user-related questions, may lead to totally new solutions and even revolutionize an industry. This is what Apple managed to do with the iPhone, or what the introduction of the microwave oven decades ago did to cooking. There is an abundance of examples. Not spending time on finding a new logic, when appropriate, only leads to more of the same, and not to a unique new way of serving customer-held purposes.

Finally, the *process* of designing for service should be attended to. Here the following questions should be answered:

- How to support the user's processes and goals?

- What resource constellations to use for providing this support?

- How to design the process, and people, systems and artefacts functioning in the process?

When developing the service process and designing the many kinds of resources involved, it is important to take a broad enough look at the process. There are often a whole host of resources and processes involved in providing service. If a required resource or sub-process is neglected and not properly designed, the whole service may fall apart, leading to a dissatisfied and, in the worst case lost, customer. Moreover, when developing and designing resources and processes, their effect on both the *technical quality* (the outcome of the service process; *what* the customer is left with) and the *functional quality* (*how* the process is perceived) have to be taken into account.

All resources and processes must be developed such that they *function as service*. They have to be *servicized*, which means that they are designed and managed in a way that indeed serves the customers. At a minimum the following kinds of resources and processes normally exist in a service process and have to be included in the design process:

Service employees: Employees in customer contacts and in support functions serving internal customers must be trained to do their job technically, but also motivated to perform in a customer-focused and service-oriented manner. Through their leadership managers and supervisors must support such behaviour (*internal marketing*; see Chapter 14).

Goods and artefacts in the service process: Such resources can be servicized, for example by making them easy to use, easy to maintain, and easily and nicely incorporated in the service process.

Recognized service activities: Activities in a customer relationship which are recognized as service, such as repair and maintenance service and call centres, must be developed so that they successfully support the customer process for which they are designed.

Hidden services: These are service activities that normally are not consider service but administrative, legal, economic, logistical or operational routines, such as complaints handling, invoicing, order-taking and deliveries. Well designed and handled hidden services can have a profound impact on customers' perception of the service provider and its service. Neglected hidden services, for example resulting in continuous delays in deliveries and unclear or supplier-focused invoices which create problems for customers, can destroy customer relationships and cause much negative word of mouth and discussion in social media.

Servicescapes: The environment where the service process takes place, or the servicescape, includes artefacts, atmosphere-enhancing elements such as music and colours, as well as people, both employees and customers. The way the servicescape looks and functions must be carefully designed to enhance the service experience.

Customers: On the one hand, customers are part of and form the servicescape. On the other hand, customers participate actively in the service process. When designing for service, both these customer roles have to be taken into account. For example, fellow customers must not disturb or in the worst case destroy the service experience of a focal customer, and customers can be given some active roles in service production, such as in Internet banking or self-service stores, or when operating vending machines and digital healthcare control devices.

The goal here is to design and develop a service process that indeed serves the customer. Apple's iPhone mentioned above is an example of a design and development process where thorough attention was paid to each part of the designing for service process. Another example is the development of a unique elevator system by the Finland-based global elevator company, Kone Corporation. This elevator system serves builders and owners of buildings better than traditional ones. By realizing the need for architects and builders to use as little space for the elevator system as possible, Kone changed the underpinning logic of the elevator concept and came up with the machine room-free system, where the machinery is built into the elevator. This freed space for other use in a building, and in addition it has positive effects on maintenance as well. From only being an elevator and escalator manufacturer, Kone is today known as a service business 'dedicated to people flow'.

DEVELOPING A SERVICE OFFERING IN THE MARKETSPACE

Today, an ever-increasing number of offerings of goods and services are marketed over the Internet and mobile phones. A large *virtual marketspace* has developed alongside the traditional physical marketplace. Regardless of whether they are related to physical goods or services, the purchase and consumption of Internet offerings can be described as process consumption and can be seen to reflect the key characteristics of service and service consumption.

The customer has to be able to operate the system in order to be able to get information about goods or services, to order them, to pay for them or arrange for payment, as well as possibly to make detailed inquiries and receive responses to those, and to perform a number of other activities related to the offering that is considered, and in many cases to use the service. In the end this process should of course lead to an outcome as in the case of any service. The quality of an Internet offering is dependent on the perceived quality of the process (the functional quality dimension) of using the Internet as a purchasing and sometimes also consumption instrument as well as on the perceived quality of the outcome (the technical quality dimension). As can be concluded from the description above, *the offering of any physical good or service over the Internet is a service.* Therefore, marketers who wish to use the Internet to offer their goods or services to customers should take care to design their offerings as service offerings that customers perceive and evaluate as service.

In the following sections the augmented service offering is developed into a service offering for the Internet, called the *NetOffer model.*[19]

THE NETOFFER MODEL

In this section the full NetOffer Internet offering model is described. The elements of the *basic service package,* i.e. the core service as well as the *enabling* and *enhancing* services, are similar to those in the original model. However, the augmentation elements of the Internet offering are different, because accessibility and interaction aspects of the process cannot be kept apart. Instead, they merge into one communication element in the augmentation process. The NetOffer model is illustrated in Figure 7.3.

The *service concept* is the foundation for the service package and for the augmentation of the package into an Internet offering. However, unless there is an easy-to-understand and easy-to-use website, i.e. a well-functioning interface between the user and the firm, there is no access to the Internet offering. Therefore, compared with the model for the traditional marketplace, an additional element termed *user interface* (UI) is included in the service package. The technical as well as the functional quality dimensions of the offering are dependent on the design and functionality of this interface. If the interface between the customer and the computer is not functional, the service that the firm is trying to supply is unusable and therefore worthless. The *user interface* consists of every aspect of the computerized interaction. The site must be easy to navigate and all the links must be clear and logical. The colours and graphics must be attractive and the text easy to process. Moreover, the speed of the server must be sufficient and the types of fonts must be appropriate. These are all issues that concern the quality of this interface.

The UI is part of the service package, because it more or less has to sell the offering itself. It has to be visually appealing and technically functioning. There are no marketers present who can convince the potential customer about the superiority of the offering. It is easy for a customer to switch to

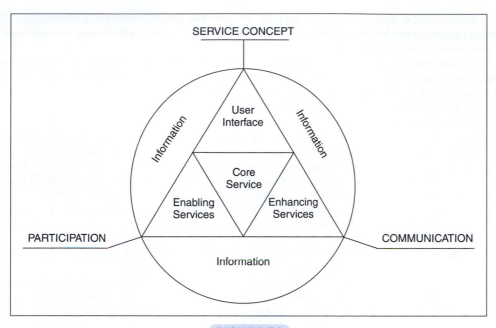

FIGURE 7.3
The NetOffer model.
Source: Grönroos, C., Heinonen, F., Isoniemi, K. & Lindholm, M., The NetOffer model: a case
example from the virtual marketspace. *Management Decision*, **38**(4); 2000: p. 250.
Reproduced by permission of Emerald Insight.

another website, and therefore a visually uninteresting or difficult-to-grasp interface quickly makes a
potential customer leave the site. In that case a sales opportunity is lost.

In an offering on the Internet, *information* is a critical element. Therefore, the inner triangle in the
figure illustrating the service package is placed within a circle of information. This circle represents
the information supply that has to be provided when offering goods or services on the Internet.
Information is a vital part of any such offering and it is a part of all the different elements of the model.
Information provided by the firm as well as by the customer is the fuel that makes the core, enabling
and enhancing services function and that drives the UI.

As Figure 7.3 shows, the augmentation of the service package includes two elements instead of the
three in the original augmented service offering model. These elements are:

1. Customer participation.

2. Communication.

Customer participation denotes the skills, knowledge and interest of customers as far as operating the UI
is concerned, i.e. as co-producers of the service, so that they can make a purchase, ask questions and
make complaints, receive responses, or go to links offered on the website. Customer participation can
also relate to discussion group activities involving customers and potential customers and other users of
a given website. Through an easily manageable UI and supportive information about various aspects

of the system and the parts of the service package, the firm can assist customers in participating. Thus, customer participation becomes partly a co-production activity, partly a co-creation of a solution for the customer's value-creating process.

On the Internet, accessibility and interaction involve communicating. Getting access means communicating with the website using the navigation system of the UI, and interacting with the website means communicating with the system through e-mail or other parts of the system. Interacting becomes part of communicating. Hence, interaction and accessibility in the original augmented service offering model merge into one element, where the common denominator is *communication*. Sometimes communication is two-way, as in the case of inquiries through e-mail. Sometimes it is one-way, as in the case of making a direct purchase or giving credit card information when paying for goods or services. The communication element of the Internet offering illustrates the dialogue that can occur between the service provider and the customer. This dialogue can include all possible media of communication, for example by e-mail, telephone, letters, message boards, etc.

By facilitating user-oriented communication, the Internet marketer helps the customer to purchase and consume goods and services offered on the Internet. Through this communication and assuming appropriate customer participation skills, the functional quality of the Internet offering (the *how* dimension) is enhanced and the customer is able to perceive the technical quality of what is offered (the *what* dimension). Good total perceived quality and value are created.

Finally, when goods and services are bought on the Internet, it is not enough that the Internet offering functions well and creates an acceptable perceived service quality. The purchases have to be delivered to the customer as well in a quality-enhancing way. Sometimes the delivery can take place electronically, as in the case of electronic airline tickets that can be printed by the consumer. Sometimes the goods are delivered in the physical marketplace.

CASE STUDY

DEVELOPING AN AUGMENTED SERVICE OFFERING ON THE INTERNET: THE PALACE

The Service Package

The Palace is a firm selling tickets to movies and it is also a group of movie theatres. The service concept can be formulated as follows: 'To offer tickets to movies supported by interesting and value-adding information related to current and future films immediately and easily accessible for a customer at a place chosen by and at any time convenient to him or her.'

The *core* service, i.e. the reason for being on the market, has changed from the traditional selling of tickets to the firm's group of cinemas to 'an Internet-based way of providing tickets to movies any time of the day'. The added value of introducing an Internet-based offering lies in the fact that, after having reserved and bought the tickets on the Internet, when coming to the movie theatre the customer knows for certain that there is a given seat available for him. Traditionally customers have had two options: either to call the movie theatre and make a reservation, in which case the ticket has to be picked up to 30 minutes in advance, or to go to the ticket booth and buy the ticket, if any tickets are available at that time.

In a traditional service offering the ticket purchase encounter is an example of enabling services. Also in the virtual surrounding of the Internet-based offering such mandatory enabling can be found, e.g. information about which movies are playing as well as information about dates, times and specific movie theatres where a given film is showing. As tickets have to be paid for, there are links to three different Internet banks. If a customer has access to them he can make the purchase. These features of the offering are typical enabling services, because without them customers cannot use the core service. For example, persons who are customers of any other than these three banks or who do not have access to their Internet payment systems cannot purchase tickets, because for them this enabling service is missing.

Also, *enhancing* services exist. In fact, there are few limits to what can be done on an Internet website. Links, competitions, games, gimmicks, etc. can be introduced. The Palace has introduced a number of such services that are not enabling the purchase of tickets but are used to enhance or differentiate the service package. Customers wanting information regarding various movies can join a mailing list and receive information about the movies at their e-mail addresses. At best, a service like this may create an interactive relationship based on e-mail communication between the company and its customers, which if effectively used can create advantages over the competitors. However, such interactive relationships are becoming so common in virtual marketspaces that they themselves do not automatically provide a competitive edge unless they are constantly updated and developed. The users must perceive that they receive essential information in a convenient way through the system. Otherwise it becomes an ineffective enhancing service.

On The Palace site there is news about the movies, the actors/actresses and off-screen activities that may be interesting to customers. This is an important supporting service, too, but probably not equally important as interactive relationships. In this case the customer has to log on to the website in order to read the news. Trailers and soundtracks are also examples of supporting services offered by The Palace. Such supporting services seem appealing, but in practice they are more gimmicks than effective marketing tools. In addition, the customer can get information about and listen to some of the soundtracks of the films shown in the movie theatre. The soundtracks belong to the same category as the trailers, initially attractive but probably of limited importance. In the beginning, when a trailer or a soundtrack system is new and technically better than what competitors can offer, the differentiating and value-adding effect of such enhancing services can be considered better. Over time, when the advantage is lost, such services are likely to become less interesting to users of the website and thus less effective as enhancing elements in the service package.

Augmentation of the Service Package

There is only one aspect of the offering that can be categorized clearly as a distinct *accessibility* issue. That is the fact that a virtual store is open 24 hours a day. This, however, is not something that distinguishes The Palace from other firms on the Internet. Accessibility is a common feature of virtual stores, because physically they are always accessible. This type of accessibility is not an issue in the marketspace; it is always there and can therefore be neglected as a distinguishing means of competition.

The absence of direct interactions with employees means that the website itself must perform the functions of employees. The site has to be technically advanced enough and functionally easy to operate by the customer so that he can get access to the service package. At the same time as this is a matter of *accessibility*; it is an *interaction* issue. The customer has to be able to understand the complexity of a website and to be able to *communicate* either in a one-way mode or in a two-way mode using an e-mail option (or sometimes the telephone).

In The Palace case, e-mail is the most important means of communicating with the firm. In this way the customer can also make complaints and get responses to them or to inquiries that he may have made. However, the e-mail system is also, simultaneously, an accessibility and interaction element of the service package.

The navigation system in The Palace example has a clear logic and is easy to use. This makes the service package easily accessible at the same time as it provides for good interactions between the user and the website. No access to employees is offered or even needed, but in other cases, if the user encounters problems, a contact to a helpdesk could be provided by the system for example. In such situations person-to-person communication and not only person-to-system communication occurs. Both accessing a system and interacting with it means communicating with the system.

Customer participation is also an important element in the augmentation of the service package on the Internet. In order to be able to operate the website of The Palace, the users need appropriate knowledge of how to use the navigation system, e-mail and other elements of the system. An easy-to-understand and easy-to-use navigation system assists the customer in purchasing tickets and in making use of supporting services available on the site. The Palace also provides the users of its website with the opportunity to log on to discussion groups, where they may exchange views on different films, movie stars and other movie-related topics with friends or strangers interested in the same issues. This is a way of creating a forum for customer participation through customer-to-customer communication. At the same time it supports word-of-mouth, or rather word-on-line communication about the Internet ticket sales service between customers and potential customers, who also may visit the website and take part in the activities of the discussion group.

Source: Grönroos, C., Heinonen, K., Isoniemi, K. & Lindholm, M. (2000) The NetOffer model: a case example from the virtual marketspace. *Management Decision*, **38**(4); 2000: 243–252. Reproduced by permission of Emerald Insight.

SUMMARY

This chapter discussed the need to develop a service offering in a systematic way. As service is a complicated phenomenon, service offerings are also complicated. The augmented service offering model was introduced as a conceptual model of the total offering customers perceive when consuming or using a service. The model includes a basic service package and an augmentation of the package into a holistic augmented service offering. The need for supportive marketing communication and positive image as well as for internal marketing to prepare the organization to perform according to the requirements of the augmented service offering was also explained. The starting point for the process of developing the offering is a clear understanding of the benefits customers want and the formulation of easily understood service concepts. As part of the presentation of how to successfully develop an augmented service offering, the issue of service guarantees was briefly touched upon. Then, how to design for service was explored and a model for designing for service was presented. Finally, a model for the development of services in the virtual marketspace was discussed.

QUESTIONS FOR DISCUSSION

1. Why has a service package to be further developed into an augmented service offering in order to be truly customer-oriented?

2. What are the elements of a basic service package?

3. How is the basic service package developed to be an augmented service offering?

4. What is the role of the service concept in the development of service offerings?

5. How does an augmented service offering for the virtual marketspace differ from an offering for the traditional marketplace?

6. What can be achieved internally and externally with the introduction of service guarantees?

7. What is the difference between service design and designing for service? When designing for service what questions should be asked?

8. Analyse the service, in general or a given service, offered by your organization, using the augmented service offering model, or develop a hypothetical service offering using the model.

NOTES

1. See Grönroos, C., *Service Managing and Marketing. Managing the Moments of Truth in Service Competition*. Lexington, MA: Lexington Books, 1990. In the service management and service marketing

literature, surprisingly little attention has been devoted to the understanding and conceptualization of service or service offerings. An example of one of the few attempts is Storey, C. & Easingwood, C.J., The augmented service offering: a conceptualization and study of its impact on new service success. *Journal of Product Innovation Management*, **15**(4), 1998, 335–351.

2. There is a limited but growing number of publications on the design and development of new services. See, for example, de Brentani, U., New industrial service development: scenarios for success and failure. *Journal of Business Research*, **32**(2), 1995, 93–103; de Brentani, U. & Ragot, E., Developing new business-to-business services: what factors impact performance? *Industrial Marketing Management*, **25**(6), 1996, 517–530; Edvardsson, B., Quality in new service development: key concepts and a frame of reference. *Internal Journal of Production Economics*, **52**(1–2), 1997, 31–46; Edvardsson, B. & Olsson, J., Key concepts for new service development. *The Service Industries Journal*, **16**(2), 1996, 140–164; Martin Jr., C.R. & Home, D.A., Service innovations: successful versus unsuccessful firms. *International Journal of Service Industry Management*, **4**(1), 1993, 49–65. See also Kokko, T., *Offering Development in the Restaurant Sector – A Comparison between Customer Perceptions and Management Beliefs*. Helsingfors, Finland: Hanken Swedish School of Economics, Finland, 2005.

3. See, for a few early examples, Normann, R., *Service Management*, 2nd edn. New York: John Wiley & Sons, 1991; Langeard, E. & Eiglier, P., *Servuction. Les Marketing des Services*. Paris. John Wiley & Sons, 1987; Lehtinen, J.R., *Quality-oriented Services Marketing*. University of Tampere, Finland, 1986.

4. This point of view goes back to the argument put forward by Theodore Levitt: 'Having been offered these extras, the customer finds them beneficial and therefore prefers doing business with the company that supplies them.' See Levitt, T., After the sale is over. *Harvard Business Review*, Sept–Oct, 1983, 9–10.

5. Lovelock, C., Competing on service: Technology and teamwork in supplementary services. *Strategy & Leadership*, **23**(4), 1995, 32–47. Recently this model has been studied and updated in Frow, P., Payne, A. & Ngo, L., Diagnosing the supplementary services model: empirical validation, advancement and implementation. *Journal of Marketing Management*, **30**(1–2), 2014, 138–171.

6. Gronroos, 1990, *op. cit.* and Grönroos, C., Developing the service offering – a source of competitive advantage. In Surprenant, C. (ed.), *Add Value to Your Service*. Chicago, IL: American Marketing Association, 1987.

7. I am grateful to Anton Molander and Daniela Voullième, two students in my Service Management and Marketing class, who in a project presentation made the point that the terms *enabling*

and *enhancing* services better communicate the meaning of the underlying constructs than the terms *facilitating* and *supporting* services which were used in previous editions of this book.

8. Grönroos, 1990, *op. cit.* and Grönroos, 1987, *op. cit.* In the service development literature, especially customer involvement has been studied. See, for example, Carbonell, P., Rodriges-Escudero, A.I. & Pujari, D., Customer involvement in new service development: an examination of antecedents and outcomes. *Journal of Product Innovation Management*, **6**(5), 2009, 536–550.

9. See Prahalad, C.K. & Ramaswamy, V., *The Future of Competition: Co-Creating Unique Value with Customers*. Boston, MA: Harvard Business School Press, 2004 and Wikström, S., Value creation by company–consumer interaction. *Journal of Marketing Management*, **12**, 1996, 359–374.

10. The relationship between image as brand image and firm reputation and service offerings have been studied in Cretu, A.E. & Brodie, R.J., The image of brand image and company reputation where manufacturers market to small firms: a customer value perspective. *Industrial Marketing Management*, **36**(2), 2007, 230–240.

11. Bitner, M.J., Brown, S.W. & Meuter, M.L., Technology infusion in service encounters. *Journal of the Academy of Marketing Science*, **28**(1), 2000, 138–149. See also Kristensson, P., Matthing, J. & Johansson, N., Key strategies for successful involvement of customers in new technology-based services. *Journal of Service Industry Management*, **19**(4), 2008, 474–491.

12. Although this case is not new, it clearly demonstrates the potential of the augmented service offering model.

13. Ostrom, A.L. & Hart, C., Service guarantees. Research and practice. In Swartz, T.A. & Iacobucci, D. (eds), *Handbook in Services Marketing & Management*. Thousand Oaks, CA: Sage Publications, 2000, pp. 299–313 and Hart, C.W.L., The power of unconditional guarantees. *Harvard Business Review*, **66**(Jul–Aug), 1988, 54–62.

14. Ostrom, A.L. & Iacobucci, D., The effects of guarantees on consumers' evaluation of services. *Journal of Services Marketing*, **12**(6), 1998, 362–378. See also Wu, C.H.J., Liao, H-C., Hung, K-P. & Ho, Y-H., Service guarantees in the hotel industry: their effects on consumer risk and service quality perceptions. *International Journal of Hospitality Management*, **31**(3), 2012, 757–763, and McCollough, M.A., Service guarantees: a review and an explanation of their continued rarity. *Academy of Marketing Studies Journal*, **14**(2), 2010, 27–54.

15. See, for example, Patricio, L., Fisk, R.P., Falcao de Cunha, J. & Constantine, L., Multilevel service design: from customer value constellation to service experience blueprinting. *Journal of Service Research*, **14**(2), 2011, 180–200.

16. See Kimbell, L., Designing for service as one way of designing services. *International Journal of Design*, **5**(2), 2011, 41–52. See also Meroni, A. & Sangiorgi, D., *Design for services*. Surrey: Gower Publishing Ltd, 2011.

17. Moreover sometime, for example, designing for artistic goals may be designing for service. For instance, a painting serves the owner or any viewer by its artistic qualities.

18. Wetter-Edman, K., Sangiorgi, D., Edvardsson, B., Holmlid, S., Grönroos, C. & Mattelmäki, T., Design for value co-creation: exploring synergies between Design for Service and Service Logic. *Service Science*, **6**(2), 2014, 106–121.

19. Grönroos, C., Heinonen, K., Isoniemi, K. & Lindholm, M., The NetOffer model: a case example from the virtual marketspace. *Management Decision*, **38**(4), 2000, 243–252.

FURTHER READING

Bitner, M.J., Brown, S.W. & Meuter, M.L. (2000) Technology infusion in service encounters. *Journal of the Academy of Marketing Science*, **28**(1), 138–149.

Carbonell, P., Rodriges-Escudero, A.I. & Pujari, D. (2009) Customer involvement in new service development: an examination of antecedents and outcomes. *Journal of Product Innovation Management*, **6**(5), 536–550.

Cretu, A.E. & Brodie, R.J. (2007) The influence of brand image and company reputation where manufacturers market to small firms: a customer value perspective. *Industrial Marketing Management*, **36**(2), 230–240.

de Brentani, U. (1995) New industrial service development: scenarios for success and failure. *Journal of Business Research*, **32**(2), 93–103.

de Brentani, U. & Ragot, E. (1996) Developing new business-to-business services: what factors impact performance? *Industrial Marketing Management*, **25**(6), 517–530.

Edvardsson, B. (1997) Quality in new service development: key concepts and a frame of reference. *Internal Journal of Production Economics*, **52**(1–2), 31–46.

Edvardsson, B. & Olsson, J. (1996) Key concepts for new service development. *The Service Industries Journal*, **16**(2), 140–164.

Frow, P., Payne, A. & Ngo, L. (2014) Diagnosing the supplementary services model: empirical validation, advancement and implementation. *Journal of Marketing Management*, **30**(1–2), 138–171.

Grönroos, C. (1987) Developing the service offering – a source of competitive advantage. In Surprenant, C. (ed.), *Add Value to Your Service*. Chicago, IL: American Marketing Association.

Grönroos, C. (1990) *Service Managing and Marketing. Managing the Moments of Truth in Service Competition.* Lexington, MA: Lexington Books.

Grönroos, C., Heinonen, K., Isoniemi, K. & Lindholm, M. (2000) The NetOffer model: a case example from the virtual marketspace. *Management Decision*, **38**(4), 243–252.

Hart, C.W.L. (1988) The power of unconditional guarantees. *Harvard Business Review*, **66**(Jul–Aug), 54–62.

Kimbell, L. (2011) Designing for service as one way of designing services. *International Journal of Design,* **5**(2), 41–52.

Kokko, T. (2005) Offering Development in the Restaurant Sector – A Comparison between Customer Perceptions and Management Beliefs. Helsingfors, Finland: Hanken Swedish School of Economics, Finland.

Kristensson, P., Matthing, J. & Johansson, N. (2008) Key strategies for successful involvement of customers in new technology-based services. Journal of Service Industry Management, **19**(4), 474–491.

Langeard, E. & Eiglier, P. (1987) Servuction. Les Marketing des Services. Paris: John Wiley & Sons.

Lehtinen, J.R. (1986) Quality-oriented Services Marketing. University of Tampere, Finland.

Levitt, T. (1983) After the sale is over. Harvard Business Review, Sept–Oct.

Lovelock, C. (1995) Competing on service: technology and teamwork in supplementary services. Strategy & Leadership, **23**(4), 32–47.

Martin Jr., C.R. & Horne, D.A. (1993) Service innovations: successful versus unsuccessful firms. *International Journal of Service Industry Management*, **4**(1), 49–65.

McCollough, M.A. (2010) Service guarantees: a review and an explanation of their continued rarity. *Academy of Marketing Studies Journal*, **14**(2), 27–54.

Meroni, A. & Sangiorgi, D. (2011) *Design for services,* Surrey: Gower Publishing Ltd.

Normann, R. (1991) *Service Management*, 2nd edn. New York: John Wiley & Sons.

Ostrom, A.L. & Hart, C. (2000) Service guarantees. Research and practice. In Swartz, T.A. & Iacobucci, D. (eds), *Handbook in Services Marketing & Management*. Thousand Oaks, CA: Sage Publications, pp. 299–313.

Ostrom, A.L. & Iacobucci, D. (1998) The effects of guarantees on consumers' evaluation of services. *Journal of Services Marketing*, **12**(6), 362–378.

Patricio, L., Fisk, R.P., Falcao de Cunha, J. & Constantine, L. (2011) Multilevel service design: from customer value constellation to service experience blueprinting. *Journal of Service Research*, **14**(2), 180–200.

Prahalad, C.K. & Ramaswamy, V. (2004) *The Future of Competition: Co-Creating Unique Value with Customers*. Boston, MA: Harvard Business School Press.

Storey, C. & Easingwood, C.J. (1998) The augmented service offering: a conceptualization and study of its impact on new service success. *Journal of Product Innovation Management*, **15**(4), 335–351.

Wetter-Edman, K., Sangiorgi, D., Edvardsson, B., Holmlid, S., Grönroos, C. & Mattelmäki, T. (2014) Design for value co-creation: exploring synergies between Design for Service and Service Logic. *Service Science*, **6**(2), 106–121.

Wikström, S. (1996) Value creation by company–consumer interaction. *Journal of Marketing Management*, **12**, 359–374.

Wu, C.H.J., Liao, H-C., Hung, K-P. & Ho, Y-H. (2012) Service guarantees in the hotel industry: their effects on consumer risk and service quality perceptions. *International Journal of Hospitality Management*, **31**(3), 757–763.

CHAPTER 8
MANAGING PRODUCTIVITY IN SERVICE ORGANIZATIONS

> ❝ *The productivity of service operations is not an internal affair. In service customers decide what is high productivity and what is not.* ❞

INTRODUCTION

The productivity concept as it has been developed for manufacturing firms cannot readily be used in service contexts. In this chapter the problem is discussed in detail. The shortcomings of a traditional manufacturing-based productivity concept are analysed, and a service productivity concept is developed. It is observed that in service organizations decisions based on traditional productivity measurements will almost always lead in the wrong direction. Internal and external consequences have to be taken into account simultaneously if productivity is to provide management with meaningful guidance. In the final sections of this chapter the possibility of creating measurement instruments is explored. No final calculation models can yet be offered. The theoretical understanding of service productivity has to be developed further before robust measurement models can be developed. After reading this chapter the reader should understand the problems of a traditional manufacturing-oriented productivity concept in service contexts and the pitfalls of using productivity measurements based on such a concept. The reader should also understand the nature of service productivity and how service productivity measurements could be made and, finally, know how continuous learning in a relationship contributes to productivity.

PRODUCTIVITY: MANAGING PROFITS, NOT COSTS

In many organizations managers seem to misunderstand the meaning of productivity. Frequently, productivity is more or less seen as cost efficiency, and productivity management only or predominantly as the management of internal efficiency. Productivity as a concept comes from product manufacturing and from a closed system without external interference. Customers are not influencing the manufacturing processes, and moreover, are not exposed to such processes and influenced by how they are organized and function.

In conventional productivity models, the objective is to ensure effective management of profits. In practice, it is assumed that when input resources into the processes are changed, and for example, less expensive resources or production processes are introduced, the quality of the production output, the products, can be controlled. Therefore, in situations where more cost-efficient resources or processes are used, revenues generated by production outputs can be expected to remain unchanged but unit costs of production go down. Costs are variable, revenues are fixed. In conventional manufacturing this means that by managing cost efficiency, productivity is managed at the same time. Productivity management becomes a shortcut to profit management, and *internal efficiency of the firm's processes becomes a proxy for profit effectiveness*.

Problems occur when this shortcut to profit management is used in business environments where production is not a system closed to customers. What functions well in a closed system does not function in an open system, as a service organization is. When new input resources and processes are introduced in service operations, the production outcome, and its technical quality dimension, and the service process, and its functional quality dimension, do not remain unchanged. When managers in service operations mistake cost efficiency for productivity, and concentrate on managing internal efficiency only, disaster is around the corner. In service, it is imperative to realize that *productivity management indeed is profit management*, and no shortcuts exist. This creates a need for new knowledge and new productivity models.

THE PRODUCTIVITY DILEMMA: BALANCING REVENUES AND COSTS

Although some publications on service productivity have been published during the past decade or so, productivity as a concept has been largely neglected in service research.[1] It is often claimed that productivity is low in many service organizations and that service is produced using excess resources and at unnecessarily high cost. With another resource structure the service provider could cut costs and still produce as much as before. For example, banks are urging their customers to use ATMs, PCs and the Internet to take care of regular bank affairs instead of visiting a bank and occupying the bank employees' time. Insurance companies have established websites on the Internet and call centres for customer service, so that customers can interact over the Internet or telephone instead of by visiting customer service employees. Airlines are forcing their customers to turn to self-service check-in systems. The reason for these changes in resource structures is of course to shift from expensive resources in the service process to cheaper resources. If customers perceive that they receive the same quality as before, or perhaps even better quality, these changes have been successful.[2] They have been *cost-effective* and at the same time maintained or improved the firm's *revenue-generating capability*.

However, cost-cutting changes in the resources used may well have the opposite effect. Perceived quality may deteriorate and customers may become dissatisfied and start to look for other options. The service provider's revenue generating capability thus declines.

The problem with being an effective service organization is that productivity and perceived quality are inseparable phenomena.[3] Therefore, managers in service organizations must never revert to cost efficiency management only. As Anderson *et al.*[4] observe, improving customer satisfaction and productivity may turn out to be incompatible goals. Improving productivity may have a neutral or positive impact on quality, but equally it may damage perceived quality. If the latter happens, satisfaction with quality declines and the risk that the firm will lose customers increases. Revenues go down, and this may have a negative effect on the firm's overall financial results, even though costs may also have been reduced. As productivity is a proxy for profitability, or profit, this development is in reality not a productivity improvement.

This is the dilemma in service processes. Improved internal efficiency following the introduction of more cost-effective production resources and processes does not necessarily lead to better economic results. In fact, while using a traditional productivity terminology, what is considered to bring about an increase in productivity – that is, improved internal efficiency – often has the opposite effect in service organizations. This leads to decreasing service quality and, as a consequence, to lost revenues. The obvious conclusion is that in service contexts productivity cannot be understood without simultaneously considering the interrelationship between internal efficiency and perceived quality (external effectiveness).[5] Hence, internal efficiency, which equates to cost efficiency, cannot be managed separately from external effectiveness, that is a firm's capability of producing a certain level of perceived service quality with a given resource structure.[6] Especially in service processes where the role of the employees is essential, 'if a firm improves productivity by "downsizing", it may achieve an increase in productivity in the short term, but future profitability may be threatened if customer satisfaction is highly dependent on the efforts of personnel'.[7]

Because the quality of the production output in manufacturing is not impacted by cost-saving changes in the production system, the revenue side can be neglected in the productivity equation. In service the quality level is impacted by such actions and therefore revenues are influenced as well. Both costs and revenues are variable. Hence, effects on revenues of cost-saving actions must always be included in productivity models and measurements.

In conclusion, following a traditional productivity concept firms are used to treating the management of productivity as an internal issue where revenue effects can be omitted from the calculations. They measure the level of productivity from an internal efficiency perspective and, because of a *constant-quality assumption*, take for granted that the external effects on quality are under control. The constant–quality assumption implies that production inputs can be changed without a negative impact on the quality produced. However, in service the situation is the opposite. Productivity is not evaluated internally by managers, but externally by the customers, *who make external judgements of the productivity of a service operation*. This, of course, does not exclude the importance of taking into account the internal efficiency aspects of service productivity as well. However, because the *constant-quality assumption* does not apply in service, *the customers have the last word*.

To clarify the discussion of service productivity, Table 8.1 describes central concepts and terms as they are used here. Some have been discussed and defined in previous chapters.

SHORTCOMINGS OF MANUFACTURING-BASED PRODUCTIVITY CONCEPTS AND REQUIREMENTS OF A SERVICE-BASED CONCEPT

The goal of productivity management is to create *profit effectiveness* – in other words, to *manage the economic results*. Because, by increasing productivity, an unchanged or even improved customer perceived quality is produced using fewer resources or using resources in a more efficient way, the economic results are assumed to improve. As long as this is the case, managing productivity makes sense. If improved productivity does not lead to better economic results, there is no profit effectiveness, and in that case increasing productivity does not make sense.

Existing productivity models and productivity measurement instruments are based on assumptions of *closed systems*, where consumption and production are separate processes and customers do not

TABLE 8.1

Definition and description of central concepts and terms used.

Concept/term	Definition and/or description
Productivity	Efficiency and effectiveness in the process of transforming input resources in a service or manufacturing process into customer value and hence also into *profitable operations.* Productivity is *profit management.*
Traditional productivity concept	The conversion of production resources into output, or the ratio between output from the production process and input into that process, given a constant quality level (the *constant-quality assumption*).
Internal efficiency	How efficiently outputs can be produced using a given amount of production resources and a given production process.
Cost efficiency	Synonym for internal efficiency; capability to manage costs.
External effectiveness	How effectively perceived service quality can be produced using a given amount of production resources.
Revenue effectiveness	Synonym for external effectiveness; capability to manage revenues.
Revenue-generating capability	The degree to which the perceived service quality capability enables the service provider to generate sales and revenues.
Capacity efficiency	How efficiently the production capacity is used for serving customers (excess supply lowers capacity efficiency; excess demand may affect perceived service quality negatively).
Profit effectiveness	How efficiently and effectively production resources are used, blending external effectiveness and internal efficiency, and capacity utilized, to produce economic results. *Profit effectiveness* is the ultimate *internal* goal for productivity-improving actions and programmes; *value for customers* is the ultimate *external* goal.

participate in the production process as co–producers. In traditional manufacturing,[8] these assumptions make sense of course. In service contexts, where the service production process is largely an *open system,* they create confusion, give rise to misleading measurements and guide decision–making in the wrong direction. In Table 8.2 assumptions underpinning the traditional manufacturing-oriented productivity concept and characteristics of service are summarized.[9]

The characteristics of service and the assumption underlying the traditional productivity concept make traditional productivity models and measurement instruments less useful *as such* for service orga–nizations. For example, how raw materials are used in a restaurant to produce a given number of meals can be calculated using manufacturing-oriented productivity methods, and this information is undoubtedly valuable for the restaurant. However, it has nothing to do with the productivity of the

> **TABLE 8.2**
>
> **The service productivity dilemma.**

Assumptions included in the manufacturing-oriented productivity concept	Characteristics of service affecting productivity in service contexts
Production and consumption are *separate*; productivity measured in a *closed system* → perceived quality is dependent on outcome only (technical quality).	Production and consumption are partly *simultaneous processes* with quality-influencing interactions, i.e. an *open system.* → perceived quality is dependent on both outcome and process (technical and functional quality). → difficulties in separating production input from output.
Customers *do not participate* in the production process (closed system) → perceived quality is not influenced by the production process.	Customers *participate* in the service process (open system). → uncertainty of customer-induced input in the service process; their effects vary from situation to situation. → customer-induced input affects the efficiency of firm-induced input in the process. → perceived quality is also influenced by the service (production) process (the functional quality dimension).

Source: Adapted from Ojasalo, K., *Conceptualizing Productivity in Services*. Helsinki, Helsingfors: Hanken Swedish School of Economics, Finland/CERS, 1999, p. 59. Reproduced by permission.

total restaurant operation. A totally different approach to productivity has to be taken to measure how well a service provider uses resources to create output in the form of acceptable perceived quality and support to customers' value creation, and hence to create profitable operations and an improved economic result. In service processes, where a firm provides customers with a highly standardized infrastructure, such as a telephone receptionist or a fast-food cash register, the service provider comes close to a closed production system resembling manufacturing. As long as the infrastructure functions without problems and the customers know how to operate it, traditional assumptions for understanding and measuring productivity apply to a large extent. However, in most service processes, even in high-tech services, the characteristics of service in Table 8.2[10] apply. There, traditional productivity models and measurement instruments are more misleading than valuable.

Because the service production process and consumption are partly simultaneous processes, where customers actively participate as co-producers, the resources used to produce service cannot be totally standardized. It is difficult to relate a given number of inputs, in volume or value terms, to a given number of outputs. Frequently, it is even difficult to define 'one unit of service'. The traditional manufacturing-based productivity concept can be described with the following formula:

$$\text{Productivity} = \frac{\text{Output produced}}{\text{Input used}} \bigg| \text{Constant quality}$$

In traditional manufacturing inputs used can be measured in monetary terms as cost of production, and because of the constant quality assumption, a decrease of the cost level equals improved productivity. Because the output quality can be kept constant, revenues will not be affected by changes in input resources and processes. Therefore, from a commercial point of view, in traditional product manufacturing, the productivity formula takes the following form:

$$\text{Productivity (manufacturing)} = \frac{\text{Fixed revenues}}{\text{Variable costs}}$$

Only if the quality of the production output is constant can productivity be measured using traditional methods. This *constant-quality assumption* is normally taken for granted and, therefore, not explicitly expressed. As an unfortunate consequence, the critical importance of this assumption is easily forgotten. However, traditional productivity measurements only make sense in service contexts when the constant-quality assumption applies. *In most service processes it does not apply.* Consequently in service the productivity formula takes the following form:

$$\text{Productivity} = \frac{\text{Output produced}}{\text{Input used}} \bigg| \text{variable quality}$$

In situations where the constant-quality assumption can be taken for granted in productivity management, *revenue effectiveness* is not an issue. A stable quality level is a guarantee of stable revenue streams. For service providers, however, revenue effectiveness considerations cannot be omitted, and therefore they become an integral part of productivity management. If they are not taken into account, productivity as profit effectiveness is not managed, only internal cost efficiency. From a commercial standpoint, *service productivity* can be illustrated with the following formula:

$$\text{Productivity (service)} = \frac{\text{Variable revenues}}{\text{Variable costs}}$$

In service, it is not only the input that is difficult to calculate, it is also difficult to measure output. Output measured as a volume is only useful if customers are willing to buy this output. Unlike in manufacturing, in service we do not know whether customers will purchase the output produced using a different input structure or not. It depends on the effects on perceived process-related functional and outcome-related technical quality of the new inputs used. Hence, the interrelationship between the use of input or production resources and the perceived quality of the output produced with these resources has to be taken into account in service productivity.[11] In other words, the interrelationship between internal efficiency (cost efficiency) and external effectiveness (revenue effectiveness) is critical for service productivity.

In the limited number of publications on productivity in service that exist, the authors normally suggest that service productivity is managed as internal efficiency only, and somehow related to the management of service quality.[12] However, this is not according to the fundamental idea of the productivity concept as an instrument for managing profit effectiveness. Moreover, such an approach does not guarantee that perceived quality effects are properly taken into account. In a recently published article, Parasuraman concluded that strategies to improve productivity and service quality, and also innovation, are likely to be suboptimal, if they are pursued in isolation. Instead integrated strategies should be developed.[13] Therefore, we present a service productivity concept which incorporates both internal efficiency (costs) and external effectiveness (perceived quality, revenues) and strives to integrate them into one model.

THE INTERRELATIONSHIP BETWEEN PRODUCTIVITY, QUALITY, CUSTOMER PARTICIPATION AND DEMAND

Because customers participate as co-producers in the service process and influence the process and its outcome, the customer's role in productivity is also different in service contexts to that in manufacturing (see Table 8.2). We can distinguish between:

- Provider-induced contribution to productivity.

- Customer-induced contribution to productivity.

- Interaction-induced contribution to productivity.

The first contribution is *provider participation* in the service process. For example, for a hair stylist, his professional and communication skills, time available, the equipment, physical products used in the process, enhancing services and goods such as coffee, tea and magazines form the provider participation in the process.

The customer and fellow customers provide *customer-induced contributions* to productivity, such as information, self-service activities, inquiries and complaints. In the hair stylist example, the accuracy of the customer's requests and her ability to provide correct information to guide the hair stylist in cutting her hair are customer-induced contributions to the process. The customers' actions do not only give the input needed to produce the service, they also influence the way the employees and technologies in the service process function. Depending on how well the hair stylist and the customer can relate to and communicate with each other, the interactions that occur will contribute more or less to the perceived quality of the process, and sometimes also to the internal efficiency. This is an *interaction-induced contribution* to productivity.

The provider-induced, customer-induced and interaction-induced contributions do not only influence service productivity but quality as well.[14] *Quality and productivity are thus two sides of the same coin.*

In addition, productivity is influenced by *demand*. If demand is low, the service provider's resources will be underutilized, which means that internal cost efficiency decreases, with a negative effect on productivity. A given cost level produces fewer revenues and the operation turns less profitable. In manufacturing, inventories can be used to offset this effect. In service, this is not possible. When there is a demand that meets the provider-induced resources in the service process, internal efficiency improves and a positive effect on productivity is created. When demand starts to exceed what can be managed with existing resources, external effectiveness decreases, which has a negative effect

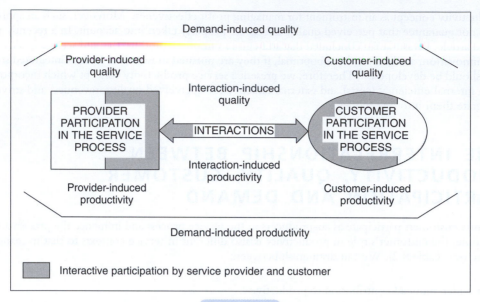

FIGURE 8.1

**Productivity, quality, customer and provider participation and demand
as productivity factors in service contexts.**
Source: Gummesson, E., Productivity, quality and relationship marketing in service
operations. *International Journal of Contemporary Hospitality Management*, **10**(1);
1998. p. 5. Reproduced by permission of Emerald Insight.

on perceived service quality and on revenues and profits. Hence, demand is also a critical productivity factor in service. In Figure 8.1[15] the interrelated factors in service productivity are illustrated schematically.

The shaded areas of the provider participation and customer participation boxes depict the parts of the provider's resources and the customer's resources that are used in interaction with each other (in service encounters). Part of provider participation takes place in a back office, where internal service is produced. On the other hand, customer participation sometimes also takes place outside the interactions with the service provider. For example, when making a telephone call the service is produced by two customers who are interacting with each other. The telephone operator only indirectly supports the service process by providing the telephone infrastructure. For example, IKEA, the Swedish furniture chain, provides its customers with packaged furniture in a box which includes parts, bolts and tools and instructions for assembly. The customer is then expected to continue the service process which started in the shop by assembling the furniture at home. Here again the service provider only indirectly supports the service process in the customer's home by providing tools and instructions.

From a managerial point of view, the following aspects are important in productivity management in service organizations:

- When the service provider designs its input into the process, an optimal balance between perceived service quality and the firm's revenue–generating capability (external effectiveness) on the one hand and cost efficiency of resources used (internal efficiency) on the other hand must be maintained.

- The service provider's resources (provider participation) must contribute to interactions with customers in the service process in a way that creates an optimal balance between perceived quality and internal efficiency.

- Customers must be chosen, educated, motivated and informed in such a way that they, through their participation in the service process, contribute positively to customer-induced quality and productivity as well as to interaction-induced quality and productivity.

- Demand must be managed so that a balance can be maintained between perceived quality and internal efficiency and thus also between revenues and costs.

The crucial point here is to pay attention to how changes in internal efficiency affect perceived service quality (external effectiveness). Longer waiting times and less customer attention from personnel may be the results of a change which increases cost efficiency in the resource structure. These effects can easily have a negative impact on the functional quality of the service process and perhaps also on the technical quality of the outcome. If this is the case, customers may be lost, revenues decline, and in the end the *profit effectiveness* of the service provider deteriorates. Then the ultimate goal for productivity improvements, a better economic result and improved profitability, is not achieved.[16]

On the other hand, actions that improve cost efficiency may have a neutral or even positive effect on perceived service quality. New configurations of inputs and a move to a new technology level may improve cost efficiency and have a positive effect on perceived quality as well. For example, a restaurant may offer a salad bar instead of serving salad at the table, to decrease its input resources. For those customers who appreciate this alternative the perceived quality is maintained or perhaps even improved. For the restaurant this shift has probably led to a more cost-efficient use of resources. In this case, both internal efficiency and external effectiveness, and hence also profit effectiveness, have improved, which is the ultimate internal goal for productivity-improving actions.

In conclusion, cost efficiency and managing costs form an important part of the management of productivity in service, as they do in manufacturing. However, because of the characteristics of service, cost efficiency is a more complicated issue in service contexts. In the next section we shall turn to the management of costs in service as one aspect of productivity management.

MANAGING COSTS IN A SERVICE CONTEXT

In a turnaround process in the 1980s that received a lot of international publicity in service industries and in service management literature, SAS (Scandinavian Airlines System), using a non-accounting language, introduced a useful division of costs. The costs of operating and administrating the firm were divided into *good costs* and *bad costs*.[17] These cost concepts are not related to conventional terminology, such as fixed and variable costs, but they are managerially relevant and helpful tools for calculating cost efficiency and for service productivity management.[18]

Good costs are productive costs, because they improve an organization's capability to produce high-quality service and thus enhance revenue. The costs of maintaining service encounters and back-office operations are mostly good costs. Also, the costs of training personnel, goods and service development, are examples of good costs. The connection between such costs and the enhancement of external effectiveness is obvious. *Bad costs* are costs that follow from unnecessary bureaucracy, heavy middle and top management layers, overstaffed departments and unnecessarily complicated and time-consuming operational and administrative routines. Changes in resource structure that decrease bad costs will have a positive effect on internal efficiency and at the same time either a neutral or sometimes even a positive effect on customer perceived quality and external effectiveness.

If management wants to improve productivity, achieve better results, or just cut costs as a means of enhancing the competitiveness of the firm, what is usually done? Far too often the main actions are to save costs of service encounter operations or back-office operations. Other staff and the management layers are left untouched. It is much easier to cut costs in operations than costs in other parts of the organization. If a firm is facing hard times with poor financial results, personnel training, product development efforts and external marketing activities are also often affected by cutbacks. What management does is to *cut good costs leaving bad costs untouched*. From this it follows that internal efficiency may or may not improve, but external effectiveness and customer perceived quality may be damaged, and the net effect is all too often negative. The firm's situation is not improved, and the competitive position of the firm is worsened. The firm becomes a victim of the *strategic management trap* discussed in Chapter 3.

A clear distinction between good costs, bad costs and mandatory costs has to be made before any cost-saving actions are considered. Even if the firm is suffering from financial hardship, good costs, following from efforts such as improving the skills of customer contact employees or investing in new technology in service encounters, may have to be increased so that its competitiveness is improved or at least not damaged. Good costs should not be cut. Instead, bad costs should be focused on by management. *Bad costs, not good costs destroy profits*. First, bad costs and the sources of such costs have to be identified. Second, actions to eliminate or decrease bad costs should be taken.

The point is that all costs are not equal wherever they occur. Until a particular cost is identified as good or bad, action must not be taken to eliminate or decrease it.

PITFALLS WHEN USING A PRODUCTIVITY MODEL FROM MANUFACTURING

As mentioned, using a productivity model from manufacturing with its *constant-quality assumption* and concentrating on the cost side only may cause problems for a service organization and even lead to the opposite effect to what was intended. In Figure 8.2 the effects of using a manufacturing productivity model in product manufacturing and in service, respectively, are illustrated.

To the left in Figure 8.2, the manufacturing case is depicted. When increasing productivity is measured as internal efficiency only, due to the constant-quality assumption the quality of the outcome, the physical products, can be expected to remain unchanged. Therefore, the level of revenues is maintained and, because of the internal efficiency gains, costs go down and profit goes up. The right part of the figure illustrates what typically happens in a service organization. When productivity gains are sought through internal efficiency increases without paying attention to quality effects, perceived service quality tends to deteriorate. Because lower quality probably leads to lost revenues, the expected profit increase due to cost savings is not achieved. Lost revenues offset the cost savings, and in the end instead of going up, profit goes down.

In reality the development is not always as bad as illustrated above. Especially in situations where service firms operate in a bureaucratic manner, both the internal efficiency and customer perceived quality (external effectiveness) may be improved by streamlining the way the firm operates. Then bad costs are found in the service encounters as well. In a situation like this, using a manufacturing-based productivity model may very well at the same time benefit the firm as well as its customers, and hence also lead to improved profits. Also, in situations where new technology to be used in service processes is available, both internal efficiency gains and improved perceived service quality can be achieved. Using the Internet and IT technologies and other digital means may be ways of rising to a

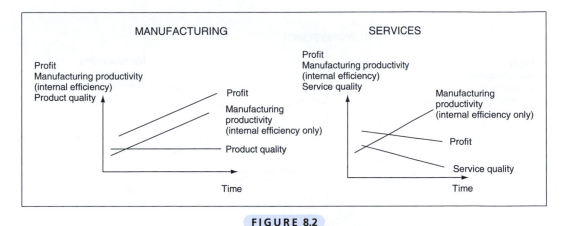

MANUFACTURING   SERVICES

FIGURE 8.2

The relationship between manufacturing productivity (internal efficiency only), product and service quality and profitability.

new and more cost-efficient technology level. As in the case of Internet banking, customers may not always immediately appreciate the new service processes, but in the end the service quality advantages of the introduction of new technologies are normally accepted by most, if not always all, customer segments. However, when the old-fashioned or bureaucratic service processes have been streamlined and/or the new technology has been adopted, and if the firm continues to cut costs, the problems with using a manufacturing model to achieve additional productivity gains demonstrated in Figure 8.2 will start to occur.

In Figure 8.3 the challenge for a service firm looking for improved profits through productivity improvements is illustrated. As long as the service processes are unclear and bureaucratic or a new technology has not yet been adopted, a manufacturing productivity model may very well be effective. Internal efficiency is improved and because the streamlined service process or the new technology is appreciated by the firm's customers, perceived service quality increases as well. Hence, costs go down and revenues go up, resulting in improved profit. However, eventually a *turning point* is reached. This breaking point, illustrated by the vertical dotted line in the figure, means that *the manufacturing-like situation no longer exists* and further developments require new, service-oriented productivity concepts and models. If the firm attempts to achieve further cost savings through internal efficiency improvement without paying due attention to how the quality of its service develops, the economic result and profitability easily starts to decrease. The actions that lead to a positive development before the *turning point* was reached become counterproductive. As illustrated in the right part of Figure 8.3, after the turning point perceived quality starts to deteriorate. The service process and the functional quality perception are probably hurt first, but eventually the outcome and the technical quality perception may also be impacted. When this happens, as was illustrated on the right side of Figure 8.2, the additional cost savings sought after the turning point are soon offset by the lost revenues that follow from a deteriorating service quality.

It is important for management in a service organization to realize that even if traditional manufacturing-oriented productivity models work at first, inevitably at some stage a turning point is reached. When this occurs, one must turn to new productivity concepts that are based on characteristics of service and service processes. Otherwise, what started as a favourable productivity and

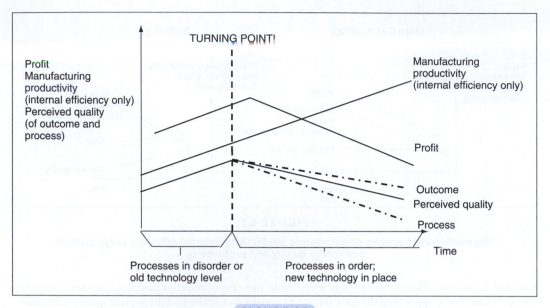

FIGURE 8.3

Effects of using a manufacturing productivity model in service organizations.

profit improvement process soon turns into a disaster. A problem exists in that there seem to be no models indicating when the turning point is reached – and managers are easily blinded by the initially occurring good results. Only by following how customers perceive the service process and the technical and functional quality of the service can one find out when the turning point has been passed and new approaches to productivity management are needed. Moreover, increasing turnover in the customer base and growing dissatisfaction among customer contact employees may be other signs indicated that the turning point has been passed.

In the following sections of this chapter a service-oriented approach to understanding productivity in service organizations will be explored and discussed.

A SERVICE PRODUCTIVITY MODEL

The discussion so far in this chapter has demonstrated that it is meaningless to develop a productivity concept for service organizations based on the management of *internal efficiency (cost efficiency)* and quantity of output only. Because of the characteristics of service and the service process, the management of *external effectiveness (perceived service quality)* of the quality of output has to be an integral part of a service productivity concept. Managing external effectiveness and perceived service quality is a matter of *revenue effectiveness*, because better quality normally means more sales and increased revenues, and vice versa. A third element of a service productivity model is the management of demand or *capacity efficiency.* This is because service providers cannot use inventories to cope with excess capacity or excess demand, as goods manufacturers can.

Hence, a service productivity concept can be described in the following way:

1. Service productivity $= f$ (internal efficiency, external effectiveness, capacity utilization) or
2. Service productivity $= f$ (cost efficiency, revenue effectiveness, capacity efficiency).

As we have seen, because in manufacturing quality is considered to remain constant and therefore no revenue effects of changes in input will occur in product manufacturing, external or revenue effectiveness can be eliminated from the productivity function. Because firms can use inventories as a buffer between excess demand and excess supply, within limits even capacity efficiency can be eliminated. In service this does not work. The service productivity model is illustrated in Figure 8.4.[19]

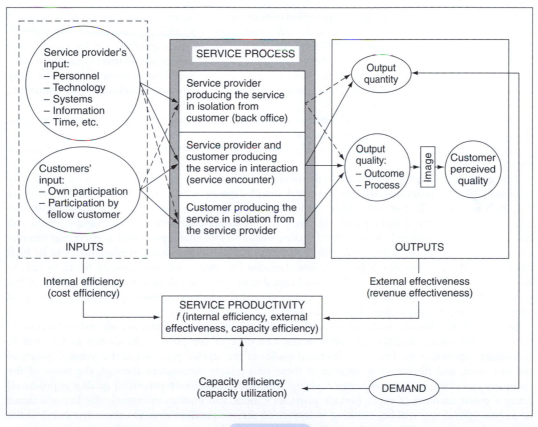

FIGURE 8.4

A service productivity model.
Source: Based on Ojasalo, K., *Conceptualizing Productivity in Services*. Helsinki: Hanken Swedish School of Economics, Finland/CERS, 1999, p. 71. Reproduced by permission.

From a productivity perspective the *service process* can be divided into three separate processes:

1. The service provider produces service *in isolation* from the customer.

2. The service provider and the customer produce service *in interactions* (service encounters).

3. The customer produces service *in isolation* from the service provider.

The *service provider-induced inputs* into the service process (personnel, technology, systems, information, use of time, etc.) influence the first two processes *directly* and, for example by providing the infrastructure for service consumption as in telephone communication, the third process *indirectly* (as illustrated by the black and dotted arrows, respectively). The *customer-induced inputs* (customer's own participation and fellow customers' participation as co-producers) *directly* affect the second and third processes, and *indirectly* affect the first, for example by providing information to back-office processes.

The more efficiently the service organization uses its own resources as input into the processes and the better the organization can educate and guide customers to provide process-supporting input to produce a given amount of output, the better the *internal* or *cost efficiency* of the service process will be. From the provider's point of view, how customers produce service in isolation from the service provider has no direct effect on internal efficiency, but has a decisive impact on service productivity through customers' perceptions of service quality and their corresponding willingness to contribute to the firm's revenues.

Finally, the service provider and the customer influence the interactive part of the service process, leading to an *interaction-induced* contribution to productivity.

The *output* of the service process is twofold: quantity of output (volume) and quality of output (outcome and process).

The *quantity produced* is dependent on demand. If demand meets supply, the utilization of capacity or *capacity efficiency* is optimal. If there is excess demand, capacity is utilized to the full extent, but there may be a negative effect on the quality of the output. If demand is lower than potential output, the capacity is underutilized and capacity efficiency will be lower than optimal. For example, if the call centre staff is underutilized, the perceived quality of the service that is produced is good, but internal efficiency is low. On the other hand, if the call centre is understaffed, internal efficiency may be high but perceived service quality is probably low, because customers will have to wait for their calls to be answered and the employees will have a limited time for each call (low functional quality of the process). In addition, they may not have the time required to solve customers' problems or give good advice, resulting in low technical quality as well.

Because of the characteristics of service, the quality of the output is partly manifested in the process (interaction-induced quality) and partly in the outcome of the process. As shown in Chapter 4, customers experience quality as the *functional quality* of the service process and the *technical quality* of the outcome, and filter the experiences of these two quality dimensions through the *image* of the company, resulting in *customer perceived quality*. The more effectively perceived quality is produced using a given amount of input (service provider's input and customers' input), the better *external* or *revenue effectiveness* will be, resulting in improved service productivity. On the other hand, if the perceived service quality goes down, because the available input is functioning in a less service-oriented way or the resource structure is altered in a way that decreases quality, external effectiveness is reduced and the firm's revenue-generating capability is lowered. This has a negative impact on service productivity.

In conclusion, internal efficiency and the cost-efficient use of resources is one side of service productivity, and external effectiveness (perceived service quality) and the revenue-generating capability following the use of resources is another. In addition, the efficient utilization of resources so that demand and supply meet as much as possible has a positive impact on service productivity. As the service productivity functions shown at the start of this section illustrate, high service productivity requires that the three efficiency and effectiveness factors are blended in an optimal way. Increasing (internal) cost efficiency may have the opposite effect on (external) revenue effectiveness. On the other hand, improved internal efficiency following new ways of producing a service (for example, using the scenario at the beginning of this chapter, going from performing everyday bank services in bank offices to customers using ATMs, home banking, the Internet and mobile devices), may very well lead to an improved quality perception and thus to improved revenue-generating capability and external effectiveness at the same time as it lowers costs. In addition, how capacity is utilized (capacity efficiency) has to be taken into account.

This blending of the three types of efficiency is illustrated in Figure 8.5. The highest possible service productivity is achieved in the shaded area of the figure. However, achieving this may not always be possible, because higher external effectiveness and revenue-generating capabilities may require lower internal efficiency and cost efficiency. The optimal combination is dependent on the blend of revenue-generating capability and cost efficiency that optimizes the firm's economic result, also taking into account the effect of the capacity efficiency that can be achieved.

In conclusion, to manage productivity in service organizations, an integrated service productivity concept, and realizing that a constant-quality assumption does not apply, is the only meaningful productivity concept. How to measure productivity based on a service productivity concept is another issue, which we shall turn to in the last section of this chapter.

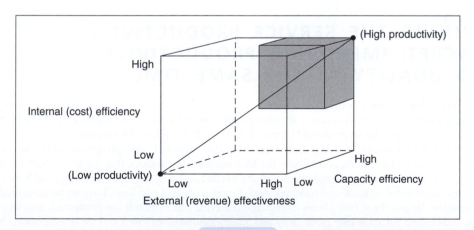

FIGURE 8.5

Service productivity as a function of internal efficiency, external effectiveness and capacity efficiency.
Source: Ojasalo, K., *Conceptualizing Productivity in Services*. Helsinki: Hanken Swedish School of Economics, Finland/CERS, 1999, p. 161. Reproduced by permission.

LONG-TERM PRODUCTIVITY COUNTS

In order to produce acceptable quality, the service provider may have to invest in new technology and in training its personnel to be more customer-oriented. In the short run, say, for the first 12 to 36 months, this may increase costs more than it will generate additional revenue. However, this short-term perspective must not guide management decisions. In Western companies there is an established inclination to demand quick results and to reject actions that only pay off in the long term and show no short-term benefits. This is a devastating approach, the negative effects of which should be avoided as much as possible.

By such a strategy the long-term profitability of a firm could be sacrificed in the pursuit of quick revenues, often without management and shareholders even realizing it. However, a short-sighted outlook can easily lead to deteriorating customer perceived quality, which in turn leads to dissatisfied customers and lost business. If a firm's market share is to be maintained, huge increases in its budget for traditional external marketing are then required, and in the long run even this may not help. A long-term perspective should, therefore, guide management decisions. *If there is ever a conflict between short-term revenue and quality, quality considerations should come first.* Focusing too narrowly on finances makes managers lose their long-term perspective and quality improvements that may be needed will not be achieved. By focusing first on quality, better financial results will follow. As Patrick Mene, Corporate Director of Quality and TQM co-ordinator of the Malcom Baldrige Quality Award-winning Ritz Carlton Hotel Company, once said: 'You cannot improve a company's financial performance merely by focusing on finances.'[20]

An investment programme such as the one illustrated in this section will probably pay off in more internally efficient operations after, say 12 to 36 months. Applying a service productivity concept to improve productivity requires a long-term approach. Managers who do not realize this easily revert to a manufacturer-oriented productivity concept, which carries a high risk of making the wrong decisions for the long-term survival of the firm.

APPLYING THE SERVICE PRODUCTIVITY CONCEPT: IMPROVING PRODUCTIVITY AND QUALITY AT THE SAME TIME

As has been shown here, contrary to what is commonly thought, it is a mistake to believe that improving productivity and increasing service quality cannot be done simultaneously. All steps taken to improve service productivity should be based on (1) a thorough understanding of what constitutes good service quality, as perceived by customers, and (2) an equally thorough analysis of the firm's processes and customer interfaces, and of how the firm operates to produce that quality; which resources (human, physical, technological and customer) are needed and which are unnecessary, and how effective or ineffective the systems and routines used. Good costs and bad costs have to be identified and kept separate. When these two pieces of research (external and internal) are compared, a strong basis will be established for *improving productivity and quality simultaneously* in a service organization. Next, ways of simultaneously improving service quality and service productivity will be discussed.

IMPROVING EMPLOYEES' TECHNICAL SKILLS

High-quality service means, among other things, that employees know how to do things correctly. If they have inadequate skills, the technical quality of the outcome of the service process will be damaged. However, at the same time, customers will probably have to wait longer, and be more proactive themselves, to receive an acceptable technical quality. Moreover, they will perceive the lack of skills on the part of the employees. All these aspects of interactions with the firm lower the perception of the functional quality of the interaction process. At the same time, this lack of skills and the need for corrective action and the repetition of activities affect productivity. Consequently, improving the technical skills of a firm's personnel may be a means of simultaneously improving quality and productivity.

SERVICE ORIENTATION OF ATTITUDES AND EMPLOYEE BEHAVIOUR

Unfriendly and negative attitudes and behaviour by personnel has a significant negative impact on the functional aspect of perceived service quality. Moreover, this has a backlash effect on productivity. Angry customers, by their reaction, tend to create problems for employees, which slows down the service process. Moreover, angry and dissatisfied customers may complain either on the spot or later, which creates extra work and lowers productivity. Service-oriented employees, on the other hand, enhance quality perception and thus enhance productivity. Of course, if, for example, employees spend an unnecessarily long time with each customer, which does not pay off even in the long run, a productivity problem may occur.

INTERNAL VALUES SUPPORTIVE TO GOOD SERVICE PRODUCTIVITY

Internal value systems in organizations that honour conventionality, risk aversion and behaviour inhibition may have an unfavourable impact on service productivity.[21] The development of internal values that support good service, on the one hand, and make employees aware of the need to use resources intelligently, on the other, is a means of improving service productivity. At the same time, employees will have to understand the interplay between internal efficiency (costs) and external effectiveness (revenues) of their actions and behaviour in the service processes. Managers and supervisors have a decisive role in this process of forming internal values and culture (see Chapter 14 on internal marketing and Chapter 15 on service culture).

MAKING SYSTEMS AND TECHNOLOGY MORE SUPPORTIVE TO EMPLOYEE AND/OR CUSTOMER CO-PRODUCTION

If the operational systems and routines used are considered complicated, or difficult to handle or to understand, this may create problems for employees, customers or both. For example, if a customer service helpdesk receives too many inappropriate phone calls – for example, requests for general information – productivity and quality problems occur. For employees, this creates barriers to meeting customer service specifications and thus they are unable to care enough for the customers. For customers, it often means a long waiting time for help. Productivity and service quality are damaged. In this situation, a front-end automated device using modern call-centre technology that directs phone calls to the correct destination could be an appropriate solution. Thus, both service quality and productivity could be influenced favourably. Moreover, self-service technologies which customers find complicated and/or which do not consistently function properly also damage productivity (and perceived service quality). Self-service check-in at airports currently seems to be an example of this.

INDUSTRIALIZING THE SERVICE OPERATION

Applying manufacturing-like methods of operations as a means of improving service had already been suggested in the 1970s.[22] Generally, industrializing a service means to substitute technology and automation for people. ATMs, insurance vending machines, Internet banking and Internet shops and automatic check-in machines in airports are examples of such an approach. In some cases industrialization is an appropriate way of improving both service quality and productivity. Today, when retail banks offer ATMs to customers who want to withdraw cash from their accounts with the convenience this provides but offer personal service when they want to discuss financial problems and opportunities, this way of industrializing the service works well. However, problems can arise if industrialization is offered for all types of service to all segments of customers in all situations, which is often the case. Productivity measured by internal measurements may increase, but service quality may decrease, and this may have a negative effect on the firm's economic result, both in the short term and the long term. Hence, industrialization as a means of improving productivity and quality always demands extremely careful internal as well as external quality impact–oriented analyses to avoid errors.

USING THE INTERNET, DIGITAL SOLUTIONS AND INFORMATION TECHNOLOGY

The Internet and other digital means and information technology offer many opportunities for creating service processes which demand fewer resources from the service provider and at the same time are perceived as improved service quality by customers. Electronic commerce, Internet shopping and banking are examples of service processes with a different input configuration that lower costs and for many customers provide a high quality service. TV shopping is another example of how an information technology-based resource structure can be used to decrease costs and at the same time provide high-quality service to customers who appreciate this form of shopping. Mobile commerce-based telecommunication and digital TV have enormous potential to offer similar opportunities.

INCREASING CUSTOMER PARTICIPATION IN THE SERVICE PRODUCTION PROCESS

Another way of improving productivity and quality is to look at customer impact on the service process. There are, in principle, two ways of doing this. First, more *self-service elements* can be introduced. However, it is extremely important that this is not done simply for internal efficiency reasons. Customers have to see that benefits arise from participating in self-service processes. If they do not find those benefits, perceived quality suffers. Customers have to be rewarded for taking part in self-service elements, and they have to be motivated to do so. The other aspect of improving productivity and quality by paying attention to customer participation is to *improve the participation skills* of customers. Sometimes customers do not know exactly what they are supposed to do or say, how documents are to be filled out, and so on. This has a negative impact on the functional quality aspect; it may also affect the technical quality of the outcome. In addition to this, more of the employee's time is required to ensure that customers fulfil their role in the service process. Thus, productivity is affected. Better-informed customers feel more secure, make fewer mistakes and need less unnecessary attention from employees. Consequently, they are more satisfied with the service. At the same time, there is a twofold effect on productivity. The customers speed up the service production process – by their input into the process they improve productivity, and employees can serve more customers, which also enhances productivity.

REDUCING THE MISMATCH BETWEEN SUPPLY AND DEMAND

Physical goods can be kept in stock, if demand is low; service cannot. If the demand curve has high peaks and corresponding troughs, service quality will probably be good in the latter situations, but at peak times too many customers present at the same time will lead to long queues, longer waiting times, less personal attention, and so on. At the same time, productivity is low, because too often the firm will have idle resources and low capacity efficiency. Hence, reducing the mismatch between supply and demand is a way of making quality more consistent and of simultaneously improving productivity. Using part-time employees may be one way of doing this, but it is not always successful. For example, when retailers replace professional sales clerks with part-time personnel without sufficient training, motivation and supervision, service quality suffers permanently, at slow times as well as at peak times. Another way of matching supply and demand is to attempt to manage the flow of customers. Offering better prices during slow periods and making customers change their consumption habits by means of communication are ways of doing this using traditional marketing activities.

In addition to these means of simultaneously improving service quality and productivity, there are other methods that can sometimes be used. Reducing the service level (quantity or quality), introducing new services (smartcards instead of credit cards or bus tickets) and substituting goods for services (new data transfer equipment replacing cable and mail services) are examples.

SERVICE PRODUCTIVITY AS A LEARNING RELATIONSHIP

Individual customers as well as organizations frequently engage in ongoing relationships with service firms, and manufacturers who face service competition also engage in relationships with customers where a range of services are included in a total offering to them. Hence, service productivity is frequently dependent on how the relationship proceeds. Relationships are *learning experiences* where both parties get used to each other and learn how to interact with each other so that errors, service failures, quality problems, information problems, etc. can be minimized. In other words, both the service provider and the customer gradually learn how to avoid errors and problems that create unnecessary costs for both parties, and have a negative impact on perceived service quality.[23] These effects of *learning relationships* on service productivity are illustrated in Figure 8.6.

Figure 8.6 demonstrates how the customer (in the upper part of the figure) gains experience of a service provider and the service process (or processes) as the relationship continues. It also shows how this has effects in two directions, on the ability to participate more effectively in the service process, thus improving internal efficiency (to the left in the figure) and on the perception of service quality, thus improving external effectiveness (to the right in the figure).

Following the upper part of the figure to the left, one can see an internal efficiency-improving learning process. More knowledgeable customers have what could be called a *narrower competence gap* than customers in earlier stages of the relationship, because their knowledge of how to act and, for example, what information input to provide, make the service process quicker and smoother. This enables more intense customer participation and co-production, which in turn results in higher internal efficiency (cost efficiency) and may also lead to improved external effectiveness (perceived quality and revenue effectiveness). Following the upper part of the figure to the right, one can see

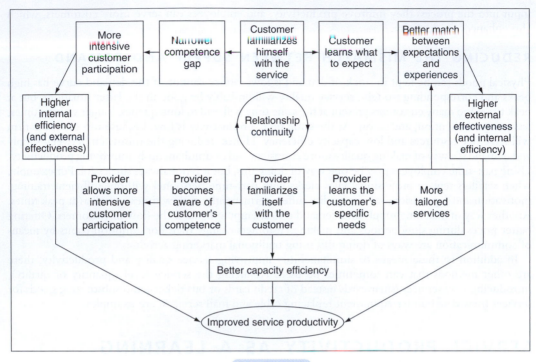

FIGURE 8.6

Effects of learning relationships on service productivity.
Source: Based on Ojasalo, K., *Conceptualizing Productivity in Services*. Helsinki: Hanken Swedish School of Economics, Finland/CERS, 1999, p. 194. See also Grönroos, C. and Ojasalo, K., Service productivity as mutual learning. *International Journal of Quality and Service Sciences,* Vol. 7, 2015 (forthcoming). Reproduced by permission.

external effectiveness–improving effects of the same learning process. Customers become more aware of exactly what to expect and this creates a better match between expectations and experiences, which in turn improves external effectiveness (perceived quality and revenue effectiveness). It may also have a positive effect on internal efficiency (cost efficiency).

In the lower part of Figure 8.6 one can see how the service provider, when it learns more about a customer, becomes more aware of the customer's competence and can allow more intensive customer participation, and learns more about the their specific needs, wishes and expectations, and therefore can better tailor service for the customer. These processes make it possible for the service provider to adjust to the customer and take actions that improve both internal efficiency and external effectiveness. At the same time, due to this learning process, the service provider can try to persuade its customers to use its service in a way that levels out demand peaks and troughs, and can adjust its resources to account for customer demand so that capacity better meets demand. In this way the utilization of capacity (capacity efficiency) improves as well. *The end result is improved service productivity.*

From a productivity point of view, longer customer relationships are preferable, because they allow for mutual learning. Due to the learning effect, the more often relationships are broken and lost customers have to be replaced by new ones, the lower service productivity will be. Hence, customer retention is important for service productivity, and productivity in service is a *learning experience*.[24]

MANAGING SERVICE PRODUCTIVITY

Service productivity theory has been developed only to a very limited extent. However, some guidelines for productivity management in service businesses can be presented. These guidelines are still quite rudimentary, but nevertheless helpful for management:

1. The first step is to *distinguish between quality-enhancing good costs and bureaucracy-maintaining bad costs* in the service processes. This information provides a starting point for making decisions about how to improve service productivity. Resources and processes which include good costs must be treated differently to bureaucracy-maintaining resources and processes.

2. Then *clarify and systematize processes which include overlapping activities and unclear purposes*, such that these processes are streamlined and double-work is avoided. In this way unnecessary cost-creating work can be avoided, and at the same time customers probably perceive the change as quality-enhancing. The customers' experiences with streamlined service processes especially have a positive impact on the functional quality perception.

3. If possible, *move to a new technology level*. Introduction of more advanced technologies in service processes may have a positive effect on the customers' perception of service quality (e.g. Internet banking) and at the same time improves the firm's internal efficiency and lowers the cost level.

4. Also if possible, *move activities which customers consider interesting and are willing to perform to the customers' sphere*. Self-service processes increase customers' quality perception provided that they do not create unnecessary perceived sacrifice for them (increase relationship costs). Moving to self-service enables the firm to be more cost efficient. However, the customers must accept the self-service requirement and find it quality-enhancing, otherwise it does not work.

All these service productivity-improving actions aim at simultaneously increasing the internal efficiency (cost efficiency) as well as the external effectiveness (perceived service quality) of the service provider, which is at the heart of service productivity. However, one should remember that especially those actions which require customers to change their behaviour are not necessarily immediately accepted. Customers may have to be educated. However, if the customers do not eventually accept a suggested new role for them in the service process, this new self-service process will not be productivity-enhancing. It may lower the cost level, but may also hurt the firm's revenue-generating capability even more, and may also have a negative impact on the firm's image.

MEASURING SERVICE PRODUCTIVITY

In the final sections of this chapter, approaches to developing instruments for measuring service productivity will be discussed. As Parasuraman notes, metrics for measuring service productivity as an integrated concept are largely lacking.[25] No final solutions are provided, because there is not yet enough research available on how to measure service productivity to make this possible. However, suggestions for how to think and in which direction to go will be made.[26]

In traditional manufacturing the *constant-quality assumption* makes it relatively easy to measure productivity. A measure of output is compared with a measure of input. If the ratio grows following alterations in the resources or resource structure used in production, productivity improves. Parts of the total service production process can be measured in a similar way. For example, the number of delivery trucks loaded in a warehouse per day, the number of phone calls that a call centre can handle in an hour or the percentage of seats in a restaurant occupied at any given point in time are examples of such *partial productivity* measures. They give management an idea of how efficiently these processes function from an internal perspective, which may sometimes be a useful piece of information. However, such measures must never be used to judge the overall productivity of these processes. Instead, measures of, for example, the number of calls received must always be accompanied by measures of the time spent with customers and the quality of the outcome of the call.[27] In service, productivity measurements must always include a measure of how a given input in the form of resources and resource structures affects perceived service quality and the revenue-generating capability of the organization. In addition, considerations of how well capacity is utilized must also be taken into account.

Because service productivity includes both cost efficiency and revenue effectiveness, the development of a *global or total* productivity measure has to incorporate both phenomena. A concept which includes both revenues and costs is, of course, profit. When capacity efficiency is included we get close to the profitability of the service operations. Capacity efficiency influences costs but also revenues where excess demand has a negative impact on quality. The interrelationship between quality, productivity and profit is complicated, but clear. In a previous chapter we discussed the *relationship cost* concept, which demonstrates how improved service quality as perceived by customers can decrease the cost level of the service provider, thus having a positive effect on both revenues and costs. In Figure 8.7 the complicated interrelationship between quality, profit and productivity is illustrated.

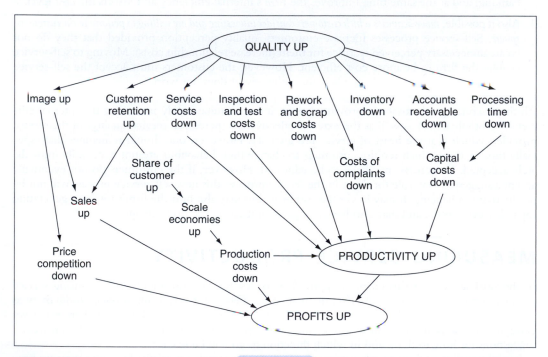

FIGURE 8.7

The interrelationship between quality, productivity and profit.
Source: Gummesson, E., Productivity, quality and relationship marketing in service operations. *International Journal of Contemporary Hospitality Management*, **10**(1); 1998: p. 6. Reproduced by permission of Emerald Insight.

The figure is based on the fact that goods and service activities almost always appear in a symbiotic relationship. As the figure indicates, improved quality can be expected to have a number of internal and external effects, all of which have a positive impact on productivity. The same positive effects of improved quality also lead to a higher profit level. The effects of improved quality on revenues are shown in the left section of the figure, on cost in the middle section and on capital employed in the right section. As Evert Gummesson observes, quality, productivity and profitability form 'triplets', the parts of which are all related to the same phenomenon, the welfare of the organization, although they approach this from different perspectives.[28]

Figure 8.7 demonstrates how the effects of quality and productivity improvements eventually lead to improved profit. As was concluded previously, as productivity is a proxy for profit the ultimate goal of productivity management is to achieve better profit effectiveness and economic results. Theoretically, *the correct way of measuring global productivity is to measure how changes in production inputs impact on the level of perceived quality and how this, in turn, affects profits*. In traditional manufacturing, due to the constant quality assumption, effects on revenue generation can be excluded from productivity measurement instruments. Therefore, measurements are reduced to cost–efficiency calculations. In service, where the constant quality assumption does not apply, effects on revenues have to be included. Hence, measuring service productivity becomes more complicated.

The next section will discuss various ways to measure service productivity and will suggest ways to develop service productivity measurement instruments.

HOW TO DEVELOP SERVICE PRODUCTIVITY MEASUREMENT INSTRUMENTS

Because external effects on perceived quality have to be taken into account in service productivity, a measurement instrument has to include the customer's perspective as well. Taking an internal organizational perspective is not enough. This, of course, makes the development of measurement models much more complicated in service contexts than in traditional manufacturing, where paying attention to internal efficiency is sufficient.

As was said before, it can sometimes be useful to measure partial productivity, but only global or total productivity measurements give real information on how a service provider is performing. Table 8.3 gives three basic alternatives for productivity measurements.

TABLE 8.3

Alternative ways of measuring service productivity.

	Physical measures	Financial measures	Combined measures
Partial productivity (output/one input)	e.g. $\dfrac{\text{customers served}}{\text{employee-hours}}$	e.g. $\dfrac{\text{revenues}}{\text{labour costs}}$	e.g. $\dfrac{\text{revenues}}{\text{number of employees}}$
Total productivity	e.g. $\dfrac{\text{customers served}}{\text{total resources}}$	e.g. $\dfrac{\text{revenues}}{\text{cost of resources}}$	e.g. $\dfrac{\text{revenues}}{\text{level of resources}}$

Source: Ojasalo, K., *Conceptualizing Productivity in Services*. Helsinki/Helsingfors: Hanken Swedish School of Economics, Finland/CERS, 1999, p. 133. Reproduced by permission.

Physical measures are the traditional way of measuring productivity in general. The normal way of measuring service productivity has been to also use physical measures. This is natural, but misleading because there was in the past no theory of service productivity and firms therefore had to borrow the manufacturing productivity concept. In an attempt to cope with the obvious problems of using physical measures in service operations, combinations of physical and financial measures have also been used. For example, in a restaurant the revenue per service employee or restaurant seat has been used to calculate partial productivity of personnel or physical outlets. The ratio between the number of customers served per period and the costs of operating the restaurant have also been used to find total productivity.

Using physical measures by themselves is misleading, because neither cost nor revenue effects are included. Using combination measures is also misleading, because they either omit cost considerations or exclude revenue effects. Other types of combination measures have also been suggested; one proposed measure that comes close to a pure financial measure is calculating 'process value productivity', which is the market value of what is produced minus the costs of the resources purchased, divided by the number of employee-hours per period used in the service process.[29]

Purely financial measures are not normally used for measuring service productivity. This is probably because it seems difficult to calculate the value of the output of the service process. First, because of the heterogeneity of production inputs and customer participation in the service process, it is difficult to standardize output and assess a market value. Second, price fluctuations make it harder to use financial measures of output.[30] Table 8.4 shows the pros and cons of physical, financial and combined measures of service productivity.

Regardless of the problems involved, the only theoretically correct and seemingly practically relevant approach to measuring service productivity is to base productivity calculations on financial measures. In principle, the correct way of measuring service productivity as a function of cost efficiency (internal), revenue effectiveness (external) and capacity efficiency is the following measure:

$$(1) \text{ Service productivity} = \frac{\text{Revenues from a given service}}{\text{Costs of producing this service}}$$

As a global or total productivity measure of the operations of a service provider, the following measure can be used:

$$(2) \text{ Service productivity} = \frac{\text{Total revenues}}{\text{Total costs}}$$

Hence, service productivity more or less equals the economic profit and profitability, and whenever possible productivity in a service organization is best assessed by measuring profitability or the economic result of an operation.

The perceived service quality following from a given resource structure as an input in the service process creates sales at a certain level. If the resource structure is changed, the cost level changes along with perceived quality and the revenue-generating capability of the service provider. A change in cost efficiency leads to a change in revenue effectiveness, and the result of this can be measured as the ratio between revenues and costs. This is a true measurement of productivity in service organizations.

TABLE 8.4

Characteristics of alternatives for measuring service productivity.

Physical measures	• Heterogeneity and intangibility aspects of services make physical measures inappropriate.
	• Physical measures ignore variations in quality.
	• Total productivity is difficult to measure because it is problematic to combine quantities of input resources.
	• Difficult to get precise information on quantities.
Financial measures	• Financial measures signal heterogeneity and intangibility aspects of services.
	• No price indices are needed because both the numerator and denominator of the productivity measure are monetary values of the same period.
Combinations of physical and financial measures	• The same problems are experienced as with physical measures.
	• Price indices are needed because neither numerator nor denominator is expressed in monetary values.

Source: Ojasalo, K., *Conceptualizing Productivity in Services*. Helsinki/Helsingfors: Hanken Swedish School of Economics Finland/CERS, 1999, p. 137. Reproduced by permission.

If revenues increase more than costs, productivity goes up. On the other hand, if a cost reduction leads to lost revenues, but the decline in revenues is less than the cost savings that have been achieved, productivity still improves. However, this may be a dangerous strategy, because in the long term it may lead to a negative image and unfavourable word of mouth, which in turn can have a further negative effect on revenues. Finally, cost reductions may lead to a bigger drop in revenues than is made up for by cost savings. If this is the case, service productivity declines.

Service-oriented productivity measures should be derived from the two formulae above. However, one should bear in mind that there are problems with financial measures that should be observed. Revenue is not always a good measure of output, since price does not always reflect perceived service quality. It may also be difficult to assign capital costs correctly to respective revenues. Table 8.5 summarizes the advantages and limitations of revenue to cost ratios for measuring service productivity.

In conclusion, service productivity is much more complicated than traditional manufacturing productivity, because the constant quality assumption does not apply to service. In service, it is not possible to make use of the shortcuts for measuring productivity that can typically be used in traditional manufacturing. Examples of such shortcuts are excluding revenue measures from the productivity formula and using physical and combined measures. Service organizations have to take the long route to understanding and measuring productivity.

TABLE 8.5

Advantages and limitations of using the revenue/cost ratio for measuring service productivity.

Advantages	Limitations
1. Easy to compute and understand.	1. Cannot be used in non-profit service sector.
2. Data from company records are easy to obtain.	2. Revenues do not always provide a reliable illustration of output quality (cf. point 4 in left column), since prices do not always tend to reflect the perceived quality, especially for services which have been paid for in advance. Also, if the business is subsidized by government, if prices are regulated, or if competition is monopolistic, revenues may be a poor measure of output quality.
3. Takes into account all quantifiable output and input factors, and provides an accurate representation of the real economic picture of a service firm on an aggregate level.	
4. Output quality tends to be *better* taken into account than in volume-based measures (cf. point 2 in the right column).	3. Does not have the ability to explain reasons for changes in productivity or to show bottlenecks in performance.
5. Reflects the level of capacity utilization, since all costs are incorporated in the denominator.	4. Assigning costs of capital correctly to respective revenues may be difficult, particularly at a detailed level.
6. Shows changes in productivity directly; no price indices are needed for comparisons.	5. Data for computations are relatively difficult to obtain on service and customer levels, unless data collection systems are designed for this purpose.
7. Easy to compare a firm's productivity at any given moment with its past performance and objectives; and easy to compare separate units of a firm with each other.	

Source: Ojasalo, K., *Conceptualizing Productivity in Services*. Helsinki/Helsingfors: Hanken Swedish School of Economics, Finland/CERS, 1999, p. 143. Reproduced by permission.

SUMMARY

This chapter concluded that using traditional productivity measurement instruments from manufacturing is not possible in service organizations. Applying a productivity concept geared to traditional manufacturing does not provide management with any useful information. Basically, this follows on from the facts that the constant–quality assumption of the traditional productivity concept does not apply in service contexts, and the ratio between production inputs and outputs varies from one customer served to another and from one 'unit of service' to another. When input resources in service processes are altered, the perceived quality of the service changes. Therefore, quality has to be included as an integral part of a service productivity concept. Based on this, a service productivity concept including internal or cost efficiency, external or revenue effectiveness, and capacity efficiency was introduced. Then service productivity as a learning process was discussed. A number of ways of improving productivity in service was presented, and finally, problems in measuring service productivity were explained.

QUESTIONS FOR DISCUSSION

1. What is meant by the constant-quality assumption in the traditional productivity concept from manufacturing, and why does this not apply in service contexts?

2. Discuss the differences in measuring productivity in closed and open systems.

3. Why is it more difficult to measure productivity in an open system?

4. What should be taken into account in a service productivity concept?

5. What are the challenges involved in the development of productivity measurement models in service?

6. Discuss service productivity as a learning process. How does this apply to service offered in your organization?

7. Discuss the factors that influence the service productivity of service processes in your firm, or in any given service operation.

NOTES

1. Grönroos, C., *Service Management and Marketing. Managing the Moments of Truth in Service Competition.* Lexington, MA: Lexington Books, 1990; Filitrault, P., Harvey J. & Chebat, J.C., Service quality and service productivity management practice. *Industrial Marketing Management,* **25**(3), 1996, 243–255. Publications from the last 10 to 15 years include Parasuraman, A. Service quality and productivity: a synergistic perspective. *Managing Service Quality,* **12**(1), 2002, 6–9; Grönroos, C. & Ojasalo, K., Service productivity: toward a conceptualization of the transformation of inputs into economic results in services. *Journal of Business Research,* **57**(4), 2004, 414–423; Rust, R.T. & Huang, M-H., Optimizing service productivity. *Journal of Marketing,* **76**(2), 2012, 47–66; Calabrese, A., Service productivity and service quality: a necessary trade-off? *Internal Journal of Production Economics,* **135**, 2012, 800–812; Rust, R.T. & Huang, M-H., Optimizing service productivity. *Journal of Marketing,* **76**(2), 2012, 47–66; Grönroos, C. Service Productivity. In Dahlgaard-Park, S.M. (ed.), Encyclopedia of Quality and the Service Economy, New York:

Sage, 2015. See also Carlborg, P., Kindström, D. & Kowalkowski, C., A lean approach for service productivity investments: synergy or oxymoron. *Managing Service Quality*, **23**(4), 2013, 291–304, where the authors discuss how a lean approach could improve service productivity without hurting customer value.

2. It is often said that quality and productivity cannot be improved at the same time. This may sometimes be the case, but as a general rule this is not true. Quite frequently new technology, a new production system using resources in a new way or an altered customer participation pattern can contribute to better productivity and improved service quality at the same time. For one example, see Truitt, L.J. & Haynes, R., Evaluating service quality and productivity in the regional airline industry. *Transportation Journal*, **33**(4), 1994, 21–32. For a more recent discussion, see Calabrese, *op. cit.*

3. Grönroos & Ojasalo, *op. cit.* See also, for example, Parasuraman, *op. cit.*, and Calabrese, *op. cit.* Johnston, R. & Jones, P., Service productivity. Towards understanding the relationship between operational and customer productivity. *International Journal of Productivity and Performance Management*, **53**(3), 2004, 201–213.

4. Anderson, E.W., Fornell, C. & Rust, R.T., Customer satisfaction, productivity, and profitability: differences between goods and services. *Marketing Science*, **16**(2), 1997, 129–149: 'if a firm improves productivity by "downsizing", it may achieve an increase in productivity in the short-term, but future profitability may be threatened if customer satisfaction is highly dependent on the efforts of personnel' (p. 129).

5. Anderson, Fornell & Rust, *op. cit.*, 129.

6. Grönroos, C., *op. cit.*

7. Anderson, Fornell & Rust, *op. cit.*, 129.

8. The phrase 'traditional manufacturing', is used because in modern manufacturing, through CAD/CAM techniques and Internet-mediated solutions, the customer is often involved in design and production. In such cases the manufacturing processes become partly open processes and start to resemble service processes. However, the existing productivity concept and measurement instruments are based on a traditional manufacturing context.

9. The table is based on Ojasalo, K., *Conceptualizing Productivity in Services*. Helsinki/Helsingfors: Swedish School of Economics, Finland/CERS Centre for Relationship Marketing and Service Management, 1999; Sumanth, D.J., *Total Productivity Management: A Systematic and Quantitative Approach to Compete in Quality, Price and Time*. Boca Raton, FL: St. Lucie Press, 1997; Grönroos, 1990, *op. cit.*

10. In modern manufacturing processes this does not always hold anymore.

11. Grönroos, 1990, *op. cit.* See also Haynes, R.M. & DuVall, P.K., Service quality management: a process control approach. *International Journal of Service Industry Management,* **3**(1), 1992, 14–24; Chase, R.B. & Haynes, R.M., Service operations management: a field guide. In Swartz, T.A. & Iacobucci, D. (eds), *Handbook of Services Marketing & Management.* Thousand Oaks, CA: Sage Publications, 2000, pp. 455–471, where the authors demonstrate the interrelationship between productivity and service quality, although they use a traditional manufacturing-oriented productivity concept. See also Vuorinen, I., Jarvinen, R. & Lehtinen, U., Content and measurement of productivity in the service sector. A conceptual analysis with an illustrative case from the insurance business. *Internal Journal of Service Industry Management,* **9**(4), 1998, 377–386; Parasuraman, A., *op. cit.*; Rust & Huang, *op. cit.*; and Calabrese, *op.cit.*, where the author discusses the need to combine the company-oriented and customer-oriented perspectives on productivity.

12. See, for example, Parasuraman, *op. cit.*; Calabrese, *op. cit.;* and Rust & Huang, *op. cit.*

13. Parasuraman, A., Service productivity, quality and innovation: implications for service-design practice and research. *International Journal of Quality and Service Sciences,* **2**(3), 2010, 277–286. The challenge to integrate productivity and quality strategies in service has also been observed within the area of service science. See Maglio, P.P. & Spohrer, J., Fundamentals of service science. *Journal of the Academy of Marketing Science,* **36**(1), 2008, 18–20. See also Luria, D., Yagil, G. & Gal, I., Quality and productivity: role conflict in the service context. *The Service Industries Journal,* **34**(11–12), 2014, 955–973, which discusses employees' ways of coping with the double messages that decisions about quality on one hand and productivity on the other hand send.

14. See Gummesson, E., Productivity, quality and relationship marketing in service operations. *International Journal of Contemporary Hospitality Management,* **10**(1), 1998, 4–15.

15. Figure 8.1 is influenced by a figure in Gummesson, *op. cit.*, 9.

16. See Kontoghiorges, C., Examining the associations between quality and productivity performance in a service organization. *The Quality Management Journal,* **10**(1), 2003, 32–43 and Dobni, D., A marketing-relevant framework for understanding service worker productivity. *Journal of Services Marketing,* **18**(4–5), 2004, 303–312, where the authors analyse the relationship beween quality and productivity in service organizations from different angles.

17. See Grönroos, *op. cit.*

18. In a study of service productivity Katri Ojasalo added *mandatory costs* as a third category. Mandatory costs are unavoidable, even though they may not have an effect on external effectiveness and customers' service experiences. Insurance is an example of such costs. See Ojasalo, 1999, *op. cit.*

19. This Service Productivity model is slightly modified and further developed from a service productivity concept developed in a large study of the productivity in services by Katri Ojasalo. See

Ojasalo, 1999, *op. cit.* Her study of service productivity is the largest and most innovative and thoughtful contribution to this field published so far. See also Grönroos, C. & Ojasalo, K., *op. cit.*

20. Partlow, C.G., How Ritz-Carlton applies 'TQM'. *The Cornell H.R.A.: Quarterly*, Aug, 1993, **22**.

21. Dobni, D., Ritchie, J.R.B. & Zerbe, W., Organizational values: the inside view of service productivity. *Journal of Business Research*, **47**(1), 2000, 91–107.

22. Levitt, T., A production-line approach to service. *Harvard Business Review*, Sept/Oct, 1972. See also Bowen, D.E. & Youngdahl, W.E., 'Lean' service: in defense of a production-line approach. *International Journal of Service Industry Management*, **9**(2), 1998, 207–225.

23. Ojasalo, 1999, *op. cit.* See also Grönroos, C. & Ojasalo, K, Service productivity as mutual learning. *International Journal of Quality and Service Sciences*, **7**(2-3), 2015.

24. Compare Reichheld, F.F., *The Loyalty Effect. The Hidden Force Behind Growth, Profits and Lasting Value.* Boston, MA: Harvard Business School Press, 1996. More generally the relationship between learning and productivity in product and service contexts is discussed in Argote, L. & Miron-Spektor, E., Organizational learning: from experience to knowledge. *Organization Science*, **22**(5), 2011, 1123–1137.

25. Parasuraman, 2010, *op. cit.*

26. Typically, attempts to study productivity in services take only partial productivity into account, and usually only measure internal variables. See, for example, Dobni & Zerbe, *op. cit.*, who in a very interesting study of the productivity impact of employees measure perceived role behaviour, organizational commitment and employee affect.

27. See Coates, R., Measuring service productivity. *Small Business Reports*, **16**(3), 1991, 22–25, where the interrelationships of quantity and quality in measuring productivity in services is discussed.

28. Gummesson, 1998, *op. cit.* This proposition was originally put forward in a seminal paper on service productivity presented by Evert Gummesson at the 2nd International Research Seminar in Service Management arranged by l'Institut d'Administration des Enterprises d'Université d'Aix-Marseille in France in June 1992. See Gummesson, E., Service productivity: a blasphemous approach. In Gummesson, E. (ed.), *Quality, Productivity & Profitability in Service Operations.* Conference Papers from the QP&P Research Program 1992–1994. Stockholm University/ Marketing Technique Centre, 1995, pp. 8–22.

29. Edvardsson, B., Thomasson, B. & Øvretveit, J., *Quality of Service.* Cambridge: McGraw-Hill, 1994.

30. For example, in Jones, P., Quality, capacity and productivity in service industries. In Johnston, R. (ed.), *The Management of Service Operations.* London: IFS Publications, 1988, pp. 309–321, the author argues against the use of financial measures.

FURTHER READING

Anderson, E.W., Fornell, C. & Rust, R.T. (1997) Customer satisfaction, productivity, and profitability: differences between goods and services. *Marketing Science*, **16**(2), 129–149.

Argote, L. & Miron-Spektor, E. (2011) Organizational learning: from experience to knowledge. *Organization Science*, **22**(5), 1123–1137.

Bowen, D.E. & Youngdahl, W.E. (1998) 'Lean' service: in defense of a production-line approach. *International Journal of Service Industry Management*, **9**(2), 207–225.

Calabrese, A. (2012) Service productivity and service quality: A necessary trade-off? *Internal Journal of Production Economics*, **135**, 800–812.

Carlborg, P., Kindström, D. & Kowalkowski, C. (2013) A lean approach for service productivity investments: synergy or oxymoron. *Managing Service Quality*, **23**(4), 291–304.

Chase, R.B. & Haynes, R.M. (2000) Service operations management: a field guide. In Swartz, T.A. & Iacobucci, D. (eds), *Handbook of Services Marketing & Management*. Thousand Oaks, CA: Sage Publications, pp. 455–471.

Coates, R. (1991) Measuring service productivity. *Small Business Reports*, **16**(3), 22–25.

Dobni, D. (2004) A marketing-relevant framework for understanding service worker productivity. *Journal of Services Marketing*, **18**(4–5), 303–312.

Dobni, D., Ritchie, J.R.B. & Zerbe, W. (2000) Organizational values: the inside view of service productivity. *Journal of Business Research*, **47**(1), 91–107.

Edvardsson, B., Thomasson, B. & Ovretveit, J. (1994) *Quality of Service*. Cambridge: McGraw-Hill.

Filitrault, P., Harvey, J. & Chebat, J.C. (1996) Service quality and service productivity management practice. *Industrial Marketing Management*, **25**(3), 243–255.

Grönroos, C. (1990) *Service Management and Marketing. Managing the Moments of Truth in Service Competition*. Lexington, MA: Lexington Books.

Grönroos, C. (2015) Service Productivity. In Park-Dahlgaard, S.M. (ed.), *Encyclopedia in Quality and the Service Economy*. New York: Sage.

Grönroos, C. & Ojasalo, K. (2004) Service productivity: toward a conceptualization of the transformation of inputs into economic results in services. *Journal of Business Research*, **57**(4), 414–423.

Grönroos, C. & Ojasalo, K. (2015) Service productivity as mutual learning. *International Journal of Quality and Service Sciences*, **7**(2-3).

Gummesson, E. (1995) Service productivity: a blasphemous approach. In Gummesson, E. (ed.), *Quality, Productivity & Profitability in Service Operations*. Conference Papers from the QP&P Research Program 1992–1994. Stockholm University/Marketing Technique Centre, pp. 8–22.

Gummesson, E. (1998) Productivity, quality and relationship marketing in service operations. *International Journal of Contemporary Hospitality Management*, **10**(1), 4–15.

Haynes, R.M. & DuVall, P.K. (1992) Service quality management: a process control approach. *International Journal of Service Industry Management*, **3**(1), 14–24.

Johnston, R. & Jones, P. (2004) Service productivity. Towards understanding the relationship between operational and customer productivity. *International Journal of Productivity and Performance Management*, **53**(3), 201–213.

Jones, P. (1988) Quality, capacity and productivity in service industries. In Johnston, R. (ed.), *The Management of Service Operations*. London: IFS Publications, pp. 309–321.

Kontoghiorges, C. (2003) Examining the associations between quality and productivity performance in a service organization. *The Quality Management Journal*, **10**(1), 32–42.

Levitt, T. (1972) A production-line approach to service. *Harvard Business Review*, Sept–Oct.

Luria, D., Yagil, G. & Gal, I. (2014) Quality and productivity: role conflict in the service context. *The Service Industries Journal*, **34**(11–12), 955–973.

Maglio, P.P. & Spohrer, J. (2008) Fundamentals of service science. *Journal of the Academy of Marketing Science*, **36**(1), 18–20.

Ojasalo, K. (1999) *Conceptualizing Productivity in Services*. Helsinki/Helsingfors: Hanken Swedish School of Economics, Finland/CERS Centre for Relationship Marketing and Service Management.

Parasuraman, A. (2002) Service quality and productivity: a synergistic perspective. *Managing Service Quality*, **12**(1), 6–9.

Parasuraman, A. (2010) Service productivity, quality and innovation: implications for service-design practice and research. *International Journal of Quality and Service Sciences*, **2**(3), 277–286.

Partlow, C.G. (1993) How Ritz-Carlton applies 'TQM'. *The Cornell H.R.A.: Quarterly*, August, 16–24.

Reichheld, F.F. (1996) *The Loyalty Effect. The Hidden Force Behind Growth, Profits, and Lasting Value*. Boston, MA: Harvard Business School Press.

Rust, R.T. & Huang, M-H. (2012) Optimizing service productivity. *Journal of Marketing*, **76**(2), 47–66.

Sumanth, D.J. (1997) *Total Productivity Management: A Systematic and Quantitative Approach to Compete in Quality, Price and Time*. Boca Raton, FL: St. Lucie Press.

Truitt, L.J. & Haynes, R. (1994) Evaluating service quality and productivity in the regional airline industry. *Transportation Journal*, **33**(4), 21–32.

Vuorinen, I., Jarvinen, R. & Lehtinen, U. (1998) Content and measurement of productivity in the service sector. A conceptual analysis with an illustrative case from the insurance business. *International Journal of Service Industry Management*, **9**(4), 377–386.

CHAPTER 9
MANAGING MARKETING OR CUSTOMER-FOCUSED MANAGEMENT

> *Full-time marketing specialists are required to make promises and find customers, but without skilful part-time marketers promises will not be kept, and the total marketing process collapses.*

INTRODUCTION

This chapter will discuss the nature and content of the marketing process in a service business. As the chapter title indicates, the traditional view of marketing management may not apply where services are concerned. A relationship approach to marketing is suggested, and the scope and content of the total marketing process is discussed in detail. The concepts of *part-time marketers*, *interactive marketing* and the *customer relationship lifecycle* are discussed. Furthermore, *a relationship marketing model* is presented. Two types of marketing strategies, relationship marketing and transaction marketing, are analysed on a *marketing strategy continuum*, and their implications for management and marketing explored. Finally, it is concluded that for service, marketing is better characterized as market-oriented or customer-focused management than as marketing management in the traditional functionalistic sense. After having read the chapter the reader should understand the role and scope of marketing in a service context, and realize the importance of the interactive marketing process to the total marketing process of a service organization as well as understand the nature of a relationship marketing approach and the consequences of adapting a relationship marketing strategy for a firm.

THE ROLE AND SCOPE OF MARKETING

The marketing process includes four main parts:

1. *Understanding the market and individual customers* by market research and segmentation analysis as well as by using database information on individual customers.

2. So that *market niches, segments and individual customers can be chosen.*

3. For *which marketing programmes and activities can be planned, implemented and followed up.*

4. Also, to *prepare the organization* so that marketing programmes and activities are successfully implemented (*internal marketing*).

This approach is based on the so-called *marketing concept*, which describes marketing as a philosophy. This concept holds that the firm should base all its activities on the needs and desires of customers in selected target markets. At the same time, of course, societal restrictions (laws, norms, industry agreements, etc.) have to be recognized. This is also known as a *market-oriented* view, in contrast to a *production-oriented* view, where the firm's activities are geared to existing technology, products or production processes.

The fourth part of the marketing function is traditionally not included. Normally, it is taken for granted that once marketing decisions are made they are executed as planned. However, this may be a dangerous assumption. Especially in service – both service firms and product manufacturers adopting a service logic – marketing programmes and activities have to be marketed *internally* to those who are expected to actively implement them *externally*.

Traditionally, marketing as a business activity is thought of as a separate function that is taken care of by specialists organized in a marketing department or marketing and sales departments. By and large, the rest of the organization, with few exceptions, has no responsibility for the customers or for marketing. Employees in other departments are not recruited or trained to take a customer focus and to think about marketing; nor are they supervised in a way that would make them feel any marketing responsibilities, or responsibility for customers. Such an approach demands that marketing specialists are the only people who have an impact on the customers' views of the firm, on their preferencs and buying behaviour. In many consumer packaged goods contexts, where consumption can be characterized predominantly as *outcome consumption*, this has always been the case. If the product is a pre-produced item with no need for service or other significant contact between a firm and its customers, only marketing (and sales) specialists are needed. Good market research, packaging, advertising campaigns and pricing and distribution decisions by marketing specialists lead to good results.

Figure 9.1 demonstrates the traditional place of marketing according to most marketing textbooks. The arrow pointing up indicates that the marketing specialists acquire information about the market (such as demand and buying behaviour analyses) through market research. The downward arrow illustrates the planning and implementation of marketing activities. However, as soon as we leave the area of consumer packaged goods, new elements appear in the relationship between buyer and seller. Many durables need delivery, installation, complaints handling and service. As soon as this happens, the prerequisites of Figure 9.1 are not valid any more, because more and more *process consumption* characteristics can be seen in the consumption process (see Chapter 2 about process and outcome consumption).

In service, the interface between the firm and the customer grows. This was first pointed out in 1974 in a service marketing book by John Rathmell.[1] Moreover, the customer no longer acts passively, but takes an active part in the service production process. This is often the case in industrial or business-to-business marketing as well. The more services that are introduced or the more hidden services that are actively used as service (e.g. claims handling, billing procedures, etc.) in customer relationships, the more important it is for companies engaged in business-to-business marketing to understand service competition and service management and marketing.

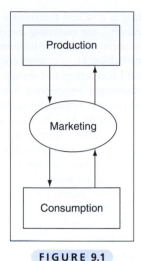

FIGURE 9.1

**The traditional role
of marketing.**

WHAT IS MARKETING?

Marketing as a phenomenon can be approached in many ways. Far too often marketing is considered to be only a set of tools and techniques and mostly in a marketing mix context. This is a dangerous way of introducing marketing into any organization, but especially into a service organization. If marketing is considered to be a set of tools, marketing remains the sole responsibility of a group of marketing specialists who are familiar with these tools and know how to handle them. The rest of the organization (for example, people involved in operations, deliveries, maintenance, the design and development of technology and systems) are not concerned with marketing, and with the firm's customers, which means that, although they may have customer contacts, they are not focused on their customers, their desires and wishes.

Marketing has been described variously as a *philosophy* and a *craft*. Focusing on the tools and techniques of marketing is to concentrate on marketing as a craft. However, we have to view marketing in a much larger context. A well-designed and executed advertising campaign will not lead to good results if campaign promises are not fulfilled by operations staff or delivery personnel. If this happens, the tool (advertising) may have been used successfully, viewed in isolation from other activities of the organization, but the marketing objective still fails (in the next chapter this particular issue will be discussed in more detail).

Marketing exists on at least three levels:

- Marketing as a *philosophy* and an *attitude of mind* or way of thinking.

- Marketing as a *way of organizing* the various functions and processes of a firm.

- Marketing as a *set of tools, techniques and activities* to which customers are exposed.

Marketing as a way of thinking. Marketing is first and foremost a *philosophy* or a mindset and a *way of thinking* in an organization. This philosophy, the *marketing concept*, has to guide all people, processes, functions and departments of an organization. It has to be understood and accepted by everyone, from top management to the most junior staff alike. Hence, marketing should, first of all, be an *attitude of mind*. This is the foundation of successful marketing and should be a basis of all decision-making.

However, it should be noted that customer perspective is not the only perspective to take into account in decision-making. For example, the economic realities and demands of other groups of stakeholders are aspects that cannot be forgotten. Also, technological development and what is sometimes labelled 'product or production orientation' must not be neglected. Normally, product orientation is not good for a firm. However, in some cases this perspective is more important than the customer perspective, because customers cannot always foresee the likely future developments of products and services based on technological advances. For example in the mobile phone business smartphones were not asked for by customers. Market research does not always give enough input to product development. This is of course most important in situations where rapid or complicated technological advances are taking place. For example, based on marketing research only, microwave ovens and text messaging (sms) had not been introduced. No one identified this as a need area. Instead, the skills and innovation of engineers and other specialists gave us these new means of cooking and communicating. Of course, in the final analysis, the customers decide whether an innovation is successful or not.

Marketing as a way of organizing. Second, successful marketing requires an appropriate *way of organizing* the firm. Various departments involved in making and fulfilling promises have to be able to compare notes and co-ordinate plans, and they have to be willing to do this. Traditional disputes and lack of willingness to collaborate between departments are examples of situations in which firms are not organized for optimal marketing. In firms where such turf fights exist, the *marketing attitude of mind throughout the organization* does not exist, and from the customers' point of view successful marketing will probably not be implemented.

Parts of customer relationships, normally traditional marketing and sales efforts, will be taken care of in a customer-oriented way. Other parts of the relationships, normally those related to interactions with customers, will be less well handled, and hence the total marketing effect, or how well customer relationships are managed over time, will be worse, often critically worse. For example, in a study of the relationship between the pulping industry and suppliers of service and components to firms in that industry, the customers talked about a 'tail-light or rear light syndrome'. They said that as long as negotiations on a deal continued, the supplier, and particularly the sales representative, showed an interest in the customers and their needs and requirements. However, as soon as the deal was closed the customers felt that they only saw the 'tail-lights' or 'rear lights' of the salesperson and the supplier as they left. After that they were dealt with by departments such as deliveries, invoicing and claims handling who apparently did not have a customer focus and consequently did not seem to consider the customers very important.

In today's competitive situation, firms cannot afford to maintain barriers between departments and organizational silos. The marketing philosophy has to be spread throughout the organization, and organizational solutions will have to support the acceptance of this philosophy. *Marketing is a set of ideas which must be integrated throughout the entire organization and overseen by top management.* This makes marketing a top management responsibility.[2]

In many situations a firm may be dependent on a network of partners to solve the problems of its customers. In such situations the management of this *marketing attitude of mind* often becomes even more complicated. With the growth of virtual or network organizations, new challenges to instil this marketing mindset emerge.

Marketing as a set of tools and activities. Finally, marketing is a *set of tools, techniques and activities*. This is, of course, an important aspect of marketing, because it is the one to which customers are exposed. But this is also the reason for much of the misunderstanding in many practical situations, where marketing as a phenomenon is predominantly or only thought of as these tools, and predominantly as marketing mix tools planned and implemented by marketing specialists. In reality, *the activities performed by many business functions have marketing effects*.

OBJECTIVES OF MARKETING AND LEVELS OF CUSTOMER COMMITMENT

Traditionally, acquiring customers and achieving sales are considered the main objectives of marketing. This has been labelled *transaction marketing*. For more than 40 years, research into *relationship marketing* has pointed out the importance of retaining customers. As service, with its often continuous interactions between the service provider and its customers, is inherently relational, in most cases an approach other than a transactional one should be taken by service organizations. Marketing activities should aim not only at acquiring customers but also, and in most cases probably more so, at keeping and further developing the customer contacts that have been established. Hence, three levels of marketing objectives can be identified:

1. Acquire customers.

2. Keep customers.

3. Grow customers into customer relationships.

The objectives of marketing on these three levels and the commitment of customers sought are summarized in Table 9.1.

TABLE 9.1

Marketing objectives and levels of customer commitment.

Level	Marketing objective	Customer commitment
Level 1: Acquire customers	To make customers choose the firm's offerings (goods, services) over those of the competitors.	Trial purchase.
Level 2: Keep customers	To make customers satisfied with what they have bought so that they decide to buy again.	A share of the 'customer's wallet'.
Level 3: Grow customers	Create a trusting relationship and an emotional connection with the customers, so that they feel committed to the firm and continuously patronize it.	In addition, a share of the 'customer's heart and mind'.

Transactional marketing aims at achieving the first level. Even if customers have bought from the same provider previously, they are approached by activities aiming at customer acquisition, such as advertising campaigns, price offers or sales calls. Each new purchase is like a new trial purchase. In situations where the firm and its customers interact on a regular basis, the firm can attempt to develop its customer contacts during service processes in a way that impacts the customers favourably and influences them to continuous purchasing. This requires that a customer focus is extended to all employees with whom the customers interact. This is called *interactive marketing* and will be discussed further in a later section of this chapter. In this way the firm can capture a continuous share of these customers' purchases in a certain category (*'a share of the customer's wallet'*).

Here it is important to realize that although these customers seem to be in a relational mode, a real relationship does not necessarily exist. Due to their continuous purchasing behaviour, these customers look relational, but in fact they may only be *bonded* to the firm in a non-committing way (customer bonds were discussed in Chapter 5).[3] The reason for their behaviour may be a lack of alternatives. A retailer may be the only one that for the time being is conveniently located or a supplier of equipment may be the only one that for the time being has the required technology to offer. As soon as an alternative with a better or equal location, or offering a better price or an improved technology enters the scene, the customer may be gone.

To develop a true relationship with a customer the firm has to strive to reach the third level, where the customer feels emotionally committed to the firm, which then also has managed to capture *'a share of the heart and mind'* of such a customer.[4] Here a *real* customer relationship has emerged, where a customer feels a trusting relationship and some level of an emotional connectedness with the firm. This does not mean that this customer could not stop patronizing a given firm at some stage, but it makes the customer less prone to shop around. To achieve this third level the firm has to take a relational approach in its marketing. In a subsequent section, the differences between a transactional and relational approach to marketing is discussed in detail.

THE CUSTOMER RELATIONSHIP LIFECYCLE

Far too often customers are viewed and treated as an anonymous mass. Customers are seen in terms of numbers. When someone stops being a customer, there are always new to take their place. From the customers' point of view, however, every single customer forms a latent relationship with the seller, which the firm should develop and maintain. However, customer relationships do not just happen by magic; *they have to be earned*. The same goes for relationships with distributors, suppliers and other partners.

It may be useful to view the development of a customer relationship as a lifecycle.[5] The concept of the *customer relationship lifecycle* is illustrated in Figure 9.2. The lifecycle consists of three basic phases:

- Initial phase.
- Purchasing phase.
- Consumption (or usage) phase.

A potential customer who is unaware of a firm and its offerings is in the *initial stage* of the lifecycle. If this individual, or an industrial customer, has a need which he feels that the firm may be able to satisfy, the customer may become aware of the firm's service and move into the second stage of the lifecycle, the *purchasing process*.

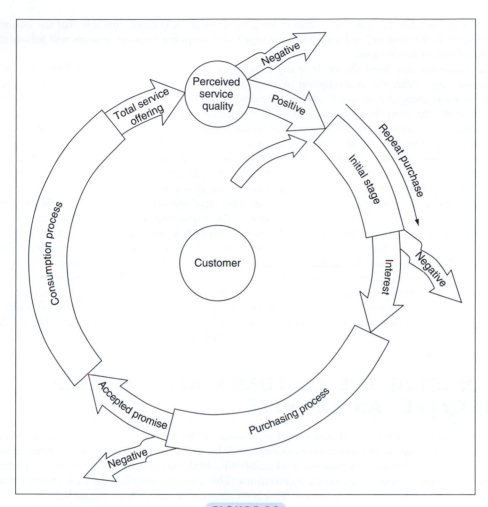

FIGURE 9.2

The customer relationship lifecycle.
Source: Grönroos, C., *Strategic Management and Marketing in the Service Sector.*
Cambridge, MA: Marketing Science Institute, 1983, p. 70. Reproduced by permission of
the Marketing Science Institute.

During the purchasing process the potential customer evaluates the service in relation to what he is looking for and is prepared to pay for. If the outcome of this process is positive, the customer decides to try the service, so he makes a *first purchase*. This takes the customer into the third stage of the lifecycle, the *consumption process* (or *usage stage*, which may be a more appropriate term in a business-to-business context). During this process the customer may observe the firm's ability to take care of his problems and to provide service, which the customer perceives have a level of outcome-related technical and process-related functional quality. If the customer is satisfied with the perceived quality and considers the value it enables to be good enough, it is more probable that the customer relationship will continue, and a new or prolonged consumption or usage process will follow than would otherwise be the case.

The customer may leave the circle at any stage, or may stay within the circle and progress to the following stage. After the consumption or usage process the customer may either leave or decide or to continue using the service provider. Obviously, the marketing efforts of the firm will have an impact on the decision the customer makes. The objectives of the firm's marketing programme and the marketing activities to be used depend on which phase of the customer relationship lifecycle the customer is in. The firm should therefore recognize (1) where in the customer relationship lifecycle a given customer is or its various groups of target customers are, and (2) which resources and activities are effective from a marketing point of view at the different stages of the lifecycle, so that the relationship with a given customer is managed as effectively as possible.

The position of a customer in the lifecycle has substantial marketing consequences. At each stage the marketing *objective* and the *nature of marketing* – the marketing resources and activities that are effective – will be different (see Figure 9.3). At the *initial stage* the marketing objective is to *create interest* in the firm and its service. At the second stage, the *purchasing process*, the general interest should be turned to sales by making promises which are accepted by the potential customer. The potential customer (an individual customer or an industrial buyer) should realize that *accepting the promises* concerning the future problem-solving offering of the firm is a good option. During the *consumption (usage) process* the customer should receive *positive experiences* of the firm's ability to take care of his problems. At this stage the promises that the customer has accepted should be fulfilled. Thus, resales, cross-sales and enduring customer relationships should be achieved.

MANAGING THE CUSTOMER RELATIONSHIP LIFECYCLE: AN EXAMPLE

As an illustration of long-range management of customer relationships, let us consider the efforts of a transportation company offering transportation service by sea. The firm operates in a consumer market as well as in a business-to-business market, offering both transportation service and conference arrangements for businesses and other organizations. This example describes how customer relationships are managed for conference service. This is illustrated schematically in Figure 9.3.

Through advertising and various promotional activities and its website, and occasional personal selling, the company attempts to make potential customers interested in it as a possible conference operator. In addition, the company relies heavily on word of mouth and social media to influence potential customers and on references promoting the idea of using its ships as conference sites. In this *initial* stage, marketing activities are mostly traditional, supported by indirect promotion drawing on the firm's reputation and word-of-mouth communication in various channels.

When a potential customer contacts the transportation company, activities are more specifically directed towards the unique processes and needs of that customer. The *purchasing process* starts. At this stage a conference service that corresponds to the customer's needs and to the customer's conference budget must be designed. Here the output of the process, accepted promises and a first purchase, is to a great extent the result of personal selling efforts. The salesperson will have clarified the customer's conference-related processes and needs to find out what the customer really wants. His ability to negotiate is considered critical to success at this point. The customer should be offered a conference design that will satisfy him both during and after the conference, rather than simply a minimum

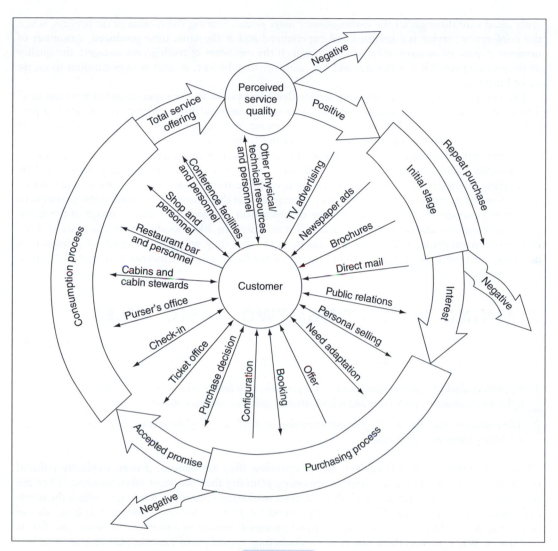

FIGURE 9.3

The customer relationship lifecycle of a transportation company.
Source: Grönroos, C., *Strategic Management and Marketing in the Service Sector*. Cambridge, MA: Marketing Science Institute, 1983, p. 75. Reproduced by permission of the Marketing Science Institute.

budget design that may seem to correspond to the customer's initial needs but which in the long term will turn out to be a disappointment.

If the purchasing process is successful, the potential customer will accept the promises made by the transportation firm and buy a conference service. The firm cannot, however, stop considering the customer as soon as the purchase decision is made. The customer relationship has to be managed with equal care throughout the *consumption* or *usage process*. During the consumption process, when the conference service is consumed and experienced and at the same time produced, a number of moments of truth, or moments of opportunity, occur. If the moments of truth go unmanaged, the quality of the service probably deteriorates and the customer may be lost, as well as opportunities to create more business.

The company attempts to produce a service that corresponds to the expectations of the customer. The conference facilities, arrangements for meals and accommodation, and the appearance and performance of the personnel on board are of the utmost importance to the success or failure of the company as a conference operator in the mind of the customer.

By appropriately designing the conference facilities as well as other aspects of the servicescape[6] – for example, cabin design, access to the Internet, telephones and computer equipment – and by conducting internal training programmes to improve the customer-oriented performance and service-mindedness of its employees, the firm tries to guarantee that the customer, the conference participants and other passengers leave the ship in a state of satisfaction and with a favourable image of the transportation company and its service in mind. This increases the likelihood that the customer and the conference participants will return. It is also expected that they will have a considerable impact on potential customers through word of mouth, social media, resulting in increased interest in the firm and its service.

DEFINING MARKETING: TWO BASIC RULES

Before discussing various approaches to marketing, two basic assumptions about marketing have to be established. These are basic guidelines for the development of marketing that are almost axiomatic:[7]

1. *Regardless of which organizational process or department they belong to, resources and activities of a firm that influence a customer's preferences and behaviours are marketing resources and activities.*

2. *The customers of a firm, not the firm nor its marketers, decide which of the firm's resources and activities are marketing resources and activities.*

These assumptions seem self-evident, but nevertheless they are seldom, if ever, explicitly pointed out in the marketing literature. And in marketing planning they are most often violated. They are somehow disguised behind the much more abstract marketing concept, according to which the needs and wants of customers should be the starting point for a firm's decision-making. The basic idea of marketing is to relate a firm to its current and potential customers and make it meaningful for its customers. What pursues these objectives is marketing, regardless of existing planning or organizational and budgeting structures. In the final analysis, only customers can decide what has an impact on them and which of a firm's resources and activities influence their preferences. What has an impact on customers will vary from industry to industry, firm to firm, situation to situation, customer to customer, from culture to culture and even from time to time. Therefore, a marketing approach cannot be based on a set of predetermined decision-making areas. Such a list will not fit all customers or customer groups in all situations, and moreover, *as the circumstances change it will become obsolete.*

Before we discuss and compare a conventional and a service-oriented marketing approach – the marketing mix and relationship marketing – in the following sections, generic views of what marketing is and how it can be defined will be presented. They are based on the view of *marketing as a value-supporting process*, which in contemporary discussion is considered the *reason d'être* for marketing.[8]

As a philosophy marketing can be described as follows:

Marketing is a set of ideas which must be integrated throughout the entire organization and overseen by top management.

Marketing is an attitude of mind which must be spread throughout an organization, wherever contacts with external customers or internal customers occur. Because marketing, therefore, exists outside the group of marketing specialists of the marketing department, only top management can take responsibility for the creation and maintenance of such a customer-focused attitude.

On the most general level:

The ultimate meaning of marketing is to make the firm meaningful for its customers.[9]

This, of course, goes for all kinds of organizatons and all stakeholder groups. By its actions, the firm should make its customers realize that it is indeed supporting their everyday processes, and ultimately their life or business, in a value–creating way. This is achieved by a customer focus throughout the firm which makes the whole organization function in a customer-centric, service-providing fashion. In this way the firm becomes meaningful for its customers.

On a somewhat more explicit level, from the meaning of marketing expressed above the following goal for marketing can be derived:

The goal for marketing is to engage the firm with its customers' processes with an aim to support value creation in those processes, and ultimately in the customers' life processes (business-to-consumer) and business processes (business-to-business), thus enabling value capture for the firm.[10]

Engaging with the customers' processes means that the firm understands these processes well enough to be able to support them in a way that is meaningful for the customers. How the firm can engage with its customers to support their value creation is further captured in the following, even more explicit definition, based on a *promise management* view of marketing:

Marketing is a customer focus that permeates organizational functions and processes and is geared towards making promises through value propositions, enabling the fulfilment of individual expectations created by such promises, and fulfilling such expectations through assistance to customers' value-creating processes, thereby supporting value creation in the firm's as well as its customers' and other stakeholders' processes.[11]

A *value proposition* is a promise made by a firm, suggesting what benefits or what value a customer can expect if buying and using this firm's offering. Basically, value proposition is a synonym of *value promise*. The value proposition term was originally introduced by the McKinsey Corporation as a concept which should guide and support all actions of a firm when communicating and providing value to customers.[12] It is important to realize that a value proposition is just that, a proposition, not realized value. Lately the value proposition term has been used extensively in the service and marketing literature.[13]

For example, the customer relationship lifecycle model demonstrates the importance of *keeping promises* made in the initial and purchasing stage – i.e. fulfilling value propositions – through value-supporting actions in the consumption stage. If promises made are not kept, customers will perceive a lower level of service quality, become unsatisfied, and perhaps leave. Because the implementation of marketing depends on the context at hand, the promise management definition does not say anything about how promises are made, enabled, and kept through the fulfilment of expectations created by promise making. Decisions on the resources and actions are contextually bound. However, schematically it works in the following way:

- *Making promises*: traditional external marketing activities, such as marketing communication and promotional campaigns, pricing and price offers, product design and packaging, and sales, are the main tools to make promises.

- *Keeping promises through fulfilment of expectations*: the way the resources and processes customers use and interact with, such as products and service processes, as well as hidden services (such as invoicing, service recovery and complaints handling), service employees, technologies and systems, function and support the customers' processes, and how they facilitate value creation in those processes, and in life and business processes, determine how well promises are kept.

- *Enabling promises*: promise making and keeping are enabled by preparing appropriate resources for the value-creating support to the customers' processes, such as service and product development, resource and systems development, and internal marketing. Internal marketing aims at ensuring that employees in customer contacts know how to successfully keep promises, and are motivated and have the required skills and knowledge to perform in a customer-focused way (internal marketing is further discussed in Chapter 14).

In Table 9.2, the levels of marketing are summarized.

TABLE 9.2

A hierarchy of marketing definitions.

Marketing as a philosophy:

Marketing is a set of ideas which must be integrated throughout the entire organization and overseen by top management.

The meaning of marketing:

The ultimate meaning of marketing is to make the firm (or any organization) relevant for its customers (and other stakeholders).

The goal for marketing:

The goal for marketing is to engage the firm with its customers' processes with an aim to support value creation in those processes, and ultimately in the customers' life processes (business-to-consumer) and business processes (business-to-business).

Implementing this goal as promise management:

Marketing is a customer focus that permeates organizational functions and processes and is geared towards making promises through value propositions, enabling the fulfilment of individual expectations created by such promises, and fulfilling such expectations through assistance to customers' value-creating processes, thereby supporting value creation in the firm's as well as its customers' and other stakeholders' processes.

DEFINING MARKETING: THE MARKETING MIX APPROACH

In this and subsequent sections we will discuss how marketing in practice can be managed in service competition. The marketing concept is transformed into marketing in practice in the standard literature on *marketing management*, which is essentially geared towards consumer goods contexts. There are dozens of textbooks covering this topic. In this approach to marketing, the core of marketing is overwhelmingly the *marketing mix*. The marketer plans various means of competition and blends them into a 'marketing mix',[14] so that a profit function, based on the goods profit logic (see Chapter 3), is optimized. When Neil Borden first introduced the idea of the marketing mix in the 1950s, he offered a list of 12 variables as a guideline and said that they would probably have to be reconsidered in any given situation. The marketing mix was soon reformulated as the '4Ps', with four standardized categories of marketing variables.[15]

Traditionally, the 4Ps are *product*, *place*, *price* and *promotion*. In a later definition from 1985 marketing, according to the marketing mix approach, is described as follows: 'Marketing is the process of planning and executing the *conception*, *pricing*, *promotion* and *distribution* of ideas, goods and services to create exchanges and satisfy individual and organizational objectives [emphasis by this author].'[16] During the last two decades, marketing researchers have increasingly found that the list of 4Ps is too restrictive and more categories of marketing variables have been suggested, most often in the form of additional 'Ps', such as people, processes and physical evidence[17] as well as public relations and politics.[18] As a consequence, in the 2000s the American Marketing Association made two attempts to renew this definition. The importance of value creation and marketing as a process is recognized, but other than that the resulting definitions are still overshadowed by a marketing mix toolbox.[19]

Defining marketing according to the marketing mix approach is like using a list of tools, or categories of tools, as a definition. Such a way of defining a phenomenon can never be considered the most valid. A list can never include all relevant items, it will not fit all situations, and it becomes obsolete. Increasing the number of Ps does not offer a fundamental improvement to the definition The need to add new categories of marketing variables or Ps is a symptom of the weakness of the marketing mix approach, and demonstrates that, as *a general marketing model*, the marketing mix approach has failed.[20] Moreover, the marketing mix approach is an inside–out oriented model, where managing marketing mix variables easily becomes more important than understanding the customers' everyday activities and processes.[21] Customers become objects for the marketer to whom something is done, instead of being subjects, with whom and for whom solutions are developed.[22] Still, it may well be helpful in many contexts, such as for consumer packaged goods where the products are standardized. In the competitive situation after World War II, with increasing demand and growing markets, the marketing mix and its 4Ps formed an effective marketing approach. In a relationship-oriented approach to marketing, many elements of the marketing mix toolbox are still highly necessary, because it includes variables, for example promotion and pricing, that are clearly important in service competition.[23] However, as a general marketing approach, and especially outside the consumer goods area, the marketing mix method hardly makes a firm meaningful for its customers anymore, and as all other stakeholders are depending on the firm's customers, this does not make the firm relevant for them either.

In a situation where service competition dominates, markets are more and more mature and competition more intense, the shortcomings of marketing mix management and its 4Ps are becoming evident. As the starting point of this approach, in practice, is marketing as a predetermined set of decision-making areas; other decision-making areas are outside the scope of marketing. The process nature of marketing as illustrated, for example, by the *customer relationship lifecycle* model is largely neglected. Marketing activities may be seen as processes, for example when executing a promotional campaign, but the firm's relationship with its customers is not viewed in that way.

Moreover, although it is not inherent in traditional models, marketing has become a function that sits alongside other business functions, delegated to a separate group of marketing specialists and frequently organized in the form of a marketing department. It is symptomatic that in the marketing literature, 'marketing' and 'marketing department' are often used interchangeably. Frequently, the customer relationship is managed with a marketing approach only or mainly to the extent that the marketing specialists (and salespeople) are involved.[24]

It is ironic that the people who by definition have a marketing attitude of mind, the full-time marketing specialists of the marketing departments, are the people who frequently have limited or no customer contact. Those who interact with customers during the consumption or usage stage of the customer relationship lifecycle (in service processes, deliveries, repair and maintenance, customer training, complaints handling, billing, etc.) normally do not have marketing training or a genuine interest in the customer.

As a consequence of these deficiencies of the marketing mix management approach, the following conclusions can be drawn:

1. Marketing has become a function for marketing specialists, and therefore a marketing attitude of mind is not easily instilled throughout the organization.

2. Because of the lack of marketing training throughout large parts of the organization, the customer's interests are given high priority only in some parts of the customer relationship lifecycle (mainly the initial and purchasing phases), whereas during the consumption or usage process the relationship is managed by staff without a customer focus and without taking customer considerations properly into account.

3. Furthermore, because of the decision variable orientation of the marketing mix, marketing and marketing planning have become preoccupied with making and refining decisions which, according to the marketing mix, are considered marketing decisions. At the same time the process of taking customers through the relationship lifecycle and ensuring that customers stay in the lifecycle, which may require that other decision-making areas are included in marketing planning as well, is neglected.

4. Finally, as a consequence of the three previous points, both 'ground rules' of marketing put forward above are violated. In service competition, particularly for service firms and in business-to-business markets, the marketing mix approach frequently does not cover all resources and activities of the stages of the customer relationship lifecycle. As can be seen in Figure 9.3, during the consumption process especially there is a range of contacts between the service firm and its customer which are outside the traditional marketing function as defined by the 4Ps of the marketing mix. Managing and operating these contacts (for example, the conference facilities, the cabins, the restaurants, and managing the employees on board) are the responsibility of operations and other non-marketing departments. Nevertheless, these contacts – buyer–seller interactions or service encounters – have an immense impact on the future buying behaviour of the customers as well as on comments on social media and word of mouth; that is, they have marketing implications, and should therefore be considered as marketing resources and activities and managed as such.

DEFINING MARKETING: A RELATIONSHIP APPROACH

In Chapter 1 we discussed the relationship perspective on marketing and the management of customer relationships as marketing. It was noted that this marketing perspective fits service competition well. The *marketing concept* as the basic philosophy guiding marketing in practice still holds, although the customer perspective has to be focused on in a much more customer value-oriented way.[25] To make firms relevant for their customers and enable them to engage with their customers' processes to support their value creation, marketing should be defined in a service-based, relationship-oriented way.

A relationship definition of marketing can be formulated as follows:

The purpose of marketing is to identify and establish, maintain and enhance, and when necessary terminate relationships with customers (and other parties) so that the objectives regarding economic and other variables of all parties are met. This is achieved through a mutual making and fulfilment of promises.[26]

Such relationships are usually long term, but they do not necessarily always have to be. In this context we are mainly discussing customer relationships, but the same approach can also be used when dealing with other parties, such as suppliers, distributors, co-producers of customer solutions, financial institutions and political decision-makers. It may be necessary for a firm to establish relationships with such parties to supply its customers with appropriate solutions.[27]

In the relationship marketing literature there are several definitions similar to the one presented here.[28] Parvatiyar and Sheth[29] present an excellent overview of the discussion in the literature of relationship marketing definitions as well as in the domain of relationship marketing. Evert Gummesson has presented a definition which is somewhat different, but nevertheless has the same process orientation: relationship marketing is *marketing seen as relationships, networks and interactions.*[30]

This definition points out the central phenomena in marketing according to the relationship perspective (the *relationship* itself) and the key processes in the relationship (the *interactions*) as well as the fact that relationship marketing often takes place in *networks* of co-operating partners. The view that exchange is the focal phenomenon in marketing[31] is not included in these definitions. Although exchange still takes place, focusing on exchange makes marketing transaction-oriented and draws the marketer's attention away from what is essential, namely the interactions with customers that form relationships in which exchanges from time to time take place.[32]

Long-term customer relationships mean that the main objective of marketing is to seek enduring relationships with customers. Of course, in some situations short-term sales based on *transaction marketing* may be profitable. Generally, however, retaining customers in the long term is vital to profitable business. In a relationship, transactions concerning goods, services, knowledge, information or any other asset of value to the customer must take place. Profitability cannot be measured immediately as a result of the first transaction. Profitability is a long-term measurement, which should develop from an ongoing and enduring relationship. However, the link between longer customer relationships and profitability is not automatic. In some cases costs of retaining customers may be high and long-standing customers may over time demand more attention and service followed by increasing costs of serving such customers.[33] Hence, firms must attempt to follow up the profitability of their customers over time, so that they are not surprised by customer relationships that gradually turn unprofitable.

Identifying and *establishing*, *maintaining* and *enhancing* customer relationships implies, respectively, that the process of marketing includes the following:

1. Market research to *identify* potentially interesting and profitable customers to contact.

2. *Establishing* the first contact with a customer so that a relationship starts to emerge.

3. *Maintaining* an existing relationship so that the customer is satisfied with the perceived quality and the value created and is willing to continue to do business with the other party in the relationship (getting a 'share of the customer's wallet').

4. *Enhancement* of an ongoing relationship so that a trusting relationship and an emotional connection between the customer and the provider is emerging, and the customer decides to expand the content of the relationship by, for example, purchasing larger quantities or new types of goods and services from the same seller (getting a 'share of the customer's heart and mind' and expanding the 'share of the customer's wallet').

5. *Terminating* a relationship; sometimes a firm will have to cope with the situation when a customer decides to discontinue the relationship *or* the firm may find it necessary to discontinue a relationship with a customer. Both these situations should be managed so that the relationship can be re-established in the future. We will, however, not discuss this fifth situation here.[34]

These situations are all different from a marketing point of view. In short, establishing the first contact demands good communication and sales skills. Favourable word of mouth and a well-known image help. Maintaining and enhancing customer relationships requires other types of tools and activities. To maintain a relationship the perceived quality of goods, service activities, information, personal contacts and all other types of service elements present in a given customer relationship have to be good. In addition, good selling skills may be required to enhance a relationship. Good selling does not only, or even mainly, mean good sales performance by professional salespeople, but also good sales and communication skills by customer contact employees interacting with customers as part of the service process. From the supplier's or service provider's point of view:

- Establishing a relationship involves *making promises*.

- Maintaining a relationship is based on *fulfilment of promises*, and finally,

- Developing or enhancing a relationship means that *a new set of promises is made with the fulfilment of earlier promises as a prerequisite*.

THE DARK SIDE OF RELATIONSHIPS

Although long-term relationships can normally be considered favourable for both the supplier or service provider and the customer, over time negative consequences of stable relationships may occur for both parties. This may be especially important in business-to-business relationships. The customer may become lazy and neglect developments in the marketplace. A competing supplier may have developed a new and better technological solution, but this has gone unnoticed by the customer who is engaged in a stable relationship with another supplier. On the other hand, the supplier may be satisfied with having customers buying existing solutions and as a consequence neglect to invest in developing new and improved technologies and solutions. For both parties this type of neglect can turn out to be fatal.

The above-mentioned negative consequence of stable relationships is only one of several possible unfavourable long-term effects that can occur. Possible negative effects include:[35]

- Either party or both neglect developments in the marketplace.

- The customer's choices are restricted by a long-term relationship.

- Suppliers may be excluded from serving other customers that compete with the one in the relationship.

- The customer may become connected to unwanted business partners who belong to the supplier's network of relationships.

- The trust in one party in a relationship may be misused by the other party, especially when problems occur.

These 'dark sides' of relationships[36] must be observed, otherwise what starts as a win–win situation may eventually turn into a burden for one of the parties, or sometimes even for both.

CASE STUDY

MARKETING AS A PASSION OR COST

Some firms view marketing just as a cost, and they do not drive their business with passion. Others see marketing as an opportunity and that makes them passionate about their business. I have worked for both types of firms. The first firm was a start-up company, where no restrictions were set for the marketing budget, neither for external nor interactive marketing and customer interactions. The costs of everything else were strictly monitored. The other firm had a totally different mindset. Marketing was considered just a necessary evil, and marketing focused only on external activities. We employees could feel this in our skin, and it hurt motivation. Two years after I left, the first firm, which had started from scratch, had grown to a prospering business which operates in six of the biggest cities in the world. The other firm still struggles with customers who are reluctant to buy its products, and it has not grown at all.

Source: This case was written by Mia-Maja Korhonen, based on her work experience.

PROMISE THEORY

An integral element of the relationship marketing definition is the *promise concept* based on *promise theory*.[37] According to this, the responsibilities of marketing do not only include making promises and thus persuading customers to act in a given way. A firm that is preoccupied with making promises may attract new customers and build new relationships to begin with. However, if promises are not fulfilled, the evolving relationship cannot be maintained or enhanced. Keeping promises is equally important as a means of achieving customer satisfaction, retention of the customer base, and long-term profitability. It is also important to notice that promises are made, and should be fulfilled, mutually. Finally, the firm has to take action to make sure that it, either by itself or together with network partners, has the resources, knowledge, skills and motivation to keep promises. Sufficient efforts to *enable promises* have to be made.[38] This will be discussed in Chapter 14 in the context of internal marketing.

MARKETING RESOURCES AND ACTIVITIES ACCORDING TO THE RELATIONSHIP DEFINITION

The relationship definition of marketing *does not* state that the traditional means of competition of the marketing mix, such as advertising using new or old media, personal selling, pricing and conceptualizing of the product are any less important than earlier. However, it does demonstrate that there is *much more* to marketing. What is important is that it represents a fundamental shift in the way of looking at marketing as a phenomenon as compared with the marketing mix. The relationship approach to marketing is based on a service logic and therefore truly *process-oriented*. It views marketing as a process of taking the customer through the customer relationship lifecycle and keeping the customer there in order to reach the mutual objectives of the firm and the customer. The exchange of promises indicated in the relationship definition may be of any kind and may concern any type of activities. The resources to which the customer is exposed and interacts with may also be of any type, and they may vary from customer to customer depending on whether the relationship is in the establishment, maintenance or enhancement phase. They cannot be predetermined or categorized, as marketing resources and decision-making areas are according to the marketing mix.

In practical situations, for teaching in classroom settings as well as for marketing planning in organizations, the relationship definition is not as easy to use as the marketing mix. This is natural, because the main virtue of the marketing mix is its simplicity, not its proven capability to capture certain marketing situations. The relationship definition does not provide users with an easy-to-implement list of categories of marketing variables or means of competition. Instead, *it forces users to think for themselves and to analyse the marketing situation at hand*, as well as develop an understanding of the resources and activities required to establish, maintain or enhance – and of course, when necessary, terminate – a relationship with a specific customer or group of customers.

To sum up, according to the relationship approach, *marketing is a process rather than a function*[39] and it is the concern of every function and department in an organization. A marketing mindset is required by everyone with a direct or indirect impact on how customers perceive the firm, its goods and services and its way of taking care of its customers, regardless of what responsibilities a person may have within the organization. The relationship perspective is, of course, not the only market-oriented way of honouring the marketing concept. It is, though, an approach well suited for understanding, as well as planning and implementing, marketing in service contexts and in service competition.[40]

Relationship marketing is a newer paradigm and school of thought in marketing, alongside the traditionally dominating marketing management school. In his analysis of relationship marketing, Adel El-Ansary goes as far as to postulate that it will 'continue to be a dominant school of thought in marketing, thus replacing the traditional marketing management school of thought'.[41]

Relationship marketing cannot be implemented by a marketing department alone. An understanding of customer relationships and relationship marketing should permeate the whole organization and employees from departments other than marketing are responsible for serving customers and thus for making customers either willing to continue buying from the same supplier or service provider or not willing to do so. In a subsequent section such employees are termed *part-time marketers*. If this is not the case, marketing will not succeed. Hence, a relationship perspective on a firm's customer management includes three levels:

1. Relationship perspective as a culture and an attitude.
2. Relationship perspective as a strategy.
3. Tactical consequences on the operational level of the relationship perspective.

A relationship-based view of how to take care of customers involves the whole company. Therefore, an *attitude among employees on all levels including top management* that honours a relationship approach to customer management is essential to successful planning and implementation. A culture that appreciates relationship marketing is required.[42] In Chapter 15 the development of a service culture, based on a relationship approach to marketing, will be discussed.

Secondly, a relationship approach to customer management has to *influence the strategic decision-making* in the firm, and not only on a separate marketing strategy level. Because one way or the other the whole organization is responsible for the implementation of a relationship approach to managing customers, *the firm's business strategy has to be relationship-focused*. Otherwise problems will occur on the third and final level. A firm with a non-relational strategy will never be able to practise a relational approach in its customer management. In essence, its marketing will remain transactional. The traditional marketing efforts may become more relational, such as an extended use of direct response activities and loyalty programmes and customer clubs, but other than that customers will not be treated in a relational manner. Relationship marketing requires that a customer is managed in a relationship-based fashion throughout the customer relationship lifecycle. It requires a focus on customers and on service in every corner of the organization.

Finally, *tactical consequences on an operational level* follow from taking a relationship perspective. All processes and functions where customer contacts occur, either directly or indirectly, have to be geared towards the development, maintenance and enhancement of relationships with customers and other stakeholders such as distributors and retailers. This probably requires changes in operational plans, policies and procedures in organizations that are used to a situation where customer management is the responsibility of marketing and sales departments only.

In Figure 9.4 a *relationship marketing model* is illustrated. The two outer circles represent processes, which the firm controls, except for word of mouth and social media on the outermost circle. The circle in the middle represents the customer's processes and, due to the firm's actions on the two outer circles, how value emerges for the customer.

The two outer circles demonstrate the two different processes that build up the relationship. The *communication process* includes communication messages which are planned and where separate and distinct planned communication media are used. Sales and all types of communication media are effective in this context (for example, TV commercials, newspaper ads, brochures, direct mail, Internet sites and adverts, sales calls, exhibition stands and sales promotions; in Figure 9.4 a limited number of examples are indicated as illustrations only). In addition, word of mouth and discussions on social media also influence the customer. Basically, here *promises are made* about how the customer's processes will be supported and what perceived quality and value this support should lead to.

The *interaction process* is a real process in the sense that through interactions *promises made are kept* and the customers perceive how the firm supports their value creation in reality. The customers' real interactions with physical products, service processes, hidden services, customer contact employees, systems and technology, e-commerce processes, administrative and financial routines, etc. occur in this process. Of course, an episode in this process includes also an element of communication. And word of mouth and social media comments are triggered by what customers experience in various episodes.

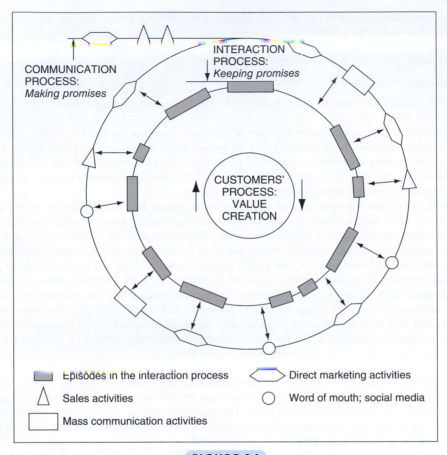

FIGURE 9.4

A relationship marketing process model.
Source: Grönroos, C., Relationship marketing: the Nordic School perspective.
In Sheth, J.N. & Parvatiyar, A. (eds), *Handbook of Relationship Marketing*.
Thousand Oaks, CA: SAGE, 2000, p. 107. Reproduced by permission of SAGE
Publications Inc.

   Successful relationship marketing requires that both the communication and interaction processes
are properly planned and executed. Only focusing on relationship-oriented communication activities,
such as direct marketing, and customer loyalty programmes creates expectations, but how such expectations are fulfilled remains unplanned. According to promise theory and the promise management
view of marketing, expectations must be fulfilled by keeping promises made. In a straightforward
consumer goods marketing situation, a standardized product will keep promises made and fulfil expectations created by such promises. However, in situations where the customer interface is broader and
may continue over a longer period of time, such as in service and relationship marketing, there is no
one standardized item which takes care of this. *All the episodes on the interaction circle and the flow of these
episodes equals the standardized product in the marketing mix of consumer goods.*

The double-headed arrows between the two outer circles in Figure 9.4 indicate that to avoid overpromising and the creation of the wrong expectations, communication activities on the communication circle must be geared to the various episodes on the interaction circle.

MARKETING FUNCTIONS AND PROCESSES

As demonstrated by the *customer relationship lifecycle* model and also the relationship marketing model, in a service context marketing is by no means only an intermediate function building a bridge between production and consumption or usage, as it is supposed to be in conventional marketing. Marketing is an integral part of producing and delivering service, especially during the *consumption (usage) process*. In other words, managing the moments of truth in the *service encounters* is a marketing task as well as a responsibility for operations, personnel, human resources management and other departments which have contact with customers or influence such contacts. The separation of marketing, production, human resource management and other processes may well be logical in traditional manufacturing, where customers order and use the products far away from the place of production. It is not appropriate for service systems where the production of service, delivery and consumption is simultaneous.[43]

There is, however, a distinct difference between handling the interactions of the moments of truth as a marketing task and executing traditional marketing activities such as advertising, personal selling and sales promotion. Normally the latter are planned *and* implemented by marketing and sales specialists, whereas the former are implemented by specialists in other areas. Moreover, they are frequently planned and managed by non-marketing managers and supervisors; people who are neither aware of their marketing responsibilities nor interested in customers or marketing.

The employees involved in marketing, who are not marketing specialists, are *part-time marketers* as opposed to *full-time marketers*, to use a term introduced by Evert Gummesson.[44] They are, of course, specialists in their own areas. At the same time, they must learn to perform their tasks in such a way that customers will want to return, thus strengthening the customer relationship. Hence, they will have to learn to act in a customer-focused and marketing-oriented fashion, and their managers and supervisors will have to learn to think in terms of marketing and customer impact as well.

To sum up, the marketing process can be divided into two separate functions or sub-processes: a specialist function, taking care of many traditional marketing mix activities and market research; and a marketing function, related to the buyer–seller interactions of the simultaneous service production and consumption processes, where marketing tasks are performed by part-time marketers, supported by, and sometimes (as in telecommunications or Internet banking) replaced by, customer-oriented physical resources, technology and systems. The two functions or sub-processes of marketing are the *traditional external marketing process* and the *interactive marketing process*.

In Figure 9.5 the two marketing functions of service organizations are schematically illustrated. The shaded areas represent the marketing functions. The *traditional marketing function* is separate from other functions. It involves market research, advertising, Internet and mobile communication, pricing, sales promotions and other activities traditionally considered to be part of marketing. This traditional marketing function is also frequently labelled *external marketing*. For consumer service, the traditional marketing function is a *mass marketing function*. However, in business-to-business relationships personal sales contacts by salespeople are also involved and most often dominate this function.

The interface between production and consumption represents the buyer–seller interactions or service encounters, where the *moments of truth* or moments of opportunity occur. Because the marketing impact of these interactions occurs in interactive processes, this part of marketing has been called the *interactive marketing function*[45] in the service marketing literature since the late 1970s. Interactive marketing, or marketing outside the marketing department, occurs at the moment when the

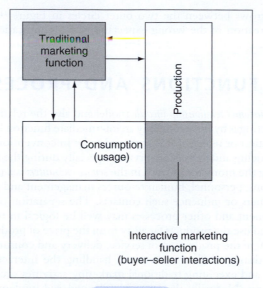

FIGURE 9.5

Two marketing processes.
Source: Grönroos, C., *Strategic
Management and Marketing in the Service
Sector*. Cambridge, MA: Marketing Science
Institute, 1983, p. 62. Reproduced by
permission of the Marketing Science
Institute.

customer and service provider interact. The service is actually delivered and the foundation laid for resales through activities in the buyer–seller interactions of the service encounters.

The customer's opinion of a service is influenced both by the means of production (i.e. the production facilities, human and other production resources and the servicescape) and by the service production process (i.e. the behaviour of the employees, the manner in which the production facilities are used, and the way physical resources, technology and systems support the production and consumption of the service in a customer-oriented fashion). The interactive marketing function recognizes that every component – human and non-human – in producing a service, every production resource used, and every stage in the service production and delivery process should be handled as a marketing issue, and not considered as merely an operations or administrative issue. In addition, customers are not only consumers or users of a service but also *co-producers* of that service. In this respect customers are also a resource in the interactive marketing process. The marketing consequences of every resource and activity involved in interactive marketing situations have to be acknowledged in the planning process, so that the production resources and operations support and enhance the organization's attempts to develop and maintain long-term relationships with its customers.

The *co-production willingness* of customers cannot be taken for granted. When necessary, customers have to be educated and advised about how to best co-operate in the service process in a way that supports their perception of service quality. In addition, especially when new technology for customer self-service is introduced, considerable efforts to not only educate customers, but also to motivate them to make use of the new technology may be required.[46]

To sum up, *the marketing resources used in the interactive marketing process are totally different from those used in the traditional external marketing function.* While the latter are *'full-time marketing resources'*, the resources of interactive marketing are only *'part-time marketing resources'*. The dual role of the part-time marketers has already been discussed, but the same applies to other resources as well. Physical resources, technology and systems used in the service process and to build up the servicescape should function well to produce the service in a technical sense and should also keep internal efficiency at an optimal level. However, when planning how such resources should be used, a customer-focused approach has to be taken simultaneously. Resources in the service process should function in inter-actions with customers in a way that creates good process-related functional quality, and thereby has a good interactive marketing effect. When investing in these resources, both internal efficiency (the cost-effective use of resources) and external effectiveness (impact on perceived service quality) must be taken into account at the same time by the service provider. Customers have dual roles, too. They consume the service, but they also contribute to how the service process proceeds.

WHAT IS MORE IMPORTANT – TRADITIONAL EXTERNAL MARKETING OR INTERACTIVE MARKETING?

Interactive marketing can be characterized as the heart of marketing in service competition. Regard-less of how customer-focused and well-planned and implemented traditional marketing activities such as advertising campaigns are, *if interactive marketing fails, marketing fails*. Moreover, because it is the way normal operational and administrative efforts are implemented, interactive marketing always exists. *In the minds of the customers, interactive marketing may be good or bad, but it is always present.*

In situations where the service provider has a stable customer base with satisfied customers who continuously patronize the firm and through positive word-of-mouth referrals bring in new cus-tomers, in principle nothing else than pricing is needed. Because of a customer-focused service process and consequently a successful interactive marketing process, the customers patronizing the firm are satisfied enough to return and to bring in new business. This is typically the case for a small pub or restaurant or a street corner retailer, but also large service firms can perform successfully without much traditional external marketing support. For example, in 2004 in Sweden the advertising expenditure of Handelsbanken, one of the four large nationwide operating banks in the country, was only 7% of that of the competitor that spent the most, and only slightly more than one-tenth of what the two other banks in that category spent. Still, this bank managed to outperform the others in terms of market share growth.[47] Ten years later the percentage is still clearly under 10%. On top of this, customer satisfaction ratings and profitability for this bank have, over the years, constantly been the highest or among the highest in the industry.

However, in most situations service organizations need both interactive marketing and traditional external marketing. Especially in situations where a firm launches new service or wants to enter a new market or customer segment, traditional marketing campaigns are needed. Furthermore, sometimes a competitor's campaign has to be matched by traditional marketing efforts. However, the better the interactive marketing functions, the less need for that. To assess the effectiveness of a service firm's total marketing in a stable market situation, the following ground rule can be used *as a first indicator* of how customer-focused the firm is: *the higher the advertising expenditures, the less service-focused the firm is likely to be and the less customer-focused its interactive marketing performance probably is*. Of course, this does not have to be the case in all situations, and further analyses should always be done. In a highly competitive market environment even a very customer-focused service provider with a good inter-active marketing performance may have to invest more in traditional external marketing campaigns. However, it is typical that less customer-focused service firms compensate a lack of service orientation in their operations with higher advertising budgets. To replace the unsatisfied customers who have left, new customers are lured to take their place. In the long run this is not an effective strategy.

THE INTERNET AND MARKETING

The Internet, and to a growing extent also mobile technologies, have become more frequently used in marketing. The Internet is, for example, used for selling, communication, market research and making payments. These are all ways of using it to perform traditional marketing activities. However, *the Internet is also an interactive marketing vehicle*, because a variety of service interactions can be initiated and also performed over the Internet. For example, by providing e-mail connections to helpdesks or other functions of a firm, the Internet becomes part of the service process. The way it functions influences the interactive marketing impact of the firm. This of course requires that the firm manages to assume its role as an interactive partner in the virtual environment. Finally, digital service is developing, for example in games, where the service is produced digitally as well.

The Internet is a service- and relationship-oriented medium, even though it is often only used as a communications and sales tool. It is important to keep in mind, though, that normally it is not the firm that makes the first contact with a customer over the Internet; it is the customer or potential customer who initiates the contact. If this contact can be developed into a service process with interactions between the firm and the customer, a relationship may emerge. Because it is so easy to jump from one website to another, creating a relationship-oriented service interaction with a given customer may be an effective way of maintaining a given customer's interest in the firm and creating ongoing business.

In conclusion, the Internet does not only offer a means of carrying out traditional marketing activities, it is also an interactive process instrument which has an important role in the interactive marketing function. Mobile technologies and cellular phones can be used both for communicating with customers and making offers and as an interactive marketing tool. However, increasingly they also function as a platform for service consumption, for example for playing games.

CASE STUDY

WWOZ RADIO: THE SOUND OF NEW ORLEANS – THE INTERNET IN THE SERVICE OF MUSIC BROADCASTING

WWOZ radio (90.7 FM) is based in the New Orleans Jazz National Historical Park in New Orleans, Louisiana, USA. Playing blues, jazz, calypso, zydeco, gospel, Brazilian, Caribbean, Irish music and a lot more, WWOZ keeps the music and musical heritage of the Crescent City alive. A listener-supported, volunteer-operated, non-profit radio station, WWOZ uses sophisticated technology to deliver its services to a global audience. In addition to broad-casting live to listeners in the south-eastern Louisiana area, WWOZ broadcasts live on the Internet (http://www.wwoz.org) and can be heard from anywhere in the world.

The New Orleans Jazz & Heritage Foundation, Inc. owns WWOZ and also produces the New Orleans Jazz & Heritage Festival (JazzFest). WWOZ broadcasts start-to-finish coverage of JazzFest. In 1999, six hours of the 56 hours of WWOZ's live JazzFest coverage were uplinked by satellite to a network of public radio stations organized by WWOZ. In addition, it does numerous live broadcasts from music clubs throughout the year via its mobile recording studio. WWOZ also offers selected downloadable MP3 music files from the WWOZ website.

Source: This case example was developed by Raymond P. Fisk, Texas State University.

THE THREE-STAGE MODEL

Marketing is a dynamic process, where traditional external marketing activities and interactive marketing resources and activities co-operate so that profitable long-term customer relationships may be developed and maintained. The *customer relationship lifecycle* model illustrated how enduring customer relationships are created through a three-stage process. The *three-stage* model demonstrates this long-term marketing approach, as illustrated by Figure 9.6. At each stage the *objective* of marketing and the *nature of* marketing – the marketing function to be used – will be different.

At the *initial stage*, when potential customers have no clear view, or perhaps old-fashioned or out-of-date views, of the firm and its service, the objective of marketing is to *create interest* in the organization and its offerings. This is best achieved by the *traditional marketing function*. Advertising, websites, sales promotions and public relations are appropriate means of competition. Sometimes sales

Stage	Objective of marketing	Marketing function
Initial stage	To create interest in the firm and its services	The traditional marketing function
Purchasing process	To turn general interest into sales* (first purchase)	The traditional and the interactive marketing functions
Consumption (usage) process	To create resales, cross-sales and enduring customer relations**	The interactive marketing function

* Making promises
** Fulfilling promises

FIGURE 9.6

The three-stage model.
Source: Grönroos, C., *Strategic Management and Marketing in the Service Sector*. Cambridge, MA: Marketing Science Institute, 1983. Reproduced by permission of the Marketing Science Institute.

is also needed, especially in business–to–business markets. One should also not overlook the potential power of favourable word–of–mouth communication.

At the second stage, the *purchasing process, general interest should be turned into sales*. More specifically, *promises* about future commitments on the part of the seller are made and should, one hopes, be accepted. Here again the *traditional marketing* activities, including sales, can be used. However, *interactive marketing* activities can also be applied whenever the customer contacts with the firm's production resources before he has made a final purchase decision.

During the *consumption (usage) process*, resales, cross-sales and enduring customer relationships should be achieved. At this stage, *promises have to be kept*, so that customers realize that the firm can satisfy their needs and that it can be trusted. At this final stage in the lifecycle the traditional marketing activities have only a slight chance, if any, of influencing the preferences of the customers towards the service. Here the *interactive marketing process* is responsible for success or failure. The marketing orientation and service-mindedness of the service process and the resources in the production process are of vital importance if customers are not to be lost at this stage.

Often the firm may be excellent at making promises, but these promises may be kept in a much less marketing-oriented way, and low perceived quality follows. Marketing may be managed successfully during the first two phases of the customer relationship lifecycle, but in the third phase, the consumption or usage process, nobody seems to be responsible for marketing and customers any more.

Marketing has to be planned and implemented throughout the lifecycle as a continuous process, otherwise too many customer relationships are broken, which leads to bad word of mouth. Moreover, lost customers have to be replaced by new customers, which requires an increased budget for traditional marketing.

THE MARKETING STRATEGY CONTINUUM

As we have seen, relationship marketing means that the firm uses a marketing strategy that aims at maintaining and enhancing ongoing customer relationships. Although getting new customers is still important, the main strategic interest is to market to existing customers. In a relationship marketing strategy, interactive marketing becomes essential. If the moments of truth of the buyer–seller interactions are badly taken care of, thus literally wasting moments of opportunity, no traditional marketing efforts can ensure that the customers will stay with the firm. A relationship marketing approach and excellent interactive marketing capabilities are essential in service competition. Without these elements a service strategy often collapses.

Of course, relationship marketing is not the only marketing strategy option in service competition, although the importance of such a strategy is increasing all the time. It can be useful to think about possible marketing approaches or strategies along a *marketing strategy continuum*.[48] As a strategy, relationship marketing can be considered one end of such a continuum. At the other end of the continuum, the strategy would be to concentrate on one transaction at a time with any given customer, without deliberately trying to develop any enduring relationship with that customer. This type of marketing strategy is often called *transaction marketing*. As marketing strategies can be placed on a continuum, where these two types of strategies are the extremes, there are, clearly, situations where firms can combine elements of the two strategies. A relationship type of strategy or a transaction type of strategy may dominate. The *marketing strategy continuum* and its consequences for a number of marketing issues are illustrated in Figure 9.7.

Marketers of consumer packaged goods will probably benefit most from a transaction-type strategy, although this is not necessarily the case. Service firms and product manufacturers adopting a service

The strategy continuum	Transaction marketing	Relationship marketing
Unit of analysis	Single exchange	Relationship
Time prespective	Short-term focus	Long-term focus
Dominating marketing function	Marketing mix	Interactive marketing (supported by marketing mix activities)
Price elasticity	Customers tend to be more sensitive to price	Customers tend to be less sensitive to price
Dominating quality dimension	Quality of output (technical quality dimension) is dominating	Quality of interactions (functional quality dimensions) grows in importance and may become dominating
Measurement of customer satisfaction	Monitoring market share (indirect approach)	Managing the customer base (direct approach)
Customer information system	*Ad hoc* customer satisfaction surveys	Real-time customer feedback system
Interdependency between marketing, operations and human resource management	Interface of no or limited strategic importance	Interface of substantial strategic importance
The role of internal marketing	Internal marketing of no or limited importance to success	Internal marketing of substantial strategic importance to success

FIGURE 9.7

The marketing strategy continuum.
Source: Adapted from Grönroos, C., From marketing mix to relationship marketing: towards a paradigm shift in marketing. *Management Decision*, **32**(2); 1994: p. 11. Reproduced by permission of Emerald Insight.

logic, on the other hand, would normally be better off by applying a relationship-type strategy. Manufacturers of consumer packaged goods have mass markets but no immediate contact with their ultimate customers, while service firms almost always have such contacts, sometimes on a regular basis, sometimes only at discrete points of time. Therefore, the interface between the service firm and its customers is expanded far outside the departments of marketing and sales specialists. However, the development of information technology has made it possible for marketers of consumer packaged goods to create databases which enable them, too, if they find this effective and justified from an economic standpoint, to treat each and every customer as an individual.

In consumer durables the customer interface is broader than for consumer packaged goods, and a pure transaction-type strategy is not the only available option. The durables have to be delivered to customers and often also installed. Industrial goods, ranging from mass-produced components to complex machines and projects, would probably fit best between consumer durables and services. However, in many business–to–business marketing situations the customer relationships are similar to many service contexts, and here no distinctions between business–to–business marketing and service marketing can be made on the continuum.

CONSEQUENCES FOR MARKETING OF THE STRATEGY CONTINUUM

In this section nine different consequences of a relationship marketing strategy and a transaction marketing strategy will be discussed (see Figure 9.7):

1. Unit of analysis.
2. Time perspective.
3. Dominating marketing function.
4. Price elasticity.
5. Dominating quality dimension.
6. Measurement of customer satisfaction.
7. Customer information system
8. Interdepartmental collaboration.
9. Role of internal marketing.

The unit of analysis and the time perspective. The time perspective of marketing differs depending on where on the continuum a firm is. As transaction marketing means that the firm focuses on single exchanges or transactions at a time, the time perspective is rather short. The unit of analysis is a single market transaction or exchange. Profits are expected to follow from today's exchanges. In relationship marketing the time perspective is much longer. The marketer does not plan primarily for short-term results. His objective is to create results in the long term through enduring and profitable relationships with customers. In some cases, single transactions that take place in the relationship may even be unprofitable as such. Thus, relationships and how they develop through continuous *interactions* to facilitate transactions which create satisfaction for both parties are the units of analysis.

Dominating marketing function. Because of the lack of personal contact with their customers and their focus on mass markets, firms pursuing a transaction-type strategy will probably benefit most from a traditional *marketing mix* approach. The 4Ps model will give guidance in most cases; this model was originally developed for consumer-packaged goods marketing where transaction marketing is most appropriate.

For a firm applying a relationship strategy the marketing mix is often too restrictive. The most important customer contacts from a marketing success point of view are those outside the realm of the marketing mix and the full-time marketers. The performance of the *part-time marketers*, the customer orientation of information technology, operating systems, industrialized service routines, such as vending machines, ATMs and home banking systems, and the willingness of customers to perform as co-producers in the service process, are critical ingredients in a relationship-oriented strategy. The marketing impact of the customer's contacts with people, technology and systems and other non-marketing functions determines whether he (or the organizational buyer) will continue doing business with a given firm or not. All these customer contacts are interactive to a certain extent. These resources form the *interactive marketing function*. This marketing function can also be described as all the marketing activities outside the marketing mix and outside a marketing (and sales) department. In relationship marketing interactive marketing becomes the dominating part of the marketing process. Of course, variables in the marketing mix, such as traditional external marketing activities, are important here as well, but to a much lesser degree and they merely support interactive marketing activities. In other situations the support of salespeople is needed, for example to close a new deal or to provide continuous attention during the consumption (usage) phase.

Price elasticity. In transaction marketing there is not much more than the core product (goods or services) and sometimes the image of the firm or its brands, to keep the customer attached to the seller. When a competitor introduces a similar product, advertising and image may help to keep customers, at least for some time, but price usually becomes an issue. A firm that offers a lower price or better terms is a dangerous competitor, because in transaction marketing the price sensitivity of customers is often high. A firm pursuing a relationship marketing strategy, on the other hand, may have created more value for its customers than what is provided by the core solution alone. Such a firm develops tighter ties over time with its customers. If, say, a financial service arrangement is complicated, an Internet grocery store provides its customers with easy-to-use ordering systems, consistent quality of goods, information and deliveries, or a supplier provides its customers with a complex solution, the buyer and seller grow together due to the various ties that have been established over time. Such ties or *bonds* may, for example, be variously technological, knowledge-related or information-related, geographical or social in nature. If they are well handled they provide customers with value; something that is not provided by the core solution itself. Of course, price is not unimportant but is often much less of an issue here. Thus, relationship marketing makes customers less price-sensitive.

Dominating quality dimension. The way quality is perceived by customers will typically differ, depending on the strategy used by a firm. In transaction marketing the customers' contact with the firm is limited to the product and exposure to other traditional marketing mix variables. The benefits sought by customers are imbedded in the technical solution provided by the product. The customer will not receive much else that will create value in his processes. Hence, the technical quality of the product, or what the customer gets as an outcome, is the dominating quality-creating source in transaction marketing.

The situation is different in relationship marketing. The customer interface is broader, and the firm has opportunities to provide its customers with value of various types (technological, information, knowledge, social, etc.). When several firms can provide a similar technical quality, managing the interactions of the service processes also becomes imperative from a quality perception perspective. Thus, in relationship marketing the *functional quality dimension* grows in importance and often dominates. Of course, this does not mean that technical quality can be neglected. It is a prerequisite for good total quality, but it is no longer the only quality dimension to be considered.

Measurement of customer satisfaction and customer information systems. A normal way of monitoring customer satisfaction and success is to look at *market share* and to do *ad hoc* customer satisfaction surveys. For a consumer-packaged goods marketing firm, which would typically apply a transaction marketing strategy, there is no way of continuously measuring market success other than by *ad hoc* customer satisfaction studies. A service firm and many business-to-business marketers, on the other hand, who could more easily pursue a relationship marketing strategy, have at least some kind of interaction with almost every single customer, even if they serve mass markets. Thus, customer satisfaction can be directly monitored. A firm that applies a relationship-type strategy can study customer satisfaction by directly monitoring its customer base.

Managing the customer base means that the firm has at least some kind of direct knowledge of its customer satisfaction levels. Instead of thinking of numbers, or of market share only, management thinks in terms of individuals with personal reactions and opinions. Instead of getting information about marketing success from customer satisfaction studies, the marketer judges success by information direct from customers. This requires a means of gathering the various types of customer feedback that are constantly obtained by a large number of employees in large numbers of customer contacts. In combination with market share statistics, such an intelligence system focusing on customer satisfaction, needs and desires forms a valuable source of information for decision-making. Of course, traditional customer satisfaction studies can be made from time to time to complement the data gathered from daily customer contacts.

Consequently, in a relationship marketing situation the firm can build up an *on-line, real-time information system*. This system will provide management with a continuously updated database of its customers and information about the degree of satisfaction or dissatisfaction among customers. This can serve as a powerful management tool. In a transaction marketing situation it is more difficult to build up such a database, although thanks to available information technology this is not impossible any more.

The strategic importance of interdepartmental collaboration. The level of interdependency between processes and departments in an organization depends on whether the firm has chosen a transaction-type strategy or a relationship-type strategy. In transaction marketing, most or all of the firm's customer contacts are related to the product itself and to traditional marketing mix activities. Marketing and sales specialists are responsible for total marketing; no part-time marketers are involved. Thus, from a marketing point of view the internal interface between functions has no, or very limited, strategic importance to the firm.

In relationship marketing the situation is different. The customer interface is much broader, often involving a large number of part-time marketers in several different departments. This is the case, for example, in most services marketing and business-to-business marketing situations. A successfully implemented interactive marketing performance requires that all parts of the firm involved in taking care of customers can collaborate, co-operate and support each other in order to provide customers with good total perceived quality. Thus, for a firm pursuing a relationship marketing strategy the internal interface between marketing, operations, human resource management and other departments is of strategic importance to success.

The role of internal marketing. Part-time marketers have to be prepared for their marketing tasks. *Internal marketing* is needed to ensure the support of traditional non-marketing staff. They have to be committed, prepared and informed, and motivated to perform as part-time marketers. This does not apply only to customer contact employees and back-office employees. It is, of course, equally important that supervisors, middle-level and top-level managers are equally committed and prepared.

Internal marketing as a process has to be integrated with the total marketing process. The traditional marketing and interactive marketing performance starts from within the organization. A thorough and ongoing internal marketing process is required to make relationship marketing successful. If internal marketing is neglected, interactive marketing in particular will suffer or fail.

MARKETING MANAGEMENT OR MARKET-ORIENTED/CUSTOMER-FOCUSED MANAGEMENT?

In conventional marketing literature, which is mainly based on the context of consumer packaged goods, the concept of marketing management is used to describe the practical applications of the marketing concept. In a consumer goods context this is perfectly appropriate. However, in situations where the typical customer relationship is extended far beyond the straightforward and impersonal relationship between a marketer and a buyer of consumer breakfast cereals, toothpaste or soap, this straightforward view of how to manage marketing does not hold any more. When marketing is geared to the management of customer relationships, the situation changes.

In business-to-business marketing contexts the marketing management approach becomes awkward. Many customer relationship issues are the concerns of departments other than the marketing department. The interrelationships between departments make planning, co-ordination and implementation much more complicated than a traditional marketing and sales department can handle. In a service context the situation is often even more complex. Marketing activities – traditional and interactive marketing activities – are spread throughout the organization; therefore, the whole organizational structure has to be supportive of marketing. Because of the extreme interdependence between the various departments of a service firm and marketing, a *marketing attitude of mind* is needed throughout the organization. Furthermore, as George Day[49] observes, the *hearts and minds* of the entire organization have to be engaged.

Customers have to be considered in planning and implementing most activities in a firm, regardless of whether those activities are labelled production and operations, human resource management, finance or any other traditional function. In other words, marketing considerations are one aspect, among others, to be observed in decision-making throughout an organization. For the full-time marketers, marketing is the main or only consideration to bear in mind, but for other functions and processes marketing is only one of many aspects to take into account. However, in the final analysis it is a firm's success in the marketplace which is crucial. Hence, market-oriented management and customer-focused performance throughout the organization is needed rather than marketing management being the responsibility of one department only.

Top management alone has the necessary overview of the organization, and the authority to manage the total marketing process; therefore, ultimate marketing responsibility has to be held sufficiently high up in the organization. A marketing department can plan and implement some marketing tasks, but total management of the marketing process has to be an integral part of overall company management. Hence, even for psychological reasons, market-oriented or customer-focused management is what it is all about, not marketing in the traditional functionalistic sense. Marketing, therefore, becomes an integral part of service management. This is also the reason why the title of this book is *Service Management and Marketing*. In fact, because in service contexts it is more a question of market-oriented, customer-focused management than just marketing management, the term 'service management' was originally introduced as a synonym for service marketing.

SUMMARY

In service competition, marketing is not restricted to marketing specialists. It is spread throughout the organization, and part-time marketers almost invariably outnumber specialists in, for example, market research, marketing communication and sales. The traditional models of marketing management, therefore, do not fit very well in a service context. The traditional approach to marketing, the so-called marketing mix, is too restrictive and simplistic to be very useful. Moreover, its approach to marketing as a function, with well-defined areas of marketing decision-making, guides management interest away from the process nature of customer management. Instead, in this chapter a relationship approach to marketing was suggested, and a relationship definition of marketing was presented.

The total marketing process is divided into two sub-processes, the traditional external marketing process and the interactive marketing process. The interactive marketing process is especially important during the consumption or usage process of the customer relationship lifecycle. Of course, traditional external marketing efforts are still important, but more in the form of support activities and mainly in the initial and purchasing phases of the lifecycle. The relationship marketing model illustrates the two processes – a communication process making promises and an interactions process keeping promises – which have to be included in relationship marketing planning and implementation. The concept of a marketing strategy continuum was introduced, and two distinct marketing strategy options, relationship marketing and transaction marketing, were analysed in relation to this strategy continuum. In service contexts, the nature of marketing makes this much more a top management process than it is normally considered to be. Hence, it is actually more accurate to talk about market-oriented, customer-focused management than marketing management in the traditional sense of the term. Therefore, marketing becomes an integral part of any theory of service management.

QUESTIONS FOR DISCUSSION

1. Why does marketing have to be a concern of all the departments of a firm in service contexts?

2. What is the difference between traditional external marketing and interactive marketing? Why is interactive marketing considered so critical to the marketing process of service providers?

3. What is the difference between full-time marketers and part-time marketers? Why are the latter especially important to marketing success in service competition?

4. Define the various groups of part-time marketers of your firm, or any given firm, and analyse their importance to the total marketing process. What are the problems with the contribution of the various part-time marketers to the interactive marketing process?

5. In view of the marketing strategy continuum, how does a relationship marketing strategy differ from a transaction marketing strategy?

6. Why is 'market-oriented management/customer-focused management' a better term than 'marketing management' in service contexts?

7. Discuss the role of making, keeping and enabling promises in marketing.

8. Using the relationship marketing model, analyse the way in which customers in your firm, or any given firm, are taken care of. Is a relationship marketing strategy implemented?

NOTES

1. Rathmell, J.M. (1974) *Marketing in the Service Sector*. Cambridge, MA: Winthrop.

2. See Strandvik, T., Holmlund, M. & Grönroos, C., The mental footprint of marketing in the boardroom. *Journal of Service Management*, **25**(2), 2014, 241–252. See also Klaus, P. & Edvardsson, B., The road back to relevance – how to put marketing back on the CEO's agenda. *Journal of*

Service Management, **25**(2), 2014, 166–170, and this whole issue of the *Journal of Service Management*, which is devoted to how to put marketing back as the firm's core strategy. If marketing is not considered a strategic issue, customer-based metrics about the market performance of the firm do not reach the boardroom, and remain unused in strategic decision-making. See Ambler, T., *Marketing and the Bottom Line. The Marketing Metrics to Pump Up Cash Flow*. London: Prentice-Hall, 2003, where this problem is discussed at length.

3. For an extensive study of positive, neutral and negative bonds in commercial relationships see Arantola, H., *Relationship Drivers in Provider–Consumer Relationships. Empirical Studies of Customer Loyalty Programs*. Helsinki: Hanken Swedish School of Economics, Finland, 2002.

4. See Storbacka, K. & Lehtinen, J.R., *Customer Relationship Management*. Singapore: McGraw-Hill, 2001, where the authors discuss the role of getting a growing share of the customer's 'wallet' as well as of their 'heart and mind' in relationship marketing.

5. The customer relationship lifecycle concept was originally introduced in Grönroos, C., *Strategic Management and Marketing in the Service Sector*. Cambridge, MA: Marketing Science Institute, 1983.

6. Bitner, M.J., Servicescapes: the impact of physical surroundings on customers and employees. *Journal of Marketing*, **56**(Apr), 1992, 57–71.

7. Compare Grönroos, C., What can a service logic offer marketing theory. In Lusch, R.F. & Vargo, S.L. (eds), *The Service-Dominant Logic of Marketing. Dialog, Debate, and Directions*. Armonk, NY: M.E. Sharpe, 2006, pp. 357–358.

8. See Sheth, J.N. & Uslay, C., Implications of the revised definition of marketing: from exchange to value creation. *Journal of Public Policy & Marketing,* **26**(2), 2007, 302–307, and many earlier sources, one of the most prominent being Alderson, W., *Marketing behavior and executive action*. Homewood, IL: Richard D. Irwin, 1957.

9. Grönroos, C. & Gummerus, J., The service revolution and its marketing implications: service logic versus service dominant logic. *Managing Service Quality*, 2014, **24**(3), 206–229.

10. Grönroos, C., Promise management: regaining customer management for marketing. *Journal of Business & Industrial Marketing*, **13**(5–6), 2009, 353. The value capture aspect has been added to the definition.

11. Adopted from Grönroos, C., On defining marketing: finding a new roadmap for marketing. *Marketing Theory*, **6**(4), 2006, 407.

12. Lannings, M.J. & Michaels, G., *A business as a value delivery system*. New York: McKinsey Paper No. 4, 1988.

13. See, for example, Payne, A. & Frow, P., Developing superior value propositions: a strategic marketing imperative. *Journal of Service Management*, **25**(2), 2014, 213–227.

14. The view of the marketer as a mixer of ingredients was first expressed by James Culliton in a study of marketing costs in 1948 and in the 1950s, based on this expression, Neil Borden created the notion of a marketing mix. See Borden, N.H., The concept of the marketing mix. *Journal of Advertising Research*, June, 1964.

15. The 4P model was first introduced in a major marketing textbook by McCarthy in 1960 (see McCarthy, E.J., *Basic Marketing*. Homewood, IL: Irwin, 1960). Since then it seems as if marketing textbooks, especially in North America, have had to be organized around the 4Ps of the marketing mix.

16. In a definition from 1985 marketing, according to the marketing mix approach, is described as 'the process of planning and executing the *conception, pricing, promotion* and *distribution* of ideas, goods and services to create exchanges and satisfy individual and organizational goals', and in a definition from 2004 the following is offered: 'Marketing is an organizational function and a set of processes for creating, communicating and delivering value to customers and for managing customer relationships in ways that benefit the organization and its stakeholders' (definition by the American Marketing Association). For a critical discussion of this updated definition, see Grönroos, C., On defining marketing: finding a new roadmap for marketing. *Marketing Theory*, **6**(4), 2006, 395–417.

17. These are the three new service-oriented categories in a 7P marketing mix for services suggested Booms, B.H. & Bitner, M.J., Marketing strategies and organization structures for service firms. In Donnelly, J.H. & George, W.H. (eds), *Marketing of Services*. Chicago, IL: American Marketing Association, 1982.

18. These two additional categories were suggested by Philip Kotler in the context of megamarketing. See Kotler, P., Megamarketing. *Harvard Business Review*, Mar–Apr, 1986.

19. The newest marketing definition by the American Marketing Association, approved in 2013, reads: '*Marketing is the activity, set of institutions, and processes for creating, communicating, delivering, and exchanging offerings that have value for customers, clients, partners, and society at large.*' See https://archive.ama.org/Archive/AboutAMA/Pages/DefinitionofMarketing.aspx (6 March 2014). As a contrast the Chartered Institute of Marketing (CIM) in the UK defines marketing strictly as a process: '*Marketing is the management process responsible for identifying, anticipating and satisfying customer requirements profitably.*' See http://www.getin2marketing.com/discover/what-is-marketing (6 March 2014).

20. See also Constantinides, E., The marketing mix revisited: towards the 21st century marketing. *Journal of Marketing Management*, **22**(3–4), 2006, 407–438, where the author offers a comprehensive critical analysis of the marketing mix approach, and also Möller, K., Comment on the

marketing mix revisited: towards the 21st century marketing. *Journal of Marketing Management*, **22**(3–4), 2006, 439–450, where the author points out positive aspects of the marketing mix.

21. Because of the inside-oriented nature of the marketing mix approach we have metaphorically labelled it a 'production-oriented' approach to marketing. See Grönroos, C., Defining marketing: a market-oriented approach. *European Journal of Marketing*, **23**(1), 1989, 54.

22. Dixon, D.F. & Blois, K., *Some Limitations of the 4Ps as a Paradigm for Marketing*. Marketing Education Group Annual Conference. UK: Cranfield Institute of Technology, July, 1983.

23. Gummesson, E., *Total Relationship Marketing. Marketing Management, Relationship Strategy, CRM, and a New Dominant Logic for the Value Creating Network Economy*. Oxford: Butterworth Heinemann, 2008, p. 325.

24. Some authors go so far as to conclude that a traditional marketing perspective, with the management of the marketing mix and its 4Ps as the central part, had by the end of the 20th century deprived the marketing phenomenon of its importance and made decision-makers in business lose interest in the development of marketing in firms. Only marketers themselves may not have fully realized the need for a reorientation of their discipline. So, for example, says Ian Gordon: 'Busy attending to the practice of marketing, marketers may not have noticed that marketing is, for all its practical purposes, dead . . . Today, marketing attracts neither interest nor patience from the investor community, except to the extent basic marketing skills must be demonstrated by the enterprise. Marketing rarely achieves its promise of differentiating and developing enduring, competitively superior value' (p. 1). He sees a hope for a revitalization of marketing in the relationship marketing philosophy. See Gordon, I., *Relationship Marketing*. Toronto: John Wiley & Sons, 1998.

25. Compare Hoekstra, J.C., Leeflang, P.H. & Wittink, D.R., The customer concept: the basis for a new marketing paradigm. *Journal of Market-Focused Management*, **4**(1), 1999, 43–76. In this article the authors formulate a new marketing concept, which they label the *customer concept*, and 'is mainly based on the realization of superior customer values where the individual customer is the starting point' (p. 43). For a study of the importance of a customer value-based approach in interactive service relationships, see Chen, S.-C. & Quester, P.G., Developing a value-based measure of market orientation in an interactive service relationship. *Journal of Marketing Management*, **21**(7–8), 2005, 779–808.

26. This definition is further developed from definitions first presented in Grönroos, C., 1989, *op. cit.*, p. 57 and further developed in, for example, Grönroos, C., Value-driven relational marketing: from products to resources and competencies. *Journal of Marketing Management*, **13**(5), 1997b, 407–420.

27. Evert Gummesson has, in a relationship marketing context, discussed a large number of relationships with various partners. See Gummesson, 2008, *op. cit.*

28. In 1999 Harker published an analysis of the then existing definitions of relationship marketing and concluded that the one suggested in the present book seems to be the most commonly accepted. See Harker, M.J., Relationship marketing defined? An examination of current relationship marketing definitions. *Marketing Intelligence & Planning*, **17**(1), 1999, 13–20. His analysis still seems to be valid.

29. Parvatiyar, A. & Sheth, J.N., The domain and conceptual foundations of relationship marketing. In Sheth, J.N. & Parvatiyar, A. (eds), *Handbook of Relationship Marketing*. Thousand Oaks, CA: Sage Publications, 2000, pp. 3–38. See also Agariya, A.K. & Singh, D., What really defines relationship marketing? Review of definitions and general and sector-specific defining constructs. *Journal of Relationship Marketing*, **10**(4), 2011, 203–237. See also the discussion of relationship marketing as a school of marketing thought in El-Ansary, A.I., Relationship marketing management: a school in the history of marketing thought. *Journal of Relationship Marketing*, **4**(1–2), 2005, 43–56. The author concludes that 'in a global and macro sense, Relationship Marketing is a culture. In a micro and managerial sense, it is a managerial practice' (p. 51). Because of its managerial aspect he suggests that this marketing school of thought should be labelled 'relationship marketing management' and proposes that ' . . . it will continue to be the dominant school of thought in marketing, thus replacing the traditional marketing management school of thought' (p. 53). In O'Malley, L., Relational marketing: development, debates and directions. *Journal of Marketing Management*, **30**(11–12), 2014, 1220–1238, a recent discussion of the relationship marketing paradigm is provided.

30. Gummesson, *op. cit.*, p. 5.

31. See Bagozzi, R.P., Marketing as exchange. *Journal of Marketing*, **39**(Oct), 1975, 32–39.

32. Grönroos, C., Adopting a service logic for marketing. *Marketing Theory*, **6**(3), 2006, 317–333. See also Sheth, J.N. & Parvatiyar. A., Relationship marketing in consumer markets: antecedents and consequences, in Sheth, J.N. & Parvatiyar, A. (eds), *Handbook of Relationship Marketing*. Thousand Oaks, CA: Sage Publications, 2000, pp. 171–208, where the authors conclude that exchange theory perhaps should be given up. Ballantyne and Varey state that 'interactions over time may be the enactment of the exchange process'. See Ballantyne, D. & Varey, R.J., Introducing a dialogical orientation to the service-dominant logic of marketing. In Lusch, R.F. & Vargo, S.L. (eds), *The Service-Dominant Logic of Marketing: Dialog, Debate, and Directions*. Armonk, NY: M.E. Sharpe, 2006, pp. 224–235. Sheth & Uslay, *op. cit.* suggest that exchange should be replaced by value creation.

33. Ryals, L., Making customer relationship management work: the measurement and profitable management of customer relationships. *Journal of Marketing*, **69**(4), 2005, 252–261. See also Reinartz, W. & Kumar, V., The mismanagement of customer loyalty. *Harvard Business Review*, Jul, 2002, 86–94, who claim that 'no company should ever take for granted the idea that managing customers for loyalty is the same as managing them for profits' (94).

34. Research into the issue of termination on dissolution of relationships is in its infancy. However, it seems to be a topic which will quickly grow. An early study in a business-to-business context is reported in Halinen, A. & Tähtinen, J., *Towards a Process Theory of Relationship Dissolution*. Finland: Working Paper No. 9, Turku School of Economics and Business Administration, 1999.

35. See, for example, Håkansson, H. & Snehota, I., The burden of relationships or who's next? In Naudé, P. & Turnbull, P. (eds), *Network Dynamics in International Marketing*. Oxford, UK: Elsevier Science, 1998, pp. 16–25; Vigon, M. & Hertz, S., The burden of key customer relationships. *Journal of Customer Behavior*, **2**(2), 2003, 269–287; Pressey, A. & Tzokas, N., Lighting up the 'dark side' of international export/import relationships: evidence from UK exporters. *Management Decision*, **42**(5–6), 2004, 694–708; Anderson, E. & Jap, S.D., The dark side of relationships. *Sloan Management Review*, **46**(Spring), 2005, 75–82; Holmlund-Rytkönen, M. & Strandvik, T., Stress in business relationships. *Journal of Business & Industrial Marketing*, **20**(1), 2005, 12–22.

36. Anderson & Jap, *op. cit*. See also Villena, V.H., Revilla, E. & Choi, T.Y., The dark side of buyer-seller relationships: a social capital perspective. *Journal of Operations Management*, **29**(6), 2011, 561–576, Fang, S-R., Chang, Y-S. & Peng, Y-C., Dark side of relationships: a tension-based view. *Industrial Marketing Management*, **40**(5), 2011, 774–784, and Frow, P., Payne, A., Wilkinson, I.F. & Young L., Customer management and CRM: addressing the dark side. *Journal of Services Marketing*, **25**(2), 2011, 79–89.

37. Henrik Calonius was probably the first marketing researcher who argued for the explicit integration of promises in marketing models. See Calonius, H., A market behaviour framework. In Möller, K. & Paltschik, M. (eds), *Contemporary Research in Marketing*. Proceedings from the XV Annual Conference of the European Marketing Academy. Helsinki: Helsinki School of Economics and Hanken Swedish School of Economics, Finland, 1986, pp. 515–524; Calonius, H., A buying process model. In Blois, K. & Parkinson, S. (eds), *Innovative Marketing – A European Perspective*. Proceedings from the XVIIth Annual Conference of the European Marketing Academy. Bradford, UK: University of Bradford, 1988, pp. 86–103. The promise concept was probably first used in a relationship marketing definition in Grönroos, 1989, *op. cit.*, 57. Calonius offered the following general promise-based definition: 'Marketing is a set of human activities directed at facilitating and consummating exchanges of promises' (1986, p. 522). Promise theory has not been adopted very much in management and marketing yet. However, see Price, R.F. & Schultz,

D.E., *Reliability Rules: How Promises Management Can Build Your Company Culture, Build Your Brand, and Build Your Bottom Line*. Chicago, IL: Racom Communication, 2008.

38. The expression 'enabling promises' was in this context introduced by Mary Jo Bitner (Building service relationships: it's all about promises. *Journal of the Academy of Marketing Science*, **23**(4), 1995, 246–251.

39. As Moorman and Rust conclude in an analysis of the role of marketing: 'Looking broadly at the marketing literature and practice, it appears that during the past ten years there has been a movement toward thinking of marketing less as a function and more as a set of values and processes that all functions are participating in implementing' (180). See Moorman, C. & Rust, R.T., The role of marketing. *Journal of Marketing*, **63**(Special Issue), 1999, 180–197.

40. Service marketing textbooks are typically based on a customer relationship approach. See, for example, Zeithaml, V.A. & Bitner, M.J., *Services Marketing. Integrating Customer Focus Across the Firm*, 2nd edn. New York: McGraw-Hill, 2000. In general, it is interesting to note that full-scale textbooks on service marketing (not just text and reference volumes) now being published in English are more and more organized around a genuinely service-oriented perspective. See, for example, Zeithaml & Bitner, *op. cit.*; Bateson, J.E.G., *Managing Services Marketing*. New York: Dryden Press, 1995; Lovelock, C., Vandermerwe, S. & Lewis, B., *Services Marketing: A European Perspective*. London: Prentice-Hall Europe, 1996; Kasper, H., van Helsdingen, P. & de Vries Jr, W., *Services Marketing Management. An International Perspective*. New York: John Wiley & Sons, 1996; McGuire, L., *Australian Services Marketing and Management*. South Yarra, Australia: Macmillan Education Australia, 1999. The marketing mix approach no longer dominates the structures of these textbooks. An early textbook pioneering such an approach in English is Cowell, D., *The Marketing of Services*. London: Heinemann, 1985, which was organized around the 7P framework. In other languages such genuinely service-based textbooks have existed since the early 1980s.

41. El-Ansary, *op. cit.*, 53.

42. Compare El-Ansary, *op. cit.*

43. Lovelock, C., Functional integration in services. Understanding the links between marketing, operations, and human resources. In Swartz, T.A. & Iacobucci, D. (eds), *Handbook in Services Marketing & Management*. Thousand Oaks, CA: Sage Publications, 2000, pp. 421–437.

44. Gummesson, E., The new marketing – developing long-term interactive relationships. *Long Range Planning*, **20**(4), 1987, 10–20 and Marketing-orientation revisited: the crucial role of the part-time marketer. *European Journal of Marketing*, **25**(2), 1991, 60–67.

45. See, for example, Grönroos, C., Designing a long range marketing strategy for services. *Long Range Planning*, April, 1980.

46. See, for example, Meuter, M.L., Bitner, M.J., Ostrom, A.L. & Brown, S.W., Choosing among alternative service delivery modes: an investigation of customer trial of self-service technologies. *Journal of Marketing*, **69**(Apr), 2005, 61–83.

47. Storbankernas reklamhaveri (The advertising flop of big banks). *Resumé*, May, 2006, 30–31. In Swedish.

48. See Grönroos, C., From marketing mix to relationship marketing – towards a paradigm shift in marketing. *Managing Decision*, **35**(4), 1997, 322–339. An earlier version was introduced in Grönroos, C., The marketing strategy continuum: a marketing concept for the 1990s. *Management Decision*, **29**(1), 1991, 7–13.

49. Day, G.S., Managing market relationships. *Journal of the Academy of Marketing Science*, **28**(1), 2000, 24–30.

FURTHER READING

Agariya, A.K. & Singh, D. (2011) What really defines relationship marketing? Review of definitions and general and sector-specific defining constructs. *Journal of Relationship Marketing*, **10**(4), 203–237.

Alderson, W. (1957) *Marketing behavior and executive action*. Homewood, IL: Richard D. Irwin.

Ambler, T. (2003) *Marketing and the Bottom Line. The Marketing Metrics to Pump Up Cash Flow*. London: Prentice-Hall.

Anderson, E. & Jap, S.D. (2005) The dark side of relationships. *Sloan Management Review*, **46**(Spring), 75–82.

Arantola, H. (2002) *Relationship Drivers in Provider–Consumer Relationships. Empirical Studies of Customer Loyalty Programs*. Helsinki: Hanken Swedish School of Economics, Finland.

Bagozzi, R.P. (1975) Marketing as exchange. *Journal of Marketing*, **39**(Oct), 32–39.

Ballantyne, D. & Varey, R.J. (2006) Introducing a dialogical orientation to the service-dominant logic of marketing. In Lusch, R.F. and Vargo, S.L. (eds), *The Service-Dominant Logic of Marketing: Dialog, Debate, and Directions*. Armonk, NY: M.E. Sharpe, pp. 224–235.

Bateson, J.E.G. (1995) *Managing Services Marketing*. New York: Dryden Press.

Bitner, M.J. (1992) Servicescapes: the impact of physical surroundings on customers and employees. *Journal of Marketing*, **56**(Apr), 57–71.

Bitner, M.J. (1995) Building service relationships: it's all about promises. *Journal of the Academy of Marketing Science*, **23**(4), 246–251.

Booms, B.H. & Bitner, M.J. (1982) Marketing strategies and organization structures for service firms. In Donnelly, J.H. & George, W,H, (eds), *Marketing of Services*. Chicago, II: American Marketing Association.

Borden, N.H. (1964) The concept of the marketing mix. *Journal of Advertising Research*, June.

Calonius, H. (1986) A market behaviour framework. In Möller, K. & Paltschik, M. (eds), *Contemporary Research in Marketing*. Proceedings from the XV Annual Conference of the European Marketing Academy, Helsinki: Helsinki School of Economics and Hanken Swedish School of Economics, Finland, pp. 515–524 also published as Calonius, H. (2006) A market behaviour framework. *Marketing Theory*, **6**(4), 419–428.

Calonius, H. (1988) A buying process model. In Blois, K. & Parkinson, S. (eds), *Innovative Marketing – A European Perspective*. Proceedings from the XVIIth Annual Conference of the European Marketing Academy. Bradford, UK: University of Bradford, pp. 86–103.

Chen, S.-C. & Quester, P.G. (2005) Developing a value-based measure of market orientation in an interactive service relationship. *Journal of Marketing Management*, **21**(7–8), 779–808.

Constantinides, E. (2006) The marketing mix revisited: towards the 21st century marketing. *Journal of Marketing Management*, **22**(3–4), 407–438.

Cowell, D. (1985) *The Marketing of Services*. London: Heinemann.

Day, G.S. (2000) Managing market relationships. *Journal of the Academy of Marketing Science*, **28**(1), 24–30.

Dixon, D.F. & Blois, K. (1983) *Some Limitations of the 4Ps as a Paradigm for Marketing*. Marketing Education Group Annual Conference, UK: Cranfield Institute of Technology, July.

El-Ansary, A.I. (2005) Relationship marketing management: a school in the history of marketing thought. *Journal of Relationship Marketing*, **4**(1–2), 43–56.

Fang, S-R., Chang, Y-S. & Peng, Y-C. (2011) Dark side of relationships: a tension-based view. *Industrial Marketing Management*, **40**(5), 774–784.

Frow, P., Payne, A., Wilkinson, I.F. & Young L. (2011) Customer management and CRM: addressing the dark side. *Journal of Services Marketing*, **25**(2), 79–89.

Gordon, I. (1998) *Relationship Marketing*. Toronto: John Wiley & Sons.

Grönroos, C. (1980) Designing a long range marketing strategy for services. *Long Range Planning*, **13**(Apr), 36–42.

Grönroos, C. (1989) Defining marketing: a market-oriented approach. *European Journal of Marketing*, **23**(1), 52–60.

Grönroos, C. (1996) Relationship marketing logic. *Asia-Australia Marketing Journal*, **4**(1), 7–18.

Grönroos, C. (1997a) From marketing mix to relationship marketing – towards a paradigm shift in marketing. *Managing Decision*, **35**(4), 322–339.

Grönroos, C. (1997b) Value-driven relational marketing: from products to resources and competencies. *Journal of Marketing Management*, **13**(5), 407–420.

Grönroos, C. (1999) Relationship Marketing: the Nordic School Approach. In Sheth, J.N. & Parvatiyar, A., eds. *Handbook of Relationship Marketing*. Thousand Oaks, CA: Sage, pp. 95–118.

Grönroos, C. (2006a) What can a service logic offer marketing theory? In Lusch, R.F. & Vargo, S.L. (eds), *The Service-Dominant Logic of Marketing. Dialog, Debate, and Directions*. Armonk, NY: M.E. Sharpe, pp. 354–364.

Grönroos, C. (2006b) Adopting a service logic for marketing. *Marketing Theory*, **6**(3), 317–333.

Grönroos, C. (2006c) On defining marketing: finding a new roadmap for marketing. *Marketing Theory*, **6**(4), 395–417.

Grönroos, C. (2009) Promise management: regaining customer management for marketing. *Journal of Business & Industrial Marketing*, **13**(5–6), 351–359.

Gummesson, E. (1987) The new marketing – developing long-term interactive relationships. *Long Range Planning*, **20**(4), 10–21.

Gummesson, E. (1991) Marketing revisited: the crucial role of the part-time marketer. *European Journal of Marketing*, **25**(2), 60–67.

Gummesson, E. (2008) *Total Relationship Marketing. Marketing Management, Relationship Strategy, CRM, and a New Dominant Logic for the Value Creating Network Economy*. Oxford: Butterworth Heinemann.

Håkansson, H. & Snehota, I. (1998) The burden of relationships or who's next? In Naudé, P. & Turnbull, P. (eds), *Network Dynamics in International Marketing*. Oxford, UK: Elsevier Science, pp. 16–25.

Halinen, A. & Tähtinen, J. (1999) *Towards a Process Theory of Relationship Dissolution*. Working Paper No. 9, Turku School of Economics and Business Administration, Finland.

Harker, M.J. (1999) Relationship marketing defined? An examination of current relationship marketing definitions. *Marketing Intelligence & Planning*, **17**(1), 13–20.

Hoekstra, J.C., Leeflang, P.H. & Wittink, D.R. (1999) The customer concept: the basis for a new marketing paradigm. *Journal of Market-Focused Management*, **4**(1), 43–76.

Holmlund-Rytkönen, M. & Strandvik, T. (2005) Stress in business relationships. *Journal of Business & Industrial Marketing*, **20**(1), 12–22.

Kasper, H., van Helsdingen, P. & de Vries Jr., W. (1996) *Services Marketing Management. An International Perspective*. New York: John Wiley & Sons.

Klaus, P. & Edvardsson, B. (2014) The road back to relevance – how to put marketing back on the CEO's agenda. *Journal of Service Management*, **25**(2), 166–170.

Kotler, P. (1986) Megamarketing. *Harvard Business Review*, Mar–Apr.

Lannings, M.J. & Michaels, G. (1988) *A business as a value delivery system*. New York: McKinsey Paper No. 4.

Lovelock, C. (2000) Functional integration in services. Understanding the links between marketing, operations and human resources. In Swartz, T.A. & Iacobucci, D. (eds), *Handbook in Services Marketing & Management*. Thousand Oaks, CA: Sage Publications, pp. 421–437.

Lovelock, C., Vandermerwe, S. & Lewis, B. (1996) *Services Marketing. A European Perspective*. London: Prentice-Hall Europe.

McCarthy, E.J. (1960) *Basic Marketing*. Homewood, IL: Irwin.

McGuire, L. (1999) *Australian Services Marketing and Management*. South Yarra, Australia: Macmillan Education Australia.

Meuter, M.L., Bitner, M.J., Ostrom, A.L. & Brown, S.W. (2005) Choosing among alternative service delivery modes: an investigation of customer trial of self-service technologies. *Journal of Marketing*, **69**(Apr), 61–83.

Möller, K. (2006) Comment on the marketing mix revisited: towards the 21st century marketing. *Journal of Marketing Management*, **22**(3–4), 439–450.

Moorman, C. & Rust, R.T. (1999) The role of marketing. *Journal of Marketing*, **63**(Special Issue), 180–197.

O'Malley, L. (2014) Relational marketing: development, debates and directions. *Journal of Marketing Management*, **30**(11–12), 1220–1238.

Payne, A. & Frow, P. (2014) Developing superior value propositions: a strategic marketing imperative. *Journal of Service Management*, **25**(2), 213–227.

Pressey, A. & Tzokas, N. (2004) Lighting up the 'dark side' of international export/import relationships: evidence from UK exporters. *Management Decision*, **42**(5–6), 694–708.

Price, R.F. & Schultz, D.E. (2008) *Reliability Rules: How Promises Management Can Build Your Company Culture, Build Your Brand, and Build Your Bottom Line*. Chicago, IL: Racom Communication.

Rathmell, J.M. (1974) *Marketing in the Service Sector*. Cambridge, MA: Winthrop.

Reinartz, W. & Kumar, V. (2002) The mismanagement of customer loyalty. *Harvard Business Review*, July, 86–94.

Ryals, L. (2005) Making customer relationship management work: the measurement and profitable management of customer relationships. *Journal of Marketing*, **69**(4), 252–261.

Sherry Jr., J.F. (1998) The soul of the company store: Nike Town Chicago and the emplaced brand-scape. In Sherry Jr., J.F. (ed.), *Servicescapes: The Concept of Place in Contemporary Markets*. Chicago, IL: NTC/Contemporary Publishing Company, pp. 109–146.

Sheth, J.N. & Parvatiyar, A. (2000) Relationship marketing in consumer markets: antecedents and consequences. In Sheth, J.N. & Parvatiyar, A. (eds), *Handbook of Relationship Marketing*. Thousand Oaks, CA: Sage Publications, pp. 171–208.

Sheth, J.N. & Uslay, C. (2007) Implications of the revised definition of marketing: from exchange to value creation. *Journal of Public Policy & Marketing*, **26**(2), 302–307.

Storbacka, K. & Lehtinen, J.R. (2001) *Customer Relationship Management*. Singapore: McGraw-Hill.

Strandvik, T., Holmlund, M. & Grönroos, C. (2014) The mental footprint of marketing in the boardroom. *Journal of Service Management*, **25**(2), 241–252.

Vigon, M. & Hertz, S. (2003) The burden of key customer relationships. *Journal of Customer Behavior*, **2**(2), 269–287.

Villena, V.H., Revilla, E. & Choi, T.Y. (2011) The dark side of buyer-seller relationships: a social capital perspective. *Journal of Operations Management*, **29**(6), 561–576.

Zeithaml, V.A. & Bitner, M.J. (2000) *Services Marketing. Integrating Customer Focus Across the Firm*, 2nd edn. New York: McGraw-Hill.

https://archive.ama.org/Archive/AboutAMA/Pages/DefinitionofMarketing.aspx (6 March 2014).

http://www.getin2marketing.com/discover/what-is-marketing (6 March 2014).

CHAPTER 10
MANAGING INTEGRATED MARKETING COMMUNICATION AND RELATIONSHIP COMMUNICATION

Everything communicates something about a firm and its offerings – regardless of whether the marketer takes this into account and acts upon it or not.

INTRODUCTION

This chapter addresses the issue of marketing communication and demonstrates the need for a total communication or integrated marketing communications approach where communication messages from a number of different sources are integrated. The *communication circle* concept is described, and the impact of various time horizons on the effects of marketing communication campaigns is analysed. Some guidelines for managing marketing communications in service are also presented. In the final sections of the chapter we discuss the *relationship dialogue* concept and how total integrated marketing communication and relationship marketing relate to each other. A relationship communication model is presented, where communication messages sent by a firm are considered facilitators of the customers' creation of meaning out of these messages. After having read the chapter the reader should understand the importance of taking a holistic approach to marketing communication and know how to integrate communication activities of different natures; planned, as well as product and service, and unplanned, messages. The reader should also understand how marketing communication has an impact on several target groups and on several levels along a time span. Finally, the reader should realize the importance of the customer as a creator of meaning out of communication messages in his temporal and situational context.

MARKETING COMMUNICATION: A TOTAL COMMUNICATIONS ISSUE

Marketing communication is a substantial part of the marketing process. Conventional marketing includes market communication activities such as sales, advertising, sales promotion and communication over the Internet. However, communication is also an integral part of the interactive marketing process and relationship marketing. What employees say, how they say it, how they behave, how service outlets, machines and other physical resources look, and how they function all communicate something to the customers. The communication effect may be positive, such as 'they really care for me here', 'they have modern and efficient equipment', 'this website is easy to use and provides useful interactions with the firm' or 'the employees are nicely dressed'. It may also, of course, be less favourable, such as 'how rude their people are', 'what a sloppy office they have', 'how can it always take so long to get things done here' or 'why do they not keep me informed about the developments?'

There is an important difference between the communication of the traditional marketing function and that involved in the interactive marketing process. The latter type of communication is related to reality as customers perceive it. They communicate *what really is* as far as consumers are concerned. The *relationship marketing model* in Chapter 9 shows communication effects of activities in the *interaction process*. The former type of communication, such as advertising, is always on an abstract level for customers. It relates to the planned *communication process* of this relationship marketing model. Planned communication involves information that may or may not be true; however, as far as the customer or potential customer is concerned, the validity of this must still be tested. Hence, this communication is a *promise* about what hopefully will happen in the future. Testing takes place when the customer meets reality. There is an obvious connection here with how service quality is perceived. Marketing communication efforts like advertising and sales predominantly impact the *expected* service, whereas the communication effects of the interactive marketing process influence the *experienced* service.

For example, a retailing chain that advertises a certain product at a special price communicates a positive promise of good value. If the product is not available in the shop, or if it has already sold out, a negative communication message is created: 'They do not advertise honestly' or 'They just want me to come to the shop to buy stuff. They probably only had a limited number of the advertised low-price products in stock in the first place.' The negative communication impact of the latter is much more forceful, because it is caused by the actual performance of the retailer. Moreover, it changes the favourable effect of the first type of communication into an unfavourable image of the retailing chain.

The size of the gap between expectations and experiences determines the quality perception, as discussed earlier. Hence, here there is a truly *total communication impact*;[1] almost everything the organization says about itself and its performance and almost everything the organization does that is experienced in the service encounters or elsewhere has an impact on the customer. Moreover, the various means of communication and their effects are interrelated. These communication effects, together with other factors such as the technical quality of the service, shape the *image* of the organization in the minds of customers, and potential customers. We shall return to the issue of *image management* and *branding* in the next chapter.

INTEGRATED MARKETING COMMUNICATIONS

The *integrated marketing communications* notion emerged as an approach to understanding how a *holistic* communications message could be developed and managed.[2] As the *total communication concept*, it is based on the notion that it is not only planned communication efforts using separate and distinct communications media, such as TV, print, direct mail, the Internet, or social media, etc., that communicate a message about the firm and its offerings to customers and potential customers. Although these are communication activities that can easily be planned and implemented by the marketer, other aspects (for example, how the service process functions, what resources are used and what physical products are used in the process) include an element of communication. The messages that these parts of the customer relationship send may be more effective than those that the customer receives from advertisements, brochures and other traditional marketing communications media. However, to an overwhelming extent the literature on integrated marketing communication only includes communication media where communication activities can be planned distinctly as communication.

Furthermore, as conventional marketing communication is basically a firm-driven process, what is communicated is expected to be perceived more or less as intended. Obviously, in reality it may not be like this. A customer-driven communication approach is presented later in this chapter.

As a true total communications approach, integrated marketing communications, which is still firm-driven though, can be defined as follows:[3]

Integrated marketing communications is a strategy that integrates traditional media marketing, direct marketing, public relations and other distinct marketing communications media as well as communications aspects of the delivery and consumption of goods and services and of customer service and other customer encounters. Thus, integrated marketing communications has a long-term perspective.

According to this definition, *communication messages* can originate from several sources. Duncan and Moriarty distinguish between four kinds of sources of communication messages:[4]

1. Planned messages.

2. Product messages.

3. Service messages.

4. Unplanned messages.

Planned messages are the result of a planned marketing communications campaign where separate communications media, such as TV, print, direct mail, the Internet, social media, etc., are used to send a message. Sales representatives also communicate planned messages. Generally, these messages are the least trustworthy, because people know that they are planned by the marketer to persuade customers and potential customers in a certain direction.

Product messages are messages about the firm and its offerings that follow from the physical products in an offering: how a physical product is designed, how it functions, how it can be disposed of, etc.

Service messages are messages that result from service processes. The appearance, attitude and behaviour of service employees, the way systems and technology function, and the servicescape all send service messages. Interactions between customers and service employees in the service process include a substantial element of communication. Not only can the customer get valuable information in these encounters, he may also develop a sense of trust in the firm based on such interactions. On the other hand, the effects may also be negative. How the systems function and how the servicescape supports the service process also communicate something and may build up trust in the firm. One might say that service messages are more trustworthy than planned messages and product messages, because customers know that it is more difficult to manage the resources that create such messages than it is with planned messages and product messages.

Least credible			Most credible	
←			→	
PLANNED MESSAGES	**PRODUCT MESSAGES**	**SERVICE MESSAGES**	**UNPLANNED MESSAGES**	**ABSENCE OF COMMUNICATION**
Mass communication (e.g. advertising) Brochures Direct response Sales Web sites etc.	Appearance Design Usefulness Raw materials Production processes etc.	Interactions with service processes Deliveries Invoicing Claims handling Information etc.	Word of mouth referrals References News stories Gossip etc.	No information or feedback to customers, for example when an unexpected delay or service failure has occurred, or in any situation when the customer feels he is out of control of the situation

FIGURE 10.1

Sources of communication messages.
Source: Developed from Duncan, T. & Moriarty, S., *Driving Brand Value.*
New York: McGraw-Hill, 1997.

Finally, there are *unplanned messages*, which are considered to be the most trustworthy. Unplanned messages about the firm and its offerings are sent by fellow customers who interact with a given customer during the service process or who make comments in social media and convey good or bad word–of–mouth communication or, for example, by articles in newspapers, magazines or in TV programmes.

In Figure 10.1 these four types of sources of communication messages, as well as examples of the various types of messages, are summarized. To the far right in the figure a fifth source of communication message has been added. As Henrik Calonius[5] suggested, *absence of communication* in critical situations, such as when service failures or other unexpected events have occurred, can have a profound influence on the customer's perception of service quality. If the marketer does not say anything, for example, about how long a delay can be expected to take or when a delayed shipment can be expected to arrive, customers are kept out of control of the situation. This almost always has a negative effect on perceived service quality, adds psychological relationship costs and hurts a relationship.

As is illustrated in Figure 10.2, the sources of these four types of messages, in addition to absence of communication, can be described as '*What the firm says*' (in planned communications messages), '*What the firm does*' (creating product and service messages) and '*What others say and do*' (fellow customers in the service process, word of mouth, social media comments and conservations, and media coverage in the form of articles and TV programmes).

A major problem in marketing communication is the fact that only the least trustworthy source of messages about the firm and its offerings – planned messages ('What the firm says') using distinct communications media – is normally planned as part of the marketing communications programme. Product messages may partly be planned, whereas the more trustworthy sources, service messages and unplanned messages ('What the firm does' and 'What others say and do') are largely ignored. The fact that these types of messages are not part of an organized marketing communications process and not covered by a budget for marketing communications does not mean that their communications impact would be low. However, firms tend to neglect them, because they are difficult to plan. It is much easier to spend even more money on developing planned messages and using advertising, direct mail, sales promotions and other traditional means of marketing communication as well as the Internet and other new media. The effect of such a communications strategy is not guaranteed.

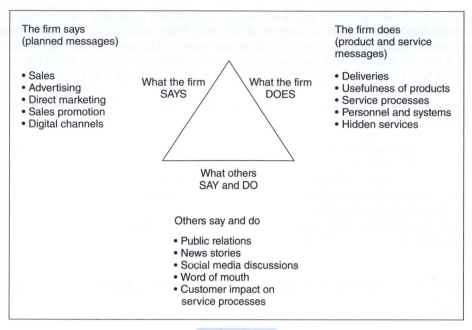

The firm says
(planned messages)

- Sales
- Advertising
- Direct marketing
- Sales promotion
- Digital channels

What the firm
SAYS

What the firm
DOES

The firm does
(product and service
messages)

- Deliveries
- Usefulness of products
- Service processes
- Personnel and systems
- Hidden services

What others
SAY and DO

Others say and do

- Public relations
- News stories
- Social media discussions
- Word of mouth
- Customer impact on
  service processes

FIGURE 10.2

The total communication/integrated marketing communication triangle.
Source: Adapted from Grönroos, C. & Lindberg-Repo, K., Integrated marketing
communications. The communication aspect of relationship marketing. *Integrated
Marketing Communications Research Journal*, **4**(1); 1998: 10.

The challenge to a firm is to manage all sources of messages about the firm and its offerings and all the communication media and their effects in an integrated way. Otherwise, customers will receive different, possibly contradictory, signals from the various types of communication. A salesperson may promise one thing while a personalized sales letter may promise something else (both planned communication messages), and a third communication effect may emerge when the customer perceives reality in the service encounter when consuming the service (effect of service messages). Furthermore, somewhere along the line there may be an *absence of communication*, either deliberate or accidental, which adds to the confusion of the total communication effect.

On the other hand, the organization that masters total communication management can achieve a powerful market communication impact, which adds substantially to the performance of the total marketing process. It is a way of boosting image and has a significant effect on *word-of-mouth communication.*

THE ABSENCE OF COMMUNICATION

As mentioned, there is a fifth source of message or type of communication that has to be considered when planning total communication, and that is the *absence of communication.*[6] This is often mistaken for lack of communication, where nothing is communicated.

The absence of communication may send messages as effectively as planned communication does. When a firm decides *not to inform* its customers about, say, a delay or a quality fault, this is *not* simply a lack of communication. Instead, *there is a distinct message involved*. This is perceived either immediately or later. It tells the customer that the service provider or supplier does not care about the customer and that the firm cannot be trusted. Absence of communication is frequently perceived as negative communication.

When a customer observes that there is a problem – for example, a flight does not leave on time or delivery of merchandise does not arrive on time – and the firm remains quiet, he loses control of the situation. Customers consider it important to be in control.[7] Being in control of a negative situation such as a delayed shipment makes a customer more trusting towards the supplier than not knowing what has happened. Also, keeping the customer informed about problems and deviations from what was expected is a way of showing respect. Openly recognizing a service failure is also the first step in a service recovery process and, as we have discussed previously, successful service recovery is a criterion of good functional quality.

In conclusion, the absence of communication may send a dangerous negative message about the firm. Normally, *even negative information is better than no information*.

WORD OF MOUTH AND THE COMMUNICATION CIRCLE

The marketing impact of *word-of-mouth communication* is usually huge, frequently greater than that of planned communication. This impact has been growing exponentially due to the Internet and since the introduction of social media. Word of mouth means messages about the organization, its credibility and trustworthiness, its ways of operating, its offerings and so on are communicated from one person to another, or through digital media to groups of other persons. As service is often based on an ongoing customer relationship, it is useful to understand word of mouth in a relationship context:

Word of mouth communication from a relational perspective is based on consumers' long-term experiences and behavioral commitment. Their word of mouth communication reflects the nature and value of their perception of relationship episodes or service encounters, as well as psychological comfort/discomfort with the relationship. It varies depending on how strong the relationship is.[8]

In the eyes of a potential customer, a person who has had personal experience with the service provider is an objective source of information. Consequently, *if there is a conflict between the word-of-mouth message and, say, an advertising campaign, advertising will lose.*

If a strong relationship develops with a given customer, *advocacy bonds* between the firm and the customer may also develop. Such customers recommend the firm to their friends, colleagues, etc., and on social media even to complete strangers, whereby they thus invite others to share the service experience with them.[9] They become *advocates* of the service offering. When offering word of mouth referrals customers with only one or a few experiences from a service will probably emphasize the price of the service, whereas long-standing customers are more likely to talk about the value of the service.

The amount of word-of–mouth referrals also seem to correlate positively with the relative growth of a firm in its industry. The more a firm's customers enthusiastically recommend the firm and its products to others, the better the growth rate of that firm. As growth can often be expected to be

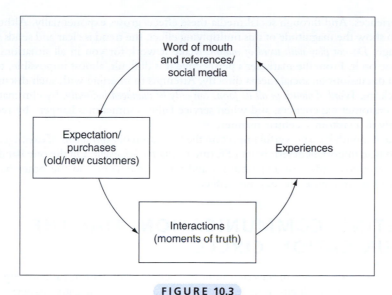

FIGURE 10.3

The communication circle.

a key driver of profitability, a large number of advocates on the market who refer the firm to other people also makes sense from a business profitability point of view.[10]

We will not go into word of mouth in any further detail here. Instead, we will turn to the *communication circle*, in which word of mouth in all its forms plays a critical role. This circle is illustrated schematically in Figure 10.3.

The communication circle consists of four parts, *expectations/purchases*, *interactions/service encounters*, *experiences* and *word of mouth and references/social media*. A potential customer or existing customer has developed certain *expectations* and therefore may decide to make a purchase; new business is created or an ongoing customer relationship thus continues, respectively. Having done so, he moves into the consumption stage of the customer relationship lifecycle. At this point, the customer gets involved in *interactions* with the organization and perceives the technical and functional quality dimensions of the service rendered. These interactions usually involve a high number of *moments of truth* or *moments of opportunity*. Here the customer is exposed to the *interactive marketing* efforts of the firm and receives service and product messages. The way the employees perform and systems function communicates a number of messages about the firm, its trustworthiness, its interest in customers, etc.

Now, the *experiences* that follow from a customer being involved in interactions in the service encounters and perceiving the quality dimensions multiply several times by means of *word of mouth* and comments and conversations on social media. If the message thus communicated is positive, customer expectations develop favourably. The customer with positive experiences is more inclined to return or continue to use the service on an ongoing basis. New potential customers become interested in the organization and its offerings. *References* (and *testimonials*) represent an active way for the firm to use positive word of mouth in its marketing, thus capitalizing more effectively on potential sources of good word of mouth.

The multiplier effect of word of mouth varies between industries and situations. It is frequently claimed that negative experiences tend to multiply by word of mouth quicker and more often than do positive experiences. And through social media these effects grows exponentially. Although there is no research to show the magnitude of this multiplying effect, the trend is clear and sends the marketer a blunt message. *Do not play with word of mouth*. Make it work for you in all situations, and always try to capitalize on it. From the marketer's perspective it is difficult, almost impossible, to steer word of mouth and discussions on social media directly. Attempts to interfere with such discussions almost invariably backfire. *Word of mouth in all its forms can only be managed indirectly*, by eliminating mistakes and negative customer experiences, and when service failures sometimes happen, by recovering the failure properly in a customer-centric manner.

Thus, word of mouth has a powerful impact on the formation of *expectations* of existing and potential customers and is an important determinant of future *purchasing behaviour*. On the one hand, good word of mouth has a positive effect on expectations and future purchases. On the other hand, negative word of mouth has, of course, the opposite effect.

MARKETING COMMUNICATION AND THE COMMUNICATION CIRCLE

It is important that the existence of the communication circle be understood and its implications fully appreciated by the marketer. If customer interactions create too many negative experiences and negative word of mouth follows, the customer builds up a *resistance to active marketing communication*. The more negative word of mouth there is, the less effective advertising campaigns, direct communication and sales efforts will be, and the less inclined people will be to look at the firm's website. More has to be invested in these types of communication if the negative impact of word of mouth is to be nullified. If too many negative messages are communicated by word of mouth and the image of the organization suffers severely, no increase in the marketing communication budget will be enough to save the situation, at least not in the long run.

Positive word of mouth, on the other hand, decreases the need to spend so much on marketing communication, through, for example, advertising and sales. It also draws customers and potential customers to Internet sites, either because they are looking for solutions to a problem, or simply out of curiosity. Good experiences and favourable word of mouth take care of much of the new business that is needed. In theory, *excellent interactions*, including good customer perceived quality and interactive communication, *make mass communication less necessary and allow more freedom in pricing*. Only when totally new services are launched may mass communication such as advertising campaigns be needed. There are numerous examples of small local firms that operate successfully in this way, and larger firms operating in larger areas can do the same. One of the leading banks in Scandinavia, Svenska Handelsbanken, has pursued such a communication strategy for over 40 years, and it has worked well; the profitability of the bank as well as customer satisfaction have constantly been well above average.

Whatever communication strategy the organization adopts, the key to successfully executed marketing communication is how the *interactions* between the organization and its customers have been geared to the needs and wishes of customers and to producing excellent perceived quality and building up supportive word of mouth. If the communication aspects of interactions are neglected, the interactive communication impact will not be as good, and could even be negative. As a consequence, more money will be needed for other types of communication, and even this may not be enough.

If marketing communication efforts sending planned messages through, for example, personal selling, mass communication and direct mail are developed without being geared to the communication effects of the service encounter (service messages) and word of mouth, the risk of overpromising and, consequently, of building up quality gaps grows substantially. Customers will then meet a reality that does not correspond to their expectations. This, in turn, destroys the communication circle, and three types of negative consequences may follow:

1. Word of mouth and references will become negative; negative discussions on social media are triggered.
2. The trustworthiness of the organization's communication messages suffer.
3. The firm's image is damaged.

On the other hand, if all elements of the communication process and customer perceptions of the service encounters are good, the corresponding effect is, of course, the opposite. Good word of mouth is built up, the credibility of the marketing communication efforts increases, and image improves.

To sum up, only a *total communication management* approach, where the effects of various sources of communication messages are integrated as well as possible, will be effective and justified from a management point of view. The effects of all types of communication, including the absence of communication, have to be taken into consideration. Integrating the different types of marketing communication and sources of messages is not an easy task. This is, however, not a valid excuse for not trying to integrate as much as possible. However, there is sometimes a structural obstacle in firms. Marketing communication is normally managed on a low level in the organizational hierarchy, where, for example, a marketing communication manager or even a marketing manager cannot integrate more than the planned communication messages.

PLANNED AND UNPLANNED COMMUNICATION

Unplanned messages were discussed in a previous section. These are messages from sources that cannot be planned or are difficult to plan. There is also another aspect of the planned/unplanned issue. Even planned messages may go partly unplanned. Hence, we can talk about *unplanned communication* as well as planned, depending on how well the marketer manages to plan all aspects of a planned message, or of a product or service message.

Unplanned communication, as opposed to planned communication, has a distinct effect just like the absence of communication.[11] There are often a number of situations where communication effects occur, although these situations have not been planned from a communication point of view. Such unplanned communication effects may be caused by planned messages in sales negotiations, advertising or some other distinct communications media, or they may be related to product or service messages.

Unplanned communications can easily have a negative impact on customer perceptions. Therefore, it is important to analyse all sources of communication and their possible effects, planned as well as unplanned. In Table 10.1 examples taken from various situations illustrate how unplanned communication effects may occur.

In practical situations it is, of course, seldom possible to exclude all sources of unplanned communication. However, successful total communications management requires that as many as possible of the potential communication situations be planned and the risk of unfavourable unplanned communication at least minimized.

TABLE 10.1

Planned and unplanned communication.

Type of communication	Planned	Unplanned
Personal selling	Good travel plans Good advice	Sloppy dress Uninterested in our values
Mass communication	Target-group directed advertising Informative menus	Communicates values that offend the customer
Direct communication (direct mail)	Correct address Personalized content	Wrong first name Irrelevant information
Websites	Easy to find interesting links & e-mail contact opportunities	No or delayed answers to e-mails
Communication in service encounters (service messages)	Good manners Pleasant servicescape Effective systems	Snooty Badly maintained premises Complicated technology
Communication by physical products in service processes (product messages)	High-class amenities in a hotel room	Plastic chairs in an outdoor café
Absence of communication	'We don't give any information unless it is correct' 'We'll inform you as soon as we know more, and let you know the situation every 10 minutes anyway'	Neglecting to inform customers about delays

THE SHORT-, MEDIUM- AND LONG-TERM EFFECTS OF MARKETING COMMUNICATION

Frequently, marketing communication is only used to achieve short-term goals. Sometimes efforts are made to create more enduring effects, for example, corporate advertising campaigns or image communication programmes. Too often, however, such long-term efforts are planned separately from other campaigns. Every communication activity, whether short-term or long-term, has effects on *customers*, as well as on *potential customers* and *employees* in a number of different time perspectives.

We are here going to distinguish between three time perspectives and their impacts on how an organization is perceived in the marketplace:

1. A marketing communication impact in the short term.

2. A marketing impact in the medium term.

3. An image impact in the long term.

Every communication effort, such as an advertising campaign, an Internet site, the behaviour of service employees, or the ease with which an ATM is operated, has an instant, *short-term communication impact as a communication activity*. This may be very effective as a means of communication; for example, a well-planned and executed advertising campaign that makes potential customers believe in the promises made. However, over a longer period the effects may be less clear, even negative. Another thing that is important to bear in mind is that mass communication has an impact on several target groups, even though it may be planned for and directed at only, say, potential customers. Existing customers and the firm's employees are also exposed to such communication. For example, potential customers to whom the firm may promise discounts or special benefits if they make a purchase may be impressed, whereas the firm's existing customers may be annoyed. Such problems should be recognized by the marketer in advance and avoided from the beginning in the planning process.

In Table 10.2 the possible effects of such an effective advertising campaign (or any type of communication effort) involving overpromising are illustrated: '+' denotes a favourable effect, '−' a negative

TABLE 10.2

Effects of an effectively executed communication campaign involving overpromising in three time periods at three levels.

Effect/period of time level	Target groups		
	Existing customers	Potential customers	Employees
Short term: effect of campaign as *communication*	+ or 0 'Maybe they really mean it!'	+ 'This sounds good!'	0 'I doubt it!'
Medium term: effect of campaign as *part of marketing*	− 'I should have known better! Cheated again!'	0 or − 'Wasn't it more than this?' or 'This is not what I expected!'	− 'It's as I thought and I have had to explain why we cannot fulfil our promises!'
Long term: effect of campaign *on image formation*	−− 'They never do what they say they are going to do!'	−− 'They just talk and promise.'	−− 'I'm looking for another employer.'

TABLE 10.3

Effects of realistic market communication in three time periods at three levels.

Effect/period of time level	Target groups		
	Existing customers	Potential customers	Employees
Short term: effect of campaign *as communication*	+ 'They have something new to offer.'	+ 'It sounds interesting.'	+ 'We are prepared!'
Medium term: effect of campaign *as part of marketing*	++ 'What a good service!'	+ 'They really fulfilled their promises.'	+ 'It works out well.'
Long term: effect of campaign *on image formation*	++ 'That's my service provider!'	++ 'You can really trust them.'	++ 'This is the best employer I've ever worked for.'

effect and '0' a neutral effect or no effect. Three target groups for this campaign, customers, potential customers and employees, are identified and the impact on these groups indicated. In reality there may be more target groups. In Table 10.2 and then in Table 10.3 traditional planned communication is used to exemplify the various effects of marketing communication. Similar analyses can, and should, be conducted for product and service messages, and also for unplanned messages and even for absence of communication.

As can be seen from Table 10.2, this hypothetical advertising campaign obviously includes promises that cannot be fulfilled. For *potential customers* and even for *existing customers*, the effects of this campaign may be positive in the short term seen as a communications effect only, if it is well executed. However, *employees*, who know they cannot possibly fulfil such promises, react differently. If this is the first time such overpromising takes place, they will probably react in a neutral way and the campaign will have no effect. However, if such overpromises have been made in the past, their reactions will be negative.

Over a longer period of time, as customers and potential customers get involved in interactions with the organization, the perception of this advertising campaign changes. They realize that reality has not met their expectations and the promises made by the campaign. The combined impact of the advertising campaign as a traditional marketing effort and the interactive marketing effect of the buyer–seller interactions in the service encounters, which are inconsistent with the campaign, thus changes the positive effect of the campaign. This combined effect is the impact of the total marketing process, including traditional as well as interactive activities, and it is probably negative. The customers feel cheated, and justifiably so. Hence, in the medium term, the marketing effect of a campaign, which judged in isolation may seem good and effective, can be poor or directly negative.

As far as the employees are concerned, the medium-term effect is definitely negative, because they will have to cope with customers who have unrealistic expectations and may get angry and sometimes even nasty towards them. Personnel are put in an awkward position, which damages employee motivation and good interactive marketing performance.

Finally, we can stretch the time perspective even more, and observe the possible *long-term effects* of this advertising campaign. If the campaign runs for a longer period of time, or is followed by other campaigns which also overpromise, *customers* and *potential customers* will learn that the organization is not trustworthy. Over the long term, single communication campaigns that, again judged in isolation, look like good communication may have a very negative impact on the image of the organization.

Of course, *employees* react as strongly as customers. Dissatisfied customers can normally leave a company with little or no notice, whereas it may be less easy for many employees to find a new employer. In the long run employee motivation suffers badly.

The effects of a trustworthy communication campaign that does not involve overpromising are, of course, totally different. Table 10.3 illustrates the effects that can be expected to occur when, for example, an advertising campaign is run which makes realistic promises. Customers exposed to the messages of this campaign experience a reality that corresponds to the promises, if they decide to buy and consume service provided by the organization.

The effects demonstrated in Table 10.3 are totally different from those in Table 10.2. In the short term, existing and potential customers and employees can be expected to react positively. This initial favourable effect is enhanced by the fact that the service production process is perceived to be in line with the campaign. Interactive marketing in the service encounters and the market communication campaign support each other. In the long term, image is improved by the fact that the organization consistently gives a good impression, by marketing communication as well as by reality and interactive marketing performance. In terms of the relationship marketing model in Chapter 9, activities in the *planned communication process* (planned messages) and in the *interaction process* (product and service messages) support each other. As a consequence, this will trigger positive unplanned communication (word of mouth, comments on social media, news stories). The employees also react favourably. In the long term, they will probably consider their employer the best possible, if other internal activities or policies do not destroy this impression.

As these examples demonstrate, it is imperative that every communication effort is judged not only on its virtues as a communication effort, but in a much larger perspective, otherwise unwanted effects may occur.

GUIDELINES FOR MANAGING MARKET COMMUNICATION

Some general guidelines for managing market communication can be identified.[12] Here 12 guidelines are discussed:

1. Direct communication efforts to employees.
2. Capitalize on word of mouth.
3. Provide tangible clues.
4. Communicate intangibility.
5. Make the service understood.
6. Provide communication continuity.

7. Promise what is possible.

8. Observe the long-term effects of communication

9. Be aware of the communication effects of the absence of communication.

10. Integrate marketing communication efforts and messages.

11. Customers integrate communication messages with their previous experiences as well as with their life experiences and expectations.

12. In the end, it is the customers who create messages for themselves out of a firm's communication efforts.

Direct communication efforts to employees. All advertising campaigns and most other mass communication efforts that are planned for various segments of existing and potential customers are also visible to employees. Employees are therefore an important 'second audience' for these campaigns. Promoting the position of employees in external communication campaigns is a way of internally enhancing the employees' roles and adding to their motivation.

Capitalize on word of mouth. As demonstrated by the discussion of the *communication circle* and the vital role of word of mouth and customer references, good word of mouth makes customers more receptive to external marketing communication efforts, and vice versa. Moreover, good word of mouth can be considered the most effective communication vehicle. Therefore, if a firm has created good word of mouth, which is a message from an objective source (satisfied customers), it is a good idea to use the objective nature of word of mouth in marketing communication. Testimonials are examples of this.

Provide tangible clues. As services are intangible, communicating information about a service, especially to an audience of potential customers, can be very difficult. The intangible service can easily become even more abstract. Therefore, it is a good idea to try to make the service more concrete. For example, a firm may illustrate or demonstrate tangible items that are either involved in the service production process or relate to the service. This is a way of demonstrating the quality of the service. Showing the physical comfort of first class travel on an airline in an advertisement may be a more effective way of giving potential customers something tangible to relate to and remember than an abstract visualization of luxury.

Communicate intangibility. Although it is often possible to offer tangible clues to a service, one should bear in mind that service is intangibly perceived. Emphasizing a tangible component in the service process, such as silverware and flatware for a first class or business class airline service, may not always differentiate a service in a meaningful way. Instead, the challenge is sometimes to be able to cope with the intangibility of the service, because the differentiating appeal may be found in some aspect of the intangibility of the service. Showing parts of the service process, for instance, a customer enjoying his leisure time at a beach while being on an inclusive vacation or presenting testimonials of satisfied customers, are examples of how to communicate intangibility of services.[13]

Make the service understood. Because of the intangible nature of service, special attention has to be paid to making the benefits of a particular service clearly understood. Using abstract expressions and superlatives may not lead to a good communication effect. The service and what it can do for the customer remains unclear. Therefore, it is important to find good metaphors that clearly communicate the service.

Provide communication continuity. Once more, because service is intangible, and because mass communication about service is difficult for the audience to grasp, there has to be continuity in communication efforts over time. A common tune in a TV or radio commercial or a common layout, picture or phrase in a newspaper advert, which continues from one campaign to the next, may be a way of making the audience realize more quickly what is advertised and what the message is. Typically, marketers feel that a communication theme is out of date and ready to change, just when the target audience has started to realize what the message is all about. In service, the marketer needs more patience than in the communication of physical products.

Promise what is possible. If promises given by external market communication are not fulfilled, the gap between expectation and experience is widened, and customer perceived quality decreases. It is often said that keeping promises is the most important single aspect of good service quality. Clearly, avoiding overpromising is essential in managing marketing communication. This has a clear connection with the next guideline.

Observe the long-term effects of marketing communication. As the discussion in the previous section demonstrated, a communication campaign that seems to be effective may have unexpected, negative effects when viewed over the long term. If promises that cannot be fulfilled are made, the short-term effects on sales may be good, but customers will become dissatisfied as they perceive reality. They will not return but will create bad word of mouth. Over the longer term, the image of the organization is damaged. The effects on employees are similar. Hence, a long-term perspective must always be taken when external marketing communication is planned and executed.

Be aware of the effects of the absence of communication. If there is no information available in a stressful situation, customers often perceive this as negative information because they lose control of the situation. It is usually better to share bad news with customers than to say nothing.[14]

Integrate marketing communication efforts and messages. As a previous discussion in this chapter demonstrated, customers are exposed to a number of different communication messages. These messages may be conflicting, thus creating a confusing impact. If communication messages through, for example, advertising, direct mail and the messages the service process are sending are contradictory, the effect is not trustworthy and the image of the firm may be damaged. Hence, it is important for the marketer to try to integrate all types of communication messages – planned, product, service and unplanned – so that customers know what the firm stands for and can develop a trusting relationship with it.

Customers integrate messages with their previous experiences and life expectations. No communication message exists in a vacuum. A customer has experiences of the firm or its services or goods from before and he may even feel that there is at least some kind of relationship with the firm. The perception of the communication message from, for example, an advertisement or service interaction is merged with these previous experiences and the image of the firm and its solutions that have developed in the customer's mind. The message that is formed in this way is probably at least somewhat different from what the firm intended it to be and it may even be vastly different.[15] Likewise, the customer's life situations, history and expectations will probably have an impact on the message he perceives. This impact may even be profound. This means that different customers will interpret the same communications effort, for example an advertisement, in very different ways.[16]

In the end it is the customers who create the message out of a firm's communication efforts. Most marketing communications models state that, except for the distorting effect of some *noise* in the communication flow, the message sent by the marketer equals the message received by the customer. Marketers often tend to act as if the message sent is also the message understood by customers. In reality *it is the customer who constructs the message for himself.* Every message is personal. It is highly questionable whether one can even say that marketers send messages. What marketers perhaps do is create inputs of various sorts for each and every customer's personal message creation mechanism. This mechanism is in the mind of the customer, and the creation process depends on the relationship history and future expectations of a given customer as well as his life history and expectations. Furthermore, it depends on environmental effects, for example what a competitor does at a given moment or changes in the customer's life situation.[17] For example, in the case of service interactions the service contact employees can attempt to take a customer's personal situation, his relationship history and expectations, and possibly even his life situation, into account as much as possible. In this way the communication effect of the interaction will probably improve. In direct communication, for example using direct mail, this is also possible to some extent. In mass communication, to improve the effect of communication efforts, the marketer will have to make use of information about customer segments.

DEVELOPING A RELATIONSHIP DIALOGUE

In an ongoing relationship context it is not only the firm that is supposed to talk to the customer, and the customer who is supposed to listen. It is a two-way street, where both parties should communicate with each other. In the best case a dialogue develops.[18] A dialogue can be seen as an interactive process of *reasoning together*.[19] In the words of Ballantyne and Varey, 'marketing's unused potential is in the *dialogical* mode'.[20]

The purpose of a dialogue is for two parties to develop a better mutual understanding of a problem and eventually to solve this problem. Hence, two business parties should reason together in order to understand a problem, and if possible find a solution to it. The process of reasoning together includes the *willingness of both parties to listen* and an *ability to discuss and communicate* for the sake of achieving a common goal. As Ballantyne and Varey conclude, 'in a dialogue participants speak and act *between* each other, not *to* each other'.[21]

A connection between the firm and the customer has to be made, so that they find they can *trust* each other in this dialogue or reasoning process. The intent of this process is to build *shared meanings*, and develop insights into what the two parties can do together and for each other through access to a *common meaning* or shared field of knowledge.[22]

A dialogue requires *participation* of the parties involved.[23] Participation takes place not only in interactions between the firm and its customers, but also through one-way communication efforts, such as advertisements, brochures and direct mail as well as one-way Internet communication. Messages through these traditional communication media using old and new technologies should, however, contribute to the development of shared meanings and common fields of knowledge. When such messages through impersonal media *and* interactions between the customer and the firm support each other, *the two parties are reasoning together*.

There is a difference between one-way and two-way communication through impersonal media as part of a dialogue. One-way communication has a sender and a receiver of messages sent. A dialogue requires the participation of the parties involved, and hence, in a dialogue there are no senders or receivers, only *participants in the dialogue process*. Therefore, a dialogue resembles a discussion more than communication in a traditional sense.

Sometimes marketers send out a direct marketing letter where they invite a response from the receiver. If the receiver reacts by responding, this is taken as the beginning of a dialogue or even as the manifestation of a dialogue. However, creating a dialogue between a firm and a customer takes much more effort than this. A dialogue is an ongoing process, where information should be exchanged between the two parties in a way that makes both the firm and the customer ready to start or continue doing business with each other. Both parties have to be *motivated to develop and maintain a dialogue*, otherwise no real dialogue will develop.[24] Instead of a dialogue, two parallel monologues or perhaps only one monologue without a listener will take place. This, of course, goes for individual consumers as well as for firms.

To maintain a dialogue not all communication contacts between the parties have to include an invitation to respond. An informative brochure or even a plain TV commercial may be part of an ongoing dialogue, provided that the customer perceives that it gives information which is valuable for him to proceed in the relationship: for example, it tells the customer what piece of advice to ask for or gives him information needed to make the next purchase. It is also important to remember that it is not only planned communication through planned communication media (TV commercials, newspaper ads, brochures, direct mail, Internet communication, sales representatives, etc.) that maintains a dialogue. In a relationship the other sources of communication which were discussed earlier in this chapter (product and service messages, unplanned messages such as word-of-mouth referrals and public relations and the absence of communication) also send messages which influence the dialogue. Goods, service processes and interactions with fellow customers during the various service encounters contribute to the firm's total communication message, and thus are all forms of input into an ongoing relationship dialogue.

In the *relationship marketing model* in Chapter 9 (see Figure 9.4) two parallel processes – a *communication process* and an *interaction process* – constitute the relationship process. Using this model, a relationship dialogue can be illustrated, and the quality of such a dialogue can also be analysed. For example, a customer calls a helpdesk because he has been advised to do so in a newspaper ad or in a brochure, and he receives attentive service and the required information. This is a good two-step sequence of distinct communication (advert or brochure) and service messages (helpdesk support), which favourably supports the development of a relationship dialogue. A customer may also have answered a direct mailing and in return received a brochure describing quick and attentive service. Following this sequence of dialogue-oriented distinct communication messages with the customer's response in between the two messages, the customer decides to purchase the service and enters into interactions with employees and systems in a service process. There he realizes that the service does *not* fulfil the promise of quick and attentive service. There are, for example, too few customer contact employees and they do not have the time or desire to show a genuine interest in the customer's problem. What started out as a positively developing dialogue is damaged by the negative message following the customer's bad experiences with the service encounter. Messages from the communication process and the interaction process have not supported each other and, consequently, no favourable relationship dialogue developed in the long run.

A successful development of a relationship requires that the two (or more) parties continuously learn from each other. The supplier or service provider acquires a constantly growing understanding of the customer's needs, values and consumption or usage habits. The customer learns how to participate in the interaction processes in order to get quick and accurate information, support, personal attention, well-functioning service, etc. This process can be characterized as a *learning relationship*.[25]

An ongoing dialogue supports the development of a learning relationship. However, if the collaboration between a supplier and a customer does not include elements of learning, a relationship dialogue will not develop. In fact, no real relationship will develop where the parties involved do not feel that a mutual way of thinking exists. The customer may still continue to buy from the same supplier or service firm, at least for some time, perhaps because the seller offers a low price, has a technological advantage over competing firms, or is conveniently located. However, this relationship is much more vulnerable to changes in the marketplace, to new competitors and to new alternative solutions that may become available.

INTEGRATED MARKETING COMMUNICATION AND RELATIONSHIP MARKETING

Simply planning and managing marketing communication through distinct communications media, even as a two-way process, is *not* relationship marketing and probably does not create a dialogue, although communication efforts may look relational, such as personally addressed letters inviting a customer response. The marketer and the customer are not *reasoning together* to build up a *common meaning*. *Only the planned integration of distinct planned communication and interaction processes into one systematically implemented strategy creates relationship marketing*. A true integration of the various marketing communication messages with each other and with the outcomes of the interaction process is required for the successful implementation of relationship marketing. Only in this way can an ongoing relationship between the firm and its customer dialogue, which is a key element of relationship marketing, be maintained.

As the relationship proceeds, the different types of messages develop in a continuous process and their effects accumulate in the minds of customers. If the distinct communication process with its planned marketing communication is supported by the product and service messages created in the interaction process, favourable unplanned communication *resulting in positive word-of-mouth communication* will occur.[26]

Both the firm and the customer should be motivated to communicate with each other. The customer should feel that the firm which sends a message is interested in him and argues convincingly for their service. In such a situation the planned communication efforts and the communication aspects of the interaction process merge into one single two-way communication process, which constitutes a relationship dialogue with the customer and the supplier or service provider as participants. The nature and content of word-of-mouth referrals will probably differ depending on how long the customer has been involved in the interaction process. It can be assumed that referrals by a long-standing customer will include more holistic expressions (such as 'It's a great company') than detailed experiences, and more value-oriented than price-related expressions.[27]

RELATIONSHIP COMMUNICATION

In order to develop a relationship with its customers the firm has to turn to a long-term dialogical communication approach. When the firm and its customer 'reason together' about how the customer's everyday activities and processes can best be supported and a mutual knowledge about how this can be done is emerging, the likelihood increases that a mutual understanding and commitment develops between the customer and the supplier or service provider. The possibility of reaching the marketing objective of getting not only a 'share of the customer's wallet' but also a 'share of his heart and mind' grows. In Figure 10.4 a trimodal conceptualization of relationship communication is illustrated.[28] The model includes three levels: *planned communication*, *contact* and *connectedness*.

The relationship communication process proceeds from a low level of interaction between the seller and buyer towards higher levels of interaction. In the first phase, communication activities are mostly *planned communication* using distinct communication media, for example, advertisements, brochures and direct mail as well as sales negotiations. As the process moves on the customer becomes involved in interactions with the firm, for example interacting with service employees and various systems representing the firm or interacting with physical goods. If these interactions successfully support the customer's everyday processes, a *contact* beyond the mere planned communication messages is established. *Product and service messages* are intertwined with planned communication messages, and if the outcome is a successfully integrated message, the first steps towards dialogical communication

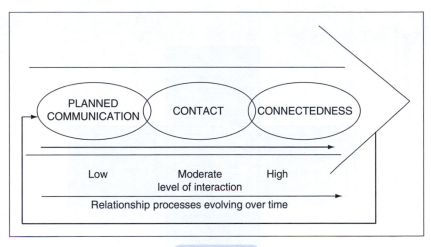

FIGURE 10.4

A trimodal relationship communication model.
Source: Reprinted from Lindberg-Repo, K. & Grönroos, C., Conceptualising
communications strategy from a relational perspective. *Industrial Marketing
Management*, **33**; 2004: p. 233 with permission from Elsevier.

have been taken. As the process moves on over time and two-way communication efforts increase, the communication that takes place can be characterized as dialogical and relational. As a result, a state of *connectedness* between the two parties is emerging. At this stage of the relationship communication process the customer's heart and mind may have been won and a true relationship established. As long as the activities taken by the other party are considered fair and supportive, the likelihood that the relationship continues is high.

A relationship dialogue is aimed at as outlined above and shown in Figure 10.4. However, *whether a communication effort is perceived as relationship communication is determined by the customer, not by the marketer*. The customer assesses what meaning *for him* there is in a message (conveyed, for example, through an advertisement, brochure or direct contact in a service encounter). What the marketer thinks is relationship-oriented communication may be something else from the customer's point of view. Finne and Grönroos suggest the following definition of *relationship communication*:[29]

Relationship communication is any type of marketing communication that influences the receiver's long-term commitment to the sender by facilitating meaning creation through integration with the receiver's time and situational context. The time context refers to the receiver's perception of the history and envisioned future of his/her relationship with the sender. The situational context refers to other elements internal or external to the receiver.

From a relationship perspective, a communication message should have a positive impact on the customer's commitment to the firm. However, whether this happens or not depends on the nature and content of the message *and* the customer's *temporal* and *contextual* reality, or rather perception of reality. This is illustrated by the *relationship communication model* in Figure 10.5.

Conventional marketing communication models, also in the context of integrated marketing communication, assume that it is the marketer who determines what meaning a message conveys. The customer as a receiver is expected to accept this meaning, only somewhat distorted by some *noise* in the communication process. The relationship communication model, on the contrary, assumes that

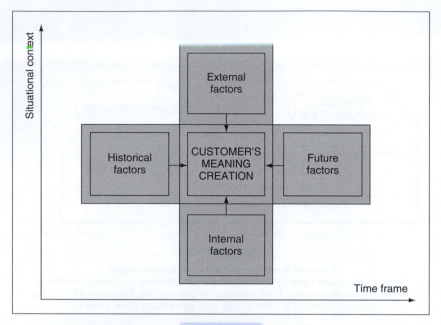

FIGURE 10.5

Meaning creation in a relationship communication model.
Source: Finne, Å. & Grönroos, C., Rethinking marketing communication: from
Integrated marketing communication to relationship communication. *Journal
of Marketing Communications*, **15**(2–3), 2009, 179–195. Reproduced by
permission of Taylor & Francis.

it is the customer who creates meaning out of communication messages. According to the model, this meaning is dependent on two factors: a temporal factor and a situational factor.[30]

The *temporal factors* relate to the customer's relationship with the firm. What are his experiences with the firm in the past, and what future expectations does he have about this relationship? The *situational factors* are either internal to the customer or external to him. *Internal* factors relate to an individual's personality, education and level of knowledge, and the individual's 'life expectations', etc. *External* factors can be culturally-situated factors or the personal context of the individual, such as family situation, economic situation and social situation, or trends, traditions, alternative choices, and also communication messages from competing firms, discussions on social media and word of mouth.

The customer relates any given communication message – an advertisement, sales call or interaction with a service employee – to the four temporal and situational factors of the model. Depending on how this assessment of the message turns out, this communication either has a positive or negative relationship-oriented meaning, or is not considered a relationship message at all. This assessment is, of course, often unconscious, but sometimes it may be very consciously conducted. From the marketer's perspective, this means that a thorough analysis of its customers' temporal and situational contexts should be done, before any communication plans are developed. Otherwise much of marketing communication may be unproductive, or even counterproductive, and relationship communication with the customers may not occur.

SUMMARY

In this chapter we dwelt upon marketing communications issues, and argued for a holistic integrated marketing communication approach. There are a number of types of sources of communication, but a need exists for a total communication approach where a sufficiently long-term perspective is taken. If this is not done, what is good marketing communication in the short term may, in the long term, have a negative marketing impact on customers, because their real experiences with physical products and services are in conflict with the promises made by, for example, an advertising campaign. Furthermore, the effect on company image the longer this continues may be even more negative. A number of guidelines for marketing communication in service were presented. Then, how total or integrated marketing communication and relationship marketing are related to each other was discussed and the development of a relationship dialogue process was explored. Finally, relationship communication was explained.

QUESTIONS FOR DISCUSSION

1. What is meant by an integrated marketing communication approach? Why is such an approach to marketing communications effective?

2. How can a marketing communication campaign (e.g. an advertisement campaign), which effectively creates awareness and generates sales, lead to a negative marketing effect and ultimately damage a firm's image?

3. Discuss how well the planned marketing communication messages given by your firm, or any given firm, are integrated with the product, service and unplanned messages about the offerings to which customers are exposed.

4. What is a dialogue? What is a relationship dialogue?

5. How can a relationship dialogue be created and maintained?

6. How can a relationship communication process be understood? How can it be used in a firm's marketing communication?

NOTES

1. This *total communication concept* was introduced in the 1980s. See Grönroos, C. & Rubinstein, D., *Totalkommunikation* (Total communication). Stockholm, Sweden: Liber/Marketing Technique Centre, 1986. In Swedish. In the early 1990s the same notion reappeared in the form of *integrated marketing communications*.

2. See Schultz, D.E., Tannenbaum, S.I. & Lauterborn, R.F., *Integrated Marketing Communications*. Lincolnwood, IL: NTC Publishing Group, 1992. For a more recent discussion of integrated marketing communication, see Kerr, G.F., Schultz, D., Patti, C. & Ilchul, K., An inside-out approach to integrated marketing communication: an international analysis. *International Journal of Advertising*, **27**(4), 2008, 511–548, and Mulhern, F., Integrated marketing communication: from media channels to digital connectivity. *Journal of Marketing Communications*, **15**(2–3), 2009, 85–101.

3. Grönroos, C. & Lindberg-Repo, K., Integrated marketing communications: the communications aspect of relationship marketing. *Integrated Marketing Communications Research Journal*, **4**(1), 1998, 10. In a definition by the American Association of Advertising Agencies, as in almost every other definition, only traditional means of marketing communication, such as advertising, direct mail, sales promotion and public relations, are included.

4. Duncan, T. & Moriarty, S., *Driving Brand Value*. New York: McGraw-Hill, 1997.

5. Calonius, H., Market communication in service marketing. In Avlonitis, G.J., Papavasiliou, N.K. & Kouremeos, A.G. (eds), *Marketing Thought and Practice in the 1990s*. Proceedings from the XVIIIth Annual Conference of the European Marketing Academy, Athens, Greece, 1989.

6. Calonius, *op. cit.*

7. Hui, M.K. & Bateson, J.E.G., Perceived control and the effects of crowding and consumer choice on the service experience. *Journal of Consumer Research*, **18**(Sept), 1991, 174–184. See also Bateson, J.E.G., Perceived control and the service encounter. In Czepiel, J.A., Solomon, M.R. & Surprenant C.E. (eds), *The Service Encounter: Managing Employee/Service Interactions in Service Businesses*. Lexington, MA: Lexington Books, 1985, pp. 67–82.

8. Lindberg-Repo, K. & Grönroos, C., Word-of-mouth referrals in the domain of relationship marketing. *The Australasian Marketing Journal*, **7**(1), 1999, 115. See also Lindberg-Repo, K., *Word-of-Mouth Communication in the Hospitality Industry*. Helsinki/Helsingfors: Hanken Swedish School of Economics, Finland/CERS, 1999. For a classical publication on word of mouth, see Arndt, J., *Word of Mouth Advertising*. New York: Advertising Research Foundation, 1969.

9. Lindberg-Repo & Grönroos, *op. cit.* For marketing in social media, see Evans, D., *Social Media Marketing. An Hour a Day*. Indianapolis, IN: John Wiley & Sons, 2012.

10. Reichheld, F.F., The one number you need to grow. *Harvard Business Review*, **81**(12), 2003, 46–55. See also Keller, E., Unleashing the power of word of mouth: Creating brand advocacy to drive growth. *Journal of Advertising Research*, December, 2007.

11. See Calonius, *op. cit.*

12. Many of these guidelines are from George, W.R. & Berry, L.L., Guidelines for the advertising of services. *Business Horizons*, July–Aug, 1981, which still today is the best discussion of how to advertise service. Even though the authors focus on the advertising of service, their guidelines are useful in a larger marketing communications context as well.

13. The need to develop advertising and other ways of communicating, based on the intangibility of service, has been proposed by Benwari Mittal, who argues that intangibility may often offer better opportunities for differentiating a service in advertising than concentrating on tangible evidence. He discusses various strategies for communicating intangibility in advertising. See Mittal, B., The advertising of services. Meeting the challenge of intangibility. *Journal of Service Research*, **2**(1), 1999, 98–116.

14. Grönroos, C., *Service Management and Marketing. Managing the Moments of Truth in Service Competition*. Lexington, MA: Lexington Books, 1990.

15. Finne, Å. & Grönroos, C., Rethinking marketing communication: from integrated marketing communication to relationship communication. *Journal of Marketing Management*, **15**(2–3), 2009, 179–195.

16. See Mick, D.G. & Buhl, C., A meaning-based model of advertising experiences. *Journal of Consumer Research*, **19**(Dec), 1991, 317–338.

17. Finne & Grönroos, *op. cit.*

18. See, for example, Fischer, A., Sieg, J.H., Wallin, M.W. & von Krogh, G., What motivates professional service firm employees to nurture client dialogues? *The Service Industries Journal*, **34**(5–6), 2014, 399–421, where the relationship dialogue notion is discussed and ways of enhancing a dialogue in a professional service context are explored.

19. Ballantyne, D., Dialogue and its role in the development of relationship specific knowledge. *Journal of Business and Industrial Marketing*, **19**(2), 2004, 114–123.

20. Ballantyne, D. & Varey, R.J., Introducing a dialogical orientation to the service–dominant logic of marketing. In Lusch, R.F. & Vargo, S.L. (eds), *The Service-Dominant Logic of Marketing. Dialog, Debate, and Directions*. Armonk, NY: M.E. Sharpe, 2006, pp. 224–235, p. 228.

21. Ballantyne & Varey, *op. cit.*, p. 227.

22. Schein, E.H., The process of dialog: creating effective communication. *The Systems Thinker*, **5**(5), 1994, 1–4 and Bohm, D., *On Dialogue*. London: Routledge, 1996.

23. Bohm, *op. cit.*

24. Dichter, E., How word of mouth advertising works. *Harvard Business Review*, **44**(Nov–Dec), 1966, 147–166.

25. Peppers, D., Rogers, M. & Dorf, B., Is your company ready for one-to-one marketing? *Harvard Business Review*, **77**(Jan–Feb), 1999, 151–160.

26. These word-of-mouth effects on ongoing relationships are discussed in Lindberg-Repo & Grönroos, *op. cit.*

27. Lindberg-Repo & Grönroos, *op. cit.* See also Lindberg-Repo, *op. cit.*

28. Lindberg-Repo, K., *Customer Relationship Communication – Analysing Communication from a Value Generating Perspective*. Helsinki, Finland: Hanken Swedish School of Economics, Finland, 2001. See also Lindberg-Repo, K. & Grönroos, C., Conceptualising communications strategy from a relational perspective. *Industrial Marketing Management*, **33**, 2004, 229–239.

29. Finne, Å. & Grönroos, C., *op.cit.,* 180–181.

30. The temporal and situational factors influencing customers' meaning creation are derived, respectively, from Mick & Buehl, *op.cit.* (meaning making is a function of internal and external factors influencing an individual's perception of a communication message) and from Edvardsson, B. & Strandvik, T., Is a critical incident critical for a customer relationship? *Managing Service Quality*, **10**(2), 2000, 82–91.

FURTHER READING

Arndt, J. (1969) *Word of Mouth Advertising*. New York: Advertising Research Foundation.

Ballantyne, D. (2004) Dialogue and its role in the development of relationship specific knowledge. *Journal of Business and Industrial Marketing*, **19**(2), 114–123.

Ballantyne, D. & Varey, R.J. (2006) Introducing a dialogical orientation to the service-dominant logic of marketing. In Lusch, R.F. & Vargo, S.L. (eds), *The Service-Dominant Logic of Marketing. Dialog, Debate, and Directions*. Armonk, NY: M.E. Sharpe, pp. 224–235.

Bateson, J.E.G. (1985) Perceived control and the service encounter. In Czepiel, J.A., Solomon, M.R. & Surprenant, C.E. (eds), *The Service Encounter: Managing Employee/Service Interactions in Service Businesses*. Lexington, MA: Lexington Books, pp. 67–82.

Bohm, D. (1996) *On Dialogue*. London: Routledge.

Calonius, H. (1989) Market communication in service marketing. In Avlonitis, G.J., Papavasiliou, N.K. & Kouremeos, A.G. (eds), *Marketing Thought and Practice in the 1990s*. Proceedings from the XVIIIth Annual Conference of the European Marketing Academy, Athens, Greece.

Dichter, E. (1966) How word of mouth advertising works. *Harvard Business Review*, **44**(Nov/Dec), 147–166.

Duncan, T. & Moriarty, S. (1997) *Driving Brand Value*. New York: McGraw-Hill.

Edvardsson, B. and Strandvik, T. (2000), Is a critical incident critical for a customer relationship? *Managing Service Quality*, **10**(2), 82–91.

Evans, D. (2012) *Social Media Marketing. An hour a Day*. Indianapolis, IN: John Wiley & Sons.

Finne, Å. & Grönroos, C. (2009) Rethinking marketing communication: from integrated marketing communication to relationship communication. *Journal of Marketing Management*, **15**(2–3), 179–195.

Fischer, A., Sieg, J.H., Wallin, M.W. & von Krogh, G. (2014) What motivates professional service firm employees to nurture client dialogues? *The Service Industries Journal*, **34**(5–6), 399–421.

Grönroos, C. (1990) *Service Management and Marketing. Managing the Moments of Truth in Service Competition*. Lexington, MA: Lexington Books.

Grönroos, C. & Lindberg-Repo, K. (1998) Integrated marketing communications: the communications aspect of relationship marketing. *Integrated Marketing Communications Research Journal*, **4**(1), 3–11.

Grönroos, C. & Rubinstein, D. (1986) *Totalkommunikation* (Total communication). Stockholm, Sweden: Liber/Marketing Technique Centre. In Swedish.

Hui, M.K. & Bateson, J.E.G. (1991) Perceived control and the effects of crowding and consumer choice on the service experience. *Journal of Consumer Research*, **18**(Sept), 174–184.

Keller, E. (2007) Unleashing the power of word of mouth: creating brand advocacy to drive growth. *Journal of Advertising Research*, December.

Kerr, G.F., Schultz, D., Patti, C. & Ilchul, K. (2008) An inside-out approach to integrated marketing communication: an international analysis. *International Journal of Advertising*, **27**(4), 511–548.

Lindberg-Repo, K. (1999) *Word-of-Mouth Communication in the Hospitality Industry*. Helsinki/Helsingfors: Hanken Swedish School of Economics, Finland/CERS Centre for Relationship Marketing and Service Management.

Lindberg-Repo, K. (2001) *Customer Relationship Communication – Analysing communication from a value generating perspective*. Helsinki, Finland: Hanken Swedish School of Economics, Finland.

Lindberg-Repo, K. & Grönroos, C. (1999) Word-of-mouth referrals in the domain of relationship marketing. *The Australasian Marketing Journal*, **7**(1), 109–117.

Lindberg-Repo, K. & Grönroos, C. (2004) Conceptualising communications strategy from a relational perspective. *Industrial Marketing Management*, **33**, 229–239.

Mick, D.G. & Buhl, C. (1991) A meaning-based model of advertising experiences. *Journal of Consumer Research*, **19**(Dec), 317–338.

Mittal, B. (1999) The advertising of services. Meeting the challenge of intangibility. *Journal of Service Research*, **2**(1), 98–116.

Mulhern, F. (2009) Integrated marketing communication: from media channels to digital connectivity. *Journal of Marketing Communications*, **15**(2–3), 85–101.

Peppers, D., Rogers, M. & Dorf, B. (1999) Is your company ready for one-to-one marketing? *Harvard Business Review*, **77**(Jan–Feb), 151–160.

Reichheld, F.F. (2003) The one number you need to grow. *Harvard Business Review*, **81**(12), 46–55.

Schein, E.H. (1994) The process of dialogue: creating effective communication. *The Systems Thinker*, **5**(5), 1–4.

Schultz, D.E., Tannenbaum, S.I. & Lauterborn, R.F. (1992) *Integrated Marketing Communications*. Lincolnwood, IL: NTC Publishing Group.

CHAPTER 11
MANAGING BRAND RELATIONSHIPS AND IMAGE

> ❝ *If anyone can build a brand, it is the customer. Marketers cannot do that. They can only create favourable conditions for a brand image to develop in customers' minds.* ❞

INTRODUCTION

This chapter discusses two important concepts in marketing, *brand* and *image*. First, the nature of a branding process and a definition of a brand is analysed. Taking a relationship approach, brands are seen as brand relationships, which are affected by a number of brand contacts that occur during an ongoing relationship between a customer and a supplier or service provider. In the latter sections of the chapter the image concept is explored. The functions of image on a company are discussed, along with possible reasons for a bad image, and actions that should be taken to improve image are presented. After having read the chapter the reader should understand the importance of branding for service providers and the characteristics of creating service brands and brand relationships, as well as the role of image and how image can be improved in various situations.

WHAT IS A BRAND? A TRADITIONAL VIEW

The *brand* concept is well established in marketing. The first brands in a modern marketing sense were developed a century ago. However, during the second half of the 20th century brands and branding became central issues in marketing. Most discussions of brands are related to physical products, especially consumer packaged goods. Only during the last 30 years or so has an awareness of the importance of creating service brands emerged. Now it is widely recognized that branding is a vital issue for service organizations as well.[1]

The American Marketing Association offers the following definition of a brand: *'A name, term, sign, symbol or any other feature that identifies one seller's product or service as distinct from those of other sellers.'*[2]

From a service perspective at least, two objections can be made: this definition misses the key characteristic of service as a process, and it excludes the customer.

First, it explicitly points out issues such as name, term, sign, symbol and feature, but does not address the fundamental characteristic of service, which is that *service is a process* and the consumption of service can be characterized as *process consumption*. Because service is perceived in processes in which the customer normally also participates, this service process undoubtedly creates a distinction between the service of one provider and that of another. Of course, names, terms, signs and so on may also contribute to the brand, but the service process (or service production process) has to be at the heart of service brands, because it is there that the most profound impression on the customer's view of the service is created.

Second, this definition *excludes the customer*. Brands are viewed from the marketer's point of view as something that the firm creates. Much brand development, or brand building as it is often *incorrectly* labelled, has been based on such a perspective in practice. The marketer uses a number of planned marketing communication efforts to develop a distinct brand, and the customer is expected to form an image of the brand that corresponds to the intended brand.

In reality this is of course not the case, but this view of a brand and branding is due to the normally used branding processes for physical goods, where planned marketing communication is the main instrument employed.[3] In a consumer goods context this has been a successful way of creating brands, because the good is pre-produced and already exists when the branding process starts. In reality, developing and designing the products is the first phase of a branding process, but it is seldom explicitly considered as that. The goods and their features are taken as given, and branding is thought to start from there. The goods always include the same features, and if proper market research has been done, customers like or accept these features and they correspond to the benefits the customers are looking for. A bottle or can of soft drink or a breakfast cereal cannot be developed into a successful brand if the customers do not like the taste of the soft drink or the breakfast cereal. Because in the case of goods the base for a successful brand already exists in the form of the goods themselves, the central part of the branding process automatically becomes a planned marketing communication issue using distinct communication media, such as television, newspapers, direct marketing and the Internet.

The development of social media has added a new dimension of customer influence on brands and branding. Conversations between customers and potential customers, for example on Facebook, and postings on YouTube, may have a decisive impact on customers' perceptions of brands. The tune 'United Breaks Guitars' posted on YouTube by a musician mistreated by this airline is a dramatic example of this. The Internet and mobile technologies have enabled customers to engage with, for example, hotels', restaurants' and tour operators' brands through favourable or unfavourable remarks on their websites or on those of other organizations, such as Trip Advisor. On the other hand, firms also have the potential to influence the branding process by actively using social media, and the Internet and mobile technologies.[4] This has, however, also lead to a considerable amount of fraud. Firms may make fake postings on websites, but customers also engage in fraud, for example in online auctions. The role of social media will be discussed in detail in Chapter 12.

Because a service as a process is a much less standardized base for branding, the situation changes and the importance and involvement of the customer increases dramatically. The first and often critical mistake in service branding is to consider the service process (and its functional quality) and its outcome (and the technical quality) as a given, and outside the branding process.

Finally, when working with brands and brand management one must not become too focused on branding in itself. After all, branding is only a means of doing better in a competitive situation. As Rust *et al.* point out, '*brands exist to serve (the firm's) customers*'.[5] If a firm becomes too preoccupied with branding as such, this may detract from the basic issue of developing a customer base and maintaining relationships with existing customers.[6]

BRAND IMAGE AND IDENTITY

One of the problems with the discussion of brands and branding seems to be the distinction between brand and brand image that is often made. *Brand image* is the image of the goods or service that is formed in the customer's mind. The term *brand identity* can be used as a description of the image of the brand that the marketer wants to create.[7] Keeping apart the concepts of a brand and brand image somehow gives the impression that a brand can be created and can exist without the presence of the customer.[8] According to this view, the customers form an image of a readily created brand. Following this line of thought, the misleading expression *'brand building'* has emerged. In reality, customers continuously receive inputs about the brand that is being created, and they relate to these *brand messages* on a continuous basis, to the extent that they observe them and react to them consciously and unconsciously, thus forming the brand image in their minds (compare the customers' creation of meaning in the *relationship communication model* presented in Chapter 10). This is the case with service as well as with physical goods. This can be put another way: *a brand is not first built and then perceived by the customers*. Instead, every step in the branding process, every brand message, is separately perceived by customers and together add up to a brand image, or brand for short, which is formed in their minds. As Anne Rindell points out, based on previous experiences with a firm or an offering, customers always carry with them an 'inherited' image. In brand management firms should keep this *image heritage* in mind.[9]

When including the customer in the branding process, there is no need to make a distinction between a brand and a brand image. For the customer brand is always brand image. Therefore, *the brand as a concept is always an image*. Hence, in this book when we talk about a brand, we always refer to it as an image in the minds of customers. In this way brand and brand image are synonymous.

In conclusion, the term *brand identity* can be used as a concept that describes the image of the brand that the marketer wants to create in the minds of customers. It is the goal to be achieved. A *brand* is the image that is actually formed in their minds. *Branding* is the process of creating this image.

As we have already noted in this chapter, 'brand building' is often used to mean branding. However, this is incorrect and even misleading and dangerous, because it gives the impression that the marketer can create a brand by himself. From this follows that after the brand has been 'built' it can be offered to customers. In reality, as we shall see in the following sections, the customers' role is much more active in the branding process. Whatever the marketer does, it is the customer who decides whether an intended brand is developing or not. *If anybody builds a brand, it is the customer*. As LEGO is reported to state: '*[W]e own the brand name, our customers own the brand*.'[10] The role of the marketer is to create frames for the development of a brand in the minds of customers, by providing an appropriate physical product, service process and supportive communication using various means of planned marketing communication. If the marketer has been successful in creating this branding 'frame', a brand image that corresponds to the intended brand identity is developing, otherwise it is not.

BRAND RELATIONSHIPS AND BRAND CONTACTS

When observing the customer's active role in branding, our understanding of the brand changes. It is no longer something that exists in a vacuum, something that can be transferred to customers. Rather, it is something that continuously develops and changes when the customer relates to the flow of brand messages, originating for example from employees, systems and physical product elements in the service process, from planned marketing communication, Internet websites, word of mouth and discussions in social media. In this way a *relationship* between the customer and the brand emerges and develops. *This brand relationship gives goods, services or the combination of the elements of a solution meaning in the minds of the customers.*[11] Therefore, the brand, as brand image, is the consequence of how a given customer perceives his relationship with a brand over time.

Schultz and Barnes[12] state that a brand relationship develops in a series of *brand contacts* experienced by customers, where they either experience a brand message to which they are exposed or are involved as co–producers. They define a brand contact as an image and information-bearing experience had by a customer or a potential customer, regardless of where this experience takes place or what kind of experience it is. In Figure 11.1 examples of such brand contacts are illustrated.

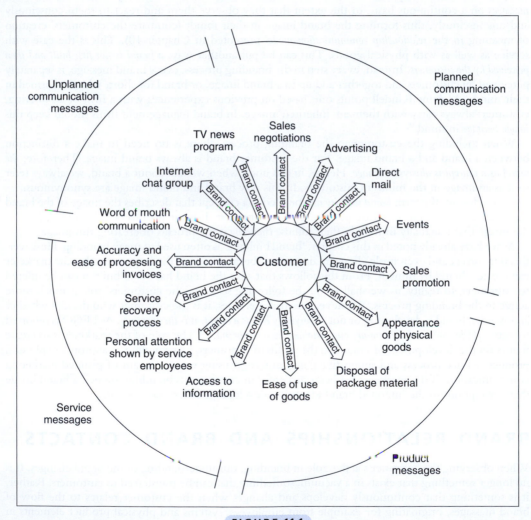

FIGURE 11.1

Brand contacts forming a brand relationship.

In the figure a number of brand contacts are depicted to illustrate the concept. Depending on the situation, the types of brand contacts experienced by a customer will differ. For a soft drink, product messages and planned communication messages dominate, although service messages and unplanned communication messages may occur in the brand relationship. The marketer may, for example, develop a waste management system to collect empty cans. This system sends a service message to consumers. For some people this message adds favourably to the brand in their minds, for others it does not. For bank service, service messages and planned communication messages dominate, but product messages, and also unplanned communication messages through word-of-mouth and conversations on social media, may occur in the brand relationship. For example, gold and platinum credit cards signal prestige, which for some consumers creates a positive extra to the bank brand in their minds. For others, such cards do not have that branding effect. In an ongoing relationship the customer experiences various kinds of brand contacts on a continuous basis.

In Figure 11.1 the time perspective is missing. In Chapters 9 and 10 we discussed the *communication process* (consisting of planned communication messages) and the *interaction process* (communicating product and service messages) and how, following a successful integration of the elements of these two processes, a relationship dialogue can be developed and maintained.

In Figure 11.2 sources of brand contacts of a retail bank is illustrated. Customers' brand relationship is based on a variety of brand contacts, indicated in the figure. Managing some well and neglecting others, thereby perhaps letting them communicate negative brand messages, creates confusion and an unfavourable brand relationship where the brand value declines. As the figure clearly demonstrates, a service brand is a function of how customers perceive a large number of communication messages originating from a variety of brand contacts, and of how they create meaning out of them.

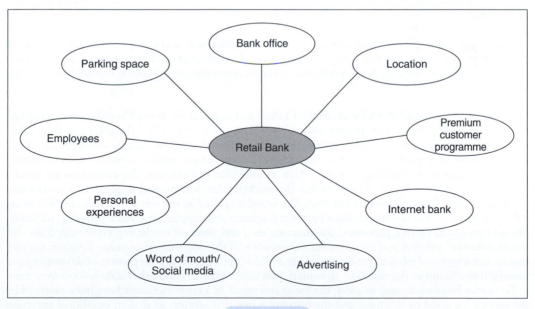

FIGURE 11.2

Retail banking: an example of brand contacts.

BRAND VALUE, BRAND EQUITY AND A RELATIONSHIP-ORIENTED DEFINITION OF A BRAND

In this context the term brand value is used as the customer's perception of how valuable a given good, service or solution is to him in comparison with other alternatives.[13] If the brand value declines over time, the customer will be more open to other solutions and more interested in communication messages from other firms. On the other hand, if the brand value increases, the likelihood that the customer will stay loyal can be expected to increase. In the same way it can be seen that brand value is important to suppliers, distributors and other network partners.

Because the brand value to customers is the basis for achieving sales and thus for creating value to the firm out of a brand, the value of brands to customers is important. However, a brand also provides value to the firm. The more customers consider a brand valuable, the more sales can be expected to be achieved. The term *brand equity* is used to describe the value of a brand to the firm. It can be defined as follows:

The differential effect that brand knowledge has on the customer response to the marketing of that brand. Equity occurs when the customer is familiar with the brand and holds some favorable, strong and unique brand associations in memory.[14]

This differential effect evolves over time and can be either positive or negative. The term *brand equity* means the value of service or a good to the firm. The higher the brand equity, the more valuable the product is to the firm.

Finally, a brand can be defined as a brand image based on the customer's perception of his brand relationship:

A brand image (often plainly called a brand) is created in continuously developing brand relationships where the customer forms a differentiating image of a physical good, a service or a solution including goods, services, information and other elements, based on all kinds of brand contacts that the customer is exposed to and engaged with.

This definition corresponds well with Ambler's short and simple definition of brand equity, according to which brand equity is *'what we carry around in our heads about the brand'*.[15] According to this definition of brand equity and the brand relationship definition above, it is meaningless to try to develop a brand without taking into account the relevant customers' and potential customers' ways of relating to and engaging with branding activities. Also, in a relationship context, the expression 'to build a brand' is inaccurate, because it implies that the marketer can initiate and implement activities that create the brand. This of course is not true. The brand is created in the mind of a customer following a flow of brand contacts – interactions between customer and supplier or service provider, including physical products, service processes, information, etc., and planned marketing communication elements, Internet websites and social media discussions – in the ongoing relationship between the two parties. *Creating brand relationships* is an accurate and descriptive term for the process of developing and maintaining a brand in the minds of customers, potential customers and other stakeholders over time.

For a true *brand relationship* to exist, the 'heart and mind' of a customer must have been captured by the service (or good or solution) and the firm providing that service, so that an emotional attraction and a state of *connectedness* have been reached. Unless this level of attraction has been created, the brand relationship is actually only a latent relationship.

If a brand relationship has been created and nurtured so that a customer feels attached to a given service and believes that this service, or any other type of offering, is different from competing service, active and favourable word of mouth can be expected to follow. The customer will feel motivated to talk about this service and make remarks on social media, and will do so. The marketer has achieved *brand involvement* from the customer.[16] Strong brand involvement means that a customer feels positively involved with the service and the service process of a given supplier or service provider. This often makes the customer himself an effective marketer of the service. A high degree of brand involvement means that a true brand relationship exists. Brand involvement can be enhanced through well-managed interactions with customers and also, for example, through brand communities on the Internet.[17]

HOW TO CREATE SERVICE BRAND RELATIONSHIPS

When branding service, two circumstances have to be kept in mind:

- There is no ready-made, standardized product to be taken as a starting point for the creation of brand relationships. Instead the service (production) processes themselves are at the heart of the branding process.

- The basis for the branding process is often the company itself and its service processes, not separate services (although firms may sometimes create service that is separable from the company itself).

In the context of physical goods the key issue in the branding process is usually planned marketing communication efforts using distinct marketing communication media (planned communication messages) implemented by the marketer, whereas the product itself is a supporting element. It should include features and benefits that the customers are interested in and relate to. Designing the product is, of course, a part of the branding process here, too, but in practice, it is often taken for granted that the product is readily designed to support the intended brand identity, and therefore it is not thought of as a part of the branding process. Marketing communication (planned communication messages) is then the most important aspect that a brand manager spends time and money on.

In the context of service, *planning and managing the service process is at the heart of the branding process*. Planned marketing communication is only a supporting element in the branding process. If the service process leads to negative brand value, planned communication efforts can seldom compensate for that. A service marketer who concentrates on planned communications as key branding activities is always at risk of failure. He may have created *brand awareness*, a knowledge of the existence of a service and perhaps also of the brand identity the firm wants to create, but this is only a promise made about the brand. This *brand promise* may not be fulfilled by the service process. If this *brand fulfilment* is missing in the mind of a customer, a brand image which corresponds to the wanted brand identity is not developing and the branding process has failed.

If the service process is not managed as part of the branding process, it may easily provide negative brand contacts which effectively counteract the planned communication efforts. As will be discussed in Chapter 15, a customer-oriented service process that consistently includes favourable brand contacts is largely dependent on the existence of a supportive service culture in the organization. If such a culture exists, the service process will effectively contribute to a planned brand identity. Thus, an intended brand emerges when the values of the customers and the values of the organization and its employees do not conflict with each other, but complement each other. In brand management the term *internal branding* is often used to describe this need to internally match the internally existing and externally wanted values of a firm as a basis for creating a favourable brand image.[19] For brand images to develop the brand identity must be marketed internally as well.[19] For many firms the internal branding issue is even more challenging than external branding.

Assuring that a firm's employees accept and embrace the firm's brand promise to its customers is also labelled *employee branding*.[20] Often this term is used interchangeably with internal branding, and also with internal marketing. Sometimes the term *employer branding* is used. One of the most important means of employee branding is a good example demonstrated by managers and supervisors. If they by their behaviour support the brand promise, customer contact employees will most likely adjust their behaviour accordingly.

The firm's intended brand, the brand identity, and the relationship of the employees to the organization is sometimes called *employee brand identification*. If a firm's employees feel alienated from the organization and its management, low brand identification by the employees is probably developing.[21] In a situation like this the employees will probably not support the promised brand through their performance as well as they would in situations where the employee brand identification is high. Employee branding and internal branding will be discussed in Chapter 14 under the rubric *internal marketing*.

In Figure 11.3 the service branding process is illustrated.[22] The starting point should be an analysis of the brand image that the firm *wants* its customers and other stakeholders, such as shareholders, financing institutions, network partners and employees, to have. This is the wanted *brand identity*. Through planned marketing communication, a *brand awareness* is then created. The purpose for doing this is *twofold*. First of all customers (and other stakeholders) are *made aware of the existence of a given service*. Secondly, provided that the planned communication efforts support and do not counteract the customers' experiences of the service firm and the service process and its outcome (the *functional*

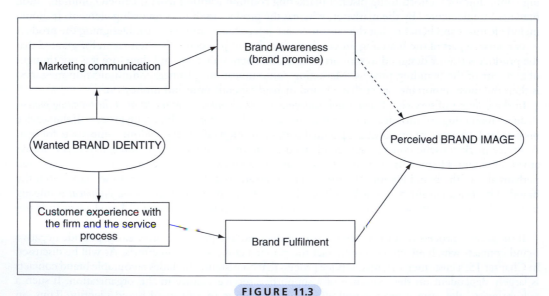

FIGURE 11.3

The service branding process.

and technical quality of the service), *these experiences are supported by the brand promise of marketing communication efforts*. In the service branding process the experiences customers have with the firm and the service process form the *brand fulfilment*. Primarily, this brand fulfilment leads to a perceived *brand image* that the customers (and other stakeholders) develop in their minds, whereas in this process the planned communication efforts are only supportive. In the figure this is indicated by the dotted line from the brand awareness box to perceived brand image.

Although the branding process illustrated in Figure 11.3 looks structured, it is only the branding process – making brand promises and creating brand-fulfilling experiences – that is manageable, the formation of the brand image is not. The brand emerges for the customer in his mind through a continuous *brand formation process*, whereas the marketer should create the right circumstances for a desired brand image to develop. Hence, if one wants to use the widely misused expression 'brand building', *it is the customers who build the brand*. The marketer can under no circumstances do that.

We can summarize the branding of service in the following way:

- The main task in the branding process is to manage the service (production) processes so that they provide the customers with positive brand contacts and corresponding brand message, which create brand fulfilment, and ultimately favourable brand relationships.

- The planned marketing communication efforts are only supportive activities in the creation of brand relationships.

- In addition, brand enabling through internal efforts (internal branding) is required to prepare and motivate employees in the organization and, for example, in distributor and other network partner organizations to actively contribute to successful brand fulfilment.

Furthermore:

- Even a good service brand concept can and will be destroyed by a malfunctioning service process.

- The service process will not contribute to the emergence of an intended brand, if the brand identity that the firm is aiming at is in conflict with the corporate culture.

- If the service process does not create a positive brand image in the minds of customers, normally this cannot be compensated for by planned marketing communication supporting a brand identity that is not manifested in the service process and in the organizational culture.

Based on the service triangle presented in Chapter 2, Brodie and his colleagues have developed a *service–brand–relationship triangle* to help researchers and practitioners alike to understand the multi-faceted aspects of branding.[23] The model is illustrated in Figure 11.4.

Leonard Berry presented a systematic view of how to 'cultivate service brands' in order to develop brand equity.[24] His suggestions, which are based on an in-depth study of a number of firms providing excellent service, include four strategic viewpoints that should be taken into account in order for the firm to cultivate brand equity and to create brand relationships that pay off:[25]

1. Be different.

2. Determine your own fame.

3. Make an emotional connection.

4. Internalize the brand.

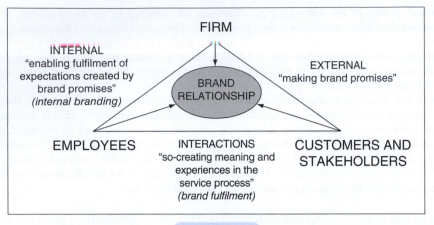

FIGURE 11.4

The service–brand–relationship triangle.
Source: Adapted from Brodie, R.J., Glynn, M.S. & Little, V., The service brand and the service-dominant logic: missing fundamental premises or the need for a stronger theory? *Marketing Theory*, **3**(3); 2006: 372. Copyright Sage Publications Ltd. Reprinted by permission.

Be different. Firms with good and recognized brands never offer their service as a commodity. It is differentiated in a way that makes it distinguishable in a way that creates an interest among current and potential customers. Such firms innovate rather than imitate existing offerings, and their service is presented in a different way compared to the competition. In this way brand relationships which differ from those of the competitors are created. In the minds of the customers of these firms, the brand is distinct and different. It creates a brand image which distinguishes the offering from competing offerings in a favourable way.

Determine your own fate. Firms with good and appreciated brands develop something that is important and valuable to their customers. Differentiating the service from that of the competitors is a necessary starting point, but it is not enough. The service must be considered valuable to the customers. If the customers do not find an offering supportive to their everyday practices, less or no value-in-use emerges for them, and no brand relationships develop. Branding is a way for firms to demonstrate their mission and organizational values to customers. Therefore, firms that determine their own fate will perform their service better than their competitors. As a consequence, good word-of-mouth is also created, and customer-to-customer discussions on social media enhance the brand.

Make an emotional connection. Good customer relationships often include an emotional bond between the firm and its customers. The customers feel an emotional connection to the firm. Service always has an emotional string attached, and therefore, firms with good brands attempt to reach beyond the mere logical and economical aspects of an offering. They develop feelings of trust, attraction, affection and closeness among their customers. Brands should reflect the customers' own core values, which often may go beyond what is purely logical from a physical or economic point of view. Of course, this does not come by itself, it has to be earned by the firm. Firms which manage to make themselves meaningful to their customers (the ultimate goal for marketing) can also make this emotional connection with them.

Internalize the brand. The brand image can be promoted by communicational efforts, such as advertising campaigns, but ultimately the brand and a brand relationship are to a large degree created in service encounters. Any kind of service encounter can either make or break the relationship. Often, but of course not always, service employees have a central role. In the service encounters employees either support or destroy the branding process. Firms with good brands invest in internalizing the brand relationship inside the organization. Therefore, firms with good brands consider internal marketing important.

In conclusion, the key to successful branding can be summarized in the following five points:

1. A brand is always an image in the minds of customers (and other stakeholders).

2. Brands cannot be built. The firm can only create favourable circumstances that facilitate the evolvement of a brand as an image in the minds of customers. ('If anyone builds the brand, it is the customer').

3. Customers' experiences with brand contacts are the key to how a brand image evolves, and managing brand contacts is at the heart of branding.

4. Marketing communication and the creation of brand awareness are only supporting activities in branding.

5. Internal branding is instrumental for successful brand management.

So far in this chapter we have discussed brand relationships and brands as brand images. In the rest of the chapter we will turn to another aspect of image, the image of a company *as an organization*. However, it should be remembered that company image and brands as images are closely related.

MANAGING COMPANY IMAGE

The image of a company or any other organization, international, nationwide or local, represents the values customers, potential customers, lost customers and other groups of people connect with the organization. The image may vary depending on which group is being considered, and may even vary between individuals. However, there is some common perception of the organization, which may be very clear and well known to some groups and unfamiliar to other groups.

Image exists on several levels. A large network organization, such as a restaurant chain, has an overall company image. In addition to this, a local organization, such as a local restaurant, has a local company image. If many outlets or offices belong to a local organization (for example, a range of car rental locations belong to the same local franchise-holder which, in turn, is part of a nationwide car rental organization), each individual outlet may very well have an image of its own, in addition to an overall local image.

Company images on different levels are interrelated. The overall image influences the perception of the local organization (i.e. the local image) and the image of an individual office or outlet to some extent depends on the local image. Moreover, the various images can affect each other in different ways. Very large customers, such as financial organizations, are more inclined to be influenced by company image. Smaller and local customers are more interested in local image. For a local firm, overall company image and local image may be virtually the same thing.

It is important from a management point of view to note that a local unit is inevitably affected by the company image of the bigger organization of which it is a part. On the other hand, service operations in many respects are local, which presents a good opportunity for a local organization to develop an image of its own among its local customers. For example, if a hotel has a bad reputation on the corporate level, a specific hotel in that chain may nevertheless develop a strong and favourable local image, which helps to attract customers.

From the company's point of view, a distinct local image may be tolerated within limits, whereas too-different local images may be harmful as far as the pursuit of a corporate strategy is concerned. If the images of local hotels are too diverse, it may be difficult to maintain a clear company image. This, of course, is a very context-specific issue.

However, again, service is local, and most customer relationships are local. Therefore, corporate-level management should not automatically try to streamline the images of all hotels. Local business environments and societies are different, and a too-streamlined local image may damage business. The issue of streamlining or differentiating local images in relation to a desired corporate image is a management concern, where the strengths of disparate local images should be compared with the need for a clear corporate image. Sometimes there is a conflict involved, sometimes not.

THE IMPORTANCE OF IMAGE

A favourable and well-known image, overall company image and/or local image, is an asset to any firm, because image has an impact on customer perceptions of the communication and operations of the firm in many respects. The role of image is at least fourfold. For the sake of simplification, no distinction between overall organizational image and local image is made here:

1. Image communicates expectations.

2. Image is a filter moderating experiences.

3. Image is a function of expectations as well as of experiences.

4. Image has an internal impact on employees as well as an external impact on customers.

First, *image communicates expectations*, together with external marketing campaigns such as advertising, direct mail and personal selling, and word-of-mouth communication. Here we will only consider customer relationships, but image works in a similar manner in relation to other stakeholders as well. Furthermore, image has an impact on expectations, and it also helps people to screen information, marketing communication as well as comments in social media and word of mouth. A positive image makes it easier for a firm to communicate effectively, and it makes people more perceptive to favourable word of mouth. Of course, a negative image has a similar effect, but in the opposite direction. A neutral or unfamiliar image may not cause any damage, but it does not increase the effectiveness of communication and word of mouth either.

Second, *image is a filter* that moderates experiences and influences the perception of the performance of the firm. Technical quality and functional quality are both seen through this filter. If the image is good, it becomes a shelter. Minor problems, even occasional more serious problems of a technical or functional quality nature, can be overlooked due to this sheltering effect. However, this only works for a short period. If such problems continuously occur, the effect of this shelter diminishes, and the company image will change. This filter has the opposite effect as well. An unfavourable image makes customers feel more dissatisfied and angrier with bad service than they would otherwise be. A neutral or unfamiliar image does not cause any harm in this respect, but it does not provide a shelter either.

Third, the *image is a function of the experiences as well as of the expectations of customers*. When customers develop expectations and experience reality in the form of the technical and functional quality of the service, the resulting perceived service quality changes the image. If the perceived service quality meets the image or exceeds it, image is reinforced or even improved. If the firm performs below image, the effect will be the opposite. Also, if the image is not clear or well known to customers, it is developed and given distinct positive or negative features by customer experience.

There is a fourth effect of image that is important to management. Image has an internal impact on employees as well as the external effect on customers. The less clear and distinct the image is, the more this may affect employee attitudes towards the organization as an employer. This, in turn, may have a negative influence on the employees' performance and thus on customer relationships and perceived quality. On the other hand, a positive image of, say, a firm with excellent service, communicates clear values internally and may thus strengthen positive attitudes towards the business among its employees. Such a firm easily attracts good employees, too.

DEVELOPING IMAGE

Frequently we hear managers say that the image of their firm is poor or unclear or old-fashioned. Far too often they try to solve this problem without analysing it and the reasons behind the unfavourable image. This, in turn, leads to poor decisions and actions. For example, cosmetic actions, such as corporate image advertising campaigns or actions involving other means of mass communication, are often turned to in situations where they will not solve the actual problem. Such actions have a limited positive effect, or in the worst case a negative effect.

There is a well-known saying that *image is reality*.[26] Therefore, image development or image improvement programmes have to be based on reality. If the company image is unknown, but the firm performs well, there is a need for planned marketing communication. But if its image is bad and the firm does not perform well, the basic problem is different. The organization faces a real problem, not only a communication problem.

First, one has to analyse why there is an image problem. Basically, there are two possible reasons: the organization is known but has a bad image; or the organization is not well known and, therefore, has an unclear image or an out-of-date image based on old customer experiences.

If the image is negative in one way or the other, *the experiences of the customers are probably bad*. There may be problems with technical and/or functional quality. In such a situation, if management calls upon an advertising agency to plan an advertising campaign offering the message that the firm is service-oriented, customer-conscious, modern or whatever the message may be, the result may be fatal. At best, the campaign will be a waste of money; however, there are cases where such actions have had much more serious consequences. A national retail chain in a European country suffered from a poorly service-oriented image. It invested extensively in a corporate advertising campaign which communicated good service, customer-conscious employees, a pleasant shopping atmosphere in its retail outlets, and so forth. In the short term, sales improved, but in the long term, sales decreased again to where they had been and even fell below this level. The organization's already bad image was further damaged.

The lesson is that because image is reality, if market communication does not fit reality, reality normally wins. An advertising campaign that is not based on reality only creates expectations that will not be fulfilled. If expectations are higher than they used to be, but reality has not changed, the perceived service quality is affected in a negative way, and the company image will be damaged.

If the image problem is a real problem, only real action will help. Real problems with the performance of the firm, its technical and/or functional quality, cause an image problem. If the poor image is to be improved, internal actions to improve the performance of the firm are needed.

If the company's image is unknown, there is a communication problem. The firm may be entering a new market, where it is unknown, or the nature of its business may lead only to sporadic customer contacts, which means that customers never develop an in-depth image of the firm based on experience. Also, the firm's reality may have changed so that it is, say, more customer-conscious and service-oriented than before, but this has not yet been fully appreciated by its customers. Therefore, the image is not yet as good as it should and realistically could be. The image will improve eventually, when enough customers become sufficiently experienced with the new reality. However, if the firm communicates this change to the market, this process will probably take less time. In these situations an image problem is really a communication problem, and improved marketing communication offers a solution.

Furthermore, it is always possible to support a company's image using various means of planned communication. The layout of websites, advertisements, brochures, packages and letterheads and the design of offices and delivery trucks may support a given image if they are in line with it. On the other hand, modern office design and advertisement layouts do not improve a firm's image if the performance of the firm is perceived as being old-fashioned and bureaucratic.

In summary, it is important to realize that image portrays what exists in reality; image is not what is communicated through planned marketing communication if the communicated image does not correspond with reality. When there is an inconsistency between real performance and communicated image, *reality wins*. The planned communication of the firm is perceived as untrustworthy, which damages image even more. If there is an image problem, management should analyse the nature of the problem thoroughly before taking action. A communication problem can and should be solved by improved communication. However, if there is a real problem, if the negative or otherwise unfavourable image is due to bad performance, the image can be improved only by internal action, the objective of which is to improve performance. Only in a second phase can planned communication be used, when the real performance-related reason for the poor image has been removed.

SUMMARY

In this chapter the issues of branding and image in service contexts were discussed. A brand develops as a brand image in the minds of customers as a result of accumulated experiences of various brand contacts. In service, the service processes, and various brand contacts, are at the heart of branding. Unlike physical products, planned marketing communication does not form a central instrument in the development of brands. Such communication can be seen as supportive activities in a branding process. If service processes do not function in a way that customers want to relate to, planned marketing communication cannot compensate for this. It was noted that customers can be understood to have brand relationships with ongoing service processes or relationships with a supplier or service provider, including ongoing interactions related to physical products, service processes, information, etc.

In the second part of the chapter the concept of image was explained. It was noted that image exists on an overall organizational level as well as on a local and branch office level. When managing an image, it is important to realize that planned communication efforts cannot improve the situation if a poor image is caused by problems in the service processes. Only actions that improve the quality of the service can improve the image.

QUESTIONS FOR DISCUSSION

1. What is a brand? What is the difference between brand, brand image and brand identity?

2. Which are the most critical aspects in the development of service brands?

3. What characterizes the branding processes of excellent service providers?

4. Identify brand contacts, analyse the brand in the minds of customers, and discuss the brand value and brand equity of a given service offering provided by your organization, or any organization.

5. How do conversations on social media and website postings impact the branding process?

6. What is the relationship between a brand and a company image?

7. What could be the reasons for a poor image? How should a poor image be improved?

8. What are the functions of a company image and a local image?

NOTES

1. Berry, L.L., Cultivating service brand equity. *Journal of the Academy of Marketing Science*, **28**(1), 2000, 128–137 and Brodie, R.J., Whittome, J.R.M. & Brush, G.J., Investigating the service brand: a customer value perspective. *Journal of Business Research*, **62**(3), 2009, 345–355.

2. Bennet, P.D., *Dictionary of Marketing Terms*, 2nd edn. Chicago, IL: American Marketing Association, 1995.

3. See, for example, Rindell, A. & Strandvik, T., Brand evolution – brands evolving in consumers' everyday life. *European Business Research*, **22**(3), 2010, 276–286 and Rindell, A. & Iglesias, O., Context and time in brand image constructions. *Journal of Organizational Change Management*, **27**(3), 2014, 756–768.

4. The role of social media, the Internet and mobile technologies in branding and various possibilities for their use in general and in service branding are discussed in de Chernatory, L., McDonald, M. & Wallace, E., *Creating Powerful Brands*, 4th edn. Oxford: Butterworth Heinemann, 2011.

5. Rust, R.T., Zeithaml, V.A. & Lemon, K.N., Customer-centered brand management. *Harvard Business Review*, **82**(Sept), 2004, 110.

6. Rust, Zeithaml & Lemon, *op. cit.*

7. Aaker, D.A. & Joachimsthaler, E., *Brand Leadership*. New York: The Free Press, 2000.

8. Rindell & Strandvik, *op. cit.*

9. Rindell, A., Image Heritage. *The Temporal Dimension in Consumers' Corporate Image Constructions*. Helsinki/Helsingfors: Hanken School of Economics, Finland, 2007. See also Rindell & Iglesias, *op. cit.*

10. See Gyrd-Jones, R.I. & Kornum, N., Managing the co-created brand: value and cultural complementarity in online and offline multi-stakeholder ecosystems. *Journal of Business Research*, **66**(9), 2013, 1484–1483, where the branding process in Lego is studied.

11. See Schultz, D.E., Barnes, B.E., Schultz, H.F. & Azzaro, M., *Building Customer-Brand Relationships*. Armonk, NJ: M.E. Sharpe, 2009.

12. Schultz & Barnes, *op. cit.*, p. 46.

13. In the literature brand value is often referred to as the value of a brand to a firm. See, for example, Melo, T & Galan, J.I., Effects of corporate social responsibility on brand value. *Journal of Brand Management*, **18**(6), 2011, 423–437.

14. Keller, K.L., Conceptualizing, measuring and managing customer-based brand equity. *Journal of Marketing*, **57**(Jan), 1993, 1–22. See also Keller, K.L., *Strategic Brand Management: Building, Measuring and Managing Brand Equity*, 2nd edn. Englewood Cliffs, NJ: Prentice-Hall, 2003. However, sometimes brand equity is also related to the value for customers of a brand. See, for example, Aaker, D.A., *Managing Brand Equity: Capitalizing on the Value of a Brand Name*. New York: The Free Press, 1991, where brand equity is defined as 'the set of assets (and liabilities) linked to a brand's name and symbol that adds (or subtracts from) the value provided by a product or service to a firm *and/or that firm's customers*' (p. 16; emphasis added).

15. Ambler, T., *Marketing and the Bottom Line: The New Metrics of Corporate Wealth*. London: Financial Times/Prentice-Hall, 2000, p. 14.

16. See Lindberg-Repo, K. & Grönroos, C., Word-of-mouth referrals in the domain of relationship marketing. *Australasian Marketing Journal*, **7**(1), 1999, 109–117. See also Andersen, P.H., Relationship marketing and brand involvement through web-enhanced brand communities: the case of Coloplast. *Industrial Marketing Management*, **34**(1), 2005, 39–51, where the author discusses the evolvement of brand involvement on the Internet.

17. See Andersen, *op. cit.*

18. See Schultz, M. & de Chernatony, L., The challenges of corporate branding. *Corporate Reputation Review*, **5**(2–3), 2002, 105–112.

19. Mitchell, C., Selling the brand inside. *Harvard Business Review*, **80**(Jan), 2002, 99–106.

20. King, C. & Grace, D., Examining the antecedents of positive employee brand-related attitudes and behaviours. *European Journal of Marketing*, **46**(3–4), 2012, 469–488. See also Miles, S.J. &

Mangold, W.G., Positioning Southwest Airlines through employee branding. *Business Horizons*, **46**(6), 2005, 535–545, and, for example, Kimpakorn, N. & Tocquer, G., Service brand equity and employee brand commitment. *Journal of Services Marketing*, **24**(5), 2010, 378–388, and Schlager, T, Bodderas, M, Maas, P. & Cachelin, J.L., The influence of employer brand on employee attitudes relevant for service branding: an empirical investigation. *Journal of Services Marketing*, **25**(7), 2011, 497–508.

21. See Hurrell, S.A. & Scholarios, D., 'The people make the brand': reducing social skills gaps through person-brand fit and human resource management practices. *Journal of Service Research*, **17**(1), 2014, 54–67, and Löhndorf, B. & Diamantopoulos, A., Internal branding: social identity and social exchange perspectives on turning employees into brand champions. *Journal of Service Research*, **17**(3), 2014, 310–325.

22. See Berry, L.L., *Discovering the Soul of Service*. New York: The Free Press, 1999, p. 200, where a service brand meaning model illustrating a similar process is presented.

23. Brodie, R.J., Glynn, M.S. & Little, V., Brands and relationships and the service dominant logic. *Marketing Theory*, **3**(3), 2006, 363–379.

24. Berry, *op. cit.*

25. Berry, 1999, *op. cit.* See also Berry, 2000, *op. cit.*

26. See Bernstein, D., *Company Image & Reality*. Eastbourne: Holt, Rinehart and Winston, 1985.

FURTHER READING

Aaker, D.A. (1991) *Managing Brand Equity: Capitalizing on the Value of a Brand Name*. New York: The Free Press.

Aaker, D.A. (1996) *Building Strong Brands*. New York: The Free Press.

Aaker, D.A. & Joachimsthaler, E. (2000) *Brand Leadership*. New York: The Free Press.

Ambler, T. (2000) *Marketing and the Bottom Line: The New Metrics of Corporate Wealth*. London: Financial Times/Prentice-Hall.

Andersen, P.H. (2005) Relationship marketing and brand involvement through web-enhanced brand communities: the case of Coloplast. *Industrial Marketing Management*, **34**(1), 39–51.

Bennet, P.D. (1995) *Dictionary of Marketing Terms*, 2nd edn. Chicago, IL: American Marketing Association.

Bernstein, D. (1985) *Company Image & Reality*. Eastbourne: Holt, Rinehart and Winston.

Berry, L.L. (1999) *Discovering the Soul of Service*. New York: The Free Press.

Berry, L.L. (2000) Cultivating service brand equity. *Journal of the Academy of Marketing Science*, **28**(1), 128–137.

Brodie, R.J., Glynn, M.S. & Little, V. (2006) The service brand and the service-dominant logic: missing fundamental premises or the need for a stronger theory? *Marketing Theory*, **6**(3), 363–379.

Brodie, R.J., Whittome, J.R.M. & Brush, G.J. (2009) Investigating the service brand: a customer value perspective. *Journal of Business Research*, **62**(3), 345–355.

Calonius, H. (1986) A market behaviour framework. In Möller, K. & Paltschik, M. (eds), *Contemporary Research in Marketing. Proceedings from the XV Annual Conference of the European Marketing Academy*. Helsinki: Helsinki School of Economics and Hanken Swedish School of Economics, Finland, pp. 515–524.

de Chernatory, L., McDonald, M. & Wallace, E. (2011) *Creating Powerful Brands*, 4th edn. Oxford: Butterworth Heinemann.

Duncan, T. & Moriarty, S. (1997) *Driving Brand Value*. New York: McGraw-Hill.

Gyrd-Jones, R.I. & Kornum, N. (2013) Managing the co-created brand: value and cultural complementarity in online and offline multi-stakeholder ecosystems. *Journal of Business Research*, **66**(9), 1484–1483.

Hurrell, S.A. & Scholarios, D. (2014) 'The people make the brand': reducing social skills gaps through person-brand fit and human resource management practices. *Journal of Service Research*, **17**(1), 54–67.

Keller, K.L. (1993) Conceptualizing, measuring and managing customer-based brand equity. *Journal of Marketing*, **57**(Jan), 1–22.

Keller, K.L. (2003) *Strategic Brand Management: Building, Measuring and Managing Brand Equity*, 2nd edn. Englewood Cliffs, NJ: Prentice-Hall.

Kimpakorn, N. & Tocquer, G. (2010) Service brand equity and employee brand commitment. *Journal of Services Marketing*, **24**(5), 378–388.

King, C. & Grace, D. (2012) Examining the antecedents of positive employee brand-related attitudes and behaviours. *European Journal of Marketing*, **46**(3–4), 469–488.

Lindberg Repo, K. & Grönroos, C. (1999) Word of mouth referrals in the domain of relationship marketing. *Australasian Marketing Journal*, **7**(1), 109–117.

Löhndorf, B. & Diamantopoulos, A. (2014) Internal branding: social identity and social exchange perspectives on turning employees into brand champions. *Journal of Service Research*, **17**(3), 310–325.

Melo, T & Galan, J.I. (2011) Effects of corporate social responsibility on brand value. *Journal of Brand Management*, **18**(6), 423–437.

Miles, S.J. & Mangold, W.G. (2005) Positioning Southwest Airlines through employee branding. *Business Horizons*, **46**(6), 535–545.

Mitchell, C. (2002) Selling the brand inside. *Harvard Business Review*, **80**(Jan), 99–106.

Rindell, A. (2007) *Image Heritage. the Temporal Dimension in Consumers' Corporate Image Constructions*. Helsinki/Helsingfors: Hanken School of Economics, Finland, 2007.

Rindell, A. & Iglesias, O. (2014) Context and time in brand image constructions. *Journal of Organizational Change Management*, **27**(3), 756–768.

Rindell, A. & Strandvik, T. (2010) Brand evolution – brands evolving in consumers' everyday life. *European Business Research*, **22**(3), 276–286.

Rust, R.T., Zeithaml, V.A. & Lemon, K.N. (2004) Customer-centered brand management. *Harvard Business Review*, **82**(Sept), 110–118.

Schlager, T, Bodderas, M, Maas, P. & Cachelin, J.L. (2011) The influence of employer brand on employee attitudes relevant for service branding: an empirical investigation. *Journal of Services Marketing*, **25**(7), 497–508.

Schultz, D.E., Barnes, B.E., Schultz, H.F. & Azzaro, M. 2009, *Building Customer-Brand Relationships*. Armonk, NJ: M.E. Sharpe.

Schultz, M. & de Chernatony, L. (2002) The challenges of corporate branding. *Corporate Reputation Review*, **5**(2–3), 105–112.

CHAPTER 12
SOCIAL MEDIA IN SERVICE MANAGEMENT AND MARKETING

Written by Johanna Gummerus

> *In social media, a firm is just as good as its customers think it is – the truth leaks out one way or another.*

INTRODUCTION

This chapter looks at the role of social media in service management and marketing. Also, different types of social media are discussed. Then, the chapter presents the social media communication circle, after which the influence of social media on service marketing and management will be explained. After reading the chapter the reader should know what kinds of social media there are, how they function, and how firms can adapt their marketing to various social media.

BACKGROUND TO SOCIAL MEDIA

Social media refer to all those new online media that allow actors to generate and share content with others on a large scale. The content can be text, pictures, video, or audio. The social media platforms enable and encourage sharing, meaning that the content spreads fast to a wide online audience, causing an enormous ripple effect. In essence, then, social media constitute a new way with which people connect to each other.

From a marketing perspective, the most important aspect of social media is their *pervasiveness and influence in people's lives*. Most people are today connected to some social media, be it social networking sites[1] such as LinkedIn and Facebook, microblogging services such as Twitter, communication apps such as WhatsApp and Kik, content sharing communities such as YouTube, SlideShare, Instagram and Pinterest, crowd sourcing or crowd funding platforms,[2] different online forums or blogs, or virtual worlds such as Second Life or Habbo Hotel. As consumers are continuously connected to different social media, they share with others their everyday life, including their interactions and experiences with firms. Because of the mass sharing of information, consumers are also better informed and thereby they become more empowered[3] – they can more readily find and evaluate service providers, brands, or products. Also, because consumers are increasingly able to learn from each other, they may question expert opinions based on the information they have accessed online. The pervasiveness and continuous mass sharing of experiences in social media further leads to transparency of firm actions, as both positive and negative firm activities spread out far quicker and to a wider audience than before, and many firms perceive an increasing lack of control of what is being said about them. Quite frequently, customer stories spread from social media to traditional media e.g. through journalists who skim through social media content to find appealing stories.

Another important aspect relates to the content that is created and shared by people in social media, the *user generated content (UGC)*, which refers to the content that is created voluntarily by ordinary users and not by professionals. This content can vary from a simple grade given for a product, brand or firm on a review site to complex information or creative efforts such as music, videos or virtual items. A single consumer can, in social media, get his voice heard by millions of listeners. Customers often create content that in one way or another relates to companies. It may be positive, for example praise for a company or a brand, or negative, such as sharing a bad experience. The social media review sites such as YELP! (www.yelp.com) collect and aggregate consumer opinions and experiences, and as they offer a continuously updated pool of information, these assessments influence customer decision-making and behaviour. Review sites may also act as middlemen as TripAdvisor does (www.tripadvisor.com), or concentrate on assessing firms from an employee's viewpoint, as done at Glassdoor (www.glassdoor.com). Importantly, customers find the content generated by other users more trustworthy and interesting than the content firms put online.[4] In particular more creative content, such as music, spreads quickly in social media. The Disney film *Frozen*, for example, has inspired video bloggers to create videos on how to get the perfect look of the main characters in the film, and these can be found on, for example, YouTube, where other users can grade and comment on them. The viewer numbers and grades then influence how high up the content appears on the site, emphasizing popular content. Another well-known example is that of the Canadian country singer Dave Carroll, whose guitar was damaged when he flew with United Airlines. After almost a year-long battle to get the damages covered, the airline turned down Carroll's request for compensation. The upset musician then wrote a song about his experiences and put it on YouTube, from where it spread virally to millions of viewers and was caught up by journalists and taken up in other media.[5] The video resonated with customers who had been maltreated by United and other big airlines, and led to United Airlines share prices plunging.[6]. Because of the video, Carroll became a popular breakfast show guest and has toured talking about airline quality, written a book about his experiences entitled *United Breaks Guitars*, and finished a trilogy of songs about his United Airlines experience. The side effect of UGC is that because of the astounding amount of content that competes with firm-generated content, gaining visibility in social media may be challenging.

A third important aspect of social media is that *customers tend to opt-in in these media*, that is, they choose and become engaged in sub-groups within different social media that by default involve a particular interest. Such sub-groups may, for example, be brand sites on Facebook, groups in LinkedIn, blogs specializing in different topics, YouTube channels, pinned interests, or online discussion fora. Furthermore, the users who have opted-in tend to be experts or highly involved in the topic. This means that many social media platforms enable firms to reach particular niche segments of customers who have signalled that they are interested and willing to learn more about a particular topic.

Fourthly, social media *offer a platform where firms and customers may interact*. Consequently, manufacturers and suppliers who have not necessarily traditionally had any direct contact with end customers are able to listen to and engage in dialogues with the end customers in social media. One such case is the Finnish dairy company Valio, that has used social media to develop new protein-rich and low-fat quark products together with the weightlifting community.[7] Similarly, social media make consumer opinions more visible for companies, as they are able to monitor what is said about them and respond directly to customers.

Fifthly, social media may *have a direct influence on the service experience during consumption*. Tweeting with others while watching a TV show or being engaged in any service process has the potential to change both the collective service experience and the experience of the individual consumer. Sharing impressions and thoughts about the service between like-minded persons changes the service experience. For example, the experience of a TV show may, through this use, change considerably from what was intended by the producer. In this way social media lifts the service experience to a new level, and offers risks and opportunities for the service provider. Kai Huotari, who has studied the impact of social media on service experiences, calls this phenomenon *experientializing*.[8] An interesting and challenging aspect of experientializing is the fact that it takes place outside the direct reach of the service provider.

Finally, social media space is fast-moving and therefore requires a totally *new type of communication from companies*. Consequently, in many cases the most efficient service and relationship-building activities require the ability to quickly react to unplanned activities taking place. One such instance happened during the 2013 Super Bowl power blackout, when Oreo biscuits were quick to tweet 'You can still dunk in the dark', referring to dunking the biscuit to liquid in order to enjoy it. This quick, snappy remark raised a wave of positive reactions among the public, journalists and marketing professionals.[9] The main winning factor was not the ingeniousness of the message, but rather the quick reaction to the disruption. Thus, the companies that are agile in the social media environment are the ones most likely to benefit from them.

Next, we will discuss the different social media types.

DIFFERENT TYPES OF SOCIAL MEDIA

Social media can be understood by looking at the different characteristics they have. The early versions of social media, virtual communities, referred to groups of people who interacted with each other because they were either enthusiastic or knowledgeable about something. Consequently, virtual communities were divided based on whether the users focused on information exchange or on social interaction, and whether the interactions were freely accessible by everybody or took place within a closed circle of people.[10] Of late, differentiations between information exchange and social interaction are difficult to make, because the information exchange itself has become a social activity.

More recently, another way to understand how the social media platforms differ has been introduced, based on media content, and the role of the participant. Media content concerns the social presence/media richness. Social presence/media richness reflects the medium's ability to provide information to decrease uncertainty and replicate real-life sensory cues.[11] The second aspect that takes up the role of the participant refers to the degree of self-presentation/self-disclosure to which the participants engage in divulging personal information.[12] Virtual worlds such as Second Life or Habbo Hotel are examples of social media with high self-presentation/self-disclosure, because people are able to create avatars that impersonate them. The virtual world participants are able to interact with others with the help of the avatars, expressing their personality with clothing, use of words, and different symbols that represent their interests. Virtual worlds are also high in social presence/media richness because the verbal and visual cues ameliorate ambiguity. If self-disclosure is high, the interactions within the media are more personal and consumers may find it easier to connect with each other, and with the firm.

Another way of understanding social media is through the *half-life and the depth of information*. The half-life of information refers to how long the information is available[13] on the screen, and social media differ in this aspect. On Kik for example, the messages come up and disappear. Facebook postings are more long-lived as they can be found on the news feed or the person's or firm's site that posted them. The depth of information in turn means how rich, numerous, and diverse the viewpoints presented on a topic are. It can vary between shallow information depth in, for example, blogs that, although they may be rich, represent mainly one person's (the blogger's) perspective and are thus classified as shallow, to the deep information presented in specialized communities that aggregate several people's views.

A challenge in many social media applications is that information emerges and then disappears in the flow of new posts. Therefore, customers may be exposed to firm postings to different degrees, some noticing all of them, some only few and some none. Consequently, firms need to understand social media in terms of media richness, participant self-presentation/self-disclosure, information depth and information longevity.

COMPANY PARTICIPATION IN SOCIAL MEDIA

In order to interact with potential, current and past customers, companies can either establish their own social media platforms, such as corporate blogs or company-sponsored communities, or employ external social media platforms.[14] Company-owned virtual communities are valuable because the company is able to set the rules for the community, direct activities and gather data from the users. However, setting up own communities may be costly, and what is even more crucial, it may be difficult to gain visibility and attract participants to them.

Companies may also choose to tap into the extant social media platforms that already have a wide audience. Most social media platforms offer firms the opportunity to establish company sites, or include their own content on the platform. If companies establish presence in external social media sites, they have to follow the rules and regulations of the platform owner. Planning activities may however be challenging because the social media platform owners may change the rules after innovative marketing campaigns. For example, the Swedish furniture company IKEA launched a Facebook campaign to promote their new store in Malmo. During the campaign, the store manager posted, within a two-week period, twelve pictures of IKEA catalogue-type photos on Facebook. On the photos, the customers could tag[15] pieces of furniture. Whoever tagged the furniture first would win it. The marketing campaign received a huge amount of 'likes' and spread among people who recommended the campaign to their peers. However, Facebook soon banned these types of campaigns.

To illustrate the contingency of company participation in social media, Figure 12.1 depicts how company–customer interaction takes place in social media.

Figure 12.1 shows how customer activities, company activities, and social media platforms together create the sphere where customer–company interactions take place in social media. The three areas are interdependent. Both firm and customer activities are dependent on the social media platform. For example, Twitter allows only 160 characters in the messages sent, which forces users to compress messages and use hashtags (# and the connecting word) to link their message to other messages where the word that has been tagged is used. The customer activities of creating, sharing and consuming also influence what firms are able to do. For example, customers' tendency to share company-related content defines how easy and costly it is to spread messages in social media. Customers may also have differing expectations about how firms are allowed to act in different social media. In general, social media that are not owned by the company are mainly meant for customer-to-customer interaction,[16]

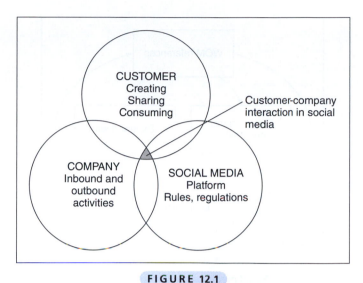

FIGURE 12.1

Customer–company interaction in social media.

and consumers may not be positively attuned to company participation. Customers generally tend to think that firms should openly admit if they are behind marketing messages. Unfortunately, not all companies do this. Companies may seed content and comments to enhance information spreading among customers, evoke interest among them, or encourage discussions without telling that they are behind this.

Because of the special media characteristics and the interdependence between company and customer activities, social media impact the traditional communication circle. This will be discussed next with the help of the social media communication circle.

SOCIAL MEDIA COMMUNICATION CIRCLE

Social media challenge the traditional communication circle, for several reasons: the communication speeds up, the customers may already during the service encounter share their experiences with others and the firm, and the customers may seek social support during the encounter. For example, a customer may, while waiting to be seated in a restaurant or during a meal, comment on the service or take photos of the food and the interior, and share them in social media. Figure 12.2 depicts the social media communication circle that is modified from the traditional communication circle.

The basic elements of the social media communication circle are the same as in the traditional communication circle: customer expectations, interactions, experiences, and word of mouth (WOM). In the traditional communication circle, expectations, interactions, experiences, and WOM follow each other, and the circle closes as the WOM influences expectations. However, in social media, as the customer is constantly connected to social media, the interactions and WOM may take place simultaneously. Because of this, as the concept of experientializing mentioned earlier demonstrates, WOM may even become a part of the interaction and the final service experience. For example, a

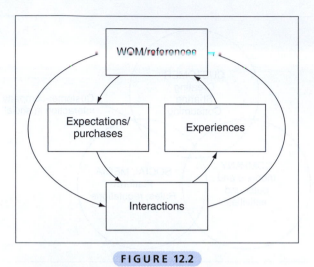

FIGURE 12.2

Social media communication circle.

customer may go to a shop to buy a new outfit for a family occasion and, while in the shop, take a photo of the dress and send it to her WhatsApp list to receive feedback from family members, and depending on the response, ending up buying the dress or not. The response may also shape how the customer experiences the whole shopping spree as either immensely humiliating ('How could you even consider that horrible rag?') or as delightful ('Where on earth did you find that lovely outfit!'). Consequently, the WOM and the service interaction become intertwined and interdependent when social media communication is involved.

THE INFLUENCE OF SOCIAL MEDIA ON SERVICE MARKETING

A number of aspects in service management and relationships become highlighted due to social media.

First of all, as both positive and negative experiences of customers will spread, the importance of making, enabling and keeping promises is accentuated. Firms must make sure that the promises they make are really kept and fulfilled, because any problems in service quality will be communicated quickly in the social media space. This means that it is crucial to prevent the negative word of mouth from emerging by removing the causes for dissatisfaction. Essentially, firms need to acknowledge even more than before that customer-to-customer communications are beyond their control. In fact, many brands have hate websites that collect negative customer experiences.[17] The existence of such communities and of any type of word of mouth can also be seen as a positive sign – the brand evokes feelings and is not within customers' sphere of indifference, which may be far more dangerous. The role of part-time marketers[18] in particular becomes pivotal, as they influence customer satisfaction directly and will be referred to in online reviews. Consequently, social media also influence how firms should organize their activities internally. The personnel need to have a clear understanding of what is expected of them, that is, role divisions, such as who is responsible; how quickly and often to respond; and how to deal with different types of issues that arise online. It is important that the personnel are allowed to show their personality in their communications with customers. All in all, the firm will have to rely on more direct communication, showing authenticity and identity. Thus, firms should encourage the employees to use their own genuine, personal interaction style.

Secondly, the agility of the social media landscape has consequences for firms. Since consumers are connected to social media, firms are able to instantaneously serve their customers. This is particularly useful in cases where unexpected situations arise, or when companies need to access customers quickly. In emergencies, when company web pages or contact centres would not manage the large number of customer contacts, different social media can be utilized to communicate with customers, as they can be updated quickly and are technically fit for mass communication. Also, through social media, marketers may find possibilities for reacting quickly to other more mundane real-life events and engage the audience in a dialogue, for example take part in conversations taking place in the general press. The instantaneous visibility of the customers' service experiences also means that firms can monitor their service performance online in real time. With the help of online monitoring tools and feedback systems, firms can reach and respond instantly to negative customer feedback, and identify and correct flaws in service processes. For example, the Finnish airline company Finnair screens customers' Twitter postings to recognize glitches in customer flight experiences, after which they analyse the underlying causes of these service failures and, when applicable, correct internal service processes. Firms may also find it easier to manage the perishability of face-to-face services by promoting the service in social media at times when the service would otherwise go unsold, for example during off-season or if demand otherwise fluctuates.

Thirdly, the new types of communications in social media including audio, video, and pictures have several implications for the communication between customers and between customers and the firm. Customers are able to provide evidence in the form of pictures and video to back up any claims they make about the firm. The social media interactions that are supported by visual evidence are more tangible than traditional word of mouth that consists mostly of verbally communicated stories. Consequently, experience services that the customer is only able to evaluate after consumption[19] may become higher in search qualities (aspects that can be evaluated before consumption). Also, this content is stored and stays online, to be found even years after the initial incident. On the one hand, firms are challenged by heightened requirements for quality management since deviations from acceptable levels of quality have even more powerful consequences due to widely spreading electronic word of mouth. On the other hand, the firms excelling in customer service will reap benefits from positive reviews and customer experiences.

Fourthly, social media also make it possible for customers to show their engagement to the firm or brand in multifaceted ways that entail both purchase and non-purchase behaviour.[20] Customer engagement captures customers' positive firm-related behaviours. It includes both consumer-to-firm interactions and consumer-to-consumer communications about the firm or the brand. Engagement behaviours may include discussing, commenting, information searching and taking part in opinion polls, as well as communicating through brand communities, blogging and other social media. When customers engage in different activities, they also derive different benefits. The benefits that firms try to create with customers may be economic (for example through lotteries, discounts), entertainment-related (for example games and videos), and social benefits (for example recognition, discussions with peers).[21] In many cases, customers engage in multiple behaviours. Customer community engagement behaviours such as content liking, reading and commenting on messages influence the benefits that customers receive from their engagement with the community. Companies should, however, be careful if they focus on economic benefits such as bonuses or lotteries, because they may not influence customer satisfaction or loyalty in a positive way. Rather, they may attract bargain-hunters who seek out cheap offers but have no intention of purchasing for full price. Also, people may become accustomed to low prices, waiting for the next offer and only buying then.

Fifthly, firms need to reconsider the division of work and whether to employ the 'wisdom of the crowds',[22] particularly when it comes to service innovation. In innovation work, companies may employ customers in several areas – externalizing activities may pay off in idea generation, developing the ideas further, or commercializing them.[23] These types of activities, where the company views innovation work more broadly in a network setting, are labelled 'open innovation'. Open innovation includes both importing innovative ideas into the company and exporting intellectual capital.[24] Crowdsourcing can extend from innovation work to any redivision of labour, so that a company can renegotiate the roles taken by its customers and other interest groups. Although customers often happily engage in service development work, the company needs to make sure that the innovation process is perceived as being fair and transparent, and that the customers are satisfied with the innovation outcome.[25] In some cases, the customer involvement may be rather straightforward, such as inviting customers to test a new concept or become brand ambassadors by displaying them while using the brand. For example, the Finnish online yoga service provider Yoogaia (www.yoogaia.com) has been using Facebook for developing and launching its service.

Sixthly, as in other media, companies need to connect with customers and support them in their daily activities, but the particularity of social media is that companies need to consider why customers would engage in word of mouth or act as advocates online. For example, companies who wish to encourage private bloggers to spread word of mouth about the company need to consider why such individuals blog in the first place. Some reasons include blogging because the activity itself is rewarding, because bloggers feel that the content they produce is valuable, and because of social connectivity to the readers of the blog.[26] Consequently, if the company is able to help the blogger to reach such benefits, for example by helping them to get exclusive content, improve their blogging skills, or help them in communicating with the readers, the blogger is more likely to accept collaboration. In the same manner, end customers value company social media activities that help them to achieve their own goals, such as to receive recognition, to be entertained, or to acquire economic benefits.[27] In some cases, such as when involving the firm's fans, the task may be quite straightforward – fans are likely to accept and share content further in their network. For example, many sports fan clubs share information about coming events, players or league news, allow fans to post content, promote events, and arrange contests for fans.

Finally, it is noteworthy that companies have different degrees of closeness to the customers. For example, companies that typically use third-party suppliers, such as manufacturers of consumer goods, have in social media a direct channel through which they can communicate with the end customers. However, their challenge, as they do not own the customer data, is to figure out whether social media marketing campaigns in fact have an effect on customer behaviour or not. The providers of experiential services that are not typically able to be evaluated beforehand, such as travel, music, or theatre, can encourage customers to spread word of mouth and thus make the service more appealing for potential clients. Similarly, services that require physical contact such as car repair, health care or hairdressers, can encourage the customers to share their experiences to reduce potential customers' risk perceptions. Manufacturers of products that require long production processes, particularly if they have highly-involved customers, may again interact with customers and make the product distinguishable for them by opening up the firm-internal production processes. Such an approach would mean that the provider invites the customers to get acquainted with the firm's daily activities.

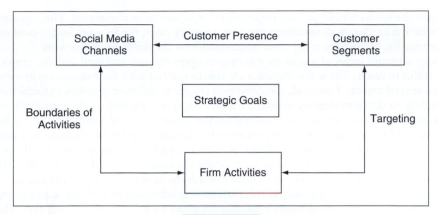

FIGURE 12.3

Company social media strategy triangle.

FIRM ACTIVITIES IN SOCIAL MEDIA

Figure 12.3 demonstrates how firms should plan their social media activities.

The model consists of four parts: strategic goals that define what should be achieved, the choice of the social media channels, the customer segments that one wishes to reach, and the firm activities that are undertaken to reach the strategic goals. These four parts are all interdependent and interlinked with the environment. For example, the choice of appropriate strategy is dependent on the customer market that is targeted, and therefore different markets may have different strategic goals. For example, a firm that has only just entered a new market will likely aim for becoming more well known, whereas an established player on the market will more likely be interested in serving current customers or learning from them. The same logic applies for different sub-markets. For example, a company may have as a strategic goal branding their hotel chain as the most appealing option for business travellers.

Firms should, if they decide to participate in social media, start by setting their strategic goals. Setting measureable goals is important, because this allows the follow-up of how well different actions lead to desired results. Also, well-defined goals allow the selection of customer segments that will be targeted, the choice of appropriate tactics, and the measurement of success/failure.

General strategic goals for social media comprise increasing brand awareness, serving customers, generating traffic or profits, and collecting customer inputs. Brand awareness is important, because it means that the company is within the customer's consideration set, and it is particularly relevant to reach in new markets where the company is poorly known. Brand awareness can be evaluated with relatively simple measures such as the number of content viewers, and how these evolve over time. Serving customers in social media offers an important opportunity to engage in dialogue with customers and support them before, after, and during service use. Increasing traffic to the company website is perhaps the most straightforward goal, because it can be defined and measured effectively. Collecting customer inputs or 'listening in' to understand customers better is an important goal. However, this goal is difficult to measure, as it not only refers to noticing customer inputs but also learning from and acting upon them.

The social media channel choice is closely interlinked with the type of users that they have and the type of company activities that they enable. Social media vary in terms of who the consumers are that use them; how widely they are used; what type of content is published and shared; the consumer activities that the media enable; and the degree of involvement from companies. The company has to consider where it can reach its customers the best. In many cases, media agencies are used to choose appropriate media, but the company must understand how the different media work.

Company activities in social media are contingent upon the channel used and the customers the company wants to reach. The way companies are able to interact with their customers in social media depends on several aspects. First of all, the customers engage in different activities in social media, and may be willing to different degrees to interact with companies. Notably, only a minority of people create content, but their contribution is central for the vitality of social media, and it can become a form of viral marketing when customers promote the company and/or its offerings. For this reason, it is important to encourage and acknowledge customer content creation. It should be kept in mind that for each person that contributes, there are typically ten people who lurk, that is, follow the social media content. These lurkers may be just as loyal towards the brand as the active participants.[28] Thus, it is dangerous to assume that it is only worth maintaining relationships with the active participants.

From a firm perspective, social media platforms are often tricky because they are typically owned by a third party that sets rules and regulates what is possible. The third parties also charge for the use of the social media space, making this medium costly. The companies often differentiate between earned media, which is essentially non-paid visibility, and paid media, which refers to paid visibility. In social media, although most word of mouth is organic (that is, stems from the participant interest and spreads around on its own), firms may need to seed content and pay for initial visibility.

One of the greatest challenges in social media is the measurement of outcomes. One central question is to what degree firms can differentiate between traditional marketing, communication, and customer service, and often the difficulty is that in social media, all these three areas come together.[29]

CASE STUDY

FINNAIR IN SOCIAL MEDIA

The Finnish airline company, Finnair, uses social media to support marketing, communication, and customer service activities. Finnair has been actively using social media for its strategic goals of increasing brand awareness, listening to customers, serving customers, and supporting sales. One challenge at Finnair has been that the roles of marketing, communications and customer service become blurred. Traditionally, marketing has been more campaign-driven and interested in measurable short-term results, whereas the communications department has aimed at increasing earned media, in other words creating positive word of mouth. Nevertheless, in social media the different departments need to be aligned. For example, the communications department will need the marketing department's support in spreading the content that they create.

At Finnair, the role of employees has been emphasized as content creators in social media. The Finnair policy is that all employees are allowed to produce content in social media, and the personnel are increasingly seen as brand ambassadors. For example, Finnair has launched an internal campaign of becoming 'the most tweeting airline company in the world', where Finnair employees are encouraged to tweet about their daily work.

A long-term example of Finnair's social media activities is the Quality Hunters programme, which started as a public relations campaign but has evolved into a service development programme. The idea with Quality Hunters originally, in 2010, was that four people at Finnair were selected to travel across the world and blog about what constitutes quality in the travel industry and how it could be improved. The Finnair customers could then vote for their favourite improvement ideas and at the end, the most successful idea was selected based on customer ratings. Subsequently, the campaign has developed into a community-based service development project where customers are able to participate in service development through, for example, workshops.

In social media, the company is able to create mechanisms that enable customers to talk about and to the company. However, even social media success relies on the core business performance: as Aku (Anna-Kaisa) Varamäki, Finnair's Social Media Manager states: 'Good customer service is the best marketing there is.'

SUMMARY

In this chapter, we first discussed what characterizes social media. Then, the social media communication circle was described, showing how customer–company interactions and word of mouth become entangled and take place simultaneously, influencing each other. Finally, a company social media strategy triangle was presented, depicting how strategy, social media channel choice, customer segments and firm activities are interrelated.

QUESTIONS FOR DISCUSSION

1. What characterizes social media in comparison to other service channels?

2. How does customer–firm interaction change if the customer uses social media during the service encounter?

3. Which aspects should a manager consider while choosing social media channels?

4. Should firms always engage in social media, regardless of their offering, size, customers, or market contingencies?

5. Discuss the fit of different social media channels to reach different strategic goals.

6. Discuss the pros and cons of social media for different types of companies.

NOTES

1. According to Boyd and Ellison (2007), social networking sites are sites that 'allow individuals to (1) construct a public or semi-public profile within a bounded system, (2) articulate a list of other users with whom they share a connection, and (3) view and traverse their list of connections and those made by others within the system'. Boyd, D.M., & Ellison, N.B. (2007) Social network sites: definition, history, and scholarship. *Journal of Computer-Mediated Communication*, **13**. Retrieved from http://jcmc.indiana.edu/vol13/issue1/boyd.ellison.html

2. Crowdsourcing entails the engagement of large numbers of individuals to conduct tasks (Howe, 2008), whereas crowd funding refers to the collective actions of people within a network to gather money for a purpose that other people or organizations have defined (Ordanini, 2009). Howe, J. (2008). *Crowdsourcing: Why the Power of the Crowd is Driving the Future of Business*, New York: Random House. Ordanini, A. (2009). Crowd funding: customers as investors. *The Wall Street Journal*, 23 March, 3.

3. Kucuk, U.S., & Krishnamurthy, S. (2007) An analysis of consumer power on the Internet. *Technovation*, **27**, 47–56.

4. Lawrence, B., Fournier, S. and Brunel, F. (2013) When companies don't make the ad: a multi-method inquiry into the differential effectiveness of consumer-generated advertising, *Journal of Advertising*, **42**, 292–307.

5. http://www.theguardian.com/world/2009/jul/23/united-airlines-guitar-dave-carroll

6. http://www.dailymail.co.uk/news/article-1201671/Singer-Dave-Carroll-pens-YouTube-hit-United-Airlines-breaks-guitar–shares-plunge-10.html

7. http://www.slideshare.net/rouenbs/netnography-by-joonas-rokka

8. See Huotari, K. (2014) *Experientalizing – How C2C communication becomes part of the service experience. The case of live-tweeting and TV viewing.* Helsinki: Hanken School of Economics, Finland.

9. http://www.360i.com/work/oreo-super-bowl/

10. Kozinets, R. (1999) E-tribalized marketing? The strategic implications of virtual communities of consumption. *European Management Journal*, **17**, 252–264.

11. Kaplan and Haenlein applied the social presence theory of Short, Williams, & Christie and the media richness theory of Daft & Lengel to classify social media, varying from low media such as blogs, medium level media richness of social networking sites, and high level media richness of virtual social worlds, such as Second Life or the Finnish teenager virtual world Habbo. Kaplan, A.M. and Haenlein, M. (2010) Users of the world, unite! The challenges and opportunities of social media. *Business Horizons*, **53**, 59–68.

12. Kaplan and Haenlein (2010).

13. Weinberg, B.D. and Pehlivan, E. (2011). Social spending: managing the social media mix, *Business Horizons*, **54**, 275–282.

14. Porter suggests that communities can be divided into organization and customer communities. Organization-sponsored communities can be divided into commercial, non-profit, and governmental communities. Porter, C.E. (2004) A typology of virtual communities: a multi-disciplinary foundation for future research. *Journal of Computer-Mediated Communication* [online], **10**.

15. Tagging refers to the act of putting labels on items in social media, for example people in photographs can be tagged to connect their figure with their Facebook profile.

16. Fournier, S. and Avery, J. (2011) The uninvited brand. *Business Horizons*, **54**, 193–207.

17. See e.g. http://www.ihateryanair.org/; http://www.ihatesbux.com/forum/

18. Gummesson, E. (1991) Marketing orientation revisited: the crucial role of the part time marketer. *European Journal of Marketing*, **25**(2), 60–75.

19. Nelson, P. (1970) Information and consumer behavior. *Journal of Political Economy*, **78**, 311–329.

20. van Doorn, J., Lemon, K.N., Mittal, V., Nass, S., Doreén, P., Pirner, P. and Verhoef, P.C. (2010). Customer engagement behavior: theoretical foundations and research directions. *Journal of Service Research*, **13**(3), 253–266.

21. Gummerus, J., Liljander, V., Weman, E. and Pihlström, M. (2012). Customer engagement in a Facebook brand community. *Management Research Review*, **35**(9), 857–877.

22. Kozinets, R.V., Hemetsberger, A., Jensen Schau, H. (2008). The wisdom of consumer crowds: collective Innovation in the age of networked marketing. *Journal of Macromarketing*, **28**(4), 339–354.

23. Muller, A., Hutchins, N. and Pinto, M.C. (2012). Applying open innovation where your company needs it the most. *Strategy & Leadership*, **40**(2), 35–42.

24. Chesbrough, H.W. (2003). A better way to innovate. *Harvard Business Review*, **81**(7), 12–13.

25. Gebauer, J., Füller, J. and Pezzei, R. (2013). The dark and the bright side of co-creation: triggers of member behavior in online innovation communities. *Journal of Business Research*, **66**(9), 1516–1527.

26. Sepp, M., Liljander, V. and Gummerus, J. (2011) Bloggers motivations to produce content – a uses and gratifications theory perspective. *Journal of Marketing Management*, **27**(13–14), 1479–1503.

27. Gwinner, K.P., Gremler, D.D. and Bitner, M.J. (1998) Relational benefits in service industries: the customer's perspective. *Journal of the Academy of Marketing Science*, **26**(2), 101–114.

28. Shang, R.-A., Chen, Y.-C. and Liao, H.-J. (2006) The value of participation in virtual consumer communities on brand loyalty. *Internet Research*, **16**(4), 398–418.

29. Gummerus *et al.* 2012.

REFERENCES

Boyd, D.M., and Ellison, N.B. Social network sites: definition, history, and scholarship. *Journal of Computer-Mediated Communication*, 2007, **13**.

Chesbrough, H.W. A better way to innovate. *Harvard Business Review*, **81**(7), 2003, 12–13.

Fournier, S. and Avery, J. The uninvited brand. *Business Horizons*, **54**, 2011, 193–207.

Gebauer, J., Füller, J. and Pezzei, R. The dark and the bright side of co-creation: triggers of member behavior in online innovation communities. *Journal of Business Research*, **66**(9), 2013, 1516–1527.

Gummerus, J., Liljander, V., Weman, E. and Pihlström, M. Customer engagement in a Facebook brand community. *Management Research Review*, **35**(9), 2012, 857–877.

Gummesson, E. Marketing orientation revisited: the crucial role of the part time marketer. *European Journal of Marketing*, **25**(2), 1991, 60–75.

Gwinner, K. P., Gremler, D. D. and Bitner, M. J. Relational benefits in service industries: the customer's perspective. *Journal of the Academy of Marketing Science*, **26**(2), 1998, 101–114.

Howe, J. *Crowdsourcing: Why the Power of the Crowd is Driving the Future of Business*. New York: Random House, 2008.

http://www.dailymail.co.uk/news/article-1201671/Singer-Dave-Carroll-pens-YouTube-hit-United-Airlines-breaks-guitar–shares-plunge-10.html

http://www.ihateryanair.org/; http://www.ihatesbux.com/forum/

http://www.slideshare.net/rouenbs/netnography-by-joonas-rokka

http://www.theguardian.com/world/2009/jul/23/united-airlines-guitar-dave-carroll

http://www.360i.com/work/oreo-super-bowl/

Huotari, K. *Experientalizing – How C2C Communication Becomes Part of the Service Experience. The Case of Live-Tweeting and TV Viewing.* Helsinki: Hanken School of Economics, Finland, 2014.

Kaplan, A.M. and Haenlein, M. Users of the world, unite! The challenges and opportunities of social media. *Business Horizons*, **53**, 2010, 59–68.

Kozinets, R. E-tribalized marketing? The strategic implications of virtual communities of consuption. *European Management Journal.* **17**, 1999, 252–264.

Kozinets, R.V., Hemetsberger, A., Jensen Schau, H. The wisdom of consumer crowds: collective innovation in the age of networked marketing. *Journal of Macromarketing*, **28**(4), 2008, 339–354.

Kucuk, U.S. and Krishnamurthy, S. An analysis of consumer power on the Internet. *Technovation*, **27**, 2007, 47–56.

Lawrence, B., Fournier, S. and Brunel, F. When companies don't make the ad: a multimethod inquiry into the differential effectiveness of consumer-generated advertising. *Journal of Advertising*, **42**, 2013, 292–307.

Muller, A., Hutchins, N. and Pinto, M.C. Applying open innovation where your company needs it the most. *Strategy & Leadership*, **40**(2), 2012, 35–42.

Nelson, P. Information and consumer behavior. *Journal of Political Economy*, **78**, 1970, 311–329.

Ordanini, A. (2009) Crowd-funding: customers as investors. *The Wall Street Journal*, 23 March, 3.

Porter, C.E. A typology of virtual communities: a multi-disciplinary foundation for future research. *Journal of Computer-Mediated Communication*, **10**, 2004.

Sepp, M., Liljander, V. and Gummerus, J. Bloggers motivations to produce content – a uses and gratifications theory perspective. *Journal of Marketing Management*, **27**(13–14), 2011, 1479–1503.

Shang, R.-A., Chen, Y.-C. and Liao, H.-J. The value of participation in virtual consumer communities on brand loyalty. *Internet Research*, **16**(4), 2006, 398–418.

van Doorn, J., Lemon, K.N., Mittal, V., Nass, S., Doreén, P., Pirner, P. and Verhoef, P.C. Customer engagement behavior: theoretical foundations and research directions. *Journal of Service Research*, **13**(3), 2010, 253–266.

Weinberg, B.D. and Pehlivan, E. Social spending: managing the social media mix. *Business Horizons*, **54**, 2011, 275–282.

FURTHER READING

Culnan, M.J., McHugh, P. & Zubillaga, J.I. (2010) How large U.S. companies can use Twitter and other social media to gain business value. *MIS Quarterly Executive*, **9**(4), 243–259.

Grace-Farfaglia, P., Dekkers, A., Sundararajan, B., Peters, L., & Park, S. (2006) Multinational web uses and gratifications: Measuring the social impact of online community participation across national boundaries. *Electronic Commerce Research*, **6**, 75–101.

Gummerus, J., Liljander V. & von Koskull C. (2014) The Role of E-Health Information in the Empowerment of Customers. In Kandampully, J. (ed.) *Service Management in Health & Wellness Services*. Dubuque, IA, US: Kendall Hunt Publishing Company.

Heinonen K. (2011) Consumer activity in social media: managerial approaches to consumers' social media behavior. *Journal of Consumer Behaviour*, **10**(6), 356–364.

Heller Baird, C. & Parasnis, G. (2011) From social media to social customer relationship management. *Strategy & Leadership*, **39**(5), 30–37.

Hennig-Thurau,T., Malthouse, E.C. Friege, C., Gensler, S., Lobschat, L., Rangaswamy, A. & Skiera, B. (2010) The impact of new media on customer relationships. *Journal of Service Research*, **13**(3), 311–330.

Hoffman D.L. & Fodor, M. (2010) Can you measure the ROI of your social media marketing? *Sloan Management Review*, **52**(1), 41–49.

Hoffman, D.L. & Novak T.P. (2012) Toward a deeper understanding of social media. *Journal of Interactive Marketing*, **26**, 69–70.

Hollebeek, L.D., Glynn, M.S. & Brodie R.J. (2014) Consumer brand engagement in social media: conceptualization, scale development and validation. *Journal of Interactive Marketing*, **28**(2), 149–165.

Jahn, B. & Kunz, W. (2012) How to transform consumers into fans of your brand. *Journal of Service Management*, **23**(3), 344–361.

Kietzmann J.H., Hermkens K., McCarthy I.P. & Silvestre B.S. (2010) Social media? Get serious! Understanding the functional building blocks of social media. *Business Horizons*, **54**(3), 241–251.

Lipsman, A., Mudd, G., Rich, M. & Bruch, S. (2012) The power of 'Like': how brands reach (and influence) fans through social-media marketing. *Journal of Advertising Research*, **52**, 40–52.

McQuarrie, E.F., Miller, J. & Phillips, B.J. (2013) The megaphone effect: taste and audience in fashion blogging. *Journal of Consumer Research*, **40**(1), 136–158.

Michaelidou, N., Siamagka N.T. & Christodoulides G. (2011) Usage, barriers and measurement of social media marketing: an exploratory investigation of small and medium B2B brands. *Industrial Marketing Management*, **40**, 1153–1159.

Sashi, C.M. (2012) Customer engagement, buyer-seller relationships, and social media. *Management Decision*, **50**(2), 253–272.

Weinberg, B.D. & Pehlivan, E. (2011) Social spending: managing the social media mix, *Business Horizons*, **54**, 275–282.

CHAPTER 13
CUSTOMER-FOCUSED ORGANIZATION: STRUCTURE, RESOURCES AND SERVICE PROCESSES

The firm should turn the organizational pyramid upside down – mentally and structurally. Its customers have done so long ago.

INTRODUCTION

This chapter discusses how to structure a service organization and manage service processes such that the service provider becomes customer-focused. The first half of the chapter concentrates on structural issues, such as the use of marketing departments or other organizational solutions, so that a total marketing process can best be facilitated. The rest of the chapter discusses how to plan and manage the service (production) process so that the interactive marketing process of a service provider is successful. A *service system model* and an *extended servicescape model* are presented. After having read the chapter the reader should understand the problems involved with organizing marketing in a traditional way in service contexts and how to find new service-oriented solutions, and know how to develop the service process so that a good marketing impact is achieved.

THE MARKETING PROCESS AND THE MARKETING DEPARTMENT

In conventional marketing thinking, which is based mainly on experience from consumer packaged goods, a marketing department is the organizational unit responsible for planning and implementing marketing activities. The logic behind this solution is, of course, that marketing can best be planned and implemented if all marketing activities are concentrated on and taken care of by a group of specialists. If marketing is seen as a function, as usually has been the case in the past, this also makes sense. However, such logic requires that marketing as a process be separated from the other business processes and activities of the firm in a logical and manageable way. In mainstream marketing this way of organizing for marketing is considered appropriate. At the same time, however, an increasing amount of criticism of this has emerged over the last 40 years.[1] According to this criticism, in the emerging business environment marketing cannot remain a specialist function or be delegated to one department where the specialists plan and implement all marketing activities of the firm. This need for marketing to break free from the marketing department was recognized very early in service marketing research, especially in the Nordic School of service marketing thought.[2] The traditional highly-structured military model with its hierarchical charts-and-box structure is seen as old-fashioned in today's business environment. Process organizations and project organizations have been used as a way of overcoming the problems in these functionalistic organizational solutions.

The development of *virtual* or *network organizations* also shows how traditional rigid solutions are becoming less effective. Such an organization[3] includes a nucleus which puts together and manages a network of other organizations and actors, and its assets, processes and people critical to the success of the business exist and function both inside and outside the conventional borderlines of the organization. In such organizational solutions, relationships and the process nature of marketing are natural ingredients.[4]

Nevertheless, a brief look at standard marketing textbooks and journals reveals that the traditional marketing department is still most often offered as the standard solution. The same is true for the practice of marketing. However, when moving the focus from the established areas of marketing, such as consumer goods marketing, to newer areas, such as business-to-business relationship marketing and service marketing, one can see another picture, where marketing departments are less dominating or there are no formal marketing departments at all. The long-term marketing perspective and the recognition of the characteristics of long-term customer relationships of service firms and business-to-business marketing demonstrate that marketing is not solely the responsibility of marketing specialists, but that *marketing activities are carried out throughout the entire organization*.[5] We thus have an *organizational dilemma* created by the fact that those who produce and deliver service carry out marketing activities for that service as *part-time marketers*,[6] whether they know it or not and whether they accept it or not.

Figure 13.1 illustrates the position of marketing in a professional service firm, as in any service organization. The dotted areas indicate the marketing responsibilities of various functions. For example, the president, divisional and regional directors, consultants and assistants as well as all other employees have marketing responsibilities as part-time marketers, because what they say and do and how they do it may have an important impact on the future buying and consumption behaviour of customers. Simultaneously, they have responsibility for operations as well. In addition, people outside the formal organization may also make a marketing impact on behalf of the service provider. In the figure, clients and former employees are examples of such people. To take a bank as an example, the managing director, regional directors, loans director and tellers are employees who have similar marketing duties as part-time marketers.

The status of most employees in service operations is complicated. They have dual responsibilities because clearly a cashier, bank teller, waiter, hotel receptionist or maintenance technician must first be able to take care of his technical duties. However, at the same time most employees have to realize that the way in which they do their duties is a marketing task. Marketing activities are carried out by every employee who influences the customers of the organization directly or indirectly. In every service organization there are a large number of *part-time marketers* who have *dual responsibilities*: to perform their tasks well in a technical sense and at the same time in such a way that they create a good

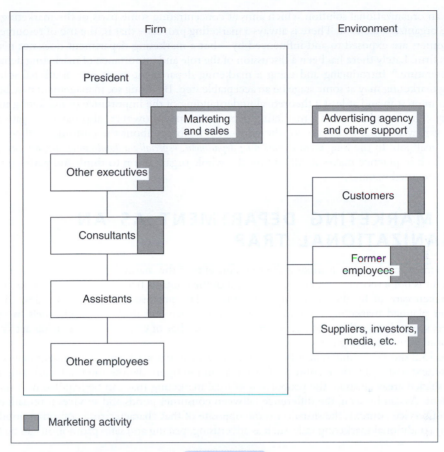

FIGURE 13.1

**The simultaneous responsibility for marketing and operations among
the personnel of a service provider.**
Source: Adapted from Gummesson, E., The marketing of professional services –
an organizational dilemma. *European Journal of Marketing*, **13**(5); 1979: p. 311.
Reproduced by permission of Emerald Insight.

marketing impact. In many service organizations these part-time marketers outnumber marketing specialists in the marketing department many times over. In the words of Evert Gummesson, this is because 'marketing and sales departments (full-time marketers) are not able to handle more than a limited portion of the marketing *as their staff cannot be at the right place at the right time with the right customer contacts*' (emphasis added).[7]

The main problem in most situations is the fact that the *marketing department* is mistaken for the much larger concept of a *marketing process*. *The marketing process includes all resources and activities that have a direct or indirect impact on customer preferences and the establishment, maintenance and strengthening of customer relationships, irrespective of where they are in the organization.* The marketing department, on the other hand, is an organizational solution which aims at concentrating some parts of the marketing process into one organizational unit. There is always a marketing process – that is, the use of resources which the customers are exposed to and influenced by – but a marketing department does not necessarily exist in a firm. Lately there has been a discussion of the role and importance of marketing departments in the literature.[8] Introducing and using a marketing department as an organizational solution to handling marketing may at some stage be an acceptable step. By doing so, management may be able to create an interest in and at least a theoretical understanding of the importance of marketing to service providers. The introduction of a marketing department may, however, also have a negative effect, because it may become an excuse for the employees to forget about the customer and concentrate on their 'real' job. In the long term *a marketing department, especially a dominating one, can easily become a trap*, which in practice makes it difficult for the whole organization to think and perform in a true customer-focused manner.[9]

THE MARKETING DEPARTMENT AS AN ORGANIZATIONAL TRAP

In a consumer goods context, mixing the two concepts of the marketing process and the marketing department is not a serious mistake, because most of the contacts between the firm and its customers can be taken care of by the marketing department. The pre-produced product, sales, advertising and other planned marketing communication efforts, price and distribution channels, is what the customers see and are influenced by. A very limited number of customer-influencing activities take place outside the marketing department.

Figure 13.2 shows the differences between the coverage of a marketing department in a consumer goods context and in a service context. The circles in the figure denote the total marketing process, and the shaded areas illustrate the proportion of total marketing that can be handled by a marketing department. As can be seen, the difference between consumer goods and services is remarkable.

In most service contexts the situation is the opposite of that characterizing consumer goods. Normally only traditional marketing tasks such as advertising, pricing and sales promotion can be handled

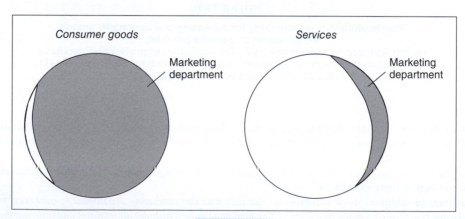

FIGURE 13.2

The marketing department versus the total marketing process.

by a typical marketing department, whereas other marketing activities carried out as part of operations and other functions are outside the realm of this department. A large part of the marketing process is carried out by part-time marketers outside the marketing department. Nevertheless, growing service firms have, in the best consumer goods tradition, often been inclined to establish a marketing department, in order to maintain or even strengthen the market orientation of the firm. However, the long-term effect of this may easily be the opposite of that intended.

A traditional marketing department cannot usually be responsible for the total marketing process of a service provider. The introduction of such departments, on the contrary, easily influences the organization in an unfavourable direction. People working in other departments, performing, for example, operational or administrative tasks, stop worrying about their customer-related responsibilities and concentrate on handling what they see as their 'real' job. The reason for this is clear. The firm now has marketing specialists in the marketing department; why should people in other departments bother any longer to do the marketers' job? There is someone else to blame if things go wrong. The result is an increasing inward orientation and a less customer-focused performance. The marketing department solution becomes *an organizational trap*.[10]

The above problem is very real. As one executive of a large insurance company recognized:

Our corporate marketing department has become an organizational trap. Employees working in various operational departments and account servicing and administration concentrate on handling operations rather than focusing on their customer influencing activities. These customer influencing activities are thought of as being the responsibility of the corporate marketing department. Although these employees realize that they do have responsibility for maintaining customer satisfaction, they tend to focus on the technical aspects of their job. Performance is measured quantitatively and quality is enforced by penalties for mistakes.

If the negative effects of a marketing department are further reinforced by performance measurement systems and reward systems that focus on aspects of jobs other than customer relationship-building and maintenance, the problems increase. In such situations these negative effects are not only psychological, but actual. Concentrating solely on the technical aspects of a job instead of paying attention to customer relationship aspects gives more credit to the employee; the reverse discredits the employee in the eyes of his superiors. Internal efficiency is seen as being more important than external effectiveness and the delivery of good service quality to customers.

In summary, in service organizations it is often counterproductive to introduce marketing departments as *the* ultimate solution to problems where a market orientation is lacking or insufficient.[11] Sometimes they can, however, be used as an intermediate solution. However, there are good examples of firms that have either closed down or drastically reduced the size of their marketing departments and become successful in the marketplace. In a later section of this chapter a case study illustrating such a development is described.

Marketing departments may be helpful for planning, market research and executing corporate-wide campaigns. Customer-influencing activities should, however, be actively planned and implemented *as part of the total marketing process* in the line organization, where the immediate responsibility lies for rendering service. A marketing department should always be introduced very carefully, so that no one in the organization misunderstands its role. Furthermore, it should never be given a dominant position. If and when such departments are introduced, careful attention should always be paid to the measurement and reward systems used for the *part-time marketers* outside the marketing department. A *marketing department is not an excuse for the rest of the organization to stop being responsible for customers.*

ORGANIZING FOR MARKET ORIENTATION: INVERTING THE PYRAMID

A service organization should not be unnecessarily bureaucratic or have a large number of hierarchical levels. Customer orientation requires thoroughly understood and accepted responsibility for customers and the authority to take action to serve them. Large staff with substantial planning and decision-making authority may not have sufficient knowledge and/or the ability to make decisions quickly enough to serve customers well. The organizational hierarchy or pyramid should therefore have as few layers as possible between the customers and top management.

The customer contact personnel create value for customers. The rest of the organization, the back-office functions, management and staff, form a support for buyer–seller interactions in service encounters. This support creates the necessary back-up for the service encounters, i.e. for the successful handling of the numerous moments of truth, such that they become well-utilized moments of opportunity which reinforce the customer relationships.

Management should not be directly involved in operational decision-making on an everyday level, but it should give the strategic support and resources necessary to pursue a service strategy. In a traditional military structure, top management is often far removed from reality. In addition, top management is often surrounded by a staff organization which seals it off from the rest of the organization, including the service encounters and the customers. This, of course, may have a harmful effect on strategic decision-making. Among other things it tends to draw attention away from external effectiveness aspects and make top management overemphasize internal efficiency instead.

The old traditional view of the organization and the modern service-oriented organizational framework are schematically illustrated as pyramids in Figure 13.3. The transition in organizational thinking, which is the result of a change in strategic thinking according to the principles of service management, means three things. First of all, priorities are changed. This is demonstrated by the fact that *the organizational pyramid is turned upside down.*[12] Top management is not the apex of the pyramid and thus the part of the organizational structure that immediately determines whether the strategy of

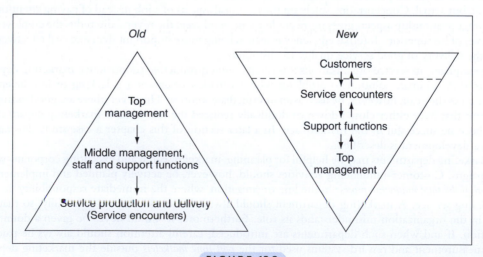

FIGURE 13.3

Service-oriented organizational structure.

the firm will be a success or failure. Instead, interactions with customers during service encounters, including personnel, physical resources, information technology and operational systems, are at the top of the organizational hierarchy. The organization's performance in service encounters determines whether it will be successful and profitable or not. Staff, other support functions and management are a prerequisite for success.

Second, the responsibility for customers and for operational decisions is moved from management to staff involved in the service encounters and thus those immediately responsible for the moments of truth. Third, the new thinking means that the organizational pyramid has to be flattened. This follows from the transition of responsibilities and authority to service encounters. Fewer intermediate levels are needed.

THE RELATIVE SIZE OF ORGANIZATIONS

Flattening the organizational pyramid and the decentralization of decision-making authority are necessities if service organizations are to become truly customer-focused. Strategic decisions should be taken by top management at the bottom of the pyramid. Another rule is that decision-making should not be transferred from the service encounters in the pyramid. Some operational decisions have to be taken by middle management, but as much as possible decisions should be taken where the reason for a decision occurs.

It could be argued that a small service firm is frequently more customer-oriented than a big firm. In a smaller organization operational decisions are made more quickly and closer to the customers. It is easier to develop good interactive marketing performance and to provide better functional quality in such situations. Internal marketing is less time-consuming and troublesome. On the other hand, there is more potential strength in large firms. In a bigger firm more resources can be used in order to develop technical quality.

Invisible systems and support functions, to which local branches can easily gain access, can often be developed centrally. This may give economies of scale as well as improve the efficiency of the total service system. It is also sometimes easier to attract better trained people to leading positions in a larger organization, although this is not always the case. Economies of scale can be achieved in production, administration, finance departments and so on, which are invisible to the market.

In summary, one may argue that *a growing service firm, in order to remain customer-oriented and be successful, will have to combine the strengths of being a small firm with the strengths of belonging to a large organization*. However, there is much evidence that demonstrates that this may be difficult to do. As an organization grows and tries to achieve the advantages of being a large company, far too often it destroys the potential strength of being a small company.

CASE STUDY

SUCCESSFUL ORGANIZATIONAL DEVELOPMENT: SCB BANK

The SCB Bank is a major bank operating nationwide in Scandinavia. In the past it suffered from low profitability and production-oriented attitudes among its personnel, including branch managers and other middle management. Marketing was handled by a large marketing department at head office. In order to turn the bank into a customer-oriented and profitable firm, it was decided that it should concentrate on profitable services and market segments. An organizational development process was also initiated. This process included several stages, where each stage followed on from customer orientation problems perceived at the previous stage.

At the first stage, the central marketing department was closed down and a *customer contact development office* established. This office was only staffed by a few people, and reported directly to the managing director. The bank was divided into regional banks, and responsibility for marketing, including selling to individual households and organizational, was delegated to local branch managers. Marketing consultants were located at the regional level, to give marketing assistance to local managers. At the same time the bank stopped all national advertising, because management felt that purchase decisions are made locally and should be influenced by the performance of the local branch offices.

However, the local branch offices remained production-oriented, and did not actively take over marketing tasks. When the branch manager felt he should do some marketing, he called upon the regional marketing consultant. When the regional marketing consultants left the local office, interest in customer-oriented activities decreased again. Nevertheless, the situation had improved because the customer contact development office created guidelines for local planned marketing communication and sales campaigns and developed training programmes for employees. These training programmes were intended to help employees handle customer contacts and communication with customers.

In order to further improve customer orientation on the local level, the regional marketing consultants were removed, and the total responsibility for marketing was given to local branch managers. The local offices operated as profit centres. When the regionally located marketers were gone, and there was no central marketing department to turn to, the interest in marketing and customer consciousness among the branch managers increased; they had no choice but to start focusing on their customers. The profit centre responsibility, accompanied by a higher decision-making authority, obviously supported this change of attitude.

The customer contact development office supported the branch office managers in training their personnel and in developing planned marketing communication and local sales efforts. Slowly, customer-orientation improved. The bank also became one of the most profitable in Scandinavia and has remained so.

INTERNAL SERVICE PROVIDERS AND INTERNAL CUSTOMERS

Traditionally, customers are thought of as people or organizations external to a company. Such *external customers* have to be served in such a fashion that their needs are fulfilled and they are satisfied with the firm's performance. However, there are user–service provider relationships inside an organization as well and also between network partners. The customer contact employees and departments in a firm have to be supported by other people and departments in the firm, if they are to give good service to customers. For example, goods cannot be delivered in a service-oriented way if the warehouse does not supply the truck driver with the correct items, in good condition, and on time.

Every service operation is full of such *internal service functions* which support one another and the customer contact employees and departments interacting with external customers. Frequently, there may be many more internal service functions than external customer service functions.

To sum up, if internal service is poor, the externally rendered service will be damaged. However, it is often difficult for people involved in internal service functions supporting other departments to realize the importance of their performance to the final service quality. They rarely see 'real' customers, and they can easily feel that those whom they serve internally are somehow just fellow employees and that the service they get does not affect external performance in any way.

A way of tackling the attitudinal problem of those who should serve 'somebody else' (other than the ultimate customers) is to introduce the concept of *internal customers*.[13] This concept brings customer–service provider relationships inside the organization, as illustrated by Figure 13.4. There may be one or a whole range of internal service functions, each illustrated by a box within the larger box in the figure. These functions are *internal customers* to other internal service providers; they are also *service providers* to other internal customers. Finally, in the service process, the ultimate output is the external service received and perceived by the ultimate external customer. In a network context or in a virtual organizational constellation, the difference between what is internal and what is external becomes blurred. However, the same type of service provider–internal customer chains exist and have to be managed in the same customer-oriented manner, so that the final, ultimate external customer receives good service.

When the existence and importance of internal customer relationships are realized by personnel, it is much easier to change attitudes among employees. The concept of internal customers gives a totally new dimension to the tasks performed inside an organization. It is more easily realized that 'a satisfied customer' should not only refer to individuals or organizations external to the firm.

Sometimes the internal customer–service provider relationships may be straightforward. However, frequently they can be complicated, with relationships in which both parties serve each other, or when the outcome of one department depends on the internal service provided by two or more other

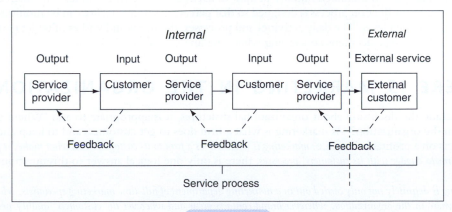

FIGURE 13.4

Internal service functions and internal customers.

departments. It is mandatory that *such internal customers are served as well as external customers are expected to be served*. This means that generating quality into service is not the exclusive duty of departments visible to external customers. For example, the perceived quality of delivery service depends just as much on the performance of the warehouse as it does on the performance of the delivery function. Therefore, *the responsibility for producing good service quality is spread throughout the organization as well as in a network of co-operating organizations throughout the network*.

In many cases two or more departments may be directly involved with customers. Then it is of vital importance that these parallel processes are co-ordinated and perceived by customers as one single service process, otherwise service quality will deteriorate. If there is no one responsible for the customer in such situations, the customer may be sent from one person to another in a disorganized way. The organization does not take responsibility for the service, and the customer is forced to take over the responsibility for getting service. This is bad quality.

The service production process is built up by interrelationships and interdependencies between a number of sub-processes. The external customer only gets in touch with part of a company's sub-systems. There is a *line of visibility*[14] dividing those parts of the process that customers immediately see and perceive from those parts that only indirectly influence the service quality perception. Psychologically, this sometimes causes internal problems. Because in many cases these interdependencies between internal service providers and internal customers are not discussed and stressed enough by management, this is often understandable. *However, almost all employees have customers to serve, although many customers may be internal ones.*

When developing a service production system, various strategies can again be used. The part of the total system that is on the visible side of the line can be limited to, say, only one or two persons. Customers only contact them, and most of the service production process is taken care of internally. For example, an insurance company that directs all of its contacts through one single agent uses such a strategy. Such a strategy is applied, of course, to make it as easy as possible for customers to deal with the firm. In other situations the visible side of the line consists of a system or physical resource only, as in Internet shopping where the customer interacts with a website. Another strategy is to expose customers to many sub-processes. A restaurant, for instance, is normally forced to apply such a strategic approach. In this case the customer relationship is broader and more vulnerable. Mistakes that may occur do so under the eyes of the customer. Fewer problems can be taken care of as internal affairs. Of course, there are an unlimited number of options between these two examples. The main thing is that the service production process is designed so that perceived service quality can be monitored and kept at an intended level. The daily activities and processes, the needs and wishes of target customers should guide strategic decisions concerning where the line of visibility is drawn.

WHERE IS MARKETING IN THE ORGANIZATION?

To conclude the discussion about organizational structures, it is appropriate to ask: 'Where is marketing in the organization?' As marketing is what a firm does to get customers and to keep and grow customers on a profitable basis, i.e. *marketing is what relates a firm to its customers* and *what makes it possible for the firm to engage with its customers' processes*, there is only one logical answer to this question:

Marketing is definitely not only carried out in a marketing department of full-time marketing specialists. Marketing is everywhere in the organization, wherever brand contacts occur and wherever the customers' quality perception is formed as a basis for their willingness to continue their relationship with the service provider. Marketing is also wherever internal customers are served in internal back-office operations.

Because marketing is everywhere and is the responsibility of no one single department, there is an obvious risk that in the end marketing is nowhere and nobody takes responsibility for it, and consequently that no one takes responsibility for customer focus in the organization either. Indeed, service providers in practice often establish separate functionalistic marketing departments to take care of the marketing process, so that they can see where marketing is concentrated. Soon enough they realize that this does not work. *Marketing is everywhere in the sense that there has to be a marketing aspect in all roles, tasks and departments of a service organization; a customer focus throughout the organization.* In other words there has to be an appreciation of the customer in all tasks that are performed in the organization. *Part-time marketers* can be found in operations, finance, administration, logistics, research and development, human resource management, and all other departments. Furthermore, technology and systems that have an interactive marketing impact are also all around the organization and should be treated as *part-time marketing resources*, for example, when investment decisions are made.

Of course, service providers also need someone who takes responsibility for market research, planned marketing communication (to the extent this is needed), pricing issues and other traditional marketing activities. Therefore, most service organizations need some *full-time marketers* to take care of the *traditional external marketing processes*. Full-time marketers should also be instrumental in internal marketing processes, normally working closely with human resource management. However, to organize them into a 'marketing department' may be detrimental and ineffective. Such a department can make promises, and can do so effectively, but it cannot contribute to the fulfilment of promises. Finally, the better the organization takes care of its customers and provides them with good service quality and value support, the less work there is for full-time marketers.

The only person who can be responsible for the total marketing process is the CEO or managing director, or locally the regional director, and more locally the outlet/branch manager. A marketing manager who is responsible for a department of full-time marketers can only be responsible for this department. However, a marketing manager is a customer specialist and should have an active role in the total marketing process as an internal consultant to top management.

Another conclusion to be drawn is that *marketing cannot be totally organized in a service firm. Marketing can only be instilled in the organization.* However, it has to be systematized in some way. Here are a few guidelines:

1. Instilling a *marketing attitude of mind* in people in all departments and enabling customer-focused performance as well as supervisory and reward systems that reinforce such performance is one aspect of how to organize marketing in a service firm.

2. Clarifying the responsibility for the customer of top management and all line managers is another aspect of marketing.

3. The service provider may of course also need to use traditional external marketing efforts to some extent, and to do market research. Therefore, resources for doing this internally and/or externally should be secured. Many traditional marketing activities can be taken care of by the local line organization, but a central marketing group or staff with full-time marketers may be required as well.

4. It is important to make sure that this central group does not become a dominant marketing department that psychologically has a negative effect on the customer focus of employees in other departments and functions.

5. Full-time marketers have an important role in the marketing process, but it is the part-time marketers and the interactive marketing process that are at the heart of marketing in service organizations.

In conclusion, when organizing marketing in a service firm the following should be kept in mind:

- Successful marketing requires a *marketing attitude of mind* throughout the organization, because the central part of marketing takes place in the service encounters, and in back-office support to service encounters, through customer-oriented *part-time marketers* and service-oriented systems and technologies (the *interactive marketing process*).

- Responsibility for marketing lies within the line organization, and the managing director has to accept the ultimate responsibility for marketing.

- Many of the traditional external marketing activities that may be needed can be handled locally in the line organization, but a central marketing staff of *full-time marketers* may sometimes also be required to take responsibility for centrally implemented marketing activities as well as to act as internal consultants to top management in customer-related issues and in internal marketing.

The aim of installing marketing as such a holistic concept in an organization is, of course, to make a firm customer-centric, where the management mindset as well as the planning and execution of service processes are customer-focused. The ultimate goal is to gear the firm's management approach from inside-out management to *outside-in management* (see Chapter 1).[15]

The following sections of this chapter look more closely at what one needs to know about customers, and at the service process, and discusses how the latter can be developed so that a good interactive marketing effect can be achieved.

WHAT DO WE NEED TO KNOW ABOUT OUR CUSTOMERS?

What makes a given customer want a certain type of service? What makes the customer purchase it from a certain service provider? The reactions of customers are based on their *expectations*, but these are a function of a whole range of internal and external factors.

First of all, the service provided by goods or service activities purchased has to fit the *customer's value-creating processes*, so that it supports value creation in his everyday activities and processes (or those in the organization he represents). For example, a firm that looks for a sales supporting database system wants a solution that makes it possible to easily find out, save, change and retrieve information about customers in order for the sales representatives to develop an understanding of the needs, values and internal processes of customers and offer them service that suit their needs. Any solution that does not fit this process will not interest the firm, because it will not create the value they want. *Customers' everyday activities and their value-creating processes are the most important thing for a firm to know about its customers*, if possible on an individual basis, otherwise on a segment-by-segment basis.

It is, however, essential to realize that the value-creation processes alone do not determine what kind of service a person looks for. Many service providers can usually produce an acceptable solution that could offer adequate support to a customer's value generation. In addition, customers also have certain *wishes* in relation to *how* they want the service provider to treat them. This normally narrows the scope of options available. For example, almost any retailing bank can provide an individual with banking service, but not every bank manages to treat customers in a way they are pleased with (compare the *technical* and *functional* dimensions of customer perceived service quality). This is also related to *the customer's value system*, which determines what kinds of solutions to a problem are considered acceptable and what is considered out of the question. Environmental concerns are examples of aspects in the value system that exclude some otherwise possible need-satisfying solutions. Some consumers do not want to use cosmetics that have been developed using animal testing, and they will not buy such products. In conclusion, *a customer's everyday processes, in combination with his value system, determine what kind of solutions are of interest to him.*

The *needs* of a customer follow from his value-creation process and how he wants his values to be supported. They direct expectations towards a certain type of solution. An organization may form its needs in a more complicated way than a single customer or a household. In principle, however, an organization's or a person's need is some sort of a problem that requires a solution. This solution may be solved in a number of ways. For example, house cleaning can be managed by buying proper equipment and by a do-it-yourself approach, or one can take care of it by purchasing a service. In both cases there are a number of options available in relation to what to buy, and where to buy the necessary equipment or service. *A customer's needs, combined with his value system, determine what kind of solutions or offerings are acceptable to him.* Finally, *a customer's everyday processes and his perceptions of his needs determine what kind of solutions he is looking for.* This could be labelled *the customer's game plan.*

To sum up, in order to thoroughly understand customers and potential customers the marketer needs to acquire information about the following (see Figure 13.5):

- The customers' everyday processes and *value-creating processes.*
- The customers' value systems.
- The customers' needs that follow from their value-creating processes and value systems.

Traditionally, customer needs are the main focus of market research. Such studies are still important, but today it is even more crucial to develop a thorough understanding of customers' everyday processes which influence their value creation. It is also more or less impossible to market anything to customers that violates their value system. However, the most important task for market research today is to study the customers' everyday processes and what kind of solutions would support them in a value-creating way. Today, firms normally know the least about such everyday processes, what customers are doing in their everyday lives, and why, and what they are trying to achieve, or what

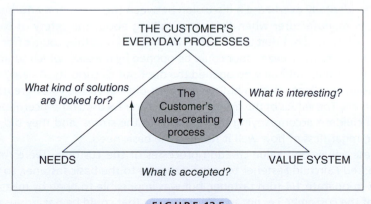

FIGURE 13.5

The customer's gameplan: what do we need to know about the customer?

they would like to achieve. Much more research about these issues is needed. Here, traditional methods are of limited value. Instead various *ethnographic methods* should be used, where the researcher in various ways gets close to the customers ('lives with the customers') and tries to understand what they are doing, why and for what purpose.

Customers' needs, wishes, value systems and value–creating processes are of vital importance for the development of *customer expectations*. However, expectations are also formed by external factors (this was discussed in more detail in previous chapters). For example, what family acquaintances and business associates say about a given service provider (word–of–mouth communication) has an impact on the formation of the expectations as well as what newspapers and trade magazines write about the service firm and its service and what is discussed in social media. This is often of great importance. Moreover, planned marketing communication activities, such as personal selling and advertising campaigns, influence expectations. Finally, the overall company image and local image also influence expectations.

CASE STUDY

SELLING 1/4-TURN FASTENERS, BUT NOT ANY 1/4-TURN FASTENERS

Dennis Holmlund, sales representative of Unilink Co., marketing Fairchild Fastener products and specialty fastening systems to industrial markets, had negotiated for some time with a major customer in the industrial freezer market about fastening solutions for the customer's freezers for supermarkets. The machinery of the freezers is accessible through a small door which should be easily opened and closed. He had offered 1/4-turn fasteners that were very easy to operate. The buyer was not convinced that this was a good solution, which puzzled Mr Holmlund, because he knew that an easier-to-use fastener did not exist on the market, and that price should not be a problem. The fastener he suggested clearly fulfilled the needs of the customer.

Then he accidentally overheard a discussion between the buyer and another executive of the freezer manufacturer when they were talking about the safety of toddlers and small children. It turned out that the customer did not feel that they could offer freezers to supermarkets where the freezer door could be opened by mistake, which could therefore be hazardous to small children who opened the door out of curiosity. An easy-to-operate fastener was an excellent solution but nevertheless did not fit the value-creating process of the customers. The values of the freezer manufacturer focused on concern for the safety of the small children accompanying their parents in the stores, and they did not accept the fastener, regardless of how well it fulfilled the basic need.

When these values and value-creating processes of the customer were revealed, Mr Holmlund asked Fairchild Fastener to make a change to the basic fastener, so that it was still an easy-to-operate 1/4-turn fastener, but was impossible to open by mistake. Hence, the values of the customer, i.e. not to offer solutions that could be hazardous to toddlers and small children in supermarkets and grocery stores, were met.

CUSTOMER SEGMENTS AND TARGET GROUPS

Customers have differing needs and/or wishes about how they want to be treated. An organization can, therefore, very seldom satisfy the needs of every potential customer in a similar manner. It should not even try to solve everyone's problems or support everyone's value-creating processes. Customers have to be divided into homogeneous *segments*, which are sufficiently different from each other. One or a few such segments are then chosen as *target groups* of customers. In service contexts it is often difficult to satisfy target groups of customers with too widely varying needs and wishes. Because customers frequently meet and interact with each other, they influence fellow customers' perception of the service. For example, a family having a picnic on a Saturday afternoon in the park does not mix well with a bunch of beer drinkers. If the firm goes for segments that are very different from each other, it is usually a good idea to keep them apart. Finally, it should be observed that a service production system cannot usually take care of satisfying too diverse needs and wishes. This follows from the fact that service is a complicated phenomenon and service production is a complicated task.

It is also important to remember that customers in a relationship with a service provider often want to be recognized and treated as individuals, even though they are part of a larger segment. Therefore, the firm should not be blinded by the fact that it may have mass markets and may use the segment concept for analytical purposes. Customers often want to be treated as *segments of one*.[16] Direct customer contacts occur naturally in most service contexts and they give a good starting point for the individual treatment of customers. In addition, the information technology available to firms today also supports individualistic treatment of customers.

RELATING THE SERVICE PACKAGE TO THE CONSUMPTION PROCESS

We now turn to the issue of how the customer and the consumption process can be incorporated into the service process. Doing this is of utmost importance because of the nature of service and the inseparability of large and critical parts of production and consumption. The service consumption process can be divided into three phases:[17]

1. Joining phase.
2. Main consumption phase.
3. Detachment phase.

The *joining phase* is the first stage of the consumption process, where the customer gets in touch with the service provider in order to buy and consume a core service, for example, elevator maintenance. In this phase facilitating services are mainly required, for example, telephone contact with the elevator maintenance firm in order to get hold of a service technician. Some enhancing services may be used, for example a toll-free number or an easy-to-use website, which makes it easy for the customer to get in touch with the maintenance firm. A customer's perception of service quality and his value creation start already during this phase.

The *main consumption phase* is the main stage of the total service consumption process. In this phase the needs of the customer have to be satisfied, and his value-creating process has to be supported.

Hence, the core service is consumed at this stage. For example, the elevator is serviced. Furthermore, there may be some enabling services (for example, a shelter surrounding the work space) and

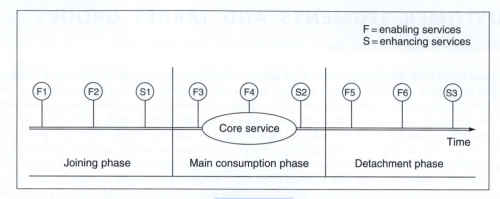

FIGURE 13.6

The service package and the service consumption process.
Source: Lehtinen, J., *Quality Oriented Services Marketing*. University of Tampere,
Finland, 1986, p. 38. Reproduced by permission of Tampere University Press.

enhancing services (for example, instructions to people normally using the elevator directing them to the stairs and telling them when the job is expected to be finished). In the *detachment phase* the customer leaves the service process. This often requires some enabling services (for example, the service technician fills in a report and hands it over to the caretaker or another representative of the customer). Enhancing services may be used here, too. It is important to realize that this phase also contributes to the customers' perception of service quality and supports their value creation. Because the detachment phase includes the customers' final experiences with the service, what happens during this phase *may be especially important for them and their quality perception.*

In Figure 13.6 the service consumption process and the types of services related to the three phases of the process are illustrated schematically. If, for example, we look at a full-service restaurant, the *joining phase* may include table reservations (F1) and cloakroom services (F2) as *enabling services*, and valet parking (S1) as an *enhancing service*. During the *main consumption phase* the core service, which may be a three-course dinner, is consumed. The table setting (F3) and the performance of the waiting staff (F4) are *enabling services*, and live music (S2) may be an *enhancing service*. In the *detachment phase*, when the customer leaves the restaurant, some *enabling services* are needed, for example, paying the bill (F5) and again the cloakroom services (F6). Valet parking (S3) may be used as an *enhancing service* again at this stage. Depending on how the enabling services function, they may operate in a service enhancing manner as well.

It should be observed, however, that this model only takes into account the components of the basic service package (core service as well as enabling and enhancing services and goods). The next step is to take the components of the augmented service offering (see Chapter 7); that is, *accessibility*, *interactions* and *customer participation*, into account so that the functional quality dimension of the process is also covered.

THE SERVICE SYSTEM MODEL

The service system model illustrated in Figure 13.7 can be used for analysing and planning the service process.[18] In this figure the various quality-generating resources are combined in a systematic way. The large central square illustrates the service-producing organization *from the customer's perspective*.

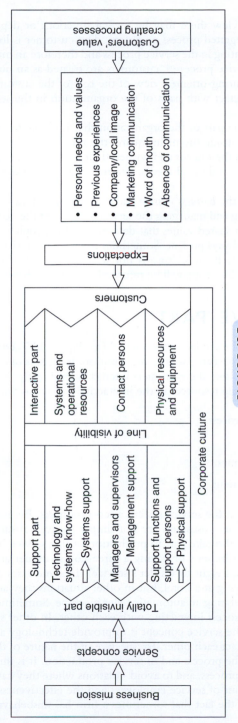

FIGURE 13.7

The service system model.

From the producer's point of view there may be several functions or departments involved, but the customer sees it as one integrated process or system. The customer is located inside the square because he is a resource participating in the service process and therefore an integral part of the service system model. Yet, in most service processes, customers are treated as an outside factor only. This, of course, is due to a manufacturing-oriented view of the role of the customer. However, they are inside the organization and interact with parts of the organization in the service process and are a service production resource.

The *line of visibility* divides the part of the organization that is visible to customers from the part that is invisible. To the right, outside the main square, the means of influencing the *expectations* of customers are illustrated, such as their needs and wishes, their previous experiences, overall company and local image, word of mouth and social media, external planned marketing communication and absence of communication.

To the left of the square are the *business mission* and the corresponding *service concepts* which, like umbrellas, should guide planning and managing the service system. At the bottom of the main square is the *corporate culture*; that is, the shared values that determine what people in the organization think and appreciate. This culture is always present. Sometimes it has a substantial impact on the employees, sometimes it is more vague. If the culture is not service-oriented, it creates problems for an organization providing service. This issue will be returned to later in Chapter 15.

THE INTERACTIVE PART

The visible or *interactive part* of the service system model (see Figure 13.7) corresponds to the service encounter where the customer meets the service organization. It consists of customers and the rest of the quality-supporting resources that the customers interact with directly. Here the *moments of truth* take place. The quality-supporting resources in the interactive part are as follows:

- Customers involved in the process.

- Customer contact employees.

- Systems and operational routines.

- Physical resources and equipment.

Customers are directly involved in the service system as co-producers. Because of the nature of service production and consumption, customers are not simply passive consumers. At the same time they consume the service, they also take part in production of that service in an active way; sometimes more (as when at the hairdresser's or having a three-course dinner at a gourmet restaurant), sometimes less (as when using a freight forwarder's service). In some cases customers interact with a large service system when staying at a hotel, but in other situations they are in touch with only a limited sub-system, as when operating an automatic teller machine. Sometimes several customers are present simultaneously in the process interacting with each other. In other situations, as in the case of telephone communication, the service concept is to provide technology and a system that makes it possible for customers to contact each other. Irrespective of the nature of the situation, customers, however, actively take part in the process and in service production. It is important to analyse how customers influence the service process, and to avoid situations where they have a negative impact on the process, and on the behaviour of service employees and the effectiveness of systems used in the process. One must be aware of the fact that sometimes a firm has misbehaving customers, and that there is a readiness in the firm to handle such customers. Furthermore, service processes are sometimes designed in a way which triggers customer misbehaviour.[19]

Customer contact persons are employees directly interacting with the customers. Sometimes they are also called 'service employees' or 'frontline employees'. Anyone can be a contact person, irrespective of which position or job he may have in the hierarchy. Interactions that take place may be face-to-face contacts or interactions over the telephone or even by e-mail, fax or letter. A manager or supervisor may also be a contact person if direct customer contacts, on a regular or irregular basis, are part of his job. Frequently, contact personnel are the most crucial resource for a service provider. Systems, technology and physical resources are a valuable support, but most service organizations depend more on their contact staff than on other resources. Contact persons are in a position to recognize the wishes and demands of customers in the moments of truth by watching, asking questions and responding to the customers' wishes, worries and behaviour. Furthermore, they are able to instantly follow up on the quality of the service rendered and undertake corrective action as soon as a problem is observed. However, more and more service processes are designed so that no contact persons are present, at least not on a regular basis. This makes the process more vulnerable when service failures occur.

Systems and routines consist of all operational and administrative systems as well as work routines of the organization. Queuing systems, call centre systems, how to cash a cheque in a bank, how to operate a vending machine or how to make purchases on a website are examples of such systems. There are a vast number of systems and routines that influence the way of consuming the service and performing various tasks. The systems can be more or less service-focused. A complicated document that customers are supposed to fill in forms a system that is not service-focused. This normally means that the perceived service quality is poorer than it otherwise would be. A manufacturer of goods has a range of such systems, which may be performed as administrative tasks without taking the customer into account *or turned into service-focused processes*. Such systems include research and development, the installation of machines and equipment, deliveries, customer training, quality control at the customer's premises, claims handling, billing or the service of a telephone receptionist.

These systems and routines have a double impact on service quality. First, they *directly influence the quality perception of customers*, because customers have to interact with systems. If they feel comfortable with a certain system, it is probably service-oriented. If they feel that they are forced to adjust to a system, however, there is room for improvement. Quality is destroyed or damaged by the system. Second, the systems and routines have *an internal impact on employees*. If a certain system is considered old-fashioned, complicated or not service-focused, employees who have to live with the system will get frustrated. This, of course, influences motivation in a negative way.

Physical resources and equipment include all kinds of resources used in the service system. Computers, documents and tools belong to this category. Some of these physical resources are a prerequisite for the good technical quality of the output. However, they also influence functional quality because customers may find it more or less easy to use them in self-service tasks and they make a favourable or less favourable impression on customers. Other physical resources only have an impact on functional quality. The interior of waiting rooms is an example of such physical resources. Physical resources and equipment used in the service process have an internal effect on employees similar to that of the systems. Physical resources and equipment form the *servicescape*[20] of the service process, where customers, contact persons and systems and resources work together. The servicescape can also include objects, music and even aromas that support a positive perception of the ambience and physical elements of the service encounter. All these elements form the visible part of the service process. Every single part, including the customers, has to match the total system if good quality is to be perceived.

THE IMPACT OF THE SUPPORT PART

Behind the interactive part, where the customer directly encounters the service organization, there is the *line of visibility* (see Figure 13.7). Customers seldom see what is going on behind this line, and they often do not realize the importance of the service production that takes place there. This causes at least two types of problems for the service provider. First, what takes place behind the line is not always appreciated as much as it should be by customers. Because of this, customers do not realize how much the service production there contributes to service quality and value support. Irrespective of whether good quality, especially good technical quality, is produced here, customers probably perceive a bad service quality if the interactive part adds mediocre or worse quality. What often happens is that good technical quality produced behind the line of visibility is damaged by bad functional quality produced in the service system in front of this line. On the other hand, good service intentions by contact persons can also be hindered by low-quality support from back offices.

Second, customers may not understand why a given service has a certain price, because they do not realize how much is done behind the line of visibility. It may be difficult to explain why the price is so high, when the visible service production process may seem uncomplicated and therefore in the minds of customers should not justify the high price level.

The service provider, on the other hand, may interpret the importance of the supporting back office in another way that is equally wrong. Because the service provider knows how much of the total value support is produced in the back office invisible to customers, he can assume that customers also know and appreciate this, and consequently enough attention is not paid to the customer orientation of the visible and interactive part of the service process. This may turn out to be a serious mistake.

COMPONENTS OF THE SERVICE SYSTEM BEHIND THE LINE OF VISIBILITY

What happens in the supporting and invisible part of the organization has an impact on what can be accomplished by the interactive part. This support is sometimes a major prerequisite for good service. There are three kinds of support to the interactive service production (see Figure 13.7):

1. Management support.

2. Physical support.

3. Systems support.

The most important type of support is *management support*, which every manager and supervisor should provide to their staff. Managers and supervisors maintain corporate culture, and if the firm wishes to be characterized by a *service culture*, they will have to support the values of such a culture. They are responsible for shared values and ways of thinking and performing in their work groups, teams and departments. If employees are to be expected to maintain service-focused attitudes and behaviours, managers are the key to success. The manager is the leader of the troop. If the boss does not provide his team with a good example, and if he by his leadership is not capable of encouraging them to be service-minded and customer-conscious, the organization's interest in its customers and in giving good service will decrease. From this follows deteriorating functional quality of the service production process and perhaps even difficulties in maintaining the technical quality of the outcome of the process.

Contact personnel often have to rely on *physical support* provided by functions and departments invisible to the customers. These *support employees* have to consider customer contact personnel as their *internal customers*. In the supporting part there may be a range of support functions, for example, behind each other as discussed previously in this chapter. Support staff have to be treated as internal customers by support functions further behind in the service system. *Internal service* has to be as good as the service to ultimate customers, otherwise the perceived service quality will be damaged. Calculating background data for offering an insurance policy and loading trucks in warehouses are examples of physical support.

The third type of support is *systems support*. This is of a somewhat different nature. Investments in technology, for example, computer systems, information technology, buildings, offices, vehicles, tools, equipment and documents, form the systems support from behind the line of visibility. If the organization invests in an unreliable, slow computer system that does not permit prompt answers to customers' questions or rapid decision-making or that regularly crashes, or a database that does not provide contact personnel with easily and quickly retrievable information about customers, the service system lacks good systems support. If a contact person cannot provide good service because of existing management regulations, there may be another type of inadequate system support – *rules and regulations* that are too rigid.

There is also another kind of systems support. The knowledge employees have of operating various systems is *systems know-how*. The organization must invest in employees who know how to operate and make best use of the company's systems and technology, and should provide training.

Behind the support part is the *totally invisible part* of the organization. This part is in a way outside the service system. It consists of functions that do not influence the service offering or service quality, either directly or indirectly. Internal bookkeeping is an example. Frequently, analysing an organization shows that there are surprisingly few parts that are totally invisible.

THE BLUEPRINTING MODEL

Service blueprinting is a well-known model of planning the service process as a system. The model was originally introduced by Lynn Shostack.[21] During the past few years this planning model has been used extensively.[22] In the blueprinting model sub-processes and activities in a service process are depicted and the relationship between them is established and related to the customer's contact points with the various processes. In this way the interrelationships between activities in the interactive part of the service process in front of a *line of visibility* and activities in a supportive back office behind this line are established, and a blueprint of the whole process is developed. In this way it is possible to analyse how a service process can best be designed to support good customer perceived service quality.

CASE STUDY

THE SERVICE SYSTEM MODEL: ELEVATOR REPAIR AND MAINTENANCE

We now consider the development of the service system in a major elevator repair and maintenance operation. This service is provided by one of the major manufacturers – the service, maintenance and modernization operations of which count for more than half of their total invoicing. The first part of this case was presented in Chapter 2 to illustrate customers' perception of service quality. In that context it was observed that customers, although they were satisfied with the technical quality of the outcome of the firm's service processes, did not appreciate the functional quality of the process, and therefore considered the total quality of the service to be low. Customers did not like the fact that almost every time the elevator needed maintenance or there was a need for repair, a new service technician arrived to take care of the job. The successive technicians did not develop a hands-on knowledge of the elevators and did not get to know the customers. The customers, in turn, did not get to know the service technicians, which made communication difficult. Moreover, the customers did not understand why the service technician often left an unfinished job, especially as no information on the reasons for this nor when the technician could be expected to return was given. Moreover, problems were experienced with the punctuality of the service and the flexibility of the firm.

The technology already existed to create a good outcome of the repair and maintenance processes. However, the systems (as well as the attitudes and skills of the employees) necessary for implementing the process were lacking. Hence, a new service system was developed and implemented. The subsequent changes in the interactive and support parts of the service system and their impact on the service process are presented and discussed in this part of the case study.

Systems and operational resources. Previously, the supervisor of a regional or local service group (covering a smaller city or part of a bigger city) allocated each day's repair and maintenance jobs to the service technicians available that morning, without considering the previous history of the various customers or whether a given service technician had any previous experience of the customers and elevators that were assigned to him. In this way no relationship between a given customer and a given service technician could develop. Moreover, service technicians did not develop a knowledge of, or responsibility for, any of the customers. This was now changed, so that every service technician was given long-term responsibility for the same set of customers. A back-up system to be used in case the regular technician was sick was also developed.

In order for the company to change its operational system, specific systems knowledge had to be developed. This was not an easy process because of the history of organizing workflow in the company. However, by developing a new understanding of how operational systems should function, a *systems support* was created that enabled the service technicians to get a far better knowledge of the history of the elevators they were responsible for as well as to feel more responsible for the customers to which they had been assigned.

Physical resources and equipment. Previously, the service technicians had a limited stock of spare parts and a limited assortment of tools in their vans. If they needed a tool they did not carry, they had to leave the job and get the missing spare part or tool from a central depot. This was one of the reasons why customers were left wondering where the service technician had gone and why he had left the job unfinished. Now the decision to invest in new and bigger vans and to keep more spare parts and tools in stock was taken (a decision to renew the car-park had already been taken, but instead of purchasing the vans that had been planned originally, the company bought bigger vans). This made it possible for service technicians to finish almost all jobs without interruption. Hence, this decision not only increased the usefulness of the physical resources used in the service process, it also had a favourable impact on the operational systems used in the process.

By changing the technology used, the company created an additional *systems support* that made it possible for the service technicians to perform in a more customer-oriented fashion.

Contact personnel. It was obvious that service technicians concentrated on the outcome of the repair and maintenance tasks, and were much less concerned with the way they did their jobs and with their interactions with the customers. Operational systems and management support from supervisors had been outcome-focused and had not encouraged an interest in the process itself. An *internal marketing* process was initiated, where the objective was to focus the interest of service technicians as well as their supervisors and managers on the quality perceptions of the customers, especially on the importance of the functional quality perception of the process. The reasons for these changes in systems and equipment were explained. By this internal marketing process, management wanted to achieve a change in all employees' attitudes towards the customers and towards their jobs, so that a more customer-focused performance would be achieved.

Traditionally, supervisors and managers had focused on the outcome of the service process, while the understanding of how to support and manage the process of repair and maintenance from a quality perspective had been neglected. Elevator repair and maintenance had been thought of as solely outcome consumption. However, in reality the customers perceived it as *process consumption*. Now a process perspective was taken, supported by the internal marketing process. Hence, *management support* by supervisors and managers was created.

A support function responsible for information about customers already existed. Through more customer-oriented market research, more accurate *support* in the form of better customer information was achieved.

Customers. The new service system was intended to make it easier for the customers to interact with the service technicians. Customers would realize that their viewpoints were recognized and that they more easily got answers to their questions. Their time could be expected to be used more effectively, because unnecessary breaks in the repair and maintenance jobs could be avoided in future.

The starting point for the change process was a strategy decision, according to which the service concept was redirected towards supporting people's movement within buildings, during and outside elevator maintenance and repair activities.

The results of the development of the service system were positive. Fewer customers left the company, while the company managed to maintain its premium price level. The business became profitable.

THE SERVICE PROCESS LANDSCAPE: THE SERVICESCAPE AND THE EXTENDED SERVICESCAPE MODEL

The service process and the service encounter take place in an environment that is partly planned and controlled by the service provider. External environmental conditions, such as the weather and competitors' actions, are not under the firm's control and in some situations the service is provided in the customer's premises. However, in most cases the immediate environment in which the service process takes place can be, and should be, carefully designed and developed by the firm. Otherwise, the number of uncontrolled factors grows. In order to help service organizations manage the physical setting of the environment for the service process, Bitner introduced the *servicescape* model.[23] When presenting the model she also makes the point that 'interestingly, in service organizations the same physical setting that communicates with and influences customers may affect employees of the firm'.[24]

THE SERVICESCAPE FRAMEWORK

The servicescape framework is based on the idea of a landscape for the service process. In this landscape the service encounters take place and the service contact personnel and the customers interact during the service process. However, according to the framework, customers and employees are not part of the service landscape, but their behaviour is influenced by it. The model has been criticized on this very point, that it does not – as integral parts – include the people acting in the physical setting. According to this criticism the physical setting is formed by the people who are in this setting and act and interact in it.[25] Moreover, the servicescape framework has been criticized on the grounds that it fulfils an instrumental role only,[26] and it excludes people's cultural perception and their experiences,[27] behavioural intentions when entering the physical setting for the service encounter[28] and social interactions.[29]

In spite of this criticism, the servicescape model provides a basic model for understanding the physical setting of a service and its influence on employees and customers. The model is illustrated in Figure 13.8.

The servicescape framework in Figure 13.8 is fairly self-explanatory. Hence, it will be commented upon only briefly here. The elements or typology of the framework are three *environmental dimensions* – that is, ambient conditions (temperature, air quality, music, noise, odour, etc.), *space and function* (layout, equipment, furnishings, etc.) and *signs, symbols and artefacts* (signage, style of décor, etc.) – the perceived servicescape as a *holistic environment, moderators* that affect employee and customer responses, respectively, three *internal response factors* (cognitive, emotional and physiological – see the figure for details that impact employee and customer responses, respectively), and *behaviour*. A behavioural element is, of course, the *social interaction among employees and customers*. However, because it has an instrumental influence on these social interactions, a main effect of the servicescape framework is the way people react to the physical setting. The framework includes two opposite ways of reacting: *approach* (affiliation, exploration, stay longer, commitment, carry out plan) and *avoid* (defined as the opposite of approach).

The servicescape model is certainly helpful for designing the physical setting of a service process and service encounters, and it indicates what factors could be observed when assessing the effectiveness of such a physical setting. However, as the criticism of the framework pointed out previously indicates, to explain the interactions between the customer and employees and other resources in the setting, it may be too structured and the social and behavioural context is lacking.

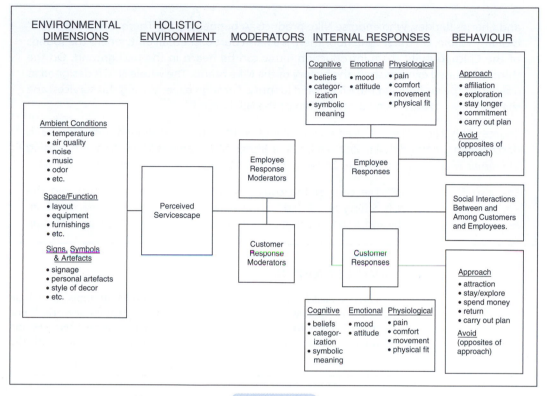

FIGURE 13.8

The servicescape model.
Source: Bitner, M.J., Servicescapes: the impact of physical surroundings on customers and employees. *Journal of Marketing*, **56**(Apr); 1992: p. 60. Reproduced by permission of the American Marketing Association.

CASE STUDY

A SERVICESCAPE EXAMPLE: NIKE TOWN CHICAGO

Nike Town Chicago (NTC) is a three-storey showcase displaying the total range of Nike products. The objective of the concept is to support the Nike brand, rather than achieve immediate sales. Customers entering NTC are invariably struck by the huge assortment of products. The ground floor simulates a small-town shopping district with cobblestone streets. When entering the store the customers or curious visitors encounter statues and framed photos of well-known people wearing Nike products as well as large fish tanks and display cases containing Nike products and memorabilia. When moving further into the showcase they are greeted by framed pictures of sports celebrities such as Michael Jordan and Charles Barkley, who endorse Nike products. A banner saying 'There Is No Finish Line' is clearly visible. On the second floor there is a half-court basketball unit, where the sounds of the Chicago Bulls' team introduction music can be heard in the background. On the third floor cased exhibits show the history of the Nike brand. The whole NTC is designed as a servicescape embodying the Nike brand identity. Through experiencing this servicescape the customer creates his own perception of the Nike brand.

Source: This Nike Town Chicago example of a thoroughly designed servicescape is described in greater detail in Zeithaml, V.A. & Bitner, M.J., *Services Marketing. Integrating Customer Focus Across the Firm*, 2nd edn. Boston, MA: Irwin McGraw-Hill, 2000, p. 264.

See also Sherry Jr., J.F., The soul of the company store: Nike Town Chicago and the emplaced brandscape. In Sherry Jr., J.F. (ed.), *Servicescapes: The Concept of Place in Contemporary Markets*. Chicago, IL: NTC/Contemporary Publishing Company, 1998, pp. 109–146.

THE EXTENDED SERVICESCAPE MODEL

In Figure 13.9 an *extended servicescape model* is illustrated. This extended model attempts to include aspects of the physical setting as *a social meeting place* that are lacking in the original framework.[30] For the sake of readability, the detailed factors that are similar to the ones in the original servicescape framework are not explicitly listed in the figure. The reader may want to consult Figure 13.8 (the original framework).

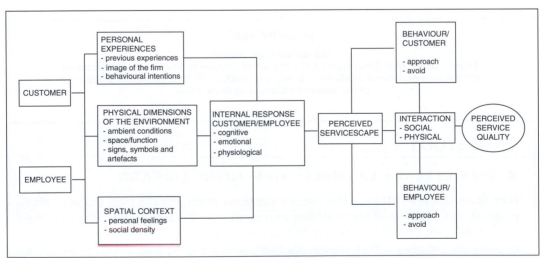

FIGURE 13.9

The extended servicescape model.
Source: Sandbacka, L., *Tjänstelandskap. Teoretisk bakgrund och praktisk tillämpning i tjänste Företag, (Servicescape. Theoretical background and implementation in practice.)* Helsinki: Hanken Swedish School of Economics, Finland, 2006. Reproduced by permission.

Customers and service employees are both part of the *extended servicescape* framework; by their presence and behaviour at the same time as they are affected by the physical setting of the service, they also form it. *Perceived service quality* is included as the final outcome of the model. The physical setting and the interactions taking place in it should be designed so that, in the final analysis, customers perceive favourable service quality that makes them want to continue using the same service provider's offerings. Moreover, not only social interactions between people in the servicescape but also interactions with the elements of the physical setting itself are included in the framework (physical interactions). Customers, and employees, do not only interact with each other but also with physical resources, systems and other tangible elements in the physical setting. Hence, in addition to the *social interactions* these *physical interactions* influence the customers' perception of service quality. At the same time, the customer contact employees also perceive such physical interactions and, in addition to the social interactions with customers, these interactions affect them as well. Both the social and physical interactions affect their feeling of well-being as well as their motivation to be customer focused, and their proneness to provide customers with good service and in the end good service quality.

To the *physical dimensions of the service environment*, such as ambient condition, space, signs, symbols and artefacts (see Figure 13.8 for details), two factors influencing the servicescape have been added – *personal experiences* and *spatial context*. The customers as well as the employees bring their *previous experiences* from the physical setting at hand and other servicescapes, *their image of the service provider* and their *behavioural intentions* to the service process. All this affects the perceived servicescape and therefore also their behaviour in it. In addition, the spatial context of the physical setting has to be taken into account. The number of people, fellow customers and also employees in the environment, i.e. the *social density*, and the *personal feelings* towards the type of spatial context they become involved in also influence the customers', and employees', perception of the servicescape.

As in the original model the *internal responses* of customers and employees are *cognitive*, *emotional* and *physiological* (see Figure 13.8 for details). From these responses the *perceived servicescape* emerges. Customers and employees *interact socially and with the physical elements* of the servicescape and their behaviour in the servicescape can be characterized either as *approach* or *avoid* behaviour (see Figure 13.8 for details). Finally, a customers' perception of *service quality* is formed.

In conclusion, the *extended servicescape* model brings the social context including personal experiences and the spatial context as well as both customers' and employees' interactions with the physical setting into the framework. Moreover, it explicitly points out that the ultimate goal for the customers' and employees' either approach or avoid behaviour in the physical setting, and the social and physical interactions taking place in it, is to create favourable perceived service quality for the service provider's customers. Alone and especially together with the *service system model* in Figure 13.7, the *extended servicescape model* provides a useful framework for planning service processes. Together with the *service style/consumption style model* presented in the next section (see Figure 13.10), they form a comprehensive framework for planning service encounters and buyer–seller interactions, and therefore also for planning the service organization's interactive marketing process.

FITTING RESOURCES IN THE SERVICE SYSTEM TO THE SERVICE CONSUMPTION PROCESS

The quality-supporting resources – personnel, systems, goods, technologies and physical resources, and customers – have to be carefully planned so that a competitive functional quality is produced in the service process. If good quality is produced, an excellent interactive marketing impact is also created. In Figure 13.10 the nature of this issue is illustrated schematically.

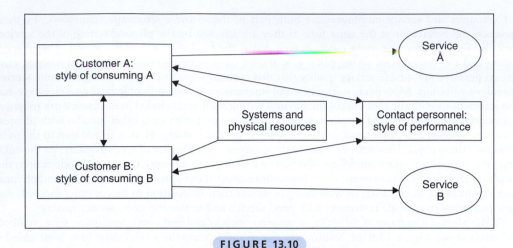

FIGURE 13.10

The service style/consumption style model.
Source: Lehtinen, J., *Asiakasohjautuva palveluyritys (Customer-oriented service firm)*.
Espoo, Finland: Weilin+Göös, 1983, p. 81.

The model demonstrates the need for achieving a balance between the resources involved. In the service encounter and its moments of truth, *contact personnel* emerge as one critical resource. Every contact person has a specific way of performing, which can be called their *service style* or *style of performance*.[31] For example, a dental receptionist and a dentist have their own way of doing and saying things and of performing their tasks. This style is, of course, partly due to their professional skills, but partly also due to their attitude towards patients.

This style of performance has to be geared to the corresponding *style of consuming* of the customers, here the dentist's patients. If there is a misfit between these two styles, perceived service quality will probably be damaged. Since many different customers are frequently present at the same time, their styles of consuming must also fit. For example, a nervous patient in the waiting room may scare other people waiting to see the dentist. In a restaurant, a group of people drinking beer and a family having lunch may not get along well in the same servicescape. The perceived service quality deteriorates.

The *systems and physical resources* used in the service production process will also have to fit the style of performance of contact staff as well as customers' style of consuming. Inappropriate systems make this unnecessarily complicated and even frustrating for contact persons to do their job. Also, if there is a misfit between the systems and the customers' style of consuming, they will not want to adjust to the systems and they will find it awkward to take part in the process. The perceived service quality is again damaged. For example, the treatment procedures and the equipment of the dentist, as well as registration and recall systems and waiting room facilities, have to fit the dentist and the other contact persons as well as the patient. The circles 'Service A' and 'Service B' in Figure 13.10 indicate that Customers A and B may perceive slightly different service, irrespective of whether or not the basic service package is the same. In conclusion, the availability of quality–generating resources as such does not automatically lead to good customer perceived service quality. Sufficient and properly designed resources are a prerequisite, whereas the fit between them determines success.

Figure 13.10 illustrates a case involving external customers. The same applies for internal customers too. The style of performance of supporting staff will have to match the style of consuming of contact staff as internal customers. If there is a misfit, the internal climate will suffer and contact personnel will feel that they get bad support – that is, insufficient internal service – from the support function. Moreover, the systems and physical resources of the support function will have to fit into the service process in a similar manner.

THE SERVICE SYSTEM IN A NETWORK OF SYSTEMS

In previous sections the service system model has been viewed as a single organizational unit. This is, of course, not always the case. Frequently a total system is built up through a network of separate service systems. This, in the minds of customers, is normally perceived as *one* service system.[32]

For example, a hotel chain may have a hotel reservation system, which is geographically located away from the hotels. Customers who make their reservations themselves through this system on one date and stay at a hotel at a later date judge the two service processes (the reservation system and the hotel's service production system) separately, but they *also* view the reservation system as a part of the hotel's system. If the reservation system fails, the customer will not make a reservation at the hotel, and consequently, the total service process system (reservation and hotel together) fails. In principle, the same holds true if the customer makes his reservation through a travel agent not affiliated with the hotel chain. From a management point of view, it will probably be more complicated to manage the total service system, since the other system of this *network*, reservation through an independent travel agent, is an independently managed organization.

Sometimes the situation becomes even more complicated because the relationships between the parties in a network are often mutual. In the previous case, the hotel's service system depends on that of the travel agent. But the service system of the latter also depends on that of the hotel. If the travel agent directs a customer to a hotel that turns out to be unsatisfactory, the customer will blame not only the hotel but also the travel agent. In this situation the travel agent can be considered a subcontractor of the hotel. However, they are both part of a network that consists of the service systems of both parties, and the customer will judge not only the systems of the two parties separately, but the total service system of the network.

In manufacturing, firms often outsource various service activities to sub-contractors. For example, independent delivery firms transport goods to customers, and independent firms are used to handle installation, technical service and repair and customer training. In these situations, similar networks to those above emerge, where the manufacturer is often judged by the performance of the service system of its subcontractor.

From a management point of view, it is essential to observe the existence of these networks of independent or affiliated service systems, and to realize the impact of one system on another and on the success of the total system. For example, bad performance by one party, say an insurance broker, in the network may damage, or even destroy, the other party, in this case the insurance company. On the other hand, excellent service provided by a partner in the network, say, by a delivery and transportation firm, may substantially enhance the image of the manufacturer in the minds of its customers.

SUMMARY

This chapter discussed how to organize marketing in a service organization. It was observed that in a service firm marketing cannot really be organized. *Marketing has to be instilled by creating a customer-focused mindset in everyone throughout the organization at every hierarchical level.* Most of the marketing process takes place outside the responsibility and reach of a traditional marketing department and is implemented by *part-time marketers* who belong to other departments and functions. The role of marketing specialists or full-time marketers is more of a supportive nature. In the latter part of the chapter a *service system model* and an extended servicescape model were presented and discussed. Depending on how well such a system is designed, interactive marketing will be more or less successful.

QUESTIONS FOR DISCUSSION

1. What does 'marketing cannot be organized in a service firm, but instead has to be instilled in the organization' mean?

2. Why does a service organization have to be able to combine the strengths of a large and small company? What results can be achieved by doing so effectively?

3. Why is there a difference between the marketing process and the marketing department?

4. How can a service package be related to the consumption process?

5. How should a service system be designed so that a good interactive marketing impact is created?

6. How does the extended servicescape model differ from the original servicescape model?

7. Analyse, using the service system model, a service of your organization, or a service of any organization, in order to detect the strengths and weaknesses of the system. What are the marketing effects of such strengths and weaknesses? How should the system be developed in order to create a better marketing effect?

8. Discuss how the service system, the extended servicescape and the service style/consumption style models can be used as a comprehensive framework to plan the service process and the service encounters of your or any organization with a goal of creating effective interactive marketing performance.

NOTES

1. In the 1980s, Haller and Piercy predicted that marketing as a separate function and marketing departments as organizational solutions would disappear. See Haller, T., Strategic planning: key to corporate power for marketers. *Marketing Times*, No. 2, 1980 and Piercy, N.F., *Marketing*

Organization. An Analysis of Information Processing, Power and Politics. London: George Allen & Unwin, 1985.

2. See, for example, Gummesson, E., The marketing of professional services – an organizational dilemma. *European Journal of Marketing*, **13**(5), 1979; Grönroos, C., An applied service marketing theory. *European Journal of Marketing*, **16**(7), 1982, 30–41; Grönroos, C., *Strategic Management and Marketing in the Service Sector*. Cambridge, MA: Marketing Science Institute, 1983. See also Grönroos, C., On defining marketing: finding a new roadmap for marketing. *Marketing Theory*, **6**(4), 2006, 395–417.

3. See Hedberg, B., Dahlgren, G., Hansson, J. & Olve, N.-G., *Virtual Organizations and Beyond: Discovering Imaginary Systems*. London: John Wiley & Sons, 1997. Also, see Piercy, N.F. & Cravens, D., The network paradigm and the marketing organization. *European Journal of Marketing*, **29**(3), 1995, 7–34.

4. See, for example, Achrol, R.S. & Kotler, P., Marketing in the network economy. *Journal of Marketing*, **63**, Special Issue, 1999, 146–163. The authors distinguish between *internal, vertical, intermarket* and *opportunity networks*.

5. The first researcher to point this out in the context of service marketing was Evert Gummesson. See Gummesson, 1979, *op. cit.*

6. Gummesson, E., Marketing revisited: the crucial role of the part-time marketer. *European Journal of Marketing*, **25**(2), 1991, 60–67.

7. Gummesson, 1991, *op. cit.* p. 72.

8. See, for example, Rust, R.T., Moorman, C. & Bhalla, G., Rethinking marketing. *Harvard Business Review*, 88, Jan–Feb, 2010, 94–101, where the authors advocate for 'customer departments' replacing 'marketing departments'. See also Leeflang, P., Paving the way for 'distinguished marketing'. *International Journal of Research in Marketing*, **28**(2), 2011, 76–88, where the author discusses a new role of marketing in the organization.

9. Grönroos, 1983, *op. cit.*

10. The notion of marketing departments as organizational traps for service providers was first introduced in Grönroos, 1983, *op. cit.*, based on a large study in the service sector in Scandinavia.

11. Grönroos, 1983, *op. cit.* See also Simon, H., *Hidden Champions*. Boston, MA: Harvard Business School Press, 1996; Piercy, N.F., *Market-Led Strategic Change*. Oxford: Butterworth-Heinemann, 1992.

12. Jan Carlzon, former managing director and president of SAS (Scandinavian Airlines System), who in the 1980s successfully turned around this airline to a highly service-oriented and profitable firm,

used the notion of inverting the organizational pyramid. See Carlzon, J., *Moments of Truth*. Cambridge, Ma: Ballinger, 1987. Translated into English, the title of the Swedish original was 'Tear down the Pyramids'. Recently, the idea of turning the organizational pyramid upside down has been reinvented. See Jacobson, M.D., *Turning the Pyramid Upside Down. a New Leadership Model*. New York: Diversion Books, 2013.

13. The concept of *internal customer* was introduced to the service and relationship marketing context by Gummesson. See Gummesson, E., *Total Relationship Marketing. Rethinking Marketing Management*. Oxford: Butterworth-Heinemann, 2008.

14. The *line of visibility* concept was introduced in the service marketing literature by Lynn Shostack as part of her service blueprinting model. See Shostack, G.L., Designing services that deliver. *Harvard Business Review*, Jan–Feb, 1984.

15. There is a discussion of customer centricity and customer–centric organizations in the literature. See, for example, Harris, J.E., Customer centricity: what it is, what it isn't, and why it matters. *Journal of Consumer Marketing*, **29**(5), 2012, 392–393, and Shah, D., Rust, R.T., Parasuraman, A., Staelin, R. & Day, G.S., The path to customer centricity. *Journal of Service Research*, **9**(2), 2006, 113–124. See also Galbraith, J.R., *Designing the Customer-centric Organization: A Guide to Strategy, Structure, and Process*. Hoboken, NJ: John Wiley & Sons, 2011.

16. See Peppers, D. & Rogers, M., *Enterprise One-to-One*. London: Currency/Doubleday, 1997, who discuss the issues of identified individual one person segments by creating interactive interfaces with customers and by mass customizing solutions to them.

17. See Lehtinen, J., *Quality-oriented Services Marketing*. The University of Tampere, Finland, 1986, which introduced this three-stage approach.

18. Grönroos, C., *Service Management and Marketing. Managing the Moments of Truth in Service Competition*. Lexington, MA: Lexington Books, 1990.

19. See Fellesson, M., Salomonson, N. & Åberg, A., Troublesome travelers – the service system as a trigger of customer misbehavior. *International Journal of Quality and Service Sciences,* **5**(3), 2013, 256–274, and also Daunt, K.L. & Harris, L.C., Linking employee and customer misbehavior: the moderating role of past misdemeanours. *Journal of Marketing Management*, **30**(3-4), 2014, 221–224, where the authors expand the topic to include misbehaving employees.

20. Bitner, M.J., Servicescapes: the impact of physical surroundings on customers and employees. *Journal of Marketing*, **56**(Apr), 1992, 57–71.

21. See Shostack, *op. cit.*

22. See, for example, Bitner, M.J., Ostrom, A.L. & Morgan, F.N., Service blueprinting: a practical technique for service innovation. *California Management Review*, **50**(3), 2008, 66–94, and

Kostopoulos, G., Gounaris, S. & Boukis, A., Service blueprinting effectiveness: drivers of success. *Managing Service Quality*, **22**(6), 2012, 580–591.

23. Bitner, *op. cit.* See also Brüggen, E.C., Foubert, B. & Gremler, D.D., Extreme makeover: short- and long-term effects of a remodeled servicescape. *Journal of Marketing*, **75**(5), 2011, 71–87, and Rosenbaum, M.S. & Massiah, C., An expanded servicescape perspective. *Journal of Service Management*, **22**(4), 2011, 471–490.

24. Bitner, *op. cit.*, p. 57. See also Baker, J., Berry, L.L. & Parasuraman, A., The marketing impact of branch facility design. *Journal of Retailing*, **10**(2), 1988, 33–42.

25. Clarke, I. & Schmidt, R.A., Beyond the servicescape. The experience of place. *Journal of Retailing and Consumer Services*, **2**(3), 1995, 149–162; Rowley, J. & Slack, F., The retail experience in airport departure lounges: reaching for timelessness and placelessness. *International Marketing Review*, **16**(4–5), 1999, 363–375.

26. Aubert-Games, V., Twisting servicescapes: diversion of the physical environment in a re-appropriation process. *International Service Industry Management*, **8**(1), 1996, 26–41.

27. Arnould, E.J., Price, L.L. & Tierney, P., Communicative staging of the wilderness servicescape. *Service Industries Journal*, **18**(3), 1998, 90–115.

28. Hightower, R., Brady, M.K. & Baker, T.L., Investigating the role of the physical environment study of sporting events. *Journal of Business Research*, **55**, 2002, 697–707.

29. Tombs, A. & McColl-Kennedy, J.R., Social-servicescape conceptual model. *Marketing Theory*, **3**(4), 2003, 447–475.

30. The *extended servicescape model* was developed at Hanken Swedish School of Economics Finland by Lotta Sandbacka. See Sandbacka, L., *Tjänstelandskap. Teoretiska bakgrund och praktisk tillämpning i tjänsteföretag* (Servicescape. Theoretical background and implementation in practice). Unpublished master's thesis. Helsinki: Hanken Swedish School of Economics, Finland, 2006. In Swedish.

31. This approach to understanding the balance between resources in the service process was developed by Jarmo Lehtinen. See Lehtinen, *op. cit.* See also Gwinner, K.P., Bitner, M.J., Brown, S.W. & Kumar, A., Service customization through employee adaptiveness. *Journal of Service Research*, **8**(2), 2005, 131–148, where the authors found that the employees' amount of customer knowledge and some personality dispositions and the intrinsic motivation of the employees influence their propensity to adapt their service style and even the service offering to better suit the customers.

32. See Gummesson, E., Quality, service-dominant logic, and many-to-many marketing. *The TQM Journal*, **20**(2), 2008, 143–153.

FURTHER READING

Achrol, R.S. & Kotler, P. (1999) Marketing in the network economy. *Journal of Marketing*, **63**, Special Issue, 146–163.

Arnould, E.J., Price, L.L. & Tierney, P. (1998) Communicative staging of the wilderness servicescape. *Service Industries Journal*, **18**(3), 90–115.

Aubert-Games, V. (1996) Twisting servicescapes: diversion of the physical environment in a re-appropriation process. *International Service Industry Management*, **8**(1), 26–41.

Baker, J., Berry, L.L. & Parasuraman, A. (1988) The marketing impact of branch facility design. *Journal of Retailing*, **10**(2), 33–42.

Bitner, M.J. (1992) Servicescapes: the impact of physical surroundings on customers and employees. *Journal of Marketing*, **56**(Apr), 57–71.

Bitner, M.J., Ostrom, A.L. & Morgan, F.N. (2008) Service blueprinting: a practical technique for service innovation. *California Management Review*, **50**(3), 66–94.

Brüggen, E.C., Foubert, B. & Gremler, D.D. (2011) Extreme makeover: short- and long-term effects of a remodeled servicescape. *Journal of Marketing*, **75**(5), 71–87.

Carlzon, J. (1987) *Moments of Truth*. Cambridge, MA: Ballinger.

Clarke, I. & Schmidt, R.A. (1995) Beyond the servicescape. The experience of place. *Journal of Retailing and Consumer Services*, **2**(3), 149–162.

Daunt, K.L. & Harris, L.C. (2014) Linking employee and customer misbehaviour: the moderating role of past misdemeanours. *Journal of Marketing Management*, **30**(3–4), 221–224.

Fellesson, M., Salomonson, N. & Åberg, A. (2013) Troublesome travelers – the service system as a trigger of customer misbehaviour. *International Journal of Quality and Service Sciences*, **5**(3), 256–274.

Galbraith, J.R. (2011) *Designing the customer-centric organization: a guide to strategy, structure, and process*. Hoboken, NJ: John Wiley & Sons.

Grönroos, C. (1982) An applied service marketing theory. *European Journal of Marketing*, **16**(7), 30–41.

Grönroos, C. (1983) *Strategic Management and Marketing in the Service Sector*. Cambridge, MA: Marketing Science Institute.

Grönroos, C. (1990) *Service Management and Marketing. Managing the Moments of Truth in Service Competition*. Lexington, MA: Lexington Books.

Grönroos, C. (2006) On defining marketing: finding a new roadmap for marketing. *Marketing Theory*, **6**(4), 395–417.

Gummesson, E. (1979) The marketing of professional services – an organizational dilemma. *European Journal of Marketing*, **13**(5), 308–318.

Gummesson, E. (1991) Marketing-orientation revisited: the crucial role of the part-time marketer. *European Journal of Marketing*, **25**(2), 60–75.

Gummesson, E. (2008) Quality, service-dominant logic, and many-to-many marketing. *The TQM Journal*, **20**(2), 143–153.

Gummesson, E. (2008) *Total Relationship Marketing. Marketing Management, Relationship Strategy, CRM, and a New Dominant Logic for the Value-creating Network Economy*. Oxford: Butterworth-Heinemann.

Gwinner, K.P., Bitner, M.J., Brown, S.W. & Kumar, A. (2005) Service customization through employee adaptiveness. *Journal of Service Research*, **8**(2), 131–148.

Haller, T. (1980) Strategic planning: key to corporate power for marketers. *Marketing Times*, **2**.

Harris, J.E. (2012) Customer centricity: what it is, what it isn't, and why it matters. *Journal of Consumer Marketing*, **29**(5), 392–393.

Hedberg, B., Dahlgren, G., Hansson, J. & Olve, N.-G. (1997) *Virtual Organizations and Beyond: Discovering Imaginary Systems*. Chichester: John Wiley & Sons.

Hightower, R., Brady, M.K. & Baker, T.L. (2002) Investigating the role of the physical environment study of sporting events. *Journal of Business Research*, **55**, 697–707.

Jacobson, M.D. (2013) *Turning the Pyramid Upside Down. A New Leadership Model*. New York: Diversion Books.

Kostopoulos, G., Gounaris, S. & Boukis, A. (2012). Service blueprinting effectiveness: drivers of success. *Managing Service Quality*, **22**(6), 580–591.

Leeflang, P. (2011) Paving the way for 'distinguished marketing'. *International Journal of Research in Marketing*, **28**(2), 76–88.

Lehtinen, J. (1983) *Asiakasohjautuva palveluyritys* (Customer-oriented service firm). Espoo, Finland: Weilin & Göös. In Finnish.

Lehtinen, J. (1986) *Quality Oriented Services Marketing*. The University of Tampere, Finland.

Peppers, D. & Rogers, M. (1997) *Enterprise One-to-One*. London: Currency/Doubleday.

Piercy, N.F. (1985) *Marketing Organization. An Analysis of Information Processing, Power and Politics*. London: George Allen & Unwin.

Piercy, N.F. (1992) *Market-Led Strategic Change*. Oxford: Butterworth-Heinemann.

Piercy, N.F. & Cravens, D. (1995) The network paradigm and the marketing organization. *European Journal of Marketing*, **29**(3), 7–34.

Rosenbaum, M.S. & Massiah, C. (2011) An expanded servicescape perspective. *Journal of Service Management*, **22**(4), 471–490.

Rowley, J. & Slack, F. (1999) The retail experience in airport departure lounges: reaching for timelessness and placelessness. *International Marketing Review*, **16**(4–5), 363–375.

Rust, R.T., Moorman, C. & Bhalla, G. (2011) Rethinking marketing. *Harvard Business Review*, **88**(Jan–Feb), 94–101.

Sandbacka, L. (2006) *Tjänstelandskap. Teoretiska bakgrund och praktisk tillämpning i tjänsteföretag* (Servicescape. Theoretical background and implementation in practice). Unpublished master's thesis. Helsinki: Hanken Swedish School of Economics, Finland. In Swedish.

Shah, D., Rust, R.T., Parasuraman, A., Staelin, R. & Day, G.S. (2006) The path to customer centricity. *Journal of Service Research*, **9**(2), 113–124.

Shostack, G.L. (1984) Designing services that deliver. *Harvard Business Review*, Jan–Feb.

Simon, H. (1996) *Hidden Champions*. Boston, MA: Harvard Business School Press.

Tombs, A. & McColl-Kennedy, J.R. (2003) Social-servicescape conceptual model. *Marketing Theory*, **3**(4), 447–475.

Zeithaml, V.A. & Bitner, M.J. (2000) *Services Marketing. Integrating Customer Focus Across the Firm*, 2nd edn. Boston, MA: Irwin McGraw-Hill.

CHAPTER 14
PEOPLE MANAGEMENT: INTERNAL MARKETING AS A PREREQUISITE FOR SUCCESSFUL CUSTOMER MANAGEMENT

> 66 *Without good and well-functioning internal relationships, external customer relationships will not develop successfully. Engaging and motivating employees – on all levels – is a true test of managing an organization.* 99

INTRODUCTION

In service businesses in particular the role of employees is paramount for success. In spite of the growing importance of technology, customer-centric and service-minded employees are needed for high-quality service experiences. Therefore, successful people management is a prerequisite for successful customer management. This chapter will discuss a phenomenon that was originally highlighted by the research into service marketing; that is, *internal marketing*.[1] Throughout this book, the issue of internal marketing has emerged in several contexts. The term was coined as an umbrella concept for a variety of internal activities and processes that are not new but, focused upon as here, offer a new approach to developing a service orientation and an interest in customers and marketing among an organization's personnel. Internal marketing starts from the concept that employees are a first, internal market for the organization. If a service perspective, goods, services, planned marketing communication, new technologies and operational systems cannot be marketed to this internal target group, marketing to ultimate, external customers cannot be expected to be successful either. Internal marketing is a prerequisite for successful external and interactive marketing. The latter part of the chapter will focus upon two concepts that are closely related to internal marketing, *empowering* and *enabling employees*. After reading this chapter the reader should understand the role of internal marketing in service management and know how to develop an internal marketing process, as well as understand the opportunities for empowerment and the risks related to half-hearted empowerment processes.

INTERNAL MARKETING: A SUMMARY

Internal marketing is not a new phenomenon, and it was not new when the term was first used in the service marketing literature in the 1970s.[2] Firms have always used morale-boosting activities and campaigns, and employees' attitudes and motivation have long been a concern of management and human resources staff. However, the notion of internal marketing has brought three new aspects to human resources management in a firm:

1. The employees are a first, internal market for the firm's offerings to external customers as well as for its external marketing programmes.

2. An active, co-ordinated and goal-oriented approach to all employee-oriented efforts, which combines these internal efforts and processes with an external orientation of the firm (that is, with creating a preparedness and motivation for good interactive marketing behaviour and provision of good perceived service quality).

3. An emphasis on the need to view people, functions and departments internal to the firm as internal customers, to whom internal service has to be provided in the same customer-focused manner as to external customers.

The first observation is important, because it points out the fact that everything the service provider does for its external customers (planned marketing communication, service offerings, etc.) is first perceived and evaluated by its own personnel. If employees do not believe in the promises made by external marketing activities and campaigns, do not know how to implement a service offering or how to make use of technology or systems in the service process – if they do not accept them, or feel that they do not have the skills to perform according to what is required of them, they will not 'buy the offering'. In that case they will not be able or willing to perform as effective *part-time marketers* and contribute to a good *interactive marketing* impact and successful brand fulfilment. *The employees form an internal market that should be attended to first.*

The second notion is equally important, because it emphasizes the fact that *all internal efforts, programmes and processes have to be geared towards maintaining or improving external effectiveness and the firm's external performance.* Human resource management is not only an internal matter, but is also a matter of making sure that employees contribute to the service provider's external performance. Such efforts and processes have to be planned and implemented with a similar approach as external marketing, that is, in a *co-ordinated*, active and *goal-oriented* way.

The third observation – that internal customers exist and that they have to be treated in the same way as external customers – has an important impact on the internal relationships of an organization.[3] Fellow employees must not be provided with slow, inattentive and careless service and support, because if this is the case their ability to provide the firm's 'real' customers with good service and to create high perceived service quality is seriously jeopardized.

Internal marketing studies[4] have emphasized a need to view people in an organization not only as individuals but as relationship partners, and moreover pointed out that people management has to reach out to people in relationships with other organizations in the network as well.[5]

> **TABLE 14.1**
>
> **What is required of the employees in a customer-focused and service-oriented organization.**
>
> *General requirements*:
>
> - Understand the full relationship the firm has with its customers (or other stakeholders).
> - Understand and accept their role and obligations in maintaining these relationships.
> - Be customer-focused in their work environment.
>
> *Specific requirements*:
>
> - Have the *skills* to interact and communicate with customers (or other stakeholders).
> - Be *motivated* to interact and communicate.
> - Feel *rewarded* for interacting and communicating in ways that support customer-focused behaviour and thus successful interactive marketing performance.

The first observation emphasizes the need to view employees not as subordinates but from a win–win partnering perspective, where people feel that they are working for an organization that provides them with something in return, such as opportunities to develop, an encouraging environment, access to skills, information and support from a knowledge-generating team, and of course an acceptable salary.[6]

The second observation demonstrates that the borderline between what is inside an organization and what is outside it becomes blurred. The distinction between relationships with employees internal to a firm or to a network and relationships with customers and other stakeholders becomes blurred as well. Suppliers, service providers and their customers become one interactive organization, where value for customers is created jointly in interactive relationships.

Recent research into internal marketing has pointed out that the notion of motivating employees and creating motivated employees, which has been suggested as a key goal of internal marketing, easily becomes an obstacle for lifting people management onto a strategic level in an organization.[7] Neither top management nor marketing specialists tend to consider motivating employees part of their responsibilities, or even an issue they should be concerned about. As a consequence motivating employees remains a tactical issue in the firm. This observation is important, because the internal marketing approach to people management considers motivating employees for customer-focused and service-minded behaviour of such importance to success that it should be given strategic attention.

In Table 14.1 what is required of employees for a service firm to be customer-focused and service-oriented is illustrated. These requirements can be divided into general requirements and specific requirements. In subsequent sections, means of achieving the goals set by these requirements will be discussed at length.

INTERNAL MARKETING: A STRATEGIC ISSUE

The term *internal marketing* was originally derived from the notion of the internal market of employees, and from this point of view internal marketing is a logical term. However, it can be argued that this term is not very appropriate. Often employees who have no marketing training and who do not consider themselves part of marketing, and normally have not been appointed to be concerned with customers as part-time marketers, have a negative view of marketing and do not want to be involved in anything labelled marketing. Why should they want to be involved in something called 'internal *marketing*'? If the term becomes a problem internally, one can always choose another name for this phenomenon for internal use. Many firms have done so, and any term or slogan that functions well will do. However, the term *internal marketing* is used to describe this approach to people management *in principle*, what it includes and how it can be implemented. Therefore, the term internal marketing is used in this book as well.

Human resources form a strategic resource for any firm. With employees who are inadequately trained, have poor attitudes towards their job and towards internal and external customers, and who get inadequate support from systems, technologies, internal service providers and their managers and supervisors, the firm will not be successful. Therefore, *internal marketing is a management strategy*.[8] It is a strategic issue, in spite of the development of information technology and the growth of high-tech service. *If top management does not understand the strategic role of people and consequently also of internal marketing, money invested in internal marketing efforts and processes will not pay off.* In that case money invested in information technology and systems often does not pay off very well either. The active and continuous support of top management, not merely lip service to the importance of employees, is a necessity for successful internal marketing.

In internal marketing the focus is on good internal relationships between people at all levels in the organization, such that a service-oriented and customer-focused mindset is created among customer contact employees, support employees in internal service processes, team leaders, supervisors and managers. However, such a mindset is not enough. Adequate skills (for example, for how to interact and communicate with customers) and supportive systems and leadership are also required. If employees do not have the knowledge and skills needed to provide good service and create a favourable marketing impact, they will not be motivated to perform in that way.

Top management, human resource management and marketing all contribute to the implementation of internal marketing processes. They do so in close collaboration with service operations and other departments, where part-time marketers work.[9] As will be seen later in this chapter, on a tactical level many of the activities of internal marketing already exist in firms. It is only a matter of refocusing, co-ordination, and active and goal-oriented implementation. However, on a strategic level the role and importance of internal marketing is often not yet properly recognized.

Internal marketing thus operates as a holistic management process to integrate multiple functions of the firm in two ways. First, it ensures that employees at all levels in the firm (including management) understand the importance of a *customer focus* in the business and its various processes, activities and campaigns. Second, it ensures that all employees have adequate knowledge and skills for complete customer support and are prepared and motivated to act in *a service-oriented* manner.

THE INTERNAL MARKETING CONCEPT

The emerging importance of service to almost every business has enhanced the notion that a well-trained and service-focused employee, rather than raw materials, production technology or the products themselves, is the *most* critical resource. These employees will be even more critical in the future in an increasing number of industries. The more information technology, automated and self-service systems are introduced in service processes, the more important will be the service orientation and customer-consciousness of the employees who remain. The customer contacts that occur from time to time will have to be consistently perceived favourably by the customers. In such service processes, the high-tech processes are largely taken for granted, whereas contacts with service employees, when they occur, either make or break the customer relationship.

Marketing specialists in the marketing department are not the only human resource in marketing; often they are not even the most important resource. In customer contacts, these full-time marketing specialists are almost always outnumbered by employees whose main duties are production and operations, deliveries, repair and maintenance services, claims handling or other tasks traditionally considered non-marketing. However, the skills, customer focus and service-mindedness of these individuals are all critical to customers' perception of the firm and to their future patronage. Hence, customer focus and a willingness to serve customers in a marketing-oriented fashion and to provide customer satisfaction have to be spread throughout the organization, to every department and work group.[10]

The internal marketing concept states that:

The internal market of employees is best motivated for service-mindedness and prepared for customer-focused performance by an active, goal-oriented approach, where a variety of activities and processes, on a strategic as well as operational level, is used internally in an active, marketing-like and co-ordinated manner. In this way, internal relationships between people in various departments and processes (customer contact employees, internal support employees, team leaders, supervisors and managers) can best be enhanced and geared towards service-oriented management and implementation of external relationships with customers and other parties.

Internal marketing is the management philosophy of treating employees as customers.[11] They should feel satisfied with their job environment and relationships with their fellow employees on all hierarchical levels, as well as with their relationship with their employer as an organization. Human resource management (HRM) and internal marketing are not the same thing,[12] although they have a lot in common. HRM offers tools that can be used in internal marketing, such as training, rewarding, hiring and career planning, and adds more tools. Internal marketing offers guidance on how these and other tools should be used, that is, to improve interactive marketing performance through customer-focused and skilful employees. Successfully implemented internal marketing requires that marketing and HRM work together.[13]

What is new with the internal marketing concept as described in this chapter is the introduction of a unifying concept for more effectively managing a variety of interfunctional and well-established activities as part of an overall process aimed at a common objective. *The importance of internal marketing is the fact that it allows management to approach all of these activities in a more systematic and strategic manner and gear them towards the external performance of the firm.* Internal marketing is not legitimated by its methods – any activity could be part of internal marketing – but by its purpose of gearing internal personnel-oriented processes towards their external customer-focused effects (or internal customer-oriented effects).[14]

TWO ASPECTS OF INTERNAL MARKETING: CHANGING ATTITUDES AND COMMUNICATING CHANGES

Internal marketing means two types of management processes, *changing attitudes* (attitude management) and *communicating changes* (communications management). First of all, the attitudes of employees and their motivation for customer-focus and service-mindedness have to be managed. This is often the predominant part of internal marketing.

Second, managers, supervisors, contact people and support staff need information to be able to perform their tasks as leaders and managers and as service providers to internal and external customers. They need information about job routines, goods and service features, promises given to customers by, for example, advertising campaigns and salespersons, and so on. They also need to communicate with management about their needs and requirements, their views on how to improve performance, and their findings of what customers want. This is the *communications* requirement of internal marketing.

Both attitude management and communications management are necessary if good results are to be expected. Too often only the communications issues are recognized, and perhaps only as a one-way information task. In such cases, internal marketing typically takes the form of campaigns and activities. Internal brochures and booklets are distributed to personnel, and staff meetings are held where written and oral information is given to the participants and very little communication occurs.[15] Also, managers and supervisors typically take limited interest in their staff and do not recognize their need for feedback information, two-way communication, recognition and encouragement. The employees receive an abundance of information but very little encouragement. As a result, there is not much mutual understanding

This, of course, means that much of the information they receive has no major impact on the staff. The necessary change of attitudes and enhancement of motivation for good service and customer consciousness is lacking, and employees are, therefore, not receptive to the information.

If the need for and the nature of the attitude management aspect of internal marketing is recognized and taken into account, *internal marketing becomes an ongoing process* instead of a campaign or series of campaigns, and the role of managers and supervisors, on every level, is much more active. Also, much better results are achieved.

Changing attitudes always includes an element of reinforcing newly instilled attitudes, and is, therefore, *a continuous process*, whereas communications management may be more of a discrete process including activities at appropriate points in time. However, these two aspects of internal marketing are also intertwined. Naturally, much or most of the information shared with employees has an effect on attitudes. For example, customer contact personnel who are informed in advance about an external advertising campaign develop more positive attitudes towards fulfilling the promises of that campaign. The tasks of managers, supervisors and team leaders include, as integral and often inseparable parts, both communications management aspects and attitude management aspects.

CASE STUDY

CHANGING ATTITUDES IN AN ORGANIZATION IN THE PUBLIC SECTOR

A consultancy firm focusing on change processes shared the following experiences about the process of changing attitudes in a Scandinavian public sector organization with several thousand employees. First, the general manager requested that the consultants, together with middle-level management, should implement and inform employees throughout the organization about substantial changes underway in the manner the organization would work. However, the consultant quickly realized that if this change was going to be successfully implemented, top management had to act as a role model and supporter of the process. Top management had to meet the employees. In the end, the organizational change was introduced through a big 'tour', containing two big buses, cameramen, supporters, and of course top management. The goal was to visit hundreds of employees at their different workplaces and tell them about the changes and ask for their opinion. Meanwhile, the entire tour was broadcast live online, such that every employee could be informed about the changes and the discussions with top management that were taking place. In this way the attitude and communication management aspects were integrated, and the change process was lifted onto a strategic level.

The tour was a great success. The response the consultants received afterwards from employees was remarkable: 'I have a feeling that I have been heard', 'I feel much more informed regarding what we are supposed to do', and 'I got the feeling that the managers at the top listen to us and take us seriously.' After six months the organizational change had been implemented successfully. Top management realized that they had to have more direct and in-depth contact with their employees to be able to secure their support for effective implementation of any decisions and changes that influenced employees. They also realized that attitude change and communication go hand in hand.

PURPOSE AND OVERALL OBJECTIVES OF INTERNAL MARKETING

Internal marketing has almost always been described as a means of *motivating* employees to be customer-focused and service-minded in their customer contacts. This makes sense, but given that internal marketing should be on top management's agenda as a strategic issue, and that top management does not usually take an explicit interest in motivating employees, defining internal marketing in this way does not seem appropriate. Instead, as Laura Cacciatore[16] suggests in her study of the subject the lack of adequate knowledge and skills, which is a major reason for lack of motivation for customer-focused and service-minded behaviour among employees, could be the key focus of internal marketing. The competence level and the development of appropriate knowledge, skills and abilities among the employees are issues which have the potential to draw top management's attention and turn internal marketing into a strategic issue.

A main reason why employees are not motivated to perform in a certain manner – customer-focused, service-minded, or any other way – is a lack of knowledge and skills that would be required for them to feel comfortable with a given behaviour. Provided that a wanted behaviour is considered generally acceptable by the employees, closing this competence gap can be expected to create motivation and a willingness to perform. However, as will be discussed in subsequent sections of this chapter, closing such a competence gap is a continuous process, where a number of strategic and tactical issues have to be considered. On a general level the purpose of internal marketing can be defined as follows:[17]

The purpose of internal marketing is to close the gap between the skills, knowledge and competencies that employees need to successfully provide customers with good service, and the current competence level (e.g. knowledge and skills) and support provided (e.g. management, information and physical support) in the organization.

Closing the competence gap can be expected to contribute to the desired motivation for a wanted behaviour. There are of course also other reasons for a lack of motivation. However, as will be shown in subsequent sections, creating, reinforcing and maintaining adequate knowledge and skills demand a set of actions which address other motivators as well, such as management and supervisory behaviour, communicating with employees and ways of disseminating information, and ways of including employees in planning processes.

Based on the purpose of internal marketing formulated above, from a relationship perspective, the objective of internal marketing is:

. . . to create, maintain and enhance internal relationships between people in the organization, regardless of their position as customer contact personnel, support personnel, team leaders, supervisors or managers, so that they have the skills and knowledge required as well as the support needed from managers and supervisors, internal service providers, systems and technology to be able to provide service to internal customers as well as to external customers in a customer-focused and service-minded way, and feel motivated to perform in such a manner.[18]

Such internal relationships can only be achieved if employees are comfortable with what is required of them and feel that they can trust each other, and above all trust the firm and its management to continuously provide the physical and emotional support required to perform in a customer-focused and service-minded way.[19]

From the relationship-oriented objective of internal marketing, four more specific overall objectives can be derived:

1. To ensure that employees are motivated for customer-focused and service-minded performance and thus successfully fulfil their duties as *part-time marketers* in the interactive marketing process.

2. To attract and retain good employees.

3. To ensure that internal service is provided in a customer-oriented manner in the organization or between partners in a network.

4. To provide people who render service internally or externally with adequate managerial and technological support, which enables them to fulfil their responsibilities as *part-time marketers*.

The main objective is, of course, to create an internal environment and implement internal actions, processes and programmes so that employees feel motivated to carry out part-time marketing behaviour. However, the second objective follows on from the first one: the better its internal marketing works, the more attractive the firm is considered as an employer. The third objective is, of course, only an extension of the first one, and the fourth objective is a requirement for maintaining a motivation for customer orientation as well as for making it possible to perform well in a practical situation as a part-time marketer. These overall objectives can be developed into more specific goals depending on the situation at hand. This will be discussed in the following sections.

THE THREE LEVELS OF INTERNAL MARKETING

In principle, three different types of situation can be identified where internal marketing is called for:

1. When *creating a service culture* in the firm and a service orientation among personnel as the fundamental requirement for the existence of customer-focused and service minded behaviour among employees on all levels.

2. When *maintaining a service orientation* among personnel.

3. When *introducing a service perspective, new goods and services or external marketing campaigns and activities or new technologies, systems or service process routines* to employees.

These situations represent three levels of internal marketing. Each of the situations will be discussed below.

CREATING A SERVICE CULTURE

As will be discussed in more detail in Chapter 15, a *service culture* exists when a service orientation and an interest in customers are the most important norms in the organization.

In many firms a service culture is lacking or weak. Internal marketing is a powerful means of developing a service culture in connection with other activities. In Chapter 16 service culture and how to create such a culture is discussed. In general, internal marketing goals in this situation are:

1. To enable employees – managers, supervisors, customer contact employees and support employees – to understand and accept the service perspective and business mission, strategies and tactics as well as the goods, services, external marketing campaigns and processes of the firm.

2. To create positive relationships between people in the organization.

3. To develop a service-oriented management and leadership style among managers and supervisors.

4. To teach all employees service-oriented communications and interaction skills.

It is essential to achieve the first goal, because one cannot expect employees to understand why service, service orientation and customer consciousness are important and why they have responsibilities as part-time marketers, unless they are aware of what the firm wants to achieve, and accept this. The second goal is important, because good external relationships with customers and other parties are dependent on the internal climate in the organization. The third and fourth goals are important because service-oriented management methods and communication and interaction skills are fundamental requirements of a service culture.

MAINTAINING A SERVICE CULTURE

The second situation where internal marketing can be useful is when a service culture should be maintained. Once such a culture has been created it has to be maintained in an active manner, otherwise employees' attitudes will easily revert to a culture where non-service norms and a lack of customer focus dominate. Internal marketing goals for helping to maintain a service culture include the following:

1. To ensure that management methods are encouraging and enhance the service-mindedness and customer focus of employees.

2. To ensure that good internal relationships are maintained.

3. To ensure that an internal dialogue is maintained and employees receive continuous information and feedback.

4. To continuously market new goods and services as well as marketing campaigns and processes to the employees before they are launched externally.

The most important internal marketing issue here is *the management support of every single manager and supervisor*. Management style and methods are of extreme importance at this point. Employees seem to be more satisfied with their jobs when supervisors concentrate on supporting how problems for customers are solved rather than enforcing existing rules and regulations.

Because management does not have the ability to directly control service processes and the moments of truth of the service encounters, it has to develop and maintain *indirect control*. Such indirect control can be established by maintaining a culture that makes employees feel that service should guide their thinking and behaviour.[20] In this continuous process, every single manager and supervisor is involved. If they are able to encourage their staff, if they can open up communication channels – both formal and informal – an established service culture can be expected to continue. Managers and supervisors are instrumental in maintaining good internal relationships.

INTRODUCING NEW GOODS, SERVICES, EXTERNAL MARKETING ACTIVITIES, CAMPAIGNS AND PROCESSES

Internal marketing initially emerged as a systematic way of handling problems when firms planned and launched new goods, services or marketing campaigns without properly preparing their employees. Contact employees especially could not perform well as part-time marketers when they did not know what was going on, did not fully accept new goods, services or marketing activities, or learned about new services and advertising campaigns from newspaper adverts or TV commercials or, even worse, from their customers.

It should be noted that this third level of internal marketing is interrelated with, and reinforces, the other two. These introductions, however, form an internal marketing task in their own right. At the same time, they enhance the maintenance of an established service culture or support the establishment of such a culture. The internal marketing goals for helping with these introductions of new goods, services and external marketing campaigns and processes include the following:

1. To make employees aware of and accept new goods and services being developed and offered to the market.

2. To make employees aware of and ensure their acceptance of new external marketing campaigns and activities.

3. To make employees aware of and accepting of new ways – utilizing new or renewed technologies, systems, routines, etc. – in which various tasks influencing internal and external relationships and interactive marketing performance are to be handled.

PREREQUISITES FOR SUCCESSFUL INTERNAL MARKETING

If internal marketing activities are implemented purely as isolated programmes or campaigns, or, even worse, as separate activities without connections to other management factors, the risk that nothing enduring will be achieved is overwhelming. The organizational structure and the strategy of the firm have to support the establishment of a service culture. Moreover, management methods and the management and leadership style of managers and supervisors have to be supportive if they are to be expected to fulfil their tasks in internal marketing.

The three prerequisites for successful internal marketing are:

1. Internal marketing has to be considered an integral part of *strategic* management.

2. The internal marketing process *must not be counteracted* by the organizational structure of a firm or by lack of management support, or systems and physical support.

3. Top management must constantly *demonstrate leadership* and active support for the internal marketing process.

In order to be successful, internal marketing starts with *top management*. Next, *middle management* and *supervisors* have to accept and live up to their role in a marketing process. Only then can internal marketing efforts directed towards *contact employees* and *support employees* be successful. Employees' ability to function as service-minded *part-time marketers* depends to a large extent on the support and encouragement they get from supervisors. Genuine customer-focused leadership at all levels in the organization is a necessity if customer contact and support employees are expected to be committed to good service.

In conclusion, all other categories of employees have to be involved as well. The *contact personnel* form a natural target market for internal marketing. They have the immediate customer contacts and are instrumental in the interactive marketing process. However, they often depend on support from other employees and departments in the firm. The ability of contact employees to perform their interactive marketing tasks depends to a large extent on the service-mindedness of employees who do not come into contact with customers themselves. Such groups of employees, the *support personnel*, should perform in a customer-focused manner when they serve their *internal customers* (for example, contact employees). They are *part-time marketers* as well, although their customers are internal and not external. In summary, the four main target groups for internal marketing are:

1. Top management.

2. Middle management and supervisors.

3. Customer contact personnel.

4. Support personnel.

It should be noted that the same person may occupy several positions. A support person may sometimes be a contact person. A supervisor who, for example, is supposed to support and encourage contact people may be a contact person serving customers, or a support person serving internal customers, regularly or occasionally. Middle or top management may also have customer contacts. When they have such contacts they, too, are *part-time marketers* in the firm's marketing process.

STRATEGIC AND TACTICAL INTERNAL MARKETING

As internal marketing is part of strategic management, and therefore should be a management philosophy, implementing internal marketing includes strategic aspects as well as tactical ones. On a *strategic level* internal marketing requires that management creates a job environment which is encouraging and motivating for customer-focused and service-minded behaviour.[21] On a *tactical level*, internal marketing activities which aim at implementing a customer-focused, service-minded behaviour are planned and executed.

STRATEGIC INTERNAL MARKETING

In order for management to create a motivating and encouraging environment for service-oriented and customer-focused behaviour, four management areas are important. These are:

1. Motivating leadership and management support.
2. Motivating human resource policy.
3. Motivating training policy.
4. Motivating planning systems.

In the following sections we shall discuss these in some detail.

MOTIVATING LEADERSHIP AND MANAGEMENT SUPPORT

Training is an important internal marketing activity. However, no training programme alone is enough in an internal marketing process. In order to achieve continuity in such a process, the role of top management, middle management and supervisors is paramount. Managers, supervisors and team leaders have to show leadership, not only administrative 'managing and controlling'.

Management support can be of various types, for example:

- *Continuity* of formal training programmes by everyday management actions.
- Demonstrating an active interest in customers and in providing good service.
- Actively *encouraging* employees as part of everyday management tasks.
- *Empowering employees* by giving them decision-making authority, and thereby showing trust in them.
- *Involving* employees in planning and decision-making.
- *Feedback* to employees and flow of *information* and *two-way communication* in formal and informal interactions.
- Establishing an open and encouraging *internal climate*.
- Creating trusting relationships among employees.

Frequently, employees returning from a course or a training session have no follow-up on the course message. Their supervisor is not interested in what they have learned or how to make use of new ideas and knowledge. Employees are usually left alone to implement what they have learnt. Sometimes employees get the impression that the fact they have been away for training has only created problems, for example with undercapacity. Nobody seems to care about any positive and potentially useful learnings. In such situations, employees are alienated, any new idea and favourable attitude effects are rapidly destroyed.

Instead, the manager or supervisor should encourage employees to implement new ideas and help them to realize how they could be applied in their specific environment. Recognition is a critical

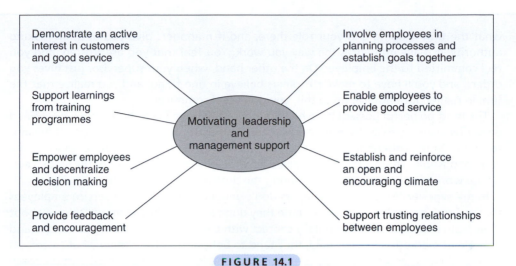

FIGURE 14.1

Strategic internal marketing: Motivating leadership and management support.

part of management support. The management style demonstrated daily by managers and supervisors has an immediate impact on the job environment and internal climate, thus management style is an internal marketing issue.

Joint planning and decision-making with the employees involved is a means of achieving commitment in advance to further actions that emerge from the planning process. Customer contact employees have valuable information and knowledge of the needs and desires of customers, so the involvement of these employees in the planning process leads to improved decision-making.

The need for information and feedback has been discussed already in this book. Here, managers, especially supervisors, have a key role. Moreover, they are responsible for creating an open climate where service-related and customer-related issues can be raised and discussed in a relationship-enhancing internal dialogue.

Management support and internal dialogue are the predominant tools of the attitude management aspect of internal marketing, but they are also key ingredients of communications management.

Key aspects of *motivating leadership and management support* as part of strategic internal marketing are summarized in Figure 14.1.

CASE STUDY

EXPERIENCES OF A SERVICE EMPLOYEE

From my job experience, it really makes a difference if the employee feels that he is an important part of the business, and really believes in what the firm is doing. I have worked for firms where I have felt important and felt that the managers believed in what I was doing, and in other firms where I have felt absolutely unimportant. If you understand what the firm is doing and your role there, and if managers give you decision-making authority, it really influences the way you work. You feel that you are trusted, and you feel committed to the employer. On the other hand, when your supervisor just gives you orders, and you'll have to make customers believe in one thing, and you realize that the firm in reality does not live up to this, you don't feel committed.

The most powerful bosses I have had during my life have been those who have gained power by giving it away, by empowering their employees and only been support persons to them. On the other hand, I have had bosses who have tried to control as much of my work as possible. These bosses have gained little real power in the minds of the employees, whose work efforts have decreased during the time they worked for them.

In my experience, so many managers don't understand the role of service employees for the firm's marketing impact. Because they don't see this, they seem not to care about their team members who are in daily contact with customers. And if they do understand the role of marketing in their field, they tend to believe that they know what customers need and want, and don't listen to the contact employees who get firsthand feedback from the customers.

The problem here is that these managers seem to think that their team members are not to be trusted or capable of taking responsibility. I have seen so many big deals lost, because the employees working directly with customers did not have proper information and authority to respond quickly to customers' inquiries and demands.

Source: This case was written by Tyrsky Ylppö from Finland, based on her work experience

MOTIVATING HUMAN RESOURCE POLICY

The human resource management approach must motivate the employees to take a customer-focused and service-oriented approach when pursuing their tasks. This includes:

- Hiring policies which encourage service-oriented persons to apply.
- Job descriptions which encourage a service orientation and customer focus.
- Career plans that encourage a service orientation and customer focus.
- Reward systems that appreciate service-orientation and customer-focused behaviour.

These aspects of human resource management aim at supporting a service culture and an interest in internal and external customers. If they are mismanaged, the culture will not enable a service orientation and an interest in customers, which are prerequisites for successful interactive marketing and customer-focused part-time marketer behaviour.

It is essential to hire and keep the right kind of employees in a firm. Successful internal marketing starts with recruitment and hiring. This, in turn, requires proper job descriptions where the part-time marketer tasks of contact and support employees are recognized. Job descriptions, recruitment

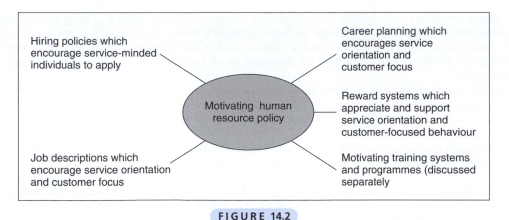

Hiring policies which encourage service-minded individuals to apply

Career planning which encourages service orientation and customer focus

Motivating human resource policy

Reward systems which appreciate and support service orientation and customer-focused behaviour

Job descriptions which encourage service orientation and customer focus

Motivating training systems and programmes (discussed separately

FIGURE 14.2

Strategic internal marketing: motivating human resource policy.

procedures, career planning, salary, bonus systems and incentive programmes, as well as other HRM tools, should be used by the organization to pursue internal marketing goals.

None of the HRM-related tasks is new. However, they are often used passively, more like administrative procedures than as active marketing tools to achieve internal objectives. The external marketing implications of these tasks are also all too often neglected. Because of the traditional management approach, most employees are considered costs only, and not revenue-generating resources, and the human resource policy is developed accordingly.

Rewarding employees for good service is also an important internal marketing instrument.[22] People should know that good service is appreciated by the firm and this should be recognized in the reward system. Far too often cost-efficiency achievements and other internal efficiency factors are the basis for reward systems. If a high number of phone calls dealt with is considered good and rewarded in spite of the fact that customers may be dissatisfied because they feel that they received too little attention, good service is not encouraged.

In many service businesses, the important customer contact jobs are placed in the hands of the newest, least-trained employees, who are often hired on a part-time basis only. Quite often they are unskilled and paid little. Their job can be monotonous. No positive relationships with the employer can develop under such circumstances, although such employees can have a major influence on customer experiences of service quality. Their impact on profits can be equally important.[23]

Key aspects of *motivating human resource policy* as part of strategic internal marketing are summarized in Figure 14.2.

MOTIVATING TRAINING POLICY

Educating employees and training programmes are part of human resource management. However, because of the central importance of training for successful internal marketing, training policies and programmes are discussed in a separate section. Training is the most frequently used internal marketing activity, and it is almost always required. However, the *training policy* is of strategic importance. Strategically, it has to be geared towards the creation and maintenance of a service culture, which enables and reinforces service-mindedness and a customer focus within the organization. A lack of understanding of the firm's strategies and of the importance of part-time marketers' responsibilities is almost always present. 'Service knowledge' and adequate skills are lacking. This is partly due to insufficient or non-existent knowledge of the meaning of a service strategy, of the nature and scope of marketing in a service and relationship context, and of the employees' role with dual responsibilities in the firm. This often goes for managers on all levels as well as for contact and support employees.

Partly, this is an attitude problem. Indifferent or negative attitudes have to be changed. On the other hand, attitude problems normally follow on from a lack of understanding of facts and a lack of adequate skills. Therefore, the tasks of improving employees' knowledge and changing attitudes are intertwined.

Training, either internal or external, is most frequently needed as a basic component of an internal marketing process. Three types of training tasks can be included:

1. Developing a *holistic* view of a service strategy and of the total customer management or marketing process, as well as of the role of each individual in relation to other individuals and processes in the firm, and in relation to customers.

2. Developing adequate technical knowledge and skills about how to provide good service and how to handle customer contact situations.

3. Developing and enhancing *favourable attitudes* towards a service strategy, a customer focus and *part-time marketer* performance.

4. Developing and enhancing *communications*, *sales* and *service skills* among employees.

Training, together with internal communication support, are the predominant tools of the communications management aspect of internal marketing. However, at the same time they are also part of the attitude management process. If the first type of training goal is overlooked, it will be very difficult or impossible to create conditions for favourable attitudes towards service and part-time marketing responsibilities, or to make employees interested in acquiring the skills required to perform as good part-time marketers. An individual who does not recognize and appreciate the whole picture will not understand why he should change his behaviour towards fellow employees and customers and bother to acquire new skills unrelated to his traditional tasks. Because employees need to feel that there is a trusting relationship between fellow employees and management as well as customers, training programmes must also include elements focusing on the fair treatment of both employees and customers.[24]

Key aspects of *motivating training policy* as part of strategic internal marketing are summarized in Figure 14.3.

MOTIVATING PLANNING SYSTEMS

Often employees feel frustrated because they cannot influence how work routines and processes are developed. They know from experience and firsthand customer feedback what could be improved. Therefore, employees on many levels in an organization should be actively involved in the planning of their work environment and job routines. The employees have knowledge and insights which are often valuable for planning their jobs. Of course, suggestions based on such knowledge must be evaluated in accordance with the firm's strategy. In a later section, a relationship-mediated model of internal marketing relying on a motivating planning system will be described.

Firms seldom make use of the firsthand knowledge of customer processes, needs and expectations held by customer contact employees. As a consequence, actions needed to correct or improve service processes and employee skills are not taken, or processes and skills are developed in a less than optimal

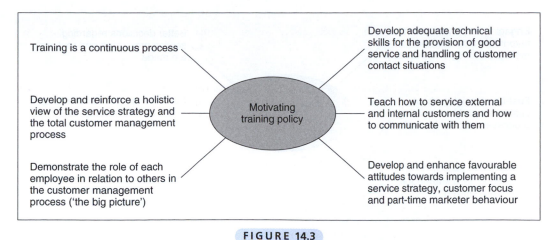

FIGURE 14.3

Strategic internal marketing: motivating training policy.

way, sometimes in a counterproductive direction. This is also true in the case of internal processes, where the insights of support employees go unnoticed.

Including employees in planning processes has at least the following benefits:

- Knowledge of how service processes function and problems with practical implementation, and about opportunities to improve them, is used.

- Knowledge about internal and external customers' views of existing processes and how such processes could be improved is used.

- Tacit knowledge as well as explicit knowledge is recognized and can be used.

- Employees who have been actively involved in planning and development processes easily feel more committed to executing new plans than other employees.

From an internal marketing perspective, the main reason to include employees in planning processes is to create and reinforce customer-centric and service-oriented attitudes in the organization. However, at the same time, better insights into how existing processes work (and why they sometimes do not work well) and knowledge about the firm's customers are obtained to improve existing processes. These insights exist in the form of tacit knowledge, which is made explicit only by deliberate actions. Furthermore, employees who have been engaged with planning processes which they are part of can be expected to commit themselves to implementing these processes more wholeheartedly than otherwise.

Engaging employees with planning processes can of course be done in many ways, both through formal routines and in informal ways. Whenever possible formal planning routines can be used, but informal contacts between a manager or supervisor and contact employees may often both enhance motivation for good service and reveal useful insights about customers and how service processes function and could be improved.

Key aspects of *motivating planning processes* as part of strategic internal marketing are summarized in Figure 14.4.

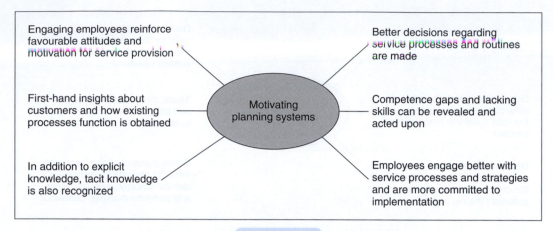

FIGURE 14.4
Strategic internal marketing: motivating planning systems.

INTERNAL MARKETING ACTIVITIES ON THE TACTICAL LEVEL

There is no exclusive list of activities that should belong to an internal marketing process. Almost any activity that has an impact on internal relationships and on the service-mindedness and customer focus of employees can be included.

Typical internal marketing activities can be identified, however. The following list is not intended to be inclusive, nor does it distinguish between activities to be used in developing or maintaining a service culture or in introducing new goods, services and marketing campaigns internally. Many of the activities are common to two or three of these situations.

TRAINING

As mentioned above, training is the most frequently used tactical internal marketing activity, and is almost always needed. However, it is important to remember that training is seldom enough to achieve lasting, or even short-term, results. Training must always be supported by other actions, out of which leadership and management support are most important. Training was discussed extensively in the context of strategic internal marketing, and will therefore not be discussed here any further.

INTERNAL MASS COMMUNICATION AND INFORMATION SUPPORT

Most managers and supervisors realize that there is a need for them to inform employees about new service-oriented strategies and new ways of performing in internal and external service encounters, and to make them understand and accept new strategies, tasks and ways of thinking. However, many people do not know *how* to do this. Therefore, it is important to develop various kinds of support materials. Computer software, PowerPoint presentations and other audio–visual and written material explaining new strategies and ways of performing can easily be used by managers during staff meetings.

Brochures, internal memos and magazines, as well as other means of mass-distributed communications material, can of course also be used in internal marketing.

HUMAN RESOURCE MANAGEMENT

HRM activities are also part of an internal marketing process. However, such tasks were discussed in the section on a motivating human resource policy and will therefore not be discussed any further here.

EXTERNAL MASS COMMUNICATION

The internal effects of any external mass communication are seldom fully recognized. However, employees almost always form an interested and responsive target audience for advertising and other marketing communication campaigns. Such activities and campaigns, and the customer promise inherent in them, should be presented to employees before they are launched externally. This may create commitment and decrease confusion. One step further would be to develop such campaigns in co-operation with the employee groups affected by the external communication effort. This can be expected to commit employees to the fulfilment of promises made in planned external marketing communication.

DEVELOPING SYSTEMS AND TECHNOLOGY SUPPORT

The development of customer information databases, systems for effective internal service support, and other types of systems and technologies that make it possible for the contact employees to provide good service are important parts of internal marketing. If such support is lacking, even the most customer-focused and service-minded employees will eventually start to feel frustrated and lose interest in being good part-time marketers.

Information technology and the development of intranets have had a tremendous impact on internal processes and provided an effective support system in internal marketing. Through easy access to databases, websites and e-mail, and also social media, people and internal processes can reliably and quickly connect to each other. The feeling of being connected to the same body of information as everyone else may create a commitment to a mutual cause among employees, which has a positive influence on internal relationships.[25] However, there is also a risk that the use of e-mail and intranets may alienate employees from each other and from the work community. It is too easy to be antisocial and only communicate using information technology. Such negative aspects of this technology are also enhanced by a surplus of information, much of which may be totally irrelevant.[26]

INTERNAL SERVICE RECOVERY

From time to time customer contact employees and support employees face service encounters where a service failure has occurred, or have to interact with customers who are having a bad day. The situation may be frustrating and sometimes also humiliating for the contact person. Furthermore, the less empowered they are, the more they may experience feelings of low perceived control of the tricky situation and helplessness in dealing with the service failure. The customers may have been emotionally upset, frustrated or angry. Internal customers may react in similar ways. Contact persons who have had to cope with situations like these may need help to recover from the mental stress they suffer following such encounters and from the pressure that they have been under. The firm must actively address these issues to help employees to recover. Bowen and Johnston call this *internal service recovery.*[27] Managers and supervisors have a decisive role in handling such internal recovery situations. Support from the whole work group can be valuable for fellow employees in such stressful circumstances. Management may need to a create a system which guarantees that a support network exists and functions.

MARKET RESEARCH AND MARKET SEGMENTATION

Both internally and externally, market research can be used to find out, for example, attitudes towards part–time marketing tasks and service–oriented performance. Market segmentation can be applied in order to find the right kind of people to recruit for various positions in the organization.

In Table 14.2 internal marketing activities are summarized.

TABLE 14.2

Internal marketing activities.

Training

- Target groups: employees on all levels from top management to middle management, supervisors and support and contact personnel.

- Understanding of the employees' role in the total relationship with a customer and of each and everyone's role and tasks in maintaining and enhancing this relationship.

- Interaction and communication skills.

Leadership and management/supervisory support

- Leadership and management/supervisory support is a continuation of training sessions, which either brings the messages of such sessions alive or kills them.

- Top management must personally demonstrate customer-focused and service-oriented attitudes and behave accordingly.

- Every manager/supervisor must live up to customer- and service-focused standards.

- They must support and not counteract the motivation of and possibilities for their people to perform in a customer-oriented and service-focused manner.

Internal communication and dialogue

- No memos must be used.
- As little one-way information as possible.
- As much personal contact as possible.
- As much dialogue as possible.
- Use intranets for key information.
- E-mail can be used, but avoid overload and if appropriate enable e-mail response.

Make use of internal effects of external communication

- The employees are always an eager audience for external communication.
- Emphasize the role of your employees in advertising and in other external campaigns.

Involve your employees in planning

- Your employees are a source of tacit knowledge about customer preferences and customers' everyday activities, expectations and requirements.
- Involvement has a motivating effect.
- The marketing communication effort that is developed can be better than it would have been otherwise.

Reward your employees for successful performance

- Encourage employees, show respect for them and acknowledge good performance.
- Correct mistakes and give advice for the future in a positive and encouraging manner.
- Although encouragement and job satisfaction are good motivators, bonuses and rewards are also supportive.

Develop supportive technologies and systems

- Make sure that support systems, databases and physical instruments required in the service process are supportive to service-focused and customer-oriented behaviour and performance and do not become a hindrance to such behaviour.

Use human resource management instruments

- Use HRM activities in an active way that not only helps create job satisfaction and a satisfying work environment, but at the same time directs the interests of employees towards customers and customer-focused behaviour so that they become good part-time marketers.

Do internal market research and segmentation

- Job satisfaction usually correlates with customer satisfaction.
- Study the employees' attitudes and preferences towards the work environment, their tasks and the challenge of customer-focused and service-oriented behaviour.
- Use qualitative as well as quantitative methods; make use of information and feedback from encounters that managers and supervisors have with their team members.
- Remember that employees also form a heterogeneous group and therefore may have to be segmented into subgroups that in some respects are approached in different ways.

CASE STUDY

HG HARDWARE

In the Scandinavian market, computer hardware competition has been fierce, and many firms have suffered. Forced to stay out of his office because of a broken leg, Mr Sam Hardman, marketing director of HG Hardware, a regional chain with 15 stores, a central warehouse and some 120 employees, took the time to develop an internal marketing concept to increase employee commitment to the employer and to good service. According to this concept, the attention of everyone in the firm – for example, managers, office personnel, sales clerks, drivers of delivery trucks, warehouse workers and cleaners – should be drawn to the economic performance of the firm, and everyone should be rewarded if its financial result exceeded a set level.

An easy-to-understand chart showing how costs and revenues lead to a Return of Investment (ROI) measure was developed, and an equally easy-to-read booklet about how everyone's performance contributed to costs and revenues was distributed to employees. In this booklet it was demonstrated how the level of service to customers over the counter contributed to revenues, how the work of office employees in the warehouse and stores and in deliveries affected costs, on the one hand, and the opportunity to serve customers well created revenues, on the other hand. The expected impact on costs and revenues of employees paying increased attention to their tasks and to serving internal and external customers was explained in detail and in an understandable way. Each and every employee, regardless of his position in the firm and area of responsibility, could see how the way he did his job influenced costs and revenues, and eventually had an effect on ROI. They could also see how changes in the way they did their job had an impact on ROI, either positively or negatively.

The firm invested in an extensive training programme, the objective of which was to teach employees to understand the economic consequences of the way they did their jobs and to help them realize how they all contributed to ROI, regardless of their tasks.

HG Hardware's management set a modest ROI target of 15% for the first year, and informed the employees that, provided this target was achieved, the owner would take 7.5% to cover their ROI objectives and for future investment in the business, and the rest of the achieved ROI would be split equally between the owners and the employees. On the 15th of every month the ROI figure for the end of the previous month was displayed in all luncheon and coffee rooms and other social areas, so that everyone could follow how their performance had paid off. This created interest in the firm's financial results. After the first year the target had been exceeded. Mr Hardman said, 'It worked. People became interested in the economic consequences of how they took care of their tasks, and we got a commitment to good service. Our customers seemed to have noticed it, too.'

A RELATIONSHIP-MEDIATED APPROACH TO INTERNAL MARKETING

In his research David Ballantyne has taken a relationship approach to internal marketing, where he views it as knowledge renewal.[28] Groups of customer contact employees have accumulated knowledge about customers' behaviour and preferences as well as about how, and with what means, to best serve customers and create a good service quality perception. However, this knowledge has the form of *tacit knowledge*, which is not documented in formal procedures or even known to management. And it is probably not known to everyone who serves customers and perhaps not widely used in the organization. This knowledge may be actively used or, if restricted by company policies, reward systems or supervisory control, not used other than marginally or not at all. If that is the case, it probably frustrates the employees and has a negative impact on their service orientation and customer consciousness. According to Ballantyne, this tacit knowledge has to be interpreted and codified, and if found useful as explicit knowledge circulated in the organization for use by everyone serving internal or external customers. If based on strategy and cost–benefit considerations found appropriate, this tacit knowledge made explicit could change company policies. In the best case scenario the new explicit and authorized knowledge about how to serve customers becomes part of the corporate culture and as tacit knowledge steers the employees' attitudes and behaviours.

According to Ballantyne, this process of knowledge renewal has four stages.

1. *Energizing*: revealing common knowledge by exploring tacit knowledge.

2. *Code breaking*: discovering new knowledge by turning tacit knowledge into explicit knowledge.

3. *Authorizing*: making cost–benefit and policy considerations and transforming tacit-made-explicit knowledge into explicit knowledge that from a strategic and commercial perspective can be put to use.

4. *Diffusing*: integrating the new explicit knowledge with corporate culture and behaviour by disseminating the new explicit knowledge in the organization.

In the first phase of the process, the *energizing* phase, groups of employees are gathered to discuss customer service and various means of servicing customers as well as obstacles and challenges related to this. Such obstacles can be related to anything, for example, existing skills, IT and physical support, atmosphere, company policies, reward systems and supervisory control. The groups are given the opportunity to meet regularly and discuss freely. This first energizing phase should not necessarily lead to any conclusions or suggestions yet. At the same time as *tacit knowledge held by the participants is explored* it is *a socialization process where the participants should create a willingness to pass on to other group members the knowledge and experiences they have gathered in their job.* A mutual trust among the participants should develop, otherwise discussions and knowledge transfers will be constrained.

In this and the next phase of the process discussions, role play and group-based dialogue could be used. Of course, any other way of comparing experiences and making knowledge and thoughts explicit could also be used.

After the initial phase the *code breaking* phase follows. There, when the group members have already familiarized themselves with other participants and developed a trust in each other, the main task is *to discover knowledge that, based on their experience, the members have gained* and perhaps made use of. Old codes should be broken and new opportunities explored. In this way the *tacit knowledge held by the group members is turned into explicit knowledge*. As the participants know that their task is to develop new ways of serving customers (or of performing any task), a mutual obligation to drive the task through should keep the process going.

In the *authorization* phase the *developments and suggestions created in a group are analysed from a company policy and cost–benefit point of view*. This analytical task can to some degree be done in the group, but other than in special cases, the final analysis and decisions have to be made on a management level. This is, of course, due to the fact that company strategies, budget restrictions and other management considerations have to be taken into account. This is a process where tacit-made-explicit knowledge about service procedures and cost–benefit and policy considerations are brought together. Through this process, *explicit knowledge created by the groups is further developed into new procedures and routines to be used in the organization*. It is probable that some developments and suggestions by the group cannot be transformed into new procedures. This can be due to, for example, cost–benefit considerations and company strategies or policies that would be violated, and according to management should not be changed.

In the final stage of the process, the *diffusing* phase, *the new authorized knowledge is integrated with corporate culture through, for example, new designs, support systems and procedures as well as training programmes and new supervisory methods and leadership*. The goal is not only to make the new knowledge and the changes in the organization known to everyone concerned, but also to achieve personal commitment by the employees. In this way *the new explicit knowledge is transformed back into tacit knowledge* that consciously and unconsciously steers the behaviours of the employees in the organization. It is integrated with and reinforces the company culture and in some cases even alters it.

Input to this internal marketing process is the *personal knowledge* of employees, possibly supported by *market intelligence*. The output can be expected to be a higher level of *customer consciousness* in the organization and, as a consequence, improved customer-perceived *service and relationship quality* as well as enhanced *market performance* of the firm.[29]

EMPOWERING AND ENABLING EMPLOYEES

Two concepts that are closely related to internal marketing are *empowering* and *enabling*. An understanding of both concepts and their meaning is important for the effective implementation of internal marketing.

Empowering employees means to give people in an organization, some of whom are customer contact employees, the authority to make decisions and take action in a large number of potentially problematic situations.[30] The main reason for empowerment is the employee motivation effect that can be achieved.[31] There will probably be limits on how far this authority can go, and these limits must be carefully determined. For example, decisions where legal matters have to be considered and/or large sums of money are at stake probably need to be taken to a higher management level. Management must set clear and acceptable boundaries for frontline employees' service recovery latitude.[32] The main thing is that the contact (or support) employee knows his responsibilities and is encouraged to perform more effectively and in a more customer-focused fashion. The ultimate goal is, of course, to improve the part-time marketing performance of the customer contact and support employees.

Correctly implemented empowerment as part of an internal marketing process can have a decisive impact on the job satisfaction of employees, which in turn may improve the part-time marketing impact of employees in customer contacts. Through improved customer retention and more cross-sales this can be expected to have a positive effect on profit.[33]

The empowerment concept has, however, also been criticized. It has been claimed that little real empowerment take place,[34] and that change programmes which aim at empowering employees are full of inner contradictions that have a negative impact on motivation. Managers consciously and unconsciously by their actions and attitudes counteract efforts to empower personnel. In practice they rely more on standardized processes that steer the performance of the employees in a predetermined direction. This does not create an environment for self-governance or for motivated employees to take responsibility for their actions, especially for actions that deviate from the normal route.

However, if empowerment is successfully introduced, the results can be good. Empowerment demands a continuous nurturing of trusting relationships between management and employees.[35] Managers must show that they respect employees' authority to analyse situations and make decisions. In this way a mutual trust between management and employees can be instilled. It is also important to realize that empowerment cannot happen overnight. Rather, management must create and maintain the conditions needed so that an employee can feel that he has power and can use his power in customer interactions.[36] The *enabling* concept is part of the process of creating the conditions required for empowerment.

Bowen and Lawler[37] put empowerment in a larger context. They claim that empowering employees means (1) providing them with information about the performance of the organization, (2) rewarding them based on the organization's performance, (3) creating a knowledge base that makes it possible for employees to understand and contribute to the performance of the organization, and (4) giving employees the power to make decisions that influence organizational directions and performance.

Empowerment cannot function without simultaneously *enabling* employees so that they are prepared to take the responsibility that goes with the new authority. Much of the concern about empowerment in the literature seems to be due to lack of enabling. The employees must understand what *goals* they should be aiming at by making empowered decisions, and feel that they have the *capacity and knowledge* required for such behaviour. Enabling means that employees need support to be able to make the independent decisions effectively in the service process. Without such support, proper conditions for empowered employees do not exist. Enabling includes:

1. *Management support*, so that supervisors and managers give information and also take over decision-making when needed but do not interfere unnecessarily with the decision-making authority given to employees.

2. *Knowledge support*, so that employees have the skills and knowledge to analyse situations and make proper decisions.

3. *Technical support*, from back-office support staff, systems, technology and databases that provide contact employees with information and other services and tools required for handling a wide variety situations.

It is important to realize that *empowerment without enabling creates more confusion and frustration than job satisfaction and motivation among employees*. People who are required to take responsibility for customers but who are not enabled to do so will feel confusion, frustration and anger, and they will probably make bad decisions. The connections between empowerment and internal marketing can easily be seen. Among the objectives of internal marketing is the development of management support, knowledge support and technical support so that empowered employees have the tools and assistance they require and will feel motivated to perform effectively as part-time marketers.

The benefits of empowerment of service employees are as follows:[38]

1. *Quicker and more direct response to customer needs in the service process*, because customers will not have to wait for a decision until a supervisor can be found in unusual situations. At the same time,

customers will experience a feeling of spontaneity and willingness to help which has a positive effect on perceived service quality.

2. *Quicker and more direct response to dissatisfied customers in service recovery situations*, again because customers will not have to wait for a decision until a superior can be found, or will not have to file a formal complaint in situations that do not warrant such a complicated procedure.

3. *Employees are more satisfied with their job and feel better about themselves*, because they take ownership of their job and know that they are trusted employees. This may also decrease absenteeism and employee turnover.

4. *Employees will treat customers more enthusiastically*, because they are more motivated to do their job. This of course requires that they have been made aware of their part-time marketing responsibilities.

5. *Empowered employees can be a valuable source of new ideas*, because they have direct customer contacts, see the problems and opportunities experienced in service encounters, and the customers' behaviours, needs, wishes, expectations and values. As empowered employees they are more inclined to notice these problems and opportunities and to share the findings and ideas they get from them with supervisors and managers.

6. *Empowered employees are instrumental in creating good word-of-mouth referrals and positive comments in social media, and increasing customer retention*, because they can be expected to serve customers in a quick, skilful and service-oriented manner, thus surprising customers and making them more inclined to spread the word and stay with the same service provider.

Empowerment does not mean that managers and supervisors should have less managerial responsibility.[39] The nature of this responsibility will change, however: there will be more leadership orientation instead of mere managing, more independent judgement instead of managing by the book, and a clear understanding when decisive action on the part of the manager or supervisor is required.

Sometimes empowering employees may incur some extra costs. Additional employee training may be required and it may be necessary to pay empowered employees better. There is also, of course, the risk that empowered customer contact employees will make bad decisions that may cost the firm money and perhaps also have a negative effect on customers. This can, however, be avoided by recruiting and enabling personnel carefully. It should also be remembered that not all employees can be empowered, because not everyone will want to have the responsibility that goes with it. Some seemingly unnecessary costs that make customers happy, for example, in service recovery situations, will probably pay off in the long run.

CASE STUDY

EMPOWERMENT AT NORDSTROM

Nordstrom, the upscale North American department store chain whose headquarters are in Seattle, Washington State, has a long-established reputation for empowering its sales associates. In turn, the chain also has a phenomenal reputation for fervently loyal customers.

Nordstrom's sales associates have an 'empowered state of mind', and they feel more control over how to perform the job, more *awareness* of the business context in which the job is performed and more *accountability* for performance outcomes. Nordstrom accomplishes this through management practices that confer significant amounts of power, information, knowledge and rewards upon them. As to power, the associates have the discretion to do whatever it takes to please the customer. The Nordstrom policy manual essentially consists of two sentences: 'Use your good judgement in all situations. There will be no additional rules.' Information on products and sales performance is widely shared. Knowledge refers to training, and Nordstrom relies on extensive on-the-job training, rather than formal classroom training. Finally, as to rewards, sales associates can earn well above the industry average through commissions on sales. There are also numerous status rewards such as being elected as Employee of the Month or being nominated to the V.I.P. Club. It is this empowerment that industry analysts claim accounts for the high level of employee sales, customer satisfaction and profits that make Nordstrom a benchmark in retailing.

AN APPROACH TO MOTIVATING EMPLOYEES

Berry and Parasuraman[40] offer a number of guidelines for firms that want to practice internal marketing effectively:

1. Compete for talented employees.

2. Offer a vision that brings purpose and meaning to jobs.

3. Make sure that employees have the skills and knowledge needed to do their job excellently.

4. Create teams of people who can support each other.

5. Leverage the freedom factor.

6. Encourage achievements through measurement and rewards.

7. Base job design decisions on research.

These seven guidelines make good sense; however, it is not always easy to implement them.[41] Employees need to be empowered to perform, but they also need the support of good management, support systems, technology and information. They also need training so that they have the skills needed to perform effectively. Most people feel motivated to perform better if they have the freedom to think, analyse, make decisions and act. To be able to do that they need knowledge and skills, so that they feel secure in an empowered position. It all starts with recruitment procedures. The better people the firm can hire from the outset, the more effectively they will perform as part-time marketers and in their other duties. In spite of all its technology, a firm is only as good as its people. However, how often do firms violate some or all of these guidelines when hiring and managing customer contact employees or support employees and their supervisors and managers?

HOW TO IMPLEMENT AN INTERNAL MARKETING PROCESS

When starting to plan and implement an internal marketing process, a few guidelines should be observed. First of all, the *internal focus* of internal marketing has to be recognized and fully accepted by management. Employees sense that management considers them important when they are allowed to participate in the process, both in an internal research process and in planning their work environment, the goals and scope of their tasks, information and feedback routines and external campaigns. When employees realize that they are able to involve themselves in improving something that is important to them, they will be more inclined to commit themselves to the business and the goals of the internal marketing strategy.

However, the *external focus* of an internal marketing strategy process should never be forgotten. Improving the work environment and tasks for the employees is, of course, an important objective in its own right. It is, nevertheless, the external marketing impact of every employee that is the ultimate focus of internal marketing. The ultimate objective is to improve customer consciousness and service mindedness and thus, in the final analysis, the *interactive marketing* abilities and the *part-time marketing* performance of the employees. Consequently, *the internal and the external focus of internal marketing go hand in hand*.

Furthermore, it should always be remembered that *if the internal marketing process is viewed as being simply tactical* and initiated only at the customer contact level involving only contact employees, *it will fail*. This level alone cannot breed a service culture for the organization, nor reach the many support employees who also have to function as part-time marketers internally. Only in a situation where a solid service culture has been established can the internal marketing of, for example, an advertising campaign or a new service be directed towards a specific target group of, say, contact employees in a certain department. In all other situations, internal marketing has to involve everyone in the organization, and start with top management and include middle management and supervisors. As has been said, continuous management support, not only by paying lip service to internal marketing, but by active involvement in the process, is an absolute necessity.

Finally, internal marketing is a *continuous process*. The organization needs constant attention from management. Changes in strategy, in technologies used in service processes and in external marketing must always be carefully introduced to the organization. Changing a corporate culture in a service-oriented direction takes time, and management must understand that it has to be given the time it takes. After that the service culture has to be continuously nurtured.

SUMMARY

Internal marketing is an umbrella concept for a range of internal activities and processes, the objective of which is to develop a service orientation, service-minded attitudes and an interest in part-time marketer behaviour among the personnel. It is, therefore, first a management philosophy and second a set of tools. As a management philosophy it emphasizes the pivotal role of the employees as a first internal market. In this chapter the importance of internal relations was emphasized. Three levels of internal marketing were discussed: (1) developing a service culture; (2) maintaining a service orientation among the personnel; and (3) introducing new goods, services, marketing campaigns and activities, systems and technologies in service processes to the personnel. Then, marketing on strategic and tactical levels were explained.

A number of typical activities that can be part of an internal marketing process were also described. In the final part of the chapter, the concepts of empowerment and enabling employees were presented and discussed at some length.

QUESTIONS FOR DISCUSSION

1. Why has a need for internal marketing emerged in service firms?

2. What does it mean to take a relationship approach to internal marketing?

3. Which are the levels of internal marketing? Which processes and activities can be expected to function well as part of internal marketing at each of these levels?

4. What is empowerment? What is the role of empowerment in internal marketing?

5. Why is it dangerous to empower employees without simultaneously considering the need for enabling employees?

6. Discuss the relationship-mediated approach to internal marketing. How could it be implemented in your firm?

7. Analyse the level of service orientation in your firm, or in any given firm, and determine the need for internal marketing. Also, discuss which internal marketing processes and activities might function well for your firm.

NOTES

1. The ultimate idea of internal marketing, to make sure that employees make a good impression on a firm's customers and support customers' perception of quality, is growing in importance. Internal marketing has been the subject of continuous academic research. For some recent publications where internal marketing is studied in various contexts, see for example Peltier, J.W, Schibrowski, J.A. & Nill, A., A hierarchical model of the internal relationship marketing approach to nurse satisfaction and loyalty. *European Journal of Marketing*, **47**(5-6), 2013, 899–916; Ting, S-C., The effect of internal marketing on organizational commitment: job involvement and job satisfaction as mediators. *Educational Administration Quarterly*, **47**(2), 2011, 353–382; and Papasolomou, I., Kountouros H. & Kitchen, P.J., Developing a framework for successful symbiosis of corporate social responsibility, internal marketing and labour law in a European context. *The Marketing Review*, **12**(2), 2012, 109–123.

2. The observation of the existence of an internal market and of the need for service firms to market their campaigns and offerings internally was probably first made by Eiglier and Langeard

in France in a working paper published in 1976 (Eiglier, P. & Langeard, E., *Principes politique marketing pour les enterprises des services*. Working Paper, Institute d'Administration des Enterprises, Université d'Aix-Marseille, December, 1976), although they did not explicitly use the phrase 'internal marketing'. In the same year Sasser and Arbeit addressed the issue of 'selling jobs to the employees' and discuss recruitment, training, motivation, internal communication and retention of service-minded personnel as aspects of this internal task (Sasser, W.E. & Stephen P., Selling jobs in the service sector. *Business Horizons*, **19**(3), 1976, 61–65). In the 1970s, Christian Grönroos also pointed out the need for internal marketing (Grönroos, C., A service-orientated approach to the marketing of services. *European Journal of Marketing*, **12**(8), 1978, 588–601). Leonard Berry was another early proponent of internal marketing (Berry, L.L., The employee as customer. *Retail Banking*, March, 1981).

3. In some publications on internal marketing the relationship between internal suppliers and internal customers (that is, the marketing of goods and services internally in the organization) is considered the main or only domain of internal marketing. See, for example, Ling, I.N. & Brooks, R.F., Implementing and measuring the effectiveness of internal marketing. *Journal of Marketing Management*, **14**, 1998, 325–351 and Reynoso, J.F. & Moores, B., Internal relationships. In Buttle, F. (ed.), *Relationship Marketing: Theory and Practice*. London: Paul Chapman Publishing, 1996, pp. 55–73. In this book, the authors have a much broader perspective.

4. See, for example, Voima, P., *Negative Internal Critical Incident Processes. Windows on Relationship Change*. Helsinki: Hanken Swedish School of Economics, Finland, 2001 and Ballantyne, D., A relationship-mediated theory of internal marketing. *European Journal of Marketing*, **37**(9), 2003, 1242–1260.

5. Varey, R.J., Internal marketing: a review of some inter-disciplinary research challenges. *International Journal of Service Industry Management*, **6**(1), 1995, 40–63; Voima, P. & Grönroos, C., Internal marketing – a relationship perspective. In Baker, M.J. (ed.), *The IEBM Encyclopedia of Marketing*. London: International Thomson Business Press, 1999, pp. 747–751; Gummesson, E., Internal marketing in the light of relationship marketing and virtual organizations. In Lewis, B. & Varey, R.J. (eds), *Internal Marketing*. London: Routledge, 2000; Voima, P., Internal relationship management – broadening the scope of internal marketing. In Lewis, B. & Varey, R.J. (eds), *Internal Marketing*. London: Routledge, 2000.

6. Gummesson, *op. cit.* See also Ballantyne, D., Internal marketing for internal networks. *Journal of Marketing Management*, **13**(5), 1997, 343–366.

7. Cacciatore, L., *När företagets och servicepersonalens uppfattning om det riktiga i företagets strategi kolliderar. En studie i användningen av intern marknadsföring för att motivera kontaktpersonalen i en bank i Finland*. Helsinki: Hanken School of Economics, Finland, 2014.

8. Grönroos, C., *Service Management and Marketing. Managing the Moments of Truth in Service Competition.* Lexington, MA: Lexington Books, 1990 and Piercy, N.F. & Morgan, R.A., Internal marketing – the missing half of the marketing program. *Long Range Planning*, **24**(2), 1991, 82–93, and more recently, for example, Awwad, M.S. & Agti, D.A.M., The impact of internal marketing on commercial banks' market orientation. *International Journal of Bank Marketing*, **29**(4), 2011, 308–332.

9. Bowen, D.A., Schneider, B. & Kim, S.S., Shaping service cultures through strategic human resource management. In Swartz, T.A. & Iacobucci, D. (eds), *Handbook of Services Marketing & Management.* Thousand Oaks, CA: Sage Publications, 2000, pp. 439–454. Also, from an HRM perspective, the internal marketing requirement of close collaboration with other business functions is an opportunity which, according to Schneider and Bowen, helps HRM to 'avoid the HRM trap'. See Schneider, B. & Bowen, D.A., *Winning the Service Game.* Boston, MA: Harvard Business School Press, 1995.

10. Compare Gilmore, A. & Carson, D., Managing and marketing to internal customers. In Glynn, W.J. & Barnes, J.G. (eds), *Understanding Service Management.* Chichester: John Wiley & Sons, 1995, pp. 295–321, where internal marketing is defined as the task of spreading the responsibility for marketing across all departments in a firm.

11. Berry, L.L. & Parasuraman, A., *Marketing Services: Competing Through Quality.* New York: The Free Press, 1991, p. 151.

12. Rafiq, M. & Ahmed, P.K., The scope of internal marketing: defining the boundary between marketing and human resource management. *Journal of Marketing Management*, **9**, 1993, 219–232. Pitt and Foreman claim that the question of whether internal marketing is synonymous with good human resource management has not been studied thoroughly enough. See Pitt, L.F. & Foreman, S.K., Internal marketing's role in organizations: a transaction cost perspective. *Journal of Business Research*, **44**(1), 1999, 25–36. Varey and Lewis suggest that internal marketing should incorporate organizational development (see Varey, R.J. & Lewis, B.R., Beyond the popular conception of internal marketing. In Fisk, R. & Glynn, L. (eds), *Jazzing into the New Millennium: 1999 SERVSIG Services Research Conference.* Chicago, IL: American Marketing Association, 1999, pp. 44–51).

13. Compare Bowen, Schneider & Kim, *op. cit.*

14. Ballantyne, D., The strengths and weaknesses of internal marketing. In Varey, R.J. & Lewis, B.R. (eds), *Internal Marketing.* London: Routledge, 2000.

15. This can typically be the case in situations where internal communication is handled by human resource management alone. See Mitchell, C., Selling the brand inside. *Harvard Business Review*, **90**(Jan), 2002, 99–106.

16. Cacciatore, *op. cit.*

17. Cacciatore, *op. cit.*

18. This relationship-oriented definition of internal marketing is adapted from Voima & Grönroos, *op. cit.*, p. 748. In the latter part of the 1990s, following intense interest in relationship marketing, there was a revival in research into internal marketing, but from a relationship perspective.

19. A lack of trust internally has been shown to have a negative effect on internal relationships. See Herriot, P., Manning, W.E.G. & Kidd, J.M., The content of the psychological contract. *British Journal of Management*, **8**(2), 1997, 151–162. See also Bowen, D.E., Gilliland, S.W. & Folger, R., HRM and service fairness: how being fair with employees spills over to customers. *Organizational Dynamics*, **27**(3), 1999, 7–23.

20. See Bowen, D.E. & Schneider, B., Service marketing and management: implications for organizations. *Research in Organizational Behavior*, **10**, 1988.

21. Over the years the relationship between internal marketing and job satisfaction has been demonstrated in several studies. For a recent study in the educational sector, see Ting, S-C., The effect of internal marketing on organizational commitment: job involvement and job satisfaction as mediators. *Educational Administration Quarterly*, **47**(2), 2011, 353–382.

22. See Lovelock, C., Functional integration in services. Understanding the links between marketing, operations, and human resources. In Swartz, T.A. & Iacobucci, D. (eds), *Handbook of Services Marketing & Management*. Thousand Oaks, CA: Sage Publications, 2000, pp. 421–437. As Lovelock observes, '*reward systems* send powerful messages to all employees as to what kind of organization management seeks to create and maintain, especially as to desired attitude and behavior' (p. 426).

23. Katzenbach, J.R. & Santamaria, J.A., Firing up the front line. *Harvard Business Review*, May/June, 1999.

24. Bowen, Gilliland & Folger, op. cit.

25. Smith, S., Internal affairs. *Marketing*, 7 August, 1997, 24–25.

26. As Gummesson points out, technology is only supportive when put to constructive use. See Gummesson, *op. cit.* See also Hallowell, E.M., The human moment at work. *Harvard Business Review*, Jan–Feb, 1999.

27. Bowen, D.E. & Johnston, R., Internal service recovery: developing a new construct. *International Journal of Service Industry Management*, **10**(2), 1999, 118–131.

28. Ballantyne, 2003, *op. cit.*

29. Ballantyne, 2003, *op. cit.*, p. 1251.

30. The psychological antecedents and meaning of empowering have largely been discussed. See, for example, Wang, G. & Lee, P.D., Psychological empowerment and job satisfaction. An analysis

of interactive effects. *Group & Organization Management*, **34**(3), 2009, 271–296, and Maynard, M.T., Gilson, L.L. & Mathieu, J.E., Empowerment – fad or fab? A multilevel review of the past two decades of research. *Journal of Management*, **38**(4), 2012, 1231–1281.

31. See Conger, J.A. & Kanungo, R.N., The empowerment process: integrating theory and practice. *Academy of Management Review*, **13**(3), 1988, 471–482.

32. Bowen, D.E. & Lawler III, E.E., Empowering service employees. *Sloan Management Review*, **36**(4), 1995, 73–84.

33. Oakland, J.S. & Oakland, S., The links between people management, customer satisfaction and business results. *Total Quality Management*, **9**(4–5), 1998, 185–190.

34. Argyris, C., Empowerment: the emperor's new clothes. *Harvard Business Review*, **76**(May–Jun), 1998, 98–105.

35. Khan, S., The key to being a leader company: empowerment. *Journal of Quality and Participation*, **20**(1), 1997, 44–50.

36. Harari, O., Stop empowering your people. *Management Review*, **86**(2), 1997, 48–51. The author expresses concerns about empowering when used without proper care. See also Edvardsson, B., Larsson, G. & Setterlind, S., Internal service quality and the psychosocial work environment: an empirical analysis of conceptual interrelatedness. *The Service Industries Journal*, **17**(2), 1997, 252–263, where the authors show that the psychosocial work environment has an impact on the service orientation of employees.

37. Bowen, D.E. & Lawler III, E.E., The empowerment of service workers: what, why, how, and when. *Sloan Management Review*, Spring, 1992, 31–39.

38. Bowen & Lawler, *op. cit.*

39. Eccles, T., The deceptive allure of empowerment. *Long Range Planning*, **26**(6), 1993, 13–21.

40. Berry & Parasuraman, *op. cit.*

41. Cahill, D.J., *Internal Marketing. Your Company's Next Stage of Growth*. New York: The Haworth Press, 1996.

FURTHER READING

Argyris, C. (1998) Empowerment: the emperor's new clothes. *Harvard Business Review*, **76**(May–Jun), 98–105.

Awwad, M.S. & Agti, D.A.M. (2011) The impact of internal marketing on commercial banks' market orientation. *International Journal of Bank Marketing*, **29**(4), 308–332.

Ballantyne, D. (1997) Internal marketing for internal networks. *Journal of Marketing Management*, **13**(5), 343–366.

Ballantyne, D. (2000) The strengths and weaknesses of internal marketing. In Varey, R.J. & Lewis, B.R. (eds), *Internal Marketing*. London: Routledge.

Ballantyne, D. (2003) A relationship-mediated theory of internal marketing. *European Journal of Marketing*, **37**(9), 1242–1260.

Berry, L.L. (1981) The employee as customer. *Retail Banking*, March.

Berry, L.L. & Parasuraman, A. (1991) *Marketing Services: Competing Through Quality*. New York: The Free Press.

Bowen, D.E. & Johnston, R. (1999) Internal service recovery: developing a new construct. *International Journal of Service Industry Management*, **10**(2), 118–131.

Bowen, D.E. & Lawler III, E.E. (1992) The empowerment of service workers: what, why, how, and when. *Sloan Management Review*, Spring, 31–39.

Bowen, D.E. & Lawler III, E.E. (1995) Empowering service employees. *Sloan Management Review*, **36**(4), 73–84.

Bowen, D.E. & Schneider, B. (1988) Service marketing and management: implications for organizations. *Research in Organizational Behavior*, **10**.

Bowen, D.E., Gilliland, S.W. & Folger, R. (1999) HRM and service fairness: how being fair with employees spills over to customers. *Organizational Dynamics*, **27**(3), 7–23.

Bowen, D.A., Schneider, B. & Kim, S.S. (2000) Shaping service cultures through strategic human resource management. In Swartz, T.A. & Iacobucci, D. (eds), *Handbook of Services Marketing & Management*. Thousand Oaks, CA: Sage Publications, pp. 439–454.

Cacciatore, L. (2014) *När företagets och servicepersonalens uppfattningom det riktiga i företagets strategi kolliderar. En studie i användningen av intern marknadsföring för att motivera kontaktpersonalen i en bank i Finland*. Helsinki: Hanken School of Economics, Finland.

Cahill, D.J. (1996) *Internal Marketing. Your Company's Next Stage of Growth*. New York: The Haworth Press.

Conger, J.A. & Kanungo, R.N. (1988) The empowerment process: integrating theory and practice. *Academy of Management Review*, **13**(3), 471–482.

Eccles, T. (1993) The deceptive allure of empowerment. *Long Range Planning*, **26**(6), 13–21.

Edvardsson, B., Larsson, G. & Setterlind, S. (1997) Internal service quality and the psychosocial work environment: an empirical analysis of conceptual interrelatedness. *The Service Industries Journal*, **17**(2), 252–263.

Eiglier, P. & Langeard, E. (1976) *Principes politique marketing pour les enterprises des services*. Working Paper, Institute d'Administration des Enterprises, Université d'Aix-Marseille, December.

Gilmore, A. & Carson, D. (1995) Managing and marketing to internal customers. In Glynn, W.J. & Barnes, J.G. (eds), *Understanding Service Management*. Chichester: John Wiley & Sons, pp. 295–321.

Grönroos, C. (1978) A service-orientated approach to the marketing of services. *European Journal of Marketing*, **12**(8), 588–601.

Grönroos, C. (1990) *Service Management and Marketing. Managing the Moments of Truth in Service Competition*. Lexington, MA: Lexington Books.

Gummesson, E. (2000) Internal marketing in the light of relationship marketing and virtual organizations. In Lewis, B. & Varey, R.J. (eds), *Internal Marketing*. London: Routledge.

Hallowell, E.M. (1999) The human moment at work. *Harvard Business Review*, Jan–Feb.

Harari, O. (1997) Stop empowering your people. *Management Review*, **86**(2), 48–51.

Herriot, P., Manning, W.E.G. & Kidd, J.M. (1997) The content of the psychological contract. *British Journal of Management*, **8**(2), 151–162.

Katzenbach, J.R. & Santamaria, J.A. (1999) Firing up the front line. *Harvard Business Review*, May–Jun.

Khan, S. (1997) The key to being a leader company: empowerment. *Journal of Quality and Participation*, **20**(1), 44–50.

Lovelock, C. (2000) Functional integration in services. Understanding the links between marketing, operations, and human resources. In Swartz, T.A. & Iacobucci, D. (eds), *Handbook of Services Marketing & Management*. Thousand Oaks, CA: Sage Publications, pp. 421–437.

Maynard, M.T., Gilson, L.L. & Mathieu, J.E. (2012) Empowerment – fad or fab? A multilevel review of the past two decades of research. *Journal of Management*, **38**(4), 1231–1281.

Mitchell, C. (2002) Selling the brand inside. *Harvard Business Review*, **90**(Jan), 99–106.

Oakland, J.S. & Oakland, S. (1998) The links between people management, customer satisfaction and business results. *Total Quality Management*, **9**(4–5), 185–190.

Papasolomou, I., Kountouros H. & Kitchen, P.J. (2012) Developing a framework for successful symbiosis of corporate social responsibility, internal marketing and labour law in a European context. *The Marketing Review*, **12**(2), 109–123.

Peltier, J.W, Schibrowski, J.A. & Nill, A. (2003) A hierarchical model of the internal relationship marketing approach to nurse satisfaction and loyalty. *European Journal of Marketing*, **47**(5–6), 899–916.

Piercy, N.F. & Morgan, R.A. (1991) Internal marketing – the missing half of the marketing program. *Long Range Planning*, **24**(2), 82–93.

Pitt, L.F. & Foreman, S.K. (1999) Internal marketing's role in organizations: a transaction cost perspective. *Journal of Business Research*, **44**(1), 25–36.

Rafiq, M. & Ahmed, P.K. (1993) The scope of internal marketing: defining the boundaries between marketing and human resource management. *Journal of Marketing Management*, **9**, 219–232.

Reynoso, J.F. & Moores, B. (1996) Internal relationships. In Buttle, F. (ed.), *Relationship Marketing: Theory and Practice*. London: Paul Chapman Publishing, pp. 55–73.

Sasser, W.E. & Stephen, P. (1976) Selling jobs in the service sector. *Business Horizons*, **19**(3), 61–65.

Schneider, B. & Bowen, D.A. (1995) *Winning the Service Game*. Boston, MA: Harvard Business School Press.

Smith, S. (1997) Internal affairs. *Marketing*, 7 August, 24–25.

Ting, S-C. (2011) The effect of internal marketing on organizational commitment: job involvement and job satisfaction as mediators. *Educational Administration Quarterly*, **47**(2), 353–382.

Varey, R.J. (1995) Internal marketing: a review of some interdisciplinary research challenges. *International Journal of Service Industry Management*, **6**(1), 40–63.

Varey, R.J. & Lewis, D.R. (1999) Beyond the popular conception of internal marketing. In Fisk, R. & Glynn, L. (eds), *Jazzing into the New Millennium: 1999 SERVSIG Services Research Conference*. Chicago, IL: American Marketing Association, pp. 44–51.

Voima, P. (2000) Internal relationship management – broadening the scope of internal marketing. In Lewis, B. & Varey, R.J. (eds), *Internal Marketing*. London: Routledge.

Voima, P. (2001) *Negative Internal Critical Incident Processes. Windows on Relationship Change*. Helsinki: Hanken Swedish School of Economics, Finland.

Voima, P. & Grönroos, C. (1999) Internal marketing – a relationship perspective. In Baker, M.J. (ed.), *The IEBM Encyclopedia of Marketing*. London: International Thomson Business Press, pp. 747–751.

Wang, G. & Lee, P.D. (2009) Psychological empowerment and job satisfaction. An analysis of interactive effects. *Group & Organization Management*, **34**(3), 271–296.

Wasmer, D.J. & Bruner II, G.C. (1991) Using organizational culture to design internal marketing strategies. *Journal of Services Marketing*, **5**(1), 35–46.

CHAPTER 15
MANAGING SERVICE CULTURE: THE INTERNAL SERVICE IMPERATIVE

> " *A functioning service culture requires that providing good service is second nature to everyone within the organization.* "

INTRODUCTION

In this chapter the concept of service culture will be discussed. First, two broader concepts are presented, corporate culture and climate, and their importance to the attitudes and behaviour of people in an organization. Next, the issue of a service culture and the need for such a culture is covered. Prerequisites for a service culture are analysed and ways of creating such a culture are described. Finally, barriers to and opportunities for developing such a culture are discussed. After reading this chapter the reader should understand the importance of a service culture for service providers, know the prerequisites for a service culture and know how such a culture can be created.

THE IMPORTANCE OF CORPORATE CULTURE

The concept of *corporate culture* is used to describe a set of common norms and values shared by people in an organization. Hence, culture is an overall concept that explains why people do certain things, think in common ways, and appreciate similar goals, routines, even jokes, just because they are members of the same organization. Corporate culture can be defined as *the pattern of shared values and beliefs that give the members of an organization meaning, and provide them with the rules for behaviour in the organization.*[1] Culture represents values that can be thought of as residing deep within the organization. It is not easy to see it, but it is always present.[2] The existing culture in a firm is a result of its organizational past, and it provides stability, meaning and predictability in the organization.[3]

Corporate culture can be related to an internal *climate* in the organization. As discussed in the previous chapter, the organizational climate is partly dependent on how internal relationships function between people in the organization. The climate is the employees' accumulated sense of what is important in an organization.[4] Schneider, White and Paul describe service climate as a description of what happens in people's work units with regards to the service-focused policies, practices, and procedures they experience, and to what they see is expected, supported and rewarded.[5] The climate is a result of what goals employees are given to pursue in their jobs and how daily routines are handled in the organization.[6] The climate has a direct external effect on customer experiences and on perceived service quality, and may also influence customer loyalty.[7]

Service providers have to manage their internal climate so that employees who serve internal or external customers develop positive attitudes towards providing service. Such attitudes and a service-oriented climate can be expected to exist if the employees feel that organizational routines, directions for action given by policies and management and reward systems indicate that focusing on giving good service is important.[8] Because of this, the culture and climate of a firm have a vital impact on how service-oriented its employees are.[9] The terms *culture* and *climate* are often used interchangeably to mean more or less the same thing, because they are so closely related to each other.[10]

Culture is an important phenomenon to study and understand, because it is considered a potential basis for competitive advantage.[11] For service firms and manufacturers facing service competition, the development and management of a service culture is a critical task.

Internal activities or projects, such as training programmes, do not lead to expected results if they do not fit the existing culture in the firm. For example, a service-oriented training programme alone would probably have no significant impact on the thinking and behaviour of employees of a manufacturer where goods-oriented industrial norms are highly regarded, or the employees of a service firm where sales and cost-efficient operations are the only visible management priorities.[12] A much more strategically-oriented and comprehensive process would be needed if any results are to be achieved (see Chapter 14).

A weak corporate culture, where there are few or no clear common shared values, creates an insecure feeling concerning how to respond to various clues and how to react in different situations. For example, when a company has a strong culture, what to do when a customer has unexpected requests may be self-evident. On the other hand, if there is a weak culture, such a situation frequently results in inflexible behaviour by contact employees, long waiting times and a feeling of insecurity on the part of the customer. This, of course, hurts customer perceived service quality. In such a culture, employees do not have any clear norms to which to relate, for example, sales training or service skills courses, and hence they do not know how to respond to such activities.

A strong culture, however, enables people to act in a certain manner and to respond to various actions in a consistent way.[13] Clear cultural values seem particularly important for guiding employee behaviour, especially in service organizations.[14] In many cases new employees are easily assimilated into the prevailing culture.[15] A customer-focused and service-minded person with a favourable part-time marketing attitude who is recruited for a service job may quickly be brought down to earth by his new colleagues who share strong values which do not honour interest in customers or in providing good service. On the other hand, a strong service-oriented culture easily snowballs. Service-oriented employees are attracted by such an employer, and most new employees are influenced in a favourable way by the existing service culture.

When employees identify with the values of an organization, they are less inclined to quit, and customers seem to be more satisfied with the service provided. In addition to this, when there is a minimal employee turnover, service-oriented values and a positive attitude towards service are more easily transmitted to newcomers in the organization.[16]

The modern views of quality and productivity are related to corporate culture. Improving productivity and quality requires a new way of thinking in the culture of the organization.

A strong culture is not, however, always good. In situations where the surrounding world has changed and new ways of thinking are called for, a dominating culture may become a serious hindrance to change. It may be difficult to respond to new challenges. In such a situation, a strong culture does not only affect the responsiveness of employees in a negative fashion, but may also paralyse management. For example, a strong manufacturing-oriented or sales-focused culture may develop into a serious obstacle for a firm that should obviously respond to service-related changes in the market, or to a situation where keeping existing customers has become the most important way of doing profitable business. A service strategy is perhaps the obvious solution, but the management team may be too restricted by their inherited way of viewing the business. If only marginal internal activities to introduce a service strategy are implemented, old-fashioned ways of thinking among middle management and the rest of the personnel do not permit any major attitude change.

THE IMPORTANCE OF CLIMATE AND CULTURE IN SERVICE ORGANIZATIONS

In a service context a strong and well-established culture, which enhances an appreciation for good service and customer orientation, is extremely important. This follows from the nature of service production and consumption. Normally, service production cannot be standardized as completely as an assembly line, because of the human impact in the buyer–seller interactions of the service encounters. Customers and their behaviour cannot be totally standardized and predetermined. Situations vary, and therefore a distinct service-oriented culture is needed which tells employees how to respond to new, unforeseen and even awkward situations.[17] Hence, the culture makes a service-oriented strategy come alive for the employees and directs their behaviour.[18] In conclusion, it will be difficult to implement a service strategy without the existence of a service-focused culture in the organization.

It has been argued that a strong culture is of vital important in service organizations, because the attitude and performance of the employees is so visible to customers. If employees experience a service-oriented climate, the customers' experience of service quality will probably be better than otherwise expected. There seems to be a clear interrelationship between employee experiences and customer experiences.[19]

Since service quality is a function of the co-operation of so many resources – human as well as technological – a strong culture that enhances quality is a must for successful management of quality in a service context. Moreover, since it is more difficult to control quality in a service context than in manufacturing, service-oriented and quality-conscious values are necessary in the organization. In this way management can execute *indirect control by culture*.[20]

MANAGING RELATIONSHIPS REQUIRES A SERVICE CULTURE

Managing customer relationships demands that the firm adopt a service perspective, and customer relationships (as well as relationships with suppliers, distributors and other types of network partners) include a large number of service activities. Some of them, such as over-the-counter personal service, goods deliveries, maintenance and consulting services, can easily be seen by management as what they are in the minds of customers, that is, as value-creating services. Other types of services, such as invoicing, complaints handling, answering phone calls or e-mails, and a host of similar activities, which were earlier labelled hidden, unbillable services in relationships, are not as easily recognized as value-supporting services.

If the culture in a firm which has decided to give priority to the management of customer relationships (and relationships with other parties) does not honour service and a constant attention to providing good service to the other party, it will be difficult to implement the relationship-oriented strategy. The non-service culture will keep people (managers, supervisors and customer contact employees alike) from realizing the importance of all the 'hidden services', and even the more visible service elements may not be given enough attention. The values that dominate in the firm will direct people's attention elsewhere. Therefore, managing customer relationships, and relationships with other parties, requires a service-oriented culture.

PROFITABILITY THROUGH A SERVICE STRATEGY REQUIRES A SERVICE CULTURE

Adopting a service logic and a *service perspective* and implementing a *service strategy* requires the support of all employees in the organization. Top management, middle management, customer contact employees and support employees will all have to get involved and perform according to such a strategy. An interest in service and an appreciation of good service among managers and all other employees is an essential requirement. What is needed is a corporate culture that can be labelled a *service culture*. Such a culture can be described as:

. . . a culture where an appreciation for good service exists, and where giving good service to internal as well as ultimate, external customers is considered by everyone a natural way of life and one of the most important values [21]

Hence, service has to be the *raison d'être* for all organizational activities.[22] This, of course, does not exclude other values from being important, too. For example, attention to internal efficiency and cost control is still important, as well as an appreciation of sales and getting new customers. However, the service-oriented values should have a dominating position in the organization with a top-priority concern in strategic as well as operational thinking and performance, and not remain a marginal or lower-priority concern.

In a service culture all employees should be service-focused. Service orientation can be described as shared values and attitudes that influence people in an organization so that interactions between them internally and interactions with customers and other external actors are perceived in a favourable manner. Internally, a service focus can be expected to enhance the internal climate and improve the quality of internal service and support. Externally, a service focus should create good perceived quality for customers and others as well as lead to strengthened relationships with customers and other parties.

Clearly, a service orientation enhances the functional quality dimension of customer perceived service quality, and probably also supports good technical quality. As Figure 15.1 illustrates, service orientation among personnel normally fuels an important positive process within an organization. A service orientation that is a characteristic of a service culture improves service quality as perceived by customers.

Service-focused employees who take an interest in their customers do more for the customers, are more courteous and flexible, try to find appropriate solutions to customers' wishes, and go out of their way to recover a situation where something has gone wrong or an unexpected scenario has occurred.

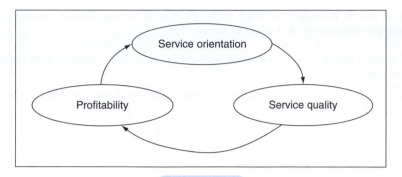

FIGURE 15.1

Effects of a service orientation.

Furthermore, we know that customer perceived quality is a key determinant of profitability, although it is not the only one. Hence, service orientation improves service quality which, in turn, positively affects profitability. This favourable process continues as an upward spiral, because better profitability provides means to maintain and further improve service-oriented attitudes among personnel. The process fuels itself.[23]

A word of warning is important here, however. Although good perceived quality can be expected to improve profitability, this requires that the service offerings provided to customers are put together in such a way that customers are prepared to pay a price which matches the cost of producing the service. There are situations where customers may be very satisfied with the perceived service quality, but they are still not profitable over time.[24] Furthermore, the positive connection between culture and profitability is often claimed to exist, and a clear service-oriented culture probably has a favourable impact on the financial performance of the firm. In Chapter 6, and especially in Figure 6.9, factors that influence the link from perceived quality to profitable customers were discussed. It is difficult to show how a service culture and service orientation leads to profitable customer relationships, because there are always so many external factors involved that it is difficult to isolate the effects of culture.[25]

SHARED VALUES

The values shared by people in an organization and the prevailing norms are the foundation of the culture. The shared values constitute guidelines for employees in performing their everyday tasks. In an organization with strong shared values three common characteristics are often present:[26]

1. The shared values are a clear guideline for task performance.

2. Managers devote much of their time to developing and reinforcing the shared values.

3. The shared values are deeply anchored among the employees.

Performance is improved by strong shared values in an organization. Managers and employees devote themselves more to issues and ways of performing that are emphasized by the shared values.

Performance is better, because people are more motivated. Strong shared values may, however, become a problem, too; for the following reasons:

- The shared values may have become *obsolete* and are therefore not consistent with current strategies and service concepts.

- Strong shared values may lead to *resistance to change*, which makes it difficult for the organization to respond to external challenges.

- New employees are formed by existing strong shared values, and in situations when the culture needs to be changed, differently thinking newcomers are easily swallowed by the existing culture.

In many firms these are highly relevant problems. Even though there may be no service culture, there may still be a strong corporate culture. The existing culture may emphasize manufacturing ideals or bureaucratic routines, or press short-term sales instead of the importance of concentrating on keeping and growing customers. In many manufacturing firms and institutions within the public sector, a strong culture that does not appreciate service is a major hindrance to change. Challenges from the market and from society may go unnoticed, or the organization may not be capable of adjusting to the need for change. The results are sometimes fatal. The effects of a single internal activity, for example a training programme that does not have a strategic foundation, will probably be counteracted by a hostile culture. Internal marketing efforts may easily fail if they are not in line with the prevailing culture, or if the objectives of the internal marketing efforts are contradictory to it. On the other hand, a long-term internal marketing process is one ingredient in a process that aims at changing an existing culture. A strategic approach to internal change is needed.

REQUIREMENTS FOR A SERVICE CULTURE

Introducing and implementing a service strategy requires a service culture. In many firms and in many organizations within the public sector, a cultural change is called for. Such a change is a *long-range process*, which demands extensive and long-range activity programmes. In the previous chapter we discussed one major ingredient in such a process, *internal marketing*. This chapter will look at general prerequisites for achieving a service culture.

The *requirements for good service*[27] are strategic requirements, organizational requirements, management requirements, and knowledge and attitude requirements.

If *all four kinds of requirements* are not all recognized, the internal change process will suffer and the result will be mediocre at best. The four different requirements above are intertwined. For example, a complicated organizational structure may make it impossible to implement a good service concept; or a service-minded, customer-focused and motivated contact employee becomes frustrated and loses interest in providing good service because he gets no support or appreciation from his boss, or finds it impossible to be service-minded because the service orientation is not derived from a strategic foundation, and therefore sufficient resources are not granted and continuous and consistent top management support is lacking. The following sections will discuss the four requirements above in some detail.

DEVELOPING A SERVICE STRATEGY

The *strategic requirements for good service* are fulfilled by developing a service-focused strategy. This means that *top management wants* to create a service-focused organisation; the management team is not just paying lip service to service orientation. Here, top management may be the CEO or the managing director and his management team, but it may also be the head of a regional or local organization or a profit centre, which can operate sufficiently well independently.

The *business mission* is the foundation of strategy formulation. Strategies are developed based on the scope and direction of the business indicated by the mission. A service strategy means that the mission includes a *service vision*. It demands that a service orientation, which of course means different things in different industries and even firms, is to be achieved. This will not be discussed here. In Chapter 3 guidelines for formulating a service-based and customer-focused business mission were presented. In short, in a generic way the *business mission* of a service-focused firm that has adopted a service perspective for its business can be described in the following way:

The business mission is to provide the customers' activities and processes with support that makes value for the customers emerge when they do those activities and run those processes.

This support could, of course, be of any kind, including goods, services, hidden services, or information, as long as when the customers make use of it, value emerges for them. For business customers this value support should ultimately have a favourable effect on the customers' business process and even on the customers' customers' processes. Although similar effects on individual customers are less obvious and more difficult to measure, in principle the support of a service provider should lead to similar effects.

However, a service strategy requires that *service concepts* related to the business mission and the strategy be defined. If service concepts are not clearly defined, the firm lacks a stable foundation for discussion of goals, resources to be used, and performance standards. As previously stated, the service concept states *what* should be done, to *whom*, *how* and with *which resources*, and *what benefits* customers should be offered. If these issues are not clarified, personnel will not understand what they are supposed to do. Moreover, goals and routines do not form a clear and understandable pattern, because there is no clear and well-known service concept to relate them to. If the service concepts are not clearly understood at the middle management level, it will be difficult to perform supervisory duties consistently.

Human resource management is an important part of strategic requirements. Recruitment procedures, career planning, reward systems and so on are vital parts of a service culture. Good service performance has to guide HRM. The more aspects other than skills and service-orientation dominate, for example recruitment procedures and reward systems, the less inclined towards service-mindedness employees will be, and a service culture will be difficult to achieve.

Good service has to be rewarded and accomplishments have to be measured in such a way that employees realise the importance of service. However, able employees are sometimes forced to do dumb things, because measurement and reward systems are wrong. Quite often only internal efficiency issues, such as the number of meals served in a restaurant or the number of phone calls dealt with, are measured and reward systems developed accordingly. If this is the case, and employees feel they are rewarded for accomplishments other than excellent service quality, any attempt to develop a service culture is bound to fail.

DEVELOPING THE ORGANIZATIONAL STRUCTURE

Development of the organizational structure creates the *organizational prerequisite for good service*. All aspects of organization design have to be geared to the service process, if high service quality is to be achieved and consistently maintained. The more complicated the formal structure is, the more problems related to giving good service will occur. The organization of a firm can be a serious obstacle to a service culture. Good service means, among other things, easy access to service and quick and flexible decision-making. It requires co-operation between various departments in designing, developing and executing service. If the organizational structure does not allow employees to perform in this way, values characterizing a service culture cannot be developed. Good intentions, even when they are based on strategy, cannot be implemented without the structure being in place. This makes people frustrated and may have a counter-effect. Employees may feel that management demands the impossible, and this only achieves negative effects as far as service-oriented attitudes are concerned.

There is also an informal organizational structure. People create a value structure and personal contacts, which make the formal structure either less or more complicated. In the former case, positive attitudes among the employees involved may make it possible to solve the problems created by a complicated structure. In the latter case, on the other hand, even a service-oriented structure may be an obstacle to good service. If people do not want to collaborate, a service culture is harder to accomplish.

Normally, a service-oriented firm requires a relatively flat organizational structure with few hierarchical levels. Decisions have to be made by employees who are close to the customers. The roles of managers change. The customer contact and support employees have more responsibility and they are expected to perform more independently. However, this does not mean that the supervisory level loses power, only that the role of supervisors changes. They are not just technical managers and decision-makers any more; instead, they are supposed to be coaches and demonstrate leadership. They will have to assist and encourage their staff and create an open climate where good service is a leading shared value.

The role of supervisors in support functions must also be clarified. Often employees who do not have immediate customer contacts regard themselves as carrying out passive functions with some administrative duties. In fact, their role in most support functions is much more active. As we have noted in previous contexts, they should see people in customer contact functions as their *internal customers*, whom they will have to serve as well as they, in turn, serve the ultimate (external) customers.

In many firms, the customer contact functions are understaffed, whereas back office and staff functions departments are overstaffed. The obvious conclusion is to strengthen the customer contact processes and streamline and redesign other departments so that they support the buyer–seller interactions in a more effective and service-focused way.

Another aspect of organizational development is the creation and improvement of operational systems, routines and work flows. Good service normally requires simplified ways of doing things, so that unnecessary delays and information breakdown are avoided. The effects of this are twofold. First of all, *customers* perceive such a development as better functional quality of the service. Second, *employees* feel that their job has become more meaningful and motivating when routines and work flows have been simplified, and unnecessary or time-consuming elements of the operational systems have been eliminated.

Information technology also provides opportunities to make changes in internal information systems and operational systems. The introduction of *intranets* can create a feeling of belonging and strengthen corporate identity among personnel. An intranet makes everyone a member of the same information system and makes it possible, for example, for every customer contact and support employee to share the same, relevant information about a given customer at the same time. If the information is easily retrievable, constantly updated and relevant, such a system supports good and timely interactions with customers and helps employees to give good service. This can contribute to a positive service culture. On the other hand, when using intranets in this way there is a danger of information overload, which must be monitored. Such overload easily counteracts the maintenance of a service culture.

DEVELOPING LEADERSHIP

The management prerequisite for good service is promoted by establishing a *service-oriented leadership*.[28] This includes managers' and supervisors' attitudes towards their role, their teams and how they act as managers. Management must be supportive, inspirational and attuned to the individuals they manage. Without active and continuous support from all managers and supervisors, the values that characterize a true service culture cannot be spread throughout the organization and maintained once they have been established. Such a managerial impact is of vital importance if service-oriented values are to be communicated to the employees, strengthened and made an integral part of the everyday life of the organization.

Managers are leaders in an organization, and by leading they also contribute to the culture. In this way managers, and supervisors, have a key role in the development of a service culture. On the other hand, a manager who is not aware of this will be led by the culture.[29] This can be a problem in a situation when the culture needs to be changed. Hence, it is very important for every manager and supervisor in the organization to be aware of the corporate culture.

Simply being a technical manager without taking on the role of coach and leader does not do much for the pursuit of a service culture. A more whole-hearted devotion to the service concepts and the employees is called for. Service is still to a large extent a human business and the result of interactions between people internally as well as externally. Management styles that do not take this into account do not fit in here.

Communication is a critical ingredient of leadership. The manager and supervisor will have to be willing, and know how to communicate with their staff. Communication is a two-way street, where the ability to listen to others is an important component. A leader should be able to create a dialogue with his team, and also be able to give clear direction and guidance, and make decisions when he is expected to take a firm stand.

One of the biggest risks involved in a process towards a service orientation is the risk of ambiguity. If the manager talks about the need for service-mindedness and customer-consciousness, but in reality does not pursue a service strategy, he *and* the service culture lose credibility. A sense of uncertainty among personnel is easily created, and the idea of service orientation and a service culture will not be taken seriously any more. Performance that is in line with good quality and the nature of a service culture as expressed by management has to be measured and rewarded. Internal efficiency and manufacturing-oriented productivity measures must not be given priority. Hence, management has to talk about the importance of good service and of pursuing a service culture, *and demonstrate by their actions* their belief in this idea. Otherwise, serious damage may easily be done to a service-orientation process that may have been initiated in good faith.

The top person in the organization, which may be a firm, a local unit, a profit centre, a strategic business unit or another well-defined organizational unit, will constantly have to give the service strategy top priority, and continuously and actively give it his strong support. Furthermore, every manager and supervisor will have to accept the role of a coach. They have to be able to encourage employees and strengthen their motivation for service-oriented performance.

Monitoring performance and results is, of course, still an integral part of management. But the traditional role of management is shifting from controlling towards guiding employees. Many managers feel that their authority is eroding as a consequence of such a change, and they cannot effectively 'manage' their people any more. However, this is not the case. The leadership-oriented management philosophy does not mean that management abdicates, but instead that it sets up goals and guidelines and delegates operational responsibility in a clear manner. Hence, the traditional role as mere technical manager is changed to a new role characterized by *leadership* and *coaching*. Another aspect of a service-oriented management style is the development of *an open internal communication climate*.

On the one hand, employees need information from management to be able to implement a service strategy; on the other hand, they have valuable information for management about customers' needs and wishes, about problems and opportunities, and so on. Feedback is required so that they see the results of their job and their actions, otherwise employees easily lose interest in what they are doing.

It is a good idea to get contact employees involved in the planning process and in decision-making concerning, say, what new services to offer and how they should be produced. Overall objectives for a group or a department can be broken down into sub-goals for that unit in co-operation with the employees who are supposed to accomplish those goals. This process is, first, a way of communicating the strategy and objectives of the firm to the employees, and second, a way of achieving employee commitment to the service strategy and to the firm's goals.

Finally, as noted in the previous chapter, management methods and the attitudes of managers and supervisors towards their employees are of pivotal importance to the long-term success of an internal marketing process.

Schneider and White summarize the impact of leadership in the following way.[30] The role of the leader is to:

- Espouse service-focus values among the employees.

- Develop policies, practices and routines that are consistent with these values.

- Ensure that those who most fully implement these procedures, to achieve a service-focused climate, are recognized for this and rewarded.

SERVICE TRAINING PROGRAMMES

By training employees, the *knowledge and attitude requirements for good service* can be achieved. However, to be effective training must be supported by the three other prerequisites for a service culture. Training employees is also an integral part of internal marketing. In organizations where existing values are not service-oriented, an attitude of resistance to change can be expected. A large portion of this resistance can be removed by creating the previously discussed strategic, organizational and management prerequisites for good service. However, this resistance is also a question of attitude and a lack of knowledge and skills. If the three requirements discussed above are not attended to, negative attitudes easily prevail or develop among the personnel. If the firm has always operated in, say, a manufacturer-oriented or bureaucratic way, it is not easy to make people think in new directions. This goes for management as well as for other employees.

If top management, middle management, and support and customer contact employees are expected to be motivated for service-oriented thinking and behaviour, they will need to know how a service organization operates, what makes up customer relationships, what their role in the operation and in customer relationships is, and what is expected of the individual. A person who does not understand what is going on and why cannot be expected to be motivated to do a good job as a contact person or an internal service provider in support functions behind the line of customer visibility.[31]

Moreover, every person should be aware of the firm's business mission, strategies and overall objectives as well as the goals of his own department and function, and his own personal goals. Otherwise, it would be unrealistic to think that an employee understands why he is told that it is important to perform in a certain way. This is even more crucial for employees in support functions than for contact employees.

In training programmes, knowledge-oriented training and attitude training are intertwined. The more knowledgeable a person is, the easier it is for that person to have positive attitudes towards a specific subject. It is essential to realise that attitudes can seldom be changed without knowledge. Pep talks may help on some occasions, but if people do not have the facts they will never create enduring service-focused attitudes. Employees need to know why the firm is a service business, or why as a manufacturer it adopts a service strategy; which requirements for performance follow from this; what their role is in relation to other functions and people, and in relation to customers; what is demanded of them as an individual, and why. And if a person feels that he does not have the required skills, he will also be reluctant to change.

Service training can be divided into three categories:

1. Developing a *holistic* view of the firm and its sub-functions as a service organization and how it operates in a market-oriented manner.

2. Developing *skills* concerning how various tasks are to be performed.

3. Developing specific *communication and service skills*.

All three types of training are needed. The first type gives a general foundation for understanding a service strategy and how to implement it. It puts every function, department and task into perspective, and demonstrates how the processes in the organization and the people performing these processes are related to each other and to a common goal of servicing customers well and creating support for their value-creating processes. The second type, vocational training, provides the skills required so that employees can perform their tasks, which may have been changed after the introduction of a service strategy, in an efficient way. The third type of training provides employees, especially customer contact employees but also support employees, with specific skills as far as communication and interaction tasks are concerned. Courses that address service-mindedness belong to this group, too. A serious mistake, which is all too common, is to believe that only the third type of training is needed to change employee attitudes. Such an approach is hardly ever successful.

DEVELOPING A SERVICE CULTURE: BARRIERS AND OPPORTUNITIES

Clearly, the task of changing the corporate culture and creating a service culture is a huge one. And it will take a substantial amount of time until any results will be observable. Getting started is often a substantial problem. There is an initial barrier to starting the process, and there is a threshold to cross on the way. Before this happens, no major changes can be seen in the internal value systems. However, once the process develops far enough it usually gains pace, provided it is constantly supported and enhanced, especially by top management. A service culture has to be maintained once it has been achieved, otherwise there is always the risk that the interest in service and in servicing internal as well as external customers will start to deteriorate.

In some situations it is easier to get started than in others. Favourable conditions for a change process are:

- *Environmental pressure*, such as increased competition, changes in customer needs and expectations, the introduction of new technologies, or deregulation or regulation of the industry.

- *New organizational strategies*, which differ from the previous ones.

- *New structural arrangements*, such as new management or a major change in the organizational structure.

All or some of these things could, of course, occur simultaneously, which would probably help the process. When times are good, and problems seem to be too far into the future or are invisible to most people in the organization, it is much more difficult to start to change the existing corporate culture. However, when altering an organization's culture, it is critical to preserve some of what has gone before and build on it to make the change. Honouring and learning from the past is important and does not have to mean that it slows down the process or counteracts it.[32] It is probably a good idea to move slowly, to set intermediate goals and to make changes gradually. Sometimes, however, there is no time for that. In most cases there is though, and trying to implement change too rapidly may lead to bad results. A cultural change means that the mindset of people has to change. The process has to be planned and executed in the same way as any important organizational task.

SUMMARY

Corporate culture and service culture is extremely complicated, and a holistic phenomenon. Developing a specific culture, therefore, requires that a whole range of internal issues be addressed. Culture cannot exist in isolation from or side by side with, for instance, the organizational structure, management approaches and methods, or the business mission and strategies of the organization. It is the result of these and other aspects of organizational life.

Hence, culture becomes a strategic matter. It does so in two ways, which are related to each other. First of all, creating a service culture requires a holistic view of the company by the decision-makers and those responsible for developing the culture; only top management holds that position. Therefore, it becomes a strategic issue that internal requirements for the creation of a service culture be developed. Second, implementing a service strategy requires, among other things, the kind of people who believe in service and who consider that it is essential in business to provide internal as well as external customers with good service. Therefore, if an organization intends to implement a service strategy, it is of vital importance that it aims for the achievement of a service culture.

QUESTIONS FOR DISCUSSION

1. Why is culture of strategic importance for the performance of an organization?

2. What is the difference between organizational climate and culture?

3. Which are the strategic requirements for a service culture?

4. Discuss the possible relationship between a service culture, service quality and profitability in a service organization.

5. Analyse how well the strategic requirements for a service culture are fulfilled in your firm, or in any given organization. What should be done to improve or strengthen the culture?

6. What are the problems related to starting to change the corporate culture?

NOTES

1. Davis, S.M., *Managing Corporate Culture*. Cambridge, MA: Ballinger, 1985. This somewhat dated definition by Davis still very accurately describes the concept of corporate culture. See also, for example, Iglesias, O., Montana, J. & Sauguet, A., The role of corporate culture in relationship marketing. *European Journal of Marketing*, **45**(4), 2011, 631–650.

2. Bowen, D.A., Schneider, B. & Kim, S.S., Shaping service cultures through strategic human resource management. In Swartz, T.A. & Iacobucci, D. (eds), *Handbook of Services Marketing & Management*. Thousand Oaks, CA: Sage Publications, 2000, pp. 439–454. See also Shein, E.H., Corporate Culture. In Vogelsang, J. *et al.* (eds.), *Handbook for Strategic HR*. Chicago, IL: AMACOM, 2013, pp. 252–258.

3. Schein, E.H., *Organizational Culture and Leadership*, 2nd edn. San Francisco, CA: Jossey-Bass, 1992.

4. Schneider, B. & Bowen, D.E., *Winning the Service Game*. Boston, MA: Harvard Business School Press, 1995.

5. Schneider, B., White, S.S. & Paul, M.C., Linking service climate and customers perception of service quality. *Journal of Applied Psychology*, **83**(2), 1998, 150–163.

6. Schneider, B., Brief, A.B. & Guzzo, R.A., Creating a climate and culture for sustainable organizational change. *Organizational Dynamics*, **24**(4), 1996, 7–19.

7. Bowen, D.E. & Schneider, B., A service climate synthesis and future research agenda. *Journal of Service Research*, **17**(1), 2014, 6, 10–11.

8. Schneider, B., The climate for service: an application of the climate construct. In Schneider, B. (ed.), *Organizational Climate and Culture*. San Francisco, CA: Jossey-Bass, 1990, pp. 383–412.

9. See also Edvardson, B. & Enquist, B., Quality improvement in governmental services: the role of change pressure by the 'market'. *The TQM Magazine*, **18**(1), 2006, 7–21, where the authors study the situation in a public sector context.

10. See Bowen, D.E. & Schneider, B., *op. cit.*, where a distinction between service climate and other concepts such as service orientation is made.

11. Barney, J., Organizational culture. Can it be a source of sustained competitive advantage. *Academy of Management Review*, **11**(3), 1986, 656–666. See also Flamholtz, E.G. & Randle, Y., Corporate culture, business models, competitive advantage, strategic assets and the bottom line: theoretical and measurement issues. *Journal of Human Resource Costing & Accounting*, **16**(2), 2012, 76–94, where the relationship between corporate culture and the competitive advantage of a firm is discussed, and Guiso, L., Sapienza, P. & Zingales, L., The value of corporate culture, *Journal*

of Financial Economics, [online, 24 May 2014] where it is shown that the relationship between corporate culture and firm performance may not be straightforward.

12. See Skålen, P. & Strandvik, T., From prescription to description: a critique and reorientation of service culture. *Managing Service Quality*, **15**(3), 2005, 230–244, where the authors study the effects of a service management programme in a public sector situation. Because the goals of the programme and the existing culture were far apart, the programme created more confusion in the organization than helped, changing the culture into a service-oriented direction.

13. Brown, S.W., The employee experience. *Marketing Management*, **12**(2), 2003, 12–16.

14. Schneider, B., Notes on climate and culture. In Venkatesan, M., Schmalensee, D.M. & Marshall, C. (eds), *Creativity in Services Marketing. What's New, What Works, What's Developing*. Chicago, IL: American Marketing Association, 1986.

15. Schein, *op. cit.*

16. Bowen, D.E. & Schneider, B., Service marketing and management: implications for organizational behavior. *Research in Organizational Behavior*, **10**, 1988.

17. Schneider, *op. cit.*

18. See Schneider, B., Hayes, S.C., Lim, B.-C. & Raver, J.L., The human side of strategy: employee experiences of strategic alignment in a service organization. *Organizational Dynamics*, **32**(2), 2003, 122–138.

19. Schneider, B., White, S. & Paul, M.C., *op. cit.*

20. Brown, 2003, *op. cit.* And for example, in a study of the airline industry it became clear that the service culture had a direct effect on service behaviour. See Zerbe, W.J., Dobni, D. & Harel, G.H., Promoting employee service behaviour: the role of perceptions of human resource management practices and service culture. *Revue Canadienne des Sciences de l'Administration*, **15**(2), 1998, 165–179.

21. Grönroos, C., *Service Management and Marketing. Managing the Moments of Truth in Service Competition*. Lexington, MA: Lexington Books, 1990, p. 244. See also, for example, Beitelspacher, L.S., Richey, R.G. & Reynolds, K.E., Exploring a new perspective on service efficiency: service culture in retail organizations. *Journal of Services Marketing*, **25**(3), 2011, 215–228.

22. To use the words of Schneider and Rentsch, service has to become 'the *raison d'être* for all organizational activities' and an '*organizational imperative*'. See Schneider, B. & Rentsch, J., The management of climate and culture. In Hage, J. (ed.), *Futures of Organizations*. Lexington, MA: Lexington Books, 1987.

23. See Gebauer, H., Edvardsson, B. & Bjurko, M., The impact of service orientation in corporate culture on business performance in manufacturing companies. *Journal of Service Management*, **21**(2), 2010, 237–259, where this relationship is discussed in a manufacturing context.

24. In a large study of the profitability of customer bases in retail banks in Scandinavia, Kaj Storbacka showed that a large number of satisfied customers had a substantial negative effect on the overall profitability of the bank. See Storbacka, K., *The Nature of Customer Relationship Profitability*. Helsingfors, Finland: Swedish School of Economics, Finland/CERS, 1994.

25. Bowen, Schneider & Kim, *op. cit.* See also Siehl, C. & Martin, J., Organization culture: a key to financial performance? In Schneider, B. (ed.), *Organizational Climate and Culture*. San Francisco, CA: Jossey-Bass, 1990, pp. 241–281. See also Edvardsson, B. & Enqvist, B., The IKEA saga: how service culture drives service strategy. *The Service Industries Journal*, **22**(4), 2002, 153–166.

26. Deal, T.F. & Kennedy, A.A., *Corporate Cultures: The Rites and Rituals of Corporate Life*. Reading, MA: Addison-Wesley, 1982.

27. Grönroos, C., 1990, *op. cit.*

28. See Schneider, B. & White, S.S., *Service Quality. Research Perspectives*. Thousand Oaks, CA: Sage, 2004.

29. Schein, *op. cit.*

30. Schneider & White, *op. cit.*, p. 118.

31. Jan Carlzon, the former managing director and president of SAS, illustrates in his book about the turnaround process of SAS in the 1980s (*Moments of Truth*. Cambridge, MA: Ballinger, 1987) the impact of a holistic understanding of the tasks people are involved in by the following anecdote:

    There is no better way to sum up my experience than with the story about the two stone cutters who were chipping square blocks out of granite. A visitor to the quarry asked what they were doing. The first stone cutter, looking rather sour, grumbled, 'I'm cutting this damned stone into a block.' The second, who looked pleased with his work, replied proudly, 'I'm on this team that's building a cathedral.'

    This anecdote is still often told in similar contexts. It is interesting to note that, in slightly different words, Mikhael Gorbachev, former leader of the Soviet Union, told it as an illustration of the *perestroika* process. See Gorbachev, M., *Perestroika – New Thinking for Our Country and the World*. New York: Harper & Row, 1987.

32. Zemke, R., Creating service culture. *The Service Edge*, 8, 1988.

FURTHER READING

Barney, J. (1986) Organizational culture: can it be a source of sustained competitive advantage? *Academy of Management Review*, **11**(3), 656–666.

Beitelspacher, L.S., Richey, R.G. & Reynolds, K.E. (2011) Exploring a new perspective on service efficiency: service culture in retail organizations. *Journal of Services Marketing*, **25**(3), 215–228.

Bowen, D.E. & Schneider, B. (1988) Service marketing and management: implications for organizational behavior. *Research in Organizational Behavior*, **10**.

Bowen, D.E. & Schneider, B. (2014) A service climate synthesis and future research agenda. *Journal of Service Research*, **17**(1), 5–22.

Bowen, D.A., Schneider, B. & Kim, S.S. (2000) Shaping service cultures through strategic human resource management. In Swartz, T.A. & Iacobucci, D. (eds), *Handbook of Services Marketing & Management*. Thousand Oaks, CA: Sage Publications, pp. 439–454.

Brown, S.W. (2003) The employee experience. *Marketing Management*, **12**(2), 12–16.

Carlzon, J. (1987) *Moments of Truth*. Cambridge, MA: Ballinger.

Davis, S.M. (1985) *Managing Corporate Culture*. Cambridge, MA: Ballinger.

Deal, T.F. & Kennedy, A.A. (1982) *Corporate Cultures: The Rites and Rituals of Corporate Life*. Reading, MA: Addison-Wesley.

Edvardsson, B. & Enqvist, B. (2002) The IKEA saga: how service culture drives service strategy. *The Service Industries Journal*, **22**(4), 153–166.

Edvardson, B. & Enquist, B. (2006) Quality improvement in governmental services: the role of change pressure by the 'market'. *The TQM Magazine*, **18**(1), 7–21.

Flamholtz, E.G. & Randle, Y. (2012) Corporate culture, business models, competitive advantage, strategic assets and the bottom line: theoretical and measurement issues. *Journal of Human Resource Costing & Accounting*, **16**(2), 76–94.

Gebauer, H., Edvardsson, B & Bjurko, M. (2010) The impact of service orientation in corporate culture on business performance in manufacturing companies. *Journal of Service Management*, **21**(2), 237–259.

Gorbachev, M. (1987) *Perestroika – New Thinking for Our Country and the World*. New York: Harper & Row.

Grönroos, C. (1990) *Service Management and Marketing. Managing the Moments of Truth in Service Competition*. Lexington, MA: Lexington Books.

Guiso, L., Sapienza, P. & Zingales, L. (online 2014) The value of corporate culture. *Journal of Financial Economics*.

Iglesias, O., Montana, J. & Sauguet, A. (2011) The role of corporate culture in relationship marketing. *European Journal of Marketing*, **45**(4), 631–650.

Schein, E.H. (1992) *Organizational Culture and Leadership*, 2nd edn. San Francisco, CA: Jossey-Bass.

Schein, E.H. (2013) Corporate Culture. In Vogelsang, J. *et al.* (eds.), *Handbook for Strategic HR*. NY: AMACOM, pp. 252–258.

Schneider, B. (1986) Notes on climate and culture. In Venkatesan, M., Schmalensee, D.M. & Marshall, C. (eds), *Creativity in Services Marketing. What's New, What Works, What's Developing*. Chicago, IL: American Marketing Association.

Schneider, B. (1990) The climate for service: an application of the climate construct. In Schneider, B. (ed.), *Organizational Climate and Culture*. San Francisco, CA: Jossey-Bass, pp. 383–412.

Schneider, B. & Bowen, D.E. (1995) *Winning the Service Game*. Boston, MA: Harvard Business School Press.

Schneider, B. & Rentsch, J. (1987) The management of climate and culture. In Hage, J. (ed.), *Futures of Organizations*, Lexington, MA: Lexington Books.

Schneider, B., Brief, A.B. & Guzzo, R.A. (1996) Creating a climate and culture for sustainable organizational change. *Organizational Dynamics*, **24**(4), 7–19.

Schneider, B., White, S. & Paul, M.C. (1998) Linking service climate and customer perception of service quality: test of a causal model. *Journal of Applied Psychology*, **83**(2), 150–163.

Schneider, B., Hayes, S.C., Lim, B.-C. & Raver, J.L. (2003) The human side of strategy: employee experiences of strategic alignment in a service organization. *Organizational Dynamics*, **32**(2), 122–138.

Schneider, B. & White, S.S. (2004) *Service Quality. Research Perspectives*. Thousand Oaks, CA: Sage.

Siehl, C. & Martin, J. (1990) Organization culture: a key to financial performance? In Schneider, B. (ed.), *Organizational Climate and Culture*. San Francisco, CA: Jossey-Bass, pp. 241–281.

Skålen, P. & Strandvik, T. (2005) From prescription to description: a critique and reorientation of service culture. *Managing Service Quality*, **15**(3), 230–244.

Storbacka, K. (1994) *The Nature of Customer Relationship Profitability*. Helsingfors, Swedish School of Economics, Finland/CERS Centre for Relationship and Service Management.

Zemke, R. (1988) Creating service culture. *The Service Edge*, **8**.

Zerbe, W.J., Dobni, D. & Harel, G.H. (1998) Promoting employee service behaviour: the role of perceptions of human resource management practices and service culture. *Revue Canadienne des Sciences de l'Administration*, **15**(2), 165–179.

Guiso, L., Sapienza, P. & Zingales, L. (online 2015) The value of corporate culture. *Journal of Financial Economics*.

Leidner, D., Kayworth, T. & Sayogo, A. (2011) The role of corporate culture in relationship marketing. *European Journal of Marketing*, 45(4), 663–666.

Schein, E.H. (1992) *Organizational Culture and Leadership*, 2nd edn. San Francisco, CA: Jossey-Bass.

Schein, E.H. (2015) Corporate Culture. In Vogelsang, J. et al. (eds.), *Handbook for Strategic HR*, NY: AMACOM, pp. 253–258.

Schneider, B. (1988) Notes on climate and culture. In Venkatesan, M., Schmalensee, D.M. & Marshall, C. (eds.), *Creativity in Services Marketing: What's New, What Works, What's Developing*. Chicago, IL: American Marketing Association.

Schneider, B. (1990) The climate for service: an application of the climate construct. In Schneider, B. (ed.), *Organizational Climate and Culture*. San Francisco, CA: Jossey-Bass, pp. 383–412.

Schlesinger, L.A. & Heskett, J.L. (1991) *Breaking the Service Cycle*. Boston, MA: Harvard Business School Press.

Schneider, B. & Rentsch, J. (1987) The management of climate and culture. In Hage, J. (ed.), *Futures of Organizations*. Lexington, MA: Lexington Books.

Schneider, B., Bro, J.A.B. & Cheung, K.A. (1990) Creating a climate and culture: an institutional approach. *Organizational Dynamics*, 17, 1–16.

Schneider, B., White, S. & Paul, M.C. (1998) Linking service climate and customer perception of service quality: test of a causal model. *Journal of Applied Psychology*, 83(2), 150–163.

Schneider, B., Hayes, S.C., Lim, B.-C., & Kmel, J. (12003) The human side of strategy: employee experiences of strategy in a service organization. *Organizational Dynamics*, 32(2), 122–138.

Schmenner, R.W. bra, M.S. (2004) *Service Quality: Research Perspectives*. Thousand Oaks, CA: Sage.

Siehl, C. & Martin, J. (1990) Organizational culture: a key to financial performance? In Schneider, B. (ed.), *Organizational Climate and Culture*. San Francisco, CA: Jossey-Bass, pp. 241–281.

Smith, R. & Schanker, L. (2015) From prescription to description: a critique and reorientation of service culture. *Managing Service Quality*, 15(3), 230–239.

Smolka, J. (1981) *The Nature of Customer Satisfaction*. Pennsylvania: Wharton School of Economics, Finland. *PhD Thesis for Relationship and Service Management.*

Zemke, R. (1988) Creating service culture. *The Service Edge*, 5.

Zeithaml, V.A., Parasuraman, A. & Berry, L.L. (1990) From training, employee service behaviour: the role of perceptions of human resource management practices and service culture. *Work Conditions de Service et d'Administration*, 15(2), 165–179.

CHAPTER 16
TRANSFORMING A MANUFACTURING FIRM INTO A SERVICE BUSINESS

> *In growing numbers customers consider manufacturers of physical products service providers, albeit often mediocre service providers. In order to maintain their competitive advantage it is time for manufacturers to start transforming themselves into service businesses.*

INTRODUCTION

In previous chapters we have discussed what it means to be a service organization, and to manage it and its customers with a customer focus in order to support the customers' activities and processes in a value-supporting way. Here the need for traditional manufacturers, such as firms in metal, forest, electronic, chemical, IT and other industries, to find new sources of competitive advantage is discussed. Transforming into a service business is one logical way of getting closer to the customers and finding new opportunities to support customers' processes in a more valuable manner than before. After reading the chapter the reader should understand the reason for manufacturers to transform into service businesses, and why this requires a strategic turnaround of the whole firm to be fully successful. The reader should also know what changes are needed to become a service business, how the product should be understood and what steps should be taken, according to the CSS (Conceptualizing, Systematizing, Servicizing) model, to make a transition.

THE CHALLENGE FOR MANUFACTURERS

It is generally agreed that markets have moved into a service economy, where the firm which can provide its customers with not only the best core solution, such as a physical product (or a core service), but also better overall value-supporting service than the competitors will survive. Product manufacturers increasingly voice a need to move into a service business mode. The traditional supplier–customer dyad has long been challenged by forces in the marketplace. To be able to support their customers, suppliers have had to move into networks with other suppliers and the customer's customer becomes a part in the chain that has to be considered. Changes in the business environment relating to business-to-business markets can have dramatic consequences for firms. A competitive advantage cannot be achieved and maintained by traditional means. A supplier who, in a competitive market, only offers the core solution to its customers in the form of a physical product, from small-scale products to large investments such as a paper machine, will, among other things, soon find that the pressure on price gradually grows from what it used to be. The reason for this is quite obvious. As customers do not perceive any other support to their processes by a supplier than what the product offers, and as there is an abundance of competing offerings on the market, it is only natural for a buyer to look at price as a major and often even *the* major purchasing criterion. What the supplier traditionally does is offer its customer a *technical solution* to a customer process, for example a production, administrative, financial, marketing or HRM process, but not explicitly a *value-creating support* to this process that has a favourable effect on the customer's business and commercial processes. The competitive advantage once created by a technological solution is in most industries long gone. And when new technological solutions are introduced, the advantage lasts less time than ever.

Furthermore, offering service, such as maintenance and upgrading, to an installed base provided by the manufacturer may provide a steady stream of revenues on top of those from delivering the product. Although the unit revenue of a single product transaction is often higher, the service-based revenue provides a continuous cash flow.

A value-creating support to a process provided by service requires, first of all, that the customer can perceive and preferably also calculate the effects on the outcome of the process that is supported. Second, a calculable longer-term effect on the customer's business process, that is, on the customer's revenue-generating capability or on its cost level, or on both, and ultimately on its profits, should at least approximately be visible for the customer. Or if for some reason it cannot be calculated, the existence of such a positive effect must at least be recognized and accepted. Otherwise the value of service remains abstract and incomprehensible, and difficult to evaluate by the buyer. If this is the case, price becomes the dominating decision-making criterion.

In order to provide more support over a longer time period than the physical product provides, suppliers often turn to various types of services, traditionally called after-sales services, or industrial services. For example, a physical product can be offered together with a service contract. This may be an improvement, but it turns out that it is often difficult to persuade customers to pay for these services. Moreover, the product as the core is often still managed and delivered with more of a product-focused than a customer-focused strategy. Hence, new visions and new actions are needed.

SERVITIZATION: INFUSING SERVICES INTO A PRODUCT OFFERING

In the management and also marketing literature the need for product manufacturers to turn to service has been recognised.[1] Oliva and Kallenberg offer a four-phase process: (1) consolidating mostly existing product-related services, (2) entering a market of servicing an installed base, and (3) expanding to services based on customer relationships and developed from existing processes. The fourth phase would cover situations where the firm takes over an end-user's operation, and for example manages a production plant.[2]

Almost invariably, the literature on how to transform product manufacturers into service businesses suggests that this transformation takes place through a gradually increasing *infusion of services into a product-based offering* (service infusion).[3] A more commonly used term for this process is *serviti-zation*. Andy Neely summarizes the discussion of what is meant by servitization with the following explanation:

In essence servitization is a transformation journey – it involves firms (often manufacturing firms) developing the capabilities they need to provide services and solutions that supplement their traditional product offerings.[4]

Hence, according to the servitization and service infusion approach, product manufacturers can move towards a service business mode, and eventually become a service firm, basically by gradually adding more service activities to their core offerings, which remain physical product-based. We *do not* believe that this would work. For this approach to be successful, a growing number of services should automatically change the overall strategy of the firm. However, if the core of the offering remains a resource, such as a physical product, there is a substantial risk that the firm's strategy will remain product-based, and the accompanying services will be treated as add-ons and the dominating culture in the firm will continue to be product-centric.

In our view, servitization and service infusion is, at best, a transition stage. For a final transformation to take place, the manufacturing firm's overall strategy has to be service-based, and the *core* of the offering has to be *value-creating support to customers*, not a physical product or any other type of resource. In the offering, products and service activities have to merge into an integrated process, which aims at supporting the customers' processes and ultimately their business processes. *Offering value-laden resources must be replaced by providing value-creating support.* This means that unlike product-based offerings which tend to be transaction based, service offerings are based on relationships. Consequently, firms which are in a true service business mode have to change their *business model* from a transaction-based model to a relationship-based model.[5]

In a study of the effects of servitization on firm value, it was observed that adding services to a core product may add to the manufacturer's value, but this requires a substantial level of service sales. It was also noted that if services offered are closely related to the core product, this effect grows.[6] However, in the recent literature the weaknesses and insufficiencies of a servitization approach are clearly recognized. In a recently reported study about European manufacturing firms it was observed that in reality product offerings are supplemented only with a limited number of services.[7] It has also been claimed that transforming into a service business mode is an evolutionary process rather than a transition from one phase to another[8] and requires strategic rather than incremental change.[9]

This chapter will discuss how to transform from a product manufacturing firm into a service business by taking a service perspective and adopting a service strategy, rather than by following a servitization process.

ADOPTING A SERVICE PERSPECTIVE: A SERVICE STRATEGY APPROACH

The question is: *What is meant by providing better service in a manufacturing industry?* We do not believe that it is enough to add better industrial services or after-sales services to the core product. In this book we have defined service as *supporting the customer's everyday activities and processes in a value-creating manner.*[10] Hence, taking a service perspective, or adopting a service logic in a manufacturing firm would mean that the supplier alone, or together with network partners, develops and implements holistic offerings that successfully support its customers' processes, for example, a production process, so that this process functions better than without the support of this offering or with the support of some other offering. Moreover, this offering should have a favourable and preferably quantifiable effect on the customers' business processes, in terms of growth and renevue-generating opportunities and/or cost savings.[11]

The next important question is: *What does this value-supporting offering include?* Does it only include industrial services such as maintenance, repair or training? The answer is definitely no. Following a service perspective, an offering with which a supplier provides service in a value-supporting manner over time cannot include only after-sales and other service elements, it has to include the total support, thus encompassing the support provided by the physical product as the core solution *as well as* by service processes, such as deliveries, installation, repair, maintenance and customer training, and *hidden services*, such as invoicing, complaints handling, extranets, product documentation and *ad hoc* interactions between people. In this way a true service offering is provided, and not a product offering accompanied by services. In Chapter 1, hidden services were defined as activities that customers are influenced by which by the firm are considered administrative, financial, legal or technical routines, without any impact on the customers' preferences. They are, therefore, treated and implemented as non-service. Badly managed and handled hidden services, such as complaints handling and invoicing, easily create emotional stress for customers and, in addition, unnecessary and unwanted sacrifice in the form of time spent, for example, on solving a service failure, checking the specification and correctness of an invoice or figuring out the meaning of product documentation, and costs created by this. In Chapter 6 such costs were discussed and termed indirect and psychological *relationship costs*.

Adding more services one by one to a product-based core offering may be counterproductive.[12] To have a major effect on a firm's competitiveness, servitization must lead to a *strategic* development of the *entire* manufacturing business into a service business, including its traditional product manufacturing part. Then a service perspective and service logic drives the whole business, both strategically and tactically.[13]

THE THIRD-PARTY THREAT

In addition to the price pressure from customers, and the fact that in most industries the technical solutions embedded in a physical product have become more or less similar, there is another threat that suppliers in manufacturing industries have to be aware of and handle. This can be called the *third-party threat*. This is illustrated in Figure 16.1.

In the upper part of the figure a traditional *supplier–customer–customer's customer* chain is illustrated. In this situation, by providing the customer with a core solution, for example, a production machine or computer hardware, more effectively than competitors also offering core solutions only, the supplier can successfully develop a working relationship with its customer. As customers have traditionally considered the technical specifications of the product the essence of a successful solution, by offering a competitive technical solution the supplier has been able to claim and keep ownership of the customer.

However, this situation is changing. In the lower part of the figure a quickly emerging situation is illustrated. Customers' preferences are changing from considering the technical specifications as the essence of a successful solution to looking at how efficiently and effectively a process, such as a production or an administrative process, runs using a given technical solution *and other support*, such as serviceability of the technical solution, repair, maintenance, training and call centre or website advice. Customers are even looking for support in operating a production line or a whole plant. Moreover, customers start to look at the effect on their business process of how well a given process functions, and at possibilities to serve their customers successfully. At this point, from having been tactical suppliers, service companies and consultants offering services that help the customer run a

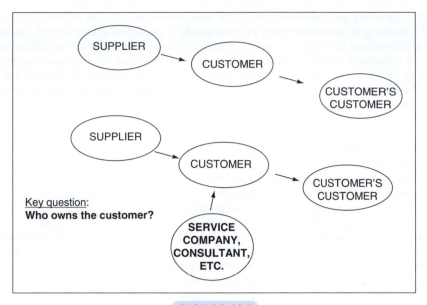

FIGURE 16.1

Who owns the customer: the third-party threat.

process successfully gradually gain a strategic position in the customer's business. When a customer decides to outsource, for example, the operation of a production line or a plant to a *third party*, such as a service company, the position of the supplier becomes shaky.

What has happened to the supplier–customer–customer's customer chain? The more the *third-party actor* gains a strategic position, the more the position of the supplier, who traditionally had this position in relation to the customer, declines and eventually becomes *merely tactical*. The supplier does not own the customer any more, the third-party actor does. This means that decisions regarding the supplier's involvement with the customer are no longer primarily taken between the supplier and the customer, but between the customer and the third-party actor. The supplier may not even be asked. Hence, ownership of the customer has slipped away from the supplier to the service firm or consultant, or whichever type of firm has taken this position. The risk grows that *the supplier becomes a subcontractor* to the third-party actor.

HOW TO MAINTAIN A SUSTAINABLE COMPETITIVE ADVANTAGE: ADOPT A SERVICE LOGIC

What can a manufacturing firm that is in the supplier's position in Figure 16.1 do? One option is to continue to compete with price. In some markets and in some customer segments it works, but a price strategy is sustainable only if the firm has a lasting cost advantage. In the long run it seldom works. Moreover, a lowest price strategy also makes it difficult for a firm to invest enough in research and development, in technology and service development.

There is also another quite obvious option. *The manufacturer can transform itself into a service company.* Instead of remaining in a manufacturing business mode it can move into a service business mode. *On top of its technological and product knowledge* it can strive to create the same capabilities as a service company and consultant as third-party actors have, and thus create an even stronger strategic position in relation to the customer than the third-party actor can ever develop. Of course this does not mean that the manufacturer has to do everything. It can very well outsource some processes, such as deliveries or maintenance, but in this case it is the supplier which is the outsourcer, not the customer who uses a third party's services. Consequently, the risk that a third-party threat develops is minimized.

Today it is seldom possible for a traditional manufacturer to create a sustainable advantage with a price strategy or based on technological development with a product strategy. The only option left is to adopt a service perspective and strategically and tactically develop into a service business.[14] This, however, is easy to say, but turns out to be very difficult to do. It normally demands changes in attitudes, business mission and strategies, organizational and operational structures and leadership approaches. *It takes a service-focused mission, service business-based strategies and a service culture.* (These issues have been discussed at length in previous chapters.) In many cases, attitudes seem to be the most problematic issue. Without a change in attitudes throughout the entire organization, none of the other required changes will take place. However, it should be noted that unless top management truly embraces a service culture first, an organization-wide cultural change will not take place.

However, what part of the business should adopt a service logic? Is it enough that a separate service operation, industrial services, is transformed into a true service business? *The answer is no.* This is servitization and service infusion into manufacturing without reaching the ultimate goal, a true service business. To achieve a sustainable competitive advantage the entire firm, including its manufacturing part and service part, has to adopt a service logic and become a service business *where the manufacturing and service operations are integrating into one business.* There are three reasons for this:[15]

1. If the industrial services part – for example, engineering, consultancy, software supply, repair and maintenance, customer training, product upgrading – is developed according to a service logic, but the manufacturing business is not, the former becomes closer to understanding its customers' value creation and geared towards supporting it (outside-in management), whereas the latter part of the business inevitably remains focused on manufacturing and the customers' technical processes (inside-out management). However, the customers are the same both for the manufactured product and for industrial services, and therefore customers easily get confused and upset by the inconsistency in approach.

2. It is difficult for two different logics and cultures to exist and thrive in an organization. Normally, the manufacturing logic which exists in a much larger part of the organization and which has much older and deeper roots in the firm and its culture will become a hindrance to the development of a much younger and stranger service culture. In the end, the service culture will fade away and the whole business will slip back to the dominating manufacturing culture. If top management is in a manufacturing mode, the risk that this will happen is overwhelming.

3. If an industrial service business has been successfully established, it easily undermines the image of the product business in the minds of the firm's customers. The service business represents solutions that are more attractive to customers than stand-alone products. The product business is perceived, relatively speaking at least, as more product-oriented and less customer-focused. Eventually customers consider stand-alone products more as commodities, which leads to an increasing price pressure.[16]

TRANSFORMING INTO A SERVICE BUSINESS—THE GAME PLAN

Being a service business means that a firm does not only provide its customers' resources, such as physical products alone or together with stand-alone services, for their use. Instead the firm *offers customers value-supporting processes, integrating a set of resources – physical products, services (including hidden services), people, systems, information – which in interactions with the customers and the customers' resources, facilitate a customer process, such as a production line or sales automation.* If this functions well, value is created in this customer process and, furthermore, *in the customer's business process as well* in the form of a better revenue-generating capacity over time, lower costs of being a customer over time (lower relationship costs), or both, and eventually improved profits.

In business-to-business markets, supporting, for example, a customer's production process in a way that has a positive effect both on the revenue side and the cost side, means that in addition to the core process, a multitude of other customer processes have to be supported in a successful way as well. Examples of such processes are the customer's warehousing, repair and maintenance, need for basic product knowledge and *ad hoc* information, payment and cost control, problem solving and failure management. Only by supporting all these and other processes, in addition to the production process, is the customer's business and commercial process backed up in a successful way. If the supplier manages to do so with adequate, customer-focused resources, a trusting relationship can be expected to emerge and the 'customer's heart and mind' can be won.[17]

As MacMillan and McGrath[18] point out in a discussion of finding ways of differentiating businesses, a supplier cannot concentrate on providing the customer with a good product only, it has to take a comprehensive look at the customer's processes. According to them, the supplier should ask the following questions:[19]

- How do customers become aware of their need for your product or service?
- How do customers find your offering?
- How do customers make their final selections?
- How do customers order and purchase your product or service?
- How is your product or service delivered?
- What happens when your product and service is delivered?
- How is your product installed?
- How is your product or service paid for?
- How is your product stored?
- How is your product moved around?
- What is the customer really using your product for?
- What do customers need help with when they use your product?
- How is your product repaired and serviced?
- What happens when your product is disposed of or no longer used?

Going through these and possibly other questions, the customer's experience is analysed. A manufacturer as a service business has to support all of the customer's processes, which are important to the customer's commercial outcome, in a satisfactory way. Some of these processes are more critical to the customer and its business process than others, and those processes have to be supported especially carefully. However, it must be realized that, in the end, all processes are important to the customer. Some activities can be outsourced, but in order for the supplier to maintain its strategic position in relation to its customers, the supplier has to stay in control of the network used and of outsourced processes.

In Figure 16.2 a typical chain of processes of a customer and a corresponding chain of processes of a supplier are illustrated. In the figure they follow each other in a chain-like order. However, in reality the order may be different, and some processes may be simultaneous or iterative. For the sake of simplicity they are depicted as a chain.

The customer chain includes awareness of needs, perception of a solution, purchasing and ordering, warehousing and installing, payment and cost control, usage, information needs, problems and complaints, upgrading and modernization and, finally, word-of-mouth referrals.

The supplier chain includes market research, sales and traditional marketing, order processing, logistics and deliveries and installation, invoicing, repair and maintenance and process operation, call centre and Internet advice and documentation, complaints handling and recovery, engineering and technology development, and public relations and marketing.

These lists are, of course, only examples. The important thing is, however, that the customer's process and the supplier's process are linked to each other and interact with each other, that is, that the supplier's activities are truly geared towards the requirements of the corresponding process on the customer side. For example, the supplier's logistical process should meet the customer's warehousing process with a delivery system that supports value creation in the customer's goods–handling processes. As another example, the supplier's invoicing system should meet the requirements of the customer's payment and book-keeping and cost control system. Developing this system includes issues such as specification of the invoice, number of invoices sent during a given period and the receiver to whom invoices are sent, and so on.

Moreover, supplier processes that, when supporting a customer's processes, need to function together or at least be informed about each other's contacts with the customer must work closely together, share information and perhaps do joint planning. Such processes are, for example, product development, repair and maintenance and modernization. Far too often people in these processes never see each other or even talk to each other, either when planning or executing.

In the supplier firm the following questions should be asked:

- Do we know which customer processes are influenced by our activities and processes?

- Do we know how these customer processes function and who is involved in them?

- Do we know how these customer processes influence the customer's business process, either through a revenue-supporting or a cost-creating effect?

- Do we know which of the customer's processes are critical to the customer's business process and commercial outcome?

- Do we know how the way we handle our activities and processes influences the customer's processes today?

- Do we know how the customer's processes could function more efficiently and effectively than today and support the business process better?

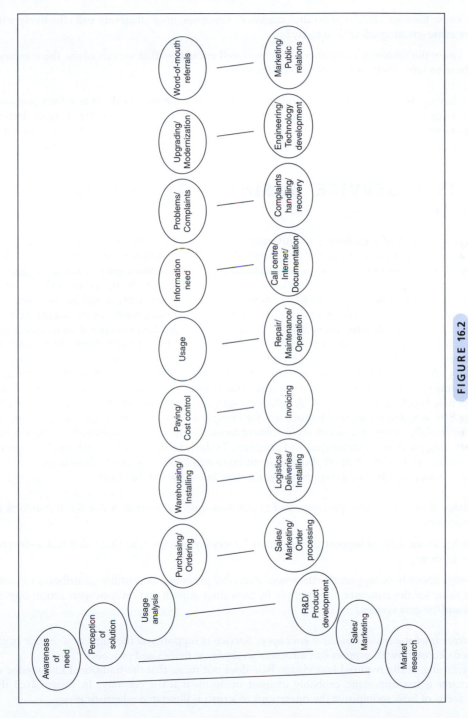

FIGURE 16.2

The customer lifecycle and supplier support chains.

- Do we know how we could support the customer's processes more efficiently and effectively with a higher value-creating effect than today?

- Do we know the customer's customers' processes well enough so that we can advise the customer about how to serve their customers better than today?

Only after having asked these questions and found satisfactory answers to them is a firm prepared to develop a comprehensive offering to support the customer in a value-supporting manner. Before finding satisfactory answers the manufacturing firm does not know the game plan for operating as a service business and probably cannot successfully service its customers in a competitive way.

WHY IS A SERVICE BUSINESS APPROACH NEEDED?

The core competence of a traditional manufacturing firm is mainly related to *how to manage manufacturing processes* and *an understanding of the customers' processes in a technical sense*. Therefore, such a firm offers its customers *a technical solution for a technical process*, for example for a production process, administrative process or sales process. This technical solution should make the customer's technical process function more efficiently. The effects on the customer's value creation and business process, not to say the processes of the customer's customers, are normally not considered in an explicit way.

A manufacturer that wants to ensure it can stay in a strategic position in relation to its customers has to be able to support the customers' various processes in a way that helps them create value in these processes (value–in–use) such that the customer's business process is also supported in a value-creating way. As the previous section demonstrated, the core solution, the physical product as a technical solution, is not enough to achieve this. Traditionally, in a manufacturing firm the main knowledge base is geared towards *knowledge about technologies, products and manufacturing processes*. This knowledge base is still of paramount importance for being a successful service business. However, to compete successfully in the new situation, in relative terms, the required *main* knowledge base is not in manufacturing processes, technologies and products. Today, the traditional knowledge base can be characterized as *a prerequisite for success*, but the main knowledge base required is elsewhere.

To compete successfully for customers today, *the main knowledge base* has to be:

- Knowledge about customers' processes and about how customers create value for themselves in these processes.

- Knowledge about how to support the customers' everyday processes, so that value (value-in-use) emerges in them.

- Knowledge about how supporting customers' everyday processes successfully contributes to commercial value for the customer, for example by providing growth and revenue-generation opportunities and/or cost savings.

This knowledge is what a service business is built upon. Service is support and the logic of a service organization is to know how to support its customers' everyday activities and processes.

This refocusing of the required knowledge base does not mean that the traditional knowledge of a manufacturer is less important, probably in most situations it is the contrary. In Figure 16.3 the change in focus of how to improve the operations of a firm is illustrated schematically.

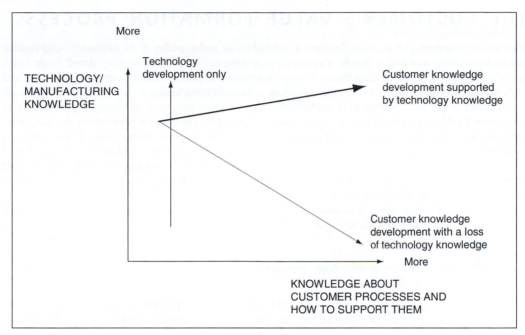

More

Technology
development only

TECHNOLOGY/
MANUFACTURING
KNOWLEDGE

Customer knowledge
development supported
by technology knowledge

Customer knowledge
development with a loss
of technology knowledge

More

KNOWLEDGE ABOUT
CUSTOMER PROCESSES AND
HOW TO SUPPORT THEM

FIGURE 16.3

Moving towards a service business knowledge base in manufacturing.

In the figure a thin line shows the traditional way of creating a competitive advantage based on a knowledge base geared towards technology and manufacturing processes. The technology knowledge deepens and the level of technology goes up, but the knowledge geared towards understanding customers' everyday processes and business process, and towards how to support them, other than with a technical solution for a technical process, remains on the same level as before. In value terms, this development is based on the idea that value for customers is embedded in the products developed and offered for the customers' use (value-in-exchange).

The dotted line illustrates the worst development that can happen. The manufacturer devotes time to create an understanding of the customers' processes, but does not maintain or when needed improve the technological knowledge. In that case the firm loses its capability to offer technical support in the form of products to its customers. The customers may like the supplier's way of interacting with them, but not the way they help them keep their processes going, for example a production or administrative process. The prerequisite for being a customer-focused service business has been lost. Such a supplier will not survive long on the market.

The thick line in Figure 16.3 indicates the way to become a service business. The manufacturer must obtain an in-depth knowledge about all its customers' processes (compare the game plan in Figure 16.2) as well as how they, and through them the business process, can be supported so that value is created in all processes. The customers are the key to value creation. They create value for themselves supported by the supplier,[20] and this value is created in the customers' processes where the support of the supplier is used (value-in use).

THE CUSTOMER'S VALUE FORMATION PROCESS

The core competence of a service business is related to *an understanding of the customer's value creation and business process and how to manage a system for supporting customer's value creation.* Based on its main knowledge base of understanding the customers' activities and processes and their value creation, and understanding how to support this value creation, a manufacturer taking a service business approach would strive to provide support to its customers' value-creating processes and business processes, and thus to total value creation. When doing so, it would probably also provide support for its customers' capabilities to serve their customers and support the customers' commercial outcome. This is achieved by offering customers, *first of all, technical solutions to technical processes,* but *in addition, by managing all of its activities and processes, including hidden services, that have an impact on the customers' total value creation,* and hence also on their preferences towards the supplier, *in a customer-focused and value-supporting manner throughout the customer relationship lifecycle.*

In Figure 16.4 a hypothetical example of how a customer's value creation is supported through a four-stage process is schematically illustrated (compare Figure 6.10 in Chapter 6). The following steps should be taken:

1. Identify customer processes which are critical to the customer's commercial result, that is, to the customer's *business effectiveness.*

2. Match the customer's key processes and the supplier's corresponding processes *(practice matching),* such that the customer's processes are successfully supported (creates *process effectiveness*),

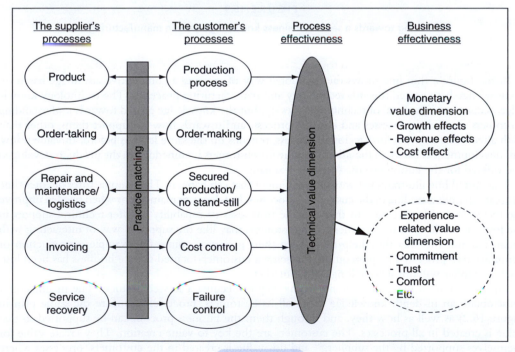

FIGURE 16.4

Supporting customers' value creation – an example.

and facilitate the customer's commercial result in a value–creating way (creates *business effectiveness*).

3. Manage the supplier processes such that the customer's identified key processes are effectively supported in a technical sense (*technical value dimension*).

4. Make sure that the technical support to the customer's processes is transformed into success-ful business effectiveness (*monetary value dimension*), and creates a favourable experience as well (*experience-related value dimension*).

In Figure 16.4 the core of the offering is exemplified with a physical product of some kind. The customer processes which are considered critical to the customer's commercial result are the following (the supplier's corresponding processes are in brackets): the production process (product), order-making (order-taking), secured production minimising stand-still time (repair and maintenance and logistics), cost control (invoicing), and failure control and correction (service recovery).

The supplier must first identify these pairs of critical processes, and thereafter initiate a *practice matching* process, where the way these processes are practised is analysed. The aim is to *align the supplier's and customer's activities, competencies and processes*, such that the customer's different processes are successfully supported. Who adapts to whom is a matter of, among other things, the two parties' strategies, power position, and also understanding of the potential of the service perspective.

Then the supplier should *integrate* support to each of the customer's key processes into *one offering*, and then manage its processes in a way which creates a *technical value*[21] in each of the customer's processes, and consequently create *process effectiveness*. This value dimension can be measured, for example, in technical, temporal, or sometimes even monetary terms, such as quality of production output, amount of scrap, time from order to delivery, or lost sales due to stand-still or delayed problem recovery. Sales often aim at supporting process effectiveness, and often the effectiveness of a core cus-tomer process only. As a consequence, technical specification and price become key sales arguments on one hand, and dominating purchasing criteria on the other hand. By taking the process one step further, sales can move the purchasing agent's interest into value for the customer on the commercial level, which leads to *value-based sales*. Sales and selling is, however, not part of the scope of this book.

The final step is to demonstrate for the customer how the combined process effectiveness in the customer's key processes leads to a monetary commercial value or *business effectiveness*: which are the effects on the revenue side through possible growth or premium pricing opportunities, and which cost savings effects can be expected to occur. In Chapter 6 on return on service and relationships we showed how these monetary effects can be calculated.

Furthermore, positive effects on business effectiveness and on the monetary value dimension can be expected to have a favourable impact on *experience-related* value dimensions, such as commitment to the supplier, and trust and comfort in doing business with this supplier.

THE BENEFIT FOR A MANUFACTURING FIRM OF TAKING A SERVICE BUSINESS APPROACH

From transforming its approach towards customers into a service business approach at least the fol-lowing benefits can be expected for a manufacturer:

- The firm becomes truly customer-focused and learns to understand not only its customers' technical processes, but how value is created in those processes and in the customers' business processes as well.

- By doing so, the firm can develop more valuable technical solutions than before as well as truly customer-focused and service-based ways of supporting all critical customer processes (warehousing, installation, maintenance, invoice processing, problem solving, etc. – compare Figures 16.2 and 16.4).

- The firm becomes more relevant for the customers' business processes than any third-party actor and can maintain a strategic position in relation to its customers.

- The firm has the potential to help their customers serve their customers in a more efficient and effective, and therefore probably also more profitable, manner.

- By developing its solutions and ways of managing its customers as a service business, the firm differentiates its offering *in a way that for competitors is substantially more difficult, sometimes almost impossible, to copy.*

- In the final analysis, a service business approach enables the firm to strengthen its customer contacts and develop them into trustworthy and sustainable relationships that are less vulnerable to competitor actions and third-party threats, and hence a source of better and more profitable business.

Of course, not all customers are interested in getting into such close contact with a supplier and are not ready to open up for a supplier. For some customers the technical solution is the only part of an offering to consider, and the price remains the most important purchasing criterion. For such customers, or sometimes even for markets dominated by such customers, a service business approach may not be effective. For all other customers and markets such an approach may even be inevitable in the future for maintaining competitive advantage or even just for staying on the market.

A service business approach can be important for any type of firm in business-to-business markets, not only for those offering tailor-made solutions in markets where there is a need for after-sales service. Standardised products are myths and commodities only exist in the minds of managers who have not had the imagination to differentiate them by developing other interfaces with the customers that inevitably always exist.[22] Offerings to customers and customer contacts with even simple products can be developed in this way. By taking a service perspective and adopting a service logic, undifferentiated, commodity-type products can be differentiated. The supplier needs to find out what would make a customer perceive the product and the supplier differently from the industry standard. There is always something in the customer relationship which a customer appreciates when it is offered and handled in a new and different way. It can relate to deliveries or delivery times, warehousing, product documentation, the invoicing system and the structure of the invoice, access to people, systems and information, or just anything that a customer may perceive as different *and* valuable compared to standard behaviour. By finding out what it is and offering it, the firm adds a customer-focused value-enhancing support to the core product. The supplier moves from a product manufacturing and delivery mode to a service business mode, *and becomes a service firm.*

TRANSFORMING INTO A SERVICE BUSINESS

In order for product manufacturers to become service businesses, two fundamental requirements have to be taken into account:

1. Becoming a service business is a *strategic choice*. There must be a strategic decision to be and perform as a service business. Such a strategic decision demonstrates top management's wish and

determination to transform the firm from a resource-delivering product business into a value-supporting service provider.

2. Performing as a service business and providing value-supporting service to customers (and other stakeholders) requires a dominating *service culture* throughout the firm. Unless such a culture can be created, the implementation of a service perspective and a service strategy will not be successful. In addition to employee training, internal communication and other efforts that may be necessary, creating and maintaining a service culture requires the continuous support through top management's leadership (see Chapters 14 and 15 about internal marketing and service culture).

The case study on the *Normet Group* at the end of the chapter clearly illustrates these requirements.

Compared with a manufacturing approach, taking a service business approach requires at least three fundamental changes in the *business logic*. These changes are:

1. Redefining the business mission and strategies from a service perspective.

2. Redefining the offering as a process.

3. Servicising critical elements in the customer relationships.

REDEFINING THE BUSINESS MISSION AND STRATEGIES FROM A SERVICE PERSPECTIVE

Being a service business means that the firm does not view its manufacturing part as one business and industrial services as another business with different strategies and planning processes. The manufacturing part must be integrated with all other activities – service processes as well as hidden services – into one total continuous support to the customers' processes over the customer lifecycle. The *business mission* is not to provide customers with excellent or high-technology resources only for their use, such as physical products as a technical solution, but *to provide customers with excellent support to their processes so that value is created in them and in the customers' business and commercial processes*. Strategies have to be formulated accordingly.

This support is formed by a continuous flow of technical solutions, products, deliveries, customer training, invoicing, service recovery when needed and handling of complaints and problems, advice, repair and maintenance service, joint product and service development, and research and development, upgrading and modernization of installed equipment, etc. (see Figures 16.2 and 16.4). This flow of activities takes place in a continuous process of supporting the customers' processes in a value-creating manner. In this way the customer is truly *served* with physical products and technical solutions, service processes (deliveries, training, maintenance, etc.), administrative and legal routines (hidden services such as invoicing and complaints handling), infrastructures (logistical systems, extranets, etc.), information (product documentation, advice, etc.) and people.

REDEFINING THE *OFFERING* AS A PROCESS

As the previous discussions of a service business-focused mission and of how customers' business effectiveness is supported demonstrated, it is not enough to just provide customers with a technical solution for a technical process. This is only one element of a process of providing customers with all the support needed for them to be able to create adequate value in their processes and for their business. Hence, the offering of a manufacturing firm, which used to be a physical product, is dead in its traditional form. The physical products still exist, of course, but from having been the *output of the manufacturer's production process* they become *one input among others into the customer's value-creating process.* The physical product becomes a resource alongside a host of other resources needed in the constant flow of supporting the customer's processes. This flow of resources and activities takes place in a continuous process. Hence, a service business's offering is the process. *This process takes the place of the traditional product.*[23]

SERVICIZING CRITICAL ELEMENTS IN CUSTOMER RELATIONSHIPS

As was shown in the previous section, a firm's productive (e.g. products), administrative (e.g. websites), financial (e.g. invoicing), legal (e.g. complaints handling) and other processes should be considered *inputs into customers' processes*, where the goal is to support value creation in those processes, and ultimately the customers' business processes. They have to be turned into true service for customers, or *servicized*. So, *servicizing* can be defined as *turning all elements in a customer relationship, regardless of their type and nature, into value-supporting inputs into the customers' processes*, i.e. turning them into service for customers. Servicizing the supplier's resources and activities makes a firm a true service business. Servicizing is not the same as servitization. The latter means that a growing number of services are added to a core product. Servicizing relates to the actions taken by a firm to transform resources and processes into a holistic offering, including products and recognized and hidden services into value-supporting processes that serve the customers' processes and business.

Servicizing requires that:

- All customer contacts and all resources and activities in those contacts, and all interactions with the customer, are analysed and the effects they have on the customer process they influence are assessed.

- If this effect is neutral or even negative, that is, no value support to a customer process is achieved, or the customer's process is affected unfavourably (unnecessary and unwanted costs are created for the customer, the customer's revenue-generating capability is hurt, or both; the value of the core solution is hurt by *value destroyers*), an assessment is made of how critical this activity is for the customer's value creation and commercial outcome (either perceptually or in financial terms, or both).

- Resources and activities with a neutral or negative effect are developed so that, in the future, they function as value-supporting service and not as value destroyers in the customer relationships.

In principle, *anything can be servicized*. It is just a matter of management attitude and the adoption of a service logic and customer focus. What in any given case should be servicized depends on what is critical for the customer, the competitive situation at hand and a long-term cost–benefit analysis. However, changing the focus and servicizing elements of the customer relationship will probably not create substantial extra costs, if any. Moreover, doing so can easily lead to cost savings for the suppliers. When the firm performs in a more service-focused manner, mistakes are avoided and unnecessary queries and complaints do not have to be attended to. Therefore, less resources, time and money are required for the unproductive processes of sorting out problems, correcting mistakes and discussing, negotiating and sometimes even quarrelling with customers. All badly-handled activities that lead to unnecessary costs for customers (rising *relationship costs*) normally at the same time also lead to similar unnecessary relationship costs for the supplier (see Chapter 6).

In Table 16.1, examples of how various systems, resources and activities in customer relationships can be servicized are described.

TABLE 16.1

Examples of how systems, resources and activities in customer relationships can be servicized.

Products	Products are traditionally seen as outputs of production processes. Servicizing products requires that they are considered inputs into the customers' processes. Tailor-making products, using CAD/CAM and other techniques and bringing customers into design and production processes, and mass customization are examples of this. Other examples are making products easier to maintain, easier to make operational, and easier to handle. However, depending on the situation and the requirements of the customers, servicizing may also mean that products are standardized. It all depends on what is the most effective way of supporting value generation for customers.
Logistics	Just-in-time logistics is a well-known means of servicizing order-making, deliveries and warehousing. By this strategy a supplier aligns its logistical processes to the customer's processes in order to minimize the customer's costs of keeping products in stock.
Deliveries	Deliveries as a separate part of logistics can be servicized, for example, by customizing timetables and by keeping customers informed about the progress of a delivery.
Information	Documentation about how to use machines, software and other solutions can be servicized by turning it into real knowledge for customers. Knowledge requires that the information is easily retrievable and understandable and can be used immediately.
Extranets and websites	Servicizing extranets and websites requires that they are designed so that users can easily navigate them and find the information they are looking for in such a format that it can easily be transformed into usable knowledge.
Managing quality problems and service failures	If there is a problem with goods quality or a mistake or service failure has occurred, servicizing requires that such incidents are managed according to the principles of *service recovery*. The customers have to perceive that the supplier or service provider cares for their situation, quickly finds a solution, and compensates for losses that they may have suffered.
Invoicing	By developing an invoicing and payment system and by designing invoices so that they are easy to understand, check and process by customers, this element of customer relationships is turned into a cost-saving service for customers. Making sure that mistakes are avoided is, of course, also part of servicizing invoicing.

TABLE 16.1

(continued)

Product and service development	Bringing customers into the processes of developing and designing new resources and processes, such as products and services, potentially makes it possible for a supplier or service provider to develop solutions that better fit customers' processes and, therefore, also more effectively support their value-creating processes. This may improve the revenue-generating capacity of customers, and reduce their costs, and is therefore an example of how to servicize the customer relationship.
R&D	Bringing customers into the processes of basic research and development may have similar effects to the ones discussed above.
Etc.	There are many more elements of the customer relationship where servicizing is possible.

As can be seen from the examples in the previous section, there are several ways of servicizing customer relationships already at least partly in use (for example, involve customers in the design and development of products and other resources and processes, just-in-time logistics and joint R&D). However, the challenge is to not just take some elements of a relationship in isolation and treat them from a value-supporting perspective. As long as other elements of a relationship are not designed in a similar manner, the customer's process may still be hurt and value destroyed.

DEVELOPING THE OFFERING AS SERVICE: THE CSS (CONCEPTUALIZING, SYSTEMATIZING, SERVICIZING) MODEL

A manufacturer that has adopted a service business logic has to develop its processes so that they support the corresponding customer processes (compare Figure 16.2). Formulated in a generic way, a business mission based on a service logic could read as follows (in Chapter 3 guidelines for developing a service-oriented business mission were discussed; see Figure 3.5):

The firm's mission is to support the customer's production process (or whichever process is concerned) and related processes (logistics, installation, maintenance, payment and book-keeping, information need, etc. depending on what is included in the customer relationship) in a way that creates value-in-use[24] for the customer, and moreover supports the customer's business process and commercial outcomes.

Hence, the business mission should not be to supply customers with, for example, the best product, but instead to support the customer's activities and processes in a value-creating manner. The difference between the two formulations is huge. The first one is based on a manufacturer's traditional main knowledge base and core competence, whereas the latter is based on a service logic and the main knowledge base and core competence of a service business.

However, once the business mission is formulated in a service-oriented manner and the manufacturing firm starts operating as a service business, the firm's offering has to be organized and developed as *one continuous flow of support* to *the customer's various processes* over the customer lifecycle. It is important to realize that service is a process, and however much this process is planned and organized, it will never become anything like a standardized product. Therefore, an idea of a 'product' must never be the ideal goal of the development of an offering. Here a three-stage approach called the CSS model is helpful. CSS stands for:

1. Conceptualizing.
2. Systematizing.
3. Servicizing.

Conceptualizing means that the firm decides what kind of support it should provide a customer with, how value should be created in the customer's processes, and how customer touchpoints should be handled and interactions with the customer's various processes should function and what they should lead to in terms of support to the customer's everyday activities and processes, and how this should affect the customer's business process commercially. Conceptualizing includes decisions about what core solutions (for example, a product, services, information, combinations of such and other resources) should be offered and how, for example, logistical, repair and maintenance, educational, advisory, invoicing, problem-solving and other activities should function in order to support value-in-use for the customer over the customer lifecycle.

In short, *conceptualizing* is to determine *what to do for the firm's customers and how to do it*.

Systematizing means that the firm should decide what kind of resources are needed in order to implement the conceptualized offering and create a structural way of putting in place the various processes of the offering. This is done so that resources are used in a rational way. Cost–benefit considerations should be taken into account in the systematizing phase. An objective with systematizing is to make sure the unnecessary or unnecessarily expensive resources are not used, or that resources are not used and processes developed in an unorganized and unco-ordinated way. *The goal of organizing resources and processes* used is to achieve a maximal effect in terms of supporting the customers' everyday activities and processes without creating unnecessary costs. *The goal of co-ordinating resources and processes* is to make sure that they are not functioning in ways that create information problems and confusion in the customer contacts and in the customer's processes.

In the systematizing phase it is important to realize that standardized packages must not be created. The customer contacts over time are not standardized. Instead, it is a question of developing organized guidelines for performance where flexibility is allowed and encouraged. However, at the same time systematizing also includes *setting the limits for flexibility*.[25] These limits are, of course, based on a cost–benefit analysis, however a *long-term* analysis of what it costs and what can be gained is required. Standardized modules that can be combined in different ways to achieve flexibility can, of course, be used, but this must not lead to stereotyped behaviour.

In short, *systematizing* is:

- *To determine what resources and processes are needed* for the firm to support customers' activities and processes in a value-creating way.
- *To organize resources and processes* that constitute the offering.
- *To co-ordinate the way various resources and processes function.*
- *To determine the limits for flexibility* in the way resources and processes function based on a long-term cost–benefit analysis.

Servicizing is the final phase of the CSS model. Once the resources and processes and the organized and co-ordinated ways of using them have been determined and the limits for flexibility set, one has to make sure that the various processes and customer contacts indeed function in a value-supporting manner. The attitudes, knowledge and skills of people, the capabilities of physical resources, systems and infrastructures to function in a customer-focused way, and the customer-focused quality of the leadership provided by managers and supervisors have to be ensured. Sometimes customers have to be educated about how to participate in the processes. The goal is to develop all resources and processes supporting the customers' everyday activities and processes, regardless of what these activities and processes are, in a way the guarantees that value-in-use is created in those processes. *Value-in-use* means that the customer perceives and wherever possible can calculate that its processes function more efficiently and effectively with the support of the supplier's activities than without them or with the support of a competitor. In the previous section, servicizing was discussed in detail and the question of what can be servicized was addressed with examples (see Table 16.1).

In short, *servicizing* is to make sure that *the planned offering including a set of resources, processes, and interactions functions in a value-supporting way*, that is, functions as service for the firm's customers, or to put it in another way, truly serves the customers.

The CSS model can often be used in two stages. First, a general conceptualizing, systematizing and servicizing of the offering to customers can be undertaken. The result is an offering that can be used as a general guideline for the business. In the next phase, if and when appropriate, applications geared towards specific customers can be created as guidelines for how a specific customer should be served.

OUTSOURCING AND BUILDING NETWORKS

Outsourcing has been mentioned a number of times throughout this book. Outsourcing (sometimes also called 'offshoring') means that a firm lets an external organization perform an activity. For example, call centres answering customers' queries about a product or a service, deliveries of goods, maintenance of products and equipment delivered, and also sometimes product development and the development of software are frequently outsourced. Sometimes outsourcing takes the form of formal networks, but the difference between building networks and outsourcing is not always very distinct. For example, in the construction industry it is normal that firms build stable or loosely-coupled networks of subcontractors that take care of parts of the construction process. Firms in the clothing industry form networks with designers, manufacturers and distributors to develop a successful business.

When, for example, product development or design of clothing are outsourced, the outsourcing firm's customers do not experience the performance and behaviour of network partners or the outsourced activities other than indirectly in the form of the final product or clothing. However, in service the situation is typically different. The way a call centre answers a call by a given firm's customer and how well it manages to solve the customer's problem have a direct impact on this customer's perception of the outsourcer's service and its quality. If the firm that handles an outsourced activity misbehaves and provides bad service, it is the outsourcing firm that suffers. This means that outsourcing must be managed carefully, and activities outsourced for the right reasons.

Today service activities are far too often outsourced for the wrong reasons. In Chapter 1 the difference between *outside-in management* and *inside-out management* was discussed (see also Figures 1.1 and 1.2). The former approach means that managers' first focus on understanding the customers' processes and the firm's revenue-generating capability, and only then on the firm's own processes and technologies and costs. The latter approach means that focus on costs and the firm's processes dominate managerial decision-making, and revenue-generating implications and the customers' processes are given less or even marginal attention, if any. Cleary, for outsourcing to be successful, the outsourced service activity should support the service quality goals. This means that the dominating reason for outsourcing, for example, call centre services or maintenance services, should be a strenuous effort to maintain the overall perceived quality of the firm's offering, and thereby strengthen or at least maintain the firm's revenue-generating capability. Of course, cost considerations should also be made, but not dominate. Outsourcing decisions should be guided by outside-in management considerations.

In reality, outsourcing decisions are often made from an inside-out management perspective. Cost considerations determine what is outsourced and how. The result is often low perceived quality, and unsatisfied customers. As a consequence, limited or no positive effect on the firm's performance is achieved through outsourcing.[26]

In conclusion, outsourcing and forming networks to serve customers may be useful. However, for service businesses one must always remember that *the outsourced service activity always has a direct impact on the customers' perceptions of the outsourcing firm's service quality, and on the firm's brand fulfilment and image.* Hence, *outsourcing decisions must not be made based primarily on cost considerations.* Instead, an outside-in management approach needs to be taken. Questions about how outsourcing a service activity to an outside firm or network partner will support the customers' processes and strengthen the outsourcing firm's revenue-generation capabilities must be asked and properly answered. Cost considerations are of course also important, but they must not dominate decision-making. An outsourcing decision which saves costs but hurts the firm's capability to generate revenues is clearly not wise, and should not be accepted from a commercial point of view.

WHAT DOES TRANSFORMATION INTO A SERVICE BUSINESS COST?

'What does it cost to transform a manufacturing firm into a service business?' and 'Does it cost considerably more to operate as a service business?' are frequently asked questions. The transformation process may require some investments in internal marketing and employee education and in development of some organizational structures, but most of all it requires intellectual effort. What is required in the transformation process is the development of a *business mission geared towards a service logic, renewed strategies* and service-focused *operational routines*, where the *resources and operational processes throughout the organization are used in a new way* that supports the customers' everyday processes and activities throughout their organizations. Moreover, *organizational structures, leadership models,* and *planning and budgeting routines* may have to be changed. Finally and above all, for a service culture to emerge *attitudes have to be changed* among everyone from top management throughout the organization. Provided that the business mission and strategies are renewed, the rest does not have to cost too much. However, if old manufacturing-oriented attitudes, missions and strategies remain, transformation attempts will start to become expensive and will probably not lead to any lasting changes.

When the transformation has taken place, *operating as a service business does not imply a higher cost level.* Normally the resources needed already existed before the transformation, and processes to take care of all necessary activities were in place. The investments that may be required are in transformation, not in operating as a service business. On the contrary, relationship costs for the supplier may decrease, and probably will do so.

CASE STUDY

NORMET GROUP: FROM PRODUCT MANUFACTURER IN THE METAL INDUSTRY TO A GLOBALLY OPERATING SERVICE BUSINESS

Normet Group is a globally operating firm based in Finland with its main production facilities in the city of Iisalmi in the northern part of the country. Ten years ago Normet was a typical product manufacturer in the metal industry, operating in three fairly different business areas. One of the businesses was subcontracting heavy equipment for the mining business to the Sweden-based global firm Sandvik. Normet's strategy at the time was formulated as 'manufacturer of rubber tired heavy duty machines'. This strategy had worked very well for years. However, in 2004 Sandvik terminated the sub-contracting agreement. In another business line Normet's own products had been delivered internationally in the thousands, but Normet had no clear idea of where they were used and how they were maintained. As Aaro Cantell, Normet Group's CEO and chair, says, 'The new situation was a major challenge for us, but also a most important opportunity to seize'. At the same time, this was also an opportunity for Normet to internationalize and grow. Today, Normet is market leader globally in its niche business areas.

During a seven-year process Normet moved from a manufacturer of products and equipment for the mining industry only to service provider, the business of which is based on understanding and supporting its customers' mining and tunnel construction operations, and its strategic goal is to facilitate value creation in the customers' processes, with over 40 offices on six continents. In that time period the turnover has grown from under €50 million per year to approx. €250 millon, and the number of employees has grown almost fivefold. Normet's new *vision* is that *through its service approach, by using its knowledge and expertise, it will be able to boost its customers' processes and support their competitive position*, and through the knowledge and level of expertise it holds, it will be able to earn the position as preferred business partner. Formally, the vision has been formulated as follows: 'To be a fast growing and innovative technology company with a passion to offer continuous improvement to our underground mining and tunnelling partners' processes for increased safety, productivity and sustainability.'

The service provided to customers typically aims at helping customers to shorten their production cycles and decrease their operating costs as well as improve environmental friendliness and work safety. Consequently, the offering has changed from mining products and equipment to consultancy, application know-how , operation support, service and maintenance, training and other customer-supporting service. Simultaneously the product elements have been enlarged to include, for example, new construction chemical products required for the customers' mining and tunnelling processes.

The main reason for Normet's growth followed from the transformation into a service provider. Aaro Cantell states: 'We realized that our holistic solution approach to support and develop the concrete spraying process in tunnel construction could also be applied to other tunnel construction processes like explosive charging and later also to injection and bolting. This helped us find new growth areas.'

Underground mining is growing, which has provided more business in Normet's traditional customer segment. In addition, tunnel construction is rising, particularly in developing countries where infrastructure (road and railroad tunnels, hydro power, etc.) is increasingly needed, and also in big cities (due to urbanisation), where lack of space forces more and more activities to be built underground (traffic, car parks, metro, water pipes, sewage, shopping centres, etc.). Furthermore, modern mechanized technologies are used more and more in underground mining and tunnelling, and therefore, the need for knowledge and consultancy supporting faster and safer operations as well as better cost efficiency and process productivity is growing. All this provides opportunities for a service provider that a pure product manufacturer finds difficult to seize.

How did all this happen? The first step was to *realize the business opportunities of providing service* to customers, instead of only delivering products. The second step was the *strategic decision* by Normet's management to become a service business and a solution provider, although in the beginning of this transformation process the products and equipment still formed the core of the offering. Without these two initial steps nothing new and, above all, nothing enduring, would have developed.

First, turning this service-based business idea into practice did not succeed well. Services were added on top of the products as after-product sales, but the distributors abroad and the customers were not impressed. As neither the distributors nor the customers saw the value of this approach, whereby Normet tried to apply servitization or service infusion through reseller channels, this attempt did not work. As Aaro Cantell afterwards concluded, 'As we had no direct contacts with our real customers, the end users, we could not provide service to them, really. We understood that we had to move close to the end users.' Consequently, Normet invested in a global network of fully-owned sales and service offices. In this way a direct link between Normet and the end users was established. This was a bold endeavour, but this network was created quickly, and it functioned well from the beginning. A major reason for the successful launch of well-performing local offices across the globe was the fact Normet managed to recruit an experienced manager, Tom Melbye, who was internationally well known and respected in the industry, to take charge of the internationalization process. Secondly, with Melbye in charge of the process, Normet managed to find skilful local individuals with good experience of the local markets to take charge of Normet's local business. Currently, Tom Melbye is the President of Normet Group.

Another reason for the successful launch of the new fully-owned sales and service network can be found in how the business mission and the corresponding strategic approach had been reformulated. Service infusion into a basically product-dominated offering had failed. Now service, instead of the products, was defined as the core of the business and the offering. The strategy *of understanding and supporting its customers' mining operations in order to facilitate value creation in the customers' processes* was crystallized. The business mission was formulated as follows: 'To improve underground mining and tunnelling processes with knowledge and technology to benefit our clients and society.' Instead of adding services to the product offering, services and products were *integrated into a service offering*, which was driven by the service perspective defined by this service strategy. Hence, a *service logic* was adopted, whereby Normet aimed at supporting customers' value creation to be able to capture value from its customer relationships in return.

An important organizational change was made in order to enable the implementation of the service strategy through the new sales and service network. Normet was divided into two separate firms, Supply Line and Front Line. However, the organization was not split in the way this often happens, that is, in a services selling and providing part and a product manufacturing, selling, and delivering part. Instead, Normet was divided into a Supply Line firm responsible for efficient and effective development and production of the products and equipment needed to provide service to customers (essentially the old Normet), and a frontline firm responsible for setting up and managing Normet's own sales and service network and *for selling and providing service, where product elements alongside consultancy, application know-how, logistics, maintenance, training and other services are integrated into a service offering*. If a customer at some point needs only a product, this is also fine. However, the product is not sold and delivered as such, but *as support to the customer's business*, and at the same time enhancing process efficiency and work safety, thereby facilitating the customer's value creation, as required by Normet's mission and strategy. In other words, *even products are sold and provided as service*.

A third reason for the successful implementation of the service strategy, and for the comparatively fast international growth, can be found in the enthusiasm and optimism demonstrated by management. Says Aaro Cantell: 'The international economic problems, following the financial crisis of 2008, hurt us and our business as well, but we considered the drop in investments being temporary and our markets as future growth markets, and felt that the biggest limitation in our growth were our own skills and human resources. During 2009 to 2010, when other firms laid off personnel, we hired 100 new employees, in spite of the fact that our turnover dropped by 16% during the same period.' This future orientation and belief in the business and its employees kept the company spirit high, spread the enthusiasm throughout the organization and motivated people to work hard.

Eventually, the ultimate reason why Normet changed so successfully into a service business was the vision of Normet Group's CEO and chair Aaro Cantell, and his enthusiasm and determination to see through the change process. 'For me this period has been an exciting adventure and a fantastic experience. But Normet's inspired professionals throughout the globe were the ones that really made it happen,' he concludes.

SUMMARY

In order to stay competitive or to create a sustainable competitive advantage manufacturers in a growing number of business-to-business markets have to redefine their business as a service business and adopt a service logic for their customer management – not only their after-sales or industrial services but their total business. Their product business and industrial service business have to be integrated into one service logic-based business. Operating with two different business logics creates confusion both for the manufacturer itself and for its customers. A service business approach requires that the business mission is redefined and, moreover, managerial, structural, operational and above all attitudinal changes have to take place. The manufacturer's processes have to be aligned with the corresponding processes of its customers. Requirements for transforming into a service business were discussed. The CSS (*Conceptualizing, Systematizing, Servicizing*) model was presented as a systematic means of developing the offering and the way of operating. The transformation into a service business mode may demand some extra costs and additional investments, but operating as a service business will not cost more than operating in a product business mode. On the contrary, it may lead to cost savings.

QUESTIONS FOR DISCUSSION

1. What are the reasons for manufacturing firms to transform into service businesses?

2. What does the third-party threat mean? How can a supplier–customer relationship be affected by such a threat?

3. How should a manufacturing firm manage its customers as a service business?

4. What changes in the business logic are required to transform into a service business?

5. What does it mean to provide value-supporting processes instead of only technical solutions to a technical process?

6. What is meant by servicizing? What can be servicized? How is a customer relationship servicized?

7. Discuss how transforming a given or hypothetical manufacturer into a service business would affect the business mission, strategies and performance of this firm.

8. Discuss how the CSS (Conceptualizing, Systematizing, Servicising) model can be used in a given or hypothetical firm.

NOTES

1. See Bowen, D.E. & Siehl, C., A framework for analyzing customer service orientation in manufacturing. *Academy of Management Review*, **14**(1), 1989, 75–95. For an overview of the early

literature on this need, see Oliva, R. & Kallenberg, R., Managing the transition from products to services. *International Journal of Service Industry Management*, **14**(2), 2003, 160–172.

2. Oliva & Kallenberg, *op. cit.*, 165ff.

3. A notable exception is Grönroos, C. & Helle, P., Adopting a service logic in manufacturing: conceptual foundation and metrics for mutual value creation. *Journal of Service Management*, **21**(5), 2010, 564–590. Typologies of service infusion strategies have been suggested in Raddats, C. & Kowalkowski, C., Reconceptualization of manufacturers' service strategies. *Journal of Business-to-Business Marketing*, **21**(1), 2014, 19–34. In Kowalkowski, C, Kindström, D, Brashear Alejandro, T., Brege, S. & Biggemann, S., Service infusion as agile incrementalism in action. *Journal of Business Research*, **65**(6), 2012, 765–772, the authors discuss service infusion and demonstrate problems with applying this concept.

4. See http://andyneely.blogspot.fi/2013/11/what-is-servitization.html. (18 March 2014).

5. See Grönroos & Helle, *op. cit.,* and also Oliva & Kallenberg, *op. cit.*, who make this observation in their four-phase model.

6. Fang, E., Palmatier, R.W. & Steenkamp, J-B.E.M., Effect of service transition on strategies and firm value. *Journal of Marketing*, **72**(5), 2008, 1–14. See also Visnjíc Kastelli, I. & Van Looy, B., Servitization: disentangling the impact of service business model innovation on manufacturing firm performance. *Journal of Operations Management*, **31**(4), 2013, 169–180.

7. Dachs, B., Biege, S., Borowiecki, M, Lay, G., Jäger, A. & Schartinger, D., Servitisation of European manufacturing: evidence from a large scale database. *The Service Industries Journal*, **34**(1), 2014, 5–23. This study also indicates that small and large firms may benefit more from servitization.

8. See Smith, L., Maull, R. & Ng, I.C.L., Servitization and operations management: a service-dominant logic approach. *International Journal of Operations & Production Management*, **34**(2), 2014, 242–269, who conclude from their research that becoming a service business is not based on a transition from one stage to another, but an evolutionary process towards a service-based mode of operations.

9. See Barnett, N.J., Parry, G. Saad, M., Newnes, L.B. & Gah, Y.M., Servitization: is a paradigm shift in the business model and service enterprise required? *Strategic Change*, **22**(3-4), 2013, 145–156.

10. See Gronroos, C., Adopting a service logic for marketing. *Marketing Theory*, **6**(3), 2006, 317–333.

11. See Grönroos & Helle, *op. cit.*

12. See Brax, S., A manufacturer becoming service provider – challenges and a paradox. *Managing Service Quality*, **15**(2), 2005, 142–155.

13. Grönroos & Helle, *op. cit.* Bowen and Siehl were one of the first, if not *the* first, to discuss the need for manufacturers to transform *their whole business* into a service business. See Bowen & Siehl, *op. cit.*

14. From a customer point of view, every business is a service business and every firm a service firm. See Webster Jr., F.E., Executing the new marketing concept. *Marketing Management*, **3**(1), 1994, 9–18 and Vargo, S.L. & Lusch, R.F., Evolving to a new dominant logic for marketing. *Journal of Marketing*, **68**(Jan), 2004, 1–17. See also Grönroos & Helle, *op. cit.*, and Eggert, A., Hogreve, J., Ulaga, W. & Muenkhoff, E., Revenue and profit implications of industrial service strategies. *Journal of Service Research*, **17**(1), 2013, 23–39, where the authors demonstrate empirically that a service-led strategy in manufacturing firms may have a positive effect on revenues and profits.

15. For an interesting discussion about the conflicts between product and service businesses in a manufacturing context see Auguste, B.G., Harmon, E.P. & Pandit, V., The right service strategies for product companies. *The McKinsey Quarterly*, **1**, 2006, 41–51.

16. See Auguste, Harmon & Pandit, *op. cit.*

17. This metaphor was used in Storbacka, K. & Lehtinen, J.R., *Customer Relationship Management*. Singapore: McGraw-Hill, 2001.

18. MacMillan, I.C. & McGrath, R.G., Discovering new points of differentiation. *Harvard Business Review*, Jul–Aug, 1997, 133–145.

19. MacMillan & McGrath, *op. cit.*, 134–137, 143.

20. See, for example, Grönroos, C. & Ravald, A., Service business logic: implications for value creation and marketing. *Journal of Service Management*, **22**(1), 2011, 5–22. See also Prahalad, C.K. & Ramaswamy, V., *The Future of Competition: Co-Creating Unique Value with Customers*. Boston, MA: Harvard Business School Press, 2004.

21. The technical value dimension has also been labelled 'functional value dimension'. See Gupta, S. & Lehman, D.R., *Managing Customers as Investments*. Wharton School, Upper Saddle River, NJ, 2005. However, in order to avoid confusion with the functional quality concept of the perceived service quality model, the expression 'functional value' is not used here.

22. See MacMillan & McGrath, *op. cit.*, 144–145, who use gasoline sales as an example.

23. Compare Storbacka & Lehtinen, *op. cit.*

24. *Value-in-use* means that the customer perceives and wherever possible can calculate how its processes function more efficiently and effectively with the support of the supplier's activities.

25. Here we can see the difference between *systematizing* and *productizing*, a commonly used concept in service businesses. Productizing views standardized products as the ideal and service as

problems. It is a matter of creating packages and eliminating flexibility as much as possible. The goal is to create standardized products out of service processes. However, the processes do not disappear anywhere. Customer-oriented flexibility is the strength of service and it is important not to eliminate that. Therefore, productizing as a concept and a term idealizing the manufactured product concept is dangerous in a service business. It is dangerous for two reasons: it is based on an impossible thought that service processes through productizing would disappear and could be reduced to a standardized thing, a package equalling a manufactured product; and psychologically it makes managers and customer contact employees alike turn their backs on the customers and focus on stereotyped behaviour instead of listening to the customers. Productizing kills a service. However, productizing aims at an important issue, the need to create organized guidelines for how service should support customers' activities and processes. The CSS (Conceptualizing, Systematizing, Servicizing) model is offered as a service-oriented alternative for achieving that goal.

26. See Gilley, K.M. & Rasheed, A., Making more by doing less: an analysis of outsourcing and its effects on firm performance. *Journal of Management*, **26**(4), 2000, 763–790, where the authors did not find significant effects of outsourcing on firm performance. If there is an effect, it depends on the firm's strategy and also on the environment.

REFERENCES

Auguste, B.G., Harmon, E.P. & Pandit, V. (2006) The right service strategies for product companies. *The McKinsey Quarterly*, **1**, 41–51.

Barnett, N.J., Parry, G. Saad, M., Newnes, L.B. & Gah, Y.M. (2013) Servitization: is a paradigm shift in the business model and service enterprise required? *Strategic Change*, **22**(3-4), 145–156.

Bowen, D.E. & Siehl, C., (1989) A framework for analyzing customer service orientation in manufacturing. *Academy of Management Review*, **14**(1), 75–95.

Brax, S. (2005) A manufacturer becoming service provider – challenges and a paradox. *Managing Service Quality*, **15**(2), 142–155.

Dachs, B., Biege, S., Borowiecki, M, Lay, G., Jäger, A. & Schartinger, D. (2014) Servitisation of European manufacturing: evidence from a large scale database. *The Service Industries Journal*, **34**(1), 5–23.

Eggert, A., Hogreve, J., Ulaga, W. & Muenkhoff, E. (2013) Revenue and profit implications of industrial service strategies. *Journal of Service Research*, **17**(1), 23–39.

Fang, E., Palmatier, R.W. & Steenkamp, J-B.E.M. (2008) Effect of service transition on strategies and firm value. *Journal of Marketing*, **72**(5), 1–14.

Gilley, K.M. & Rasheed, A. (2000) Making more by doing less: an analysis of outsourcing and its effects on firm performance. *Journal of Management*, **26**(4), 763–790.

Grönroos, C. (2006) Adopting a service logic for marketing. *Marketing Theory*, **6**(3), 317–333.

Grönroos, C. & Helle, P. (2010) Adopting a service logic in manufacturing: conceptual foundation and metrics for mutual value creation. *Journal of Service Management*, **21**(5), 564–590.

Grönroos, C. & Ravald, A. (2011) Service business logic: implications for value creation and marketing. *Journal of Service Management*, **22**(1), 5–22.

Gupta, S. & Lehman, D.R. (2005) *Managing Customers as Investments*. Upper Saddle River, NJ: Wharton School.

http://andyneely.blogspot.fi/2013/11/what-is-servitization.html.

Kowalkowski, C., Kindström, D., Brashear Alejandro, T., Brege, S. & Biggemann, S. (2012) Service infusion as agile incrementalism in action. *Journal of Business Research*, **65**(6), 765–772.

MacMillan, I.C. & McGrath, R.G. (1997) Discovering new points of differentiation. *Harvard Business Review*, Jul–Aug, 133–145.

Oliva, R. & Kallenberg, R. (2003) Managing the transition from products to services. *International Journal of Service Industry Management*, **14**(2), 160–172.

Prahalad, C.K. & Ramaswamy, V. (2004) *The Future of Competition: Co-Creating Unique Value with Customers*. Boston, MA: Harvard Business School Press.

Raddats, C. & Kowalkowski, C. (2014) Reconceptualization of manufacturers' service strategies. *Journal of Business-to-Business Marketing*, **21**(1), 19-34.

Smith, L., Maull, R. & Ng, I.C.L. (2014) Servitization and operations management: a service-dominant logic approach. *International Journal of Operations & Production Management*, **34**(2), 242–269.

Storbacka, K. & Lehtinen, J.R. (2001) *Customer Relationship Management*. Singapore: McGraw-Hill.

Vargo, S.L. & Lusch, R.F. (2004) Evolving to a new dominant logic for marketing. *Journal of Marketing*, **68**(Jan), 1–17.

Visnjíc Kastelli, I. & Van Looy, B. (2013) Servitization: disentangling the impact of service business model innovation on manufacturing firm performance. *Journal of Operations Management*, **31**(4), 169–180.

Webster Jr., F.E. (1994) Executing the new marketing concept. *Marketing Management*, **3**(1), 9–18.

CHAPTER 17
CONCLUSIONS: MANAGING SERVICE AND RELATIONSHIPS

> *Good intellectual analysis and thorough planning of a service-oriented business is valueless unless management has the determination, courage and strength needed to implement their visions and plans.*

INTRODUCTION

This final chapter will summarize the essence of service management and service strategy. First, implications for management of the *Service Profit Logic* are presented. Then, the scope of *service management and marketing* is summarized. Thereafter, consequences for marketing of the service and relationship approach are discussed, followed by seven 'rules' of service. Finally, barriers to achieving results in an organization are presented.

A SUMMARY OF MANAGEMENT IMPLICATIONS OF THE SERVICE PROFIT LOGIC

From a commercial point of view, adopting a service logic and applying service management principles in business requires a clear understanding of the *Service Profit Logic* and its implications for management. As we have demonstrated throughout this book, in a service organization the economic result is generated in a dramatically different way as compared to conventional product manufacturing. Therefore, the *Service Profit Logic* requires equally dramatic rethinking about several management issues. This rethinking, pointed out and discussed in the previous chapters, is summarized in Table 17.1.

TABLE 17.1

Managerial implications of the Service Profit Logic.

Marketing management	Holistic customer management through Promise Management instead of functionalistic marketing management.
Human resource management	Externally-oriented Internal Marketing instead of internally-oriented HRM only.
Quality management	Management of Customer Perceived Quality instead of internally-oriented quality assurance and management only.
Productivity management	Holistic externally-oriented management of profit effectiveness instead of internally-oriented cost efficiency management only.
Operations management	Customer-focused management of operations; management of service production processes as well as of systems and resources used, including customers.

AN OVERVIEW OF A *CUSTOMER*–FOCUSED SERVICE STRATEGY

In Figure 17.1 the essence of *service management and marketing* is summarized. The core of the process is the series of *moments of truth* of service encounters, where the employee and the customer, supported by systems and technology and physical resources, meet and interact. Employee–customer interactions are not always the normal form of interaction. In many cases the customer interacts with IT and other systems, infrastructures or fellow customers and only on certain occasions, such as when a failure has occurred or the customer needs advice, interactions with contact employees take place. These service encounters influence customers' value-creation. If they are not well taken care of, the *perceived service quality* (service quality as perceived by the customer) is damaged, and the service provider may lose business. *The main focus in service competition is the continuous management of the series of moments of truth in service processes, as well as adequate support from managers and supporting functions and from investments in technology, operations and administrative systems.* If the ongoing moments of truth are well taken care of, the service encounters will turn out well, and the relationship will probably develop satisfactorily and lead to continuous business and loyal customers.

Value for customers is not, of course, entirely dependent on what takes place in service encounters. Much value support may have been pre-produced by the supporting part of the organization. The final value for the customers emerges in the consumption or usage of the service. *From the customer's point of view, however, what happens in the service encounter is always decisive.* If the customer is not satisfied with what he experiences, then the pre-production efforts in back offices, or by manufacturers in factories, have been in vain.

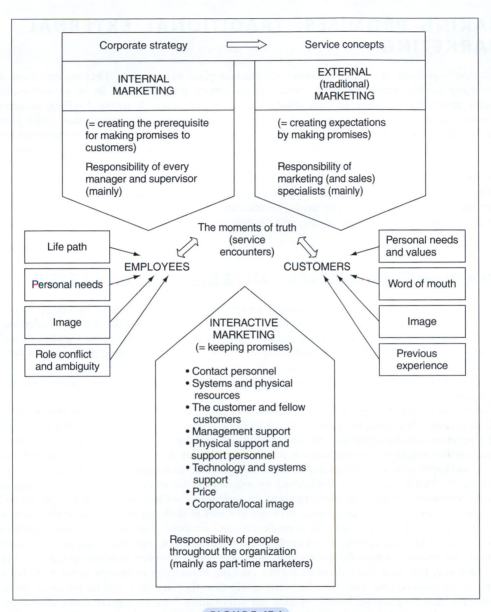

FIGURE 17.1

An overview of a customer-focused strategy.

MAKING PROMISES: TRADITIONAL EXTERNAL MARKETING

Customers' experiences of service encounters do not take place in a vacuum. They go into them with certain *expectations*, which are partly created by the service provider itself. By its *external marketing* process, involving *traditional marketing* efforts, such as market research, personal selling, advertising, Internet communication, direct mail, sales promotion and pricing, the organization *makes promises* that should correspond to the customers' everyday activities and processes and their personal needs, values and wishes. The *full-time marketers* inside the organization or outside of it (for example, in advertising agencies and market research firms) are usually responsible for this type of traditional external marketing.

These promises are enhanced or counteracted in the minds of the customers by their *previous experiences*, if they have had any, by *word-of-mouth communication,* and by postings on various websites and discussion in various social media, and by customers' conceptions of the *image* of the service provider.

ENABLING PROMISES: INTERNAL MARKETING

Employees' abilities, skills and motivation to meet the expectations of customers are backed up by *internal marketing efforts*. By creating and maintaining a service culture, as well as by actively marketing the service perspective as well as new goods and services, systems and processes to the employees, and by making use of all available means of motivating the employees and enhancing their skills for service-oriented and customer-focused performance, the organization can prepare its employees for *part-time marketing* responsibilities. Thus, internal marketing is a must for *creating the prerequisite conditions for keeping promises*.

Internal marketing is a *top management* responsibility, but it is also the responsibility of *every* manager and supervisor. Of course, the personal needs of the employees and their perceived job satisfaction and supervisors' encouragement, as well as their life path and their image of the employer, also have an impact on the employees' performance as part-time marketers. Moreover, employees are influenced by *role ambiguity*, related to, for example, what they perceive customers and the organization expect them to do. Employees are also influenced by *role conflicts*, for example, when what management says the employees should consider important in their jobs conflicts with the opportunities to live up to these intentions that management provides in terms of skills, support and incentives, and with their personal beliefs and values. Grocery retailers sometimes make promises in their advertising about products and additional service, for example cooking advice, that customers can get in the store. If there are not products left on the shelves or if employees, a large proportion of whom may be working on a low-pay, part-time basis, do not have the cooking knowledge or interest needed to give such advice to customers, who may often be better cooks than they are, they will be put in an awkward situation which they cannot handle. If they get information from customers about what they are supposed to do, which is not uncommon, the situation is even more frustrating for the employees. Bad internal relationships and bad external relationships with customers follow from this.

Another aspect of how well promises are enabled is the *support of systems and technology* – information technology and other – on which the employees depend. If customer information is difficult to retrieve from databases, or if files are not properly updated, contact employees have difficulty in providing customers with attentive, prompt and accurate service. Moreover, a lack of *systems support* also has a counterproductive impact on internal marketing processes in the organization.

Empowering employees is another key aspect of enabling promises. Employees who have the authority to handle customer contact situations themselves, and who have the technical skills and the motivation to take this responsibility, will keep promises effectively and in a customer–oriented manner. Here again, a lack of systems support can seriously diminish the potential positive effects of empowerment. However, it must always be remembered that empowerment without *enabling* does not work and may even be counterproductive and discourage employees. Enabling means that empowered employees are supported by necessary supervisory and physical support, and have been provided a required level of knowledge and skills to handle customer contact situations.

KEEPING PROMISES: INTERACTIVE MARKETING

What actually happens in the moments of truth of the service encounters, where customers and employees meet and interact, determines whether customers' experience meets their expectations. If experiences are equal to or higher than expectations, the perceived service quality is probably good; otherwise, there may be a quality problem. Good quality is a strong basis for a long-term customer relationship, including resales and cross-sales, as well as for favourable word of mouth and image.

Thus, *keeping promises* is one major aspect of the *interactive marketing process*. The customer contact employees are most often the key to success. However, information systems, operational systems and physical resources, and the customers, all influence interactive marketing performance. Although the role of the employees is most often paramount, other resources must not be neglected. First of all, there is a range of situations in which customers interact only with systems and physical resources. Using an ATM, making a local telephone call, sending a text message (SMS) from a mobile phone, playing digital games or making a purchase on the Internet are examples of such situations. Second, employees need a service-oriented operational system and proper computer technology, customer databases and other physical resources to be able to create positive moments of truth. However, one should never forget that if the technology or automatic service production system does not work, breaks down or cannot be operated, the key to recovering the situation is a service-minded and customer-focused employee. As has been discussed in previous chapters, if there is a problem of any sort, the service provider most often gets a second chance. However, in such service recovery situations the contact employees' role and responsibility for success is paramount.

The *physical support* of support personnel and functions, as well as *management support and leadership*, are critical to the service orientation of the customer contact employees and systems of the visible part of the service process. Furthermore, customers' experiences in service encounters are influenced by the corporate and/or local image of the service provider. Finally, the price level and possible price offerings have an impact on the level of customer satisfaction. This is not always altogether true, however. For example, if a manufacturer needs service and spare parts in order to keep its machines running, and if every hour of delay means thousands of euros, pounds or dollars of lost production and sales, he will probably be willing to pay almost anything to get the service.

Interactive marketing and keeping promises is almost entirely the *responsibility of operations and other traditionally non-marketing functions*. Therefore, employees involved in such functions are called *part-time marketers*, with dual responsibilities – for operations, or whatever their tasks concern, and for the marketing impact of their performance as well. To some extent, full-time marketers are also involved, but their role is marginal. Of course, in most business-to-business relationships the sales representatives have continuous responsibility for their customers. They cannot, however, do much to rescue a customer relationship if the organization has made a customer sufficiently dissatisfied with the service quality. In the short term the organization may be able to hold on to the customer's business; in the long term it loses customers.

Keeping promises is also dependent on how *productivity management* is understood. If productivity is predominantly considered a cost efficiency management issue and not a profit management issue, where external effectiveness and internal efficiency considerations are integrated in decision-making, service quality is easily hurt and the interactive marketing performance deteriorates.

FROM TRANSACTIONS TO RELATIONSHIPS IN MARKETING

Service processes are inherently relational. Normally, interactions between the customer and the service provider occur and continue for some time. In many cases, service is consumed or used on a continuous basis. The same customer meets the same service provider over and over again. Service marketing has often been difficult and considered less effective because service firms have not recognized that service is inherently relational and have instead taken a transactional approach in their marketing strategies.

There are certainly situations where a transaction marketing approach leads to good results, and there are customers who do not appreciate relationships in commercial contexts, but as a principle, a relationship approach can be expected to lead to better results in service competition. Because markets are maturing and new customers are difficult to acquire, other than by poaching them from competitors, long-lasting relationships with existing customers become exceedingly important. It is much more difficult to compete with a core solution, whether it is a physical product or a service process, than before. Firms have to develop total service offerings to support competitive value for their customers. This means that more and more businesses have become service businesses and that *service competition* has taken over. Sometimes a transaction approach can work, but generally speaking these developments require a relationship approach to managing customers (and other stakeholders, such as wholesalers, retailers and other distributors).

CONSEQUENCES FOR MARKETING IN SERVICE COMPETITION

Because of the transaction marketing traditions, the marketing mindset and mainstream marketing concepts and models do not fit service competition very well. In this section consequences for marketing in service competition of its transaction-oriented traditions and the requirements of a service and relationship-focused perspective,[1] respectively, are discussed. In Table 17.2 summarizes these consequences and requirements.

Diffusion of customer-focused activities (that is, the existence of marketing-like behaviour). Due to the transaction-oriented traditions of marketing, a customer focus normally exists only among full-time marketers and salespeople, who have been trained and appointed for marketing and sales tasks. When performing their jobs people outside these groups are generally not focused on customers. However, *a service perspective demands that a customer focus is present throughout the firm.* Wherever customer interfaces occur and customer contacts take place, a customer focus and marketing-like behaviour should exist. People who are engaged in such activities are *part-time marketers*. This goes for internal customers as much as for ultimate, external customers. All customer contacts have to be taken care of in a customer-focused or marketing-like manner, otherwise the total marketing process fails.

Dedication to customer management and a customer focus (that is, the existence of marketing attitudes in the firm). Normally, only a limited part of the organization, outside the group of full-time marketers and salespeople, takes a genuine interest in the firm's customers. A firm that faces service competition

TABLE 17.2

Consequences for marketing in service competition of its transaction-related traditions and of a service and relationship-focused perspective, respectively.

Aspect of marketing	Consequences of transaction-related traditions	Requirements of service and relationship-focused perspective
Diffusion of customer-focused activities (marketing)	A customer focus normally exists only in some of the places where customers interact with the firm.	A customer focus has to be present throughout the organization, wherever external or internal customers are present.
Dedication to customer management (marketing)	Only a limited part of the organization is engaged in customer-focused behaviours and has a customer-focused attitude.	In addition to full-time marketers and salespeople, a major part of the organization must be committed to customer-focused attitudes and behaviours.
Organising for customer mangement (marketing)	Marketing is normally a hostage of marketing and sales departments. Marketing is normally organized in marketing departments consisting of full-time marketers only.	All marketing cannot be organized in a traditional sense. Only full-time marketing can be organized in a specialized department. In part-time marketers a customer-focused (marketing) attitude can only be instilled.
Planning and preparing budgets for customer management (marketing)	Plans and budgets for customer management (sales and marketing) are normally plans of sales and marketing departments only.	Planning and preparing budgets for customer management must be part of all planning in a firm and co-ordinated in the business plan.
Commitment to internal marketing	All marketing and sales people are considered marketing professionals. Hence, no internal marketing is needed.	Part-time marketers outnumber full-time marketers several times. Hence, internal marketing is of strategic importance.

TABLE 17.2
(continued)

Aspect of marketing	Consequences of transaction-related traditions	Requirements of service and relationship-focused perspective
The term used for customer management (marketing)	For a century marketing has been used as the term for customer management.	Marketing as a term may relate too much to customer acquisition only. Moreover, part-time marketers often do not accept being involved in something called marketing. Hence, this term may be outdated and psychologically wrong and therefore not useful as an overall label for the process of acquiring, keeping and growing customers (customer management).

and adopts a service perspective has to be customer-focused throughout the organization. *Everyone who interacts with external or internal customers, including support persons whom customer contact persons are relying upon, have to be dedicated to a customer focus and have a marketing mindset.* If they are not, the customer contacts will be taken care of in an inconsistent manner and customer perceived service quality will suffer, and in the end marketing will fail.

Organising for customer management and customer-focused performance (that is, organizing marketing in a service business). In most firms marketing is the hostage of marketing departments. Firms have marketing departments staffed with full-time marketers who are highly visible in the organization and often run large external marketing campaigns. People outside the marketing department easily believe that the firm's total impact on the customers, that is, total customer management, is taken care of by that department, and by sales departments. However, a service perspective requires that almost everyone as part-time marketers take responsibility for customers. Of course, not everyone can be placed in the marketing department and report to its director. It is impossible to organize marketing in a similar manner to its traditional arrangement in consumer goods marketing firms. Only the full-time marketers, the specialists on customers, can be organized in one department totally dedicated to marketing and customer-focused behaviour. Everyone else, the customer contact employees and support employees as part-time marketers, whose main job after all is to produce a service or take care of some administrative tasks, albeit in a marketing-like fashion, belongs to their own department or processes. However, in spite of this, they have dual responsibilities. A marketing attitude of mind has to be instilled in them so that when doing their main jobs, they have the skills and motivation needed to perform them in a customer-focused manner. Hence, *marketing can only partly be organized. Mostly it is instilled in the organization as an attitude of mind.*

Planning and preparing budgets for customer management and customer-focused performance (that is, preparing marketing plans and budgets). Normally, what are called marketing plans and marketing budgets are prepared within the marketing department and mostly only cover activities planned and implemented by that department. Then the marketing plan becomes a plan for traditional external marketing only and the budget prepared for marketing becomes a budget for external marketing. In the plans governing other customer-contact activities performed in other departments and processes, that is, in plans governing the remaining parts of customer management, a customer focus is normally marginal or even lacking. Everyone knows that activities that have an impact on the firm's customers are planned in the marketing department and budgets for such activities are prepared there. Therefore, *marketing plans and budgets truly become hostages of the marketing department.* In a firm that adopts a service perspective, *a customer focus has to be present in all plans developed in the organization and in all budgets.* Hence, the plan and budget prepared by the marketing department is only a minor part of the total customer management (that is, total marketing) planning and budgeting in the firm. Ultimately, all these sub-plans have to be co-ordinated, and probably this can best be done *in the firm's business plan.*

Commitment to internal marketing. By definition, full-time marketers and salespeople are, or should be, customer-focused. They are also trained and motivated for marketing-like performance. Traditionally, no additional marketing-focused training for other people in the firm is considered necessary. However, when adopting a service perspective the firm has part-time marketers throughout the organization in a number of different organizational units and processes, who from the outset are not appointed for customer-focused behaviour and whose basic training is not related to handling customer contacts in a marketing-like fashion. Neither can they be expected to have a customer-focused attitude. However, they have customer contacts on a regular basis and they outnumber the full-time marketers several times. Hence, *internal marketing is not only a tactical issue, it is of strategic importance to the firm.* If internal marketing is lacking or less effectively managed and implemented, customer contacts will be handled badly, perceived service quality will suffer and the total marketing process fails.

The use of the term 'marketing' for customer management. Customer management, that is, being focused on customers and taking care of customers, is as old as the history of trade and commerce. The term *marketing* has been used for this process for roughly 100 years. Hence, it is a very new term. On no tablets of stone is it written that marketing, under all circumstances, is the best label to use. Indeed, marketing may turn out to be a problematic term in firms adopting a service and relationship approach, where the commitment to customers is required of a host of part-time marketers in almost every corner of an organization. First of all, this label has developed as a term describing the act of acquiring customers, persuading customers to buy and creating sales. It is an *inside-out* label. The very word 'marketing' refers to a movement, moving out onto the market. Today in service competition, when forming and maintaining longer-term relationships are a major part of customer management, customer acquisition and persuading customers to buy are still important tasks, of course, but so much else related to keeping and growing customers and creating a sense of connectedness with customers (and other stakeholders) is also important, and perhaps an even more important part of the customer management process. Hence, *the term marketing refers only to a part of what 'marketing' is today, and perhaps often to the less important part.*

Secondly, in the minds of people with part-time marketing responsibilities, marketing as a term is frequently loaded with negative associations. According to them, marketing is far too often equal to persuasion, pushing and making people buy things they do not need. And who would like to be part of that? So, *for potential part-time marketers the very term 'marketing' easily creates resistance to adopting a customer focus.* They simply do not listen to internal efforts aimed at explaining why they, as part-time *marketers*, are part of the firm's total marketing process. Therefore, for a firm in service competition to become truly customer-focused it may even be necessary to abolish the label 'marketing' for customer management. Psychologically this label is wrong and may become a hindrance for change processes, and it does not refer to the whole customer management process of acquiring, keeping and growing customers, where the latter two aspects are frequently more important than the first one (to which the term marketing originally referred).[2]

Throughout this book the term 'marketing' has been used for customer management. As a more appropriate term that would be even to some limited extent agreed upon or understood in a more or less similar way does not seem to exist, for the time being we have chosen to label the customer management process 'marketing'.[3] However, we suggest that firms seriously consider taking another, more appropriate and psychologically less problematic label for the customer management process in use.[4] Of course, this also goes for the label 'internal marketing'.

GUIDELINES FOR MANAGING SERVICE COMPETITION

In this last section of this concluding chapter a set of guidelines for service management are presented. The situation differs, of course, between firms and industries. However, some general guidelines for implementing a service strategy can be put forward. These guidelines start from the idea that people are still the critical resource and the bottleneck in most service businesses. However, information technology, the Internet, operational systems and physical resources are increasingly important. So technology and an understanding of how to use it may also be the bottleneck in a service process. As business is a social phenomenon it is, of course, incorrect to talk about any rules of service in a strict sense. Nevertheless, in order to emphasize the common characteristics of the customer relationships in most organizations in service competition, these concluding guidelines have been labelled *the seven rules of service*. The reader is asked to bear in mind that these rules are general and overemphasize the role of the employees for some situations. The fifth and sixth rules, however, focus on other aspects of service management.

The seven rules of service are as follows:

First rule: The general approach.

Second rule: Demand analysis.

Third rule: Quality control.

Fourth rule: Marketing.

Fifth rule: Technology.

Sixth rule: Organisational support.

Seventh rule: Management support.

FIRST RULE: THE GENERAL APPROACH

The importance of service elements in customer relationships grows over time and customers – business customers as well as individuals – increasingly demand individual and flexible responses from the service provider. Success in the market requires that the firm can offer advice and guidance; for example, technical advice needed to start operating a printer or a production machine, as well as small details, for example, a quick response on the telephone about airplane departure times. If employees are authorized to make their own judgements and have the knowledge needed to do that, and in addition have a service-focused approach to their job and to their customers, and if the firm is competitive in other respects, this will give good results in the marketplace. In spite of automated service systems, the increased use of information technology and the Internet, the creativity, motivation and skills of people are still the drivers behind successful development of new service, the implementation of service concepts and recovery of service failures that occur from time to time. Hence, the *first rule of service* can be expressed as follows:[5]

People develop and maintain good and enduring customer contacts. Employees ought to act as consultants, who are prepared to do their duty when the customer needs them and in a way the customer wants. The firm which manages best to do this strengthens its customer relationships and achieves the best profitability.

SECOND RULE: DEMAND ANALYSIS

Service is either rendered directly to people or organizations, or services are made on equipment owned by people (or organizations). In all cases the customer is present, extensively or occasionally, in the service process. Direct interactions between customer contact employees and customers occur, and in such situations immediate actions may have to be decided upon and taken by the contact person, or they may have to provide some information or change their way of doing the job according to the needs of the customer. Such a reaction may be, for example, changing the level of a customer training seminar to better meet the requirements or level of knowledge of the attendees, or a quick decision by a telephone receptionist about whom to put on the phone when the person a customer is asking for is absent. If corrective actions are to be taken immediately, nobody other than the person who produces the service can recognize the perhaps unexpected shift in the needs or wishes of the customer. As has been discussed in previous chapters, in such situations prompt action is called for.

Market demand can, of course, be measured in advance using standard market research. However, the changing needs and wishes of customers at the point and time of service production and consumption cannot be measured in advance. Nor can this be reacted to later on, when somebody else has detected the need for changes in the service process. If the need for a reaction is detected afterwards, the customer relationship was affected long ago. Only customer contact personnel can manage such a situation in a satisfactory manner. Hence, the *second rule of service* can be expressed as follows:

The customer contact persons producing the service in contact with customers will have to analyse the customers' activities and processes and their needs, values, expectations and wishes at the point and time of service production and consumption.

THIRD RULE: QUALITY CONTROL

According to traditional manufacturing quality control models, the quality of a product is controlled by a separate unit, which checks the pre-produced goods. This view is no longer valid in modern quality management. Everyone, in manufacturing as well as in service production, has a responsibility for quality, and producing good quality is based on the notion that things will have to be done correctly the first time. Because of the characteristics of service and the nature of service production and consumption, post-production control cannot prevent failure; it can only be observed that bad service quality has been produced *and* experienced by the customer. Moreover, if things are not done correctly the first time, the cost of correcting quality problems, which have occurred either in the back office or in the service encounter, is frequently high, especially if problems and failures are not rectified immediately. In this scenario the quality goal is often less than 100% and mistakes are therefore tolerated, and these costs easily become 'hidden costs', which are taken for granted and considered a necessary evil. It is not possible to have a separate quality control unit following every production step; instead, everyone has to control the result of his job.

In service operations this is very true. In manufacturing, one has to do things right the first time according to static specifications. In service production, as was demonstrated by the discussion of the second rule, *the specifications may change during the service process*. The customer may change his mind. Technology may break down, or almost anything may happen to change the situation and demand new or unforeseen actions.

The customer contact employee will have to check the quality of the service at the time it is produced and delivered. For example, when goods are delivered to a customer, an elevator is repaired, or a customer in a restaurant is being served, the quality of that service operation cannot be controlled and managed by anyone other than the person who has contact with the customer. Normally, there are no supervisors physically present in employee–customer interactions who can monitor quality on a continuous basis. Afterwards the quality can, of course, be checked, for example by market research, but then the mistake has already been made and the customer relationship may have been damaged.

On the other hand, the contact person must not be left totally alone. 'Common sense' may not be sufficient guidance. Management must provide employees with the knowledge, skills and directions needed to manage quality on their own with their customer contacts (internal or external). Moreover, management has to enhance the attitudes and mental capabilities of the employees to manage quality. Hence, the *third rule of service* can be expressed as follows:

The customer contact person producing the service in contact with customers will have to control the quality of the service at the same time he produces the service.

FOURTH RULE: MARKETING

In service competition the nature of marketing changes as well. Although traditional external marketing activities, such as market research, advertising campaigns, pricing, personal selling by a professional salesforce and sales promotion, are as important as ever, they are not the only activities to be performed as marketing activities. The *marketing process* is much broader and is spread throughout the organization. When ongoing relationships are to be maintained and strengthened, traditional marketing efforts are of less importance. In order to develop existing customer relationships, the exchange of goods, services and information, as well as financial and social exchange, is of critical importance. Personal selling, advertising and sales promotion activities are, of course, used in such situations, too, but their impact is often minor. Price is important at all stages of the customer relationships lifecycle.

In service competition every contact between a contact person and a representative of a customer includes an element of marketing. These contacts are the moments of truth or the moments of opportunity where the success of the service provider is determined, and resales and cross-sales opportunities can be utilized. If these moments of truth give the customer a favourable impression of the contact person, of the systems and resources used, and thus of the total organization, the customer relationship is strengthened. The probability that it will last longer and lead to further business increases. However, the opposite is also true. Badly-handled service encounters – that is, negatively experienced moments of truth – damage customer relationships and lead to lost business. They are truly missed moments of opportunity.

Any service organization has a large number of part-time marketers. However, marketing is only their second responsibility, beside the tasks they are set to perform. If the marketing aspect of their job is neglected, customers will perceive the quality of the service more negatively. Furthermore, in almost every service organization the part-time marketers outnumber the full-time marketers and salespeople several times over.[6] Consequently, the marketing impact of what they do and how they perform their tasks has to be recognized by management, because their role in the total marketing process is critical. If the interactive marketing performance of the part-time marketers fails, the marketing process fails, irrespective of whether the efforts of the salesforce or the advertising campaigns or other traditional external marketing efforts have been successful or not. This is the essence of service marketing. Marketing the service as a part-time marketer in the interactive marketing sense does not necessarily mean that the contact person would have to actively sell or offer the service, although this may also occur. Normally good part-time marketing behaviour means that the job is done skilfully, in a flexible manner, without unnecessary delays, and with a service-focused attitude. Hence, the *fourth rule of service* can be expressed as follows:

The customer contact person has simultaneously to be a marketer of the service he produces.

FIFTH RULE: TECHNOLOGY

Information technology is becoming exceedingly important for more and more service processes. If a website is designed so that users find it complicated or uninteresting, or if people using a website do not get a quick response to their inquiries, they quickly lose interest in the firm and its offerings; it is so easy to jump to the next website. Information technology should also enable contact employees to get easily retrievable and reliable information about the customers they are serving. If that is not the case, interactions between contact employees and customers are affected and bad perceived quality created.

All kinds of technology and physical resources used in service processes must be customer-friendly and reliable. A technological solution, or a physical resource that is geared to the needs and wishes of the user and that fits the situation in which it is to be used, may well enhance the quality of the service. It can improve the efficiency of operations and profitability as well. Even more frequently, technological support enables personnel to produce a better service. Appropriate technology and physical resources, such as computer systems, documents, tools and equipment, may at the same time improve working conditions and enhance the motivation of the employees to give good service. On the other hand, technology that employees do not understand or are not willing to use has a negative effect both on internal relationships in the organization and on external customer relationships. Employees need adequate *technological support*.

Hence, the *fifth rule of service* can be expressed as follows:

The impact on customers' ability and willingness to use technology, systems and physical resources (of any kind), as well as the impact of such resources on the employees in interactive and supporting parts of the organization, and on their ability and willingness to serve customers, have to be taken into account when investments in such resources are made, so that the service orientation of employees and the service quality perceived by customers are not affected in a negative way.

SIXTH RULE: ORGANIZATIONAL STRUCTURE SUPPORT

In many firms the organizational structure does not support customer-focused and high-quality service operations. Contact employees and departments that have to interact with each other in order to produce a service may be geographically or physically far apart in the organization. Often decisions concerning even minor details are made too far away from the service encounter which, of course, can have a negative impact on the perceived service. Internal regulations may restrict the flexibility of the contact staff. For example, hotels frequently have their employees say, 'No, sir, we cannot do that – management regulations, sir' to customers who ask for a service outside the normal procedures. Trousers cannot be ironed on a Sunday, or pyjamas cannot be supplied for a guest whose luggage has been left behind by an airline, or because designated exit gates are elsewhere an entry gate to an attraction cannot be opened to let an exhausted visitor out quickly. Management does not trust employees to think for themselves and make sensible decisions.

In many manufacturing firms, service elements are considered to be low priority. This means that services are not, like goods, an integral part of the total offering to the market. They receive fewer resources and less of management's time.

The employees and their managers alike often feel that service is not important. A company's organizational structure may not be geared to the demands of the new service competition. The result is inevitable, of course. Employees involved in the firm's variety of service operations feel no pride in their job, nor do they feel motivated to provide good service to customers. In order to develop their service into powerful means of competition, firms will have to adjust their structure so that the organization supports employees in their efforts to provide good service. An *organizational structure support* is needed.

Hence, the *sixth rule of service* can be expressed as follows:

The organizational structure must enable internal collaboration between employees and departments and motivate customer contact personnel and support personnel alike, such that good service can be provided to internal and external customers.

SEVENTH RULE: MANAGEMENT SUPPORT

It is well known that managers and supervisors get the staff they deserve. They have an important effect on the values that guide the overall way of thinking and behaving in the organization. In service competition this is as true as it ever was, and even more important to realize than before, because of the immediate impact that contact persons have on demand analysis, quality control and marketing.

Managers and supervisors have to be true *leaders*, not simply technical managers. There are too many rules and restrictions that managers and supervisors use as managing devices. If employees are well informed and have required skills, they are normally able to think for themselves, act spontaneously and in a flexible manner, and still make good judgements. Such service-oriented attitudes are effectively damaged by too much rules-and-regulation management and too little leadership.

Managers have to be able to motivate their people to be service-oriented and customer-focused, by, for example, their leadership style, their way of sharing information and giving feedback to people in their organizational unit, and their way of encouraging, supporting and guiding employees. They will have to demonstrate, by the way they do their job, that they, too, consider good service and satisfied customers important. It goes without saying that this attitude is required of every manager in the firm, irrespective of their hierarchical position and their own involvement in service operations.

Unclear visions and/or badly defined or undefined *service concepts* (one or several) make it difficult for managers, supervisors and support and customer contact employees to decide in which direction they should go, what leads to fulfilling goals, and what is contradictory to the objectives of the organization. If service concepts are not well stated, no clear goals can be set. In such situations there will be disarray both in planning and in the everyday implementation of plans. To sum up, the employees need the management support of their managers and supervisors. Moreover, clearly defined service concepts are a necessity if the organization is to avoid a chaotic situation where nobody knows what to do in certain situations or how to react to changes in the environment and to unexpected customer behaviour. Hence, the *seventh rule of service* can be expressed as follows:

Every manager and supervisor, and explicitly defined service concepts, have to provide the guidance, support and encouragement needed to enable and motivate customer contact persons and support persons alike to provide good service.

CASE STUDY

CREATION OF NEW AND INNOVATIVE SERVICE SYSTEMS THROUGH EMPLOYEE INITIATIVE: THE HOSPITAL MATERNITY WARD

There are significant opportunities for service and relationship marketing in the UK healthcare sector. However, realizing measurable success here is fraught with difficulties, some due to its corporate culture. However, a recent tragic event has had the effect of inspiring a radical turnaround in one maternity ward in a major regional hospital. This event was the theft of a baby from another hospital maternity ward. The subsequent public outcry made finding a solution to security issues of the utmost importance. What catalyzed service improvements in this particular organization was a series of employee-driven changes that had the effect of significantly changing both procedures and the way in which patients were treated. What was the most significant change, however, was who actually made it happen.

In almost all UK hospitals, it is the responsibility of the Estates department to take care of such matters as gardens, car parking, building maintenance, cleaning and security. Since baby theft was clearly a security matter, the Estates department acted promptly in implementing new procedures and systems. CCTV, security passes, visitor screening and so on all had the effect of making the obstetrics ward appear to be under siege. One of the new work practices was to cease rotating the cleaning staff, whose additional tasks were to help with security maintenance. As people became used to new working practices, certain problems arose. Nursing staff felt pressurized under the greater administrative load caused by the heightened security procedures. Because they were no longer regularly reassigned to different groups, cleaning staff had by then acquired, for the first time, a team ethos. This moved them to suggest ways in which they might help. Cleaners began undertaking non-medical tasks, such as serving meals to patients, managing visitor traffic and helping with admission of patients. The 'siege mentality' induced by the security regime engendered a supportive enclave of teams who expressed this support by regularly meeting to discuss ways in which their service might improve. The Estates managers were keen to give them autonomy since they were also learning and, significantly, they wanted to avoid another public relations disaster. Two small but significant changes occurred – patients were now called mothers, and the cleaners now called themselves the domestic staff. The first change was in response to the way in which the domestic staff viewed their clientele. They reasoned that unlike other hospital patients there was nothing 'wrong' with their patients, they were not ill; they freely entered into pregnancy, but did need medical support service. Mothers did not need 'fixing'; instead of commiseration there should be celebration, and so the mindset of service providers was positive. Mothers, in turn, did not see such caring and supportive service providers as simply cleaners, and the term 'domestics' was felt more appropriate to the mindset of the customer.

Domestic staff made significant strides in freeing the medical staff from the pressure of the security environment. Nursing staff, in turn, were highly supportive of their internal suppliers, expressing confidence by giving the domestics more freedom in assisting them. Domestic staff for the most part were mature women, with much experience. First-time mothers and difficult-birth mothers were routinely isolated, which may have made medical sense but made little human sense. Domestics organized their work around ensuring that no such mother was ever isolated, each spending as much time with the mothers as needed to support them psychologically, advising, alleviating fears and simply listening. Thus, the level of service, both in terms of efficiency and effectiveness, had the result of achieving a virtuous circle of self-sustaining benefits available to each member of the obstetrics department. More effective planning could be observed, administrative efficiency was optimized, staff morale was high, management input was minimal and mothers expressed far more satisfaction than at any time previously. At the heart of these beneficial effects was the emergence of a relatively autonomous empowered workforce, none of whom were very well qualified, and certainly not sophisticated intellectuals. The lucky induction of a simple Hawthorne effect impelled a highly complex series of events, the momentum of which created the conditions for a continuous quality improvement strategy.

Source: This case study was developed by Peter Murphy, University of Dundee.[7]

FIVE BARRIERS TO ACHIEVING RESULTS

The last three rules can be made more explicit by adding five additional statements that follow directly from the discussion about these rules. These statements all concern major *barriers to successfully implemented service management*. Most of these are due to an outdated management philosophy and old organizational structures, which hamper the development of sound and effective management of firms in the post–industrial society of the 21st century.[8] They are:

1. Organizational barrier.

2. Systems and regulations–related barrier.

3. Management–related barrier.

4. Strategy–related barrier.

5. Decision–making barrier.

Barrier 1 (organizational barrier). *Good service, and sound change processes towards a service culture, are effectively destroyed by an old-fashioned and obsolete organizational structure.* If an inappropriate organizational structure is left outside a change programme, much of the effort to achieve better service may be in vain. The organization simply is not suitable for service and, thus, becomes a barrier to change.

Barrier 2 (systems and regulations-related barrier). *Employees would normally like to treat their customers well and provide good service, but internal rules and regulations, the systems of operating, and the technology used may make this an impossible task.* It is only natural that most people would prefer to treat their customers well and provide good service, but if management regulations, operational or administrative systems, or the technology used counteract good service, they cannot do this. The internal infrastructure becomes a barrier to change. This typically happens when training efforts are used in isolation as the major or only means of developing a service culture in an organization, and no attention is given in the change process to this infrastructure provided by regulation, systems and technology.

Barrier 3 (management-related barrier). *How managers treat their staff is the way the customers of the organization will be treated.* If a change process focuses predominantly or only on contact and support personnel and top and middle management are left outside, there is a risk that the superiors of those involved in customer contacts will not be fully aware of what should be emphasized in these contacts and how the moments of truth should be handled and managed. Supervisors can easily encourage the wrong aspects of a task, and a role conflict emerges for the employees. They would like to implement new ideas, but their bosses have become a barrier to doing this.

Barrier 4 (strategy-related barrier). *If well-defined and easily understood service concepts are lacking, chaos will reign in the organization, and managers and customer contact and support persons alike will be uncertain about how to act in specific situations, in planning as well as in implementing plans.* If the organization throws itself into a change process without first clearly analysing the benefits sought by the customers in the organization's target segments, and decides what it should do, and how corresponding goals should be accomplished, there is no solid foundation for a consistently pursued change process. A number of projects are initiated and programmes started without anyone really knowing why this is being done and what the ultimate objectives are. In short, there is no strategic approach, and this becomes a barrier to change.

All of the four barriers above, as well as the six rules, are easy to accept, and generally it is not difficult for managers to admit that these rules have been broken and/or several barriers to change are present in their organizations. However, there is a big step from understanding a phenomenon and accepting that a problem may exist to doing something about it. Therefore, a fifth barrier is finally offered as the key to success.

Barrier 5 (decision-making barrier). *Good intellectual analysis and thorough planning is of no value unless there is the determination, courage and strength needed in the organization to implement new visions and intellectually sound plans.* To put this another way, weak management is always a barrier to implementing change processes.

SUMMARY

This chapter has illustrated the essence of management and marketing in service competition. The first sections summed up management implications of the Service Profit Logic and the customer-focused service management framework, and in the following sections consequences for marketing of a service and relationship approach and general guidelines for service management, *the seven rules of service*, were described.

The conclusions in this chapter hold true not only for so-called service firms such as hotels and restaurants, banks and financial institutions, insurance companies, transportation firms and a variety of public service. *They are equally valid for any type of organization.* This follows from the fact that in most industries the importance of service has grown dramatically. Everybody is now part of the service economy. *Every firm faces service competition to some extent.* Services can be found in any industry, and they should be an integral part of any firm's offering, irrespective of whether goods or services are the core of the business.

The traditional ways of handling demand analysis, quality control and marketing are not sufficient. The new *service competition* requires a new way of thinking, adopting a *service logic.*[9] If management cannot adjust its ways of thinking and its actions according to the new situation, the risk that the firm will suffer and lose market share will grow. *Service logic is a strategic issue, and not only an operational one.* The ways in which demand analysis, quality control and marketing have been carried out in the past are not necessarily totally outdated today. Traditional activities may still be efficient and effective, and they should be applied whenever appropriate. The main thing is that they are not sufficient any more. They have to be accompanied by new efforts, and they should be viewed from a new, more holistic perspective.

In service competition, if the firm fails to understand the characteristics of service and the critical importance of successful customer management, the firm's operations will deteriorate and be less successful. A number of moments of truth will become wasted moments of opportunity. On the operational level, every employee has to meet the demands that competition makes on them all the time. Although mistakes are bound to happen, *the objective must be to achieve 100% excellence.* Otherwise, the battle is lost before it has even begun; customers will receive inconsistent service, bad word of mouth is created, negative comments on social media occur, and the organization's image is damaged.

Inconsistency of service is perhaps the most serious problem facing service operations today. Most parts of a service process may function well, but if one or two interactions with a customer are handled badly, all the good that has been developed may be destroyed by these elements of bad service. Or the customer may be pleased with the service he receives in the service encounters he is regularly involved in, but if he has an unexpected request or a service failure has occurred, no service can be obtained. This means that his opinion of the firm's service will be revised. Whether the customer experiences bad service or a lack of willingness to give good service, the total *perceived service quality* will collapse in the mind of the customer on that occasion. The inconsistency of the service process caused by one or more badly handled moments of truth has an immense negative impact on the customer relationship. Successful service management requires an appreciation for the customers' perspective throughout the organization and consistency in the way that every customer contact is handled.

QUESTIONS FOR DISCUSSION

1. Discuss the implications for marketing of a service and relationship approach.
2. Discuss the importance of the seven rules of service.
3. In your organization, or in any organization, which of the barriers to achieving results are present? What are the reasons for the existence of these barriers? How can they be removed?

NOTES

1. See Grönroos, C., Relationship marketing: challenges for the organization, *Journal of Business Research*, **46**(3), 1999, 327–335.

2. Grönroos, *op. cit.* One of the major Scandinavian banks referred to in previous chapters of this book has long ago abolished the use of the term 'marketing' for the customer management process. In that bank the term 'active customer contact behaviour' was introduced instead. This change of terminology turned out to be successful. There are also other examples.

3. However, as the author believes that it is only fair to say that the term 'marketing' is outdated and does not fit an era of service competition and a service and relationship perspective in customer management, he would have liked to use another term which more appropriately would fit today's situation in the marketplace.

4. See Strandvik, T., Holmlund, M. & Grönroos, C., The mental footprint of marketing in the boardroom. *Journal of Service Management*, **25**(2), 2014, 241–252, where problems with the term 'marketing' are discussed.

5. The logic underpinning this general rule of service was discussed by Gösta Mickwitz in an essay on the role of service in business. See Mickwitz, G., Arbetstid och service (Working hours and service). *Ekonomiska Samfundets Tidskrift* (The Journal of the Economic Society of Finland), **38**(4), 1985, 163. In Swedish. Gösta Mickwitz is a former Professor of Marketing and Economics at Hanken School of Economics and Helsinki University in Finland and my mentor, who taught me to think laterally and seek solutions outside the limits set by the prevailing opinion.

6. Gummesson, E., Marketing revisited: the crucial role of the part-time marketer. *European Journal of Marketing*, **25**(2), 1991, 60–67.

7. Murphy, P., Front stage transactions lead to backstage relationships: a study of role repertoires in hospital service provision. Unpublished research paper. Dundee University, Scotland, UK, 2000.

8. Grönroos, C., Företagsledningens tvångströja (The management straitjacket). *Ekonomiska Samfundets Tidskrift* (*The Journal of the Economic Society of Finland*), **52**(3), 1999, 115–116. In Swedish.

9. See, for example, Grönroos, C., Adopting a service logic for marketing. *Marketing Theory*, **6**(3), 2006, 317–333, and Grönroos, C. & Voima, P., Critical service logic: making sense of value creation and co-creation. *Journal of the Academy of Marketing Science*, **41**(2), 2013, 133–150.

FURTHER READING

Grönroos, C. (1999a) Relationship marketing: challenges for the organization. *Journal of Business Research*, **46**(3), 327–335.

Grönroos, C. (1999b) Företagsledningens tvångströja (The management straitjacket). *Ekonomiska Samfundets Tidskrift* (*The Journal of the Economic Society of Finland*), **52**(3), 115–116. In Swedish.

Grönroos, C. (2006) Adopting a service logic for marketing. *Marketing Theory*, **6**(3), 317–333.

Grönroos, C. & Voima, P. (2013) Critical service logic: making sense of value creation and co-creation. *Journal of the Academy of Marketing Science*, **41**(2), 133–150.

Gummesson, E. (1991) Marketing revisited: the crucial role of the part-time marketer. *European Journal of Marketing*, **25**(2), 60–67.

Mickwitz, G. (1985) Arbetstid och service (Working hours and service). *Ekonomiska Samfundets Tidskrift* (*The Journal of the Economic Society of Finland*), **38**(4), 163.

Murphy, P. (2000) *Front Stage Transactions Lead to Back Stage Relationships: A Study of Role Repertoires in Hospital Service Provision*. Unpublished research paper. University of Dundee, Scotland, UK.

Strandvik, T., Holmlund, M. & Grönroos, C. (2014) The mental footprint of marketing in the boardroom. *Journal of Service Management*, **25**(2), 241–252.

INDEX